R E

FOR THE

ORDER

AND

DISCIPLINE

OF THE

TROOPS

OF THE

UNITED STATES.

Facsimile Edition

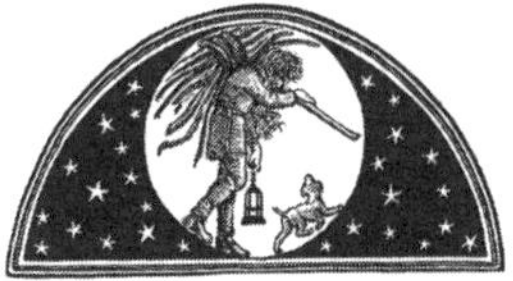

APPLEWOOD BOOKS
Carlisle, Massachusetts

Prepared by Friedrich von Steuben in 1779
as inspector general of the Continental Army
and adopted by Congress, March 29, 1779.

Originally published in 1786.

978-1-4290-9555-6

Thank you for purchasing an Applewood book.
Applewood reprints America's lively classics—
books from the past that are still of
interest to modern readers.
Our mission is to build a picture of America's
past through its primary sources.

To inquire about this edition
or to request a free copy
of our current catalog
featuring our best-selling books, write to:
Applewood Books
P.O. Box 27
Carlisle, MA 01741
For more complete listings,
visit us on the web at:
www.awb.com

10 9 8 7 6 5 4 3 2

MANUFACTURED IN THE UNITED STATES OF AMERICA

In CONGRESS, 29th March, 1779.

CONGRESS *judging it of the greatest importance to prescribe some invariable rules for the order and discipline of the troops, especially for the purpose of introducing an uniformity in their formation and manœuvres, and in the service of the camp:*

ORDERED,

That the following regulations be observed by all the troops of the United States, and that all general and other officers cause the same to be executed with all possible exactness.

By Order,

JOHN JAY, PRESIDENT.

Attest,

CHARLES THOMSON,
Secretary.

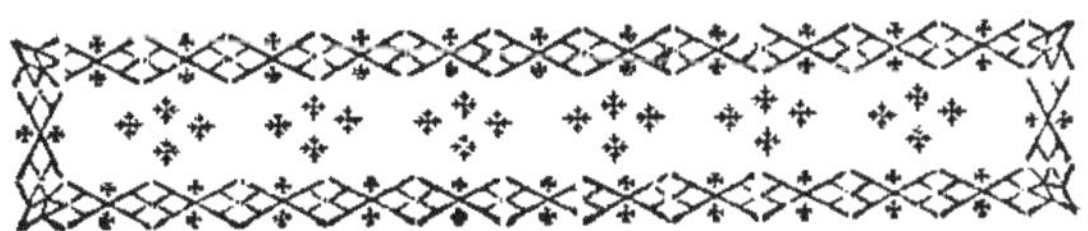

REGULATIONS, &c.

CHAPTER I.

Of the Arms and Accoutrements of the Officers, Non-Commiſſioned Officers, and Soldiers.

THE arms and accoutrements of the officers, non-commiſſioned officers, and ſoldiers, ſhould be uniform throughout.

The officers who exerciſe their functions on horſeback, are to be armed with ſwords, the platoon officers with ſwords and eſpontoons, the non-commiſſioned officers with ſwords, firelocks, and bayonets, and the ſoldiers with firelocks and bayonets..

CHAPTER II.

Objects with which the Officers and Non-commissioned Officers should be acquainted.

THE officers and non-commissioned officers of each regiment, are to be perfectly acquainted with the manual exercise, marchings, and firings, that they may be able to instruct their soldiers when necessary; they must also be acquainted with the dress, discipline, and police of the troops, and with every thing that relates to the service.

The commanding officer of each regiment is to be answerable for the general instruction of the regiment, and is to exercise, or cause to be exercised, the officers, non-commissioned officers and soldiers, whenever he thinks proper.

CHAPTER III.

Of the Formation of a Company.

A COMPANY is to be formed in two ranks, at one pace distance, with the tallest men in the rear, and both ranks sized, with the shortest men of each in the centre. A company thus drawn up is to be divided into two sections or platoons; the captain to take post

on

on the right of the firſt platoon, covered by a ſerjeant; the lieutenant on the right of the ſecond platoon, alſo covered by a ſerjeant; the enſign four paces behind the centre of the company; the firſt ſerjeant two paces behind the centre of the firſt platoon, and the eldeſt corporal two paces behind the ſecond platoon; the other two corporals are to be on the flanks of the front rank.

CHAPTER IV.

Of the Formation of a Regiment.

A REGIMENT is to conſiſt of eight companies, which are to be poſted in the following order, from right to left:

Firſt captain's.
Colonel's.
Fourth captain's.
Major's.
Third captain's.
Lieutenant colonel's.
Fifth captain's.
Second captain's.

For the greater facility in manœuvring, each regiment conſiſting of more than one hundred and ſixty files, is to be formed in two battalions, with an interval of twenty paces between them, and

and one colour poſted in the centre of each battalion; the colonel fifteen paces before the centre of the firſt battalion; the lieutenant-colonel fifteen paces before the centre of the ſecond battalion; the major fifteen paces behind the interval of the two battalions; the adjutant two paces from the major; the drum and fife-major two paces behind the centre of the firſt battalion; their places behind the ſecond battalion being ſupplied by a drum and fife; and the other drums and fifes equally divided on the wings of each battalion.

When a regiment is reduced to one hundred and ſixty files, it is to be formed in one battalion, with both colours in the centre; the colonel ſixteen paces before the colours; the lieutenant-colonel eight paces behind the colonel; the major fifteen paces behind the centre of the battalion, having the adjutant at his ſide; the drum and fife-major two paces behind the centre of the battalion; and the drums and fifes equally divided on the wings.

Every battalion, whether it compoſe the whole or only half a regiment, is to be divided into four diviſions and eight platoons; no platoon to conſiſt of leſs than ten files; ſo that a regiment, conſiſting of leſs than eighty files, cannot form a battalion, but muſt be incorporated with ſome other, or employed on detachment.

In caſe of the abſence of any field-officer, his place is to be filled by the officer next in rank in the regiment; and in order that the officers may remain with their reſpective companies, if any company officer is abſent, his place ſhall be ſupplied by the officer next in rank in the ſame company; but ſhould it happen that a company is left without an officer, the colonel or commanding officer may order an officer of another company to take the command, as well for the exerciſe as for the diſcipline and police of the company in camp.

When the light company is with the regiment, it muſt be formed twenty paces on the right on the parade, but muſt not interfere with the exerciſe of the battalion, but exerciſe by itſelf; and when the light-infantry are embodied, every four companies will form a battalion, and exerciſe in the ſame manner as the battalion in the line.

CHAPTER V.

Of the Inſtruction of Recruits.

THE commanding officer of each company is charged with the inſtruction of his recruits; and as that is a ſervice that requires not only experience, but a patience and temper not met with in every officer, he is to make choice

choice of an officer, ferjeant, and one or two corporals of his company, who, being approved of by the colonel, are to attend particularly to that bufinefs: but in cafe of the arrival of a great number of recruits, every officer, without diftinction, is to be employed on that fervice.

The commanding officer of each regiment will fix on fome place for the exercife of his recruits, where himfelf, or fome field-officer muft attend, to overlook their inftruction.

The recruits muft be taken fingly, and firft taught to put on their accoutrements, and carry themfelves properly.

The Pofition of a Soldier without Arms.

He is to ftand ftraight and firm upon his legs, with the head turned to the right fo far as to bring the left eye over the waiftcoat buttons; the heels two inches apart; the toes turned out; the belly drawn in a little, but without conftraint; the breaft a little projected; the fhoulders fquare to the front, and kept back; and the hands hanging down the fides, with the palms clofe to the thighs.

Attention!

At this word the foldier muft be filent, ftand firm and fteady, moving neither hand nor foot, (except as ordered) but attend carefully to the words of command. This

This attention of the ſoldier muſt be obſerved in the ſtricteſt manner, till he receives the word

Reſt!

At which he may refreſh himſelf, by moving his hands or feet; but muſt not then ſit down or quit his place, unleſs permitted ſo to do.

Attention!

To the Left,—Dreſs!

At this word the ſoldier turns his head briſkly to the left, ſo as to bring his right eye in the direction of his waiſtcoat buttons.

To the Right,—Dreſs!

The ſoldier dreſſes again to the right, as before.

The recruit muſt then be taught

The Facings.

To the Right,—Face! Two motions.

1ſt. Turn briſkly on both heels to the right, lifting up the toes a little, and deſcribing the quarter of a circle.

2d. Bring back the right foot to its proper poſition, without ſtamping.

To the Left,—Face. Two motions.

1ſt. Turn to the left as before to the right.

2d. Bring up the right foot to its proper position.

To the Right about,—Face. Three motions.

1st. Step back with the right foot, bringing the buckle oppoſite the left heel, at the ſame time ſeizing the cartridge-box with the right hand.

2d. Turn briſkly on both heels, and deſcribe half a circle.

3d. Bring back the right foot, at the ſame time quitting the cartridge-box.

When the recruit is ſufficiently expert in the foregoing points, he muſt be taught the different ſteps.

The Common Step

Is two feet, and about ſeventy-five in a minute.

To the Front,—March!

The ſoldier ſteps off with his left foot, and marches a free, eaſy and natural ſtep, without altering the poſition of his body or head, taking care to preſerve a proper balance, and not croſs his legs, but to march without conſtraint, in every ſort of ground: The officer muſt march ſometimes in his front, and ſometimes at his ſide, in order to join example to precept.

Halt!

Halt!

At this word the ſoldier ſtops ſhort, on the foot then advanced, immediately bringing up the other, without ſtamping.

The Quick Step

Is alſo two feet, but about one hundred and twenty in a minute, and is performed on the ſame principle as the other.

The recruits having been exerciſed ſingly, till they have a proper carriage, and are well grounded in the different ſteps; the officer will then take three men, and placing them in one rank, exerciſe them in the different ſteps, and teach them

The March by Files,

Which, being of great importance, muſt be carefully attended to; obſerving that the ſoldier carries his body more forward than in the front march, and that he does not increaſe the diſtance from his file-leader.

The Oblique Step

Muſt then be practiſed, both in the quick and common time.

In marching obliquely to the right, the ſoldier ſteps obliquely with the right foot, bringing up the left, and placing the heel directly before the toes of the right foot, and the contrary when marching to the left; at the ſame time obſerving to keep the ſhoulders ſquare to the front, eſpecially that the ſhoulder oppoſed to the ſide they march to, does not project, and that the files keep cloſe.

The recruits being thus far inſtructed, muſt be again taken ſeparately, and taught

The Poſition of a Soldier under Arms.

In this poſition the ſoldier is to ſtand ſtraight and firm upon his legs, with the heels two inches apart, the toes a little turned out, the belly drawn in a little without conſtraint, the breaſt a little projected, the ſhoulders ſquare to the front and kept back, the right hand hanging down the ſide, with the palm cloſe to the thigh, the left elbow not turned out from the body, the firelock carried on the left ſhoulder, at ſuch height that the guard will be juſt under the left breaſt, the fore-finger and thumb before the ſwell of the butt, the three laſt fingers under the butt, the flat of the butt againſt the hip bone, and preſſed ſo as that the firelock may be felt againſt the left ſide, and ſtand before the hollow of the ſhoulder, neither leaning towards the head nor from it, the barrel almoſt perpendicular. When exerciſing, he is to be very exact in counting a ſecond of time between each motion.

The MANUAL EXERCISE.

I.

Poiſe—Firelock! Two motions.

1ſt. With your left hand turn the firelock briſkly, bringing the lock to the front, at the ſame inſtant ſeize it with the right hand juſt below the lock, keeping the piece perpendicular.

2d. With a quick motion bring up the firelock from the ſhoulder directly before the face, and ſeize it with the left hand juſt above the lock, ſo that the little finger may reſt upon the feather ſpring, and the thumb lie on the ſtock; the left hand muſt be of an equal height with the eyes.

II.

Cock—Firelock! Two motions.

1ſt. Turn the barrel oppoſite to your face, and place your thumb upon the cock, raiſing the elbow ſquare at this motion.

2d. Cock the firelock by drawing down your elbow, immediately placing your thumb upon the breech-pin, and the fingers under the guard.

III.

Take Aim!—One motion.

Step back about ſix inches with the right foot, bringing the left toe to the front; at the ſame time drop the muzzle, and bring up the butt-end of the firelock againſt your right ſhoulder; place the left hand forward on the ſwell of the ſtock, and the fore-finger of the right hand before the trigger; ſinking the muzzle a little below a level, and with the right eye looking along the barrel.

IV.

Fire! One motion.

Pull the trigger briſkly, and immediately after bringing up the right foot, come to the priming poſition, placing the heels even, with the right toe pointing to the right, the lock oppoſite the right breaſt, the muzzle directly to the front, and as high as the hat, the left hand juſt forward of the feather-ſpring, holding the piece firm and ſteady; and at the ſame time ſeize the cock with the fore-finger and thumb of the right hand, the back of the hand turned up.

V.

V.

Half-cock—Firelock! One motion.

Half bend the cock brifkly, bringing down the elbow to the butt of the firelock.

VI.

Handle—Cartridge! One motion.

Bring your right hand fhort round to your pouch, flapping it hard, feize the cartridge, and bring it with a quick motion to your mouth, bite the top off down to the powder, covering it inftantly with your thumb, and bring the hand as low as the chin, with the elbow down.

VII.

Prime! One motion.

Shake the powder into the pan, and covering the cartridge again, place the three laft fingers behind the hammer, with the elbow up.

VIII.

Shut—Pan! Two motions.

1ft. Shut your pan brifkly, bringing down the elbow to the butt of the firelock, holding the cartridge faft in your hand.

2d. Turn the piece nimbly round before you to the loading pofition, with the lock to the front, and the muzzle at the height of the chin, bringing the right hand up under the muzzle; both feet being kept faft in this motion.

IX.

Charge with Cartridge! Two motions.

1ſt. Turn up your hand and put the cartridge into the muzzle, ſhaking the powder into the barrel.

2d. Turning the ſtock a little towards you, place your right hand cloſed, with a quick and ſtrong motion, upon the butt of the rammer, the thumb upwards, and the elbow down.

X.

Draw—Rammer! Two motions.

1ſt. Draw your rammer with a quick motion half out, ſeizing it inſtantly at the muzzle back-handed.

2d. Draw it quite out, turn it, and enter it into the muzzle.

XI.

Ram down—Cartridge! One motion.

Ram the cartridge well down the barrel, and inſtantly recovering and ſeizing the rammer back-handed by the middle, draw it quite out, turn it, and enter it as far as the lower pipe, placing at the ſame time the edge of the hand on the butt-end of the rammer, with the fingers extended.

XII.

Return—Rammer! One motion.

Thruſt the rammer home, and inſtantly bring

up

up the piece with the left hand to the ſhoulder, ſeizing it at the ſame time with the right hand under the cock, keeping the left hand at the ſwell, and turning the body ſquare to the front.

XIII.

Shoulder—Firelock! Two motions.

1ſt. Bring down the left hand, placing it ſtrong upon the butt.

2d. With a quick motion bring the right hand down by your ſide.

XIV.

Order—Firelock! Two motions.

1ſt. Sink the firelock with the left hand as low as poſſible, without conſtraint, and at the ſame time bringing up the right hand, ſeize the firelock at the left ſhoulder.

2d. Quit the firelock with the left hand, and with the right bring it down the right ſide, the butt on the ground, even with the toes of the right foot, the thumb of the right hand lying along the barrel, and the muzzle being kept at a little diſtance from the body.

XV.

Ground—Firelock! Two motions.

1ſt. With the right hand turn the firelock, bringing the lock to the rear, and inſtantly ſtepping forward with the left foot a large pace, lay the piece on the ground, the

the barrel in a direct line from front to rear, placing the left hand on the knee, to ſupport the body, the head held up, the right hand and left heel in a line, and the right knee brought almoſt to the ground.

2d. Quitting the firelock, raiſe yourſelf up, and bring back the left foot to its former poſition.

XVI.

Take up—Firelock! Two motions.

1ſt. Step forward with the left foot, ſink the body, and come to the poſition deſcribed in the firſt motion of grounding.

2d. Raiſe up yourſelf and firelock, ſtepping back again with the left foot, and as ſoon as the piece is perpendicular, turn the barrel behind, thus coming to the order.

XVII.

Shoulder—Firelock! Two motions.

1ſt. Bring the firelock to the left ſhoulder, throwing it up a little, and catching it below the tail-pipe, and inſtantly ſeize it with the left hand at the butt.

2d. With a quick motion bring the right hand down by your ſide.

XVIII.

Secure--Firelock! Three motions.

1ſt. Bring up the right hand briſkly, and place it under the cock.

2d. Quit the butt with the left hand, and ſeize the firelock at the ſwell, bringing the arm cloſe down upon the lock, the right hand being kept faſt in this motion, and the piece upright.

3d. Quitting the piece with your right hand, bring it down by your ſide, at the ſame time with your left hand throw the muzzle directly forward, bringing it within about one foot of the ground, and the butt cloſe up behind the left ſhoulder, holding the left hand in a line with the waiſt belt, and with that arm covering the lock.

XIX.

Shoulder—Firelock! Three motions.

1ſt. Bring the firelock up to the ſhoulder, ſeizing it with the right hand under the cock.

2d. Bring the left hand down ſtrong upon the butt.

3d. Bring the right hand down by your ſide.

XX.

Fix--Bayonet! Three motions.

1ſt and 2d motion the ſame as the two firſt motions of the ſecure.

3d. Quitting the piece with your right hand, ſink it with your left down the left ſide, as far as may be without conſtraint, at the ſame time ſeize the bayonet with the right hand, draw and fix it, immediately ſlipping the

the hand down the ſtock, and preſſing in the piece to the hollow of the ſhoulder.

XXI.

Shoulder--Firelock! Three motions.

1ſt. Quitting the piece with the right hand, with the left bring it up to the ſhoulder, and ſeize it again with the right hand under the cock, as in the ſecond motion of the ſecure.

2d. Bring the left hand down ſtrong upon the butt.

3d. Bring the right hand down by your ſide.

XXII.

Preſent--Arms! Three motions.

1ſt and 2d motion the ſame as in coming to the poiſe.

3d. Step briſkly back with your right foot, placing it a hand's breadth diſtant from your left heel, at the ſame time bring down the firelock as quick as poſſible to the reſt, ſinking it as far down before your left knee as your right hand will permit without conſtraint, holding the right hand under the guard, with the fingers extended, and drawing in the piece with the left hand till the barrel is perpendicular; during this motion you quit the piece with the left hand, and inſtantly ſeize it again juſt below the tail-pipe.

XXIII.

Shoulder--Firelock! Two motions.

1ſt. Lift up your right foot and place it by your left, at the ſame time bring the firelock to your left ſhoulder, and ſeize the butt-end with the left hand, coming to the poſition of the firſt motion of the ſecure.

2d. Bring the right hand down by your ſide.

XXIV.

Charge Bayonet! Two motions.

1ſt. The ſame as the firſt motion of the ſecure.

2d. Bring the butt of the firelock under the right arm, letting the piece fall down ſtrong on the palm of the left hand, which receives it at the ſwell, the muzzle pointing directly to the front, the butt preſſed with the arm againſt the ſide; the front rank holding their pieces horizontally, and the rear rank the muzzles of theirs ſo high as to clear the heads of the front rank, both ranks keeping their feet faſt.

XXV.

Shoulder--Firelock! Two motions.

1ſt. Bring up the piece ſmartly to a ſhoulder, ſeizing the butt with the left hand.

2d. Bring the right hand down by your ſide.

XXVI.

Advance--Arms! Four motions.

1ſt and 2d the ſame as the two firſt motions of the poiſe.

3d. Bring the firelock down to the right ſide, with the right hand as low as it will admit without conſtraint, ſlipping up the left hand at the ſame time to the ſwell, and inſtantly ſhifting the poſition of the right hand, take the guard between the thumb and fore-finger, and bring the three laſt fingers under the cock, with the barrel to the rear.

4th. Quit the firelock with the left hand, bringing it down by your ſide.

XXVII.

Shoulder—Firelock! Four motions.

1ſt. Bring up the left hand, and ſeize the firelock at the ſwell; inſtantly ſhifting the right hand to its former poſition.

2d. Come ſmartly up to a poiſe.

3d. and 4th. Shoulder.

Explanation of Priming and Loading, as performed in the Firings.

Prime and Load! Fifteen motions.

1ſt. Come to the recover, throwing up your firelock, with a ſmart ſpring of the left hand,

hand directly before the left breast, and turning the barrel inwards; at that moment catch it with the right hand below the lock, and instantly bringing up the left hand, with a rapid motion, seize the piece close above the lock, the little finger touching the feather-spring; the left hand to be at an equal height with the eyes, the butt of the firelock close to the left breast, but not pressed, and the barrel perpendicular.

2d. Bring the firelock down with a brisk motion to the *priming position*, as directed in the 4th word of command, instantly placing the thumb of the right hand against the face of the steel, the fingers clenched, and the elbow a little turned out, that the wrist may be clear of the cock.

3d. Open the pan by throwing back the steel with a strong motion of the right arm, keeping the firelock steady in the left hand.

4th. Handle cartridge.
5th. Prime.
6th. Shut pan.
7th. Cast about.
8th and 9th. Load.
10th and 11th. Draw rammer.
12th. Ram down cartridge.
13th. Return rammer.
14th and 15th. Shoulder.

N. B. The motion of recover, coming down to the priming poſition, and opening the pan, to be done in the uſual time, the motions of handling the cartridge to ſhutting the pan, to be done as quick as poſſible; when the pans are ſhut, make a ſmall pauſe, and caſt about together; then the loading and ſhouldering motions are to be done as quick as poſſible.

Poſition of each Rank in the Firings.

Front rank! Make ready! One motion.

Spring the firelock briſkly to a recover, as ſoon as the left hand ſeizes the firelock above the lock, the right elbow is to be nimbly raiſed a little, placing the thumb of that hand upon the cock, the fingers open by the plate of the lock, and as quick as poſſible cock the piece, by dropping the elbow, and forcing down the cock with the thumb, immediately ſeizing the firelock with the right hand, cloſe under the lock; the piece to be held in this manner perpendicular, oppoſite the left ſide of the face, the body kept ſtraight, and as full to the front as poſſible; and the head held up, looking well to the right.

Take Aim! Fire!

As before explained.

Rear

Rear rank! Make ready! One motion.

Recover and cock as before directed, at the ſame time ſtepping about ſix inches to the right, ſo as to place yourſelf oppoſite the interval of the front rank.

Take Aim! Fire!

As before explained.

The recruits being thus far inſtructed, the officer muſt take twelve men, and placing them in one rank, teach them *to dreſs* to the right and left; to do which the ſoldier muſt obſerve to feel the man on that ſide he dreſſes to, without crowding him, and to advance or retire, till he can juſt diſcover the breaſt of the ſecond man from him, taking care not to ſtoop, but to keep his head and body upright.

When they can dreſs pretty well, they muſt be taught *to wheel*, as follows:

To the Right,—Wheel!

At this word of command the men turn their heads briſkly to the left, except the left-hand man.

March!

The whole ſtep off, obſerving to feel the hand they wheel to, without crouding; the right hand

hand man, ferving as a pivot for the reft to turn on, gains no ground, but turns on his heel; the officer will march on the flank, and when the wheeling is finifhed, command,

Halt!

On which the whole ftop fhort on the foot then forward, bringing up the other foot, and dreffing to the right.

To the Left,—Wheel!

The whole continue to look to the right, except the right hand man, who looks to the left.

March!

As before explained.

N. B. The wheelings muft firft be taught in the common ftep, and then practifed in the quick ftep.

When the recruits have practifed the foregoing exercifes, till they are fufficiently expert, they muft be fent to exercife with their company.

CHAPTER

CHAPTER VI.

The Exercise of a Company.

ARTICLE I.

Of opening the Ranks.

Rear Rank! Take--Distance!

March!

THE rear rank steps back four paces, and dresses by the right; the officers at the same time advancing eight paces to the front, and dressing in a line; the serjeants who covered the officers, take their places in the front rank; the non-commissioned officers who were in the rear, remain there, stepping back four paces behind the rear rank.

Rear Rank! Close to the Front!

The officers face to the company.

March!

The rear rank closes to within a common pace, or two feet; and the officers return to their former posts.

ARTICLE 2.

Of the Firings.

The captain will divide his company into two or more ſections, and teach them the fire by platoons, as directed in chap. XIII. art. 1, 2.

The officers muſt give the words of command with a loud and diſtinct voice; obſerve that the ſoldiers ſtep off, and place their feet, as directed in the manual exerciſe; and that they level their pieces at a proper height; for which purpoſe they muſt be accuſtomed always to take ſight at ſome object.

The officer will often command, *As you were!* to accuſtom the ſoldier not to fire till he receives the word of command.

In all exerciſes in detail, the men will uſe a piece of wood, inſtead of a flint; and each ſoldier ſhould have ſix pieces of wood, in the form of cartridges, which the ſerjeant muſt ſee taken out of the pieces when the exerciſe is finiſhed.

When the company exerciſes with powder, the captain will inſpect the company, and ſee that all the cartridges not uſed are returned.

ARTICLE 3.

Of the March.

In *marching to the front*, the men muſt be accuſtomed to dreſs to the centre, which they will have to do when exerciſing in battalion; and for this purpoſe a ſerjeant muſt be placed ſix paces in front of the centre, who will take ſome object in front to ſerve as a direction for him to march ſtraight forward; and the men muſt look inwards, and regulate their march by him.

The captain muſt exerciſe his company in different ſorts of ground; and when, by the badneſs of the ground, or any other accident, the ſoldier loſes his ſtep, he muſt immediately take it again from the ſerjeant in the centre. The officers muſt not ſuffer the leaſt inattention but puniſh every man guilty of it.

The Oblique March

Muſt be practiſed both in the quick and common ſtep, agreeably to the inſtructions already given.

The March by Files.

Is as important as difficult. In performing it, the officers muſt be attentive that the ſoldiers bend their bodies a little forward, and do not open their files.

The

The leading file will be conducted by the officer; who will post himself for that purpose on its left, when they march by the right, and the contrary when they march by the left.

The Coun'er March.

Note. This march must never be executed by larger portions of a battalion than platoons.

CAUTION.

Take Care to counter march from the Right, by Platoons!

To the Right,—Face! March!

The whole facing to the right, each platoon wheels by files to the right about; and when the right hand file gets on the ground where the left stood, the officer orders,

Halt! To the Left,—Face!

and the company will be formed with their front changed.

ARTICLE 4.

Of Wheeling.

The captain will exercise his company in wheeling entire, and by sections or platoons, both in the common and quick step, taking care that the men in the rear rank incline a little

little to the right or left, according to the hand they wheel to, ſo as always to cover exactly their file-leaders.

ARTICLE 5.

Of breaking off, and forming by the oblique Step.

The captain having divided his company into two ſections, will give the word,

Sections! Break off!

Upon which the ſection on the right inclines by the oblique ſtep to the left, and that on the left, following the former, inclines to the right, till they cover each other, when they march forward.

Form Company!

The firſt ſection inclines to the right, ſhortening its ſtep, and the ſecond to the left, lengthening its ſtep, till they are uncovered, when both march forward, and form in a line.

Two or more companies may be joined to perform the company exerciſe, when they have been ſufficiently exerciſed by ſingle companies, but

but not till then; the inattention of the soldiers, and difficulty of instructing them, increasing in proportion with the numbers.

CHAPTER VII.

Exercise of a Battalion.

WHEN a battalion parades for exercise, it is to be formed, and the officers posted, agreeably to the instructions already given in the third and fourth chapters.

The battalion being formed, it is then to perform the manual exercise, and the wheelings, marches, manœuvres, and firings described in this and the following chapters, or such of them as shall be ordered.

N. B. When a battalion performs the firings, the six centre files (viz. three on each side the colours) are not to fire, but remain as a reserve for the colours; and the officers of the two centre platoons are to warn them accordingly.

The battalion will wheel by divisions or platoons, by word of command from the officer commanding.

By { *Platoons!* / *Divisions!* } *To the* { *Right,* / *Left,* } *Wheel!*

March!

When the battalion wheels, the platoons are conducted by the officers commanding them; the supernumeraries remaining in the rear of their respective platoons.

The colours take post between the fourth and fifth platoons.

The wheeling finished, each officer commanding a platoon or division, commands

Halt! Dress to the Right!

and posts himself before the centre, the serjeant who covered him taking his place on the right.

Forward,—March!

The whole step off, and follow the leading division or platoon; the officer who conducts the column receiving his directions from the commanding officer. When the battalion wheels to the right, the left flank of the platoons must dress in a line with each other, and the contrary when they wheel to the left.

Battalion!

Battalion! Halt!

By Platoons! To the Left,—Wheel!

March!

The wheeling finiſhed, each officer commanding a platoon or diviſion, orders

Halt! Dreſs to the Right!

dreſſes his platoon, and takes poſt in the interval; the battalion being now formed in a line.

CHAPTER VIII.

Of the Formation and Difplaying of Columns, with the Method of changing Front.

ARTICLE I.

The clofe Column formed on the Ground by the Right, the Right in Front.

Caution by the commanding officer.

Take Care to form Column by Platoons by the Right, the Right in Front!

To the Right,—Face!

THE whole face to the right, except the right platoon; at the fame time the leading file of each platoon breaks off, in order to march in the rear of its preceding platoon.

March!

The whole ftep off with the quick ftep, each platoon marching clofe in the rear of that preceding it, to its place in the column.

The officers commanding platoons, when they perceive their leading file dreffed with that of the platoon already formed, command

Halt! Front! Drefs!
and the platoon fronts and dreffes to the right.

ARTICLE 2.

Difplay of a Column formed by the Right, the Right in Front.

Caution by the commanding officer.

Take care to difplay Column to the Left!
The officers commanding platoons go to the left, in order to conduct them.

To the Left,—Face!
The whole face to the left, except the front platoon.

March!
The platoons faced, ftep off, and march obliquely to their places in the line; when the fecond platoon has gained its proper diftance, its officer commands

Halt! Front! To the Right,—Drefs!
dreffes his platoon with that already formed, and takes his poft on the right; the other platoons form in the fame manner.

ARTICLE 3.

The close Column formed on the Ground by the Left, the Left in Front.

This is formed in the ſame manner as the preceding column, only facing and marching to the left inſtead of the right. The officers will conduct their platoons, and having dreſſed them, return to their poſts on the right.

ARTICLE 4.

Diſplay of a Column formed by the Left, the Left in Front.

This column is uſually diſplayed to the right, on the ſame principles as the column formed to the right is diſplayed to the left.

ARTICLE 5.

The close Column formed on the Centre, or fifth Platoon, the Right in Front.

CAUTION.

Take Care to form Column on the fifth Platoon, the Right in Front!

To the Right and Left,—Face!

The fifth platoon ſtands faſt; the others face

to

to the centre; the officers poſt themſelves at the head of their platoons, and break off; and on receiving the word

March!

conduct them to their poſts in the column; the four platoons on the right forming in the front, and the three platoons on the left forming in the rear of the fifth platoon.

When this column is to be formed with the left in front, the four platoons on the right form in the rear, and the three on the left form in front.

In all formations and diſplayings, the officers whoſe platoons march by the left, ſo ſoon as they have dreſſed their platoons in line or column, return to their poſts on the right.

ARTICLE 6.

Diſplay of a Column having the Right in Front, from the Centre, or fifth Platoon.

CAUTION.

Take Care to diſplay Column from the Centre!

At this caution the officer of the platoon in front poſts a ſerjeant on each flank of it, who are to remain there till the platoon on which the column

column diſplays, has taken its poſt in the line, when they retire along the rear of the battalion to their platoon.

To the Right and Left,—Face!

The four front platoons face to the right, the fifth ſtands faſt, and the ſixth, ſeventh, and eighth face to the left.

March!

The four platoons of the right march to the right, the firſt platoon taking care to march ſtraight towards the point of view; ſo ſoon as the fourth platoon has unmaſked the fifth, its officer commands,

Halt! Front! March!

and it marches up to its poſt in the line; the third and ſecond platoon, as ſoon as they have reſpectively gained their diſtances, proceed in the ſame manner; and then the firſt halts and dreſſes with them; the fifth platoon in the mean time marches to its poſt between the two ſerjeants; and the three platoons of the left form by marching obliquely to their poſts in the line, as before explained.

ARTICLE 7.

The cloſe Column formed by the Right, the Right in Front, diſplayed to the Right.

When a column is formed by the right, and the

the nature of the ground will not permit its being diſplayed to the left, it may be diſplayed to the right in the following manner :

CAUTION.

Take Care to diſplay Column to the Right!

The two ſerjeants are to be poſted, as before, on the flanks of the front platoon.

To the Right,—Face!

The eighth platoon ſtands faſt, the reſt face to the right, and march, the firſt platoon keeping the line; ſo ſoon as the eighth platoon is unmaſked, it marches forward to its poſt between the two ſerjeants of the firſt platoon, left there for that purpoſe; the ſeventh platoon, having gained its diſtance, halts, fronts, and marches up to its ground; the other platoons proceed in the ſame manner, as explained in the diſplay from the centre.

ARTICLE 8.

The cloſe Column formed by the Left, the Left in Front, diſplayed to the Left.

This is performed on the ſame principles as the diſplay of the column in the ſeventh article.

A column formed either by the right, left, or centre,

centre, may, according to the ground, or any other circumſtance, be diſplayed on any particular platoon, on the principles before explained.

ARTICLE 9.

Open Columns

Are formed by wheeling to the right or left by platoons; and, *when indiſpenſably neceſſary*, by marching the platoons by files, in the following manner:

CAUTION.

Take Care to form open Column by the Right.

To the Right,—Face!

The right platoon ſtands faſt, the reſt face to the right, and break off to the rear.

March!

Each platoon marches to its place in the column, the officers taking care to preſerve the proper diſtances between their platoons.

Open columns may in the ſame manner be formed by the left, centre, or on any particular platoon, the officers taking care to preſerve their proper diſtances.

Open columns are formed again in line, either

ther by wheeling by platoons, or by closing column and displaying, as explained in the articles on close columns.

If the commanding officer chooses to close the open column, he will command

Close—Column! March!

On which the platoons march by the quick step, and close to within two paces of each other; when the commanding officers of platoons successively command

Halt! Dress to the Right!

and the column is closed.

When the commanding officer chuses to open a close column, he commands

Open—Column!

On which the front platoon advances, followed by the others successively, as fast as they have their distances.

The different manners of forming and displaying columns being the basis of all manœuvres, require the greatest attention of both officers and men in the execution. The officers must by frequent practice learn to judge of distances with the greatest exactness; as an augmentation or diminution of the proper distance between the platoons,

platoons, is attended with much confufion in forming a line. They muft alfo be very careful not to advance beyond the line, in forming battalion, but drefs their platoons carefully with the points of view.

ARTICLE 10.

Of changing the Front of a Line.

The changing the front of a platoon, divifion, or even a battalion, may be performed by a fimple wheeling; that of a brigade muft be performed by firft forming the open column, then marching it into the direction required, and forming the line.

If it be neceffary to change the front of a line confifting of more than a brigade, the fimpleft and fureft method is to form clofe columns, either by brigades or battalions, march them to the direction required, and difplay.

CHAPTER IX.

Of the March of Columns.

THE march of columns is an operation fo often repeated, and of fo much confequence, that it muft be confidered as an effential

tial article in the inſtruction of both officers and men.

ARTICLE 1.

The March of an open Column.

Column! March!

The whole column muſt always begin to march, and halt, at the ſame time, and only by order of the commanding officer. After the firſt twenty paces he ſhould command

Support—Arms!

When the men may march more at their eaſe, but keeping their files cloſe. Before the column halts, he ſhould command

Carry—Arms! Column! Halt!

Dreſs to the Right!

When marching in open column, the officer commanding will often form battalion, by wheeling to the right or left, in order to ſee if the officers have preſerved the proper diſtances between the platoons.

ARTICLE 2.

Columns changing the Direction of their March.

When a cloſe column is obliged to change the direction of its march, the front platoon muſt not wheel round on its flank, but advance in in a direction more or lefs circular, according to the depth of the column, that the other platoons may follow.

An open column changes the direction of its march by wheeling the front platoon, the others following; in doing which, the officers commanding platoons muft be particularly careful that their platoons wheel on the fame ground with the front platoon; for which purpofe a ferjeant fhould be left to mark the pivot on which they are to wheel.

ARTICLE 3.

Paffage of a Defile by a Column.

A column on its march coming to a defile, which obliges it to diminifh its front, the officer commanding the firft platoon commands

Break off!

On which thofe files which cannot pafs, break off, face inwards, and follow their platoon by files, and as the defile narrows or widens more files will break off, or join the platoon: The fucceeding platoons proceed in the fame manner.

If the defile is difficult or long, fo foon as the front have paffed and gained fufficient ground, they will halt till the whole have paffed and formed, when they will continue the march.

ARTICLE 4.

A Column croſſing a Plain, liable to be attacked by Cavalry.

When the commanding officer thinks himſelf in danger of being attacked by cavalry, he muſt cloſe the column, and on their approach, halt and face outwards; the front platoon ſtanding faſt, the rear platoon going to the right about, and the others facing outwards from their centres.

In caſe of attack, the two firſt ranks keep up a ſmart running fire, beginning as well as ending by a ſignal from the drum.

The ſoldiers muſt be told, that under theſe circumſtances, their ſafety depends wholly on their courage; the cavalry being only to be dreaded when the infantry ceaſe to reſiſt them.

When the column is to continue its march, the officer commands

Column! To the Front,—Face! March!
The platoons face to the front, and march:

ARTICLE 5.

A Column marching by its Flank.

Column! To the { *Right,* / *Left,* } *Face!*

If the column marches by the left, the officers

cers go to the left of their respective platoons.

March!

The column marches, dressing by the right.

Column! Halt! Front!

The column faces to the front.

CHAPTER X.

Of the March in Line.

ARTICLE I.

The March to the Front.

Battalion! Forward!

AT this caution the ensign with the colours advances six paces; the serjeant who covered him taking his place. The whole are to dress by the colours. The commandant of the battalion will be posted two paces in front of the colours, and will give the ensign an object to serve as a direction for him to march straight forward.

March!

The ensign who carries the colours will be

careful to march ſtraight to the object given him by the colonel; to do which, he muſt fix on ſome intermediate object.

If many battalions are in the line, the enſigns muſt dreſs by the enſign in the centre; if only two, they will dreſs by each other. They muſt be very careful not to advance beyond the battalion they are to dreſs by, it being much eaſier to advance than to fall back.

Should a battalion by any cauſe be hindered from advancing in line with the reſt, the enſign of that battalion muſt drop his colours, as a ſignal to the other battalions (who might otherwiſe ſtop to dreſs by them) not to conform to their movements; the colours to be raiſed again when the battalion has advanced to its poſt in the line.

The commanding officer of each battalion muſt be careful that his men dreſs and keep their files cloſe, and to preſerve the proper diſtances between his own battalion and thoſe on his flanks; and when he finds that he is too near the one or the other, muſt command

Obliquely,—To the { *Right!* / *Left!* }

When the battalion will march by the oblique ſtep, as ordered, till they have recovered their diſtance, and receive the command

Forward!

Forward!

Upon which the battalion will march forward, and the enfign take a new object to march to.

If the diftance is augmented or diminifhed only two or three paces, the commanding officer will order the colours to incline a little, and then march forward; the battalion conforming to their movement.

The officers commanding platoons will continually have an eye over them, immediately remedying any defect, carefully dreffing with the centre, and keeping ftep with the colours.

The officers in the rear muft take care of the fecond rank, remedying any defect in a low voice, and with as little noife as poffible.

The foldier muft not advance out of the rank the fhoulder oppofite the fide he dreffes to; he muft not crowd his right or left hand man, but give way to the preffure of the centre, and refift that of the wings; he muft have his eyes continually fixed on the colours, turning his head more or lefs, in proportion to his diftance from them.

Battalion! Halt!

The whole ftop fhort on the feet then advanced.

Drefs

Dreſs to the Right!

The men dreſs to the right, and the colours fall back into the ranks.

ARTICLE 2.

Of the Charge with Bayonets.

The line marching, the commanding officer, on approaching the enemy, commands

March! March!

On which the whole advance by the quick ſtep.

Charge—Bayonet!

The line charge their bayonets, and quicken their ſtep; the drums beat the long roll; and the officers and men muſt take care to dreſs to the centre, and not crowd or open their files.

Battalion! Slow Step!

The battalion falls into the ſlow ſtep, and carry their arms.

Halt! Dreſs to the Right!

The battalion halts and dreſſes to the right.

ARTICLE 3.

Method of paſſing any Obſtacle in Front of a Line.

When an obſtacle preſents itſelf before any diviſion,

divifion, platoon, or number of files, the officer, commanding the platoon, &c. commands

Break off!

on which the files obftructed face outwards from their centre, and follow by files the platoons on their right and left; if the platoons on the wings are obftructed, they will face inwards, and follow in the fame manner.

In proportion as the ground permits, the files will march up to their places in front, drefs, and take ftep with the colours.

ARTICLE 4.

Paffage of a Defile in Front, by Platoons.

A battalion marching and meeting with a bridge or defile, over or through which not more than the front of a divifion can pafs at a time, the commanding officer orders

Halt!

and then to the two platoons before whom the defile prefents itfelf

March!

on which they pafs the defile in one divifion. As foon as thofe two platoons have marched, the commanding officer orders

To the Right and Left,—Face!

The platoons on the right face to the left, and thoſe on the left face to the right.

March!

They march till they join, fronting the defile; when the commanding officer of the two platoons commands

Halt! Front! March!

and they paſs the defile; the reſt following in the ſame manner.

As ſoon as the front diviſion has paſſed, it will halt; and the other diviſions, as faſt as they arrive in the rear, face outwards, and march by files till they come to their proper places in battalion; when the officers commanding the platoons, order

Halt! Front! Dreſs!

and the platoons dreſs in line with thoſe already formed.

If the commanding officer does not think proper to form immediately on paſſing the defile, he may order the battalion to remain in column, march it where he thinks neceſſary, and form the line in the manner above mentioned.

ARTICLE

ARTICLE 5.

Paſſage of a Defile in Front, by Files.

If the defile will not permit more than four files to paſs, the four files before which the defile preſents itſelf enter without any word of command; the reſt face inwards, and follow them; the whole marching through by files.

As ſoon as the files which firſt entered, have paſſed, they halt; the others, as faſt as they paſs, marching to their places in battalion.

ARTICLE 6.

Of the March in Retreat.

Battalion! To the Right about,—Face!

The whole face to the right about; the officers keeping their poſts.

Forward,—March!

The colours advance ſix paces, and the whole ſtep off, dreſſing by them.

The paſſage of any obſtacle in retreat, is the ſame as in the march to the front.

ARTICLE 7.

Paſſage of a Defile in Retreat, by Platoons.

If it is at any time neceſſary to paſs a defile in

in the rear, in presence of an enemy, the line must march as near as possible to the defile; when the commanding officer orders

To the Front,—Face!
From the Wings,—By Platoons,—Pass the Defile in the Rear!

The two platoons on the wings face outwards.

March!

The two platoons wheel by files, and march along the rear of the battalion to the entrance of the defile; where joining, their officers command

Halt! To the { *Right,* / *Left,* } *Face!*

The platoon of the right wing faces to the left; the other platoon faces to the right; and both pass in one division; the other platoons following in the same manner, except those of the centre.

When all have entered but the two centre platoons, that on the right faces to the right about, and marches twenty paces into the defile; when the officer commands

Halt! To the Right about,—Face!

The officer of the other platoon, when he sees

fees them faced, will retire in the fame manner; and having paffed twenty paces beyond the platoon halted in the defile, comes alfo to the right about; they continuing in this manner to cover each other's retreat till they have paffed, when they face to the front, and cover the defile.

The three platoons of the right wing wheel to the left; thofe of the left wing wheel to the right; and having gained their proper diftances, the commanding officer orders

Halt!———Platoons!
To the Right and Left,—Wheel! March!

The right wing wheels to the left, and the left to the right; which forms the battalion.

If the defile fhould prefent itfelf behind any other part of the battalion, the platoons fartheft off muft always retreat firft; and if the defile becomes narrower than at the entrance, the platoons muft double behind each other.

ARTICLE 8.

Paffage of a Defile in Retreat, by Files.

This manœuvre is performed in the fame manner as the preceding, except that, inftead of forming at the entrance, the platoons pafs by files; and having paffed, face to the right and left,

left, march till they have their proper diſtances, and then wheel and form battalion.

The paſſage of defiles may be executed at firſt in the common ſtep, for the inſtruction of the troops; in ſervice, always in the quick ſtep.

The paſſage of defiles being difficult in preſence of an enemy, the officers muſt be particularly careful to keep the files cloſed; to be quick in giving the words of command; and not loſe any time in the execution.

This manœuvre ſhould always be covered by troops poſted on each ſide the defile, and on every advantageous piece of ground that preſents itſelf, to annoy and keep back the enemy.

ARTICLE 9.

Method of paſſing the front Line to the Rear.

The firſt line being obliged to retreat, will face to the right about, and retire in line.

The ſecond line, if not already formed in colums, will immediately, on perceiving the firſt line retire, form in that order by brigades or battalions; and the firſt line having paſſed the intervals between the columns, the ſecond line will diſplay; or, if too cloſely preſſed by the enemy,

enemy, attack in columns the flanks of the battalions which purfue, thereby giving time for the firft line to form and take a new pofition.

CHAPTER XI.

Of the Difpofition of the Field-pieces attached to the Brigades.

THE field-pieces attached to the different brigades muft always remain with them, encamping on their right, unlefs the quarter-mafter general thinks proper to place them on any advantageous piece of ground in front.

When the army marches by the right, the field-pieces muft march at the head of their refpective brigades; when it marches by the left, they follow in the rear, unlefs circumftances determine the general to order otherwife; but, whether they march in front, centre or rear of their brigades, they muft always march between the battalions, and never between the platoons.

In manœuvring they muft alfo follow their brigades, performing the manœuvres and evolutions with them; obferving that, when the clofe column is formed, they muft always proceed to the

the flank of the column oppofed to that fide their brigade is to difplay to; and on the column's difplaying, they follow the firft divifion of their brigade; and when that halts and forms, the field-pieces immediately take their pofts on its right.

CHAPTER XII.

Of the Firings.

WHEN the troops are to exercife with powder, the officers muft carefully infpect the arms and cartridge boxes, and take away all the cartridges with ball.

The firft part of the general will be the fignal for all firing to ceafe; on the beating of which the officers and non-commiffioned officers muft fee that their platoons ceafe firing, load and fhoulder as quick as poffible. The commanding officer will continue the fignal till he fees that the men have loaded and fhouldered.

ARTICLE 1.

Firing by Battalion.

CAUTION.

Take Care to fire by Battalion.

Battalion! Make ready! Take Aim! Fire!

If there be more than one battalion to fire, they are to do it in ſucceſſion from right to left; but after the firſt round, the odd battalions fire ſo ſoon as the reſpective battalions on their left begin to ſhoulder; and the even battalions fire when the reſpective battalions on their right begin to ſhoulder.

ARTICLE 2.

Firing by Diviſions and Platoons.

CAUTION.

Take Care to fire by Diviſions!

Diviſion! Make ready! Take Aim! Fire!

They fire in the ſame order as is preſcribed for battalions in Article 1.

The firing by platoons is alſo executed in the ſame order in the wings of the battalion, beginning with the right of each: that is, the firſt and fifth platoons give the firſt fire, the ſecond and ſixth the ſecond fire, the third and ſeventh the third fire, and the fourth and eighth the fourth fire; after which they fire as before preſcribed.

ARTICLE 3.

Firing Advancing.

The battalion advancing, receives the word,

Battalion! Halt!

Take Care to fire by Diviſions!

They fire as before.

ARTICLE 4.

Firing Retreating.

When a battalion is obliged to retire, it muſt march as long as poſſible; but if preſſed by the enemy, and obliged to make uſe of its fire, the commanding officer will order,

Battalion! Halt!
To the Right about,—Face!

and fire by battalion, diviſion, or platoon, as before directed.

CHAPTER

CHAPTER XIII.

Of the March of an Army or Corps.

THE greateſt attention on the part of the officers is neceſſary at all times, but more particularly on a march: The ſoldiers being then permitted to march at their eaſe, with the ranks and files open, without the greateſt care, theſe get confounded one with another; and if ſuddenly attacked, inſtead of being able to form immediately in order of battle, the whole line is thrown into the utmoſt confuſion.

The order for the march of an army being given, the adjutant general will appoint the field officers for the advanced and rear guards, and iſſue orders to the brigade majors to have ready their reſpective quotas of other officers and men for the advanced guard, which will conſiſt of the number neceſſary for the guards of the new camp. Theſe, together with a pioneer of each company, and a ſerjeant from the regiment to conduct them, muſt be warned the evening before.

At the beating of the general, the troops are immediately to ſtrike their tents, and load the waggons, which muſt then fall into the line of march for the baggage.

At this ſignal alſo all general and ſtaff officers guards, and thoſe of the commiſſaries, muſt return to their reſpective regiments.

At the beating of the aſſembly, the troops will aſſemble, and be formed in battalion on their reſpective parades.

The guards ordered, muſt then be conducted by the brigade majors, or adjutants of the day, to the rendezvous appointed for the advanced guard, where the field officers warned for that duty, will form them in battalions, or other corps, according to their ſtrength, and divide them regularly into diviſions and platoons. The officer commanding the advanced guard, muſt take care to have a guide with him, and to get every neceſſary information of the road.

The camp guards muſt at the ſame time retire to the rendezvous appointed for the rear guard, where they muſt be formed in the ſame manner.

At the ſame time alſo the quarter-maſters and pioneers of each battalion muſt aſſemble on the ground appointed for the advanced guard, where one of the deputies of the quarter-maſter general muſt form them in platoons, in the ſame order as their reſpective battalions march in the column.

Each

Each detachment will be conducted by its quarter-master, who must be answerable that it marches in the order prescribed; and the quarter-masters of brigades will conduct those of their respective brigades, and be answerable for their behaviour.

The signal for marching being given, the whole will wheel by platoons or sections, as shall be ordered, and begin the march.

The advanced guard will march at a distance from the main body proportioned to its strength, having a patrole advanced; and must never enter any defile, wood, &c. without having first examined it, to avoid falling into an ambuscade.

The pioneers are to march behind the advanced guard, and must repair the road, that the column may be obliged to file off as little as possible.

The advanced guard, besides its patroles in front, must have a flank guard, composed of a file from each platoon, and commanded by an officer, or non-commissioned officer, to march at the distance of one hundred paces on the flank, and keep up with the head of the advanced guard.

If it be necessary to have a flank guard on

each ſide, a file muſt be ſent from the other flank of each platoon to compoſe it; and as this ſervice is fatiguing, the men ſhould be relieved every hour. The like flank guards are to be detached from each battalion in the column.

For the greater convenience of the ſoldiers, the ranks muſt be opened to half diſtance during the march.

When the column meets with a defile, or any obſtacle, the commanding officer muſt ſtop till the column has paſſed it, taking care that they paſs in as great order and as quick as poſſible; and when one half have marched through, he muſt command the front to halt, till the whole have paſſed and formed, when he will continue the march.

When a column croſſes a road that leads to the enemy, the patroles or guards on the flanks of the firſt battalion muſt form on the road, and halt till the patroles of the next battalion come up, which muſt do the ſame: The others proceed in the ſame manner, till the whole have paſſed.

When the commanding officer thinks proper to halt on the march, immediately on the column's halting, the advanced, flank and rear guards muſt form a chain of ſentinels, to prevent

vent the soldiers from ſtraggling; and all neceſſaries, as wood, water, &c. muſt be fetched by detachments, as in camp.

On the beating the long roll, the whole are to form and continue the march.

On the march no orders are to be communicated by calling out, but muſt be ſent by the adjutants from regiment to regiment. The ſignals for halting, marching ſlower and quicker, muſt be given by beat of drum. (*See Chap.* XX.)

The commanding officer of the advanced guard being informed by the quarter-maſter general, or his deputy, of the ground the troops are to encamp on, will go a-head and reconnoitre it; and immediately on the arrival of the advanced guard, poſt his guards and ſentinels, as directed in Chapter XXI.

March by Sections of Four.

The roads being very often too narrow to admit the front of a platoon, and the troops being therefore continually obliged to break off, which fatigues the men; to prevent this, when the road is not ſufficiently large throughout, the battalions may be divided into ſections in the following manner:

Each

Each platoon is to be told off into ſections of four files; if there remain three files, they form a ſection; if two files, or leſs, they form one rank. At the word,

By Sections of Four!
To the Right,—Wheel! March!

they wheel by fours and march, the ſecond rank of each ſection taking two paces diſtance from the front rank. The officers commanding platoons take poſt on the left of their firſt ſection; but on the right, if the ſections wheel to the left. The file-cloſers fall in on the flanks.

The officers muſt take great care that the diſtance of two paces, and no more, is kept between the ranks. At the word,

Halt!

The front rank of each ſection ſtops ſhort, and the ſecond rank cloſes up, which gives the proper diſtance between the ſections; and by wheeling to the right or left the line is formed: or, if the commanding officer chooſes, he may form platoons by the oblique ſtep.

If a column be already on the march by platoons, and the road becomes too narrow and inconvenient to continue in that order, it may be formed into ſections of four, in the following manner:

Caution

Caution by the commanding officer.

Take Care to break off by Sections of Four!

Upon which the officers commanding platoons tell them off as before, but without halting. At the word

Sections of Four! Break off!

the ſections on the right of each platoon incline by the oblique ſtep to the left; and thoſe on the left of each platoon, following the former, incline to the right, till they all cover; when they march forward, opening the ranks as before directed. If the number of ſections in a platoon be uneven, that in the centre is to march ſtraight forward; the ſections on the right inclining to the left, and covering it in front; and thoſe on the left inclining to the right, and covering it in the rear.

CHAPTER XIV.

Of the Baggage on a March.

THE inconveniencies ariſing to an army from having too great a number of waggons, muſt be evident to every officer; and it is expected, that for the future each officer will curtail his baggage as much as poſſible.

The

The order of march for the army will always determine that for the baggage; and, whatever place it may occupy in the line of march, the waggons muſt always follow in the ſame order as their reſpective regiments.

The quarter-maſter general, or his deputy, will give the order of march for the baggage; and the commander in chief will order an eſcort, to be commanded by a field-officer, according to its ſtrength.

An officer of each battalion muſt be appointed to ſuperintend the ſtriking of the tents, and loading the waggons; he muſt ſee that the tents are properly tied up; that no proviſions or other articles are packed in them; and that the tent-poles are tied in a bundle by themſelves: he muſt not ſuffer the waggons to be overloaded, or any thing put into them but what is allowed; and when the waggons are loaded, he muſt ſend them with the quarter-maſter ſerjeant to the rendezvous of the brigade. This ſerjeant is to remain with the baggage of his regiment, to ſee that the waggons follow in order; and if a waggon breaks down, it muſt be put out of the line, that it may not impede the march of the reſt.

Each regiment will furniſh a non-commiſſioned officer to conduct the ſick and lame who are not able

able to march with their regiments. Thefe men are to repair, at the beating of the general, to the rendezvous appointed, where a fufficient number of empty waggons will be ordered to attend for the reception of their knapfacks, and their arms, if neceffary. A furgeon of each brigade is to attend the fick belonging to it.

The commanding officer of each battalion will infpect the fick before they are fent from the battalion, in order that none may be fent but thofe who are really incapable of marching with their regiments. And the officer commanding the efcort will be anfwerable that no foldiers are permitted to march with the baggage on any pretence whatever, except the quarter-mafter ferjeant of each regiment, as before directed.

No waggons are to be permitted to go between the battalions or brigades, except the ammunition waggons.

The waggons of the park, and others, are to be conducted agreeably to the foregoing directions, and the neceffary officers furnifhed to keep order on the march.

CHAPTER XV.

The Manner of laying out a Camp, with the Order of Encampment.

WHEN the quarter-maſters arrive on the ground where the troops are to encamp, the quarter-maſter general having fixed his line of encampment, will conduct them along the line, and give each brigade quarter-maſter the ground neceſſary for his brigade.

The quarter-maſters of regiments will then have their ground given them by the brigade quarter-maſters, and will mark out the place for each company and tent, and for the kitchens, &c. as deſcribed in the following order:

Order of Encampment.

The infantry will on all occaſions encamp by battalions, as they are formed in order of battle.

The front of the camp will occupy the ſame extent of ground as the troops when formed; and the intervals between the battalions will be twenty paces, with an addition of eight paces for every piece of cannon a battalion may have.

The quarter-maſter of each regiment ſhall be anſwerable

anſwerable that he demands no more ground than is neceſſary for the number of men he has actually with the regiment, allowing two feet for each file, excluſive of the officers, and adding ſixteen feet for the intervals between the platoons. He is alſo to be anſwerable that no more tents are pitched than are abſolutely neceſſary, allowing one tent for the non-commiſſioned officers of each company, and one for every ſix men, including the drums and fifes.

The tents of the non-commiſſioned officers and privates are to be pitched in two ranks, with an interval of ſix paces between the ranks, and two feet between each tent: the tents of the non-commiſſioned officers to be in the front rank, on the right of their companies, in the right wing, and on the left in the left wing of the battalion. Nine feet front are to be allowed for each tent with its interval, and twenty feet in the centre of the battalion for the adjutant; but when a regiment forms two battalions, the adjutant is to encamp with the firſt battalion, the ſerjeant-major ſupplying his place in the ſecond.

The captains and ſubalterns tents are to be in one line, twenty feet from the rear of the mens tents; the captains in the right wing oppoſite the right of their reſpective companies, and the ſubalterns oppoſite the left; and the contrary in the left wing.

 The

The field officers tents are to be in one line, thirty feet from the line of officers; the colonel's opposite the centre; the lieutenant-colonel's on the right; and the major's on the left. But if the regiment forms two battalions, the colonel encamps behind the centre of the first battalion; the lieutenant-colonel behind the second battalion; and the major behind the interval between the two battalions.

The surgeon, pay-master, and quarter-master, encamp in one line, with the front of their tents in a line with the rear of the field officers tents; the surgeon on the right, paymaster on the left, and quarter-master in the centre.

The kitchens are to be dug behind their respective companies, forty feet from the field officers tents. The suttlers tents are to be between the kitchens.

The horses and waggons are to be placed in a line, twenty feet behind the kitchens.

The drums of each battalion are to be piled six paces in front of the adjutant's tent, and the colours planted before them.

The camp guards are to be three hundred paces in front of the first line, and the same distance in the rear of the second line.

The

The quarter guard is to be forty feet from the waggons, oppoſite the interval between the two battalions who furniſh it.

The ſinks of the firſt line are to be three hundred feet in front, and thoſe of the ſecond line the ſame diſtance in the rear of the camp.

The commanding officers of regiments are to be anſwerable that no tents are pitched out of the line of encampment, on any account whatever, except for the regimental hoſpital.

The ground being marked out, the quarter-maſters will leave the pioneers, and go to meet their regiments, conduct them to their ground, and inform the colonel where they are to go for their neceſſaries.

CHAPTER XVI.

Manner of entering a Camp.

THE head of the column arriving at the entrance of the camp, the commanding officer of the firſt battalion will command,

Carry,—Arms!

On which the men carry their arms, and the drums

drums beat a march; and the officers will ſee that their platoons have their proper diſtances, cloſe the ranks and files, and each dreſs the flank on which his platoon is to wheel, with the ſame flank of the platoon preceding. The other battalions obſerve the ſame directions, and keep their proper diſtances from each other.

The general or officer commanding muſt take great care to march the troops in a direct line along the front of the camp, and at ſuch a diſtance as to give ſufficient room for the largeſt platoons to march clear of the line of tents.

As the battalions reſpectively arrive in front of their ground, they halt, form battalion, (dreſſing with the right) and order or ſupport their arms.

The adjutants immediately turn out the piquets that may have been ordered, form them in front of their reſpective battalions, and ſend them to the rendezvous appointed.

The piquets being ſent off, the commanding officers of battalions command their men to pile their arms, and diſmiſs them to pitch their tents.

As ſoon as a company have pitched their tents, the captain parades them, and they fetch in their arms.

The

The tents of the battalion being all pitched, the adjutant will form the detachments for neceſſaries, and ſend them off.

In the mean time the commanding officer of the battalion, having examined the ground, will, if neceſſary, order out a party to open the communications on the right and left; in front for the troops, and in the rear for the baggage.

CHAPTER XVII.

Neceſſary Regulations for preſerving Order and Cleanlineſs in the Camp.

WHEN a regiment enters a camp, the field officers muſt take care that the encampment is pitched regularly; that the ſinks and kitchens are immediately dug in their proper places; and that no tents are pitched in any part of the camp contrary to the order preſcribed.

At leaſt one officer of a company muſt remain on the parade, to ſee that the tents are pitched regularly on the ground marked out.

The tents ſhould be marked with the name of each regiment and company, to prevent their

 being

being loſt or exchanged, and the tents of each company numbered; and each non-commiſſioned officer ſhould have a liſt of the tents, with the mens names belonging to each.

The utenſils belonging to the tents are to be carried alternately by the men; and the non-commiſſioned officers of the ſquads are to be anſwerable that they are not loſt or ſpoiled.

Whenever a regiment is to remain more than one night on the ſame ground, the ſoldiers muſt be obliged to cut a ſmall trench round their tents, to carry off the rain; but great care muſt be taken they do not throw the dirt up againſt the tents.

One officer of a company muſt every day viſit the tents; ſee that they are kept clean; that every utenſil belonging to them is in proper order; and that no bones or other filth be in or near them: and when the weather is fine, ſhould order them to be ſtruck about two hours at noon, and the ſtraw and bedding well aired.

The ſoldiers ſhould not be permitted to eat in their tents, except in bad weather; and an officer of a company muſt often viſit the meſſes; ſee that the proviſion is good and well cooked; that the men of one tent meſs together; and that the proviſion is not ſold or diſpoſed of for liquor.

A ſu-

A ſubaltern, four non-commiſſioned officers and a drummer, muſt every day be appointed for the police of each battalion, who are on no account to be abſent during the time they are on duty.

The officer of the police is to make a general inſpection into the cleanlineſs of the camp, not ſuffer fire to be made any where but in the kitchens, and cauſe all dirt to be immediately removed, and either burnt or buried. He is to be preſent at all diſtributions in the regiment, and to form and ſend off all detachments for neceſſaries.

In caſe the adjutant is obliged to be abſent, the officer of the police is to do his duty till his return; and for that purpoſe he muſt attend at the adjutant's tent, to be ready to receive and diſtribute any orders that may come for the regiment.

The drummer of the police muſt attend conſtantly at the adjutant's tent, to be ready at all times to communicate the neceſſary ſignals; nor muſt he abſent himſelf on any account during the twenty-four hours, without leaving another drummer to ſupply his place till his return, nor then, without leave from the adjutant.

When any of the men want water, they muſt apply

apply to the officer of the police, who will order the drum to beat the neceſſary ſignal; on which all who want water muſt immediately parade with their canteens before the colours, where the officer of the police will form and ſend them off under the care of two non-commiſſioned officers of the police, who are to be anſwerable that they bring back the whole detachment, and that no exceſſes are committed whilſt they are out. Wood and all other neceſſaries muſt be fetched in the ſame manner. Except in caſe of neceſſity, not more than one detachment is to be out at a time.

The quarter-maſter muſt be anſwerable that the parade and environs of the encampment of a regiment are kept clean; that the ſinks are filled up, and new ones dug every four days, and oftner in warm weather; and if any horſe or other animal dies near the regiment, he muſt cauſe it to be carried at leaſt half a mile from camp, and buried.

The place where the cattle are killed muſt be at leaſt fifty paces in the rear of the waggons; and the entrails and other filth immediately buried; for which the commiſſaries are to be anſwerable.

The quarter-maſter general muſt take care that all dead animals, and every other nuiſance in the environs of the camp, be removed.

No non-commiſſioned officer or ſoldier ſhall be permitted to paſs the chain of ſentinels round the camp, without permiſſion in writing from the commanding officer of his regiment or battalion; which permiſſion ſhall be dated the ſame day, and ſhall, on the return of the perſon to whom it was granted, be delivered to the adjutant, who is to return it to the colonel or commanding officer, with his report.

Every detachment not conducted by a commiſſioned officer, ſhall have a written permiſſion from a field officer, or officer commanding a regiment, or the officer of the police if it be a detachment going for neceſſaries; without which they are not to be permitted to paſs the chain.

All officers whatever are to make it a point of duty to ſtop every non-commiſſioned officer or ſoldier they meet without the chain, and examine his paſs; and if he has not a ſufficient paſs, or having one, is committing any exceſs, the officer muſt conduct him to the neareſt guard, from whence he muſt be ſent, with his crime, to his regiment.

The ſentinel before the colours muſt have orders, in caſe he hears any alarm in camp, or at the advanced poſts, to acquaint the adjutant with it; who will inform the commanding officer of the battalion, or order an alarm beat, if the caſe requires it.

CHAP.

CHAPTER XVIII.

Of Roll-Calls.

THE rolls ſhall be called in each battalion at troop and retreat beating, at which times the men are to parade with their arms; and at the beating of the *reveille*, and at noon, the commanding officers of companies ſhall cauſe the rolls of their reſpective companies to be called, the men parading for that purpoſe without arms, and to be detained no longer than is neceſſary to call the roll.

The non-commiſſioned officers are to viſit their reſpective ſquads a quarter of an hour after *tattoo* beating; ſee that they are all preſent and retired to reſt; and make their report to the commanding officer of the company.

No non-commiſſioned officer or ſoldier is to be abſent from roll-call without permiſſion from the commanding officer of the company.

No commiſſioned officer is to be abſent from roll-call, without permiſſion from the commanding officer of the regiment.

CHAPTER XIX.

Of the Inſpection of the Men, their Dreſs, Neceſſaries, Arms, Accoutrements, and Ammunition.

THE oftener the ſoldiers are under the inſpection of their officers the better; for which reaſon every morning at troop beating, they muſt inſpect into the dreſs of their men; ſee that their clothes are whole, and put on properly; their hands and faces waſhed clean; their hair combed; their accoutrements properly fixed, and every article about them in the greateſt order. Thoſe who are guilty of repeated neglects in theſe particulars, are to be confined and puniſhed.—The field officers muſt pay attention to this object, taking proper notice of thoſe companies where a viſible neglect appears, and publicly applauding thoſe who are remarkable for their good appearance.

Every day the commanding officers of companies muſt examine their men's arms and ammunition, and ſee that they are clean and in good order. (*See farther Chap.* XXII.)

That the men may always appear clean on the parade, and as a means of preſerving their health, the non-commiſſioned officers are to ſee that they waſh their hands and faces every day, and oftener when neceſſary. And if any river is nigh,

nigh, and the feafon favorable, the men fhall bathe themfelves as frequently as poffible, the commanding officers of each battalion fending them by fmall detachments fucceffively, under the care of a non-commiffioned officer; but on no account muft the men be permitted to bathe when juft come off a march, at leaft till they have repofed long enough to get cool.

Every Saturday morning the captains are to make a general infpection of their companies, and examine into the ftate of the men's neceffaries, obferving that they agree in quantity with what is fpecified in the company book; and that every article is the man's who fhews it: For which purpofe, and to difcover theft, every man's things fhould be marked; if any thing is deficient, ftrict inquiry muft be made into the caufe of it; and fhould it appear to be loft, pledged, fold or exchanged, the offender muft be feverely punifhed.

That the men may not be improperly burdened and fatigued, the captains are not to fuffer them to carry any thing which is either ufelefs or unneceffary.

CHAPTER XX.

Of the different Beats of thè Drum.

THE different daily beats ſhall begin on the right, and be inſtantly followed by the whole army; to facilitate which, the drummer's call ſhall be beat by the drums of the police a quarter of an hour before the time of beating, when the drummer's will aſſemble before the colours of their reſpective battalions; and as ſoon as the beat begins on the right, it is to be immediately taken up by the whole army, the drummers beating along the front of their reſpective battalions, from the centre to the right, from thence to the left, and back again to the centre, where they finiſh.

The different beats and ſignals are to be as follow:

The *General* is to be beat only when the whole are to march, and is the ſignal to ſtrike the tents, and prepare for the march.

The *Aſſembly* is the ſignal to repair to the colours.

The *March* for the whole to move.

The *Reveille* is beat at day-break, and is the signal for the ſoldiers to riſe, and the centries to leave off challenging.

The *Troop* aſſembles the ſoldiers together, for the purpoſe of calling the roll, and inſpecting the men for duty.

The *Retreat* is beat at ſun-ſet, for calling the roll, warning the men for duty, and reading the orders of the day.

The *Tattoo* is for the ſoldiers to repair to their tents, where they muſt remain till *reveille* beating next morning.

To *Arms* is the ſignal for getting under arms in caſe of alarm.

The *Parley* is to deſire a conference with the enemy.

The SIGNALS.

Adjutant's call—*firſt part of the troop.*

Firſt Serjeant's call—*one roll and three flams.*

All non-commiſſioned officers call—*two rolls and five flams.*

To go for wood—*poing ſtroke and ten ſtroke roll.*
water—*two ſtrokes and a flam.*
proviſions—*roaſt beef.*

Front

Front to halt—*two flams from right to left, and a full drag with the right, a left hand flam and a right hand full drag.*

For the front to advance quicker—*the long march.*
to march slower—*the taps.*

For the drummers—*the drummers call.*

For a fatigue party—*the pioneers march.*

For the church call—*the parley.*

The drummers will practise a hundred paces in front of the battalion, at the hours fixed by the adjutant general; and any drummer found beating at any other time (except ordered) shall be punished.

CHAPTER XXI.

Of the Service of the Guards.

ARTICLE I.

Of the different Guards, with their Use.

THE different guards of the army will consist of

1ſt. Out poſt and piquet guards.
2d. Camp and quarter guards.
3d. General and ſtaff officers guards.

The piquet guards are formed by detachments from the line, and are poſted at the avenues of the camp, in ſuch numbers as the general commanding thinks neceſſary for the ſecurity of the camp.

The camp and quarter guards are for the better ſecurity of the camp, as well as for preſerving good order and diſcipline.

Every two battalions will furniſh a camp and quarter guard between them, to conſiſt of

Subalt.	Serj.	Corp.	Drum.	Priv.	
1.	1.	1.	1.	27.	For the camp guard.
-	-	1.	-	9.	For the quarter guard.

The camp guard of the front line is to be poſted three hundred paces in front of it, and that of the ſecond line the ſame diſtance in the rear of the ſecond line, each oppoſite the interval of the two battalions who furniſh it.

Each guard will poſt nine ſentinels, viz. one before the guard, two on the right and two on the left; theſe five ſentinels, with thoſe from the other

other battalions, forming a chain in front and rear of the camp; the ſixth and ſeventh ſentinels before the colours; and the eighth and ninth before the tents of the commanding officers of the two battalions.

In order to complete the chain of ſentinels round the camp, the adjutant-general will order two flank guards from the line, to conſiſt of a commiſſioned officer, and as many men as are neceſſary to form a chain on the flanks.

The intention of the camp guards being to form a chain of ſentinels round the camp, in order to prevent improper perſons entering, or the ſoldiers going out of camp, the commanding officers of brigades will add to, or diminiſh them, ſo as to anſwer the above purpoſe.

The quarter guard is to be poſted twenty paces in the rear of the line of waggons, and will furniſh three ſentinels, viz. one at the guard, and one behind each battalion.

The guards of the general and other officers will be as follows:

	Sub.	Serj.	Corp.	Priv.
A major-general will have	1	1	1	20
A brigadier-general -	0	1	1	12
Quarter-maſter general (as ſuch)	0	1	1	12

 Adjutant-

	Sub.	Serj.	Corp.	Priv.
Adjutant-general - -	0	1	1	12
Commiſſary-general -	0	0	1	6
Pay-maſter-general - -	0	0	1	6
Auditors - - -	0	0	1	6
Judge Advocate-general -	0	0	1	3
Muſter-maſter general -	0	0	1	3
Clothier-general - - -	0	0	1	3
Brigade commiſſary, General hoſpital, Provoſt guard	According to circumſtances.			

Any additional guard to the quarter-maſter, commiſſary, or clothier-general, will be determined by the ſtores they may have in poſſeſſion.

The different guards are all to mount at one hour, to be regulated by the commanding officer for the time being.

The camp and quarter guards are to parade before the interval of their battalions, where they will be formed by the adjutant who furniſhes the officer, and immediately ſent off to their reſpective poſts.

The guard of a major-general is to be furniſhed from his own diviſion, each brigade furniſhing it by turns; it is to be formed by the major

major of brigade, and ſent from the brigade parade.

The guard of a brigadier-general is to be furniſhed by his own brigade, and formed and ſent from the brigade parade by the major of brigade. The brigade commiſſary's guard is to be furniſhed in the ſame manner.

The other guards being compoſed of detachments from the line by brigades, each detachment is formed on the brigade parade by the major of brigade, and ſent with an adjutant to the grand parade.

All guards (except thoſe which are honorary) ſhould ordinarily be of force proportioned to the number of ſentinels required, allowing three relieves for each poſt.

ARTICLE 2.

Of the Grand Parade.

As ſoon as a detachment arrives on the grand parade, the officer, having dreſſed the ranks, commands,

Order—Firelocks!

and then takes poſt eight paces in front of his detachment; the non-commiſſioned officers fall two

two paces into the rear, except one who remains on the right of every detachment. Each detachment takes poſt on the left of that preceding it, and is examined by the brigade major of the day, as it arrives.

When the whole are aſſembled, the adjutant of the day dreſſes the line, counts the files from right to left, and takes poſt on the right.

The brigade major then commands,

Attention! Shoulder—Firelock! Support—Arms!

Officers and Non-commiſſioned Officers!

To the Centre,—March!

The officers then march to the centre, and form themſelves, according to ſeniority, in one rank, ſixteen paces in front of the guards; the non-commiſſioned officers advance and form two ranks, four paces in the rear of the officers, and with the ſame diſtance between their ranks.

The brigade major then appoints the officers and non-commiſſioned officers to their poſts; the officers in the following manner:

The

The 1st on the right of the	1st
2d on the left of the	8th
3d in the centre, on the right of the	5th
4th on the right of the 2d division, or	3d
5th on the right of the 4th division, or	7th
6th on the right of the	2d
7th on the right of the	8th
8th on the right of the	4th
9th on the right of the	6th
10th in the rear of the	1st
11th in the rear of the	8th
12th in the rear of the	5th
13th in the rear of the	3d
14th in the rear of the	7th
15th in the rear of the	2d
16th in the rear of the	6th
17th in the rear of the	4th
18th in the rear of the	5th
19th in the rear of the	1st
20th in the rear of the	8th

Platoon.

10 19 15 13 17 12 18 16 14 20 11
1.——6——4——8——3.——9——5.——7——2

The non-commiſſioned officers are poſted thus: A ſerjeant on the right of each platoon, and one on the left of the whole; the reſt as file-cloſers equally divided to each platoon.

Whilſt this is doing, the adjutant divides the guard into eight platoons, leaving proper intervals between the platoons for the officers who are to command them.

The brigade major having appointed the officers, and the battalion being divided, he commands,

Officers and Non-commiſſioned Officers!
To your Poſts!

The

The officers and non-commiſſioned officers face outwards from the centre.

March!

They go directly to their poſts in the battalion.

The brigade major then advances to the general officer of the day, informs him that the battalion is formed, and takes his directions relative to the exerciſe.

The general of the day will uſually order the manual exerciſe to be performed, and ſome manœuvres, ſuch as he thinks proper; the major of brigade of the day giving the words of command.

The exerciſe being finiſhed, the major of brigade commands,

Order—Firelocks!

The drums then beat from right to left of the parade, and paſſing behind the officers of the day, take poſt on their left.

The major of brigade then orders,

Shoulder—Firelocks! Support—Arms!

Officers and Non commiſſioned Officers!
To the Centre,—March!

They advance as before to the centre, and the brigade

brigade major appoints them to their respective guards, takes the name of the officer commanding each guard, and gives him the parole and countersign. The adjutant having in the mean time told off the guards, and divided them into platoons, the brigade major then commands,

Officers and Non-commissioned Officers!
To your Posts! March!

The officers go to their respective posts.

The brigade major then commands,

Present—Arms!

And advancing to the general, acquaints him that the guards are formed; and on receiving his orders to march them off, he commands,

Shoulder—Firelocks!
By Platoons! To the Right—Wheel! March!

The whole wheel, and march by the general, the officers saluting him as they pass; and when the whole have passed, they wheel off and march to their respective posts.

ARTICLE 3.

Of relieving Guards and Sentinels.

The guards in camp will be relieved every twenty-four hours. The guards without the limits

limits of the camp will ordinarily be relieved in the ſame manner; but this muſt depend on their diſtances from camp, and other circumſtances, which may ſometimes require their continuing on duty for ſeveral days. In this caſe they muſt be previouſly notified to provide themſelves accordingly.

The guards are to march in the greateſt order to their reſpective poſts, marching by platoons, whenever the roads will permit.

When the new guard approaches the poſt, they carry their arms; and the officer of the old guard, having his guard paraded, on the approach of the new guard, commands,

Preſent——Arms!

and his guard preſent their arms.

The new guard marches paſt the old guard, and takes poſt three or four paces on its right (both guards fronting towards the enemy) and the officer commands,

Preſent——Arms!

and the new guard preſent their arms.

The two officers then approach each other, and the relieving officer takes his orders from the relieved. Both officers then return to their guards, and command,

Shoulder

Shoulder—Firelocks!

Non-commiſſioned Officers! Forward,—March! The non-commiſſioned officers of both guards, who are to relieve the ſentinels, advance in front of the new guard.

The ſerjeant of the new guard then tells off as many ſentinels as are neceſſary; and the corporal of the new guard, conducted by a corporal of the old guard, relieves the ſentinels, beginning by the guard-houſe.

When the ſentinel ſees the relief approach, he preſents his arms, and the corporal halting his relief at ſix paces diſtance, commands,

Preſent--Arms!
Recover--Arms!

This laſt command is only for the ſentinel relieving, and the one to be relieved; the former immediately approaching with the corporal, and having received his orders from the old ſentry, takes his place; and the ſentry relieved marches into the ranks, placing himſelf on the left of the rear rank.

Front--Face!

Both ſentries face to the front. The corporal then orders,

Shoulder—Firelocks! Support—Arms! March!

and the relief proceeds in the ſame manner till the whole are relieved.

If the ſentries are numerous, the ſerjeants are to be employed as well as the corporals in relieving them.

When the corporal returns with the old ſentinels, he leads them before the old guard, and diſmiſſes them to their ranks.

The officer of the old guard then forms his guard in the ſame manner as when he mounted, and marches them in order to camp.

As ſoon as he arrives in the camp, he halts, forms the men of the different brigades together, and ſends them tö their reſpective brigades, conducted by a non-commiſſioned officer, or careful ſoldier.

When the old guard march off, the new guard preſent their arms, 'till they are gone, then ſhoulder, face to the left, and take the place of the old guard.

The officer then orders a non-commiſſioned officer to take down the names of the guard, in the following manner:

Hours

Hours they go on,	10-4, 10-4,	12-6, 12-6,	2-8, 2-8.
	Men's names.	Men's names.	Men's names.
Poſt No. 1.			
2.			
3.			
4.			
5.			
6			
7.			
8.			

Suppoſe, the guard to conſiſt of twenty-four men, and to furniſh eight ſentinels, they are divided into three relieves, and the poſts being numbered (beginning always with the guard-houſe) each man's name is put down againſt the number of the poſt he will always ſtand ſentry at during the guard, by which means an officer knows what particular man was at any poſt during any hour of the day or night.

The relief of ſentries is always to be marched in the greateſt order, and with ſupported arms, the corporal often looking back to obſerve the conduct of the men; and if an officer approaches, he is to order his men to handle their arms, ſupporting them again when he has paſſed.

The corporals are to be anſwerable that the ſentries, when relieving, perform their motions with the greateſt ſpirit and exactneſs.

A corporal who is detected in having the inſolence to ſuffer ſentries to relieve each other, without

without his being preſent, ſhall, as well as the ſentry ſo relieved, be ſeverely puniſhed.

ARTICLE 4.

Inſtructions to Officers on Guard.

On the vigilance of the officer depends not only the ſafety of his guard, but that of the whole army.

As it is highly neceſſary an officer ſhould have ſome knowledge of his ſituation, he muſt, immediately after relieving the old guard, viſit the ſentinels, and examine the ground round his poſt; and if he thinks the ſentries not ſufficient to ſecure him from a ſurprize, he is at liberty to place more, acquainting therewith the general or field officer of the day, who viſits his poſt; but without their leave he is not to alter any that are already poſted. He muſt cauſe the roads leading to the enemy and to the next poſts, to be well reconnoitred by an officer of the guard, or for want of one, by an intelligent non-commiſſioned officer and ſome faithful men, inform himſelf of every thing neceſſary for his ſecurity, and uſe every poſſible precaution againſt a ſurprize. He muſt permit no ſtranger to enter his poſt, nor ſuffer his men to talk with him. If a ſuſpicious perſon, or a deſerter from the enemy approaches, he muſt ſtop him, and ſend him to head

head quarters, or to a ſuperior officer. He muſt on no account ſuffer the ſoldiers to pull off their accoutrements, or ſtraggle more than twenty paces from the guard; and if water or any other neceſſaries are wanted for the guard, they muſt be ſent for by a non-commiſſioned officer and ſome men (with their arms if at an out-poſt) on no account ſuffering a ſoldier to go by himſelf; but never whilſt the ſentinels are relieving. He muſt examine every relief before it is ſent off; ſee that their arms are loaded and in order, and that the men are acquainted with their duty; and if by any accident a man ſhould get the leaſt diſguiſed with liquor, he muſt on no account be ſuffered to go on ſentry.

At every relief the guard muſt parade, and the roll be called; and during the night (and when near the enemy, during the day) the guard muſt remain under arms till the relief returns.

During the day the men may be permitted to reſt themſelves as much as is conſiſtent with the ſafety of the guard; but in the night, no man muſt be ſuffered to lay down or ſleep on any account, but have his arms conſtantly in his hands, and be ready to fall in on the leaſt alarm.

Between every relief the ſentries muſt be viſited by a non-commiſſioned officer and a file of men; and, when more than one officer is on guard,

 as

as often as poſſible by an officer. A patrole alſo muſt be frequently ſent on the roads leading to the enemy.

During the day, the ſentinels on the out-poſts muſt ſtop every party of men, whether armed or not, till they have been examined by the officer of the guard.

As ſoon as it is dark, the counterſign muſt be given to the ſentinels of the piquets and advanced poſts, after which they are to challenge all that approach them; and if any perſon, after being ordered to ſtand, ſhould continue to approach or attempt to eſcape, the ſentry, after challenging him three times, muſt fire on him.

The ſentinels of the interior guards of the camp will receive the counterſign, and begin to challenge, at ſuch hours as ſhall be determined in orders, according to circumſtances.

A ſentinel, on perceiving any perſon approach, muſt challenge briſkly, and never ſuffer more than one to advance, till he has the counterſign given him; if the perſon challenged has not the counterſign, the ſentry muſt call the ſerjeant of the guard, and keep the perſon at a little diſtance from his poſt, till the ſerjeant comes to examine him.

Whenever

Whenever a ſentry on an out-poſt perceives more than three men approach, he muſt order them to ſtand, and immediately paſs the word for the ſerjeant of the guard; the officer of the guard muſt immediately parade his guard, and ſend a ſerjeant with a party of men to examine the party: the non-commiſſioned officer muſt order the commanding officer of the party to advance, and conduct him to the officer of the guard; who, in caſe he is unacquainted with his perſon, and does not chooſe to truſt either to his cloathing or to his knowledge of the counter-ſign, muſt demand his paſsport, and examine him ſtrictly; and if convinced of his belonging to the army, muſt let him paſs.

If a ſentry, on challenging, is anſwered *relief*, *patrole* or *round*, he muſt in that caſe order the ſerjeant or corporal to advance with the counter-ſign; and if he is then aſſured of their being the relief, &c. he may ſuffer them to advance.

A ſentinel muſt take the greateſt care not to be ſurpriſed; he muſt never ſuffer the perſon who advances, to give the counterſign, to approach within reach of his arms, and always charge his bayonet.

The officers who mount the camp guards muſt give orders to their ſentries not to ſuffer any perſon to paſs in or out of camp, except by one of the

the guards, nor then till the officer of the guard has examined him.

In caſe one of the guard deſerts, the officer muſt immediately change the counterſign, and ſend notice thereof to the general of the day; who is to communicate the ſame to the other guards, and the adjutant general.

As ſoon as the officer of a guard diſcovers the approach of the enemy, he muſt immediately ſend notice to the neareſt general officer, call in the ſentries, and put himſelf in the beſt poſture of defence. If attacked on his poſt, he will defend it to the utmoſt of his power, nor retreat, unleſs compelled by ſuperior force; and even then he muſt retire in the greateſt order, keeping a fire on the enemy, whoſe ſuperiority, however great, can never juſtify a guard's retiring in diſorder. Should the enemy purſue a guard into camp, the officer muſt take care to retire through the intervals of the battalions, and forming in the rear of the line, wait for further orders.

When an officer is poſted at a bridge, defile, or any work, with orders to maintain it, he muſt defend himſelf to the laſt extremity, however ſuperior the force of the enemy may be, as it is to be ſuppoſed that the general who gave thoſe orders will reinforce him, or order him to retire whenever he thinks it proper. An

An officer muſt never throw in the whole of his fire at once; for which reaſon every guard is to be divided into two or more diviſions or platoons, according to its ſtrength; any number above eight and under ſeventy-eight men, forming two platoons; the eldeſt officer taking poſt on the right of the firſt platoon, the next eldeſt on the right of the ſecond platoon, and the third on the left of the whole; the non-commiſſioned officers cover the officers; the drum is to be on the right of the captain, and the ſentinel one pace advanced of the drum. If the guard conſiſts of no more than twelve men, it forms in one rank.

ARTICLE 5.

Method of going and receiving the Grand Rounds.

The general and field-officers of the day will viſit the ſeveral guards during the day, as often and at ſuch hours as they judge proper.

When the ſentry before the guard perceives the officer of the day, he will call to the guard to turn out; and the guard, being paraded, on the approach of the officer of the day preſent their arms.

The officer of the day will examine the guard; ſee that none are abſent; that their arms and accoutrements

coutrements are in order; that the officers and non-commiſſioned officers are acquainted with their duty; and that the ſentinels are properly poſted, and have received proper orders.

Not only the officers of the day, but all general officers are at liberty to viſit the guards and make the ſame examination.

The officers of the guard ſhall give the parole to the officer of the day, if demanded.

During the night, the officers of the day will go the grand rounds.

When the officer of the day arrives at the guard from whence he intends to begin his rounds, he will make himſelf known as ſuch, by giving the officer of the guard the parole.--- He will then order the guard under arms, and having examined it, demand an eſcort of a ſerjeant and two men, and proceed to the next poſt.

When the rounds are challenged by a ſentinel, they will anſwer, *Grand rounds!* and the ſentry will reply, *Stand, grand rounds! Advance ſerjeant with the counterſign!* Upon which the ſerjeant advances and gives the counterſign. The ſentinel will then cry, *Advance, rounds!* and preſent his arms till they have paſſed.

When

When the ſentry before the guard challenges, and is anſwered, *Grand rounds!* he will reply, *Stand, grand rounds! Turn out the guard! Grand rounds!* Upon the ſentinel's calling, the guard is to be turned out and drawn up in good order, with ſhouldered arms, the officers taking their poſts. The officer commanding the guard will then order a ſerjeant and two men to advance towards the round and challenge. When the ſerjeant of the guard comes within ten paces of the rounds, he is to halt and challenge briſkly. The ſerjeant of the rounds is to anſwer, *Grand rounds!* The ſerjeant of the guard replies, *Stand, grand rounds! Advance ſerjeant with the counterſign!* and orders his men to preſent their arms. The ſerjeant of the rounds advances alone, and giving the counterſign, returns to his rounds; and the ſerjeant of the guard calls to his officer, *The counterſign is right!* On which the officer of the guard calls, *Advance, rounds!* The officer of the rounds then advances alone, and on his approach the guard preſent their arms. The officer of the rounds paſſes along the front of the guard immediately to the officer (who keeps his poſt on the right) and gives him the parole. He then examines the guard, orders back his eſcort, and demanding a new one, proceeds in the ſame manner to the other guards.

ARTICLE 6.

Honors due from Guards to General Officers and others.

To the commander in chief: All guards turn out with presented arms; the drums beat a march, and the officers salute.

To major generals: They turn out with presented arms, and beat two ruffles.

To brigadier generals: They turn out with presented arms, and beat one ruffle.

To officers of the day: They turn out with presented arms, and beat according to their rank.

Except from these rules a general officer's guard, which turns out and pays honors only to officers of superior rank to the general whose guard it is.

To colonels: Their own quarter guards turn out once a day with presented arms; after which they only turn out with ordered arms:

To lieutenant-colonels: Their own quarter guards turn out once a day with shouldered arms; after which they only turn out and stand by their arms:

To

To majors: Their own quarter guards turn out once a day with ordered arms; at all other times they ſtand by their arms.

When a lieutenant-colonel or major commands a regiment, the quarter guard is to pay him the ſame honors as are ordered to a colonel.

All ſentries preſent their arms to general officers, and to the field-officers of their own regiments; to all other commiſſioned officers they ſtand with ſhouldered arms.

The preſident of congreſs, all governors in their own ſtates, and committees of congreſs at the army, ſhall have the ſame honors paid them as the commander in chief.

When a detachment with arms paſſes before a guard, the guard ſhall be under arms, and the drums of both beat a march.

When a detachment without arms paſſes, the guard ſhall turn out and ſtand by their arms.

After dark no honors are to be paid; and when near the enemy, no honors are to be paid with the drum.

CHAPTER XXII.

Of the Arms and Ammunition, with the Methods of preserving them.

THE preservation of the arms and ammunition is an object that requires the greatest attention. Commanding officers of regiments muſt be anſwerable for thoſe of their regiments, and captains for their reſpective companies.

An officer of a company muſt every morning at roll-call inſpect minutely into the ſtate of the men's arms, accoutrements and ammunition; and if it ſhall appear that a ſoldier has ſold, or through careleſsneſs loſt or damaged any part of them, he muſt be confined and puniſhed, and ſtoppages made of his pay, as hereafter mentioned: For which purpoſe ſuch officer ſhall certify to the commanding officer of the regiment, the names of the delinquents, and the loſſes or damages which ſhall appear of their arms, ammunition and accoutrements; and the commanding officer, after due examination, ſhall order ſtoppages to be made for whatever ſhall appear to have been ſold, loſt or damaged as aforeſaid. The ſtoppages to be as follows:

For a firelock, ſixteen dollars.
a bayonet, two dollars.

For

For a ram-rod, one dollar.
a cartridge-box, four dollars.
a bayonet belt, one dollar.
a fcabbard, two-thirds of a dollar.
a cartridge, one-fixth of a dollar.
a flint, one twentieth of a dollar.
a gun-worm, one-fourth of a dollar.
a fcrew-driver, one-twelfth of a dollar.

And for arms, accoutrements and ammunition damaged, fuch fums as the repairs fhall coft the ftates, to be eftimated by the brigade conductor, or, when a corps is detached, by fuch perfon as its commanding officer fhall appoint for that purpofe; provided that fuch ftoppages do not exceed one half the delinquent's pay monthly.

It is highly effential to the fervice, that the ammunition fhould be at all times kept complete; for which purpofe, as often as is neceffary, a return is to be made by each company of the number of cartridges deficient, to the quarter-mafter, that he may make out a general one for the regiment, to be figned by the commanding officers of the regiment and brigade, and no time loft in fupplying the deficiency. The like care is to be taken that all deficiencies of arms and accoutrements are fupplied without lofs of time.

All arms, accoutrements and ammunition unfit

ſit for ſervice, are to be carefully preſerved and ſent by the commanding officer of each company to the regimental quarter-maſter, who ſhall deliver the ſame to the brigade conductor, they reſpectively giving receipts for what they receive. The arms, accoutrements and ammunition of the ſick and others, when delivered up, are to be taken care of in the ſame manner. Before the cartridge-boxes are put in the arm-cheſts, the cartridges muſt be taken out, to prevent any loſs or accident.

A conductor ſhall be appointed to each brigade, who ſhall have under his immediate care and direction a travelling forge, and five or ſix armourers, an ammunition waggon, and a waggon with an arm-cheſt for each battalion, each cheſt to hold twenty-five arms, to receive the arms and accoutrements wanting repair, or of the men ſick or abſent; and when the arms delivered in by a battalion, ſhall exceed the above number, the ſurplus ſhall be ſent to the commiſſary of military ſtores.

The brigade conductor ſhall iſſue no ammunition, but by order of the commanding officer of the brigade; but may receive and deliver the arms and accoutrements of each battalion, by order of its commanding officer.

The ammunition waggon ſhall contain twenty thouſand

thousand cartridges; and in order to keep the same complete, the conductor shall, as deficiencies arise, apply to the field-commissary, or one of his deputies, for a supply, or otherwise for the necessary materials of cartridges, and to the major of brigade for men to make them up under the direction of the conductor; and for this purpose the brigade major shall order out a party of the most careful soldiers.

The non-commissioned officers of each company will be provided with gun-worms; and every day, at the noon roll-call of the company, those men who have returned from duty are to bring their arms and have their charges drawn; the first serjeant to receive the powder and ball, and deliver the same to the quarter-master.

CHAPTER XXIII.

Of the Treatment of the Sick.

THERE is nothing which gains an officer the love of his soldiers more than his care of them under the distress of sickness; it is then he has the power of exerting his humanity, in providing them every comfortable necessary, and making their situation as agreeable as possible.

Two or three tents ſhould be ſet apart in every regiment for the reception of ſuch ſick as cannot be ſent to the general hoſpital, or whoſe caſes may not require it. And every company ſhall be conſtantly furniſhed with two ſacks, to be filled occaſionally with ſtraw, and ſerve as beds for the ſick. Theſe ſacks to be provided in the ſame manner as cloathing for the troops, and finally iſſued by the regimental clothier to the captain of each company, who ſhall be anſwerable for the ſame.

When a ſoldier dies, or is diſmiſſed from the hoſpital, the ſtraw he lay on is to be burnt, and the bedding well waſhed and aired, before another is permitted to uſe it.

The ſerjeants and corporals ſhall every morning at roll-call give a return of the ſick of their reſpective ſquads to the firſt ſerjeant, who muſt make out one for the company, and loſe no time in delivering it to the ſurgeon, who will immediately viſit them, and order ſuch as he thinks proper to the regimental hoſpital; ſuch whoſe caſes require their being ſent to the general hoſpital, he is to report immediately to the ſurgeon general, or principal ſurgeon attending the army.

Once every week (and oftener when required) the ſurgeon will deliver the commanding officer of the regiment a return of the ſick of the regiment,

regiment, with their diforders, diftinguifhing thofe in the regimental hofpital from thofe out of it.

When a foldier is fent to the hofpital, the non-commiffioned officer of his fquad fhall deliver up his arms and accoutrements to the commanding officer of the company, that they may be depofited in the regimental arm-cheft.

When a foldier has been fick, he muft not be put on duty till he has recovered fufficient ftrength, of which the furgeon fhould be judge.

The furgeons are to remain with their regiment as well on a march as in camp, that in cafe of fudden accidents they may be at hand to apply the proper remedies.

CHAPTER XXIV.

Of Reviews.

ARTICLE I.

Of Reviews of Parade.

WHEN a battalion is to be reviewed, it muft be drawn up in the following manner:

The

The ranks at four paces diſtance from each other; the colours advanced four paces from the centre; the colonel twelve paces before the colours; the lieutenant-colonel four paces behind the colonel; the major on the right of the battalion in the line of officers; the adjutant behind the centre; the officers commanding platoons eight paces before their intervals; and the other officers on the ſame line equally divided in front of their reſpective platoons; the ſerjeants who covered officers take their places in the front rank of their platoons; the other non-commiſſioned officers who were in the rear, remain there, falling back four paces behind the rear rank; and the drummers and fifers are equally divided on the wings of the battalion, dreſſing with the front rank. The general officer who is to review them being within thirty paces of the battalion, the colonel orders

Battalion! Preſent—Arms!

On which the men preſent their arms, and the drums on the right wing ſalute him according to his rank; the officers and colours ſalute him as he paſſes in front of the battalion; and on his arriving at the left, the drums beat the ſame as on the right.

The colonel then commands

Shoulder—Firelocks!

And

And when the general has advanced to the front,

Rear rank! Cloſe to the Front!

On which the officers face to their platoons.

March!

The rear rank cloſes to the front, and the officers ſtepping off at the ſame time, thoſe commanding platoons take their poſts in the front rank, and the others go through the intervals to their poſts in the rear.

The colonel then commands

Battalion!

By Platoons! To the Right,—Wheel! March!

The whole wheel by platoons to the right, and march by the general; the colonel at the head of the battalion, with the major behind him, followed by the drums of the right wing; the adjutant on the left of the fifth platoon; and the lieutenant-colonel in the rear, preceded by the drums of the left wing.

The officers and colours ſalute when within eight paces of the general; and the colonel having ſaluted, advances to him.

The battalion having marched to its ground and formed, the general orders ſuch exerciſe and manœuvres as he thinks proper.

ARTICLE 2.

Of Reviews of Inſpection.

For a review of inſpection the battalion muſt not be told off into platoons, but remain in companies, at open order; the drums and fifes on the right, and the enſigns with the colours in front of their reſpective companies.

The inſpector begins with a general review, paſſing along the front of the battalion from right to left, accompanied by the field and ſtaff officers. The general review over, the colonel commands,

Rear Rank! Cloſe to the Front! March!

The rear rank cloſes to the front, the officers remaining in front.

By Companies! To the Right,—Wheel! March!

Each company wheels to the right; the captains then open their ranks, and order

Non-commiſſioned Officers! To the Front,—March!

The officers take poſt four paces, and the non-commiſſioned officers two paces, in front of their companies.

The whole then order their firelocks by word of command from their captains, except the firſt company, where the inſpection begins; when the firſt company has been inſpected, they order their firelocks, and the next company ſhoulders; the others proceed in the ſame manner till the whole are inſpected.

The field and ſtaff officers accompany the inſpector while he inſpects the companies; and when the inſpection is over, the colonel forms the battalion, and cauſes it to perform any exerciſe or manœuvres the inſpector thinks proper to order.

INSTRUCTIONS.

Inſtructions for the Commandant of a Regiment.

THE ſtate having entruſted him with the care of a regiment, his greateſt ambition ſhould be to have it at all times and in every reſpect as complete as poſſible: To do which, he ſhould pay great attention to the following objects.

The preſervation of the ſoldiers health ſhould be his firſt and greateſt care; and as that depends in a great-meaſure on their cleanlineſs and manner of living, he muſt have a watchful eye over the officers of companies, that they pay the neceſſary attention to their men in thoſe reſpects.

The only means of keeping the ſoldiers in order is, to have them continually under the eyes of their ſuperiors; for which reaſon the commandant ſhould uſe the utmoſt ſeverity to prevent their ſtraggling from their companies, and never ſuffer them to leave the regiment, without being under the care of a non-commiſſioned officer, except in caſes of neceſſity. And in order

der to prevent any man's being abſent from the regiment without his knowledge, he muſt often count the files, and ſee that they agree with the returns delivered him, ſtrictly obliging every man returned fit for duty to appear under arms on all occaſions; and if any are miſſing, he muſt oblige the commanding officer of the company to account for their abſence. In a word, the commandant ought to know upon what duty and where every man of his regiment is. To theſe points the other field officers muſt alſo pay attention.

The choice of non-commiſſioned officers is alſo an object of the greateſt importance: The order and diſcipline of a regiment depends ſo much upon *their* behaviour, that too much care cannot be taken in preferring none to that truſt but thoſe who by their merit and good conduct are entitled to it. Honeſty, ſobriety, and a remarkable attention to every point of duty, with a neatneſs in their dreſs, are indiſpenſable requiſites; a ſpirit to command reſpect and obedience from the men, an expertneſs in performing every part of the exerciſe, and an ability to teach it, are alſo abſolutely neceſſary; nor can a ſerjeant or corporal be ſaid to be qualified who does not write and read in a tolerable manner.

Once every month the commandant ſhould make a general inſpection of his regiment, examine into the ſtate of the men, their arms, ammunition, accoutrements, neceſſaries, camp utenſils, and every thing belonging to the regiment, obliging the commanding officers of companies to account ſtrictly for all deficiencies.

He ſhould alſo once every month aſſemble the field officers and the eldeſt captain, to hold a council of adminiſtration; in which ſhould be examined the books of the ſeveral companies, the pay-maſter and quarter-maſter, to ſee that all receipts and deliveries are entered in proper order, and the affairs of the regiment duly adminiſtered.

All returns of the regiment being ſigned by the commanding officer, he ſhould examine them with the greateſt care before he ſuffers them to go out of his hands.

The commandant muſt always march and encamp with his regiment; nor muſt he permit any officer to lodge out of camp, or in a houſe, except in caſe of ſickneſs.

On a march he muſt keep his regiment together as much as poſſible, and not ſuffer the officers to leave their platoons without his permiſſion; nor permit any of them, on any pretence whatſoever, to mount on horſeback. There is no fatigue the ſoldiers go through, that the officers

ficers ſhould not ſhare; and on all occaſions they ſhould ſet them examples of patience and perſeverance.

When a regiment is on a march, the commandant will order a ſerjeant and ſix men into the rear, to bring up all ſtragglers; and the ſerjeant, on his arrival in camp or quarters, muſt make his report to him.

In a word, the commanding officer of a regiment muſt preſerve the ſtricteſt diſcipline and order in his corps, obliging every officer to a ſtrict performance of his duty, without relaxing in the ſmalleſt point; puniſhing impartially the faults that are committed, without diſtinction of rank or ſervice.

Inſtructions for the Major.

THE major is particularly charged with the diſcipline, arms, accoutrements, cloathing, and generally, with the whole interior management and œconomy of the regiment.

He muſt have a watchful eye over the officers, and oblige them to do their duty on every occaſion; he muſt often cauſe them to be exerciſed in his preſence, and inſtruct them how to command their platoons and preſerve their diſtances.

He

He muſt endeavor to make his regiment perform their exerciſe and manœuvres with the greateſt vivacity and preciſion, examine often the ſtate of the different companies, making the captains anſwer for any deficiencies he may perceive, and reporting the ſame to the colonel.

He muſt pay the greateſt attention to have all orders executed with the ſtricteſt punctuality, ſo far as reſpects his regiment; and ſhould every week examine the adjutant's and quarter-maſter's books, and ſee that all returns, orders, and other matters, the objects of their reſpective duties, are regularly entered.

He muſt cauſe to be kept a regimental book, wherein ſhould be entered the name and rank of every officer, the date of his commiſſion, and the time he joined the regiment; the name and deſcription of every non-commiſſioned officer and ſoldier, his trade or occupation, the place of his birth and uſual reſidence, where, when and for what term he was enliſted; diſcharges, furloughs and courts martial, copies of all returns, and every caſualty that happens in the regiment.

He muſt be at all times well acquainted with the ſtrength of his regiment and brigade, and the details of the army, and ſee that his regiment furniſhes no more than its proportion for duty.

He

He muſt often inſpect the detachments for duty furniſhed by his regiment, ſee that they are complete in every reſpect, and formed agreeably to the regulations.

On a march he muſt often ride along the flanks of his regiment, ſee that the platoons march in order, and keep their proper diſtances.

When the regiment is detached, he will poſt the guards ordered by the colonel, often viſit them, examine whether the officers, non-commiſſioned officers and ſentinels are acquainted with their duty, and give inſtructions.

Inſtructions for the Adjutant.

THE adjutant is to be choſen from among the ſubalterns, the field officers taking care to nominate one the moſt intelligent and beſt acquainted with the ſervice.

He muſt keep an exact detail of the duty of the officers and non-commiſſioned officers of his regiment, taking care to regulate his roſter in ſuch a manner as not to have too many officers or non-commiſſioned officers of the ſame company on duty at the ſame time.

He muſt keep a book, in which he muſt every

 day

day take the general and other orders, and ſhew them to the commanding officer of the regiment, who having added theſe he thinks neceſſary for the regiment, the adjutant muſt aſſemble the firſt ſerjeants of the companies, make them copy the orders, and give them their details for the next day.

He muſt attend the parade at the turning out of all guards or detachments, inſpect their dreſs, arms, accoutrements and ammunition, form them into platoons or ſections, and conduct them to the general or brigade parade.

When the regiment parades for duty or exerciſe, he muſt count it off, and divide it into diviſions and platoons, and carry the orders of the colonel where neceſſary.

The adjutant is to receive no orders but from the field officers and officer commanding a battalion.

On a march he muſt ride along the flanks of the regiment, to ſee that regularity is obſerved, and muſt pay attention to the ſerjeant in the rear, that he brings up all ſtragglers.

On the arrival of the regiment in camp, his firſt care is to form and ſend off the guards; and when the tents are pitched, he muſt immediately

diately order out the neceſſary number of fatigue men to dig the vaults or ſinks, and open the communications where neceſſary. He will then form the detachments for wood, water, and other neceſſaries.

He muſt be conſtantly with the regiment, ready to receive and execute any orders that may come; nor muſt he go from his tent without leaving an officer to do his duty, or directions where he may be found.

Inſtructions for the Quarter-Maſter.

THE quarter-maſter, being charged with encamping and quartering the regiment, ſhould be at all times acquainted with its ſtrength, that he may require no more ground than is neceſſary, nor have more tents pitched than the number preſcribed: for both which he is accountable.

He muſt inform the regiment where to fetch their wood, water and other neceſſaries, and where to paſture the horſes.

He muſt inſtruct the quarter-maſter ſerjeant and pioneers in the manner of laying out the camp, agreeably to the order preſcribed in the regulations.

He

He is anſwerable for the cleanlineſs of the camp, and that the ſoldiers make no ſire any where but in the kitchens.

When the army marches, he muſt conduct the pioneers to the place appointed, and order the quarter-maſter ſerjeant to take charge of the baggage.

He is to make out all returns for camp equipage, arms, accoutrements, ammunition, proviſions and forage, and receive and diſtribute them to the regiment, taking the neceſſary vouchers for the delivery, and entering all receipts and deliveries in a book kept by him for that purpoſe.

He muſt pay particular attention to the preſervation of the camp equipage, cauſe the neceſſary repairs to be done when wanting, and return every thing unfit for uſe to the ſtores from which he drew them.

The preſervation of the arms, accoutrements and ammunition is of ſuch eſſential importance, that he muſt be ſtrictly attentive to have thoſe of the ſick, of the men on furlough, diſcharged, or detached on command without arms, taken care of and depoſited with the brigade conductor, as directed in the regulations.

Inſtructions for the Captain.

A CAPTAIN cannot be too careful of the company the ſtate has committed to his charge. He muſt pay the greateſt attention to the health of his men, their diſcipline, arms, accoutrements, ammunition, clothes and neceſſaries.

His firſt object ſhould be, to gain the love of his men, by treating them with every poſſible kindneſs and humanity, inquiring into their complaints, and when well founded, ſeeing them redreſſed. He ſhould know every man of his company by name and character. He ſhould often viſit thoſe who are ſick, ſpeak tenderly to them, ſee that the public proviſion, whether of medicine or diet, is duly adminiſtered, and procure them beſides ſuch comforts and conveniencies as are in his power. The attachment that ariſes from this kind of attention to the ſick and wounded, is almoſt inconceivable; it will moreover be the means of preſerving the lives of many valuable men.

He muſt divide his company into four ſquads, placing each under the particular care of a non-commiſſioned officer, who is to be anſwerable for the dreſs and behaviour of the men of his ſquad.

He

He muſt be very particular in the daily and weekly inſpections of his men, cauſing all deficiencies to be immediately ſupplied; and when he diſcovers any irregularity in the dreſs or conduct of any ſoldier, he muſt not only puniſh him, but the non-commiſſioned officer to whoſe ſquad he belongs.

He muſt keep a ſtrict eye over the conduct of the non-commiſſioned officers; oblige them to do their duty with the greateſt exactneſs; and uſe every poſſible means to keep up a proper ſubordination between them and the ſoldiers: For which reaſon he muſt never rudely reprimand them in preſence of the men, but at all times treat them with proper reſpect.

He muſt pay the utmoſt attention to every thing which contributes to the health of the men, and oblige them to keep themſelves and every thing belonging to them in the greateſt cleanlineſs and order. He muſt never ſuffer a man who has any infectious diſorder to remain in the company, but ſend him immediately to the hoſpital, or other place provided for the reception of ſuch patients, to prevent the ſpreading of the infection. And when any man is ſick, or otherwiſe unfit for duty, or abſent, he muſt ſee that his arms and accoutrements are properly taken care of, agreeably to the regulations preſcribed.

He

He muſt keep a book, in which muſt be entered the name and deſcription of every non-commiſſioned officer and ſoldier of his company; his trade or occupation; the place of his birth and uſual reſidence; where, when and for what term he inliſted; diſcharges, furloughs, copies of all returns, and every caſualty that happens in the company. He muſt alſo keep an account of all arms, accoutrements, ammunition, cloathing, neceſſaries and camp equipage delivered his company, that on inſpecting it he may be able to diſcover any deficiencies.

When the company arrive at their quarters after a march, he muſt not diſmiſs them till the guards are ordered out, and (if cantoned) the billets diſtributed, which muſt be as near together as poſſible; and he muſt ſtrictly prohibit his men from vexing the inhabitants, and cauſe to be puniſhed any that offend in that reſpect, He muſt acquaint them with the hours of roll-call and going for proviſions, with their alarm poſt, and the hour of march in the morning.

If the company make any ſtay in a place, he muſt, previous to their marching, inſpect into their condition, examine their knapſacks, and ſee that they carry nothing but what is allowed, it being a material object to prevent the ſoldier loading himſelf with unneceſſary baggage.

Inſtructions for the Lieutenant.

THE lieutenant, in the abſence of the captain, commands the company, and ſhould therefore make himſelf acquainted with the duties of that ſtation; he muſt alſo be perfectly acquainted with the duties of the non-commiſſioned officers and ſoldiers, and ſee them performed with great exactneſs.

He ſhould endeavour to gain the love of his men, by his attention to every thing which may contribute to their health and convenience. He ſhould often viſit them at different hours; inſpect into their manner of living; ſee that their proviſions are good and well cooked, and as far as poſſible oblige them to take their meals at regulated hours. He ſhould pay attention to their complaints, and when well founded, endeavour to get them redreſſed; but diſcourage them from complaining on every frivolous occaſion.

He muſt not ſuffer the ſoldiers to be ill-treated by the non-commiſſioned officers through malevolence, or from any pique or reſentment; but muſt at the ſame time be careful that a proper degree of ſubordination is kept up between them.

Although no officer ſhould be ignorant of the ſervice of the guards, yet it particularly behoves the lieutenant to be perfectly acquainted with that

that duty; he being oftener than any other officer entrufted with the command of a guard—a truft of the higheft importance, on the faithful execution of which the fafety of an army depends; and in which the officer has frequent opportunities to diftinguifh himfelf by his judgement, vigilance, and bravery.

Inftructions for the Enfign.

THE enfign is in a particular manner charged with the cleanlinefs of the men, to which he muft pay the greateft attention.

When the company parades and whilft the captain and lieutenant are examining the arms and accoutrements, the enfign muft infpect the drefs of the foldiers, obferving whether they are clean, and every thing about them in the beft order poffible, and duly noticing any who in thefe refpects are deficient.

He muft be very attentive to the conduct of the non-commiffioned officers, obferving that they do their duty with the greateft exactnefs; that they fupport a proper authority, and at the fame time do not ill-treat the men through any pique or refentment.

As there are only two colours to a regiment,

 the

the enfigns muft carry them by turns, being warned for that fervice by the adjutant. When on that duty, they fhould confider the importance of the truft repofed in them; and when in action, refolve not to part with the colours but with their lives. As it is by them the battalion dreffes when marching in line, they fhould be very careful to keep a regular ftep, and by frequent practice accuftom themfelves to march ftright forward to any given object.

Inftructions for the Serjeant Major.

THE ferjeant major, being at the head of the non-commiffioned officers, muft pay the greateft attention to their conduct and behaviour, never conniving at the leaft irregularity committed by them or the foldiers, from both of whom he muft exact the moft implicit obedience. He fhould be well acquainted with the interior management and difcipline of the regiment, and the manner of keeping rofters and forming details. He muft always attend the parade, be very expert in counting off the battalion, and in every other bufinefs of the adjutant, to whom he is an affiftant.

Inftructions for the Quarter-Mafter Serjeant.

HE is an affiftant to the quarter-mafter of the regiment, and in his abfence is to do his

his duty, unlefs an officer be fpecially appointed for that purpofe: He fhould therefore acquaint himfelf with all the duties of the quarter-mafter before mentioned. When the army marches, he muft fee the tents properly packed and loaded, and go with the baggage, fee that the waggoners commit no diforders, and that nothing is loft out of the waggons.

Inftructions for the Firft Serjeant of a Company.

THE foldier having acquired that degree of confidence of his officers as to be appointed firft ferjeant of the company, fhould confider the importance of his office; that the difcipline of the company, the conduct of the men, their exactnefs in obeying orders, and the regularity of their manners, will in a great meafure depend on his vigilance.

He fhould be intimately acquainted with the character of every foldier of the company, and fhould take great pains to imprefs upon their minds the indifpenfable neceffity of the ftricteft obedience, as the foundation of order and regularity.

He will keep the details of the company, and never warn a man out of his turn, unlefs particularly ordered fo to do.

He

He muſt take the daily orders in a book kept by him for that purpoſe, and ſhew them to his officers.

He muſt every morning make a report to the captain of the ſtate of the company, in the form preſcribed; and at the ſame time acquaint him with any thing material that may have happened in the company ſince the preceeding report.

He muſt parade all guards and detachments furniſhed by his company, examine their arms, ammunition, accoutrements and dreſs, before he carries them to the parade; and if any man appears unfit, he muſt ſupply his place with another, and have the defaulter puniſhed: For this purpoſe he muſt always warn a man or two more than ordered, to ſerve as a reſerve, who, if not wanted, will return to their companies.

He will keep the company book (under the inſpection of the captain) in which he will enter the name and deſcription of every non-commiſſioned officer and ſoldier; his trade and occupation; the place of his birth and uſual reſidence; where, when and for what term he was inliſted; the bounty paid him; the arms, ammunition, accoutrements, cloathing and neceſſaries delivered him, with their marks and numbers, and the times when delivered; alſo copies of all returns, furloughs, diſcharges, and every caſualty that happens in the company.

When

When each foldier fhall be provided with a fmall book, the firft ferjeant is to enter therein the foldier's name, a copy of his inliftments, the bounty paid him, the arms, accoutrements, cloathing and neceffaries delivered him, with their marks and numbers: For this purpofe he muft be prefent at all diftributions in his company; and as often as arms, cloathing, &c. are delivered, he muft enter them in the foldier's as well as the company's book.

The firft ferjeant is not to go on duty, unlefs with the whole company; but he is to be always in camp or quarters, to anfwer any call that may be made.

He is never to lead a platoon or fection, but is always to be a file-clofer in the formation of the company, his duty being in the company like the adjutant's in the regiment.

Inftructions for the Serjeants and Corporals.

IT being on the non-commiffioned officers that the difcipline and order of a company in a great meafure depend, they cannot be too circumfpect in their behaviour towards the men, by treating them mildnefs, and at the fame time obliging every one to do his duty. By avoiding too great familiarity with the men, they will not only gain their love and confidence, but be treated with a proper refpect; whereas by a contrary conduct they forfeit all regard, and their authority becomes defpifed.

Each ferjeant and corporal will be in a particular manner anfwerable for the fquad committed to his care. He muft pay particular attention to their conduct in every refpect; that they keep themfelves and their arms always clean; that they have their effects always ready, and put where they can get them immediately, even in the dark, without confufion; and on every fine day he muft oblige them to air their effects.

When a man of his fquad is warned for duty, he muft examine him before he carries him to the parade, obliging him to take all his effects with him, unlefs when fpecially ordered to the contrary.

In teaching the recruits, they muft exercife all their patience, by no means abufing them, but treating them with mildnefs, and not expect too much precifion in their firft leffons, punifhing thofe only who are wilfully negligent.

They muft fupprefs all quarrels and difputes in the company; and where other means fail, muft ufe their authority in confining the offender.

They

They ſhould teach the ſoldiers of their ſquads how to dreſs with a ſoldier-like air, how to clean their arms, accoutrements, &c. and how to mount and diſmount their firelocks; for which purpoſe each non-commiſſioned officer ſhould always be provided with a turnſcrew, and ſuffer no ſoldier to take his arms to pieces without his permiſſion.

On a march the non-commiſſioned officers muſt preſerve order and regularity, and ſuffer no man to leave the ranks without permiſſion of the officer commanding the platoon.

A corporal muſt teach the ſentinels to challenge briſkly, and every thing elſe they are to do in their different ſituations; and when he relieves them, muſt make them deliver the orders diſtinctly.

When a guard is relieved, the non-commiſſioned officers take the orders from thoſe whom they relieve; when ſent to viſit the ſentries, they ſhould inſtruct them in their duty. They ſhould reconnoitre the roads they are to patrol in the night, that they may not loſe themſelves. They muſt make their patrol with the greateſt ſilence and attention, and where neceſſary, ſend a faithful ſoldier a-head to look out. If they meet a detachment of the enemy ſtronger than their own, they muſt retreat in order to their own poſt. In the night they muſt ſtop all ſtrangers that approach.

proach. They muſt not ſuffer their men to make the leaſt noiſe with their arms or accoutrements, and every now and then ſtop and liſten. On their return from patroling, they muſt report to the officer what they ſeen or heard.

When a non-commiſſioned officer is a file-cloſer in an action, he muſt take care to keep the ranks and files properly cloſed, and when too much crowded, make them incline from the centre. When the files of his platoon are diſordered by the loſs of men, he muſt exert himſelf to dreſs and complete them afreſh, with the utmoſt expedition. He muſt keep the greateſt ſilence in the ranks, ſee that the men load well and quick, and take good aim. He will do all in his power to encourage the ſoldiers, and uſe the moſt vigorous means to prevent any from leaving the ranks, unleſs wounded.

Inſtructions for the private Soldier.

THE recruit having received his neceſſaries, ſhould in the firſt place learn to dreſs himſelf with a ſoldier-like air; to place his effects properly in his knapſack, ſo as to carry them with eaſe and convenience; how to ſalute his officers when he meets them; to clean his arms, waſh his linen and cook his proviſions. He ſhould early accuſtom himſelf to dreſs in the night;

night; and for that purpoſe always have his effects in his knapſack, and that placed where he can put his hand on it in a moment, that in caſe of alarm he may repair with the greateſt alertneſs to the parade.

When learning to march, he muſt take the greateſt pains to acquire a firm ſtep and a proper balance, practiſing himſelf at all his leiſure hours. He muſt accuſtom himſelf to the greateſt ſteadineſs under arms, to pay attention to the commands of his officers, and exerciſe himſelf continually with his firelock, in order to acquire vivacity in his motions. He muſt acquaint himſelf with the uſual beats and ſignals of the drum, and inſtantly obey them.

When in the ranks, he muſt always learn the names of his right and left hand men and file-leader, that he may be able to find his place readily in caſe of ſeparation. He muſt cover his file-leader and dreſs well in his rank, which he may be aſſured of doing when he can juſt perceive the breaſt of the third man from him. Having joined his company, he muſt no longer conſider himſelf as a recruit, but as as a ſoldier; and whenever he is ordered under arms, muſt appear well dreſſed, with his arms and accoutrements clean and in good order, and his knapſack, blanket, &c. ready to throw on his back in caſe he ſhould be ordered to take them.

When

When warned for guard, he muſt appear as neat as poſſible, carry all his effects with him, and even when on ſentry muſt have them at his back. He muſt receive the orders from the ſentry he relieves; and when placed before the guard-houſe, he muſt inform the corporal of all that approach, and ſuffer no one to enter until examined; if he is poſted at a diſtance from the guard he will march there in order, have the orders well explained to him by the corporal, learn which is the neareſt poſt between him and the guard, in caſe he ſhould be obliged to retire, or have any thing to communicate, and what he is to do in caſe of an alarm; or if in town, in caſe of fire and any diſturbance. He will never go more than twenty paces from his poſt; and if in a retired place, or in the night, ſuffer no one to approach within ten paces of him.

A ſentinel muſt never reſt upon his arms, but keep walking on his poſt. He muſt never ſuffer himſelf to be relieved but by his corporal; challenge briſkly in the night, and ſtop thoſe who have not the counterſign; and if any will not anſwer to the third challenge, or having been ſtopped ſhould attempt to eſcape, he may fire on them.

When on patrol, he muſt obſerve the ſtricteſt ſilence, nor make the leaſt noiſe with his arms or accoutrements.

In

In action he will pay the greatest attention to the commands of his officers, level well, and not throw away his fire; take particular care to keep his rank and file, incline to that side he dresses to, and encourage his comrades to do their duty.

When ordered to march he must not charge himself with any unnecessary baggage; he will march at his ease, without however leaving his rank or file; he should drink as seldom as possible, and never stop but when necessity obliges him; in which case he must ask leave of the commanding officer of the platoon.

When arrived at camp or quarters, he must clean his arms, prepare his bed, and go for necessaries, taking nothing without leave, nor committing any kind of excess.

He must always have a stopper for the muzzle of his gun in case of rain, and when on a march; at which times he will unfix his bayonet.

F I N I S.

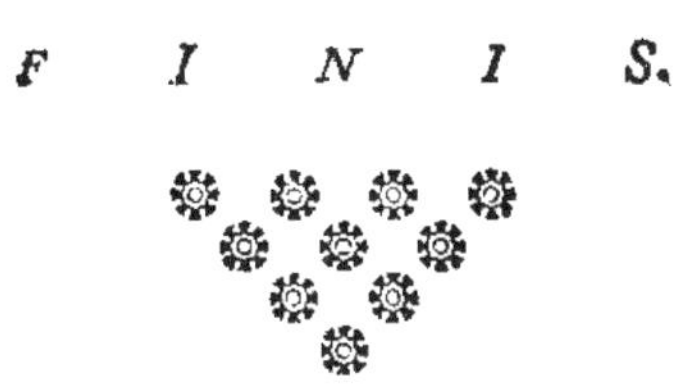

EATING THE ENLIGHTENMENT

EATING THE ENLIGHTENMENT

Food and the Sciences in Paris

E.C. SPARY

THE UNIVERSITY OF CHICAGO PRESS
CHICAGO AND LONDON

E. C. SPARY is a lecturer in the faculty of history at the University of Cambridge. She is the author of *Utopia's Garden: French Natural History from Old Regime to Revolution* and coeditor of *Materials and Expertise in Early Modern Europe: Between Market and Laboratory*, both published by the University of Chicago Press.

The University of Chicago Press, Chicago 60637
The University of Chicago Press, Ltd., London
© 2012 by The University of Chicago
All rights reserved. Published 2012.
Printed in the United States of America

21 20 19 18 17 16 15 14 13 12   1 2 3 4 5

ISBN-13: 978-0-226-76886-1 (cloth)
ISBN-13: 978-0-226-76888-5 (e-book)
ISBN-10: 0-226-76886-4 (cloth)
ISBN-10: 0-226-76888-0 (e-book)

Library of Congress Cataloging-in-Publication Data

Spary, E. C. (Emma C.)
Eating the Enlightenment : food and the sciences in Paris / E. C. Spary.
pages. cm.
Includes bibliographical references and index.
ISBN-13: 978-0-226-76886-1 (cloth : alkaline paper)
ISBN-10: 0-226-76886-4 (cloth : alkaline paper)
ISBN-13: 978-0-226-76888-5 (e-book)
ISBN-10: 0-226-76888-0 (e-book)
1. Diet—France—Paris—History—18th century. 2. Gastronomy—France—Paris—History—18th century. 3. Nutrition—France—Paris—History—18th century. 4. Paris (France)—Intellectual life—18th century. 5. Enlightenment—France—Paris—History—18th century. I. Title.
GT2853.F8S737 2012
394.1'20944—dc23

2011050358

♾ This paper meets the requirements of ANSI/NISO Z39.48-1992 (Permanence of Paper).

AUX MÂNES DE MON PÈRE

MARTIN CHARLES SPARY (1939–2008)

qui aurait été content de recevoir une dédicace en français

CONTENTS

ILLUSTRATIONS

ACKNOWLEDGMENTS

For useful interventions, interesting conversations, insightful observations, extensive or intensive commentaries, or just moral support, I am especially grateful to Guy Attewell, Vincent Barras, Maxine Berg, Melissa Calaresu, Kyri Claflin, Lucia Dacome, Raine Daston, James Delbourgo, Anne Janowitz, Nick Jardine, Colin Jones, Ursula Klein, Micheline Louis-Courvoisier, Jenny Mander, Sévérine Pilloud, Daniel Roche, Anne Secord, Daniela Sechel, Rebecca Spang, Stéphane Vandamme, Paul White, and Elizabeth Williams. I am of course indebted to many more friends and family members who for reasons of space cannot be named individually here, plus the audiences at many seminars and conferences. All translations from the French are my own, except where stated.

My thanks must also go to my colleagues at various institutions: the Eighteenth-Century Studies Centre at the University of Warwick; Abteilung II of the Max-Planck-Institut für Wissenschaftsgeschichte, Berlin; the sadly missed Wellcome Trust Centre for the History of Medicine at University College London; the Department of History and Philosophy of Science and the Faculty of History at the University of Cambridge.

This project has been slow to come to fruition. Its development coincided with the first appearance of electronic databases, search engines, and digitized media, which facilitated its wide-ranging exploration of primary materials. All those unsung heroes of digitization deserve thanks, too, as do the staff of libraries and archives in different parts of Europe. Without them, this book would not have been possible.

Last, but not least, many thanks to Karen Darling at Chicago and her team for bringing the book into the public domain.

INTRODUCTION

Like many major European capitals in the eighteenth century, Paris was a city of people fascinated with new knowledge. Visitors remarked on the fact that even servant girls were to be seen reading in the streets, while whole areas of the city were devoted to bookshops, cabinets of curiosities, and scientific demonstrations. Libraries, cabinets, and scientific devices increasingly filled the houses of literate families.[1] This book takes one particular aspect of everyday life, namely eating, to explore some of the ways in which that increasingly public culture of knowledge made a difference to the daily life of literate Parisians between 1675 and 1760. My argument in *Eating the Enlightenment* is that by attending to the history of an everyday activity such as eating, we are able to understand both "science" and "Enlightenment" in new ways.[2]

The history of food in eighteenth-century Paris is intimately bound up with the history of knowledge, and with the formation of a public space where political critique, consumption, and commerce took place, mediated by print. The classic account of the Enlightenment by Peter Gay modeled knowledge in terms of free-floating quasi-autonomous ideas hatched in the minds of great men, and transmission as a matter of influences operating upon a largely passive and undifferentiated public.[3] In recent years, historians of the book, together with historians and sociologists of science, have come to present knowledge very differently: as transaction, appropriation,

1. Bensaude-Vincent and Blondel 2007; Lynn 2006; Sutton 1995; Kennedy 1989, 38; Roche 1987, 206–9; Laissus 1986.

2. Broman 1998 makes an eloquent plea for such an endeavor, although the history of eating is perhaps not the subject he had in mind.

3. Gay 1966–69; see also, more recently, Israel 2006, 2001.

and negotiation, and so as something that is provisional and consensual.[4] Historians of science have attended to natural knowledge as the outcome of locally reliable practices and meanings; in the words of Charles Withers, "Rather than treat the Enlightenment as a corpus of self-contained ideas circulating without reference to their local sites of social making, it is possible to consider it as situated and multiple practices, concerned in different places and in different ways with different conceptions of practical reason, natural philosophy, and so on."[5]

To take such an approach is to break radically with the program of characterizing "the" Enlightenment as a movement typified by set political, social, and epistemological goals, with a named and familiar population of practitioners. Instead, it is to assume that in a culture like eighteenth-century Paris, where many consumers laid claim to knowledge of one sort or another about food and its effects on the body, the exact content of the category "enlightenment" was a work in progress, accomplished through a variety of encounters, only some of which involved famous philosophes such as Voltaire, Rousseau, or Diderot, who now constitute the "big names" of Enlightenment historiography. Laying claim to enlightenment involved self-fashioning, writing, publishing, reading, and, as this book will demonstrate, eating. My title, *Eating the Enlightenment*, thus alludes to a controversy over what, if anything, enlightenment still means for historians in the wake of that turn toward the local. Laurence Brockliss, calling on historians to attend to the Republic of Letters instead, questions how useful "the Enlightenment" can be as an analytical category; as he notes, "there is no pan-European consensus as to the movement's origin, content and membership." In this book, "enlightenment" is not treated as a movement or community amenable to prosopography. My own use of the term should be understood as an English gloss upon the French word "*lumières*," as used, for example, by Daniel Roche.[6] As Diego Venturino shows, the expression "*siècle des lumières*" as a name for an eighteenth-century intellectual movement only came into general use in the mid-twentieth century. Eighteenth-century authors deployed the metaphor of light, "*lumières*," to comment on the state of learning of their day, rather than to define one particular knowledge project or learned community. To say that an individual possessed *lu-*

4. E.g., Fish 1980; Holub 2003; Suleiman and Crosman 1980; Chartier 1987a; Johns 1998; Secord 2000.

5. Withers 2007, 64–65; see also Ophir and Shapin 1991. On practice, see, e.g., Latour 1987; Pickering 1992, 1995; Lynch 1993; Buchwald 1995; Golinski 1998; Schatzki and Knorr Cetina 2001.

6. Brockliss 2002, 8; Roche 1988.

mières did not imply membership of a coherent intellectual movement, but rather indicated that that person had publicly acknowledged expertise in some domain of knowledge. Enlightenment here—rather than "the" Enlightenment—was thus a state to which individuals might aspire, or which they might cultivate. Such a definition has heuristic value for historians in that it allows for a broad range of claimants to *lumières* to be included in a study of early modern learning. The reasons for the success or failure of particular enlightened self-presentations can be scrutinized on their own terms, freeing historians from the need to adjudicate about the legitimacy of past pretensions to a learned or expert state. Thus, while agreeing in broad terms with Brockliss's critique, I find the term "enlightenment" too useful to abandon; its use ought at the least to direct our attention to the fact that new conditions of scholarship arising in the eighteenth century would open up new routes for laying claim to a state of learning, as well as facilitating new critiques of older scholarly personae. Most prominent among these new conditions was the rise of a world of public commentary, enshrined in a flourishing print culture.[7]

The expression "siècle philosophe" was also used by eighteenth-century authors of their own time, as in Denis Diderot's article "Encyclopédie" in the eponymous work. Yet to fall back upon a category of "philosophes" on which to ground "the" Enlightenment as a cohesive social group or body of ideas offers no solution to the teleological double-bind afflicting Enlightenment historiography, for the appelation "philosophe" was equally contested and fluid. In practice, it could denote quite incompatible sets of values; in the words of Conal Condren, Stephen Gaukroger, and Ian Hunter, "disputes over philosophical problems quickly become disputes over what is to count as philosophy and what it is to be a philosopher."[8] To take the definition of rationality as something that was always already settled is to privilege the winners' interpretation of what counted as enlightenment and who could lay claim to it. Rationality and learning were attributed states, an outcome as much as a cause of past disputes. Indeed, those disputes were precisely what *created* something that could retrospectively be designated as "the" Enlightenment. So one central aim of this book is to investigate the public

7. Venturino 2002, esp. 59–76; Mah 2003, introduction. Here I distance my approach markedly from recent essentialist revivals of "the" Enlightenment such as O'Brien 2011; Robertson 2005.

8. Condren, Gaukroger, and Hunter 2006, 8. See also Sutton 1995; Bury 1996, 199–203; Yeo 2006, 257; Darnton 1996, 1979; Badinter 1999–2007; Brockliss 2002, introduction; Brewer 2002. By the 1760s the title of "philosophe" was synonymous with "atheist" for many commentators; see, e.g., Pekacz 1999, 111–12.

domain as a space in which definitions of reason and enlightenment were crafted, appropriated, and applied (or denied) to others. Only thus, I suggest, can we understand enlightenment as process, instead of constructing "the Enlightenment" in purely retrospective terms, as a movement whose content, membership, and goals were unproblematically agreed upon by all. I am concerned to ask how, in a competitive public world of learning and letters, the status of knowledgeable expert could be successfully forged by individuals.

It is this public construction of knowledgeable expertise that *Eating the Enlightenment* examines, in this case through the lens of contemporary debates over eating, food, and cuisine. How did learned individuals lay claim to a state of enlightenment themselves, or else challenge the claims of others to be learned? The question of what it meant to live a rational life, as well as the nature of the relationship between mind and body, loomed large in writings on cuisine, diet, and health. There is a peculiar irony in writing the history of eighteenth-century knowledge as a biography of disembodied ideas, which is that many philosophes in early eighteenth-century Paris understood mental function as a product of the operations of a material substance, spirit. In the English language, the word "mind" does not connote the material; both the French "*esprit*" and the German "*Geist,*" on the other hand, have multiple meanings, embracing the alimentary, the physiological, and the mental. The literal overlap between these meanings in late seventeenth- and early eighteenth-century iatrochemistry is a starting point of this book, where the word "*esprit*" appears by turns as a measure of politeness, a material substance, and a term for mind and its characteristics.[9] Among a polite readership, the operations of mind and body continued to be regarded as intimately linked, even after iatrochemical models of physiology gave way to understandings of bodily function in terms of the movement of solids and fluids, and mental function ceased to be seen as driven by a unique material substance. A new model of mental function, developed by John Locke and widely taken up by French authors during the eighteenth century, rested upon the claim that the acquisition of knowledge was itself a habit, that is to say, a physical transformation of the structure of the brain by reiterated mental actions. This enduring proximity between body and mind, matter and spirit, is one reason why so many eighteenth-century savants and philosophes, seeking to illuminate the role played by the mate-

9. Although King (1978, 124) warns against rigid categorization under the rubrics of iatrochemistry and iatromechanism, there were salient differences between chemical and mechanical accounts of digestion in early eighteenth-century France; see chap. 1.

rial world and bodily appetites in the operations of reason, interested themselves in the nature, composition, production, consumption, effects, and political or social significance of food.[10]

Despite this widespread interest, it was not self-evident to all Parisian authors that scholarship should embrace food, taste, and cuisine. On the contrary, attempts to do so were compromised throughout the period covered by this book. To take food too seriously, or to be involved in its production, was potentially to endanger both learned and polite self-presentations. On several levels, discussions of eating and cuisine were thus the crucible for controversies over the nature of mind and its relationship with body. Concerns about the formation of habits also extended to the political management of consuming publics. Certain foods previously reserved to the city's rich households, like coffee and sugar, were increasingly consumed even by the poorer ones on a daily basis. This spread of luxury consumption to large sections of the city's population over the course of the century provoked much comment from contemporaries, partly because such changes signaled an unprecedented transformation in everyday life, partly because of the social dynamic underlying that transformation, in which even servants and the poor now had a legitimate claim to luxury and exotic consumption. The city, at the hub of an increasingly global food commerce, thus became the focus of debates about how best to accommodate such changes in individual appetites and what their significance was for the nation as a whole.

The controversies that food provoked could not be so lightly dismissed, therefore. Efforts to extend the domain of reason to encompass food and appetite took place in a highly public arena, they were not uncontested, and they were understood to be political enterprises. The social significance of changing habits and the consequences and proper regulation of appetites were central questions in attempts to define the relationship between individual action and political truth. Alimentary authors wrote their advice books on the premise that they would thereby contribute to making eating choices more rational, and so improve the physical and moral condition of the nation as a whole. One reason for doing so was that the exercise of unbridled appetites threatened any project for universal enlightenment. In this sense *Eating the Enlightenment* addresses Habermas's celebrated thesis concerning the transformation of the public sphere in the eighteenth century. Habermas's work, which addressed the unprecedented development of print culture, commerce, consumption, and political engagement character-

10. Shapin and Lawrence 1998; Chisick 1984; Williams 1994; Staum 1980, chap. 2; Johns 1996.

izing eighteenth-century public life, was taken up by Anglophone historians at the end of the 1980s to underpin arguments both about the formation of a modern political public and about the rise of consumer culture. Like Habermas, I suggest that the answer to the central question of "when and under what conditions the arguments of mixed companies could become authoritative bases for political action" needs to be sought in the relationships among print, commerce, sociability, civility, and consumption in the eighteenth century.[11] However, in my account of those relationships, I proceed more along the lines of Bruno Latour's critique of Habermas, concerning myself with "the fabric of science-society tangles." For, as I hope this book will demonstrate, the entanglement of knowledge and society was a central condition of the production of successful knowledge-claims about food.[12]

This brings me to two major historical developments that have shaped this study: first, the move toward understanding enlightenment in terms of the production and circulation of written materials. *Eating the Enlightenment* approaches polite philosophy and the literate public primarily through the expanding world of writing and reading in eighteenth-century Paris. An extensive periodical and satirical literature, as well as personal memoirs, diaries, and letters, constitute its main resources, and this literature has governed the selection of authors who wrote, sometimes extensively, on food and its significance for knowledge between 1670 and 1760. In my account, enlightenment is firmly tied to the material and mundane problems of the learned life in eighteenth-century Paris. The attention paid by Darnton and other historians to book history in recent decades has done much to free eighteenth-century French history from the teleological trap of implying that certain individuals were somehow predestined to participate in "the" Enlightenment, and that the circumstances of that participation need no explanation. In Parisian literary life, all authors, whether famous, obscure, or infamous, confronted the uncertainties of politics, patronage, publishing, and the pursuit of renown.[13] *Eating the Enlightenment* investigates the hazards and predicaments of the learned and authorial life, depicting *gens de lettres* as agents, rather than members, of a state of enlightenment. It was a consciousness of the dependency of this project upon printed sources that also led me to limit its focus to those who had direct access to print—in other words, to those who were literate—rather than considering food history as a problem most relevant to the poorest sections of so-

11. Calhoun 1992, 1; Habermas 1989; Furet 1988; Baker 1990; Baker 1987; Melton 2001.
12. Latour 1992, 290.
13. Particularly Darnton 1982, 1984a, 1995, 1996; Chartier 1989; and Roche 1988.

ciety. The justification for such a move lies in the fact that this study, like most historical writing, is primarily concerned with written materials. The very poor were generally illiterate, and what was written about their dietary habits, even when it purported to have been written in their name, invariably constructed them for particular and usually polemical purposes, especially where diet was concerned.

Nonetheless, the public world of eighteenth-century Paris may still be viewed as a leveling ground in certain critical respects, for it offered all literate city-dwellers, high and low, new opportunities and formats for communication and encounter that their ancestors had lacked. To argue that the public domain offered new occasions for communication and sociability is not thereby to imply that it was socially or intellectually homogeneous: many would-be participants in Enlightenment found themselves excluded from learned credibility for one reason or another, while others never laid claim to such credibility in the first place. But even if dialogues about knowledge and expertise were not conducted on equal terms, the very possibility thereof was an innovation.

The second major historiographical development to which this book is indebted is the history of consumption. As a growing body of secondary literature has shown, significant innovations in production, commodification, selling, purchasing, and consumption emerged in European cities prior to any of the typical features of industrialization, such as factory production, mechanization, or mass consumption.[14] In 1675 there were few food shops or cafés and no restaurants on the streets of Paris. Taverns and inns served those wishing to eat and drink in public, while markets offered food that was prepared and cooked in the household.[15] Many types of foods and food products were only accessible to the very wealthy. By contrast, in 1760 Paris had hundreds of food shops, offering an increasingly diverse clientele an expanding range of luxury food products, frequently manufactured in the city's many specialist workshops. The history of knowledge, as this book attempts to show, can look very different when scientific activity is envisaged from the standpoint of a world of consumers, merchants, and artisans, and when its setting is the city as a whole, "the most direct physical and sociospatial locus of science," as Sven Dierig, Jens Lachmund, and Andrew

14. Among an extensive literature, see McKendrick, Brewer, and Plumb 1982; Reddy 1984; Campbell 1987; Brewer and Porter 1992; Poulot 1997; Pennell 1999; Roche 2000; Smith 2002; Berg and Eger 2003; Berg 2005. The term "consumers" came into general use during the mid-eighteenth century in works of political economy and in the language of government (Williams 1999).

15. Sargentson 1996; Coquery 2003; Kümin and Tlusty 2002; Brennan 1988; Abad 2002.

Mendelsohn have put it, rather than the confines of scientific institutions.[16] Paris in the eighteenth century was a porous space: as well as being a metropolis of exotic consumption, it was comparatively open to influxes of new would-be scholars and merchants. Only the city could offer suitable conditions for both social mobility and dietary change; for this reason it was here that debates over the significance of new foods for society as a whole, and over the role of scientific and medical knowledge in regulating individual action, found a particular place.

This book takes the new arena of public criticism as a key space for understanding how the sciences "worked" as a social power in eighteenth-century Paris. If the daily lives of literate Parisians were increasingly conducted in accordance with the dictates of reason and nature, what significance did this situation have for the fate of knowledge-claims outside the learned institutions with which that city was so richly endowed, even by 1700?[17] The growth of a polite readership, coupled to a rapid expansion in publishing, provided a new forum outside the capital's learned institutions for conducting controversies over natural knowledge or learned expertise. The public domain provided a very different sort of setting for such disputes, however, from the learned institution. Print and commerce had a leveling effect upon claimants to expertise, be they academicians, merchants, artisans, projectors, or consumers. Chemists, doctors, poets, and antiquaries confronted one and the same critical audience of polite readers; even Crown ministers were forced to participate on the terms of this polite world of satire, critique, and contestation.[18] Attempts to promote particular programs of alimentary knowledge took place in this highly public arena, where individuals deriving their authority from sources as diverse as guild membership, Crown service, privilege, or publishing jostled to secure the attention of readers and clients. But it continued to be the polite reading public that had the last word in matters of culinary taste and literary style, and which itself formed an expert constituency of connoisseurs where food was concerned. Savants, philosophes, and artisans, inasmuch as they too wished to count as members of polite society, were not exempt from the constraints of taste and politeness.

Looking at how authoritative knowledge about food was constituted thus leads us into the heart of the problem of how social as well as epistemologi-

16. Dierig, Lachmund, and Mendelsohn 2003, 2; also Harkness 2007.

17. The major learned establishments of the capital were Royal creations of the seventeenth century: the Académie Françoise in 1635; the Jardin du Roi in 1640; the Petite Académie, which later became the Académie Royale des Inscriptions et Belles-Lettres, in 1663; the Académie Royale des Sciences in 1666; the Observatoire in 1671.

18. Sutton 1995; see also Masseau 1994; Chartier 1997; Roche 1988, chap. 8.

cal authority was coproduced in the public domain. In the eighteenth century, there was no formal institutional setting for alimentary knowledge, and even the very possibility of such a project was questioned by contemporaries. For most of the eighteenth century, practitioners of the natural sciences and mathematicians were understood first and foremost as men of letters, though subdivisions between disciplinary groups became increasingly apparent as the century progressed. Within the world of letters, practitioners of the natural sciences possessed no supreme hegemony over explanations of food, either before or after 1760. To scrutinize the ways in which learned expertise over food was negotiated, *Eating the Enlightenment* casts a broad net, considering cooks and café proprietors, philologists and Orientalists, as well as chemists, naturalists, and physicians. For this reason, I use the term "science" and its cognates throughout the book primarily to refer to all formal learned enterprises, in the Continental European sense, not merely the natural sciences.

In attempting to construct some of the ways in which authoritative learning could be constituted over one area of everyday life, this book seeks to extend the insights of recent history of science to new domains. I began my research with the aim of exploring the ways in which early modern scientific authority could be constituted outwith such spaces as the academy, laboratory, or museum, where scientific practitioners had succeeded fairly early on in establishing particular styles of knowledge production as authoritative. This is the crux of *Eating the Enlightenment*'s engagement with the preoccupations of historians and sociologists of science since the 1980s. In their seminal book *Leviathan and the Air-Pump* (1985), Steven Shapin and Simon Schaffer broke conclusively with accounts that presented the history of science as a progression of great men, great discoveries, or great ideas. They called for the history of the sciences in the early modern period to become an investigation of the "moral geography of knowledge." Their atlas began with a map of one early modern space where scientific authority and credibility were successfully fashioned: the seventeenth-century laboratory, together with the experimental, material, literary, and social technologies for producing knowledge that were housed there.[19] The characterizing feature of eighteenth-century scientific practice, however, was not so much the appearance of new types of specialized space for scientific practice, as the consolidation of scientific authority outside them. Scientific enterprises and practitioners were still savaged by satirists, but the sciences in general were increasingly accommodated—even respected—within eighteenth-century polite society. It was in public, too, that knowledge-claims crafted within the bounds of the

19. Shapin and Schaffer 1985; Shapin 1984, 1988; Latour 1987; 1999, chap. 2.

institution could be said to become universal, shedding their association with a single space of scientific labor and becoming applicable to all.[20]

Eating the Enlightenment does not, however, offer a teleological portrait of natural scientific practitioners successfully pinning down universal alimentary truth within the public domain over the course of the eighteenth century. For one thing, such a victory has effectively never occurred. Nowadays, public authority over alimentary knowledge is wielded by nutritional scientists with an institutional training and government sanction, but within the public domain such experts continue to bemoan the power of rival dietary accounts and practices (fast food advertising or the Atkins diet, for example) over ordinary eaters.[21] Therefore, though we can speak of a consolidation of particular forms of learned authority that took place during the period covered by this book—the creation of a new kind of Orientalist expert, for example, the rise of the literary critic, the dominance of pharmacists over the other Paris guilds, or the success of physicians in deploying new definitions of the "natural" in reforming lifestyles—such transformations did not represent an ultimate victory for one particular group of practitioners over dietary habits among the polite Parisian public. In 1760, as in 1670, eaters could turn to many different sources for advice about food consumption. Even within the medical world, clients drew upon multiple sources of authority to construct lifestyle, not just the knowledge-claims of physicians. Medical authority, too, would weaken in ensuing decades with the rise of alimentary chemistry, wielded by pharmacists, and with the Revolutionary abolition of the medical faculties. The picture that emerges in regard to scientific authority within the public domain is thus one of plurality and flux, rather than stability and universality. If there was a gradual consolidation of medical and scientific expertise over the period under consideration, it did not occur because of the virtues of the scientific method, something relatively invisible to those outside scientific institutions. No single supreme scientific account of diet thus prevailed (or prevails) in the complex heterogeneity of the public domain with which consumers, like scientific and medical experts, must contend as they navigate between different dietary choices.[22]

Instead, what concerns me in this book is rather the question of how public learned authority over food could be constituted under particular local circumstances, and the wider implications of particular tendencies and

20. The conversion of local knowledge into universal knowledge is well explored in Shapin and Schaffer 1985; Latour 1988; Ophir and Shapin 1991; Withers 2007.

21. Nestlé 2002; De Knecht-van Eekelen and van Otterloo 2000.

22. Ramsey 1988; Jenner and Wallis 2007; Spary unpublished; Vess 1975.

transformations in public views of the "good" diet. Here the issue of how scientific and medical practitioners endeavored to represent their particular knowledge-claims (among a plurality of competing knowledge-claims) as the most universal and natural comes to the fore. To date, those historians of science who have studied public and polite scientific practice in the eighteenth century have rarely engaged directly with Schaffer and Shapin's questions about how early modern scientific practitioners recruited authority.[23] That is to say, new models of the conditions under which it was possible to produce authoritative knowledge-claims in a particular culture have not yet been brought together in a sustained way with new accounts of the importance of eighteenth-century publics for creating and maintaining an early modern European scientific culture. Studies of the fate of scientific truth-claims in everyday life have much to contribute to our understanding of this process. Scientific practitioners in the early modern period must be understood as social actors, fabricating social condition, kinship, sociability, and corporate allegiance, at the same time as they are understood as knowledge-makers. Commerce and consumption have rarely featured within histories of science except in relation to the instrument trade and the "popularization" of scientific knowledge, though there has been some attention to the importance of artisanal skill in early modern scientific practice. Yet these issues can be critical in explaining the form taken by scientific controversies before 1800.[24]

Specific local corporate allegiances and commercial rivalries shaped this public domain and the knowledge that was engendered within it, often in covert and unexpected ways. Among the leading claimants to expertise in knowledge about food were apothecaries, who before 1760 constituted the majority of Paris's community of chemical practitioners. Though they had better access to institutional representation than most types of merchant, apothecaries were still invested first and foremost in commerce. In the commercial world, they competed with a range of other expert corporate practitioners, such as cooks, grocers, and distillers, and they were only one of many groups of specialists in the manipulation of materials who had access to print. *Eating the Enlightenment* thus contributes to our understanding of how eighteenth-century chemistry developed into the principal science of material life.[25] In a more general sense, eating practices among the polite

23. See, however, Golinski 1992, esp. chap. 1; Stewart 1992.

24. On commerce, see, e.g., Smith and Findlen 2002; Anderson, Bennett, and Ryan 1993. On skill, see Gooding, Pinch, and Schaffer 1989; Biagioli 1993; Iliffe 1995; Sibum 1998. On artisans, see especially Smith 2004; Secord 1994a,b.

25. I take up the account in Spary unpublished; see also Klein and Spary 2010.

elite responded to the successful capture of new and highly politicized versions of the "natural" from the 1750s onward by certain physicians whose therapeutics represented a sharp break with the iatrochemistry that had dominated Parisian medicine since the late seventeenth century. By the end of the period covered by this book, dietary reform was thus comprehended within the process that Jean-Pierre Goubert once termed "the medicalisation of French society," and indirectly within the rise of programs of public hygiene that extend beyond the scope of this volume.[26]

New models of "the natural" as frugal and austere can be identified in the writings of moral and medical reformers from the start of the eighteenth century onward, long before they became general among a polite reading public in the middle of the eighteenth century. As I show in chapter 1, these reform programs were explicit responses to a political project of civility and *politesse* closely associated with the court of Louis XIV and manifested in culinary writings. This book therefore parts company with the approach of historians of cuisine, who have treated culinary writing as a self-referential, homogeneous genre and a direct precursor of the gastronomic writings of the early 1800s. Instead, my concern is with the very specific polemical (and political) purposes served by culinary writing within the literate culture of eighteenth-century Paris, including the promotion of Cartesian and iatrochemical models of taste, the working out of debates over the civilizing process and new forms of knowledge, and the accommodation of novelty. At the beginning of the period covered by this book, courtly styles of cookery were already fashionable, thanks to the success of cookbooks such as Pierre-François de La Varenne's *Cuisinier françois* (French Cook) of 1651. A culture of fine dining had emerged at the courts of Louis XIII and XIV, and during the eighteenth century many literate persons aspired to participate in courtly dining styles. Because of their association with courtly manners and with the Sun King's reign, the spread of tasteful connoisseurship and culinary knowledge through polite society was viewed by some commentators as continuous with the spread of Enlightenment and civility, and the rise of the café after 1690 was taken to be part of that process. By others, however, delicate eating would be represented as part of the general cultural hegemony of Bourbon absolutism, something to be resisted and critiqued.[27]

For the remainder of the Old Regime, French cuisine would never shed

26. Goubert 1982.

27. On French cuisine, see Flandrin, Hyman, and Hyman 1983; Mennell 1996; Spang 2000; Davis 2004; Takats 2011; Pinkard 2009. On the political function of conspicuous consumption and luxury under Louis XIV, see Burke 1992; Rothkrug 1965, pt. 1, chap. 11.

these political associations. The critique of cuisine and the values it denoted—refinement, delicacy, civilization, artifice—were integrated into an opposition politics. Cuisinc's cosmopolitanism was reformulated by its critics as a demonstration of the adverse consequences of imperialism, in which eaters' pursuit of ingesta from other parts of the globe was effected at the expense of other peoples and of their own health. Cuisine also came to denote artificiality, thanks to cooks' claims to excel in the creation of appetites through the manipulation of flavors, and their appeals to chemistry to legitimate that skill. Last, it came to signify the decline of French society, in that the delicacy required to appreciate the labors of cooks was increasingly represented as a mark of corporeal weakness and hence political incompetence. This book traces the shifting relationship between celebrating and stigmatizing cuisine in the first half of the eighteenth century.

Culinary writers legitimated their accounts of bodily function, taste, and cookery by appealing to iatrochemical models current in Paris between the 1670s and the 1730s. Early in the eighteenth century, both chemistry and cuisine could function as signs of the progress of French taste, delicacy, civility, and learning, but by 1760 they were arts that transformed or perverted that which was natural, arts that distanced people from authenticity and were symbolic of what many saw as the corruption of French society in modern times. At around the same time, new accounts of the healthy and politically fit body and a new chemistry of food were being invented. The entanglement of food and learning also raised new questions about the social purpose, relevance, and scope of knowledge in general, and about the relationship between old and new forms of knowledge. This dialectic between eating as critique and eating as knowledge—of the public sphere, of the self, and of the relationship between the two—would unfold in the decades leading up to the French Revolution.[28]

Three related historical processes were taking place during the reigns of Louis XIV and Louis XV, and it is these which set the chronological and thematic parameters for my study. Beginning in the 1660s, France actively pursued a foreign policy aimed at creating an empire founded largely on the domination of maritime trade routes and the formation or consolidation of colonies. Domestic commerce too was undergoing extensive transformation: urban settings fostered a rapid proliferation of shops and shopping, forming a new community of consumers with access to imported foods and the money to buy them. The period was thus one of rapid transformation

28. Spary unpublished takes up the history of alimentary knowledge in France from 1760 onwards.

in lifestyles and eating habits, particularly in the metropolis. Reading and learning were themselves becoming fashions, embraced by everyone with pretensions to politeness and reflected in the sharp increase in publishing and the commodification of medicine and the sciences. It is the convergence of these three phenomena that marks out the period from 1670 to 1760.

Rather than a comprehensive overview of the relations between eating and knowing, *Eating the Enlightenment* investigates a succession of specific problematics, illustrated through debates over particular foods or settings for consumption. Certain themes provide continuity throughout the book. The foods that attracted particular attention were those which contemporaries deemed to be especially potent substances. They were attributed wide-ranging powers to affect the body, nerves, and mind, to provoke or regulate appetites, and thus to transform both individual and collective lives. The fascination with foods such as spices, coffee, and liqueurs, and with the products of nouvelle cuisine in the decades up to 1750 was a sign of contemporary concern about the consumption of substances that had the power to overturn custom and tradition. Diet became a metaphor for the problems of novelty and change afflicting France in the early stages of consumption and capitalism. New knowledge, similarly, could be interpreted as threat or as potential; discourses about cuisine, appetite, spices, and spirits made plain what enlightenment and innovation might mean for the future of society.

Chapter 1 sets up the opposition that would prevail all through the period from 1675 to 1760, between culinary skill and courtly luxury on the one hand, and sobriety and reform on the other. This opposition, as chapter 6 later shows, was not fought out as a clash between social groups, such as between courtiers at Versailles and an urban middling sort. Rather, it took the form of distinct ways of life, attached to particular sets of moral, political, and health claims, and available to a generalized literate polite public of readers and eaters, of which the philosophes formed a part. In the earlier period, luxurious eating was supported by iatrochemical models of corporeal delicacy and connoisseurship, which gave way to concerns about the weakening effect of luxury, often allied to broadly iatromechanical models of the body. But it would be wrong to suggest that there was a neat dichotomy between court and city, royalist and reformist, iatrochemistry and iatromechanism. As chapter 6 demonstrates, eaters themselves freely oscillated between different models of the healthy body and mind while openly acknowledging the political stakes attached to each. Moreover, these debates had a broader significance: eighteenth-century eaters, just like those of today, were concerned with the wider implications of the free play of appetites and dietary choice. Accounts of alimentary chemistry and physiology enabled the articulation of concerns about the rapidity of change in European consumption habits, which affected both the internal structure of (particularly urban) society and the relations between European colonizing nations and the rest of the world. These were prescriptive as well as descriptive statements.

In iatrochemical accounts, certain foods, including spirits and spices, were seen as vital dietary components because they either contained or fueled the production of the animal spirits that drove mental operations. In chapters 2 and 3 I focus on coffee, a new foodstuff that was seen by many contemporaries as a key source for the production of mind, superseding older foods and drinks such as wine and facilitating new forms of sociability centered on polite conduct, which distinguished the rational eater from the rabble. Enlightenment and the cultivation of polite taste were enrolled in the coffee trade at all levels and served to justify acclimatization projects for colonial coffee production as well as the global pattern of coffee commerce. At every step, the production of knowledge about coffee was yoked to its status as a commodity, which in turn was significantly reshaped in the period 1670 to 1730, turning coffee from an exotic rarity with a small clientele into an everyday item of consumption. More than any other foodstuff in this period, coffee exemplified the dilemmas of globalization, the anxiety attached to mental powers in an age of enlightenment, and the interactions between individual habits and central policies. If in chapter 2 my concern is to move between the scales of metropolitan scientific writing, urban consumption, and global trade, chapter 3 looks more closely at the commercial world of Parisian food consumption and production, from the perspective both of clients and of merchants, a viewpoint developed further in chapter 4. In these two chapters the focus is on the café as the newest and most self-consciously enlightened of spaces for urban consumption and production both of knowledge and of food. Yet the writing that emerged from such spaces was under fire from others within the Republic of Letters, who were less convinced of the virtue of the iconoclasm and novelty that seemed to dominate modern knowledge. The whole principle of an epistemological expertise that was at once public and credible was at stake in debates over both cafés and the drinks they served.

However, Parisian cafés were not just places for the consumption of coffee. As chapter 4 argues, many were also chemical laboratories, where scientific knowledge was wielded by individuals who could pretend to the best chemical education the capital could afford. This chapter considers how institutional affiliation created a line of demarcation among city merchants—the few who entered the favored academies of Bourbon absolutism wielded a public authority to which the rest could not aspire. Yet as scientific expertise increasingly came to be put on display and tested within the public domain, how could the authority of institutional scientific knowledge be assured over that which was produced within laboratories operating outside institutional sanction? And what were the implications of that proliferation of sites for generating natural knowledge, given that institutional scientific practitioners were actively seeking to privilege their own knowledge-claims over everyday assertions about foods? Seen from a commercial viewpoint, certain disputes over epistemological authority seem driven by market competition between rival city guilds. This overturns our ordinary hierarchies of the sources of reliability and credibility of natural knowledge in the early modern period.

The question of the role and status of the skilled artisan in the manufacture of knowledge for a tasteful public of consumers resurfaces in chapter 5. Here the polite and literate elite is once again the focus of attention, in this case through a study of accounts of taste and its proper exercise. In this chapter I locate the common origin of models of spiraling consumption and theories of addiction in challenges to early eighteenth-century optimism about reason as sufficient to control appetite. Faith in reason, a philosophical commonplace in the 1740s, was giving way to more conservative views of the power of reason to reform society by the 1750s and 1760s. The conflict between these two accounts of the relations between appetite, reason, and health is the central subject of chapter 6, where the experiences of literate consumers, including the philosophes themselves, take center stage. By ending with the eaters themselves, or at least those who were in a position to choose among the various alimentary repertoires available to the literate elite, I show how different models of food, eating, and the body, stemming from chemical, mechanical, and vital accounts of health, from learned and political self-presentations, and from both secular and religious moral agendas, offered contemporaries different repertoires of alimentary conduct. In correspondence and diaries, learned and polite eaters articulated the reasons behind their choice of one set of dietary recommendations over another. This process of selection among dietary alternatives underscores claims by Jewson and others that early modern medical (and scientific) practitioners possessed no automatic public authority over matters of natural fact, especially when these concerned experiences as intimately individual as taste and health.[29] The problem of establishing and maintaining authority over diet persisted all the way down the alimentary tract of polite eaters in eighteenth-century Paris.

29. Jewson 1976.

CHAPTER ONE

Intestinal Struggles

The starting point of this inquiry into the relations between food and knowledge in eighteenth-century Paris is the stomach. In recent years, the turn toward cultural history has encouraged attention to the stomach's dominant position in the medical advice offered to men of letters.[1] Yet models of the digestion and of the physiological purpose and action of the stomach also contributed to bigger debates over the relationship between the conduct of individual bodies and the state of society as a whole. French physicians and their clients regarded the stomach as a somatic locus where digestive, moral, and even political upsets manifested themselves and through which appetite was expressed. This intense focus led to some bizarre narrative formulations by the middle years of the eighteenth century, in which individual eaters were metonymically supplanted, as it were, by their own stomachs:

> I dare say no sort of foodstuff exists which some of these difficult stomachs do not desire [*appeter*] & digest by preference & to the exclusion of all others. Most peculiar oddities have been observed in this respect, & even contradictions of a sort: one such stomach, for example, digests melon & ham very well, but will not digest peach & salt beef, even though there is undoubtedly more analogy between ham & salt beef, than between melon & ham, &c.[2]

In general parlance, "the" digestion was understood less as a physiological or anatomical system than as a single self-contained corporeal event. A

1. Vila 2005a; Williams 2007.

2. Gabriel Venel, "Digestion (Œconom. anim.)" (1754), in Diderot and d'Alembert 1751–77, 4:1002.

healthy body mastered foods in the stomach and produced a "praiseworthy chyle." In the opposite eventuality, often caused by overeating, the body failed to overcome its foods and an indigestion was the result. A badly concocted chyle full of partially assimilated nutritive principles could penetrate the body, affecting and altering the humors and the constitution. A failed digestive event gave rise to a range of disagreeable and sometimes even fatal side effects:

> Whenever one has a clear head, a fresh body, & a sound & merry mind after the meal, it is proof that one has not eaten too much: on the contrary, when one's body is heavy, one's mind incapable of application after the meal, and one suffers acid, putrid, foetid burps smelling of rotten eggs, when one experiences a swelling & sensation of fullness in the stomach, feelings of faintness, hiccups, vomiting, yawns, burning, & sweat on the face or chest, lastly when one's tongue is thick, one's mouth bad, one's head heavy, & one has a desire to spit, especially on waking in the night, it is a certain proof that one has committed excesses in drinking or eating.[3]

Both in moral and in physical terms, foods could overpower the eater. Both enduring illnesses and sudden deaths, such as that of the archbishop of Toulouse in April 1758, were explicitly attributed to indigestion.[4]

If the characteristic of a healthy body in the eighteenth century was the ability to extract the maximum nutriment from foods consumed, so, by extension, the mark of a good digestion was minimal defecation. The physician Arnulphe d'Aumont claimed that the healthy individual would produce feces infrequently and in small quantities: "this is proof that the food is being properly digested, & that it's attenuated to such an extent that little coarse matter remains to produce excrement; the superfluous part which enters the blood dissipates insensibly." For enlightened Parisians, constipation was the sign of a robust temperament: "There are people in very good health who empty their bowels no more than once a week; conversely, the weaker one's temperament, the more fecal matter one produces & the more liquid it is." Digestibility would remain a salient characteristic of foods throughout the century in political debates over the food supply between consumers and administrators, and to tar a new food with the brush of indigestibility was an easy way to undermine its reputation in the eyes of

3. Jacquin 1762, 199–200; see also Le Thieullier 1739–47, *passim*; Helvétius 1707, 33.
4. Barbier 1857–66, 7:45.

consumers and rulers alike. In fact, in cultural, political, physiological, and etiological terms, the stomach and digestion were understood very differently in the eighteenth century from the way they are understood today, and this was particularly true for the category of individuals who worked with their minds and pens to produce the writings and knowledge-claims historically associated with Enlightenment.[5]

But how did the body's mechanism for the extraction and processing of nourishment become a politically significant topic in eighteenth-century Paris? A key controversy between rival medical sects, beginning in the 1710s, offers an example of the politics of knowledge about food and its effects on the body. My approach is prompted by extensive work on the body as a site of production and reproduction of social and political truth, as well as the site of lived experience: the liminal space between the inner and outer worlds.[6] Yet much writing on the history of the body and nutrition as scientific subjects in eighteenth-century France has addressed bodily function only within the terms sanctioned by physiology texts: as part of a history of ideas rather than lifestyles. Within this literature, generation and sensibility have consistently attracted most interest, while digestion and the assimilation of food within the body have commanded comparatively little attention.[7] Eighteenth-century authors regarded digestion as a key bodily function. Digestion, appetite, and diet were of interest precisely because of their relevance for daily life, and models of their function and purpose frequently featured in prescriptive programs for individual self-conduct. Such advice seemed especially necessary in light of the sweeping changes in Parisian food habits from the late seventeenth century onward, in particular the increased consumption of exotic foods.

In the first instance, then, attention to digestion allows the production of natural knowledge to be firmly situated within the domains of the body and of everyday life. Second, controversy over such issues rehearsed contemporary conflicts about the relative power of doctors, cooks, and eaters, an issue that will be reprised in subsequent chapters. Appeals to medical and scientific authority could legitimate proposals for the reform of society

5. Arnulphe D'Aumont, "Déjection" (1754), in Diderot and d'Alembert 1751–77, 4:770–73; Spary unpublished, chap. 2.

6. See especially Kilgour 1990; Morton 1994; Lupton 1996; Lawrence and Shapin 1998; Féher, Naddaff, and Tazi 1989; Turner 1992, 1996; Featherstone and Turner 1990; Terry and Urla 1995; Forth and Crozier 2005; Stafford 1991.

7. On the animal economy, see Rey 2000; Roger 1997; Duchesneau 1982; Callot 1965; Brown 1968; on sensibility, Staum 1980, chap. 2; Haigh 1976; on generation, Roe 1981; Gasking 1967.

through dietary change, as for example in calls to abolish or restrict luxury consumption. Establishing the healthy diet thus meant working out the proper relationship between, and respective authority of, rival forms of knowledge. Digestion and indigestion were also relevant to disputes over materialistic philosophy and medical theory. Debates over digestion went right to the heart of contemporary matter theory, touching on issues ranging from theological orthodoxy—explaining the mechanism by which the body and blood of Christ, consumed at the Eucharist, entered and transformed the communicant's own body—to philosophical heterodoxy—could digestive phenomena demonstrate that matter possessed innate vital powers? It seems anomalous, therefore, that the extensive history of materialism in the Enlightenment is effectively an immaterial history; many of the disciplinary domains within which matter was actively being discussed in the period, such as chemistry or medicine, have barely registered in it.[8] Digestion and assimilation infringed philosophically problematic boundaries, after all: between living and nonliving matter, between self and other, between organized and brute, between inside and outside. The French anthropologist Claude Fischler suggests that for omnivorous humans eating is a source of anxiety precisely because it is a liminal act in this sense. By incorporating the external world into themselves, eaters constantly face the risk of perversion by the eater of the eaten. Many decisions about diet, he argues, are driven by the concern to avoid polluting the self or transforming one's identity through the inevitable act of consumption. Although Fischler's primary concern was with the nineteenth and twentieth centuries, his model also has relevance for the earlier period. Throughout the eighteenth century, digestion featured in discussions about the formation of individual character and conduct, and their relevance for the physical and moral condition of society as a whole. Digestion was thus a major area where medicine, philosophy, and theology intersected with the political praxis of daily life and the management of bodies. It provided personal experiences by which the truth-claims of philosophy and medicine could be judged to stand or fall.[9]

Accounting for digestion thus allows some of the links between individual responsibility and collective action to be explicated. More than other

8. See, e.g., Kors 1976; Yolton 1984; 1991, esp. chaps. 2 and 3; Léon-Miehe 2004; Fink and Stenger 1999. By contrast, see Thomson 1981, chap. 2; Vila 2005b. On the physical and the moral, see Williams 1994. Thomson 2008, 219, argues that the political and medical implications of materialism were separately explored.

9. Fischler 1993, chap. 3.

bodily functions, digestion and assimilation reveal the social porosity of accounts of the animal economy. The disputes addressed in this chapter exemplify in miniature the conjuncture of social and political critique, challenges to traditional authority, and appeal to natural knowledge that are often taken to typify enlightened self-understandings. But they also represent recent interest among historians of science in the moral geography of knowledge and the historical fate of knowledge-claims. Debates over digestion thus provide a useful starting point for an inquiry into the way in which medical and scientific authority over the workings of the body related to everyday practices on the one hand, and controversies over knowledge and credibility on the other.

TRITURATION AS A WAY OF LIFE

For much of the eighteenth century, there was little dispute over either the anatomical structure of the digestive organs or the fact that food transformed into chyle in the stomach and then passed via the lacteal ducts to the bloodstream. However, there was scant agreement about the phenomena of digestion and absorption. Chemical explanations predominated in accounts of digestion produced at the start of the eighteenth century, such as the *Dictionnaire des Aliments* (Dictionary of Foods) written by Louis Lémery, a leading food analyst and the son of one of Paris's most prominent chemists, who had achieved social advancement by qualifying to practice medicine in Paris. Lémery, along with other iatrochemists such as the Montpellier physician Antoine Deidier, postulated the existence of multiple ferments in the body, controlling the various stages of digestion in the stomach, intestines, and bloodstream. Ferments were either acid or alkaline in nature, with active particles that penetrated and separated out the constituent elements of foodstuffs, allowing the finest particles to be freed of the earthy matter surrounding them and absorbed into the lacteal ducts. This was a process often called "elaboration." Ferments derived from the writings of Van Helmont and Sylvius and had been made fashionable by another Montpellier physician, Pierre Chirac, newly relocated to Paris.[10]

Iatrochemists explained all health and disease in terms of good or bad ferments within the bodily fluids. Such views had only lately penetrated the most respected and ancient of Parisian scientific and medical institutions, including the medical faculty, and as early as 1709 they faced a new threat when a dispute over the mechanism of digestion broke out in the pages

10. Brockliss and Jones 1997, 144–49, 420–24.

of the *Mémoires de Trévoux*. This leading Jesuit newspaper regularly reviewed books on medicine and the natural sciences, but in previous reviews of physiology books, including Lémery and Deidier's own, digestion had had a low profile.[11] The controversy related to a theologically contentious matter: the customary right of Parisian physicians to confer individual dispensations upon their clients, freeing them from the legal requirement to fast during Lent on health grounds. Among the principal Lenten dietary restrictions was a ban on the consumption of meat and eggs. Medical and theological treatises on the healthiness or otherwise of lean foods such as fish, beans, and other meat surrogates poured from the presses. The relative authority of religious and natural laws was at stake in debates over issues such as whether fish-flavored meat, or quadrupeds with an aquatic lifestyle, could count as fish and thereby fulfill the Lenten prescriptions. Authors also reflected in general upon the health effects of abstinence, whether from meat or from food in general, whether among the clergy or in high life. In 1700 the Paris physician Barthélemy Linand had argued against Lenten dispensations on moral as well as medical grounds. Corporeal delicacy, a coveted attribute of polite eaters, was, he insisted, no adequate reason to claim dispensation, since polite consumers manufactured their own physical weakness by, wittingly or unwittingly, indulging in excess and ruining their health.[12]

The appeal to health, therefore, could be countered by presenting changing consumption habits in the modern city as a reversible evil. The solution, Linand argued, was for Catholics to exert more self-discipline: the earliest Christians had had no need of such rules, but "nowadays when the laxity of Christians is so great, one is obliged to Mr Linand for removing the vain pretexts which they use to avoid the painful duties that Religion imposes on them," as a reviewer noted. Linand also advised the delicate and valetudinarian to exercise Lenten fasting outside of the legally required period, "so that the body might accustom itself little by little to this sort of nourishment."[13]

The debate over Lenten dispensations in part concerned the opposition between two different ways of life that the well-to-do medical client might embrace: the fashionable, civilized lifestyle of pleasure, refinement, and novelty on the one hand; and on the other, a devotional lifestyle that

11. E.g., review of Lémery 1705 in *Mémoires de Trévoux* (1702), 71–91; (1705), 2053–56. The journal's official title was *Mémoires pour l'Histoire des Sciences et des Beaux Arts*. The Paris medical faculty had only founded a chair of chemical and Galenic pharmacy in 1696. Debus 2001, 26.

12. Lémery 1705, 306; Linand 1700.

13. *Mémoires de Trévoux* (1702): 32–33.

favored the cultivation of the soul, rejected the pleasures of the body, and treated the proliferation of wealth and luxury with suspicion. During the early years of the century, different medical explanations for digestion mapped onto these distinct programs for the future of French society. In 1709 Philippe Hecquet, a doctor of the Paris medical faculty, published his *Traité des dispenses du Carême* (Treatise on Lenten Dispensations), which proclaimed the moral bankruptcy of Lenten dispensations. This widely read book was rebutted the following year in an anonymous work, in fact written by Hecquet's faculty colleague and bitter enemy Nicolas Andry de Boisregard.[14] There were many parallels between the two men. Andry was just three years Hecquet's senior. Both were probably near contemporaries at the Collège des Grassins in Paris, both obtained their first medical degrees from Reims, and both entered the Paris medical faculty within a short time of one another. Both men would serve as the dean of the Paris medical faculty, Hecquet in 1712 and Andry in 1724.

Where they differed radically, however, was in their religious convictions. Before entering the Paris faculty, Hecquet had worked for a few years as the physician to the famous Jansenist religious foundation at Port-Royal-des-Champs. Here he acquired lifelong Jansenist convictions and adopted a highly visible pious lifestyle of abstinence, fasting, and self-denial. Due to ill health, however, Hecquet's association with Port-Royal was short-lived. He soon returned to Paris, entering the circle of the king's premier physician, Guy-Crescent Fagon, and acquiring a degree from the Paris medical faculty in 1697. This was one of only two ways in which a physician like Hecquet or Andry, holding a medical degree from a provincial university, could legitimately practice in the metropolis, the other being to obtain a royal privilege. Hecquet was soon honored with the title of Doctor Regent of the faculty. When the dispute commenced in 1709, he had recently been appointed personal physician to the Condé family, and was soon to obtain the post of physician to the Charité hospital.[15] By contrast, Andry's religious views were closer to the Molinism exhibited by many of the *Mémoires de Trévoux* reviewers. Both Molinism and Jansenism had originally developed as responses to the Reformation, but while the former minimized the effects of the Fall and stressed the residual goodness of human nature, the latter treated human nature as fundamentally corrupt, to be redeemed only

14. [Hecquet] 1710a, reviewed in *Journal des Sçavans* 43 (March 1710): 422–43; [Andry de Boisregard] 1710. Andry de Boisregard 1713 was a revised edition. On Andry and Hecquet's enmity, see [Lefèvre de Saint-Marc] 1740, 22–42.

15. *Biographie Universelle*, 19:20–22, 1:685–86; [Lefèvre de Saint-Marc] 1740, 8–10, 20.

by an unremitting labor of good works and self-denial. These oppositions would structure the form taken by the dispute over digestion, especially in the *Mémoires de Trévoux*, whose Jesuit editors opposed Hecquet's Jansenist heterodoxy.[16]

A major part of the service early modern physicians offered their clienteles was the prescription of suitable diets for therapeutic or prophylactic purposes.[17] Hecquet's plan to make medicine a road map for acting out and reforming the relationship between the body and faith was evident in the dietetic rules he laid down in his *Traité des dispenses du Carême* and other books. His most controversial claim was that lean foods were healthier than fat foods and also more virtuous, since they were the foods originally ordained to man by God at the Creation "in those innocent times, when man, still in his natural state, had not yet corrupted himself . . . [and] had not learnt to live in order to eat, but rather to eat in order to live." Above all, Hecquet criticized the consumption of meat as contrary to human virtue and health. "Dishes of raw vegetables, against which the world, & even savants, have allowed themselves to become so prejudiced, were formerly the ordinary nourishment of men." Other peoples had thrived for centuries on a vegetarian diet, the source of "the best part of the happiness of the golden age," and the diet of classical heroes, legislators, and philosophers. "Man was initially made to content himself with little; some fruits, [and] at most some vegetables, were to suffice for his subsistence, & everything dainty [*exquis*] & succulent was not destined for him." Representing the first men as vegetarians was a commonplace of travel accounts, medical works, and civil and natural histories. Even some cookbook authors paid tribute to the vegetable diet of the Golden Age, as celebrated in Ovid's *Metamorphoses*. Discussions of passages celebrating a vegetarian diet in the writings of the ancients—Pythagoras, Plutarch, Porphyry—appeared in print throughout the century.[18]

The controversy over digestion in which Hecquet became embroiled had its roots in these concerns about the historical significance of diet for mankind, considered as a social and natural being. Hecquet presented lean foods

16. Pappas 1957; Sgard 1991, 2:805–16; Froeschlé-Chopard and Froeschlé 2001.

17. Albala 2002.

18. [Hecquet] 1710a, 1:41, 53–54, 135; 2:2; see also Urbain de Vandenesse, "Abstinence" (1751) in Diderot and d'Alembert 1751–77, 1:44. [Marin] 1750, x–xiij specifically mentioned Hecquet's exhortation to vegetarianism; on the Golden Age, see also Ovidius Naso 1732; Denis Diderot, "Abstinence des Pythagoriciens" (1751), in Diderot and d'Alembert 1751–77, 1:44; Porphyry 1747; Dacier 1771, 57–229; Plutarch 1785.

and vegetarianism as elements of a great reformation of Catholic lifestyles, a return to an original purity of soul and body. But to advocate a restricted diet of lean foods was, as a contemporary remarked, to fly in the face of "most worldly people, who regard abstinence as the enemy of health."[19] Since the seventeenth century, fine eating had gradually become a mark of civility in French polite society. After 1700, nouvelle cuisine dishes, wine and liqueurs, and imported luxury foods such as coffee or chocolate became increasingly common dietary items in well-to-do urban households, in emulation of the custom prevailing at court. The lifestyle practiced and prescribed by Hecquet contrasted sharply with this trend, and his views on digestion were just part of a thorough-going reform of everyday practices of consumption. For Jansenists, daily life was a constant exercise in prophylactic self-denial: the pleasures of the flesh had to be put off as far as possible in an attempt to achieve a state of grace sufficient to warrant salvation. Jansenists engaged in physical self-chastisement, wore poor clothes, lived humbly, and ate a restricted diet. Meat was often absent from their tables. Hecquet was typical of the movement, giving up wine and adopting "the habit of always eating lean [foods], & of chiefly eating nothing other than Herbs & Vegetables."[20]

But to give up a luxury diet was to change not just one's eating habits but one's perceived social status, especially significant when courtly dishes held sway as the aspirational pinnacle of consumption. To give up meat was to abandon a food that was both a status symbol and increasingly regarded as a staple. Hecquet's critique, which centered on the fact that the pleasure of consuming lean foods was less than that gained from nouvelle cuisine, was accordingly perceived as a radical political gesture. In publishing his dietetics, Hecquet sought to divert French eaters from the ruinous path to luxury eating, which was destroying the nation's health and virtue. The physician, too, could be a mediator of salvation by intervening in lifestyle, on the basis of possessing privileged knowledge about the nature of foods and their effects upon the body. Thus, in Hecquet's view, the luxury foods

19. Review of [Andry de Boisregard] 1710, *Journal des Sçavans* 47 (April 1710): 427–46, quoted on 428. On lean eating as an everyday practice of certain religious orders, compare d[e Prémont,] "Au Lecteur," in Cornaro 1703, 8; Hecquet 1740, 3:371–403.

20. The ordinary diet of the famous Jansenist deacon François de Pâris "was extremely frugal: cabbage soup, a handful of rice [cooked] in water, a slice of brown bread constituted his sole daily repast, taken in the evening at six o'clock; meat appeared on his table three times a year." Taveneaux 1973, 104–5, 171–72. Details of Hecquet's own dietary practices come from [Lefèvre de St-Marc] 1740, 65; Le Sage 1715, 1:163–64. Jansenists were not the only group to practise dietary austerity; for example, Lister 1699, 136 disapprovingly noted the "little slimy nasty Fish and Herbs" that formed the diet of the traveling naturalist Charles Plumier, a Minim.

spreading through urban elite society in the 1700s were merely flavorings, not nourishment, serving to render the consumption of indigestible meats a pleasurable experience.[21]

Hecquet was not alone in having a deep suspicion of the moral and social implications of alimentary pleasure, cuisine, and luxury. Just as Louis XIV had explicitly harnessed the display of self to the exercise of political power by making certain forms of self-presentation, self-conduct, and conspicuous consumption indispensable to polite status, so opponents of the Crown raised luxury consumption to the level of a political act. Appeals for a return to primitive vigor and a new simplicity of morals and needs among the French elite were characteristic of several groups which, in one way or another, opposed Crown policies such as the revival of papal authority within France, or Louis XIV's minister Colbert's attempt to encourage international commerce and domestic production, both of which facilitated the rapid growth of shopping and luxury consumption in Paris, as we will see in later chapters. The most vocal critics came from within the French court itself during the 1690s and 1700s: Louis XIV's grandson and heir, the duc de Bourgogne, and his circle of advisors, including François Salignac de La Mothe-Fénelon, Henri de Boulainvilliers, and Louis de Rouvroy, duc de Saint-Simon. Among their reform plans were proposals for import substitution and sumptuary legislation, couched within a program for reviving the original purity of Gallic morals and reforming courtly lifestyles. This circle also inclined toward a deep skepticism vis-à-vis the sciences and arts, seen as playing a significant role in the transition to a society of global luxury consumption. Fénelon, for example, included among his "Fables composed for the education of Monseigneur le Duc de Bourgogne" an essay entitled "Voyage dans l'île inconnue," which described a veritable land of Cockayne: Pacific islands, one constructed of sugar with forests of liquorice and rivers of syrup, another of sausages, ragoûts (a hallmark of nouvelle cuisine), and pastry, where it rained wine. Although the inhabitants had mastered technologies for enhancing appetite and sleep to take advantage of the bounty around them, these corporeal pleasures were in the end spoiled by commodification and excess. The capital city, luxurious and built entirely of marble, was also against the order of nature: the women had rebelled against male dominance and taken the task of government into their own hands, leav-

21. Duncan 1705, 12–13, claimed: "Not to know [Coffee, Chocolate and Tea] is to be a Barbarian. They are in all good company." On courtly eating, see Mennell 1996, chap. 4, 108–16; Foucher-Wolniewicz 1992; Babelon 1993.

ing the men effeminately engaged in embroidery (and, Fénelon hinted, also sexually impotent). This literature was among the earliest to present the cultivation of civility, luxury, and *délicatesse* by Louis XIV, his ministers, and his court as bad politics because against the order of nature; it was by no means the last. Some or all of the policies developed by the Bourgogne circle might indeed have been implemented in law had the duc de Bourgogne succeeded to the throne, but he would die prematurely in 1712.[22]

Hecquet's inclusion of culinary reform within a political critique of court and urban society thus addressed the issue of diet and luxury from the same standpoint as other contemporary critics of the society of Louis XIV. Portraying the developing society of luxury consumption as fundamentally vicious and impious, Hecquet called for the abandonment of the art of cuisine as celebrated in publications of the late seventeenth and early eighteenth centuries, in favor of a cuisine that would assist Catholic eaters in achieving a more pious lifestyle: "The Public has been given the Royal Cook, the French Cook, &c. One ought to give to Religion and piety, the Catholic Cook." Here he was referring to two well-known contemporary cookbooks, *Cuisinier François*, a mid-seventeenth-century publication by La Varenne, and its successor, Massialot's *Cuisinier Royal*, a founding work of French nouvelle cuisine. Massialot in particular had identified cuisine as a distinguishing feature of civilized Europe and a mark of French cultural superiority:

> If [Travel] Accounts are to be believed, there are whole Peoples, who, far from having the least understanding of how to awaken appetite through ways of preparing the Foods which are suitable to nourish them, are ignorant of the excellence & goodness of most of them; and often even prefer the dirtiest [of foods] to these, or only eat them in the most disgusting manner. Only in Europe do cleanliness, good taste, & skill in the seasoning of the Meats & foods that are found there reign, & only here is justice done to the marvellous gifts that are made available to the fortunate situation of other Climates; & in France, above all, we may boast of beating all the other Nations in this regard, as we do in politeness, & in a thousand other well-known advantages.[23]

22. Fénelon 2011; see especially the analysis of this rare text by Leplâtre 2007. On the Bourgogne circle and other reforming groups, see also Galliani 1989, chap. 6; Rothkrug 1965, pt. 1, chap. 7; Steinmetz 1988, 11–14; Van Kley 1975, 22–28; Morize 1970, 63–65; Shovlin 2006, 20–21. On Louis XIV and the politics of display, see Marin 1988; Burke 1992; Mukerji 1997, chap. 6; Jones 2004.

23. [Massialot] 1698, unpaginated preface.

The art of manipulating flavors was thus one and the same with the civilizing process for this cook, who had worked for several courtiers.[24] By contrast, Hecquet, like many later authors, portrayed nouvelle cuisine as an art of deception that concealed the link between man and his Providentially supplied resource of nutrition. This tension would continue to be central in later discussions of cuisine.[25]

In linking digestion with this broader debate over the ethics of consumption, Hecquet and his supporters conferred a new theological, moral, and political relevance upon it. This was true both in terms of the dietetic recommendations that followed from Hecquet's digestive model, and in terms of the kinds of explanation for physiological processes that triturationist models sanctioned. Hecquet drew upon different learned resources, including scriptural interpretation and natural history, to defend plant foods as the most natural, healthy and virtuous diet for man. He argued that carnivores, with their claws, teeth and beaks, were anatomically marked out for a meat diet, whereas man was not.[26] However, natural historical arguments based on an appeal to a universal natural diet for mankind were full of pitfalls, as one reviewer of the *Traité des Dispenses* noted in March 1709: "From the fact that the Americans, for example, & some Africans eat human flesh & thrive on it, would one be justified in concluding that it was a very suitable foodstuff for man in general?" Hecquet also had to contend with naturalists and scriptural exegesists who claimed that nature had fallen into decadence since the Deluge, and therefore plant foods had become incapable of nourishing man. Nature, he insisted, retained her primitive vigor. The loss of longevity, health, and strength evident in eighteenth-century French bodies was, rather, the price paid for abandoning a vegetarian diet.[27]

Even more central to Hecquet's defense of lean foods was his appeal to mechanics and geometry. His iatromechanical model of digestion drew on the writings of Archibald Pitcairn, a Scottish physician trained in France, the founder of the Royal College of Surgeons. Pitcairn had sought to reform medicine by placing it wholly on a mathematical basis, as being the

24. [Hecquet] 1710a, 1:444. See also La Varenne 1651. On the civilizing process, see Elias 1983; on seventeenth-century cookbooks, Flandrin, Hyman, and Hyman 1983; Wheaton 1983, chaps. 7–8; Cowan 2007, 224–29; Rambourg 2005, 116–17.

25. On cuisine as deception, see Lévi-Strauss 1970; Morton 1994. Though Jean-Jacques Rousseau is particularly associated with this argument, in fact it was widespread among reforming circles in early eighteenth-century France.

26. On earlier English anatomical arguments for the essentially vegetarian nature of man, see Spencer 1993, chap. 9.

27. *Journal des Sçavans* 43 (March 1709): 428; [Hecquet] 1710a, vol. 1, chap. 8.

only certain route to true knowledge. This project entailed a total abandonment of iatrochemical explanation in favor of a hydraulic model of illness, now construed in terms of disruption to the circulation. Pitcairn's model suited Hecquet's theological agenda. He portrayed the body as a continuous network of pulsating vessels, a phenomenon termed "trituration." By this means, food was elaborated into chyle, chyle into blood, and blood into a subtle vapor able to penetrate the brain substance. The digestive process thus became a universal explanatory principle within the bodily economy. Living bodies were distinct from inert ones by virtue of special divine intervention, which was a recurrent theme in Hecquet's writings. Much later, in his 1733 *La médecine théologique,* Hecquet was to define nature as "nothing other than the impression of the finger of God transmitted to and remaining in the body and which a doctor sees in the least of the organs of man." This overtly theological reference, which contrasted with a general trend toward the secularization of medical knowledge in medical faculties, was what attracted supporters of trituration.[28] In 1713 a young Hecquet protégé, Philippe-Bernard de Bordegaraye, argued that trituration demonstrated God's continual presence within human bodies. The principle of movement, impressed upon infinitely extended matter and conserved to the end of the world, constituted universal nature, "the mother of everything which falls under our senses, which maintains, nourishes and perfects: it is in fact, so to speak, God himself." The whole animal economy was maintained in its existing condition by a constant principle, the arrangement of the organs destined to perform certain functions. Without this arrangement, life could not be sustained. Like all triturationists, Bordegaraye located the source of motion and order in the solids, casting the body's fluids as essentially passive. He also insisted that any comparison of the body's fibers with ordinary mechanical springs was misplaced; motion, in the case of trituration, was unique to organized bodies.[29]

Hecquet had originally presented trituration as an explicitly mechanical riposte to iatrochemical models of the body. The triturating body pulsed with an alternating motion between contraction and dilation that was set in motion by God's personal intervention and continued until the moment

28. Quoted in Murphy 1989, 328. On medical secularization, see also Jones 1989; Greenbaum 1981; on Pitcairn, see especially Guerrini 1987.

29. Procope Couteaux 1712, 1727; Bordegaraye 1713, 18, 30, 33; "Procope Couteaux, Michel Coltelli," *Biographie Universelle* 34:394. Brockliss 1978, 233n, shows that in 1707 Procope Couteaux was the first in the faculty to *defend* the notion of tritus. Possibly the Jansenist associations trituration acquired soon afterwards at the hands of Hecquet caused his later skepticism.

of death. After the publication of the second edition of his treatise on digestion, in 1729, Hecquet's recourse to a classic mechanical image—he likened the body to a divinely engineered clockwork—attracted the ire of a "teacher of natural philosophy," writing in the *Mémoires de Trévoux*, whose editors continued to campaign against trituration. The anonymous critic, drawing on a line of argument developed by natural philosophers objecting to Newtonian forces, accused Hecquet of inventing an occult cause for the oscillatory action that characterized trituration, in effect of falling back on special providence to account for the perpetual motion that characterized the animal machine. If a "deus in machinâ" had been acceptable in 1713, sixteen years later self-moving machines were more problematic, and mechanists sought other explanations for the principles of corporeal activity.[30]

Hecquet's Jansenist convictions were no secret from his contemporaries. Nicolas Andry de Boisregard's response to the *Traité des dispenses de Carême* began as a single volume, *Le régime du carême* (Lenten Regimen) of 1710, and was extended into a detailed two-volume denunciation in 1713. Here Andry addressed the most medically and theologically problematic aspects of Hecquet's claims: lifestyle, health, and corporeal strength. "The better part," he snarled, "turns on outrageous sentiments, which far from remaining limited to the wise severity of the Gospel, exceed all moderation, & sometimes extend to inhumanity."[31] In particular, he attacked as irreligious Hecquet's claim that Lenten foods were actually more healthy. The consumption of lean foods was only validated as an act of penitence if such foods were less, not more, nourishing than an ordinary diet; thus, Hecquet's claim that vegetable foods were the most nourishing of all was self-defeating. Self-starvation fulfilled the need to mortify the flesh, which Jesuits viewed as the principal purpose of the Lenten period: it served as a temporal penance for the sins of ordinary life. For Jansenists, everyday life was the setting for a continual struggle for self-discipline and the repression of the passions in the effort to transcend the inherent corruption of the flesh. Food pleasure, rather than corporeal mortification, was their target. For Molinists, by contrast, the performance of specific, customary corporeal acts, such as prayer, fasting, and celibacy, was sufficient to allow the venial sins of every day to be expiated successfully. Thus, Andry argued that God had ordained the Lenten period precisely in order to humble the body by

30. As Murphy 1989, 324–30, shows, Hecquet championed Newton's theories at the Paris medical faculty.

31. [Andry de Boisregard] 1710, 497. On Jansenist cuisine as a political and theological project, see Cottret 1983.

weakening it.[32] Similarly, though the journalists of Trévoux seem often to have endorsed calls for limited religious reform, they vehemently opposed the extreme transformations of lifestyle that Hecquet both advocated and practiced.

Molinists also tended to play up the positive side of the pleasures of the table. In 1702 a Trévoux reviewer, reflecting on the claim that fasting was "an error against civil society & even against the State," noted that:

> with this excessive diet, men would on the one hand lose table commerce, one of the most usual means of maintaining unity & friendship in civil society, & they would, on the other hand, become *soft, lazy, & incapable of working, bearing arms, trading, & fulfilling the other employments which a State cannot do without*. If this is true, one would have to be very unhappy not to prefer to take a little good cheer, rather than expose oneself to sinning against the laws of human nature, & to become, in a way, a criminal of the State.[33]

Table commerce and alimentary pleasure, in this view, were fundamental not only to the relation between God and man, but also to the social bonds that constituted the State as an entity. Within limits, individual veniality could be condoned if society as a whole benefited. Andry's versions of Lent and health were therefore more politically acceptable to the Trévoux reviewer precisely on the grounds of ecclesiastical politics: "Mr Andry always supports the practice of today's Church, against Mr Hecquet who seeks to bring fasting back to its former austerity." Where human nature was concerned, Molinists tended to support the status quo in regard both to scientific explanations and to everyday life. Dale Van Kley has observed that the practical effect of the Molinist response to Jansenism and other radical reform movements in the early eighteenth century was "to exalt, like Renaissance humanism, man's nature in its present state." Molinists were optimistic about secular society, placing a value on terrestrial existence, including political engagement and the cultivation of the sciences and arts for their secular benefits. In this sense the dispute also turned on the question of progress and change: was modern civil society an improvement upon the past, or not?[34]

32. Astruc 1711, 23–24, also rejected the possibility of conciliating health with piety through a lean diet.

33. Review of *L'Anti-Cornaro* 1702, *Mémoires de Trévoux* (1703): 596–602 (original emphasis).

34. Review of [Andry de Boisregard] 1710, *Mémoires de Trévoux* (1710): 2086; Van Kley 1975, 7–8.

RESPONSES TO HECQUET

It is no surprise, then, to find that Andry and others who responded to Hecquet's thesis treated the problem of digestion as a question of medicine, theology, and politics simultaneously. This dispute rested on incommensurable views of the phenomenon of digestion and assimilation: far from being "just" about medical theory, it addressed the role medicine might play in relation to religion in general and to individual lifestyle in particular, as well as the relationship between accounts of the body and absolutist politics. The *Mémoires de Trévoux* had begun open warfare on Hecquet's digestive model in its January 1710 issue with an article written by Raymond Vieussens, a leading Montpellier iatrochemist, a member of Paris's Académie Royale des Sciences, and a privileged physician. This meant that he was not a member of the Paris medical faculty, where Hecquet had much support. Vieussens appealed to iatrochemical ferments, which Hecquet had sought to discredit, as the source of chemical change in foods. The stomachic ferments, subtle fluids which dissolved foodstuffs in the stomach, were a "very fine extract of the various principles of the blood . . . composed of volatile parts, phlegm, sulphur, acrid saline salt, & acidic salt," secreted into the stomach and intestines.[35] For Vieussens, like many iatrochemists, the active principle of digestion was spirit. Digestion and absorption were thus described in the language of corpuscular chemistry, which explained chemical phenomena by appealing to the physical properties of particles. The finer particles of foods possessed greater activity and mobility, while the heavier, coarser, or more earthy particles were more inert. As we will see in later chapters, these appeals to spirit and to corpuscular chemistry remained characteristic of food chemistry until 1750.[36]

During digestion, Vieussens claimed, the "finest parts [of foods], & in consequence those most charged with ethereal matter, insinuate themselves through the motive force of that matter into the mass of the blood." Slightly coarser parts entered the small intestine to make chyle, which then penetrated into the body via the lacteal ducts. The digestive organs thus acted like a series of progressively finer sieves, filtering out the coarsest,

35. Raymond Vieussens, "De la nature et des proprietez du levain de l'estomac," *Mémoires de Trévoux* (1710): 134–51. On Vieussens, see Debus 1991, chap. 4, esp. 139–41; "Vieussens, Raymond," *Biographie Universelle* 43:363–64; Sturdy 1995, 376; Institut de France 1979, 498.

36. This widespread iatrochemical assertion, bolstered by the recent anatomical investigations of Thomas Willis, also had Renaissance antecedents (Albala 2002, 62–63; Johns 1996, 1998).

indigestible material, which was expelled as excrement. Eating spirit-rich foods could also speed up digestion by making the stomach more active. The proportion of spirits vis-à-vis other types of elemental particles (earth, water, or salt) contained in a given foodstuff determined the balance of principles it generated in the blood of a healthy eater. Health could be disrupted by imbalances in consumption; for example, an excessive intake of spirit-rich foods would make the blood hyperactive and more liable to ferment, rendering the eater more liable to certain diseases, particularly hot conditions like fevers. Chemical models of this sort were distinct from earlier models of the stomach as a cooking pot, gently boiling foods into a uniform, gruel-like consistency.[37]

Iatrochemical models also offered a complete contrast to Hecquet's pulsating, pounding body. Because of the centrality of mechanical movement in the triturationist model, muscular strength played a key part in the efficacy of digestion. Such claims had extensive significance for medical therapy and regimen advice. Hecquet differentiated between two types of physical weakness, organic dysfunction and muscular weakness: "Those people are called weak, whose organs are delicate rather than imperfect or badly conditioned; but muscular strength, which is less vigorous in them, always becomes adequate, when well managed. Now sobriety, with a simple regimen, contributes wonderfully to that management." Corporeal delicacy was, as mentioned above, the principal ground for according Lenten dispensations. For Hecquet, physical health, achieved and maintained by practices of self-management and self-disciplining in the form of sobriety and abstinence, was an indicator of proper religious conduct, and a good digestion a manifestation of a good life. But both, like the Jansenists' state of grace, were hard to achieve and demanded constant unremitting effort, in the form of the sacrifice of physical pleasure and comfort. By contrast, Andry denied that physical robustness was a good measure of digestive power: "A child, he says, a delicate person, digests meats that a strong & robust man cannot digest. One sees people who digest the toughest meat, & who would not be able to eat a small amount of fruit without suffering indigestions: a currant or a plum resist digestion in certain stomachs. These effects could never be explained by grinding." Andry pointed to the way in which chemical substances varied in their ability to dissolve different substances: "*eau regale*" dissolved gold but not silver, for example. By analogy, he argued, digestion

37. Vieussens (1710), esp. 147–48; trituration was critiqued in pt. 2 of the same article. On models of the stomach as a cookpot, see especially Albala 2002, 57–62.

must occur in the stomach by means of ferments, and differing abilities to digest individual foods must reflect the varying composition of the ferment rather than being an absolute measure of corporeal strength.[38]

In February 1710, in a critical review of Hecquet's *Traité des dispenses de Carême*, Father René-Joseph de Tournemine, editor of the *Mémoires de Trévoux*, invited Hecquet to respond to Vieussens. Hecquet rose to the journal's bait, publishing additional defenses of trituration and invoking the aid of colleagues in the Paris medical faculty. Over the next decade, Hecquet's allies and students used endorsements of books and thesis defenses to make public expressions of support for him personally, if not necessarily for the doctrine of trituration.[39] Political and theological factions now formed, dividing French medical practitioners over the question of digestion and the consuming body. The scientific opponents of Jansenism joined forces to counter Hecquet's claims with new epistemological resources. Jean-Claude-Adrien Helvétius, father of the famous philosophe, carried out an anatomical study of the stomach and intestinal muscles specifically to refute the triturationists. Helvétius, a royal academician and Hecquet's faculty colleague, had been Andry's favored candidate as premier physician to the king in 1718, but the post had gone to Claude-Jean-Baptiste Dodart, the son of Hecquet's close friend and fellow Jansenist Denis Dodart. Helvétius used anatomy and vivisection to argue that the amount of strength attributed to the stomach by the triturationists was a mechanical and physiological impossibility. This work denoted a significant shift in the style of proof used in the digestion dispute. Up to that point, the debate had relied upon analogical reasoning and scholastic argumentation; from Helvétius onward, modeling and anatomical dissection were invoked in addition. Hecquet's provocative thesis thus opened up a range of new avenues of inquiry into the

38. [Hecquet] 1710a, 1:425; *Mémoires de Trévoux* (1710): 2081, 2086. Corporeal delicacy was not necessarily the same as muscular weakness at this time (Bertrand 1712, 713–14; "Santé [Œcon. anim.]" [1765], in Diderot and d'Alembert 1751–77, 14:630).

39. *Mémoires de Trévoux* (1710): 284; [Hecquet] 1710b, 1712, 1730; review of [Hecquet] 1710b in *Journal des Sçavans* 48 (August 1710): 127–41. An active editor from 1701 until 1719, Tournemine frequently campaigned against Jansenism and was identified by Hecquet as the review's author, refuting views of it as a passive mouthpiece of orthodoxy (Ribard 2005; Hecquet 1712, iij; Ehrard and Roger 1965). The digestion controversy is summarized in Debus 2001, 154–62; Doyon and Liaigre 1966, 127–28; Torlais 1936, 347–52. Hecquet 1712; Bordegaraye 1713; [Lefèvre de St-Marc] 1740, 6, 47n, 92; review of Hecquet 1712 in *Journal des Sçavans* 51 (April 1712): 363–76. From such texts it is possible to construct Hecquet's network of supporters within the faculty, which probably included Raymond Finot, Alexandre-Pierre Mattot, François Maillard, and younger physicians sponsored by Hecquet, such as Bordegaraye, Antoine Pepin, François-Antoine le Dran, and Emmanuel-Maurice Duverney.

nature of food and digestion, or rather borrowed them from English natural history.[40]

Only during Andry's tenure as faculty dean, in 1730, did Helvétius finally succeed Dodart junior as premier physician to the king. In the meantime, the Crown had conducted an ongoing campaign of persecution against Jansenists. The nuns of the Port-Royal convent were evicted in 1709 and, while Hecquet was dean of the Paris medical faculty, the convent was razed to the ground. At the height of the digestion controversy, in September 1713, Pope Clement XI was induced by Louis XIV to write a bull, *Unigenitus*, condemning numerous propositions from a leading Jansenist text. Many French institutions rejected the bull: above all, the Paris *parlement*, the judicial organization whose task it was to register new laws, refused to do so in this case, while groups of clergy with Jansenist leanings and favorably disposed university faculties expressed vocal opposition. *Unigenitus* became a rallying point for both Jansenists and another clerical group seeking religious reform, the Richerists. This latter group sought a democratic reform of ecclesiastical structure, giving more power to the lower clergy and more autonomy to the French church to manage its own affairs. Collectively, these opponents of *Unigenitus* became known as appellants. During the next decades, significant skirmishes in the digestion dispute coincided with the timing of major moves in an ongoing effort to suppress appellancy involving the Crown, the Inquisition, and the papacy. Throughout, the appellants were defended by the Paris *parlement*, a bastion of resistance to the political and religious policies of the Crown since the Fronde in the 1650s.[41]

Finally, in 1722, the Regent's ministers made a decisive move, insisting that university degrees and Crown benefices be granted only to those prepared to sign a document renouncing the appeal against *Unigenitus*. Recalcitrant appellants were imprisoned during the mid-1720s, and in 1730 the Paris *parlement* finally capitulated, making the bull *Unigenitus* law. The medical faculty was among those organizations that officially appealed against this new legislation in 1726. By now, Nicolas Andry was dean. Obdurately opposed to Jansenism, he surreptitiously altered the wording of the letter of appeal written by the faculty, an act for which he was roundly

40. Helvétius 1721; Fontenelle 1721; Brockliss 2002, 141; 1998, 76–77; 1989, 142; 1987, 405–8; 1978, 235; Brockliss and Jones 1997, 422–25; Debus 1991, chap. 4.

41. On Dodart, see Sainte-Beuve 1926–32, 2:350, 6:197–98, 7:283; *Dictionnaire de Biographie Française* 11, cols. 417–18. On the Jansenist movement at this date, see Chantin 1996, chap. 2; Van Kley 1975, 22–25; on the Fronde and opposition politics, Baker 1990.

condemned by his colleagues.[42] Indeed, the faculty seems to have acquired something of a reputation for supporting appellancy. The clandestine Jansenist periodical *Nouvelles Ecclésiastiques* reported that in April 1728 a Court informer accused the faculty of covertly supporting the nationalist agendas of appellancy and Richerism by altering the wording of the admission oath sworn by students. A furious letter from the minister de Fleury to Dodart in his capacity as premier physician ensued. Threatening dire punishments, Cardinal de Fleury claimed "that for a long time it had been known at Court that the Faculty is suspect as regards Religion." At a hastily convoked meeting, faculty members signed a letter declaring their own innocence of the charge of religious sedition.

> All the Doctors signed the deliberations in a uniform manner. Only two distinguished themselves, viz., Mr Winsløw who expressed himself thus: "Not only do I profess the Roman Religion, but on that basis, I believe that it is necessary to revoke the Appeal against the Bull Unigenitus." Monsieur Andry wrote beneath this remark: *I too attest to the same thing*.[43]

Jacques-Bénigne Winsløw, Andry's fellow opponent of appellancy, was a high-profile Danish convert to Catholicism and an increasingly eminent anatomist.[44] The coincidence of important episodes in the appellancy crisis with medical controversies over matters of natural fact is highlighted by the digestion dispute. A new flurry of pamphlets arguing for and against trituration appeared in the late 1720s, a second edition of a critique of Hecquet written by Michel Procope in 1727, and another edition of Hecquet's book in 1729. In short, digestion was a good meter of the climate of political and religious opposition in Parisian medical circles between 1710 and 1730.[45]

THE INVESTIGATION OF FOOD

But how was food understood within these conflicting models of the digestive process? Iatrochemists and iatromechanists had different accounts of the nature of the alimentary substance. In the early modern body, food

42. *Biographie Universelle*, 1:685–86; Brockliss 1989, 195–96; [Hecquet] 1726b. In October 1718, Hecquet was one of forty-six appellant Faculty members.

43. *Nouvelles Ecclesiastiques* 1734, entry for April 28, 1728 (original emphasis).

44. Winsløw endorsed trituration in Hecquet 1712, but later rejected both trituration and appellancy (Grell 2007; Stroup 1990, 83–88; Helvétius 1721, 343).

45. Procope Couteaux 1727; Hecquet 1730.

was generally understood as the matter that repaired the wear and tear of everyday life. As Bordegaraye claimed, "Our machine would use itself up without fail, both by continual rubbing, & by the dissipation of its juices which evaporate like smoke, if it did not draw something to replenish that expenditure from some source." It was virtually axiomatic in eighteenth-century medical writings that the relationship between the consuming body and its food was a primary cause of both corporeal and moral disease. Both food choice and the degree of efficacy of the digestive process contributed to this. To continue in Bordegaraye's words:

> These foodstuffs also cause [the body's] ruin. They are strangers which we admit without knowing whence they come: we often do not examine their condition, number, or weight; we even accumulate them hastily & without selectivity, thus these guests, imprudently admitted, trouble our œconomy.[46]

Claude Fischler suggests that "In incorporating foods, we make them . . . attain the ultimate in interiority," characterizing the "paradox of the omnivore" as the fear that the incorporation of a foodstuff necessarily entails the incorporation of all or part of the properties ascribed to it. This is a useful model for explaining how the debate over digestion and diet in the 1710s medical world was also a commentary upon the ethics of individual conduct at this time of social and dietary transformation. At stake was not only the issue of how foods generated disease, but also the bigger question of how what people ate made them who they were, in sickness or in health—and thus the question of the extent of individual responsibility for the health of society as a whole, and how the control of appetite might contribute to or harm that.[47]

Hecquet expressed standard contemporary medical views of disease causation when he claimed that an incomplete digestive process would yield a poor-quality chyle and a blood supply clogged with unrefined alien substances: "Coarser vapors will arise, only suitable for encumbering the brain & nerves; the liqueurs will increase and thicken; the motion of the solids will slow; the play of the whole machine will be disrupted; deposits, blockages [*engagemens*] and obstructions are inevitable." His supporter Bordegaraye appealed to the quantity of foods ingested as the "primary cause" of disease, with culinary preparation and dietary choice as secondary causes

46. Bordegaraye 1713, 42–43.
47. Fischler 1993, 9.

that disrupted the muscular action of the digestive tract. Iatrochemists and iatromechanists thus differed over diet as the cause of disease, the former appealing to imbalances in the chemical composition of the humors while the latter appealed to mechanical difficulties such as obstruction or thickening.[48] It was when they were converted into practical recommendations for regimen that such differences took on a new significance for the relationship between diet, health, and piety. Ease of digestion was widely portrayed in medical writings as the principal reason why foods were healthy or unhealthy. According to Hecquet, Lenten foods, especially cereals and pulses, were easier to digest than meat because they were more readily ground up. For triturationists, digestibility was a purely mechanical property. Their dietary recommendations rested upon underlying claims that food was a homogeneous substance, identical in composition to the body itself. In the stomach, gut, and blood, trituration ground the nutritive substance finer and finer, reducing it to its microscopical component vessels. These then circulated around the body in the bloodstream and lodged in those places of the body that had been eroded away by the grind of everyday life.

Such claims by Hecquet and other triturationists were comprehensively challenged by Jean Astruc, who taught medicine at the faculties of Toulouse and Montpellier before being appointed to a chair at Paris's Collège Royal in 1731. He would be identified as a supporter of the Jesuits, admittedly for polemical ends, after the suppression of the Society of Jesus in France in 1764 and his own death in 1766. Though Astruc did not arrive in Paris until after the second wave of the digestion controversy in the 1720s, he had by then already proven himself perhaps the most redoubtable of Hecquet's iatrochemical opponents. A correspondent, and probably favored student, of Pierre Chirac at Montpellier, Astruc responded to Hecquet from Toulouse, in his reply defining corporeal phenomena, including digestion, in terms of iatrochemical ferments. A brief critique presented to the Montpellier Société Royale des Sciences in 1710 and published in 1711 was followed by a book-length elaboration of the same piece in 1714. The controversy over digestion evidently had personal significance to Astruc, for over the next decades he amassed a large collection of works dealing with both tritura-

48. *Mémoires de Trévoux* (1707): 73–74; Bordegaraye 1713, 43. Seventeenth-century iatrochemistry emphasized the balance of acids and alkalis, but this view had become unfashionable by the 1710s, as had the Renaissance model of dietary regimen as a balancing of humoral qualities—hot with cold and moist with dry. In Lémery 1705 and Astruc 1714, 364–66, stress was placed instead upon the balance between active principles (spirits and volatile salts) and tempering principles (oily and balsamic substances) which restrained the violence of the former.

tionist and fermentationist models of digestion, including medical theses, memoirs, and books.[49]

Astruc acknowledged the sweeping implications of the digestion controversy in terms of the relationship between medical knowledge and daily life.

> The interests of our health & of our own preservation ought to engage us to [discover the cause of digestion]. This is not vain nor purely speculative research, the knowledge of which only serves to enlighten the spirit, without any utility. It is a question whose decision influences daily custom & practice. The cause of Digestion, well developed, must inform us which Foods are easiest to digest . . . [and] about the choice we ought to make; it must dissipate the doubts which divide Physicians over the quality of viands; in a word, it must either confirm the ideas we already have on this matter, or disabuse us of our old errors & lead us to adopt the new regimen of living that a learned Physician has proposed.[50]

To settle this question, Astruc entered into the chemistry of alimentary matter itself. One great concern with trituration was that it could not explain the way in which human bodies differed in nature from their foodstuffs.

> Grinding . . . can only reduce the Foods we take, for example Bread, into *integral* parts, which, though very small, will always retain the nature of the Whole, from which they were detached. . . . Thus, the Chyle formed in this manner would only be a mass of bread parts. The blood & nourishing juice . . . would also be but a compound of similar parts, but finer & more divided. . . . The parts of bread of which they were composed, having lost their sensible properties only by division, would quickly recover them, once they united to nourish our bodies, & rather than changing into our substance, would turn back into bread, as they were before.[51]

If the French eater was not to be a mere man of bread, then there had to be an essential distinction between the matters of food and man. It is surely

49. This collection was used to compile Portal 1770–73, vol. 6. On Astruc, see Tourneux 1877–82, 7:38; Doe 1960; Huard et al. 1972, 9–30; Dulieu 1973; Corcos 1983; Lorry 1767; Richard 2001.

50. Astruc 1711, 3, reviewed in *Journal des Sçavans* 50 (July 1711): 65–81.

51. Astruc 1711, 6–7. Original emphasis.

no coincidence that Astruc chose bread and wine, the two foods of the Eucharist, to illustrate his argument. Contemporary theological treatises on the Eucharist sometimes resorted to natural philosophical explanations to describe the mechanism by which the Holy Spirit was transmitted to communicants with the Eucharistic meal. Astruc portrayed the digestive tract in terms akin to the miracle of the Eucharist: as the site of a genuine transsubstantiation, a "marvellous change" in the matter of foods that approximated them to our own substance, replacing the qualities they had originally possessed with radically different ones. It was this that proved the phenomenon to be a true chemical decomposition, in which the ferments of the digestive tract, beginning with saliva, broke down foods into their elementary molecules. In support of this argument, he posited two distinct types of chemical processes: those that merely disaggregated the "integral parts" while preserving the properties of the whole, and those that decomposed integral parts or molecules into their component or "principal" parts, which were those obtained in the laboratory by analysis. The latter occurred in all three forms of coction that accomplished the conversion of foods into self: chylification, sanguification, and assimilation. It was also the phenomenon taking place during fermentation, when must converted into wine, or flour into bread. However, it was a phenomenon that could not be explained by recourse to mechanics alone. Accordingly, Astruc concluded, "the foods which are most friable & most disposed to be ground or milled, are not always the most easily digested, nor the most suitable for nourishing." Without chemistry, by implication, the scientific study of food verged on materialist heterodoxy.[52]

Hecquet responded by appealing to the special nature of foodstuffs, considered as matter:

> Digestion is less a production of new substances than a release of those which are contained in food. These substances come from the animals and plants which make up [our] food: they are, consequently, materials which have already served to nourish, & which do not need to change in nature so much as in situation or place. . . . Thus food, in man, is no more than the reuse of the same matter that has nourished an animal,

52. Ibid., 3, 23; 1714, 4, 107–9, chap. 8. In the 1750s, Astruc would extend his interest in the theological implications of matter to mental physiology. See Yolton 1991, 63–66, 106–8. For contemporary discussions of transubstantiation, see, e.g., *Mémoires de Trévoux* (1702): 10, 51–60; (1730): 1570–80; Brockliss 1987, 206–7. On early modern medical models of assimilation, see Orland and Spary (in press).

> say; [and] which, after being disunited from the body parts of the latter, attaches itself to the body of the former; anything going beyond that disunion would change the nature of the foodstuff, & cause it to lose that natural & *innate* compatibility that it has with the parts it is supposed to nourish. From which it should be concluded that the digestion of foods is only a disunion, a *separation*, a *dissolution* of materials. These materials have formed vessels in the bodies of animals & plants, & through digestion they become suitable for forming vessels in man.[53]

All types of matter in the body, whether spirits or salts, solids or fluids, were of a fundamentally different order from those produced in the laboratory, which were salamanders, experimental artifacts. "The juices in our bodies are the more perfect inasmuch as they partake less of those *creatures* of fire, which *chymistry* produces, & which physics supposes."[54]

Hecquet's skepticism regarding chemistry as a heuristic tool for investigating the phenomena of the living body probably owed much to his relationship with Denis Dodart. While conducting a vast program of plant and animal analysis at Paris's Académie Royale des Sciences during the 1670s, Dodart and Claude II Bourdelin had subjected countless organized bodies, including many foods, to analysis by distilling them in an alembic over a naked flame. Their results were inconclusive and, in the experimenters' own eyes, cast doubt on the utility of chemical analysis.[55] By 1712 fire analysis was becoming a byword for the shortcomings of chemistry as a technique for exploring physiological phenomena. The grounds for this discredit were that chemical intervention destroyed the unique properties of living matter. As one physician wrote:

> The uncertainty of fire analysis for knowing the nature of mixts appears in the way it produces as many alkaline salts from saliva as from bile, whose taste & color are so different; & a very skilful Physician has remarked that the same quantity of principles is produced from very dissimilar plants, such as from cauliflower and *Solanum furiosum*; the first being a foodstuff, & the second a poison; it is the same with chervil & hemlock. It must be then that fire causes a change in the salts of one of these plants, & thus does not render them in their natural state; or else

53. Hecquet 1712, 2. Original emphasis.

54. Ibid., 413.

55. Ibid., 42–46; Stroup 1990, 92–97; Holmes 1996, 289–311; Kim 2003, chap. 1; Debus 1987, chaps. 7, 10; Moran 2005.

that it destroys the arrangement of their parts, in which their qualities consist: thus fire is not a competent judge.[56]

For Hecquet, all artificial phenomena were essentially distinct from the Hippocratic naturals, which were restricted to processes occurring within the body. Thus, no analogy could be drawn between chemistry and physiology, even by reasoning from fermentative processes such as those used in breadmaking or beer-brewing to bodily function. Chemists erred in the assumption that conditions in their apparatus were analogous to those prevailing in the human body, and Hecquet contrasted the ambitious, overreaching knowledge-claims of the chemist with the more limited and modest concerns of physicians, who only aspired to the knowledge which God had made available for man's self-preservation. By 1729, when the second edition of his treatise on digestion was published, Hecquet was presenting himself, perhaps not surprisingly, as a supporter of the German physician Georg Stahl, whose view of the animate body as governed by forces differing fundamentally from those affecting brute matter would prove so significant for later physiologists.[57]

MODELS OF DIGESTION, 1735–1755

Between 1730 and 1750, as Van Kley shows, the meaning of "Jansenism" underwent a change. From denoting a set of beliefs and practices shared by a small, if vocal, group of heterodox religious reformers, Jansenism came to stand for a generalized political opposition to the status quo, often associated with the *parlements*, the judicial bodies whose magistrate members had since the mid-seventeenth century taken it upon themselves to criticize the Crown. An allegiance between Jansenists and Gallicans was forged by the appellancy issue, such that by the 1750s the head of the Paris police, d'Argenson, could write of the Jansenists as nationalists, and of the Molinists as the *parti dévot*, the pious sect. By 1750 this originally religious dispute had metamorphosed into a broader political opposition, culminating in the suppression of the Society of Jesus in France in 1764.[58] During the same two decades, trituration lost its exclusive association with Jansenism and thus to some extent its raison d'être. Simultaneously, the attempt to explain

56. Viridet 1735, 1:59–60, 104–5, based on an account of the failure of the analysis project by a Paris medical faculty member, Le François 1723, 1:250–57; see also [de Caylus] 1719, 81. On the Académie Royale des Sciences's program of plant and animal analysis, see Stroup 1990, chap. 7.

57. On Stahl, see especially Duchesneau 1976; Debus 2001, 207–22; Cheung 2004, 2006.

58. Van Kley 1975, chap. 1; Chantin 1996, 40–45; Melton 2001, pt. 1, chap. 2.

digestion moved out of the medical faculty and into the domains of natural history and natural philosophy. This is evident in attempts by the naturalist Antoine-René Ferchault de Réaumur and the *mécanicien* or mechanical inventor Jacques Vaucanson to prove that trituration was not the mechanism of digestion. Where the medical dispute had been conducted largely on traditional scholastic lines within the Paris medical faculty, with parades of verbal bravura in a succession of pamphlets and journal articles, both Réaumur and Vaucanson addressed the problem of digestion from an experimental angle, utilizing technologies developed in natural philosophy to investigate bodily function, though both took very different approaches to the experimental study of digestion. The digestion dispute now took a new direction.

Jacques Vaucanson was a prominent figure in the Académie des Sciences until his death in 1782. He founded and maintained the academy's important collection of mechanical models of machines and scientific instruments. Himself an inventor, he moved back and forth across the boundary between the royally privileged, scientific space of the academy and the inventors' world of commercial profit, and, since he was in a position to judge the work of other inventors, he was in turn courted and attacked by them, as Liliane Hilaire-Pérez has shown. Vaucanson intervened in the digestion dispute on the back of the enormous success of his human automata. The first of these, a flautist, was demonstrated to the Académie des Sciences in April 1738 and heralded by Vaucanson as an implementation of the solid mechanical principles that the academy fostered. On Easter Monday 1739 he demonstrated two more figures: a tambourine player and a duck. The latter had the primary function of proving that the digestive mechanism of the stomach was chemical. It represented "the mechanism of the viscera destined for the functions of drinking, eating, and digestion; the Play of all the parts necessary for these actions is precisely imitated: it stretches out its neck to take grain from one's hand, swallows it, digests it, and produces it completely digested by the ordinary route." Although Vaucanson's duck invariably features in historical accounts as a case of the application of mechanistic natural philosophy to the body, in fact it served precisely the opposite purpose. It presented the digestive process as a *chemical* operation. Enshrined "in a small space" within the duck's body was a model stomach, which was "a chemical laboratory, to decompose the principal constitutive parts" of the grain which it swallowed. "Here food is digested as [it is] in real animals, by dissolution, & not by trituration, as several Natural Philosophers claim; but that is what I shall reserve to be treated & displayed on the occasion."[59]

59. Hilaire-Pérez 2000, 163; Vaucanson 1738, 19.

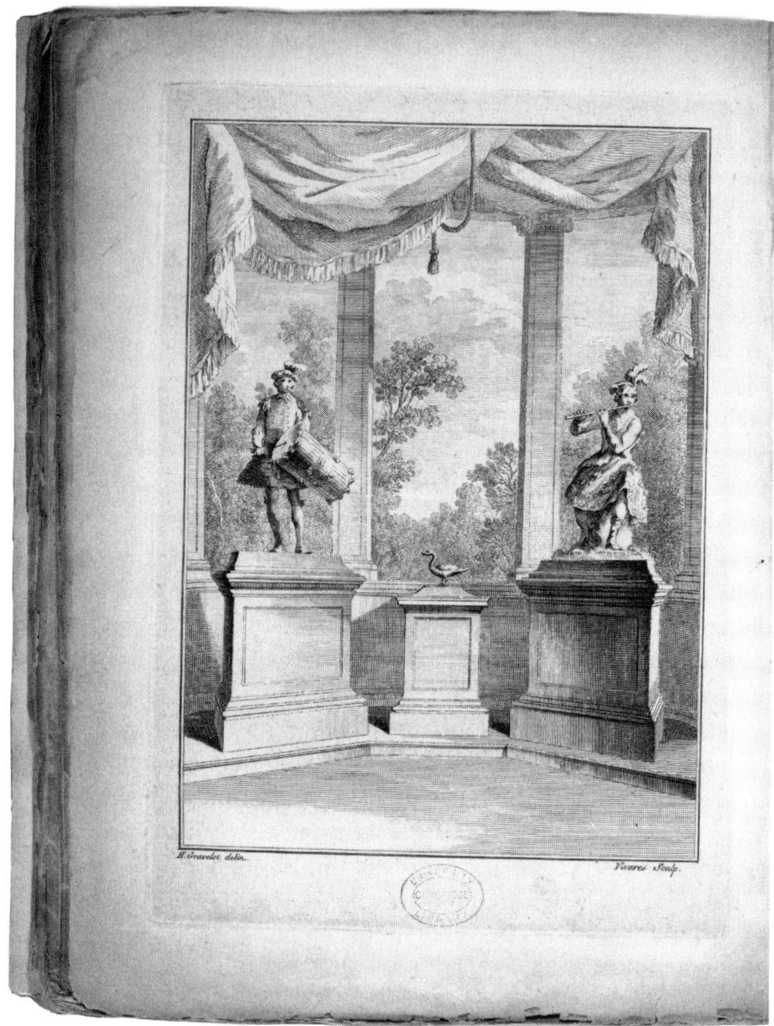

Figure 1.1. Jacques Vaucanson, *Le Mécanisme du Fluteur Automate* (Paris: Jacques Guerin, 1738), frontispiece. The famous digesting duck occupies the center pedestal. Copperplate engraving by Vivares after Henri Gravelot. Cambridge University Library.

Vaucanson warned: "I do not claim this digestion to be a perfect digestion, capable of making blood & nourishing parts for the animal's upkeep; it would be with bad grace, I think, that one would reproach me for that." While the mechanism of the duck's wings and the gears and rods in the pedestal were available for the curious onlooker to marvel at, the display of the process of digestion was much more carefully policed, for the inner workings of the duck's abdomen were not fully exposed. As late as 1781, a visitor with triturationist leanings denounced the automaton's performance of digestion as a fraud, claiming that the grain "consumed" by Vaucanson's duck lodged in a reservoir at the base of the throat, while the excrement was produced from a supply inserted into the automaton before the demonstration began. Digestion, he said, could in any case hardly occur so rapidly unless one was to adduce trituration. It is hardly coincidental to the theological issues provoking the digestion controversy that the duck made its debut on Easter Monday, as soon after the end of Lent as was legally permissible for public displays of this sort.

Vaucanson's specific interest in physiology may have begun, his chief biographers suggest, in 1731 or 1732, when he began to associate with the Rouen surgeon Claude-Nicolas Le Cat. At this time he was also contemplating entry to the Jesuit order. For the next couple of years, Vaucanson toured Normandy exhibiting animal automata; the duck or a prototype thereof was probably in existence by 1734. Subsequently, Vaucanson associated with the physician François Quesnay, who argued for a chemical foundation for physiology in the first edition of his *Essai phisique sur l'œconomie animale* (Physical Essay on the Animal Economy, 1736).[60] The capacity of natural philosophers and inventors to make credible working replicas of bodies was, as Simon Schaffer has asserted, part of the way in which they demonstrated mastery of the mechanical principles of nature and society. By theatricalizing mechanical function, they could present more persuasive accounts of these principles: as Schaffer argues, automata "were both arguments and entertainments, designed . . . to place craft skill within the setting of power, and to allow the selective entry by that power to the inner workings of art and nature." Vaucanson's was probably one of the most successful of the numerous attempts made throughout the eighteenth and early nineteenth centuries to model digestion experimentally, if only because of the high public

60. Vaucanson 1738, 19; Quesnay 1736. On claims that the duck's digestion was a fake, see Doyon and Liaigre 1966, 125–27; Cottom 1999, 69; Riskin 2003a, 608–9; 2003b, 104; Stafford 1994, 76; Dagognet 1987, 25–30; Beaune 1989; Fryer and Marshall 1979. On Vaucanson in Normandy, see Riskin 2003b, 114. On Vaucanson, Le Cat, and Quesnay's support for mechanical and hydraulic models of the body, see Doyon and Liaigre 1966, 18–19, 123–24, chaps. 5 and 6, *passim*; review of Quesnay 1748, *Mémoires de Trévoux* (1748): 822–25, 971–72; Murphy 1989. Banzhaf 2000, 533–45, presents Quesnay's model of the animal economy as iatromechanical, but Quesnay consistently rejected trituration, the only contemporary mechanistic explanation for digestion. Later, he treated digestion as the dissolution of foods by a soapy solvent, reflecting a mid-century turn toward solvent analysis of foods (Quesnay 1736, 1748; Spary unpublished, chap. 2).

visibility of the duck: the exhibition was extremely well attended. The very possibility of modeling the digestive process by mechanical and chemical means was, however, ruled out by Hecquet's version of trituration, which depended upon attributes specific to the naturals, in particular the property of perpetual motion uniquely accorded by God to living bodies.

For his part, Réaumur sidestepped such problems by performing experiments upon living birds. A highly active figure in Paris's Académie des Sciences, Réaumur was best known for his program for perfecting the arts and crafts and, from the 1740s onwards, for his interest in natural history, especially birds and insects, where he advanced a natural theological view of animal bodies as admirable Divine mechanisms. His biographer, Jean Torlais, positioned Réaumur between the religious heterodoxy of some *Encyclopédie* contributors and the extremes of Molinism. Réaumur's recourse to birds indicates the extent to which natural history and comparative anatomy could be used to challenge Hecquet's claims that mankind was vegetarian by nature, and that the human stomach operated through grinding rather than by some chemical process, whether fermentation or dissolution. Yet such arguments by analogy were not incontrovertible. Comparative anatomists could also defend the essentially vegetarian nature of man by appealing to the absence of sharp teeth and claws, or else cast man as naturally carnivorous by emphasizing the shortness of the human intestine, quite unlike the involved and convoluted digestive tract of herbivores.[61] For Réaumur, attention to structure and function was essential, however, because it allowed the theological emphasis of the digestion dispute to be relocated: the fact that the Creator had supplied a single ideal foodstuff, chyle, to nourish all animals, was more significant than the mechanism whereby chyle was obtained from foods. As he framed the question at the beginning of his presentation to the Académie des Sciences in December 1752:

> [God] has established that birds and quadrupeds should owe their growth and lifespan to a milky liqueur, to chyle which is partly prepared in the stomach. But did he want that liqueur to be extracted from foods in all animals by similar operations? We have grounds for doubt, at least, since he employed stomachs whose conformation is different.[62]

61. For a response to Réaumur's experiments as a problem of the legitimacy of analogies, see review of *Histoire de l'Académie Royale des Sciences. Année M.DCC.XLII*, *Mémoires de Trévoux* (1762): 2262; see also Spencer 1993.

62. Archives Nationales, Paris, dossier Réaumur, "Sur la maniere dont se fait la digestion," f°. 2.

A theological point was still to be made from truths about the digestion process, but the route to knowledge now lay in a logic based around experimentation and modeling. The particular strength of Réaumur's experimental program, carried out on animals from his own household, including birds, dogs, and sheep, lay in its claims to offer direct observation of events inside the digesting stomach.[63] He forcefed turkeys and a buzzard with metal and glass containers filled with barley or meat, and attached to strings that allowed them to be withdrawn at specified periods after consumption. The gizzards of the turkeys deformed and even crushed metal and glass, confirming that trituration was taking place. In the case of the buzzard, however, only the contents of the experimental vessels were dissolved away; the vessels remained intact and were eventually regurgitated, like other hard objects ingested by birds of prey. To prove the specificity of the digestive juices, Réaumur fed both raw and cooked grain to the buzzard, concluding that even when carnivorous birds of prey were driven by hunger to eat floury foods or fruits, foods they naturally shunned, their stomachic solvents were ineffective. Again, like Astruc, he appealed to a chemical analogy, the diverse effects of solvents on different metals.

Though earlier critics of trituration had claimed that the selectivity of digestion could only be explained by recourse to chemical solvents in the stomach, Réaumur was the first to design an experiment that could make visible that selectivity. The implications for dietary recommendations of a digestive model that relied upon specialized juices had been noted by Astruc in the 1710s: if the principle that digested foods acted chemically, the ideal food could not be determined from knowledge about the texture of foodstuffs. Indeed, if the digestive juices were specially designed solvents, only direct investigation of their behavior could indicate which foods were most suitable for human consumption. Unfortunately, this goal proved difficult to achieve. Réaumur attempted to extract the stomachic solvents of the buzzard on a sponge and add them to meat in a vessel, but neither this nor other in vitro digestive experiments carried out in the middle years of the century produced something that contemporaries agreed was the same as chyle. However, Réaumur was undaunted by his lack of success: like earlier

63. Schaffer 1999, 128–44; Torlais 1936, 47–48, 255–66, 347–63. The original accounts are reproduced in Réaumur 1756; one was presented to the December 23, 1752, meeting of the Paris Académie des Sciences. This experimentation revived an experimental program undertaken by Italian naturalists in the late seventeenth century, including the promoter of mechanical physick, Giovanni Alfonso Borelli, and his opponent Antonio Valisnieri. Hecquet 1712; Astruc 1714, chap. 12; anon. 1743, 2382. Holmes 1974, 141–43, claims Réaumur's investigations set the terms of digestive experimentation for several generations.

iatrochemists, he suggested that the digestive solvents, in order to penetrate and dissolve foods, must be highly volatile, and so evaporate once they were outside the body. Not until the end of the 1770s was the Italian clergyman Lazzaro Spallanzani successful in using gastric juice, extracted with a sponge, to dissolve foodstuffs outside the body.[64]

Though some subsequent commentators portrayed Réaumur's experiments as conclusive refutations of the triturationists, in practice it remained impossible to produce conclusive in vitro replications of digestion until well after the French Revolution. At the end of the eighteenth century, Spallanzani's experimental replication of digestion was not perceived to have settled the digestion dispute. The First Empire physician Armand Jenin de Montègre still claimed that the stomach's serous fluid was merely swallowed saliva, not, as many chemists asserted, an acid. But as Jansenism moved from a marginal radical theology to a mainstream style of political opposition, debates over digestion and the most suitable diet for pious eaters became less controversial, and many medical and scientific authors were happy to compromise by explaining digestion as a combination of chemical and mechanical phenomena.[65]

CONCLUSION

From the 1710s right up until the digesting duck that entertained Parisians in 1730, Hecquet's digestive model stood for one particular approach not only to natural knowledge, but also to lifestyle, religion, and politics. This chapter has described the various ways in which his medical and scientific opponents sought to counter the theological and political implications of his claims by resorting to experimentation, argument, and demonstration. Digestion enrolled the body tightly within events in the body politic and the public sphere: in tracing the evolution of this dispute, it is possible to show how the digestion controversy closely parallels the fate of Jansenism as described by Van Kley. Initially a minority religious sect, Jansenism transformed into an important political focus of opposition to absolutism. Similarly, the embrace of the frugal, sober, and natural, which Hecquet represented, would become a recurrent theme in later attempts

64. Réaumur 1756; Poncelet 1755, xj–xiv; Spallanzani 1784.

65. Holmes 1974, 143–44; Torlais 1936, 361–62. The mixed chemical and mechanical model of the Dutch physician Herman Boerhaave was especially favored, but German chemistry and Montpellier vitalist physiology also became important after 1750. See Spary unpublished, chap. 3.

to express opposition to absolutist and courtly politics through alternative lifestyles, as later chapters of this book will demonstrate. The significance of the digestion controversy for the politics of the science of food during the first decades of the eighteenth century should not be underestimated. Jansenists were far from being the only group calling for the sumptuary reform of everyday conduct as part of the creation of a new and better French nation from the beginning of the eighteenth century onward. But by carrying the call for reform into the fabric of the body itself, authors like Hecquet highlighted the political dilemmas that literate Parisians were to confront in eating and digesting in the century of Enlightenment.

By the 1750s, as later chapters of this book will show, eating as opposition had acquired even greater significance, following the social critiques of Jean-Jacques Rousseau. If the author of the *Encyclopédie*'s entry on digestion stoutly maintained that trituration was "the most ridiculous opinion ever to have disfigured the theory of Medicine," the doubts cast by its supporters on the validity of iatrochemical interpretations of food in the 1710s would resurface in later decades as French alimentary chemistry remained a contested domain.[66] The overtly religious implications of digestion, indigestion, and diet dwindled over the century, but only because their wider moral, political, and scientific significance expanded. The trituration controversy was a harbinger of the extent to which eighteenth-century men of science and letters would contribute to this process. Many scholars, indeed, saw themselves as exemplary cases of the relationship between mental or physical function, diet and national character, which was at stake in controversies such as this, for the organs of ratiocination and digestion were commonly regarded as closely connected. According to the seventeenth-century English anatomist Thomas Willis, the brain was the ultimate organ of digestive filtration, and this view was repeated in numerous French medical and philosophical works up to the 1760s.[67] But it was commonplace to suggest that digestive function affected moral conduct, as when Voltaire playfully alluded to the moral breakdown of rulers while in the grip of indigestion: "sedentary barbarians who order the massacre of a million men from the depths of their study, during their digestive period, and afterwards solemnly have God thanked for it." For iatrochemists in particular, enhancing mental function through diet was an actively pursued goal from the late seven-

66. Venel, "Digestion," 1000.

67. See, e.g., Le Camus 1769, 1:28–34, 66; Vandermonde 1756, 1:372–73; *Journal de Physique*, 2nd ed., 1772, pt. 2, 290–94; Le Cat 1767. On the relationship between mental and gastric function, see Vila 2005a; Jonsson 2005.

teenth century until around 1750. But even after the Revolution, medical authors continued to remind their readers of the close link between digestion and mental or moral function.[68]

In short, digestion was a prime locus at which matter and mind intersected in the eighteenth century. Not only did the digestive process play a role in moral conduct, it also helped to shape body and mind through its effects, good or bad, on the food that individuals ingested. Conversely, the condition of health of body and mind were exhibited in appetite and digestion, as we will see below. As the main route by which external matter determined the characteristics of the thinking self, digestion was thus a principal way in which social institutions such as cookery, political institutions such as the food supply, and natural phenomena such as climate affected the individual—a question of great importance to philosophical authors between 1670 and 1760. No wonder, then, that digestion was seen by some as crucial to the exercise of reason and the critical faculty, and so as relevant to the political critique produced by philosophes of different stripes. The trituration controversy not only concerned the proper way to generate knowledge of the animal economy, but also the nature and purpose of knowledge in general. The social and political agendas in which digestion and diet were implicated, including utility, health, and the critique of luxury, would characterize enlightened body politics in subsequent decades. Before moving on to investigate subsequent developments in the science and politics of alimentary opposition, I shall first outline the political conditions that were allowing courtly and luxurious eating to become an everyday experience for an increasing number of Paris's inhabitants, thus opening up a public space within which alimentary chemistry found social and moral relevance. Chapter 2 takes coffee, that epitome of rational consumption, to be a representative food of Enlightenment, and thus a point where debates over the relationship between food and mental function intersected with a centralizing absolutist politics that was creating the new public world of luxury consumption inhabited by the philosophes.

68. Voltaire 1752, chap. 7; compare La Mettrie 1912, 22; Cabanis Year X / 1802, 1:111.

CHAPTER TWO

From Curiosi to Consumers

The digestion debate of the early eighteenth century helped to fashion a new body politics for Paris. Successive generations of radical commentators from the 1710s onward presented alimentary hygiene as a tactic of political self-presentation. New mechanical physiologies were invoked to support calls for the cultivation of the strong body as an indispensable part of a reformed French nation, as we will see in later chapters. If one side in the conflict over diet and the politics of bodily knowledge explicitly sought the reform of the status quo, on the other side were those who not only welcomed, but even promoted the extension of European diet to foods hitherto regarded as outlandish and luxurious, and who viewed cuisine and courtly styles of consumption as desirable marks of taste and civilization. The knowledge projects associated with such positions rested upon rather different sorts of claims about the effects of foodstuffs upon body and mind, and often found favor in medical and scientific circles indebted to Crown patronage.

Perhaps the most significant difference European eating habits underwent in the seventeenth and eighteenth centuries was the increasingly generalized consumption of new and exotic foods, especially coffee, tea, chocolate, and sugar. In this chapter and the next, I take coffee as an exemplary substance for exploring one conjuncture of taste, expertise, and politics, which I want to argue was prominent in enlightened accounts of the effects of diet upon mind. Coffee, surely the drink that after wine is most associated with the French, exemplified the cultivation of reason and was therefore a valuable aid to an enlightened self-presentation. In addition, coffee stood for novelty. As an entirely new substance, not known to the ancients and not used in Paris before the 1650s, coffee provoked extensive commentary on the significance of dietary change for bodies, society, and learning. The process of converting coffee consumption from the arcane to the everyday and the process of turning it into the object of knowledge proceeded in parallel. Coffee's novel status allowed different groups to lay claim to scholarly expertise about its qualities, identity, and preparation. This makes it a useful focus for an inquiry into how knowledge about food was generated in enlightened Parisian society.[1]

Coffee entered scholarship between 1670 and 1730. The first date coincides with a historical event widely taken to mark the beginning of wider public familiarity with coffee in Paris, namely the visit of the Ottoman ambassador to the capital in 1669; the second marks the decade by which coffee had become an everyday substance for many of the capital's inhabitants. Coffee is also a microcosm of European relations with the rest of the world during a key historical period. As a commodity, coffee exemplifies contemporary transformations in world trading patterns that would fundamentally and permanently alter European tastes. What people in eighteenth-century Paris ate would from this time onward make a vast difference in very distant lands. In 1670 there was still little demand for coffee in France, except in towns with heavy concentrations of Levantine merchants, such as Marseille and Lyon. The production of coffee as a literary good thus preceded, but probably also fostered, its evolution into a major import commodity.[2] Coffee was not indigenous to the Middle East—it was probably transplanted there from Ethiopia—but by the late seventeenth century plantations at Bayt al Faqih on the Arabian peninsula supplied demand across the Ottoman empire. The crop was sold at Mocha, largely to Cairoese traders, but increasingly also to European merchants, especially the Dutch, who formed colonial plantations in Java from the 1690s onward. By the 1730s, however, the Ottoman empire had become an important client for *French* coffee, grown in colonial plantations. By the 1750s the French had overtaken their rivals, the English and Dutch, to constitute the largest European presence

1. On the introduction of coffee to Europe, see, among others, Wild 2004; Ellis 2000; Weinberg and Bealer 2001; Pendergrast 2001. The chronology of the introduction and consumption of coffee varies between sources; the scholarly rigor and thoroughness evident in Ellis 2004a has yet to be emulated for France, but see especially Turner 2004.

2. Provençal traders and traveling scholars, including Jean de Thévenot, who returned from a voyage to the East in 1659, were apparently the first Parisian coffee drinkers. By the 1660s, some coffee was already being drunk in the south of France (Turner 2004, 39; Courdurié 1980, 75; Boulanger 1980, 3). Coffee became a literary theme in the same decade; see D[u] F[our de la Crespelière] 1671, 646 (approved by the Royal censors in 1668); Franklin 1887–1902, 13:34–35 (quoting a poem of 1666).

in Smyrna, the main Ottoman port for international trade.[3] The embrace of exotic foods and of nouvelle cuisine by Parisian eaters thus mirrored a profound shift in French commercial and foreign relations between 1670 and 1730, which converted the kingdom into a major player in European imperialism and colonialism. The metropolis ceased to be a closed citadel; it was now a hub of trade and consumption, open to a growing global market in foodstuffs. Debates over the consumption of nouvelle cuisine and new or exotic foods now reflected anxieties over French national identity, as well as over European relations with the rest of the globe.[4] The period covered by this chapter thus marks a critical turning point in the history of French commercial relations with the Levant and also with the rest of the world—a turning point that denotes not only a commercial change but also a transformation in the management of natural resources. French scholarship contributed to these transformations in important ways.

For the first part of the period covered by this chapter, French merchants did not deal in coffee themselves. It was a commodity about which they knew little, a trade already dominated by the minority peoples and tributary states of the Ottoman empire—Armenians, Persians, Jews, and Syrians. The Turks generally did not conduct long-distance trade, and at Red Sea ports such as Jedda and Basra it was traders from these minorities who exchanged coffee from Mocha for luxury goods from the Far East. With their networks of contacts stretching throughout the East Indies and the Ottoman empire, such merchants probably also dominated the fledgling coffee trade to Europe.[5] The very first Constantinople coffee-house had been founded by Syrians in 1555. When the Turks knocked on the gates of Vienna, Armenian traders followed in their wake, bringing the small luxuries of the Ottoman empire to Europeans. In some accounts, the first coffee-house in Paris was founded in 1671 or 1672 by the Armenian merchant Pascal. Similar go-betweens also founded coffee-houses elsewhere in Europe, such as the Ragusan Pasqua Rosa in London and Amsterdam, and in Paris another Armenian, Maliban, a Persian merchant, Jobé Makara, and a street vendor known only as "Le Candiot," the Cretan.[6]

3. Panzac 1996, 27, 183, 198–99; Rafeq 2001, 139–40. Archives de la Chambre de Commerce de Marseille, ms. B 152, "Instructions Données a M. fabre . . . ," f°s. 374–397, reveals that between 1680 and 1706 coffee was among the most profitable goods traded from the Levant.

4. Chaudhuri 1985; Smith 2002; Abad 2002; Pennell 1999.

5. Ellis 2004a, 144; Chaudhuri 1985, chap. 8; Sandgruber 1991.

6. According to [de la Roque] 1716, 253–343. See also Hattox 1991, 76–79; Rafeq 2001; Teply 1978; Sandgruber 1994, 76–77. Numerous sources claim that Pasqua Rosee or Pasqua

The coffee trade first became a focus of interest for the French as a by-product of a larger program for reshaping commercial relations with the Levant, initiated by Louis XIV's chief minister, Jean-Baptiste Colbert. But these commercial transformations also required a changed understanding of the Levant, the colonies, the luxury trade, and ultimately of coffee itself. How did coffee come to be understood in the metropolis, as plant, drink, and commodity? What disciplines and epistemological forms existed that could encompass this new substance, of interest to ministers creating foreign policy as well as to ordinary Parisians? Precisely because coffee was a newcomer in a society with an expanding print culture and increasingly exoticized consumption habits, it lends itself to a study of the conjuncture of knowledge and consumption. This chapter shows how the agency of experts in food knowledge came to be aligned with the interests of an increasingly centralized Crown administration between 1670 and 1730. It demonstrates how different sorts of claimants to expertise—Orientalists, merchants, colonial administrators, journalists, collectors, medical practitioners, and botanists—crafted public authority over a new natural substance, in part through representing it in texts and images.

As an object of knowledge, coffee first reached Parisians via a network of Orientalist experts: collectors, curiosi, and philologists who redefined the Levant for polite readers through their travel accounts and fictional writings, even as they worked on behalf of the Crown to reshape French commercial and political relations with the Ottoman empire. A couple of decades later, coffee had become the subject of attempts to create a new maritime trading network and of the first French colonial cultivation programs. For the first time, it became a focus of scholarly interest in its own right, as well as a playful source of literary creativity. Only after this date did metropolitan botanists begin to have direct access to coffee, and they sought to reinvent it as a subject of cultivatory and botanical expertise rather than literature or philology. Paris was an important site for the promotion of new exotic foods, drinks, and drugs as materia medica. Yet until the end of the reign of Louis XIV, botanists' pronouncements on the subject of coffee did not rest upon knowledge of the living plant, and they had no involvement with colonial cultivation programs. It was not until later that they played an active

Rosa was the Ragusan servant of a Levantine merchant. He may have been the same person as Pascal (Ellis 2004b; Turner 2004, 35; Moura and Louvet 1929, 20). Makara was still trading in 1692; see Archives Nationales, Paris, V^{7} 167, dossier 4, appeal by Geoffroy de Lautel. Ragusa was a tributary of the Ottoman empire until 1684, and Crete was conquered by the Ottomans in 1669. Armenians had long dominated French imports of exotic luxury goods (Mantran 1977; Kiple and Ornelas 2000, 642–44; Meyer et al. 1991, 141).

role in translating the main site of French colonial coffee production from east to west—to France's Antillean rather than Mascarene colonies. This shift, brokered by many intermediaries, made it possible for coffee to become an everyday consumer good within the French metropolis.

The translation of coffee expertise from one field of knowledge to another thus accompanied the translation of coffee from a luxurious rarity into a commonplace beverage. In different ways, Orientalists, collectors, and botanists all interpreted and appropriated coffee to fit the needs of a centralizing absolutist State. Their expertise in the matter of coffee was a product of their ability to make their particular skills indispensable to the Crown's administrative needs worldwide. By 1730 the effects, composition, source, and public significance of coffee had become topics on which learned experts could advise both public and administrators with authority. To describe these changes, sociological models of networks, rather than the linear commodity histories or object biographies favored in most historical sources, provide the most useful model of the history of foodstuffs. In this chapter, I explore three networks, which, reflecting their geographical and commercial remit, I refer to as the Oriental, Indian, and American networks.[7]

THE "ORIENTAL" AGE OF FRENCH COFFEE

Most historians date the beginnings of Parisian coffee consumption to a visit by the Turkish ambassador, Soliman Aga, to the city in 1669. At his lodgings, elite visitors from court and city were served coffee in tiny cups by servants dressed in exotic Turkish garb. Coffee had been drunk throughout the Middle East since the second half of the sixteenth century; one hundred years later, it had become an established part of daily life in the Ottoman empire, and a leading luxury import. At the time of Soliman Aga's visit, there was a considerable French presence in Levantine and Eastern Mediterranean seaports. The French *négociants* or long-distance merchants who frequented such ports mostly originated from Marseille; such coffee consumption as occurred in France prior to Soliman Aga's visit can often be tied to these very groups. In the Ottoman empire, French merchants established ghetto settlements in port towns, represented by a royal official, a consul or (in the Porte) the king's ambassador himself. They brought minerals, precious metals, coin, New World commodities, and European manufactured goods, especially silk or wool cloth, to the vast market that was the Ottoman empire, a congeries of states sharing a common administrative

7. Spary 2005.

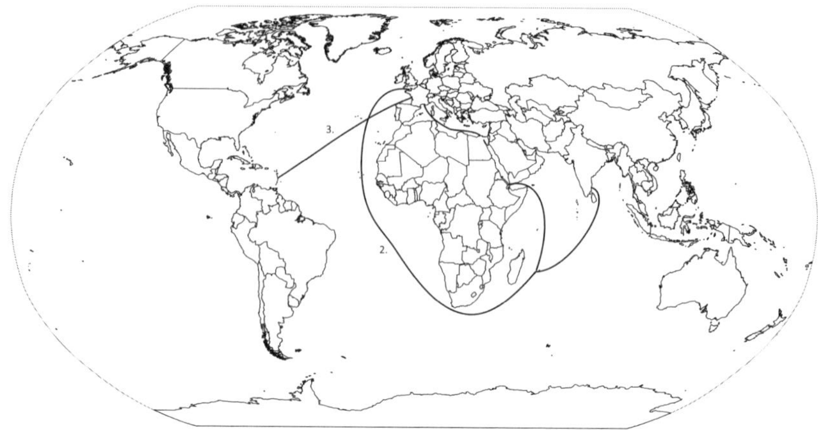

Figure 2.1. French coffee trade routes, 1670–1730. (1) The Levantine route, between Marseille and Cairo. (2) The East Indies route, from St. Malo via the Cape of Good Hope to the Mascarene Islands, the Indian trading outposts, and the Yemen. (3) The American route, between western French ports and the Antillean colonies. Prepared by the author using Inkscape software and a free downloadable map from digital-vector-maps.com.

structure but a diversity of languages, religions and ways of life. Here they exchanged their wares for goods from the East: spices, drugs, porcelain, cotton, and silk.[8]

Soliman's embassy was made possible—some even said his passage to France was paid—by the French ambassador to the Ottoman empire, Denis de la Haye Vantelet, whose embassy to the Levant coincided with a program for restoring wealth to the realm in the wake of lengthy European wars, promoted by the minister Colbert. As the latter noted in 1671, "the only extensive [international] trade conducted in France" was that with the Levant, but merchants from Marseille had contributed to the decline in French profits from this trade—and, more significantly, in France's international reputation—by passing bad coin. It was for the ambassador, a Crown employee independent of the Marseille merchant dynasties, to rectify the situation and restore trade with the Ottoman empire to its former profitability. Among de la Haye's orders from Colbert were to negotiate a renewal of the trade agreement between France and the Ottoman empire on terms more favorable to the French. In addition, Colbert sought direct trading access

8. Panzac 1996, 95, 201; İnalcık 1994; Raymond 1984, chaps. 1 and 2; 1999, vol. 1, chap. 4. The embassy of Soliman Aga is mentioned in most histories of coffee, though few discuss the circumstances outside France that led to his visit.

to the Indies via the Red Sea for French merchants, as part of an attempt to secure French global trade monopolies.[9]

With de la Haye, we are immediately plunged into the niceties of diplomacy in the age of Louis XIV. The fate of coffee as a historical and epistemological object was bound up with the changing balance of power between Europe and the Ottoman empire; as the centralized administrative apparatus of the old empire crumbled, coffee in France would shift from being an imported Oriental luxury to becoming a leading colonial product. In 1669, however, this shift was not yet apparent. De la Haye's embassy made little headway even in obtaining due ambassadorial courtesies from the Grand Vizier, chief official of the Ottoman empire, Köprülüzade Fazıl Ahmed Pacha, let alone in brokering a vital new trade agreement. Despite his attempts to portray the power and magnificence of his own monarch as on a par with those of the Grand Sultan, de la Haye thus failed to manifest French monarchical authority successfully before the Ottoman court.[10] At home this failure was viewed as damaging to Louis XIV's presentation of himself as a ruler on a par with the Roman emperors of classical antiquity. To compound matters, de la Haye encountered hostility from local French traders, who availed themselves of every opportunity to send unfavorable reports of his activities and conduct back to court. Though the ambassador was not sacked, he was given the order to withdraw from the Levant embassy. But he did not board the royal ships sent to collect him; instead, it was Soliman Aga who traveled to France in his stead. The ability to send an envoy from the Grand Turk himself back to court might well have counted in de la Haye's favor, but the Provençal merchants proclaimed Soliman Aga nothing more than de la Haye's puppet, a fake without any power to assist in negotiating the treaty that Colbert desired.[11]

From this perspective, the creation of a coffee fashion in Paris looks somewhat different. The journey by Soliman that supposedly brought coffee to the attention of Parisian and court society may well have been a tactic in de la Haye's attempt to bolster his perceived diplomatic prowess.

9. Clément 1861–82, 2:628–30, 841–49. On relations between the Ottoman empire and European traders, see Goffman 2002, esp. 197–205; Sundeen 2003. Ottoman authorities began intervening in the coffee trade to Europeans from 1696 onwards (Genç 2001).

10. On the problems diplomats faced in impersonating the monarch, see especially Jettot 2010.

11. Faroqhi 1994, 519–22, 616; Mantran 1984, chap. 4; Abdel-Halim 1964, esp. 27–81; Labat 1735, 4:127–32. This embassy and its successors received much attention in newspapers (Martino 1970, 90–91).

If the ambassador could not reach the Grand Sultan, the Ottoman empire would be brought back to France by someone who could enact Orientalism before an audience of French consumers. This event took place at a time of profound upheaval in political and commercial relations between France, other European nations, and the Ottoman empire. It is significant for our understanding of the historical relationship between politics, consumption, commerce, and culture that what is remembered of Soliman's role was not de la Haye's reputation, nor indeed some new political or commercial relationship between the Ottoman empire and France, but rather a fashion that was an apparently accidental byproduct of an attempt to stage the Ottoman empire credibly at the heart of the French court. In fact, the status of Soliman Aga and the precise nature of his relations with de la Haye were never fully clarified, either in Paris or at court. We can explore his reception in France through Molière's satire, *Le Bourgeois Gentilhomme*, a play commissioned by Louis XIV himself after Soliman's visit. Here everything turns on the theme of people who are not what they seem. The hero, originally played by Molière himself, is a wealthy bourgeois (in other words a town-dweller rather than a courtier) who hopes to appear a gentleman. To that end, he hires music, dancing, and philosophy masters, and dresses in expensive garb. But in his turn, he too is deceived when a "Turk" purporting to be the son of the Grand Sultan appears to claim his daughter's hand in marriage. For this is none other than the daughter's existing suitor, disguised as a Turk. The plot thus turns on a double deception: the impersonation of a Turk by a Frenchman, but also the impersonation of a gentleman by a rich commoner. Both events are identical transactions in one sense, for dress and manner deceive others into taking the individual for better than he is.[12]

Le Bourgeois Gentilhomme touched a nerve in French high society. Not long before, Louis XIV had imprisoned the intendant Nicolas Fouquet, whose house and lifestyle rivaled the splendor of Versailles, on charges of embezzlement.[13] Concern about the pretensions of the upwardly mobile to rank, connoisseurship, and learning, and about the role of consumption and display in that process, formed a central theme in debates about the relationship between wealth and taste from these decades onward. In the metropolis, where even poor residents rapidly learned to manipulate the trappings

12. Molière 1962; Martino 1970, 93, 227–31.

13. On the political significance of Fouquet's ostentation, see Burke 1992, chap. 4; Foucher-Wolniewicz 1992, 29–45; on his fall as part of Colbert's "cultural politics," cf. Mazauric 2007, 35.

of luxury consumption and display, critics addressed the individual and collective implications for French society of the new material goods that were flooding it. From its very beginnings, the coffee habit in Paris would be a sign of the power of consumption to permit upward mobility, to seal the success of impersonations of a higher social state. Accordingly, all histories of Soliman Aga addressed the theme of impersonation: was he merely a domestic of the Grand Sultan, or an official ambassador? His ambiguity is reflected in modern histories, which confer on him several different titles and names. The memoirs of the chevalier Laurent d'Arvieux, an equally enigmatic figure, offer an explanation that aligns with what we know of the Ottoman empire's diplomatic and administrative structure in these decades. D'Arvieux had begun life as Laurent Arviou, from the Marseille branch of a family of long-distance traders originally from Lombardy. After extensive commercial travels in the eastern Mediterranean, he became something of a general fixer for the Crown in the Levant, resolving tricky diplomatic and military issues thanks to his detailed knowledge of languages and politics in the region. The particle *de* (which implied nobility) was added to his name later, when Arviou began to move in ministerial and diplomatic circles.[14]

As with d'Arvieux, Soliman's name became corrupted. In some sources he appears as "Soliman Aga Mustapha Raca." "Mustapha Raca" was not Soliman's name but his Turkish title, "muteferaca," an administrative rank translatable as "distinguished man." From seraglio gardener, a post in the Sultan's household, the Ottoman civil servant Süleymān *Agha* had been promoted to this position which, as d'Arvieux said, "is best compared to that of Gentleman-in-Waiting to the King's household." In d'Arvieux's account, Süleymān occupied the position of a royal valet: of gentlemanly standing, certainly, but with doubtful credentials as an official political representative of the Ottoman empire. In passing, d'Arvieux also remarked that Süleymān was a native of Bosnia. The capture of children from conquered Christian states had begun as a form of tribute levied by the Ottoman empire but by the late seventeenth century was a routine means of recruiting high-ranking civil servants, educated to their posts from infancy in a special school in the Sultan's palace, the Topkapı. Bosnia, where a substantial part of the popula-

14. See Hossain 1990. D'Arvieux later became French consul at Aleppo in Syria. The editor of Molière 1962, 506 describes him as an Italian adventurer; see also Martino 1970, 228. On D'Arvieux's name, see Labat 1735, 1:iij–xvj; Pettet 2003. A royal edict of August 1669 had recently permitted nobles to undertake overseas trade, but D'Arvieux's commercial activities still threatened his social standing. See Schaeper 1983, 38–39.

tion had converted to Islam over several centuries of Ottoman rule, had supplied several prominent administrators. Thus Süleymān—the most famous Turk in French history—was not even a Turk.[15]

After Süleymān landed at Toulon, the whole affair increasingly took on the air of a comedy of errors, in which the minister for foreign affairs, Hugues de Lyonne, charged to give audience to the envoy, "was to play the Grand Vizier." He performed the role under the direction of d'Arvieux, who set the stage at Suresnes, just outside Paris, where de Lyonne, dressed in a black satin robe embroidered with silver thread, received Süleymān after "the manner in which the Grand Viziers give audience to Foreign Ministers." And there was no more appropriate way of doing so than by serving Süleymān a cup of coffee, the conventional Ottoman sign that one's audience with the Grand Vizier was now over. This dramatic reconstruction of the Ottoman court in France was undertaken for the benefit of a man who, himself, was to dramatize the Orient for the French, and the whole process was observed, through windows of Venetian glass, by "a number of persons of distinction, drawn to this ceremony out of curiosity." Throughout this game of international diplomacy, no one, in the last analysis, was what he appeared. Coffee was a commodity that embodied a culture of impersonation and parody, a political weapon from which no one in literate circles of absolutist France, not even the king and his ministers, was immune. Hence it was also a dangerous weapon; for a subsequent audience with the envoy, d'Arvieux advised the minister to conduct himself in his normal manner, since "it would have been better to receive the Envoy in accordance with French grandeur, than to stoop to adopting their [manners], while abandoning our own." The minister, in making a spectacle out of himself, was potentially compromising royal dignity. But the damage was done: "Turkish manners" had been adopted by a minister, however briefly, and they would be emulated throughout high society.

Coffee's introduction to Paris, its status as an object of knowledge, cannot be divorced from international or domestic politics in a world where

15. Labat 1735, 4:119–25, 176–81. D'Arvieux also suggested that the Divan contributed to Süleymān's predicament by sending him to France without proper authority, to see whether Louis XIV could be cowed. Many variants of "muteferaca" are given in Leclant 1951, 3–4. In Clément 1861–82, 2:491n, 849n, "Soliman Aga Mustapha Raca" is described as the director of the Seraglio gardens, who later became a valet to the Sultan. Abdel-Halim 1964, 30–32 offers almost the only fully accurate account: the problem was that the Sultan's official letters to Süleymān identified him as a servant, not an ambassador (Labat 1735, 4:148–49, 168, 174–75). On Bosnian Christians in the Ottoman civil service, see Hegyi 1989, 52; Lovrenović 2001, 121; Faroqhi 1995, 52; Kiel 2004; Zirojević 2004, 169.

the Ottoman empire was still the leading international power and European states competed for its favor. But its history is also entangled with late seventeenth-century scholarship and the culture of curiosity. Parisians drove out to Issy to watch Süleymān taking his walk, eating, and praying, and lined the streets to see him making an official entry into Paris on December 3, 1669. They came in such numbers—as if to marvel at a new exotic animal in the royal menagerie—that Swiss guards were called in "to prevent disorder."[16]

The Ottoman empire was not only the scene for debates over international trade and diplomacy, but also an important nexus in France's network of scholarly curiosi. De la Haye was still in Constantinople in 1670 to greet his successor, Charles Olier de Nointel, a Jansenist magistrate from the *parlement* of Paris. It was Nointel who in 1673 finally brokered the revised Franco-Ottoman trade agreement sought by the Crown. He was also a major collector of antiquities and Oriental curiosities, forming a cabinet that quickly ruined him, coupled as it was with his attempts to live in an ostentatious manner so as to overawe Ottoman civil servants. Recalled to France, he soon fell from Crown favor, and died in poverty.[17] But among the network of contacts and correspondents in which he participated, even among those who passed through his embassy, were scholars responsible for most of the French-language texts about coffee written before 1700. Metropolitan knowledge of coffee was largely created by this scholarly network of Orientalists and antiquarians, which had close ties to the Crown. These men were almost all experienced travelers in the Levant, who became indispensable royal aides during the execution of Colbert's foreign policy toward the Ottoman empire. Moreover, they represented a new sort of expertise: back in France, they supplanted a cohort of royal interpreters, *érudits* with a reading knowledge only of Turkish, Arabic, Greek, and Hebrew. In place of erudition, these men could offer their personal experience of the East, its languages, customs, antiquities, and politics.[18]

16. Labat 1735, 4:131–32, 135, 144–45, 150–51, 153–54; Vandal 1900, 25. French luxury fabrics were coveted import goods in the Ottoman empire; see Mantran 1986; Raymond 2002, chap. 2. On curiosity, display and power, see Wintroub 2006; Mukerji 1997; Robbins 2001; Pomian 1990; Daston and Park 1998; Evans and Marr 2006; Kenny 1998, 2004; Jones-Davies 2005.

17. Hossain 1990; Meignen 1976, 119–20; Vandal 1900, X–XI, 35–37, 111, 232–40, 256; Omont 1902, 1:198.

18. D'Arvieux was involved in the training of interpreters (Labat 1735, 4:147–50; Hossain 1990, 1992, 1993; Bléchet 1997; Ter Minassian 1997). On "Orientalism" and on European scholarly contacts with the Ottoman empire, see Dew 2009; Brentjes 1999. According to Jettot 2010, 218, the norm at this time was for French diplomats to be ignorant of all languages other than their own.

In other words, knowledge about coffee in Paris was produced by the very same people who helped to craft a new understanding of the Levant, and to invent Orientalism as a foreign policy, a literary genre, a collecting fashion, and a new domain of erudition. It was they who helped to commodify the Orient for polite society, and to process the Levant as part of a cultural politics intricately bound up with Louis XIV's attempts to represent himself as heir to a Roman imperial tradition, and with Colbert's attempts to manage the wealth of the State. The French owed that artifact "the Orient," as well as that artifact "coffee," to such individuals. The same network of philology, diplomacy, and commerce, at its other extremity, also produced the main French-language book on coffee of the seventeenth century. *De l'Vsage du Caphé, du Thé, et du Chocolate* (On the Use of Coffee, Tea, and Chocolate), published in 1671, was an immediate success, the edition rapidly selling out. *De l'Vsage du Caphé* has a complex publishing history, typical of early modern eclecticism. The work was compiled and edited by Philippe Sylvestre Dufour, a Protestant grocer-apothecary of Provençal origin, trading from Lyon. A much extended edition appeared in 1684, this time under Dufour's name, as *Traitez Nouveaux & Curieux du Café, du Thé, et du Chocolat* (New and Curious Treatises upon Coffee, Tea, and Chocolate), and a Latin translation appeared the following year.[19]

The first edition of *De l'Vsage du Caphé* consisted of little more than quotations from travelers' accounts of coffee drinking and physicians' accounts of its properties and uses. The 1684 edition, however, was a very different matter. It gave coffee substantially more coverage: in 1671 chocolate had received 91 pages, coffee 47, and tea 24, but by 1684 coffee occupied 215 pages, the bulk of the book. The reviewer of this second edition for the official learned periodical *Journal des Sçavans* noted: "There is nothing which is more fashionable nowadays than Coffee." By the 1690s, coffee towered over the other two drinks in its importance as a consumer good, and it would continue to be the focal point for literary interest in new exotic foods throughout the eighteenth century. Coffee's significance for French

19. The three editions are Dufour 1671, 1684, 1685. The authorship of the original Latin treatise is highly contested, but often attributed to Dufour's close friend Jacob Spon, albeit with little foundation; see Pommier 1993; Duval 1912; Turner 2004, 41; Vicaire 1890, cols. 2983–96; Quérard 1869, 1014; *Biographie Universelle* 40:76–78. Certainly Spon was responsible for the Latin translation in 1685. Dufour and Spon were also related by marriage (Santschi 1993; *Biographie Universelle* 11:447–48). Dufour's Provençal origins are mentioned in *Nouvelles de la République des Lettres* 3 (1685): 497. On Orientalism under Louis XIV, see especially Dew 2009.

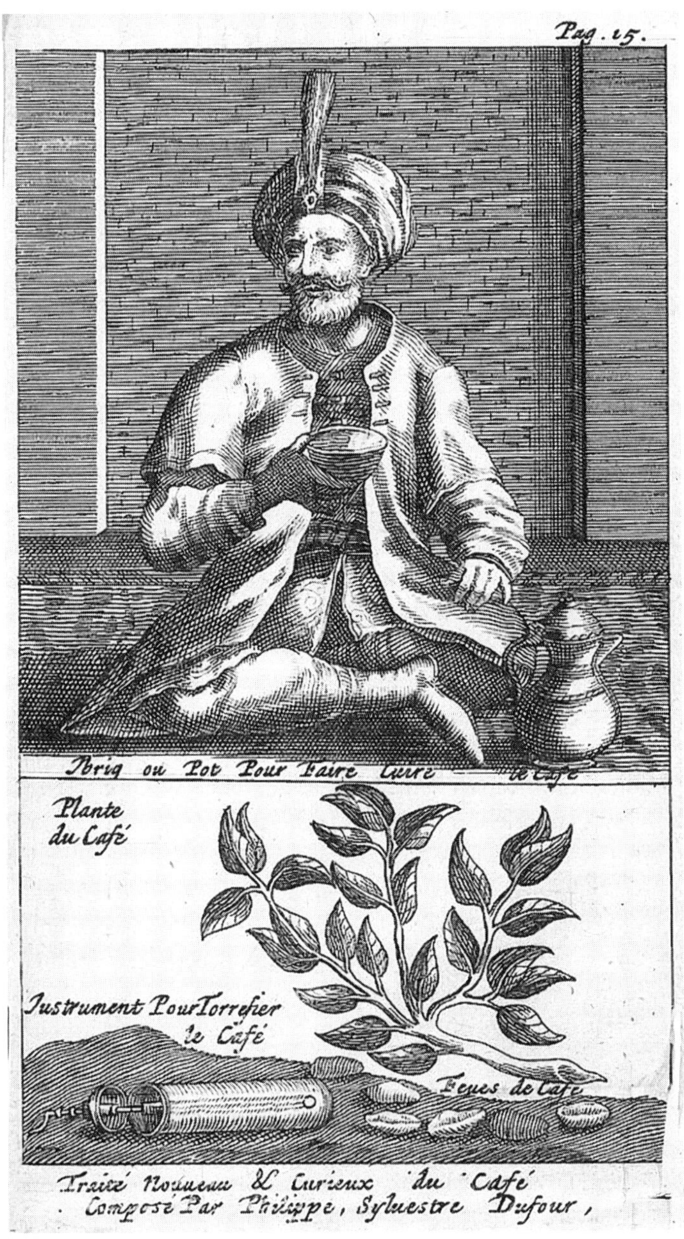

Figure 2.2. Philippe Sylvestre Dufour, *Traitez Nouveaux & curieux du café, du thé et du chocolate* (Lyon: Jean Girin & Barthelemy Riviere, 1685), plate opp. p. 1. Coffee is represented by a seated, cross-legged man dressed as a Turk, with a branch of the plant, some coffee beans, and a roasting device below. Copperplate engraving, unknown artist. British Library.

consumers led to its becoming a major symbol of the problems and possibilities of exotic and luxury consumption, as we will see.[20]

The three beverages addressed in *De l'Vsage du Caphé* have remained linked in food history ever since. Yet there is nothing self-evident about their association. In the 1680s, coffee was imported to France from the Ottoman empire, tea traveled from China or Japan, while chocolate came from the Americas via Spain. Only the pattern of European commercial relations with the rest of the world as it was shortly before 1700 makes sense of this literary geography of foodstuffs. Dufour wrote of exotic ingesta that were reasonably well known because they had become established commodities along international trade routes. Yerba, kava, betel, coca, and a host of other substances that were used recreationally elsewhere in the world did not feature in his work or the genre it created.[21] The dyad of East and West Indies constituted the commercial geography of early modern France upon which Dufour's wealth depended, and, as in Rameau's opera-ballet *Les Indes Galantes* (The Gallant Indies) fifty years later, it was unproblematic for him to amalgamate these different parts of the world into a common "exotic" encompassing Turks, Persians, Chinese, Indians, and Americans. Of the three beverages Dufour discussed, however, he only had direct access to coffee; as he explained in 1684, "I was not content to consult a great number of Savants inside & outside the kingdom who do me the honour of engaging in commerce with me. I also extended my research into the depths of the Orient, where I conduct my trade."[22] And coffee, its properties and correct usage, was the subject in which he interested himself most actively.

An important stage in the domestication of coffee within French culture involved its medicinal properties. Like other new foods and drinks, it created uncertainties that were resolved by technologies of knowledge drawn from medicine and other well-established European disciplines: case histories—cures and illnesses caused by coffee—as well as printed denunciations and defenses of its effects on the health. Dufour's primary concern was to justify coffee as a medicinal preparation, not a recreational substance. In his

20. *Journal des Sçavans* 11 (January 1685): 46. The letters of Marie de Rabutin-Chantal, Mme de Sévigné, document the fluctuating fortunes of coffee at court after 1676. Bayle (1685, 505) observed that "one hardly sees a family in Paris or Lyon above the artisans, in which the Coffee pot is not to be found by the fire after dinner every day," while the Paris grocer Pomet (1694, 143–44) claimed that coffee and chocolate had completely replaced tea in fashionable circles since the 1670s. See also Franklin 1887–1902, 13:47–58; Leclant 1951, 9–10; Lansard 1991, 130.

21. Courtwright 2001, chap. 3; Cowan 2007, 214.

22. Dufour 1684: unpaginated preface.

eyes, its history was part of a bigger history of materia medica, rather than the foundation of a new genre, the history of stimulants. All the themes he included in the 1684 treatise point toward this medicinal understanding of coffee. There was a chemical analysis of the drink, conducted by Dufour and a local apothecary, Cassaire; there were reflections on the theological significance of consuming exotica; and there were descriptions of cures effected by coffee, culled from letters sent to Dufour by physicians in Grenoble, Montpellier, and elsewhere. There was also an account of Dufour's use of coffee to treat his own migraines.[23]

The 1684 treatise also represented a much bolder project, however. It constituted Dufour's claim to be an author, and thus a member of the Republic of Letters. Many references within the book tied Dufour to the network of diplomatic antiquarians and philologists who were the acknowledged contemporary authorities on the Levant, in the eyes of Crown and public alike. Even Dufour himself felt it necessary to defend the role of author, however, for this was not a self-evident role for a merchant in late seventeenth-century France. In particular, he daringly laid claim to public expertise on the basis of his commercial experience rather than his scholarly reputation:

> The profession I make of Merchant seems to me not to be incompatible with that of Author, especially on this occasion, where it is a matter of a drug of which Merchants have given us knowledge. It is to those who have traded in the Levant, that we in France owe the discovery of Coffee. . . . For a subject of this sort, I will even cover a great many things about which a Merchant may be better informed than a Philosopher.

These facts included the source, preparation, and preservation of coffee, all areas "in which [Dufour's] correspondence makes him more instructed, than a Savant could be by all his meditations."[24]

Merchants had been used as advisors and consultants to the Crown by ministers from Colbert to the Pontchartrains. Nevertheless, Dufour's claim to be a coffee expert was cautiously received by the reviewer of his book in the *Journal des Sçavans*, the nation's most respectable scholarly periodical:

23. Dufour 1684, chap. 12; Cowan 2007, 217–18. For a discussion of stimulant history, see chapter 4 in this volume.

24. Dufour 1684, unpaginated preface. Dufour 1679, a travelers' manual, was dedicated to Jean Chardin. On the Republic of Letters, see Goldgar 1995; Daston 1991; Brockliss 2002; Bots and Waquet 1997.

> raising himself above the profession of Merchant which he wants it to be known that he practises, & reasoning as a Natural Philosopher, [the author] shows that the primary qualities [of coffee] depend on the primary parts which enter the composition of the mixts, & that the secondary [qualities] are but the effects of the latter. After having gone so far as to mock the Philosophers who assign degrees of heat or cold to different compounds, he says that things are only hot or cold relative to ourselves, or by comparing them to one another.

Though the reviewer hesitated to endorse Dufour's critique of these already rather outdated claims from humoral medicine concerning the degrees of heat, cold, humidity, and siccity to be attributed to different foodstuffs, he was nevertheless impressed by the range of witnesses, scholarly and gentlemanly, which Dufour could muster in support of his account of coffee. Dufour's correspondence with François Bernier, Gassendist physician and noted traveler in the Indies, "shows that he has taken care, as he avows, to consult the most skilful men of his acquaintance, & draw what he ought to give the public from their learning [*lumières*]." Coffee would repeatedly confront the French learned world with the same problem: it exemplified new approaches to learning, some of which were commanded by persons not within traditional spaces of scholarship or gentlemanliness. A literature about food constituted a new epistemological domain, where the likes of merchants, shopkeepers, and artisans could credibly feature alongside *érudits* and academicians. The expanding world of print permitted encounters between different knowledge experts, all of whom laid claim to be "enlightened."[25]

For the *Journal des Sçavans* reviewer, Dufour's treatise was noteworthy for the contrast between the commercial background of its author and its learned treatment of sources and etymology, values espoused by the network of French Orientalist antiquarian scholars with whom Dufour was in close contact. His production of coffee as an object of knowledge, consumption, and cure was made credible by his insertion into this network—he was himself a collector of coins and antiquities. In consequence, his corre-

25. *Journal des Sçavans* 11 (January 1685): 49. Bayle 1685 likewise viewed Dufour's coupling of commerce with learning as exceptional; see also Jeannin 1995; Julia 1995. On the recruitment of another merchant family, the Savarys, by the French Crown, see Schaeper 1983, 5–6; "Preface historique," in Savary Des Bruslons and Savary 1759–65, vol. 1, I–XXXIII. On Bernier, see Ames 2003; Dew 2009, chap. 3.

spondence placed him firmly within the Republic of Letters, which united scholars across Europe. Several of his correspondents were renowned curious travelers in the Levant, who had direct personal knowledge of Nointel or de la Haye. Dufour's close friend and translator, Jacob Spon, planned a journey around the Mediterranean area in the mid-1670s with Jean-Foy Vaillant, a royal antiquarian and numismatist also given collecting commissions by Colbert. Though they ended by traveling separately, Spon was able to admire Nointel's collection of antiquities in Constantinople. Jean Chardin, another Protestant merchant, described Dufour as "one of my Illustrious and most intimate Friends," and recommended his treatise as the authoritative source for information on coffee. Chardin's journal of his second voyage to Persia remains one of the most famous travel accounts of the period and contains a detailed account of de la Haye and Nointel's struggles to obtain trading concessions from the Ottoman empire. Laurent d'Arvieux was another of Dufour's correspondents, and he published several travel accounts, as well as providing Molière with notes on Turkish customs for *Le Bourgeois Gentilhomme.* Other well-known Levantine travelers like Jean-Baptiste Tavernier formed part of this network, whose members wrote travel accounts covering much of the Levant, including Syria, Armenia, Georgia, Persia, the Lebanon, Palestine, Greece, Italy, and Dalmatia.[26]

There was thus direct continuity between the brokers of Colbertian foreign policy in the Ottoman empire, the network of curious collectors, and the authors or translators of coffee treatises. One individual who exemplifies this was Antoine Galland, a Norman Jansenist numismatist and antiquarian who accompanied Nointel when the new consul took up his post in 1670. He returned to the Levant twice more, on the third occasion accompanying Nointel's successor, de Guilleragues (yet another Dufour correspondent). On his travels, Galland procured inscriptions, books, manuscripts, and antiquities for French scholars such as Spon and Melchisedech Thévenot, for courtiers including Colbert, and even for the king himself. The pamphlet on the "origins and progress of coffee," which he published in 1699, was based on a letter written twenty years earlier to a Parisian antiquary at whose private

26. Chardin emigrated to England in the 1680s, after acting as a translator at the Persian court thanks to his extensive knowledge of Levantine languages and etiquette (Chardin 1927, 241; 1686, esp. 1–83; Eurich 2003; Martino 1970, 56). For other travel accounts penned by Dufour's correspondents, see Spon and Wheler 1724; Galland 2002; Labat 1735; Tavernier 1679. For Dufour's other correspondents, see *Nouvelles de la République des lettres* 3 (1685): 498. Another coffee work produced by this network, no longer extant, was written by Vaillant's son Jean-François-Foy Vaillant, probably in the early 1680s (*Biographie Universelle* 42:409).

academy coffee was served in imitation of Eastern hospitality. Though generally described as a translation of an Arabic manuscript on coffee, Galland's short pamphlet included etymological and philological commentaries, as well as a detailed refutation of an earlier account published by a Marronite scholar in Rome. As such, it contributed to the program of learning pursued by his network of collectors and correspondents.[27] While in Paris, Galland maintained a tenuous foothold in high society, moving from household to household as secretary, librarian, and curator for a succession of wealthy patrons, trading on the expertise he had acquired in antiquities and matters Oriental. He would become best known as the translator of a collection of "Oriental" tales still well known as the *Arabian Nights*. After the publication of the first installment in 1704, he finally achieved public visibility as an expert on the East, and was appointed professor of Oriental languages at the prestigious Collège de France in 1709. The literary fashion for Orientalism that his writings fueled would continue into the eighteenth century with works like Montesquieu's *Lettres Persanes*.[28]

Individuals like Galland both created and capitalized upon the metropolitan taste for Orientalism after 1670, to which the habit of coffee drinking belonged. But it is also obvious that the penniless Galland was able to make a living as a scholar on the basis of his expertise in the matter of coffee and other Oriental curiosities. Once again, it is possible to see that a new domain of expertise, knowledge, and capital was being constructed, in which such novel matters as coffee could find a place. Coffee drinking in Paris between 1670 and 1700 was, first and foremost, a way of displaying a fashionable familiarity with the cutting edge of academic scholarship, of marking out one's credentials as a member of the curiosi. In turn, coffee found its cultural niche in the need for new ways of displaying hospitality that befitted a self-consciously rational public, an elite that was beginning to legitimate its status through the possession of *lumières*—enlightenment—and through forms of sociability designed to display that possession.[29]

27. Galland 1992. For the publishing history of this work, see [de la Roque] 1716, 269–71. On Nointel and Galland's collecting activities, see Vandal 1900, 49, 74–76; Omont 1902, 1:175–221; Abdel-Halim 1964; *Biographie Universelle* 15:438–41. Colbert was the first of several ministers for whom Galland and his fellow curious travelers collected in the East; see Omont 1902, 1:222; Saunders 1991; Dew 2009, 16–40. On Thévenot, see Dew 2006; 2009, chap. 2; McClaughlin 1975. On the dedicatee of Galland 1992, Chassebras de Camaille (possibly the Italian traveler Jacques Chassebras de Cramailles), see Abdel-Halim 1964, 95.

28. *Mille et une nuits* was dedicated to the daughter of Galland's deceased patron, the ambassador Gabriel-Joseph de Lavergne Guilleragues; see Cary 1963, chap. 4; Mantran 1986; Martino 1970, 29, 87, 253–79; Pomeau and Ehrard 1984, 62–64.

29. On Spon's travels, see Omont 1902, 1:197–98.

THE INDIAN OCEAN NETWORK

Colbert himself was central to this Oriental network as a collector and patron. He was also central in setting in motion a "reversal of flow" in trading patterns that would eventually make French exports to the Levant more profitable than Levantine imports to France. His interventions in the Levant trade in the 1670s had two aims: to preserve the Ottoman empire as a market for goods coming from the new French manufactures established, as Laurent d'Arvieux nicely put it, "to counterfeit the woollen cloth of England, Holland, & Venice"; and to facilitate French commerce in luxuries from the Indies currently generating profits for other European nations, primarily spices, porcelain, and silks. Coffee, with which Colbert was able to give himself insomnia before he died in 1683, would be grafted onto these enterprises.[30]

As part of his plan for the Levant, Colbert sought a guarantee from the Ottomans that the maritime commerce route into the Red Sea to the crucial ports for the East Indies trade would be protected. The Portuguese were blockading the entrance to the Red Sea in order to protect their Indies trade route around the Cape of Good Hope. Colbert's efforts to insert France into foreign trade took place with an eye to this successful diversion of the spice route from the Mediterranean to the Indian Ocean. The subsequent history of coffee as an object of knowledge is entangled with these maneuvers. Neither de la Haye nor Nointel could prevail upon the Sultan and his Grand Vizier to accord French merchant ships trading rights at Red Sea ports. As it became clear that French Levantine merchants would not be permitted to use the Red Sea route to Jedda for luxury goods from Asia and Africa, Colbert began to explore other ways of establishing a regular East Indies trade. Long-distance commerce in the Indian and Atlantic oceans became a priority for him and his successors, and in late 1669 and early 1670 he was engaged in assembling a "grand Asian fleet." Pierre Pluchon has argued that the cultivation of maritime commerce routes between the Indies and France was merely a diversion from France's colonial program. But the fate of coffee between 1670 and 1730 allows a different story to be told. This good was not one of the spices originally sought out by Europeans in the East Indies. It was a new commodity in European markets, whose precise function—spice? medicament? recreation?—was not clear for some time after it began to be consumed in the West. However, it rapidly became one of the major exotic imports and, like sugar, would become inextricably im-

30. Raymond 1999, 1:133–35, 144–57; Labat 1735, 4:204; Duncan 1705, 113.

plicated in European programs of colonization and slavery over the next two centuries, leaving a dismal legacy of problems still unresolved today. Coffee is the commodity that, more than any other, exhibits the continuities between the trading emporia system that had long dominated Asian commerce, and the spread of European colonization and the slave trade in the Americas and Africa. Its history as a traded good exemplifies this process and reveals how intricately natural knowledge was bound up in the process of empire-building.[31]

In the late seventeenth century, the principal long-distance merchants were shipowners and wealthy *négociants* from the port towns. Marseille in particular, with its Chamber of Commerce, played a prominent role as the sole French port to which coffee could legitimately be imported. Marseille hegemony over coffee was fragile, however, threatened as it was by rival programs for importing coffee via new routes or from new sources. These rivals included maritime trading companies founded by the Crown. Best-known among these merchant consortia was the Compagnie des Indes, founded in 1664, which changed hands several times during its fifty-year privilege. By 1707, at the end of the Spanish War of Succession, the consortium that had held the Compagnie's Indian Ocean trading privileges since 1683 had become mired in debt. Its inability to undertake further voyages provided an opportunity that was seized by a new consortium of investors based in the Breton port of Saint Malo, and headed by two financiers, Antoine Crozat and Samuel Bernard. This Malouin consortium, which already monopolized French South Sea commerce, was headed by Jérôme de Pontchartrain. On becoming minister of the navy in 1699, de Pontchartrain promptly secured the right to import coffee direct from Mocha by sea for his former associates. This phase of the French coffee trade demonstrates how long-distance trading activities, formerly highly regionalized, gradually came under centralized Crown control after 1700.[32]

The Malouin investors financed an initial voyage to Mocha in 1707–10, followed by a second one in 1711–13. Their new East Indies Company was

31. Savary des Bruslons and Savary 1723–30, 1:1097–1107; Clément 1861–82, 2:841–49; De Blégny 1687, 113; Ames 1990, 548; 1992; 1996, chap. 3; Pluchon 1991, 149–51. On the Red Sea trade, see Raymond 1999, vol. 1, chap. 4; on trading emporia, see Chaudhuri 1985, 209.

32. Haudrère 2005, 1:23–24; Durand 1971, 134, 330; Schaeper 1983, 51–52; Saint-Germain 1960. Jérôme de Pontchartrain succeeded his father Louis as naval minister in 1699; see Pluchon 1991, 1:114–19, 105. Antoine Crozat made a fortune speculating on the Mississippi bubble. Samuel Bernard was a member of the Crown's Conseil de Commerce and held the tobacco monopoly.

largely controlled by the Crown, which appointed its directors and part of its administration. Between 1702 and 1720, the Malouins would outfit ten voyages to Mocha and twenty-seven to the East Indies. In Pluchon's words, Saint Malo now became the "metropolis of commerce" for the South Seas, China, and the Indies.[33] The significance of this shift for the history of coffee lay in the routes by which coffee reached France. Rather than seeking to break into existing trading networks, the East Indies Company endeavored to take a short cut by exploring completely new ventures. Initially the Malouin enterprises were principally commercial in nature; in 1708 and again in 1711 ships were sent out to the port of Mocha with a view to opening up a direct trade route around the Cape of Good Hope to the Yemen, making access to the Red Sea ports superfluous.[34] One sound commercial reason for doing so was that between 1707 and 1720 the Porte imposed a ban on the export of coffee outside the Ottoman empire. The irregular nature of the coffee supply from Cairo resulting from the intermittent enforcement of this ban ensured that the activities of the Malouin consortium were highly profitable. And within a few years, the new Compagnie des Indes also added a new string to its bow. Rather than merely trading in coffee, it began to fund experiments for the introduction of coffee and other exotica to the colonies it administered, becoming a leading player in projects to naturalize exotic plants of commercial value in the French colonies. In this, the French Compagnie was following the example of the Dutch, whose colonial botanical gardens contributed to their consolidation of monopolies over the European market in nutmeg and clove. Such projects may have been a response to threats to the Compagnie's Crown privilege from other entrepreneurs. In 1711, for example, the *négociant* Vauvré had approached the king and his ministers with a plan to redress what he represented as the unpatriotic neglect of natural productions by the Compagnie des Indes on its Indian Ocean base, the Isle de Bourbon (now Réunion). Instead, he promised to produce enough pepper, cinnamon, clove, nutmeg, and coffee to supply the needs of

33. The Malouins viewed their trade as an integral part of Colbert's program for increasing French manufacturing exports and replacing ancient East Indies trade routes in luxury goods like cotton, spices, and porcelain with French long-distance maritime trade. The Dutch paid 4,000,000 livres for their Mocha coffee cargo (Archives Nationales, Aix-en-Provence, C^2 14, f°s. 206 r°.–212 r°.) On the Compagnie des Indes, see Raynal 1774, 2:144–63; Haudrère 1993; Kaeppelin 1967.

34. Haudrère 2005, 1:27–29; [de la Roque] 1716. The Yemen was at this time only partly under Ottoman control, and its sultan made trading agreements with European merchants that infringed directives from the central Ottoman administration. See Panzac 1996, 202; Raymond 1999, 1:144, 150–51.

French consumers within eight years, in return for the concession of the island and its dependencies.[35]

Horticultural knowledge now became central to coffee's colonial and metropolitan identity. During the 1710s Compagnie des Indes administrators on the Isle de Bourbon developed a plant introduction program, beginning with coffee, whose domestic profitability was already well established. This project unfolded quite independently of institutional botanical intervention, but had strong Crown ties. La Grélodière, one of the travelers on the 1711–13 Mocha voyage, negotiated a promise from the sultan of the Yemen to recognize French trading rights at Mocha and to supply young coffee plants for cultivation in the Mascarene colonies, of whose existence the sultan proved well aware. The plan came to fruition in June 1715, when the Compagnie's agent in Mocha shipped sixty young coffee plants aboard the *Chasseur*, bound for Bourbon. Just twenty of the plants reached Bourbon alive the following September, and this number dwindled to two after they were planted out in the colony. An assiduous program of cultivation and propagation nevertheless allowed the island's governor, Desforges-Boucher, to begin sending coffee back to France by the mid-1720s.[36]

From a metropolitan standpoint, acclimatized coffee created fiscal dilemmas. The Malouin merchants had a trade monopoly in goods from the East Indies, but they could only import their coffee to mainland France through the port of Marseille, where it incurred a 20 percent entry duty. This monopoly system generated conflict between rival merchant groups, but also encouraged commercial collaboration between merchants from different cities. The leading work on coffee dating from this period was written by Jean de la Roque, who may himself have participated in the 1711 voyage, even though he came from a Marseille rather than a Malouin merchant family. Like Dufour's book, de la Roque's *Voyage de l'Arabie Heureuse* (Journey to Arabia Felix, 1716) is now regarded as one of the principal resources for writing the history of coffee. A long discourse on commercial and political relations between France and the Levant is leavened by curious anecdotes about eating crocodile eggs and ceremonial encounters with

35. Lougnon 1956, 64–65; Kaeppelin 1967, 600–601; Courdurié 1980, 76; Malleret 1974, 93–99; Archives Nationales, Aix-en-Provence, C[3] 3, f°s. 83 r°.–131 v°., 179 r°.–194 v°., with quote at 98 r°. See also Wijnands 1988; Stearn 1962; Courdurié 1980, 78; Spary 2000, chap. 2; Regourd 1999; Drayton 2000. Raymond 1999, 1:175n, calculates that coffee constituted 67 percent of French Levantine purchases by 1715, so these plans addressed what was by now a substantial sector of French imports.

36. Archives Nationales, Aix-en-Provence, C[3] 3, f[os]. 209 r[o].–210 v[o].; Lougnon 1956, 73–75; *Biographie Universelle* 28:78; anon. 1798, pt. 1, 38.

governors. There follows a scholarly account of coffee, making extensive reference to all other published botanical descriptions of the coffee plant, together with an explanation of how the beans and the drink itself were prepared. Next is a treatise on the habit of coffee drinking in Europe, listing all the learned persons who had previously written on that subject. Antoine Galland supplied notes on the uses and nomenclature of coffee among the Arabs for the next essay, which also included an account of the origins of cafés in France and contemporary medical critiques of coffee. The book ends with a reprint of a poem on coffee originally published in a collection of fashionable songs, and the author's personal description of visiting the Jardin des Plantes in Paris in July 1714, in the company of Galland and a Chinese scholar, Ouange. Here Antoine de Jussieu, professor of botany at the garden, showed the three visitors the first coffee plants ever grown on French soil.[37]

In many ways, the new Indies network resembled the sort of world in which knowledge about coffee had been constituted in the 1670s and 1680s. The Compagnie's founders, Samuel Bernard and Antoine Crozat, moved between their provincial place of origin and courtly or metropolitan high society. Samuel Crozat and his brother Pierre, both rich financiers, were close to the Regent. Pierre Crozat, like Jean de la Roque's brother Antoine, was a celebrated collector. However, these collectors specialized in fine art—paintings and sculpture—rather than coins and antiquities, and in modern Italian, Dutch, or French art rather than in classical and Oriental antiquity and philology. Pierre Crozat funded a vast project to publish engravings of the Italian art collection sold by Queen Christina of Sweden to the Regent, and his cabinet was frequented by leading artists and critics. Art historians have portrayed Crozat's circle of private criticism and connoisseurship as the source of a new form of curiosity based on equality of taste, and of a new language of appreciation.[38] Collecting was an important way for wealthy financiers to exchange financial resources for cultural credit; it permitted entry into the social and literary circles of the metropolis and was one way in which financiers achieved high social status during these very

37. Carrière [1973], 1:359–74; [de la Roque] 1716; Kaeppelin 1967, pt. 5, chap. 1; Buti 2001, 227.

38. *Biographie Universelle* 36:441–42. In the secondary literature, there is confusion over the identity and relationship of the Crozats. Some write of two financier brothers, Pierre and Antoine, others of a father and son, Antoine and Joseph-Antoine, and there is disagreement over which of them was the famous collector (Scott 1995, 226; Haskell 1987, 18–57; *Biographie Universelle* 9:540–41; Banks 1977, 69–76; Crow 1985, 41; Pomian 1990, 160; Chaussinand-Nogaret 1972, 22–30).

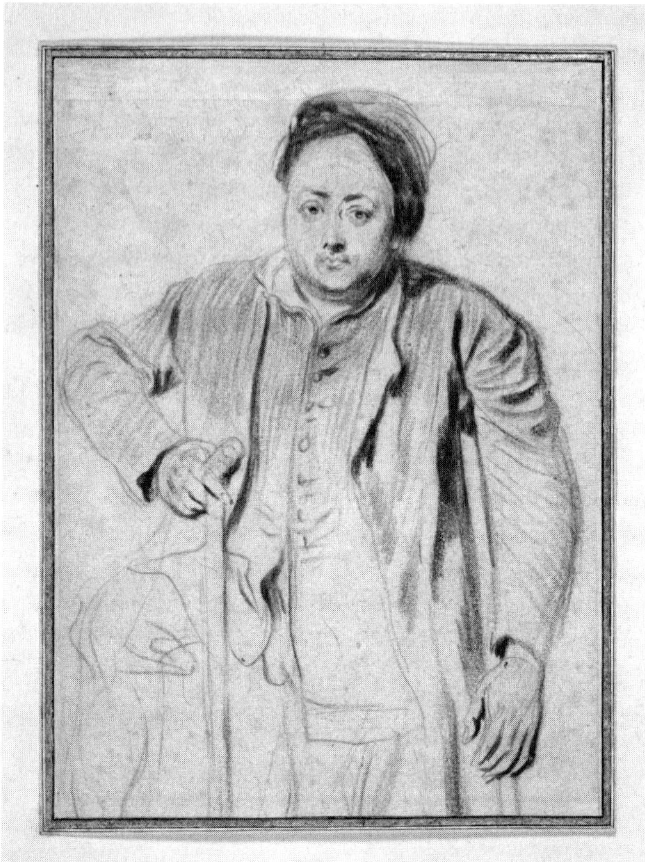

Figure 2.3. Antoine de la Roque sketched by Antoine Watteau, after 1709. Fitzwilliam Museum, Cambridge.

decades. The lucrative privilege of editing the national newspaper, the *Mercure*, was held from 1721 to 1740 by Antoine de la Roque, assisted by his brother Jean; it gave ample space to collecting. For this network, coffee was an object of commercial gain and scholarly interest in its own right, rather than an advertisement for Orientalism. Yet the new status of coffee as a subject of learned inquiry and a fuel for mental creativity was mocked by other authors. Works like Jean de la Roque's *Voyage* were seen as emanations of the new scholarship, dealing with absurd rather than elevated themes. This concern about the superficiality of fashionable knowledge arose in part from coffee's status as a marker of new wealth and upward mobility, like the financiers themselves.

In 1716 the royal treasury was declared empty. The Regent, with his trusted minister, the Scottish banker John Law, turned to private investment to rebuild French fortunes. Over the next decade, the funds invested in the Compagnie des Indes by shareholders great and small were absorbed into ministerial fundraising policies. This was also the decade in which the tax farmers' role as Crown creditors became a permanent feature of national finance, a state of affairs that would last until the fall of the monarchy. Law began his reform program by yoking the Compagnie des Indes first to the Compagnie d'Occident, then to the national bank he founded. In the process, the Malouins' monopoly was weakened. Law himself became the principal shareholder in the new merged company. With the advent of closer ties between Crown and colonial administration, new opportunities opened up for metropolitan scholars to insert themselves into the coffee trade. This brings us to the third network.[39]

THE AMERICAN NETWORK

One might remark upon the low profile that natural history had within all of this, compared to its prominence in colonial administration after about 1750. Writing in the 1740s, Pierre Barrère, traveling naturalist, would date the beginnings of coffee cultivation on the South American island of Cayenne to 1721, when "some French Deserters, who had taken refuge in *Suriname*, and afterwards returned to Cayenne, thought they could obtain an amnesty by bringing some Coffee berries with them, which the Dutch had already cultivated for some time in their Colony." Plants for political amnesty? This exchange conveys a sense of the political status that cultivatory skills, practices, and objects were acquiring in the eighteenth-century French colonial setting. It was during the eighteenth century that natural resources became an explicit focus for Crown investment and a highly politicized issue. Ministers now began to rely more heavily than ever upon the expertise of scientific practitioners, who collaborated with administrators in the effort to diversify natural resources both at home and in the colonies. Long-standing proposals for capturing lucrative global commerce in natural productions monopolized by other European powers were renewed and—quite literally—bore fruit. Thus coffee, having passed through succes-

39. Durand 1971, 449; Faure 1977; Murphy 1997; Cellard 1996; Hamilton 1991; Chaussinand-Nogaret 1972, 30–37. The Compagnie d'Occident was founded in 1717, when Samuel Bernard ceded Louisiana to the Crown, and was united to the Compagnie des Indes in 1719 (Haudrère 2005, 1:37–51; Pluchon 1991, 1:49).

sive incarnations as a curiosity and and an aid to diplomacy, would become a major commodity, an everyday recreation, and a botanical species, pretty much in that order.[40]

It is important to emphasize that the initial impetus for colonial coffee cultivation was entirely unconnected with the activities of metropolitan botanists. At the royal natural history garden, the Jardin du Roi, the professor of botany, Antoine de Jussieu, had no contact with the coffee trade prior to 1714 except via his correspondent Gaudron, a master apothecary at Saint Malo. Both Gaudron and Jean de la Roque had received their descriptions of the coffee plant from Desnoyers, a ship's surgeon on the second Mocha voyage of 1711–13. It was Gaudron who forwarded Desnoyers's memoir to de Jussieu, and the botanist relied on it for a description of coffee he presented to the Académie Royale des Sciences in November 1713, when reporting that coffee seeds sent him by the Amsterdam botanist Caspar Commelin had germinated. The following year de Jussieu received a young coffee plant from the Regent Burgomaster of Amsterdam, Pancras, a replacement for one given to the king in 1712 by de Resson, a lieutenant-general of artillery, which had died.[41] This showy, mature plant from Amsterdam was transported to the Jardin du Roi, where it flowered and fruited. Though several coffee plants in various stages of development were probably growing in Paris in 1714, this highly visible diplomatic gift became an icon for subsequent enterprises of naturalization. As late as 1788, the head gardener at the Jardin du Roi in Paris would suggest that colonial coffee production had *originated* at that metropolitan institution: "For a century the greater part of the plants introduced to France have had the Jardin du Roi for their nursery and there are some which have now become the subject of an extensive trade which has generated several million for the State, for example the revenue from coffee cultivation."[42]

40. Barrère 1743, 110. Aublet 1775, 51, dated the introduction of coffee to Surinam to 1719. According to Franklin 1887–1902, 13:106–7; Masson 1912, 165; Legrand d'Aussy 1783, 3:121, the two individuals involved were a Marseillois, de Mourgues, and one de la Mothe Aigron, a lieutenant in Cayenne. In 1713 there was a proposal to approach Guy-Crescent Fagon, intendant of the Jardin du Roi, to recommend a botanist to travel to the Yemen and supervise the gift of coffee plants from the Sultan, though nothing came of it. See Archives Nationales, Aix-en-Provence, C3 3, fos. 209 ro.–209 vo. On French colonial botany after 1750, see Regourd 1999; Spary 2000, chap. 2.

41. Turner 2004, 52; anon. 1798, 10. De Jussieu's report to the Académie Royale des Sciences, presented on November 18, 1713, is in Archives de l'Académie des Sciences, Paris, "Procès-verbaux," 1713, fo. 339 vo. [De la Roque] 1716, 239–40, identifies Desnoyers as de Jussieu's source. On Commelin, see Wijnands 1983, chap. 1.

42. Archives Nationales, Paris, AJ15 502: André Thouin, draft project for the regulation of the Jardin, September 1788. See also Gentil 1787, 14; Aublet 1775.

How then did the arrival of the coffee plant in Paris help to reconfigure botanical expertise as a necessary part of commercial and colonial profitability, given that hitherto coffee had stood for quite different domains of knowledge and expertise, other networks, and distinct spaces? No author writing before 1700 had suggested that metropolitan botanical expertise was essential to the development of the coffee trade, and naturalization projects were in the hands of merchants or colonists, not centrally driven by the Crown. In 1713 coffee was already widely drunk on the streets of Paris, but it was still not accessible to the botanists of the Jardin du Roi: it was easier for this metropolitan scientific institution to acquire a plant from the Dutch, France's old commercial and military rivals, than from the nation's own East India Company. This tells us much about the *lack* of integration of botany within colonial and commercial policy circa 1700. The transformation can be traced through de Jussieu's relationship with coffee between 1713 and 1723.

The papers presented to the Académie Royale des Sciences in 1713 were not published until 1716. In the meantime, Antoine de Jussieu had jettisoned his original account of the coffee plant to the Académie. In the published memoir, he substituted a new description and depiction of the coffee plant, as known to him through firsthand experience of the Jardin du Roi's specimen, and used this to correct the accounts of earlier authors. The epistemological transformation that coffee underwent in this three-year period is evident from its new iconography. The ability of botanists to involve themselves in the global coffee trade depended in part on a displacement of attention away from the commodity, the domain of merchants' skill, and toward the flower, the domain of botanists' expertise. De Jussieu's text was cited in later natural historical publications; significantly, it omitted any account of the Saint Malo consortium's commercial enterprise or of its plans to introduce Arabian coffee to the Indian Ocean colony of Isle de Bourbon.[43]

In 1716 de Jussieu also defended a thesis on coffee in the Paris medical faculty in which he demonstrated his support for iatrochemistry and his enthusiasm for coffee as a new exotic drug. Following the traditional format of medical theses, it asked, "Whether coffee is healthy for men of Letters?," a question resoundingly answered in the affirmative:

> [De Jussieu] vividly depicts the misfortunes of studious people, exposed by their sedentary lifestyles, dogged efforts [and] regular late nights to a

43. French medicine had been transformed by the introduction of new, high-profile remedies such as quinquina and ipecacuanha. De Jussieu's project continued this tradition (Spary 2004).

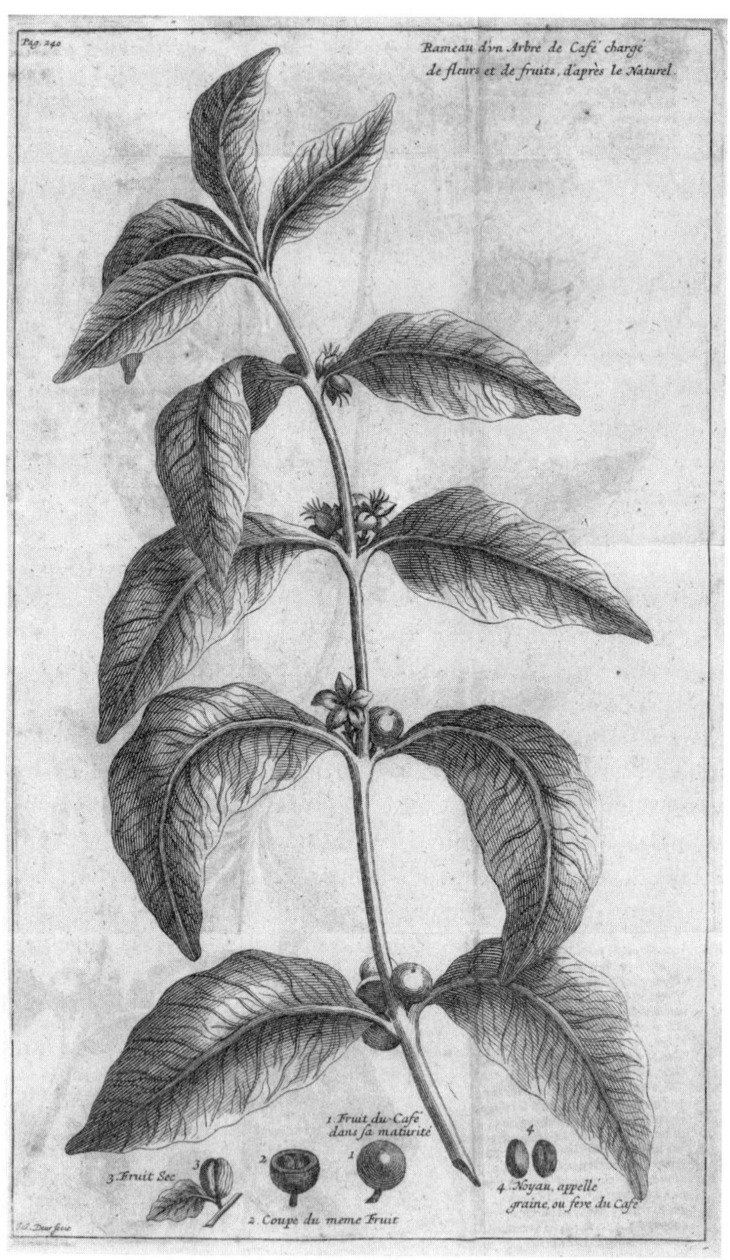

Figure 2.4. [Jean de La Roque,] *Voyage de l'Arabie Heureuse* (Amsterdam: Steenhouwer and Uytwerf, 1716), plate 3, opp. p. 240: "Rameau d'un Arbre de Café chargé de fleurs et de fruits, d'après le Naturel." Jacob Deur. Cambridge University Library.

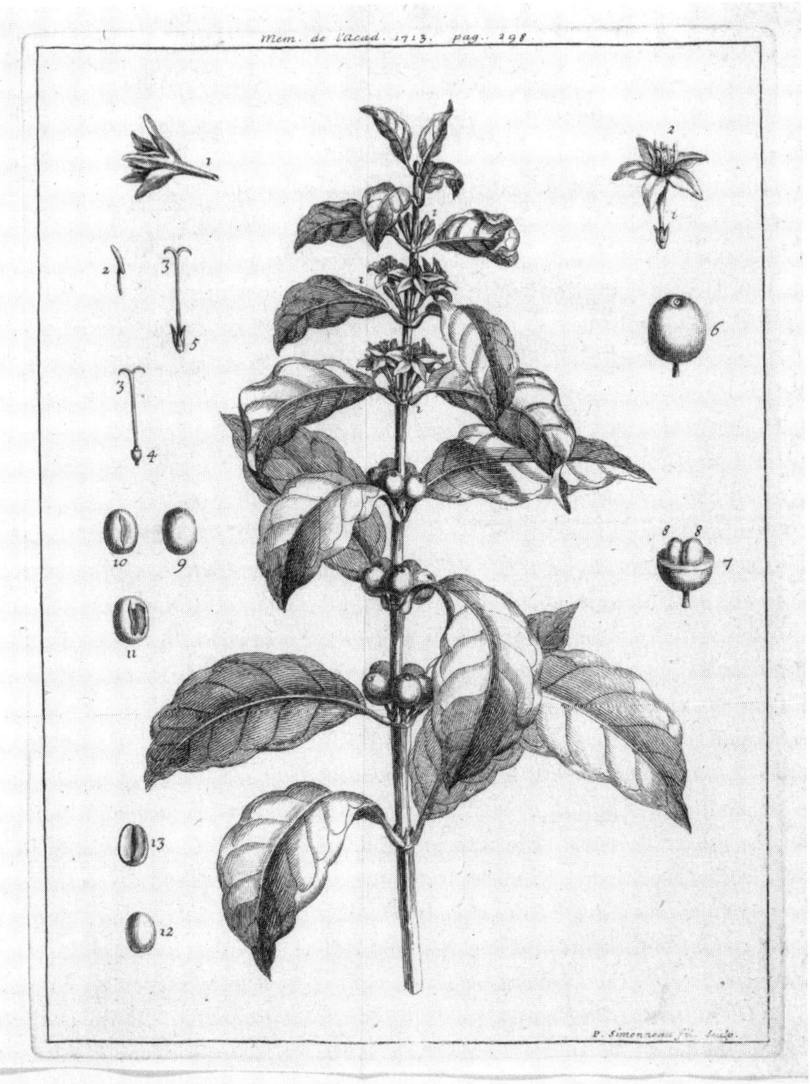

Figure 2.5. *Histoire de l'Académie Royale des Sciences. Année M.DCCXIII. Avec les Memoires de Mathématique & de Phisique* (Paris: Imprimerie Royale, 1716), "Mémoires," plate opp. p. 298, showing a branch of the coffee tree according to Antoine de Jussieu's botanical system. Copperplate engraving, P. Simonneau fils. Cambridge University Library.

> host of diseases. The exhaustion they experience from the dissipation of animal spirits is the most common cause; the loss of that precious liquor destroys them. This principle of life extracted from the purest blood, subtilises in the brain to the point of meriting the name of spirits in some sense, spreads via the nerves throughout our whole machine; an instrument of the soul, it animates the body [and] is the link uniting them.

Excessive loss of this "principle of life" weakened the link between body and soul, causing myriad health problems, beginning with stomach troubles, vomiting, and colic, and ending with thickened humors: "if one does not die, one lives with the pain of gout, nephritick, the stone, dropsy, asthma, hemorrhoids, the sorry fruits of assiduous labour." In this regard, coffee was better than tea, which provoked transpiration without increasing the levels of spirits, or chocolate, which contained an indigestibly thick oil, harmful to studious consumers. Coffee "is fortunately coming to take the place of these drinks, and to take their place to advantage; . . . it remedies all the bad effects of mental labour through its oily, saline, [and] volatile principles." The first salutary effects of coffee were experienced in the stomach; it eased digestive and circulatory processes, expedited secretion "& by giving the brain a new resource of *esprits*, sustains the body during great application & long wakefulness." Early in the century, iatrochemists viewed the mind as a corporeal reserve that could be topped up from diet. Unlike other spirit-rich foods, however, coffee was hailed as a wonder drug because its volatile salts were chemically bound in such as way as to prevent excessively violent chemical activity within the body or mind, unlike wine. According to de Jussieu, coffee "seems to cheer [the mind], make It more fit for work, recreate it and dissipate Its cares." Coffee thus exemplified a particular iatrochemical conjuncture of pleasure and learning: more than any other foodstuff, it epitomized the dietary ambitions of those aspiring to a state of enlightenment. This optimism was not universal, however. Some physicians claimed coffee had no medicinal properties at all, but was "only . . . an amusement suitable for interrupting [scholars'] work"; habitual consumption would soon cancel out any positive or negative health effects. Others cited coffee drinking as the cause of ill effects ranging from weight loss and insomnia to dysentery, and insisted that coffee was and must remain a remedy. By the 1750s certain physicians were arguing that coffee was especially unsuitable for men of letters.[44]

44. *Mémoires de Trévoux* (1716): 674–80; see also Archives de l'Académie des Sciences, Paris: "Procès-verbaux," 1715, f°s. 102r[o]–102v[o]; review of [de la Roque] 1716 in *Journal des*

De Jussieu's personal commitment to coffee as a remedy encouraged his interest in the botany of the plant and explains his attempts to promote coffee cultivation in the French colonies in the 1710s and 1720s. Unlike previous commentators on coffee, he also moved from literary representations of coffee to practical intervention in coffee cultivation. Subsequent botanical involvement in naturalization programs for other plants rested on three types of interrelated knowledge-claims, which in anachronistic terms we might characterize as "biogeographical" "replicatory," and "taxonomic": naturalists needed (1) to recruit reports concerning the distribution of species around the globe, (2) to possess the skill to preserve and propagate exotic plants in metropolis, province or colony, and (3) to proclaim their exclusive right to define classificatory boundaries and especially species identity and difference. The immediate significance of such moves became evident in the case of wild coffee.

WILD COFFEE

What excited particular interest both among botanists and within the Compagnie des Indes during these same years was the discovery of coffee plants growing wild on Bourbon itself. Louis Boyvin d'Hardancourt, a Compagnie official on an inspection tour of the Asian *comptoirs*, visited Bourbon in 1711 to find "wild coffee trees, of a height of ten to twelve feet, full of fruit" growing in the forest. "The coffee in the mature pods was falling to the ground. . . . I had as much as possible gathered up and had it made into two small bales, which I brought back to France in order to know its quality." The plants' identity was affirmed by the Bourbon settlers after comparison with the specimens recently arrived from Mocha.[45]

Back in Paris, Antoine de Jussieu only received news of indigenous coffee secondhand. Once again, it was Gaudron, his Saint Malo contact, who sent him news of the discovery, which was enthusiastically reported in the Académie des Sciences' published history for 1716: "It would be an advantage for the Kingdom to have a Colonial source for this fruit which is so much in vogue. The difference between coffee from the Isle de Bourbon and that from Yemen might be to the advantage of the former, once it is better

Sçavans 60 (September 1716): 243–53. As Franklin 1887–1902, 13:76–77, shows, there was no unanimity among medical practitioners over coffee's health effects. For a representative spectrum of views on the medicinal properties of coffee, compare Dufour 1684, 89; anon. 1696, 27–29; Duncan 1705; Lémery 1705, chap. 9; Hecquet 1710a, vol. 2, chap. 10; anon. [1711?]. On coffee as a cause of nervous disease, see also chapter 5 in this volume.

45. Quoted in Lougnon 1956, 132–33; on D'Hardancourt, see Haudrère 1989, 1:52–53, 99.

known; if not, a way of correcting it might be found." The discovery of wild coffee provoked Bourbon's administrative council to propose a systematic survey of the island's natural resources. The island's governor traveled to Paris to present specimens of wild coffee to the Company, accompanied by a Bourbon creole, Jean-Baptiste Daillau, whose father had been involved in earlier acclimatization projects.[46]

Cross-questioned at the Jardin du Roi concerning the indigenous productions of Bourbon, with a view to ensuring no other natural treasures were going to waste, Daillau claimed to recognize coffee and pepper, but not vanilla. Armed with this authentication and eager for profit, the directors of the Compagnie des Indes and the island's council joined in promoting wild coffee production. In September 1717 the Mocha plants on Bourbon flowered for the first time. The island's military commander, Henri de Justamond, reported to his French correspondents that although the flowers were similar to those of wild coffee, the "wood and the leaf" were different. Wild coffee fruited once a year, not twice, and bore much smaller crops. The fruits were oval and pointed, in contrast to those borne by the Mocha plants. Nonetheless, during the autumn of 1717, fifty pounds of indigenous coffee were sent to the Compagnie's directors in France, who congratulated themselves that the beans they had received were indeed "coffee whose cultivation will correct its small defects." Contemporary accounts show that the flavor and mode of preparation were different also. Indigenous coffee still needed to be roasted, but one-third less ground coffee was required to make the drink. It also produced a beverage that was noticeably bitter. This too was ascribed to the lack of cultivation: the bitterness dissipated after three or four years of storage, and at least one Saint Malo optimist claimed that grafting would improve the flavor until "the finest connoisseurs can in no way distinguish the natural coffee of the island from that of Mocha." By 1718 there were plans to make concessions of indigenous coffee cultivation on the island.[47]

Wild coffee flourished for a few years within an optimistic and ambitious program of inventorizing, cultivating, and improving natural resources, cen-

46. Fontenelle 1718; Archives Nationales, Aix-en-Provence, C^{3} 4, f°s. 7 r°.–36 r°. For earlier attempts by colonists to acclimatize profitable plants on Bourbon, see Lougnon 1956, 75–78; Archives Nationales, Aix-en-Provence, C^{3} 3, f°s. 75 r°.–76 v°.

47. Lougnon 1956, chap. 4, with quotations, 114, 116, 149; Archives Nationales, Aix-en-Provence, C^{3} 4, f°s. 37 r°.–43 v°. De Justamond was commander of the island and played an active part in encouraging wild coffee cultivation. Le Gentil de la Barbinais 1728, 3:98–99, similarly claimed that cultivational techniques would improve flavor.

tral to which was a portrayal of Bourbon as a natural paradise: "This island has no animal, reptile or insect which is harmful; the water, and the air are marvellous here, one can sleep on the ground everywhere, day and night, without any risk . . . everything one sows or plants from Europe and the Indies grows and fruits to perfection here." The wild coffee cultivation program was supported by the Compagnie des Indes, a body tied to John Law's financial projects. When Law's bank collapsed in 1720–21, the company's future was only secured by a Crown takeover and the extensive reforms described above. De Jussieu, who had known of the existence of the Bourbon coffee plant since 1716, again only managed to obtain specimens of wild coffee following the collapse of the Malouin monopoly. This was thanks to the intervention of the new *contrôleur général des finances*, Law's replacement. Félix Le Pelletier de la Houssaye was the son of the tax collector and *parlementaire* Nicolas Le Pelletier de la Houssaye, one of those to whom de Jussieu had personally exhibited the Jardin du Roi's coffee plant in 1714.[48]

The new minister found himself in the midst of a pitched battle. Port customs officials were confiscating wild coffee cargoes, arguing that if it was the same as ordinary coffee, it must be imported to Marseille and properly taxed. If, however, wild coffee was not the same as ordinary coffee, then there was the possibility that a fraud was being perpetrated. When a cargo of Bourbon coffee arrived at L'Orient in 1721, ministerial intervention was necessary to obtain its release from customs. This fiscal dilemma prompted the minister to turn to botanical expertise as the means of settling whether wild coffee was, or was not, real coffee. In the summer of 1722 Antoine de Jussieu thanked the minister for inducing Le Cordier, a director of the Compagnie des Indes, to send him specimens of Bourbon coffee, which he identified as a member of the coffee genus, though not the same species as the plant that produced Mocha coffee. In spite of all the ways in which wild coffee differed from Mocha coffee—morphology, flavor, yield, geographical origin—de Jussieu supported the claims of the colonists that wild coffee and Mocha coffee were both "real" coffee, and argued for the commercial viability of the indigenous crop. The minister had evidently also asked de Jussieu to indicate whether wild coffee's distinctive flavor could be disguised, for the botanist had experimented on mixtures of one part wild coffee to two parts Mocha coffee: "I can even confirm that when this coffee was presented

48. Archives Nationales, Aix-en-Provence, C^{3} 3, f°s. 75 r°.–76 v°.; compare f°s. 83 r°.–131 v°. On Le Pelletier de la Houssaye, see Lacroix 1936.

at the end of the meal to persons who had not been informed of the existence of another coffee, they were unable to perceive any difference."[49]

This last maneuver, deceiving the consuming public, in fact proved crucial to the commercial future of wild coffee, as to many subsequent state-approved surrogates. An unsigned memoir of 1722 proposed, similarly, that Bourbon coffee be sold in the East Indies in Mocha coffee wrappings. This was a way of dealing with widespread suspicion on the part of metropolitan merchants and consumers concerning the authenticity and quality of exotic drugs and spices, for unscrupulous traders commonly substituted, adulterated, or counterfeited these valuable goods. The claim that wild coffee was "real" coffee, and that its defects would be overcome by cultivation, proved difficult to sustain, however. The collapse of Law's colonial program marked the end of a transparent relationship between metropolis and colony where wild coffee was concerned. After 1722, the company's new directors pressed Desforges-Boucher to abandon wild coffee experiments and to increase the production of Mocha coffee beans on the island. Indigenous coffee, they informed him in 1725, was not wanted in France; the earlier shipments had remained rotting in the stores. The plan to wait until cultivation improved wild coffee had failed, it was implied, because the claim that wild coffee was real coffee could not be sustained among domestic vendors and consumers. Despite such injunctions, wild coffee continued to be grown on Bourbon, and was apparently mingled with the Mocha coffee crop, then shipped to Europe. Its distinct botanical identity was not made public until 1783, when Lamarck named it *Coffea mauritiana* in a botanical dictionary. Even today, this species forms a small percentage of the global coffee crop, and it has been joined by several other species and subspecies, mostly originating from Western Africa. Yet its very existence is scarcely noted in most historical treatises on coffee.[50]

A second acclimatizatory enterprise has attracted more historical attention. Young coffee plants grown from seed at the Jardin du Roi were transported to the French Antillean colony of Martinique by the botanist Michel Isambert, a protégé of de Jussieu who traveled with the official sanction

49. Archives Nationales, Aix-en-Provence, C³ 3, f°s. 75 r°.–76 v°., 83 r°.–131 v°.; Lougnon 1956, 150; Lacroix 1936, 206–14. On the Law scheme as it affected the colonies and the Compagnie des Indes, see Haudrère 1989, chap. 1; Hilaire-Pérez 1997, 217–21.

50. An exception to the general neglect is Turner 2004, chap. 1. Archives Nationales, Aix-en-Provence, C³ 4, f°s. 56 r°.–58 v°.; Lougnon 1956, chap. 10. Wild coffee still lacked a definitive botanical identity at the end of the eighteenth century. See "Caffeyer," Lamarck 1783, 550–51; anon. 1798, pt. 1, 18–19. On coffee substitutes and fraud, see Pomet 1694; Spary unpublished, chap. 8.

of the Paris Académie Royale des Sciences. The cultivation attempt failed when Isambert died soon after his arrival in July 1716. It was the intendant of the Antilles from 1719 to 1722, Charles Bénard, who finally convinced the Crown of the value of trialing coffee cultivation in French colonies. On June 25, 1720, the Conseil de marine voted to "Take [Bénard's proposal] to the Regent. It seems [coffee] could be sent from here, it not being possible to get any from Mocha." Later that year, a naval officer, chevalier Gabriel-Mathieu d'Erchigny de Clieu, was appointed by the director of the Jardin du Roi to accompany cuttings of the royal coffee plants to Martinique. Departing Rochefort that October, he famously shared his shipboard water ration with the plants, planting them out in Martinique in 1723. This journey was rapidly worked into an emblematic and oft-recounted history of naturalizatory heroism, with a trajectory from center to periphery. Its historical significance is, however, somewhat diminished by the fact that by 1724 only seed-grown plants, from several different sources, were known to exist on the island. Acclimatizing coffee was a multifocal event, involving planters, administrators, botanists, the academy, and the Crown. Only in retrospect would it be interpreted as a process driven by central botanical authority.[51]

From Martinique, coffee plants traveled to other French Antillean colonies, including Guadeloupe and, especially, Saint-Domingue, where coffee production rose with dramatic speed. Antillean coffee began to be imported to France by 1727, at first in very small quantities. By 1729 one Marseille merchant reported from Martinique that there were at least three million plants on the island, and that the plant grew "like a weed"; in 1732 he would estimate the population at some 25 million plants.[52] The Compagnie des Indes fought hard to maintain its privileges against the tidal wave of coffee, wild, naturalized, adulterated, and smuggled, which began to reach

51. Archives Nationales, Aix-en-Provence, C^{8A} 21, f°. 156; C^{8A} 26, f°s. 325 r°.–329 v°.; C^{8A} 27, f°s. 254 r°.–260 v°.; C^{8B} 4, f°. 67. Bénard was active in founding a botanic garden in the colony. De Clieu accorded the Jardin and himself a central place in coffee acclimatization, but this was not unchallenged; cf. anon. 1774. All accounts of his voyage in fact date from considerably later, e.g., [Chanvalon] 1763, 122; anon. 1773; de Clieu 1774; Cassan 1789; anon. 1798, pt. 1, xxix, 17. For secondary accounts, see Franklin 1887–1902, 13:105–6; Stella 1997, 30; Masson 1912, 165. From contemporary documents I construct a somewhat different picture of events: Archives Nationales, Aix-en-Provence, C^{8A} 33, f°. 49 v°. shows that by 1724 no adult plants existed on Martinique, though colonists had successfully germinated coffee beans brought by de Clieu as well as beans from Bourbon and Surinam. On the Jardin du Roi and early colonial cultivation, see Bourguet and Bonneuil 1999.

52. Trouillot 1982; Turner 2004, 59; Carrière [1973], 1:360–66; Courdurié 1980; Archives de la Chambre de Commerce, Marseille, ms. H 112: "Memoire," February 17, 1730. The growth in coffee imports from the Antilles after 1723 may have been encouraged by exceptionally high prices for Yemeni coffee. See Raymond 1999, 1:138–40.

French shores by the end of the 1720s. Its directors solicited the Crown to defend the company's exclusive right over the coffee trade between France and Mocha, proclaimed in 1723 and repeated in 1725.[53] But the Compagnie singularly failed in its bid to control colonial coffee commerce. One reason for this lay in the fact that colonial coffee created a legislative loophole in the tightly woven fabric of French commercial society. Colonial coffee was not covered by the existing network of monopoly legislation, which covered most trade routes, land areas, and specific commodities. The battle was already lost by the time the Compagnie des Indes made a bold bid for proprietorship in 1730, arguing that its right to import coffee from one French island, Bourbon, gave it the right to trade in coffee produced by any and all French islands. The Compagnie's claim, not surprisingly, fell foul of other legislation privileging coffee entry to the port of Marseille and also raised public concerns over the adulteration of exotic imports. A memoir defending its monopoly, which was being undermined by smuggled American-grown coffee, highlights the problem:

> For fear that merchants would mix [Bourbon] and Mocha [coffee beans], And out of concern not to interfere with Public taste, the Compagnie des Indes has hitherto adopted the policy of not selling any [Bourbon coffee] within the Kingdom, & of exporting it all. Before offering it for consumption in France, it has been waiting until the finest taste would mistake the Coffee from that Island for that from Mocha. Bourbon Coffee is on the point of reaching that degree of perfection.

As late as 1731, the Compagnie was still not selling Bourbon coffee to French consumers, but was anticipating some future moment when the semi-wild qualities of the colonial product should have been corrected by cultivation. A horticultural knowledge-claim about the important differences in flavor and quality introduced into food plants by cultivation underpinned both this organization's failure to dominate the colonial coffee trade to mainland France, and Antoine de Jussieu's advice about how to manage the potential problem of public perception created by colonial coffee. Moreover, in a commercial move quite incomprehensible in today's terms,

53. Archives de la Chambre de Commerce de Marseille, ms. H 112, "Memoire sur l'arret du Con.[l] d'Etat . . . ," October 1, 1723; *ACE* 1723; Service Historique de la Marine, Brest, ms. 50, f°s. 257–86. Archives de la Chambre de Commerce de Marseille, ms. H 112, "Memoire sur Le Commerce du Caffé," September 6, 1726, claimed that by 1726 the legitimate coffee trade accounted for less than half of the coffee consumed in France.

the Compagnie defended its policy regarding Bourbon coffee by presenting itself as the defender of French connoisseurship, protecting the drinking public against the evils of inferior-tasting coffee. Paris merchants, indeed, were asserting that Bourbon coffee "cannot call Itself coffee, as it only roughly resembles it, and is good for nothing, According to the trials that have been performed." A memoir sent to the Conseil de Commerce in 1733 is redolent of the Bourbon taste experience: "Up to now," the author commented, "the Coffee from that island which has reached Europe has smelt unripe, with a complex taste of mildew which it is impossible to remove." This author argued, however, that the problem was one of inadequate methods of preservation, rather than an innate shortcoming of the colonial product. In general, therefore, the response to Bourbon coffee was not unanimously favorable, in spite of the claim by one traveling naturalist-clergyman that "the coffee of this island is more bitter and healthier than the other [i.e., Mocha coffee]." Bourbon coffee, instead, was sold to the Dutch, where it fetched prices almost as high as Mocha coffee. The company's caution about selling Bourbon coffee within France indicates that the whole concept of a colonial coffee trade was still problematic by the 1730s, and for reasons connected with contemporary understandings of cultivation and connoisseurship. As with naturalization programs for spice plants, success depended on defending the claim that over time naturalization and cultivation would operate profound changes in the plant, enhancing its useful properties. For the remainder of the Old Regime, Parisian botanists continued to insist that the appropriate management of wild forms of particular plant species would convert them into valuable plantation crops. After 1750 colonial agriculture and experimental botany gained increasing Crown support thanks to these accounts of naturalization.[54]

It is only by considering such limiting cases, the uncertainties and hesitancies over wild coffee, colonial coffee, and adulterated coffee—goods that resembled coffee but were not quite the same, that threatened the boundaries of coffee as it was already known—that we can come to understand what coffee "was" for contemporaries. Clearly, its identity was not constant, but was the end product of many negotiations over value, meaning, and authenticity, which took place under very specific social and political circumstances. In effect, the colonial coffee offered by the Compagnie was

54. Carrière [1973], 1:366–67; Service Historique de la Marine, Brest, ms. 50, f°s. 268, 318; Archives de la Chambre de Commerce de Marseille, ms. H 112, "Coppie du Memoire presentée a Monseigneur Le Controlleur General," October 20, 1723, f°. 1 v°.; Lougnon 1939, 204–12; Spary 2000.

precisely what French consumers already knew to reject, an adulterated product. Either colonial coffee producers would need to sit out the period of time supporters of naturalization predicted it would take for the flavor of their product to improve, or else French consumers would have to compromise their connoisseurial standards.[55] In the event, it was the second of these two changes that occurred, after legislation of 1736 and 1737 finally made the sale of Antillean coffee within the kingdom of France legal.[56] The effect on the international coffee trade was rapid: according to Carrière, the trade in Mocha coffee declined in value over the course of the eighteenth century. Mocha coffee became a luxury good sold to the few, at twice the price of Antillean coffee, and preserved a "select clientele." Antillean coffee undermined the huge profitability of the Levant coffee route, but made coffee accessible to many more Parisian drinkers. During the 1750s Antillean coffee production overtook that of Bourbon, and by the end of the century Bourbon coffee was a small fraction of a market dominated by the American product. At Beaucaire fair in the South of France, for example, the total coffee trade approximately tripled between 1744 and 1789, but the market sector of Antillean coffee increased twelvefold.[57]

As cheap colonial coffee conquered the metropolis in the second half of the century, it became available to many more consumers. Coffee, as a commodity, was now priced not only by its sensory properties, such as smell or appearance, but also by its place of origin. Works of natural history, medicine, and commerce advised the literate consumer as to the best qualities of coffee on the market. The product from Saint-Domingue was known as "the common Coffee," that from Martinique was the best "Coffee of the Islands," while Levantine coffee still reigned supreme. By the 1780s Mocha coffee was still regarded as "the richest in volatile principles, the most agreeable to the [senses of] taste and smell, and the one which, generally speaking, has always been preferred up to now and probably always will be." One acade-

55. On the problem of identity and quality, cf. Stanziani 2007, 395; Spary 2005; on the effects of cultivation, Archives Nationales, Aix-en-Provence, C[3] 3, f°s. 95 v°., 98 r°.

56. *Déclaration* [1732]; *ACE* 1736; Masson 1912, 167; see also Buti 2001, 230–37. The legislation was extended to Cayenne in December 1732. There were several subsequent suspensions and reinstatements of this legislation.

57. Carrière [1973], 1:360–73; see also Raymond 1999; Lougnon 1956; Tuchscherer 2003; Meignen 1976, 130–35; Carrière and Courdurié 1975, 97; Trouillot 1982. By 1723 French merchants had virtually abandoned the land coffee route and were trading directly with Mocha by sea. See Archives de la Chambre de Commerce de Marseille, ms. H 112, "Memoire sur Le Commerce du Caffé," f°. 2 v°. The decline of the coffee trade from Mocha and Bourbon was hastened by other factors such as shipping costs, irregular supplies, and naval warfare. See Haudrère 1989, 1:318–19.

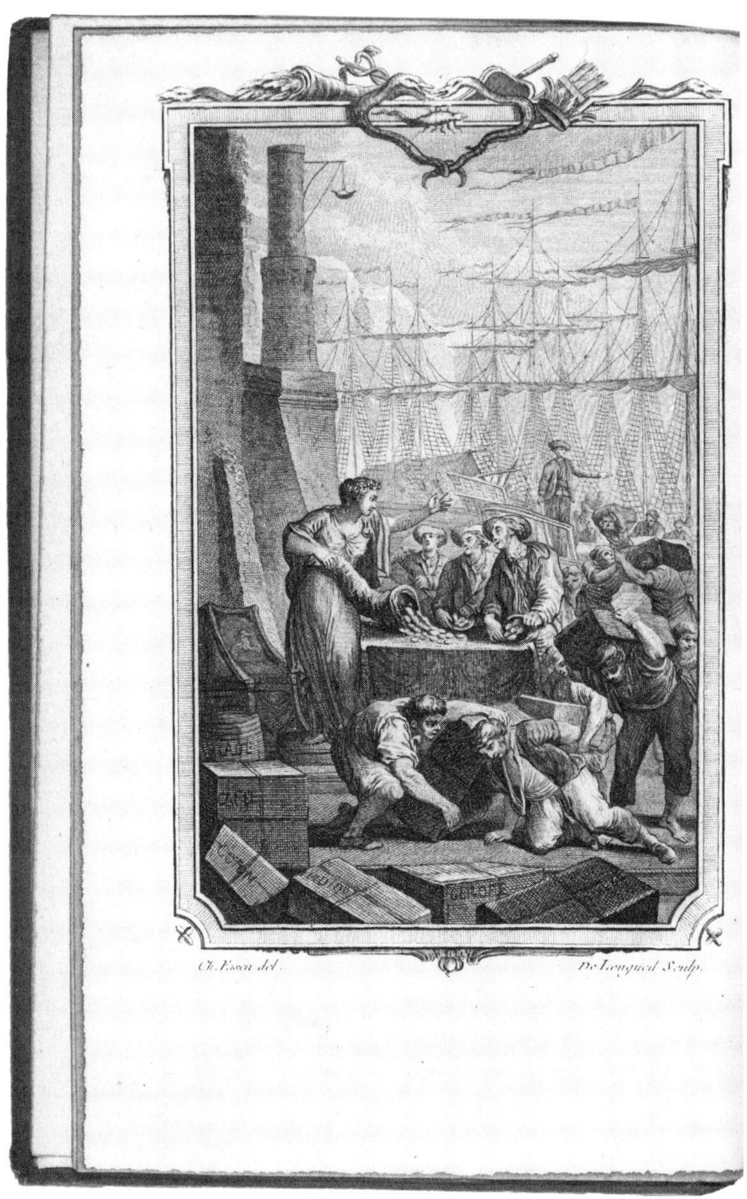

Figure 2.6. Abbé Guillaume-Thomas-François Raynal, *Histoire philosophique et politique des établissements & du commerce des Européens dans les deux Indes* (La Haye: Gosse fils, 1774), vol. 2, frontispiece. Coffee and other colonial goods being unloaded from ships in Marseille harbor. Copperplate engraving by De Longueil after Charles Eisen. Cambridge University Library.

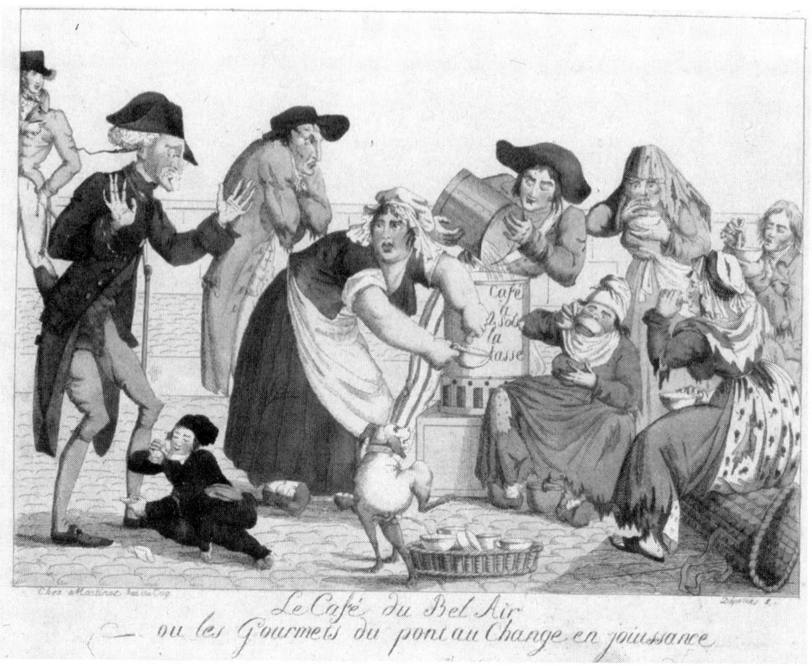

Figure 2.7. "Le Café du Bel Air ou les Gourmets du pont au Change en jouissance" (*c.* 1790). A polite consumer encounters "open air gourmets" drinking what they consider to be coffee. Note the fraudulent composition of this street "coffee" hinted at by the dog urinating into the cups. Ink and wash drawing, probably by François-Nicolas Martinet. Johann Jacobs Museum, Zürich, E87/229.

mician and traveler complained: "I left for the Indies with the prejudice that there was no difference, or at most a very slight one, between [colonial and Mocha] coffee: this prejudice, which I had acquired from experiments at the home of a person . . . at the head of the Compagnie des Indes, soon deserted me at Pondicherry."[58] In other words, well after colonial coffee had garnered a significant portion of the domestic market, it continued to suffer from a second-class reputation among eighteenth-century consumers.

As coffee consumption became ubiquitous in the city, the commodity itself was reclassified in scientific, medical, and economic texts to sustain connoisseurial hierarchies of taste and social standing, giving rise to cari-

58. Gentil 1787, 93; Le Gentil de la Barbinais 1779, 2:685–86; Legrand d'Aussy 1783, 3:123. Déjean 1759, 271, described Bourbon coffee as having "a more seductive appearance than Mocha" so that even "connoisseurs deceive themselves over it," but he observed that the other senses, smell and taste, were not similarly deceived.

catures such as that penned by the pharmacist, poet, philosophe, and spy Jacques-François Demachy in 1775.

> For a Philosophe, it will always be a singular spectacle to see, on the one hand, a woman of high society, comfortably settled in her armchair, who consumes a succulent breakfast to which mocca has added its perfume from a well-varnished tea table, in a . . . gilded porcelain cup, with well-refined sugar & good cream; & on the other, a vegetable seller soaking a bad penny loaf in a detestable Liquor, which she has been told is Café au lait, in a ghastly earthenware pot far from being new, on a willow basket; especially when that Philosophe reflects that the breakfast is, at the least, superfluous for both of them.[59]

But now, the connoisseurial judgment of the coffee drinker was classified in accordance with a hierarchy based on financial value, rather than innate discriminatory powers.

CONCLUSION

Coffee is an especially interesting historical subject, but neither because it belongs within a history of stimulants nor because its history provides us with an ancestry for modern-day coffee drinking. Instead, coffee illustrates the epistemological peculiarity of comestibles. Coffee was exotic, novel, neither food nor medicament: a troublesome matter. It was also seen as a symbol of the increasing penetration of the foreign into French ways of life. As Philippe Hecquet put it in 1710, "The Romans . . . were lost for drinking like the Greeks; the French drink like the Arabs and Chinese: isn't that to adopt a barbarous taste, & shouldn't we be worried about it?"[60] Coffee disrupted established conventions about eating and diet, and during the period covered by this book it underwent a complete transformation from a rare and foreign curiosity into an everyday and quintessentially French substance.

Ever since, coffee has been a familiar accompaniment to everyday life. It has figured in an extensive literature on the rise of European luxury consumption, commodity history, and the history of stimulants. The books and pamphlets that were written about the plant, the drink, and the habit between 1670 and 1730, and which have been the subject of this chapter,

59. Demachy 1775, 115; see also Legrand d'Aussy 1783, 3:105, 125–26; [Mercier] 1781, pt. 2, 205–6. On the hierarchization of quality, see Stanziani 2007, 407–8.

60. *Mémoires de Trévoux* (1710): 289–90.

have been plundered for "facts" about coffee, its origins and its consumption, or for colorful anecdotes. Our historical accounts of coffee are built upon these past attempts to make coffee known to Europeans, yet the status of such printed materials as the products of particular knowledge projects remains neglected. My reading frames this coffee literature within three networks, in which trade and knowledge overlapped: a Levantine network, in which antiquarian and philological experts became involved; an Indian Ocean network, in which connoisseurs of modern European art became involved; and an American network, in which botanical experts became involved. My claim is that the politics of coffee commerce and the practices of coffee consumption were entangled with the ends and knowledge-claims of these groups of learned practitioners, and vice versa.

Rather than a continuous narrative thread, a winner's history of how one stimulant entered European life, therefore, this chapter proposes a history of coffee written as a process of selective appropriations, rejections, and accommodations by various actors. This strategy calls for a different methodological approach to foodstuffs as historical subjects, at one and the same time material substances, commodities, political symbols, and epistemological categories. Such an approach must take into account the circumstances of production and circulation of the texts in which commodities were described, explained, and illustrated. In the existing secondary literature, however, the questions raised here have found little place. Within commodity history, the identity and historical continuity of individual commodities are taken for granted. This chapter shows the identity of coffee to have been a complex historical construct, built around models of metropolis and province, connoisseur and plebeian, rich and poor, natural and artificial. In his classic study of sugar, *Sweetness and Power*, Sidney Mintz gave commerce and economics priority as the real motors of changes in consumption. Both of these genres treat knowledge-claims about food as illustrative, a resource rather than the subject of historical investigation. But those who wrote about coffee were not isolated authors, passively responding to the impact of a new social practice. They were actively involved in fostering new political and scholarly meanings and identities for coffee, as well as in advancing or opposing its use. Many were members of networks of sociability, learning, trade, travel, and correspondence, the same networks that during this very period were advancing Crown agendas for the development of global trade and colonialism. Different categories of learned experts—philologists, collectors, travelers, physicians, botanists, gardeners, even merchants—were aligning their expertise with the Crown's need to relate to its subjects in new ways as consumption habits changed. Metropolitan scholarship and foreign policy came into alignment as scholarship became a resource for resolving problems of colonial government, international commerce, or foreign diplomacy. It was partly thanks to coffee that French scholars became implicated in political and commercial programs central to European global imperialism.

The new imperial France required new sorts of knowledge. Merchants could lay claim to an expertise that the Crown could not otherwise access, while traditional forms of metropolitan erudition might prove inadequate to grappling with problems such as conversing with Ottoman envoys, or preserving and propagating the coffee plant. New types of learned expert thus became useful to the Crown because they specialized in new forms of knowledge such as Orientalism, horticulture, or botany, or had new sorts of skills. The terrain of public alimentary expertise to which these scholars of coffee laid claim altered as coffee consumption spread throughout French society between 1670 and 1730. Coffee's history is thus not one of continuity, but one of transformation. Its translation from the Levant to the colonial world, marking a shift in global trade patterns, was also accompanied by epistemic shifts. Against world or global histories, with their emphasis on environmental transformation and the "big-picture narrative," against commodity histories that take the subject of circulation and exchange as a fixed datum, we need to understand past narratives that compose the good as an ontological unity in time and space as themselves historical products requiring analysis.[61]

The increasingly central place of coffee in everyday life was underlined when naval wars threatened trade routes; at such times, coffee became news. During the Seven Years' War, consumers like François-Marie Arouet de Voltaire anxiously awaited announcements of coffee cargoes captured from the enemy and auctioned in French ports by word of mouth or in the public papers. What makes coffee a commodity with distinctly modern hallmarks is the signal role it came to play in public life and a global financial market. When Jean de la Roque's father returned from his travels in the Levant with Denis de la Haye's father to drink coffee in Marseille in 1644, coffee was so rare that his supply and the associated equipment were housed in his cabinet of curiosities. Between 1670 and 1730 coffee was naturalized not only in the colonies, but also in the metropolis, where Parisian consumers came to regard it as both ubiquitous and indispensable. Public responses to shortages highlighted the ways in which habits of consumption were essentially forms of political action. As early as the 1690s an anonymous correspondent

61. Courtwright 2001, 2; Spary 2005.

of the newspaper *Mercure Galant* conferred on coffee a status akin to that of bread as a barometer of public feeling: "People are concerned with its availability & cost, & fear shortages of [coffee] as they do those of bread . . . news that it is rare & dear is upsetting news for the Public." If early modern rulers began by attempting to curb the consumption of exotica using sumptuary legislation, by the middle of the eighteenth century British and French governments were following behind the taste trend, shaping colonial policy to fit domestic demand. Rather than controlling consumption, ministers now only tried to stem the flow and ensure that the State, rather than rival nations, companies, or private individuals, would become the prime beneficiary of the growing habit for the exotic. As Raynal remarked in the closing years of the Old Regime, "The passion of Europeans for this foreign luxury has been so lively, that neither the heaviest taxes, nor the most severe prohibitions and penalties have been able to stop it. Having battled in vain against an inclination which chafed against hindrance, all governments have been forced to give way to the torrent." Contemporaries attached much significance to these overwhelming desires in the age of reason precisely because they seemed to be a social phenomenon which it was beyond the power of traditional forms of authority to control. Taste was neither static nor apolitical in the eighteenth century, but was rather a meter of profound concerns about the effects of changes in consumption upon society.[62]

As coffee became more widespread, it ceased to be an exclusive property, belonging to a narrow social elite. The social trajectory of coffee was this: it had begun as a curiosity, became a fashionable luxury, and ended as an everyday good. In the process, it also transformed the everyday. By the 1770s it had come to belong to the wider public domain of vegetable-sellers, inter alia. But by this point it was also no longer a unitary substance or good; in commercial and gustatory terms, it was stratified to accommodate multiple groups of users, each of which valued it in different ways, and that stratification was mirrored in the expanding classification of coffee and other commodities in dictionaries and encyclopedias. As the epistemological identity of "coffee" was reconfigured around the questions of authenticity raised by the introduction of colonial and naturalized coffee grades, so metropolitan consumers were likewise reclassified into connoisseurs and those who aped their habits but lacked the ability to discriminate between real and fake coffee. This identification of consumption and discrimination with personal authenticity might be, I suggested at the start, a microcosm of the fears, op-

62. Voltaire 1950, 352, 462, 548, 562; [Chanvalon] 1763, 17–18; [de la Roque] 1716, 307–11; anon. 1696; see also De Saint-Haippy 1784, 2–3; Buti 2001, 214.

portunities, and dilemmas that the rise of luxury created in French society. In this sense, coffee possesses a wider significance than just as a means for measuring how linguistic, horticultural, botanical, chemical, and gustatory knowledge shaped public and administrative relations with new foodstuffs. Rather, in the words of Natacha Coquery, the transformations of coffee and of knowledge about coffee reflect "the passage from a civilisation of rarity and a stationary economy to one of development and abundance."[63]

63. Mintz 1985, chap. 3, 2006, 4; Raynal 1774, 2:354; Coquery 2003, 190. The abandonment of sumptuary legislation after about 1720 was an effective admission by the Crown that government policy followed innovation rather than vice versa. See Roche 1983, 13; Galliani 1989, chap. 4; Schaeper 1983, 176–77; Olivier-Martin 1938, 165–67; Minard 1998, 338–40.

CHAPTER THREE

The Place of Coffee

Coffee, as a substance, emblematized the overwhelming power of the new in Parisian lives. Appeals to the pleasure, increased mental efficiency, and improved health engendered by that "dark & bitter drink" were all seemingly inadequate to explain the growing appeal of a beverage consumed by rich and poor alike.[1] Thanks to its conquest of French daily life within little more than a generation, coffee became a focus for worries about the encroachment of fashion upon traditional habits and morals. It figured in debates about social distinction and authenticity, where it stood for fears about the victory of luxury over necessity, but also—paradoxically—of poor over rich. Thus, it was central to a crucial transformation taking place during the eighteenth century, in which luxury consumption changed from being the primary means by which hegemonic social groups such as rulers and nobles manifested exclusive power, to a set of practices to which many might aspire.[2] As an exotic substance that proliferated throughout Old Regime society, coffee was a marker for the spread of global commerce and superfluous consumption. It highlighted and problematized contemporary social change and the increasingly troubled relations between old and new, indigenous and exotic. Other consumed substances raised similar concerns, as I will show in later chapters, but coffee played a leading role in the politics of consumption from the end of the reign of Louis XIV onward.

Famously, coffee also came to be particularly associated with the exercise of reason, especially in a new type of establishment that developed to house it and other exotic foodstuffs in the late seventeenth century: the coffeehouse or café. As a space of consumption, the French café served as a tem-

1. Savary Des Brûlons and Savary 1723–30, 1:515.
2. See Berg and Eger 2003b: 9; Smith 2002, esp. chap. 3; Albrecht 1988.

plate for similar establishments in other countries, just like the restaurant a century later; even the English abandoned their indigenous coffee-house for the café.[3] Though the café's origins are generally dated to the 1670s, the shops that served coffee to Parisians did not acquire the name "café" until some decades later. The history of the identification of the space with the beverage is the history of how the café came to be a center of *esprit*. I shall argue that the café's emergence depended on a specific conjuncture of guild relations and centralizing commercial policies in Louis XIV's France, then move on to consider the café as a center of learning. Along with the salon and the Masonic lodge, the coffee-house has become a familiar setting for accounts of the development of a public sphere in the eighteenth century, building upon the work of Jürgen Habermas.[4] Coffee-houses were a forum for the public presentation of knowledge and for displays of learned expertise. In Restoration England, they were spaces where natural philosophers could meet on equal terms with inventors and artisanal entrepreneurs.[5] By around 1700, they were the home of Augustan literature, as penned by the likes of Addison and Steele. Though the relative merits of Aristotelian, Cartesian, and Gassendist philosophy were debated in Parisian cafés, their principal role was as a center for the production of belles-lettres—novels, poetry, plays.[6] Philosophie and literature tended to hybridize in these sites, producing geometrical poetry and belletristic philosophy, reflecting the fact that in 1700 practitioners of the natural sciences, mathematicians, and poets shared the common title of *gens de lettres*.

French cafés prior to the Revolution had two especially salient characteristics: they were spaces of intellectual sociability, in which many types of persons laid claim to learned status, and spaces of innovation, associated both with projects for literary and philosophical reform and with new foods and beverages. Both positive and negative evaluations of their function emphasized these two characteristics in particular. The café was a site of conversation and knowledge production, and the display of learning there represented a new type of hegemony over knowledge, differing from that manifested in traditional institutions such as the Church or universities, though possessing ties to newer organizations such as the royal academies. In this sense, again like Masonic lodges and salons, cafés were sites at which

3. Spang 2000.

4. Habermas 1989; Calhoun 1992; LaVopa 1992; Mah 2000; Goodman 1992; Nathans 1990; Gordon et al. 1992; Broman 1998.

5. Johns 2006; Iliffe 1995, esp. 310–18; Stewart 1999, 1992; Ellis 2004a, 157–64.

6. Ellis 2004a, chap. 12; Cowan 2005, 229–46; Klein 1997.

the possible forms that Enlightenment might take, and the best way of displaying an enlightened condition, were being established.

In the realm of learning, cafés were sites of innovation in that they were associated with the wholesale rejection of erudition, in favor of a worldly, playful, secular knowledge. Both in the food and drink that it offered and in the literature that it generated, the café depended upon a culture of *esprit*—to be understood as wit, mind, and spirit. I shall argue that the characteristic form of café knowledge was satire; the inversions and subversions inherent in this genre formed the principal weapon of the men (and women) of letters who frequented the café, and it was with this instrument that they set about dismantling and rebuilding certain features of Old Regime society. Like the English coffee-houses, cafés were a leveling ground, where literary debate operated according to rules that superseded the social relations prescribed by rank and birth. Such rules were being worked out in the café after 1700, not without violence. Cafés were sites at which the public status of letters and science, the relationship between fame and insignificance, politeness and impoliteness, learning and ignorance, was constructed. They provide a window upon the technologies by which epistemological authority was asserted, defended, and maintained in the early eighteenth century, and I shall consider both those who became famous through such activities—philosophes like Voltaire and Diderot, who have played a key role in canonical histories of the Enlightenment—and some relatively little-known participants in the world of letters and learning, including café proprietors themselves. So, following Darnton and others, my analysis extends beyond the bounds of the small population of authors allocated roles in "the Enlightenment" by an older history of ideas, to embrace a broader range of claimants to epistemological authority in the early decades of the eighteenth century.[7] But the café's grasp on learned egalitarianism was always, I shall suggest, a shaky one.

COFFEE INCORPORATED

The history of the coffee-house in the age of Enlightenment has been told in two broadly distinct ways. On the one hand, there are studies that amass literary anecdotes about coffee drinking and cafés, and meticulously trace the locations of historic coffee-houses on the streets of European cities. More recently, this approach has given way to accounts that present the coffee-

7. See especially Gay 1966–69; Darnton 1982; Chartier 1987a; Goodman 1994.

house as an important site for sociability, intellectual exchange, and political activity—in short, as a major locus for the emerging public sphere proposed by Habermas. The coffee-houses of Restoration and Georgian London are known as places where news was broadcast by word of mouth or print, as social circles facilitating the practice of natural philosophy and as the scene of open political disagreement and discussion. The Parisian coffee-house was not identical to its London counterparts, but was considerably more literary in orientation, and at its origins indebted to the Orientalist fashion of the 1670s and 1680s.[8]

The French coffee market originated, as I showed in chapter 2, in Colbert's programs for legislative reform at home and abroad. Holding three ministerial posts, *contrôleur général*, *secrétaire d'Etat à la Marine*, and *surintendant des bâtiments du Roi*, Colbert was in charge of both domestic finance and foreign trade. In both cases, the Crown's trade policies were implemented through a system of privileges. These took the form of contracts leasing a monopoly over some particular aspect of trade to a private individual or company. Within France, many such privileges were held by companies of merchants, who thereby acquired not only trading rights, but also a shared legal and social identity as guilds. Individual guilds were often linked by dynastic ties and common commercial interests. The guild system, which dated back to the Middle Ages, would form one of the main domestic targets of Colbert's reforms, but remained highly localized and urban. In March 1673 a royal edict drawn up by Colbert commanded all Parisian merchants practicing trades that had no guild status to form a guild or *communauté* and propose regulations for their trade. As in his foreign policy, the privilege over certain trading domains and commodities was conferred upon certain merchant consortia chosen from among the contenders. These consortia were then given a legal identity and specified commercial and social rights by royal letters patent.[9]

Colbert's well-known reforms had a dual purpose: protecting domestic merchants and manufacturers from foreign competition, and raising much-needed funds for the royal exchequer. Louis XIV's *contrôleurs généraux*, be-

8. For France, see Fosca 1934; Moura and Louvet 1929; Leclant 1951; Franklin 1887–1902, vol. 13, chaps. 1–4; Funck-Brentano 1905. For Britain, see Pincus 1995; also Cowan 2005; Ellis 2004a; Ball 1991; Albrecht 1988.

9. Olivier-Martin 1938; Coornaert 1968; Sewell 1980, chap. 1; Minard 2004; Sargentson 1996, esp. chap. 1; Crowston 2001. On corporate legal identity in the Old Regime, see Durand 1971, bk. 1, pt. 1, chap. 1; Bien 1987; Crowston 2001, chap. 5; Bossenga 1988. On commerce, see Schaeper 1983; Rothkrug 1965, pt. 2, chap. 7.

ginning with Colbert, repeatedly exploited the guild system to finance the king's military enterprises against his European enemies. Constituting new monopoly guilds was an efficacious method, since consortia of merchants were eager to pay for exclusive rights to trade in some good or service. One group of Parisian merchants offered 27,000 livres for a monopoly over the preparation and sale of a variety of hot and cold beverages, ices, and preserved fruits and nuts. By letters patent of January 25, 1676, this group was erected into the guild of Paris master limonadiers and brandy merchants. After a few months of intense conflict with the older guild of brandy distillers and vendors, founded in the 1630s, the limonadiers were legally united with their erstwhile rivals. On May 15, 1676, the guild of "Master Distillers of brandy, & of all other waters, & Merchants of brandy, & of all kinds of liqueurs" was created. Colbert involved himself personally in the matter, writing a report on the union that would fix the guild's structure for the century of its existence. The limonadiers' guild was thus one of the newest corporations, and its emergence attests to the rising public consumption of exotic luxury goods in Paris.[10]

Colbert's sometime steward, Audiger, numbered among the first masters of the limonadiers' guild. Exceptionally, some details of his life survive, thanks to an autobiographical account he inserted in his widely read *La Maison réglée* (The Orderly Household, 1692), a book on household management. After an apprenticeship in France, Audiger had traveled with various employers in Spain, Holland, and Germany before reaching Rome, where he acquired a special expertise in the manufacture of fashionable liqueurs, preserves, and confections, including:

> all sorts of waters, from both flowers and fruit, with or without ice, sherbets, creams, orgeat, water of pistachios, pine-nuts, coriander, aniseed, fennel and all other kinds of seeds. . . . I also learnt how to distil all manner of flowers, fruits, seeds and other things to be distilled hot or cold, and how to prepare chocolate, tea and coffee, something that few people in France know as yet.[11]

10. Delamare 1722–38, 3:434, 797–800. See also Franklin 1877–1902, vol. 13, chap. 7; Olivier-Martin 1938, 188–201; Guery 1989; Pluchon 1991, 83–88. The limonadiers' guild was a second-ranking communauté rather than a corps (Crowston 2001, 187–96; Bourgeon 1985, 250; Clacquesin 1900; Scagliola 1943).

11. [Audiger?] 1692, bk. 4, "Traité ou la véritable manière de faire toutes sortes d'eaux." Extensive searching in the archives has thus far failed to identify this individual or confirm the attribution of authorship in Barbier 1875, 6:18. The timing of publication may be explained by the suppression of the limonadiers' guild in 1692 (see below, this chapter.)

Returning to Paris in January 1660, Audiger presented the king and a privileged few courtiers with forced peas and roses, in other words with a curious gift, whose rarity we nowadays fail to appreciate, but at the presentation of which "all exclaimed as one that nothing could be finer or more novel, and that the like had never been seen in that season in France." Rather than a monetary reward for his horticultural showmanship, Audiger requested "the privilege and permission to make and have made, sell and retail all kinds of liqueurs in the Italian fashion, both at court and in His Majesty's train and in any other town of the realm," with a ban on all rival commerce in this field. Some months of assiduous cultivation of his court contacts followed, but Audiger failed to get the letters of privilege through the final hurdle of legality—a seal imposed by the Royal Chancelier. Returning to domestic service, he entered the comtesse de Soissons's household as a liqueur-maker, and in ensuing years perambulated through various great houses, working as officier d'office or steward for the président de Maisons, for Colbert himself, and for the future duc de Beauvilliers. Finally, "I set up a limonadier's shop for myself in Palais-Royal square, where for twelve years I supplied the king's household, as well as all the great lords who demanded them, with all kinds of liqueurs."[12]

Audiger continued to work both in his own business and as an outside caterer, supplying his preserves and liqueurs for court banquets to order. Meanwhile he continued to solicit an exclusive privilege to sell liqueurs, hot and cold, and preserves, especially after the foundation of the limonadiers' guild in 1676, using his personal familiarity with Colbert to protest against guild usurpation of the rights he had sought some years earlier. The only outcome, however, was that Audiger himself was accorded—apparently for free—a mastership in the new guild. Writing in 1692, he was still bitter about the way the *communauté* had been set up: instead of a select band of 100 masters chosen for their wealth and respectability, there were 400 who were demeaning themselves by making and selling high-quality liqueurs cheek by jowl with ordinary brandy, masters who could barely raise 10,000–12,000 livres for the royal coffers and were perennially harassed by the *lieutenant de police*, Gabriel-Nicolas de La Reynie. Rather than becom-

12. Audiger's employment by Olympe Mancini, comtesse de Soissons, shows him to have been part of a particular patronage network. Mancini's uncle, the cardinal de Mazarin, had brought Audiger's teacher More from Rome to Paris with him. The comte de Soissons was among those to whom Audiger had presented his peas and flowers in January 1660. René de Longueil, président de Maisons, was one of the first hosts in France to serve coffee. Paul de Beauvilliers, duc de Saint-Aignan, was related to Colbert by marriage, later becoming the Dauphin's tutor. See [Audiger?] 1692, 531–36; Turner 2004, 35.

ing the sole proprietor of a secret for extracting large sums of money from French courtly consumers, Audiger had found himself rubbing shoulders with several hundred distillers and liqueur-makers in a novice guild with (as we will see) a slightly dubious reputation.[13]

Audiger's move from high-ranking servant in noble households to autonomous businessman on the streets of Paris has a significance beyond guild conflicts or commercial policies. From serving a single patron, Audiger was now supplying a range of goods to a paying public. Shopkeeping was, in both social and economic terms, a very different matter from private employment. The new limonadiers' guild was a large group of producers, who mostly lacked the court contacts that Audiger possessed. The fashionable confections and beverages they sold—which Audiger had sought to present as highly skilled products, elite curiosities suited to courtly connoisseurs, could now reach a wider public: access to them was secured by wealth rather than birth or status. At the same time, they ceased to be goods that were unique to a single household, becoming comestibles that were manufactured again and again to similar standards. This was the first step in a transformation of luxury goods that numerous historians have identified during the eighteenth century. In "traditional" models of luxury, the possession of luxury goods was restricted to the highest levels of society, rulers, princes, high nobles, and clergy, who used them as ways of displaying social status. In "modern" forms of luxury, such goods are accessible to many or all levels of society, so that their possession more explicitly defines economic rather than social difference. Luxuries of this sort generated an extensive debate linking consumption to morality, commerce, manufacture, the condition of the nation, and the nature of government.[14]

In effect, Colbert's guild policy, though disadvantageous to his erstwhile servant, materially aided the spread of luxury consumption to a broader section of the French public. While such goods as liqueurs and sherbets were not populuxe or semiluxury goods in the usual sense of the term, which designates products made in emulation of luxury goods using cheaper materials, nonetheless foods and beverages had a low price by comparison with garments, jewelry, or furniture.[15] Audiger's history is thus representative of wider transformations in the consumption and meaning of luxuries and

13. [Audiger?] 1692, 532–37.

14. Berg and Eger 2003b: 9. Smith 2002, chap. 3, differentiates between gentility and luxury. However, Berg and Eger's model of a shift from social distinction to economic distinction better characterises the French situation. On cuisine as social distinction, see Goody 1982, chap. 4; Bourdieu 1994.

15. See Fairchilds 1992; Spang and Jones 1999; Coquery 2003, 191n.

the social relations that formed around them. It also marks a new attitude to the commodification of skills. As a servant, a unique value was placed on Audiger as a person, including character attributes such as loyalty, industriousness, and economy. Here he received a salary reflecting his overall status and importance within the household. By contrast, in his shop, his skill was commodified in a different way: each of the goods he prepared had a specific individual value. In commercial exchanges, value was transposed from personal conduct onto a succession of physical objects that were the material, visible, and sensory evidence of the producer's skill. Inventiveness now became a tool of commerce.

During the 1650s and 1660s, fashionable cuisine had expanded particularly rapidly in culinary domains reliant on exotic comestibles, especially sugar. Combining this colonial good with spirit of wine and aromatics, such as vanilla, cacao, coffee, almonds, and extracts of fruits, spices, and herbs, cooks experimented, invented, and diversified, producing a range of beverages and sweet foods that appealed to a polite clientele for their decorative appearance as much as for their artful flavor combinations.[16] In 1705 the police commissioner Nicolas Delamare included all exotic comestibles in a single category. Eastern foods and drinks like sherbet and coffee were grouped with the "hot liqueurs"—primarily liqueurs, tea, and chocolate, consumed "since the establishment of our colonies in the Indies." The new limonadiers' guild found its market niche in precisely this domain: its members specialized in producing exotic alimentary novelties using specialized preparation methods. According to the 1676 statutes, the guild had the exclusive privilege to "compose & sell all lemonades with amber, perfumes & other iced waters, & ices of fruit & flowers, even waters of aniseed & cinnamon, & frangipani, bitter lemon, sherbet & coffee in the form of beans, powder, & drink." Limonadiers might also sell cherries, raspberries, and other fruits preserved in brandy, nuts and dragees, liqueur wines, and liqueurs.[17] Together with the grocers and the pastrycooks, the limonadiers thus exemplified the globalization of Parisian consumption. This shared specialization in exotic foods, however, caused conflict, especially between

16. Smith 2002, 97–102. The use of sugar increased, while that of spices declined; see Flandrin 1996b, esp. 667–74; Huetz de Lemps 1996; Mintz 1985, chap. 3; Pluchon 1991, 463–65.

17. Delamare 1722–38, 3:797: "Titre 47," chap. 2. The statutes of the guild are reproduced in Lespinasse 1886, 602–5. Legrand d'Aussy 1783, 3:90–91, claimed that the first Parisian lemonade vendors appeared in around 1630. "Sherbet" originally denoted a highly perfumed mixture of spices and fruit juices from the Levant. By the eighteenth century, it referred to the syrups used to make ice cream, or sorbets in modern parlance. See Calaresu in press; anon. 1798, pt. 1, 70.

limonadiers and grocers. Only minor differences distinguished the rights of each corporation to use, sell, and supply particular goods, and debates and lawsuits would continue on into the eighteenth century.[18]

Among the goods legally allocated to the limonadiers, coffee appears to have played a secondary role in the early years. It was merely one among many fancy and exotic drinks served by limonadiers in their shops. Banned from infringing the wine merchants' privileges, the limonadiers sold only a few imported and fortified wines, specializing instead in flavored beverages, spirituous and nonspirituous. In the list of commodities identified in the limonadiers' privilege by their letters patent, coffee figured after liqueur wines, liqueurs, lemonades, ices, and sherbet. The café in France thus began life as an establishment for the sale of liqueurs to seated customers. Not until the 1690s did coffee come to be viewed as the limonadiers' premier commodity, just as their establishments were coming to be generally known by the name of cafés, as in Jean-Baptiste Rousseau's play *Le Caffé* of 1694.[19]

Older guilds such as the pastrycooks and grocers competed with the neophyte limonadiers for their commercial privileges. In Legrand d'Aussy's words, "Few Corporations have suffered as many changes as this one."[20] During the 1680s, the combined guild of apothecaries and grocers obtained rulings from the Paris *parlement* supporting their claims to certain privileges that had been attributed to the limonadiers in their letters patent. This forced the closure of some limonadier businesses: for example, in June 1686 the right of the grocers to sell coffee was defended by the *parlement*, though this was overturned by the Crown's Conseil d'État in 1689 after many solicitations by the limonadiers.[21] All these machinations help us to chart the uptake of exotic foods in the metropolis. A decade after the foundation of the limonadiers' guild, coffee, tea, chocolate, and sherbet (usually ignored in histories of stimulants) had become sufficiently profitable commodities to attract the attention of members of rival guilds.

After 1690, the Crown set out to milk the assets of the Parisian corporations of arts and trades, a policy that would result in the ossification of the guild system over the long term, while in the short term creating havoc

18. E.g., Delamare 1722–38, 3:826–27; Bibliothèque Interuniversitaire de Pharmacie, registre 32, pièce 41.

19. Rousseau 1694. The name "café" does not figure in the early legislation reproduced in Lespinasse 1886, Titre XIX, and the entry "Café" in Académie Françoise 1694, 3:146–47, did not denote a place. See also Ellis 2004a, 81.

20. Legrand d'Aussy 1783, 3:91. Details from Delamare 1722–38 and Lespinasse 1886.

21. Delamare 1722–38, 3:805, *Arrêt de Parlement* (June 21, 1686); *Arrêt du Conseil d'Etat* (December 13, 1689).

within the limonadiers' guild. In March 1691 a royal edict depicted a guild system in disarray, poorly policed and malfunctioning owing to exclusivity, high entry costs, and interguild conflicts. No secret was made of the fact that one reason for reforming the guilds was to raise money for the Crown, "so that we may draw some aid in the present need, both from the product of these duties, and from the cost of the charges of masters and guards of the corps of merchants and *jurés* [officials] of the communities of arts and trades, in order to sustain military expenditure." During the next decade, the Crown proceeded to establish new privileges, mostly inspection rights, over many guilds, which were usually then allowed to buy back the rights, often by raising a huge loan from financiers. In 1692, for example, the Crown created fifty offices of "Assayers & Controllers of Brandy & Spirit-of-Wine." That same year, a different strategy for profiting from the new commodities was trialed when coffee, tea, sherbet, chocolate, and vanilla were added to a small group of substances, including salt and tobacco, already being exploited for profit by a group of financiers known as the Farmers General. François Damanne, a *bourgeois* of Paris, bought the monopoly rights over the new comestibles in January, but proved unable to meet the high charges demanded by the Crown from a Farmer General. The commercial monopoly was restored to the limonadiers in March 1693.[22]

In 1703 a financier, Jean Lescuyer, proposed that to replace the entire guild with individual privileges, allowing the purchaser to practice the trade of merchant limonadier in the capital, would raise more money for the Crown than the invention of inspectorates. In December 1704, based on this proposal, the Crown suppressed the distillers' guild and advertised 150 such privileges for sale to "persons experienced in this profession." Seven months later, the former limonadiers offered to buy all the new posts for the princely sum of 200,000 livres, to be raised as a loan. This request was initially granted, in return for an exclusive privilege "of selling all liqueurs composed of brandy, & of spirit of wine, French and foreign, & fruits preserved in brandy: as also to be the only ones to sell roasted coffee in powdered form & as a drink, to make & sell chocolate in tablets and rolls, & to sell brandy to drink in their shops." Immediately, the grocers appealed for the same rights *and* the right to inspect the distillers' shops. A royal dec-

22. Lespinasse 1886, 125, 315–16, 368, 693–94; Crowston 2001, 177–80; Delamare 1722–38, 2:684–87; 3:575–79, 627, 805–7; *ACE* [1692]. Such practices were abandoned after 1750 (Riley 1986, chap. 6; Root 1994, 121–27). On Damanne, see *Memoire* [1692?]; Archives Nationales, Paris, V[7] 167, dossier 4. I suspect that the timing of Audiger's publication was related to the Damanne episode.

laration of September 1706 did allow them and the vinegar-makers to sell *eaux-de-vie* and liqueurs, but not to offer them to seated customers. The formal distinction of the limonadier's shop from other establishments was gradually being established through these negotiations: like the *traiteurs* and wine merchants, limonadiers were specialists in serving drinks and food to be eaten on the premises. This did not preclude the sale of comestibles for home use, but it did lay particular emphasis on the limonadier's shop as a space for public consumption, and above all the consumption of luxury exotic foods and beverages.[23]

The limonadiers responded to the 1706 declaration by refusing to repay the enormous debt they had contracted to repurchase their own guild privileges in 1705, on the grounds that competition from the grocers and vinegar-makers was damaging their trade. The Crown promptly dissolved the guild once more and returned to Lescuyer's plan, this time establishing 500 privileges rather than 150. By 1713, however, it was clear that the plan was a failure. Only 138 posts had actually sold: 72 to masters from the old limonadiers' guild, 21 to grocers and vinegar-makers, and 45 to "individuals with no title," in other words no guild affiliation. The total income for the treasury was a little over half what the limonadiers had offered. The Crown cut its losses, bought back the new posts, and revived the old limonadiers' guild under financial terms favorable to the erstwhile masters, including the abolition of debts incurred prior to the suppression in 1706. The unusually high level of financial experimentation on this guild by comparison with others in the city suggests that the Crown, too, was testing the limits of profitability of the new trade.[24]

CABARET, COFFEE-HOUSE, CAFÉ?

The café was not the only public space for commercial consumption. It stands out from other contemporary eating places like the cabaret, tavern, or inn in three ways: the centrality of exotic luxury ingredients to its wares, its respectability among members of a polite urban elite, and the inclusion of learning among the entertainments it offered. The prominence of coffee among the privileged wares of the limonadiers was not only a response to changing customer tastes and the spread of the coffee habit. It also reflected a reformulation of the café's social role. Writing a century after the appear-

23. Delamare 1722–38, 3:821–23; Bibliothèque Interuniversitaire de Pharmacie, registre 32, pièces 46, 50.

24. Lespinasse 1886, 609–12; Doyle 1996, chap. 2.

ance of the first Parisian coffee-house, the pharmacist Jacques-François Demachy located the café's early success in its promise to provide novelty, exoticism, and temperance. He contrasted the orderly behavior of the literate elite who frequented the café with the debauched conduct common in taverns and cabarets. The mythology of the café's origins had come to rest upon a clearcut separation between taverns or cabarets, where wine and beer were drunk, and cafés, where coffee was drunk. In his study of drinking in Paris, Brennan warns against a literal reading of the censorious accounts of taverns penned by middling authors in the eighteenth century, and points out that contemporary portrayals of wine shops as sites of drunkenness and disorder are not borne out by surviving legal documents; the fear of inebriation, social unrest, and criminality that dogged the cabaret throughout the century were, he suggests, part of the process by which a polite elite distinguished itself from the unruly *peuple*.[25] The early history of the café confirms this role. Complaints against the cafés lodged with the police in the 1670s and 1680s undermine the general view in the secondary literature of cafés as sites of respectability and literary *politesse*.

> For some time now, many of them have been causing disorder. This was so substantial and so widespread that public tranquility & safety would certainly have been troubled, if [the matter] was not promptly resolved. The need to put an end to such disorder is ever more pressing because those who exercise this Profession, whose number has greatly increased since the year 1677, have converted their shops & houses into new cabarets of liqueurs, which stay open all night long throughout the city's quartiers & fauxbourgs, [and] these shops & houses now serve as the meeting places & dens of burglars, pickpockets & other unruly ruffians.[26]

The incorporated limonadiers of Paris responded to the threat to their livelihood implied by the curtailment of their opening hours with a xenophobic attack on the café's Orientalist origins. They threw the blame for the unrest afflicting cafés on "numerous foreigners, calling themselves Armenians, who had meddled in the trade & encroached upon the functions of the Community of the said Masters & Merchants of Liqueurs & Limonadiers of this City." The original appeal of Parisian coffee shops had stemmed from the

25. Demachy 1775, 108; Brennan 1988, introduction and chap. 1; Stallybrass and White 1986, 96–97.

26. Delamare 1722–38, 3:810, from a 1685 report by Paris's *lieutenant de police* de la Reynie; see also Leclant 1951, 8–9.

ability of such places to evoke the Orient. Proprietors played on the Eastern origins of coffee and sherbet to market their goods. By the end of the seventeenth century, Orientalism in the café was under attack. The letters patent of the limonadiers' corporation contained a clause to the effect that members must be French subjects.[27] Moves of this sort, accompanying the reform of the guilds in the last quarter of the seventeenth century, put foreign merchants under increasing pressure. Parisian limonadiers capitalized on their privilege by presenting themselves as authentically *French* vendors, distinct from the disruptive foreigners, and this self-presentation entailed the transformation of their shops from exotic venues of questionable morality into sites where the local virtues of politeness and *honnêteté* were on display.[28]

By 1700 the *honnête* ambitions of Paris's café proprietors were beginning to attract comment, at least of a satirical sort. The *Porte-feuille galant* (Gallant Portfolio), published that year, recorded: "Cafés are places frequented by *honnêtes gens* of both sexes. One sees all types of characters there: gallants, flirts, polite abbés, others who are not, fighters, newsmongers, officers, provincials, foreigners, litigants, drinkers and professional gamblers, parasites, adventurers, knights of industry, young people of fortune, old women in love, Gascons and braggarts, half-wits and authors, and many other people." This motley clientele, claimed the anonymous author, attended cafés on the pretext of drinking coffee, while in reality indulging to excess in spirits and other pleasures.[29] The author of *Diogène à Paris* (Diogenes in Paris, 1707) suggested on the contrary that the café was responsible for civilizing everyone:

> I think I can affirm that the glow of gentleness and urbanity on most faces is due to the establishment of Cafés in such large numbers in Paris. Before their establishment, everyone, or almost everyone, went to the cabaret. . . . Since the establishment of the cafés, everyone meets there, . . . Everyone is become more *honnête*, more civil in appearance.[30]

By 1723 Savary des Bruslons was able to present the café as an unproblematically *honnête* space: "The Cafés of Paris are, for the most part, magnificently outfitted haunts, with marble tables, mirrors, & crystal chandeliers, where

27. Delamare 1722–38, 3:810, sentence de police of March 12, 1695; Lespinasse 1886, 367. According to Fosca 1934, 15, the limonadiers of the Foire Saint-Germain employed waiters dressed as Armenians.

28. On *honnêteté* and *politesse*, see Pekacz 1999, 13–142; Bury 1996; France 1992a; Chartier 1987b; Muchembled 1998, 200–206; Revel 1989.

29. Quoted in Fosca 1934, 14–15.

30. Quoted in Thelamon 1992, 9.

many *honnêtes gens* of the City meet as much to enjoy conversation & to learn the news, as to drink that drink."[31] And by 1738, the abbé Antoine-François Prévost d'Exiles, writing in his newspaper *Le Pour et Contre*, could insist of the cafés that "any public assembly where the proprieties are observed, is a useful School."[32] Over thirty years, then, the café changed from being a den of drunkenness frequented by a motley array of shady clients, into an establishment that fits the image of the café celebrated by its historians. Unlike cabarets and taverns, it had been successfully reformed into a seat of luxury, politeness, and order in the first decades of the eighteenth century.

The enthronement of coffee as the principal consumer good of the limonadiers' establishments contributed to this signal transformation. While both coffee and wine shared the power to stimulate creativity, coffee was also credited with counteracting the drunkenness produced by wine. As one Regency poet, Louis Fuzelier, put it: "you capture from the God of the vine, / The drinker awakened by your charms, / And bring him back to Reason."[33] The particular association of the limonadiers' establishments with coffee drinking underlined the separation between the old tavern and the new café and signified the rise of a new public space housing new standards of politeness and temperance. This role for the café is borne out by archival sources. An account book kept during the 1770s by Beaujon, proprietor of the Café Suédois, shows that although some customers ordered coffee alone, most ordered spirits—brandy, liqueurs (rose, orange, walnut, gin, oil of Venus, and others), apricots in brandy, punch, lemonade, fortified wine, even beer—with coffee on the side. Coffee, an acknowledged antidote for drunkenness, was consumed in tandem with liqueurs, and for the specific purpose of countering inebriation.[34] It had become an integral part of a bodily technology of polite consumption that served to restore good order to the mind and conduct of the polite consumer. This gives coffee a unique place in the history of mind-altering substances. It was not taken to get high, but to stay low: it was a defining drug of Enlightenment.[35] The spirituous liqueurs also consumed in cafés would have a far more troubled history, as we will see in chapter 4.

One café proprietor in particular, Francesco Procopio dei Coltelli, known as François Procope Couteaux, helped to make the new-style café fashion-

31. "Caffé," Savary Des Brûlons and Savary 1723–30, 1:516–17. See also Liger 1715, 356.

32. *Le Pour et Contre* 14 (1738): 319.

33. Quoted in [de la Roque] 1716, 337–39; see also Vigarello 1999, 127–30.

34. Archives de Paris, D^5B^6 1635: account book of Beaujon, cafétier-limonadier, 1774. For presentations of coffee as an antidote to wine, see Audiger 1995, 565; anon. 1696, 36–37; M[ailly] 1702: "Onzieme Entretien"; anon. 1798, 107; Franklin 1887–1902, 13:62, 93.

35. Courtwright 2001, 106.

able. Procope had originally been an apprentice of Pascal, the Armenian who had founded the first Parisian café. Early on, he was an ambulant street vendor at the Saint Germain fair, one of many hundreds of peddlers and street sellers who played an important role in the city's commerce.[36] Soon after the formation of the limonadiers' guild, in 1676, Procope established a limonadier's shop in a former public baths and brothel that had belonged to his grandfather. In a legal document of the following year, he titled himself a "distiller," indicating that he had become one of the original 250 masters. As a commercial undertaking, the Café Procope, which quickly became the most celebrated of all Parisian cafés, is revelatory of the transformation that was taking place. Procope catered not to the taste for Orientalism but rather to the social aspirations of polite city-dwellers. He decked his café out with luxury goods: varnished or gilded mirrors, tapestries, marble-topped tables, chandeliers, silver cutlery and porcelain or silver cups, pots, and cutlery, marble floors, and painted ceilings. Such items drew upon contemporary Italianate styles of interior decoration that became the hallmark of the Parisian café. Similar features are still recognizable in cafés worldwide, if the coffee is now likely to be espresso and the "marble" plastic. Evidence from business inventories suggests that such luxurious outfittings characterized even the city's humbler cafés. Like the drinks served, such luxury accessories had formerly been imported from the East, but were increasingly being manufactured at home. Colbert's sponsorship of the national manufactories had enabled French artisans to produce tapestries, mirror glass, coffee, and ultimately porcelain, too. In all senses—the material, the legislative, the gustatory, and, as we shall see, the social—cafés were very innovative spaces circa 1700.[37]

THE PRODUCTION OF MIND

Throughout the seventeenth century, drinking societies frequented by men of letters and their wealthy patrons had foregathered at taverns, creating

36. Moura and Louvet 1929, 22, 40–41; "Couteaux," Jal 1872, 445–48; Fontaine 2003. On the "draws" of such establishments, cf. Isherwood 1986, chap. 6.

37. Moura and Louvet 1929, 41n, 48, 49n; Legrand d'Aussy 1783, 3:111–12; Brennan 1988, 128–32. On luxury household goods, see Schaeper 1983, chap. 6; Pardailhé-Galabrun 1988; Roche 2000; Scott 1995; Scoville 1950, esp. 113–14; Pris 1977, esp. 16–17; Cole 1964, 2:286–320. Such items remained standard café outfittings throughout the eighteenth century; see, e.g., Archives Nationales, Paris: Minutier Central, Étude XC/369: July 30, 1751; Étude LXV/381: November 18, 1773; Ellis 2004a, 203–4. A similar argument is made for the "domestication" of tea by Smith 2002, 75–76.

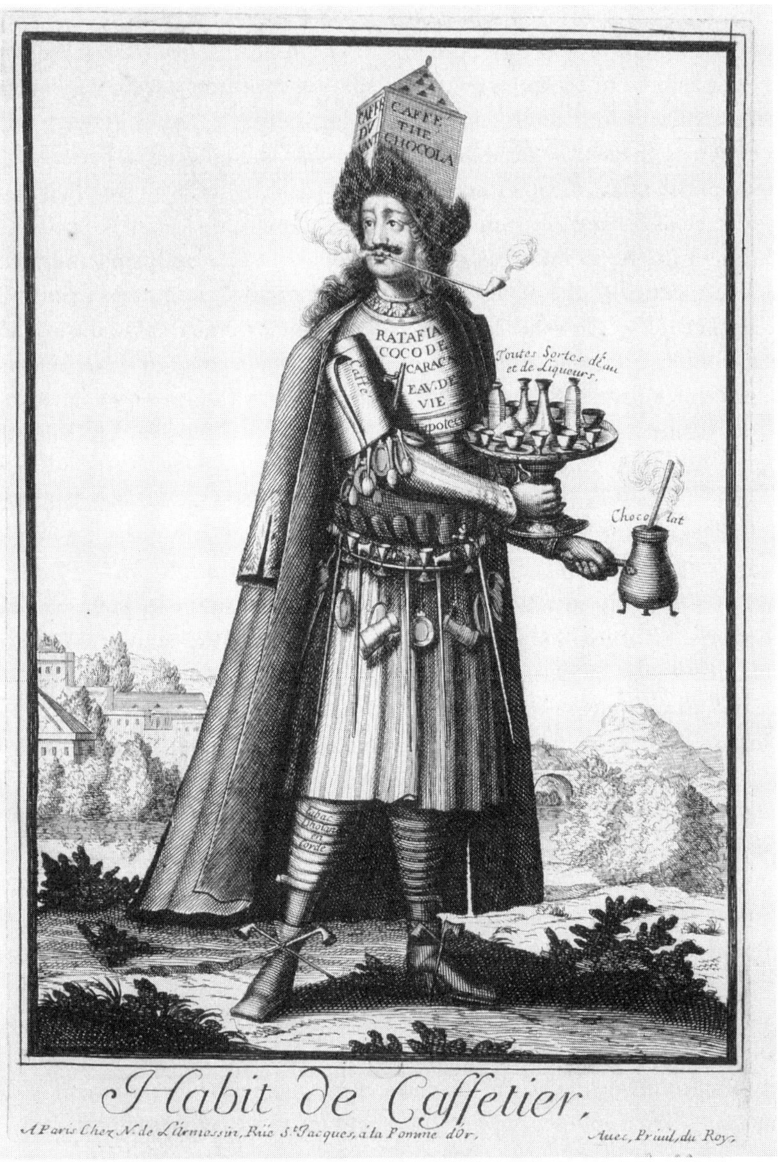

Figure 3.1. "Habit de Caffetier," from a collection of Larmessin engravings featuring grotesque costumes (Paris, 1695). Showing an ambulant street vendor of coffee whose attire is made up of the tools of his trade. Note the tray he carries labeled "All Sorts of *Eaux* and Liqueurs." Copperplate engraving after an original by Nicolas de L'Armessin or Larmessin. Bibliothèque Nationale de France, Z Le Senne-543.

a prolific genre of Bacchic literature and poetry. This long-lived tradition of drinking and writing would continue on through the vicissitudes of the Revolution and into the Napoleonic years. As cafés absorbed those who were or aspired to be *honnête*, they also took over from taverns as favored meeting places for literary and philosophical circles. The shift from wine to coffee as the source of literary creativity is exemplified in poems written in praise of the drink by authors like Louis Fuzelier, who supplied plays and librettos for the Parisian stage, or abbé Guillaume Massieu, one of the editors of the Académie Françoise's dictionary, who read his poem on coffee at a meeting of the newly founded Académie Royale des Inscriptions et Belles-Lettres in 1718.[38] As a place of sociability, literary cafés allowed the terms of worldly support for men of letters to be negotiated. Like Masonic lodges, cafés permitted talented individuals from the lower social levels, predominantly men, to encounter favorably disposed male patrons from the social élite, including financiers like the tax farmer Alexandre-Jean-Joseph Le Riche de La Pouplinière. There was a constant circulation of dependents, termed "parasites," between the lavish dinners on offer at the houses of patrons or "amphitryons," in Molière's term, and the cafés.[39]

Cafés formed one node of the social networks within which philosophes whose names are still familiar to us today as part of the canonical Enlightenment moved. As Darnton, Roche, Chartier, and others have suggested, the philosophes must be understood in the first instance as authors.[40] The role played by Parisian literary cafés as sites where crucial criteria of authorship and productivity were being worked out has received only superficial historical attention, despite growing interest in the English coffee-house as a center of activity in the letters and sciences. Yet the list of café habitués compiled by Fosca, though undoubtedly representing only a tiny fraction of the cafés' actual clientele, offers a respectable cross-section of the city's scholarly population. The Café Laurent, founded in 1690 by François Laurent, was a prominent meeting place for lovers of belles-lettres, philosophes, musicians, painters, and poets. It was frequented by Bernard le Bovier de Fontenelle, the perpetual secretary of the Académie Royale des Sciences; Antoine Houdard de la Motte, of whom more anon; abbé Pierre-Joseph Alary, the son of a rich apothecary and founder of the politically powerful Club de

38. [De la Roque] 1716, 337–39; Massieu 1740; anon. 1798; see also Franklin 1887–1902, 13:75–76, 83–92. On Bacchic literary culture, see Aguilà Sorana 1997; Level 1988.

39. On enlightened sociability, see Jacob 1991; Lilti 2005a, 102–6; on amphitryons and parasites, see Stewart 1985.

40. Darnton 1982; Roche 1988; Jacob 1991; Goodman 1994; Goldgar 1995; Chartier 1997; Broman 1998, 127; Cowans 1999; Brockliss 2002.

l'Entresol; Nicolas Boindin, a prosecutor to the *trésoriers de France*, who collected income from royal estates; Jean-Baptiste Rousseau, a poet; Louis Racine, Jansenist son of the famous playwright; Joseph Saurin and Jean-Elie Lériget de La Faye, two geometers who were both members of the Académie Royale des Sciences; and numerous other poets and playwrights.[41] This celebrity clientele deserted the Café Laurent in around 1714 for the Café du Parnasse, alias the Café Gradot, run by Poincelet, and for Procope's café near the Comédie Françoise. During the 1720s and 1730s, a new generation of learned café habitués began to appear, with the likes of François-Marie Arouet de Voltaire, Pierre-Louis Maupertuis, Jean-François Melon, and Charles Pinot Duclos mingling with survivors from the previous generation, like La Motte and Saurin. By the 1750s, many of Paris's most celebrated littérateurs, philosophes, and academicians were or had been regular clients of cafés, and so too were a throng of obscure authors who, as Darnton points out, have been omitted from most histories of the Enlightenment.[42]

During the early years of the century, the corporeal effects ascribed to coffee contributed substantially to the café's perceived function as a space of literary production and sociability. In his *Entretiens sur les Cafés* of 1702, Louis, chevalier de Mailly, a Paris nouvelliste or newsmonger, recorded a series of possibly authentic café conversations between pseudonymous speakers, ranging over foreign, legal, and private affairs, philosophy, moral character, gallant tales, and history. The café, in Mailly's formulation, was a space for dramatizing and resolving disagreements over knowledge. It was also a space for unplanned encounters with strangers and, as such, a place where the unexpected could occur. "There a number of Knights-errants come and sit at the same table without knowing one another; hardly have they glanced at one another when they are brought a certain black liqueur, which has the virtue of making them converse; & it is then that they tell one another of their adventures." The café appears as a theatricalized space of shifting attention: though separate tables were occupied by discrete groups of friends or acquaintances, the clientele as a whole eavesdropped on interesting conversations, which became the center of attention. This café audience also played an active part in the settlement of philosophical disputes. When a debate between three philosophes, an Aristotelian, a Gassendist, and a Cartesian, became heated, the Aristotelian called for a ban on teaching Cartesianism, the burning of Cartesian books, and the expulsion of Cartesians

41. *Biographie Universelle*, 4:571–72; 36:608–11; 35:47–49; 38:69–70; 22:447. On the Club de l'Entresol, founded in 1725, see Clément 2002; Alem 1900, chap. 1.

42. Fosca 1934, 42–45, 56, 59; Darnton 1982, chap. 1.

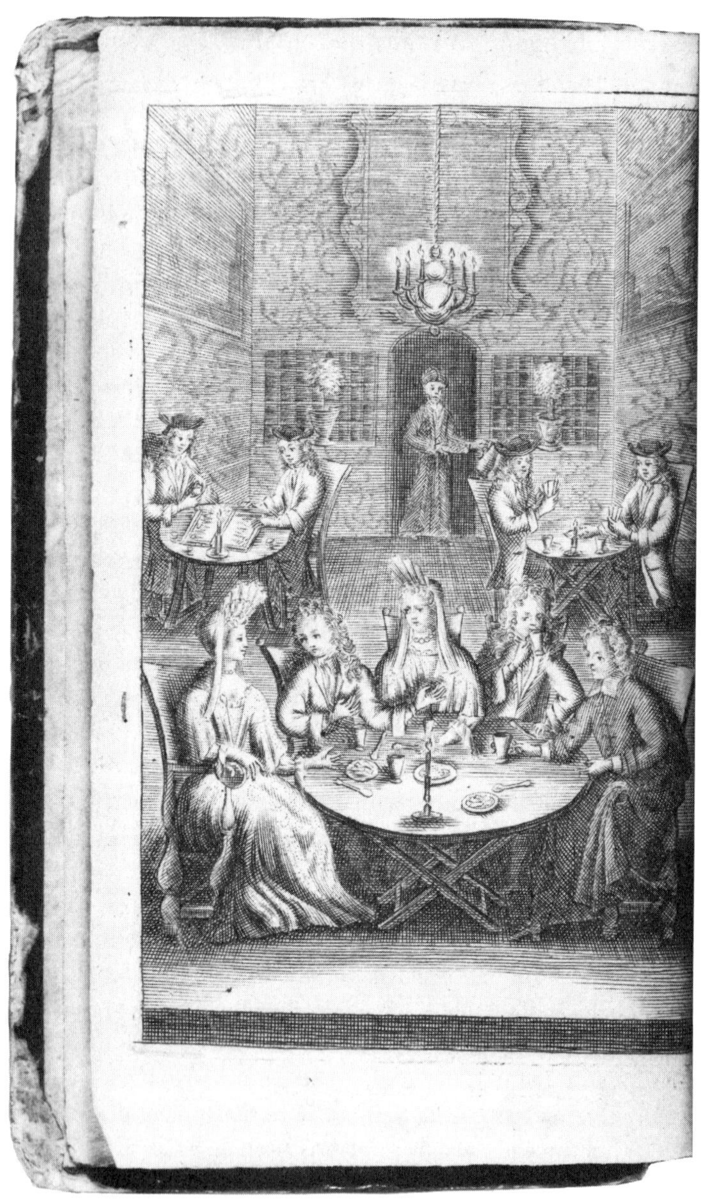

Figure 3.2. Chevalier de Mailly, *Les Entretiens des Cafés de Paris* (Trévoux, 1702), frontispiece. In this early eighteenth-century book, women are still shown as clients of the café, a situation that would change over the next decades. British Library.

from the realm as "Heretics & disturbers of public order." The café audience intervened to calm down the combatants, and to request that the philosophers' conversation be committed to writing, "on account of the learned, & curious things that had been spoken."[43]

For contemporaries, the very thought itself, the *science*, that emerged from this new social space was structured by the consumption of coffee. As the author of a Parisian travel guide explained in 1715:

> [The café] is the meeting place of Nouvellistes [newsmongers] & of some wits who meet here in order to conduct conversations on fine literature. To keep them going, all the substances which are most capable of arousing the ideas under discussion are consumed: coffee, chocolate, rossolis, claret, aniseed water, populo, & other drinks of that kind comprise [the café's] pleasures; those who go there have the choice of them.[44]

Parisian cafés often specialized in particular areas of learning. Laurent's café in rue Dauphine, run by his widow after he died in 1694, was also known as the Café des Beaux-esprits (Wits' Café), where individuals "laid on the carpet all kinds of curious and spiritual matters," while would-be men of letters could foregather at the Café sçavant (Learned Café) to hear learned persons discoursing on all subjects relating to literature. Though elite tourists like Nemeitz, a councillor to the prince of Waldeck, treated such conversations seriously, French commentators were often less than complimentary about the standards of learning on display in the café. In his Orientalist satire *Lettres Persanes*, published anonymously in 1721, the magistrate Montesquieu teased: "There is one [café] where the coffee is prepared in such a way that it bestows *esprit* upon those who drink it: at least, of all those who come out, there's not one person who doesn't believe that he has four times as much as when he went in." Even thirty years later, an article in Diderot and d'Alembert's *Encyclopédie* described cafés as "manufactories of mind, whether good or bad."[45]

43. [Rivière-Dufresny] 1709, 62–63; "Dix-Septieme Entretien," in M[ailly] 1702. Little is known of Mailly; several *galant* publications between 1697 and 1709 are attributed to him. On the nouvellistes, who rattled off memorized items of news to a café's clientele, see Funck-Brentano 1905, chap. 13.

44. Liger 1715, 356; anon. 1798, 99.

45. Nemeitz 1727, 112; [Montesquieu] 1721, 1:79: Letter 34; "Caffés" (1751), in Diderot and d'Alembert 1751–77, 2:259. On Montesquieu's familiarity with Parisian cafés, see Montesquieu 1954, 94n–96n. In Britain, a similar debate over the role of coffee in provoking wit arose in the 1680s and 1690s: see Ellis 2004a, chap. 10.

Critics agreed about several attributes of the cafés of Paris, qua sites of learning. Their knowledge standards were compromised by virtue of admitting such a mixture of types of person, "Nobles & Commoners, well-formed & flat-faced Adolescents, wits & fools." Those who put themselves on display there were rather obviously not profound thinkers: they had dubious political and philosophical views, poor reasoning abilities, and an often ludicrous literary style. In a satire of 1740, Alain-René Le Sage identified a fourfold learned constituency for the café: nouvellistes, chess-players, philosophes, and poets. In his caricature, the nouvellistes or newsmongers were loud-voiced know-it-alls, the chess aficionados absurdly sat in total silence, and the poets were prone to sham displays of violence. For their part, the philosophes reasoned emptily about scholastic platitudes such as "The whole is greater than its parts," but were never able to reach agreement since they could not agree on the terms of the debate. Le Sage here implied that debates about important philosophical and literary matters could never be settled in cafés; they were not places from which convincing new truths would ever emerge. Another satirist illustrated this shortcoming with a fictitious discussion among café wits about the nature of harmony in language, which began on January 15, 1714, and had not ended by December 22 of the same year.[46]

Though satires, such commentaries still suggest that many people probably did treat cafés as sites of learning. However, the learning on offer there took the form of public entertainment—listening in on the sparkling verbal exchanges of the philosophes, poets, and playwrights who frequented them. For these, the café served above all as a performative space. It was where literary reputations were made or broken, where authors met to hear the first public judgments on new plays, and where men of letters engaged in dazzling displays of wit, word-juggling, and erudition. This combination of stylistic innovation, performative bravura, and enlightenment is demonstrated in recorded exchanges between men of letters taking place in the café. Here the wordsmiths' skills were polished and exhibited to the ears. Their verbal displays entailed a sophisticated knowledge of poetic form, *galant* epigrams, and the architecture of jokes and satires.

The conflicts of the Republic of Letters generated a vast literature embracing the art of insult, satire, and parody. In a brilliant essay, Kristine Hecker has addressed satire as the characteristic mode of Parisian literary production in the eighteenth century, particularly exemplified in the epi-

46. [Le Sage] 1740, Letter 10; "Pantalo-Phebeana ou Mémoires, Observations et Anecdotes," in [Bel and Guyot-Desfontaines] 1750, 353.

gram, whether impromptu or deliberated, oral or written. She shows how this form, though much neglected in French histories of literature, was pervasive and powerful as an element in negotiating relations between members of the Parisian literary world and their social superiors. In the celebrated "Couplets Affair," Jean-Baptiste Rousseau was charged with writing malicious epigrams against the regular clientele of the Café Laurent in 1709 and 1710; after losing the case, Rousseau was exiled in 1712 and found refuge in Geneva. But, as Hecker notes, epigrams were an omnipresent feature of literary and political life; "rhyming went on not only in private, in restricted circles, but also in public: a steady stream of verses poured forth from court, indeed, from the whole city." Every significant event in the city and at court was marked by poems, witty, subversive, usually anonymous—in Hecker's phrase, poetry was a "situation-specific art," and versifying was itself a form of newsmongering, a commentary on politics and society.[47]

Poetry was thus a ubiquitous practice of social exclusivity, a highly skilled use of language in a form so localized that the internal references are often invisible to readers today. Hobson has argued that the appeal of much contemporary poetry lay in the game of allusion and concealment involved in reading; the ability to decode rested on the shared possession of knowledge about the subject addressed. Yet the reader was not to be so gullible as to believe in the illusion the poet created: instead, she or he was to appreciate the technical merits of a given poem as a solution to a particular problem of representation through the medium of language. With epigrams, persuasion was achieved by the aptness of the verse in question, so that this genre presupposed shared knowledge and skill on the part of both poet and audience. Menant describes epigrams as a "poetry of social unanimity" rather than an expression of personal sentiments: they pronounced society's judgment against particular individuals. So successful was this literary form that even ministers commissioned satires in order to intervene in current affairs. At the center of this world of literary output was the person of *esprit* (mind, wit, or spirit), an ideal type in polite society up to the rise of didactic nature poetry and sensible literature in the 1760s. Hecker dates a significant transformation of this particular literary model as coinciding with the "'disempowerment' of *esprit*" between 1760 and 1770, a chronology that, as we

47. Hecker 1979, 52–55; Richardot 2002, pt. 2. The couplets particularly targeted La Motte, who beat Rousseau in an election to the Academie Françoise in 1710. On satire, see Connery and Combe 1995; Highet 1962; Kernan 1959, chap. 1; Frye 1990, 223–39, 309–14; Elkin 1973, chap. 2; Adam 1920.

shall see in later chapters, is strongly supported by a range of related transformations in eighteenth-century accounts of health, wealth, and learning.[48]

Participation in café literary circles offered the promise of membership in an elite, while conferring public visibility. The would-be author was here exposed to a barrage of criticism, not only of his opus but of his personal appearance, tastes, and habits. The reportage of café conversations in print, in correspondence, or by word of mouth produced a pressure to shine in conversation and an attention to self-presentation. Literary judgment was passed not only on outside authors, but also on the café's own clientele. Voltaire described how, at the Café Laurent, new publications were dissected, and poetry and songs written. At the Procope, playwrights sat out first nights and came to drown their sorrows after bad performances. Men of letters adopted various strategies for running the gauntlet of the mercilessly brilliant, cruelly incisive outpourings of *esprit* in the café. Voltaire went disguised as a priest to hear judgment passed on his new play *Sémiramis* at the Café Procope, after its opening performance in 1748. Less fortunate was the abbé Simon-Joseph Pellegrin, who eked out a miserable living writing verse and songs; his tragedy *Pélopée* was greeted at the Procope with a note consisting of nothing more than fifteen *P*s, short for:"*Pélopée*, pathetic play presented by Pierre Pellegrin, poor paltry Provençal poet, priest, parasite, perfectly punished." In effect, cafés facilitated literary triage. Resounding put-downs of would-be men of letters' work, harsh criticisms of theatrical failures abounded. Cafés were sites where men of letters jockeyed for social prominence with words and worse. Fosca records how Piron, the playwright and poet, appeared at the Procope wearing a fine outfit, only to have Edme-François Guyot-Desfontaines hoist his doublet and announce with exaggerated admiration, "What clothes, for such a man!" Piron in turn hoisted the abbé's clerical robes to declare: "What a man, for such clothes!" The army officer turned man of letters Germain-François Poullain de Sainte-Foix, author of many plays and other publications including the *Lettres Turques* (a riposte to Montesquieu's *Lettres Persanes*), purportedly insulted a customer's choice of food, provoking a swordfight. Sainte-Foix, refusing to back down, ended the matter with an elegantly turned insult condemning his adversary as boring.[49]

48. Hobson 1982, 224; Hecker 1979, 88, 95, 99, 111–12; Menant 1981, 260–65; Bonnet 1998, 140–41; Darnton 2010, chaps. 1–9. The minister Maurepas was a renowned composer of epigrams.

49. Fosca 1934, 43, 56–62; see also Dupont 1898, 10–12 (for an entirely different version of this anecdote, see anon. 1798, pt. 1, 60–61).

Such anecdotes might appear trivial, but in fact they point to the *uses* of language between 1700 and 1750, to its role in fostering both violence and civility, and above all to the ways in which social status and literary reputation were interwoven in eighteenth-century public spaces. The literary café was a site of innovation, in the sense that it generated new exotic drinks and new literature, but it was also socially innovative, an indicator of a process of social mingling and leveling. The terms of exchange within such cafés were not those of the outside world; here, verbal skill and bravura won out over birth and rank. This situation was one that developed gradually over the early decades of the café's existence; early on, conversations often apparently ended in brawls, as clients sought to defend their honor in the face of verbal insults or philosophical disputes. Violence was a common outcome of the café conversations recorded by Mailly in 1702:

> The Glasses & Cups were smashed, the tables & Coffee-pots overturned, the Chandeliers & Mirrors broken, & for a quarter of an hour there was nothing but disorder, & blows struck on one side or another. When the fight was over, everyone left apart for the Prosecutor, who stayed behind to leave a deposit to cover the food & drink & all the uproar that had occurred.[50]

Over time, such violence became increasingly theatricalized. Writing in 1740, Le Sage satirized café poets for engaging in showily exaggerated displays of enmity and insult, passing instantaneously from rational debate to violence—but only drawing their swords when they knew they were about to be separated.[51]

The café caused problems of violence when it first began to attract polite clients because it was an unfamiliar type of place in this city and this society: a place for the free expression of opinion between persons of different social stations. Early in its existence, there was arguably little precedent for distinguishing critical commentary about literary or philosophical production from attacks upon the self, which impugned personal reputation and honor. The rules of socially acceptable literary criticism were being constituted in public spaces like these literary cafés. In Mailly's "Sixteenth Conversation," Thémiste, a courtier with a "brilliant & solid *esprit*, & an admirable discernment for all the sciences & fine literature," meets Aris-

50. M[ailly] 1702, 115.

51. [Le Sage] 1740, 70–71. A similar tension between worldly and scholarly rank within the Republic of Letters is described by Goldgar 1995.

ton, who has perfectly mastered not only the sciences and belles-lettres, but also "all the fine manners of Court. In particular, he has the gift of the most just Criticism of Works of *esprit.*" When Ariston and Thémiste are offered a satirical madrigal written by Lacon (a thinly veiled reference to François Gacon, a prolific satirist), they refuse to read it, on the basis that the victim, Perrachon (possibly the academician Charles Perrault), was a writer of genuine merit, as confirmed by the king's judgment, with a "high reputation which he had acquired through his learning & eloquence." Themiste adds that "we ought to distinguish bad pieces which interest nobody, & the reading of which should be wholly despised, from those offensive pieces, whose censure should not be neglected, while the work [itself] is scorned." Gacon's critique was thus taken as a personal attack on the king, who had implicitly endorsed Perrachon's intellectual and literary abilities by honoring him.[52]

Over time, this situation changed. The café was a crucial space for the emergence of an entirely different relation between reputation and literary production that did not depend upon official credit: literary criticism, governed by particular rules of engagement permitting nonviolent disagreement over matters of opinion. The properties of coffee itself contributed to this state of affairs; in Massieu's 1718 poem, coffee is credited with converting "odious persiflage" into a "gentle gaiety which offends no-one." Some decades later, the playwrights Le Sage and Guyot-Desfontaines expressed nearly identical views on the importance of literary criticism as a means to distinguish taste from caprice or truth from error, while sharply differentiating it from personalized satirical attacks.[53]

Cafés, as spaces where the normal social hierarchy of rank and birth was temporarily suspended according to agreed rules, allowed men of letters to express philosophical novelty, religious heterodoxy, political dissent, and personal disagreement, while being bonded and reconciled by consumption, as an insightful verse by Voltaire demonstrates:

> Once Boindain had cursed the heavens, in a surfeit of impiety;
> Once Piron had spewed his bile against Olympia;

52. M[ailly] 1702, 316–27.

53. anon. 1798, 97; [Guyot-Desfontaines and Granet ed.] 1731, vol. 2, letter 17; Le Sage-de l'Hydrophonie 1745, vij–xxxv: "Lettre preliminaire." On the identification of moderate criticism with "Old Regime ideals of monarchy and royal absolutism," cf. Pekacz 1999, 54. On journalists as the guardians of Parisian taste, see Goldgar 1992; on the origins of literary criticism, see Eagleton 1984, chap. 1; Hohendahl 1982, chap. 1; Habermas 1989, 167. On public opinion, see Ozouf 1987, 1988. Perrault's importance in the royal academic program is underlined by Mazauric 2007, 36–38.

Once Rousseau the misanthropist had philosophized,
There, Sirs, said Procope,
Do drink your coffee.[54]

NEW FORMS OF REASON

As learned spaces, cafés were heterogeneous, embracing belles-lettres, philosophie, geometry, political economy, and the natural sciences. However, the most visible output emerging from them was literature, both high and low—from belles-lettres, the polished literary product of the scholarly elite and supposedly the embodiment of French linguistic purity, to ephemera such as drinking songs, epigrams, vaudevilles, and *galant* poetry. The latter forms, in particular, were associated with the café: the eclogue, epigram, madrigal, ode, opera, and vaudeville. All addressed lighter themes, including comedy, fable, and mythology; history rarely figured, and public discussion of politics and religion was prohibited anyway. Light poetry was the leading form of literary output between 1700 and 1750. Menant reveals that the composition of poetry was universal in polite society, from the Jesuit *collèges*, where poetry was a didactic device for teaching rhetoric and the knowledge of genres and tropes, to party games in polite houses. This common educational background for all elite males, primarily centered upon the Roman satirists—Horace, Juvenal, Ovid—made poetry a ubiquitous mode of self-expression, qualifying the user as a member of polite society. Poetic skills were thus desirable for worldly persons.[55]

For this reason, light poetry attracted particular criticism from those opposed to worldly knowledge. In 1716 one satirist exhorted French poets "not to occupy yourself with trivia, & pay all your attention to the coining of some little Epigram, or the composition of some cold & dry Opera, or insipid Ode." Instead, he argued, poets should address elevated themes, something that required a combination of literary power and elegance. There was disagreement in the Regency world of letters over whether poetry constituted entertainment or elevation, worldliness or erudition, feminine triviality or masculine force. Of all the literary café habitués of the first half of the eighteenth century, none was perhaps more central to this dispute than the poet Antoine Houdard de La Motte. A hatmaker's son from Troyes, he rose from comparative obscurity to become a leading light in the literary

54. Fosca 1934, quoted 63.

55. On poetry and belles-lettres, see Menant 1981, chaps. 1 and 2; Pomeau and Ehrard 1984, pt. 2, chap. 3; Roche 1988, 99; Furet 1965, 19–21.

world, like several others in the period between the 1690s and 1720s. La Motte was a well-known figure in Parisian cafés, even in old age, when he would appear, blind and crippled, at the café Gradot on the quai de l'École.[56] His high status in the café mirrored his reputation within the Académie Françoise, the heart of Crown-supported literary enterprise in France, and the Parnassus toward which men of letters strove ("Here lies Piron who was nothing, / Not even an Academician").[57]

The first edition of the Académie's dictionary, published in 1694, gave a generally favorable reception to the types of poetry favored by the *cafétistes*. An epigram was defined as a "genre of light poetry, ordinarily consisting in a single thought, whose power is mostly in the final verses." A madrigal was not a triviality but a poetic form close to the epigram, containing "a gallant & ingenious thought in a small number of verses." Two characteristic forms, the vaudeville and the satire, were here explicitly presented as forms of social commentary: the former was a "Song which runs through the Town, whose tune is easy to sing, & whose words are usually based on some adventure or intrigue of the day." Satires were "written to remark upon [and] censure the vices, disordered passions, stupidities [and] impertinences of men," à la Horace and Juvenal; or the term referred more generally to "any saucy [or] malicious discourse." Though favorably treated in the Académie Françoise's dictionary, light poetry was elsewhere attacked as a derogation of the elite standards for heroic, moral, energetic, manly verse and prose established in the Grand Siècle, and contemporaries held that it was not insignificant that this genre could be composed in a shop setting, the café. With men like La Motte wielding power in both domains, the café seemed a sort of debased version of the Académie Françoise, and it is not surprising that they were unflatteringly yoked by satirists.[58]

La Motte was productive in a wide range of poetic forms, and the publication of his *Discours sur la Poésie* in 1707 has been taken to mark the outbreak of a new skirmish in the "*querelle des Anciens et des Modernes*," which in the late seventeenth century had pitted those devoted to classical learning against those who claimed that the moderns had improved upon the ancients. Here La Motte vehemently insisted that poetry had no elevating

56. [Limojon de Saint-Didier] 1716, 41. On La Motte, see Dupont 1898; Gevrey and Guion 2002, 9–44; Fosca 1934, 45.

57. Menant 1981, 264.

58. Académie Françoise 1694: "Epigramme," 1:378; "Madrigale," 2:2; "Satyre," 2:443; "Vaudeville," 2:615. On subversive literature in eighteenth-century France, see especially Darnton 1995, 1996.

purpose, but served merely to please. His main entanglement in the debate came after his 1710 election to the Académie Françoise, when he composed his own version of Homer's *Iliad* in response to a recent French translation by Anne Dacier, the erudite wife of one of his academic colleagues. La Motte and his *cafétiste* supporters resolutely defended the moderns: the new *Iliad* needed to improve upon Homer, correcting the ancient poet's occasional lapses into a coarseness ill-suited to La Motte's poetically expert and tasteful audience, French polite society. The presumption was, therefore, that poets and their audience coexisted on a single level of expertise. According to La Motte, "The poet should only have cultivated *esprits* in view, who are familiar with his subject and the manner in which he treats it: he is speaking a language which is unfamiliar to everybody else."[59]

Moreover, La Motte's *Iliad* exemplified a new philosophical program for the reform of poetry; in Menant's words, "at bottom, the debate turned on the legitimacy of a 'poetry founded upon reason.'" This attempt to reconcile the philosophical or geometrical spirit with poetry was oxymoronic for many commentators. La Motte's improved Homer generated a storm of controversy over the role of poetry within the world of letters. More than any other of his publications, the *Iliad* project contributed to the extremely equivocal reputation that La Motte has possessed ever since.[60] Yet Menant points out that La Motte was the most prolific of contemporary authors on poetic theory: he called for freedom from the constraints of verse form, and, abandoning erudite and theological or elevated goals to recast poetry as secular entertainment, he embraced an explicitly philosophical approach, characterized by verbal precision and exactitude. Above all, on Menant's reading, La Motte's reforms consisted of an attempt to fashion literary criticism as a sphere of mutual respect between "the critic and his reader, between a critic and his adversary." In other words, this was an attempt to generate a polite, non-erudite literary criticism, to be exercised in the world and not in the academy. Together with his friend Bernard Le Bovier de Fontenelle,

59. La Motte 1714, 1715; Dacier 1711. On the "querelle," and on La Motte's reforms of poetry as an explicitly polite undertaking, see Assaf 1987; Levine 1991, chap. 4; Létoublon and Volpilhac-Auger 1999; Cary 1963, chap. 3; Gillot 1914; Pomeau and Ehrard 1984, pt. 2, chap. 1; Dupont 1898, 33–34; Pekacz 1999, 40. On the debate over verse form up to 1750, see Menant 1981, chap. 2, with quote on 87; France 1992b.

60. Menant 1981, 51, with quote from Terrasson 1715; Hobson 1982, 224. For a typical critique of La Motte, see *Les Petits poètes* [1911]: "Avertissement des éditeurs," 7. Only recently have studies such as Hecker 1979, Menant 1981, and Gevrey and Guion 2002, 9–32, revised such portrayals.

Perpetual Secretary of the Académie Royale des Sciences, La Motte sought to rebuild literature upon the philosophical and moral certainty afforded by geometry.[61]

La Motte's poetical enterprise was certainly anathema to the tradition of careful literary exegesis and philological expertise that had developed in Parisian literary life since the 1670s, as we saw in chapter 2. This was a tradition that Dacier, the daughter of the celebrated Hellenist Tanneguy Lefèvre and herself a philological prodigy, exemplified. In her response to La Motte, Dacier invoked the café's contested role in knowledge production in order to undermine her adversary's poetic enterprise. Modern knowledge was ephemeral, fading with the vagaries of fashion; ancient learning was enduring, still familiar thousands of years after it had been produced.

> Where, then, does this difference between the fate of that [ancient] poetry and that eloquence, and that of our poetry today come from? Doesn't it just come from the fact that those orators and great poets labored and meditated, and drew upon the sources of the true and good, and that, following Cicero's example, they subordinated themselves to masters of the arts, and instructed themselves in all the sciences? While the poets of today who dishonor poetry, who have never worked seriously, [and] who have only conducted research which did more harm than good, only have cafés as a study and a Parnassus, and . . . , their heads filled with nothing but operas and novels, only have wrong ideas.[62]

Though La Motte attended salons and academies, his frequenting of the café, that innovative space for consumption and production, supplied ammunition for those who wished to discredit his literary standing, precisely because it was within the café that the moderns seemed to be especially good at winning the debate over the reform of learning. Dacier's partisan Ignace-François Limojon de Saint-Didier, a feudal landlord from the Venaissin, published a satirical essay entitled *Voyage au Parnasse* attacking La Motte as the leader of the moderns in the Paris literary scene. Here he caricatured the moderns' bizarre beliefs, lack of taste, and superficiality, and especially their presence in the café. The ancients might indeed be rough

61. Menant 1981, 59; see also Russo 2007, chap. 2. On the geometrical spirit in poetry, see Becq 1984, 1:325–29, 355–77; Pomeau and Ehrard 1984, 101–4. At just this time the term "savant" was beginning to be used pejoratively, of one who ignored greater significances in the pursuit of minute detail, as well as of a person ignorant of the rules of *honnêteté* (Pekacz 1999, 30–33, 60–61).

62. Dacier 1714, 30.

and unpolished, but that was better than bringing guttersnipe standards to the world of learning. "Where were they to have learnt good conduct? It is the polite world which confers fine manners, & they only see Libraries. The Moderns frequent Cafés and alleys; there [they] have learnt things which are not to be found in Books, & this science is worth more than all that hotchpotch of Greek & Latin. Who says *Savant*, says Pedant."[63]

The title of Limojon de Saint-Didier's book evoked, of course, both the mythological Parnassus from which poets supposedly drew their inspiration and Poincelet's famous café of the same name, much frequented by men of letters. Indeed, in this satirist's view the "black & smoking streams" consumed in the Café Parnasse could only generate "cold Works," written by new authors "who have nothing to excite them but their own opinions [*suffrages*]" and who were attracted to the café "by the gleam of marble & chandeliers." The debate over the café as a setting for new scholarship also addressed the nature of the authority to which the new breed of *gens de lettres* laid claim. Here the perceived effects of consumption and luxury on Parisian society played a central role. On the one hand were those who criticized the growing separation between savant or erudite circles and the public sphere. They welcomed the emergence of a new, worldly philosophy and literature, legitimated by the public expression of opinion, and outside the control of established sources of epistemological legitimacy, such as the Church or the universities.[64] For others, the move to make poetry philosophical seemed like a satirical inversion of its main purpose. The progressive reform of poetry proposed by La Motte and his supporters—first by orienting it toward secularity and politeness, later by abolishing rhyme and even predicting an end to poetry altogether with the progress of reason—might be seen as an exemplary case of the power of satire to undermine the very canon it purports to represent.[65]

CREDIBILITY BETWEEN CAFÉ AND ACADEMY

These subversive effects of café learning would eventually be felt even in that bastion of official learning, the Académie Françoise, where André

63. [Limojon de Saint-Didier] 1716, 91. See also, e.g., [Gacon n.d.], 99–102.

64. On programs for combining pleasure and learning, see Sutton 1995; Spencer 1984; Lynn 2006.

65. Hammer 1990; see also Knight 2004, 4–5. The concern over satire and over La Motte's reforms reveal contemporary fears that new knowledge rendered modern scholars independent of any authority outside themselves, a solipsism famously associated with Cartesian philosophy's "Cogito, ergo sum."

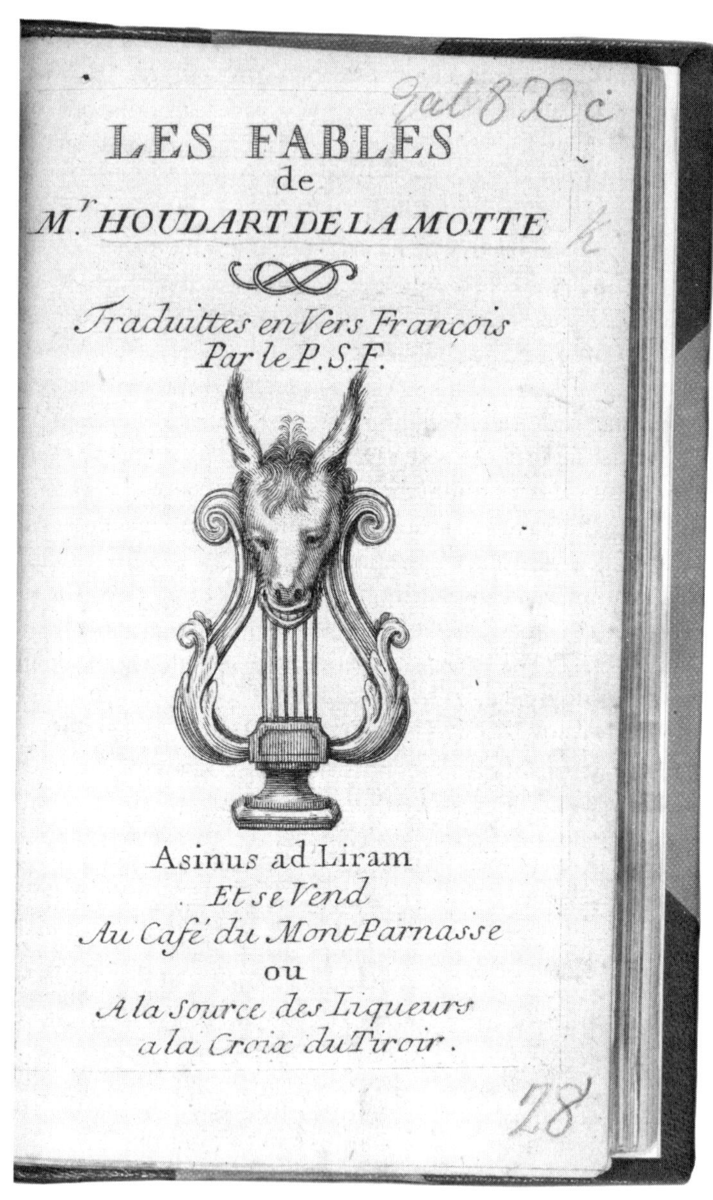

Figure 3.3. [François Gacon,] *Les Fables de M.r Houdart de La Motte Traduittes en Vers François* (Paris, 1715), title page. The title translates as "The Fables of Mr. Houdart de La Motte Translated into French Verse by F[ather] S. F." The book's place of publication purported to be the Café Parnasse, otherwise known as the "wellspring of liqueurs," which, Gacon claimed, sold "bitches of Fables" and "Dogs' Coffee." British Library.

Dacier, Mme Dacier's husband, occupied the post of Perpetual Secretary from 1713 to 1722.[66] The Académie Françoise, founded in 1635, was one of Paris's oldest royal academies and represented Crown efforts to police the use of the French language by laying down standards of linguistic purity and literary style. Election to membership among the *immortels*, as they were known, thus effectively represented a Crown endorsement of literary authority, conferring the right to legislate about the uses of language in the literary world as a whole. La Motte and his circle would become the dominant faction in the Académie Françoise in the 1720s when first Fontenelle, then La Motte, became directors of the institution; as one "ancient" outsider complained of La Motte, "The Academy adopts his Work as a body." Close to Court, La Motte became a leading public embodiment of Crown authority over literary production.[67]

Attempts by members of the Académie Françoise to claim supreme authority over the state of French learning, publicized in manifestos such as the *Harangues* or the Académie's official dictionary, were subject to satirical scrutiny alongside the epistemological projects of the cafés. An anonymous *Dictionnaire Néologique*, reprinted and updated regularly from 1726 onwards, undertook to criticize vicious allocutions and absurd fashionable jargon. It was probably the combined work of two men of letters, Guyot-Desfontaines and Jean-Jacques Bel.[68] Later editions added a short satire by Louis Fuzelier and a "Discourse of thanks pronounced by M Christophle Mathanasius, when he was received at the Académie Françoise in place of Mr ***." This pastiche of hyperbolic praise for the rationality of academic inquiry was purportedly culled from the *Harangues*, a published collection of the real eulogies pronounced by academicians to commemorate deceased *immortels*. Among the metaphors targeted were many that related to the Académie's status as an authoritative center of rational and scientific endeavor, endorsed by the Crown. The Académie was "a Star come to enlighten the whole circle of the Sciences" as well as the "abridgement, collection, extract, [and] analysis of all the most excellent & most refined

66. The Dacier–La Motte dispute thus reflected a battle for hegemony within the Académie Françoise. The moderns dominated other academies first, including the Académie Royale des Sciences and the Académie Royale des Inscriptions et Belles-Lettres. See Pomeau and Ehrard 1984, 45–48.

67. Académie Française 1970; [Limojon de Saint-Didier] 1716, 95; Pomeau and Ehrard 1984, 45–48.

68. On Bel's satire against La Motte, see Dupont 1898, 134–40, 172–73. As Krauss 1967, 780, notes, Fontenelle and La Motte "claimed the right to create new words corresponding to new facts and things"; the *Dictionnaire* may thus be seen as a specific attack against these two authors. In 1724 Bel's *Apologie de M. Houdart de La Motte* had damned the rational poet with false praise.

productions of Reason"; as we will see in chapters 4 and 5, the chemical allusions here to extracts and analyses were not arbitrary. Continuing on the spirituous theme, the Académie was a "nearly immaterial body," so much so that "one might say that in a way it was only *esprit*." It was also a "living Library" and a "learned Society, where one has found the secret of sharing *esprit*," a council for repressing eccentric and disorderly uses of language, a general council of the greatest Republicans of Letters, and the sanctuary and school of eloquence. The author also poked fun at Fontenelle's eulogies of defunct members of the Académie Royale des Sciences such as the botanist Joseph Pitton de Tournefort, who had died in 1708. Surely there was a sly allusion to La Motte and Fontenelle's views on poetry and geometry in one particular "quotation": "Metaphysics laid claim to [Tournefort] so strongly over Poetry & conic Sections, which had unjustly taken hold of him, that the latter were forced to abandon him."[69] By 1730 the quartet of geometry, poetry, Cartesianism, and iatrochemistry apparently formed a program for knowledge that Parisian theatre-goers could be expected to recognize and to mock. That year the Comédie Italienne put on the play *La Foire des Poètes* (The Poets' Fair). In scene 2 the curtain rose upon a chorus of poets seated "like Gods" in a café, singing about how coffee was their "only food." Inevitably, a dispute promptly broke out between two of their number:

> *First Poet.* I maintain that Coffee is harmful to health; Boy bring me some Lemonade.
>
> *All.* Coffee is harmful to health.
>
> *First Poet.* Yes Sirs, I'll demonstrate it to be so on Physical grounds.
>
> *Second Poet.* And I, Sir, shall prove the contrary, Geometrically.
>
> *First Poet.* Let's reason about one principle: it causes insomnia.
>
> *Second Poet.* I say it makes you sleep.
>
> *First Poet.* Sirs, mark well what Monsieur has just said: Coffee makes you sleep. You see that it acts in a different manner, & according to temperament; let's draw a conclusion; now, whether it provokes sleep, or troubles it, whether it stifles the senses, or awakens them, its effects are still prejudicial, because it makes the blood circu-

69. [Bel and Guyot-Desfontaines] 1750, 257–59, 291. The quotes parodied real Académie publications such as Fontenelle 1717 and Académie Françoise 1714–87, vol. 4, e.g., 227, 293, 389, 398, 414. Chrysostôme Mathanasius featured in a spoof work of literary criticism by Thémiseul de Saint-Hyacinthe (Dupont 1898, 134). On the role of the Académie's éloges and other historical publications, see especially Mazauric 2007.

late too rapidly, or else coagulates it; so I liken it to Tarantula, or to Opium.

Second Poet. A conclusion very wrongly drawn. For my part, I call it the universal Vehicle; if it finds the mass of the blood obstructed, its sharp points are so many lines which divide the collateral humors; if the mass of the blood is too fluid, it fills up the voids with a viscous matter which thickens it.[70]

The playwrights not only sent up poets for their total inability to reason but also (like critics before them) ridiculed the ad hoc use of Cartesian matter theory to explain the effects of foods on the body: coffee's particles, it seemed, adapted their physical properties to suit every disruption of health.[71]

Early in the century, for Mailly the café's philosophical role had been as a space for mediating between Cartesians and Gassendists, emblematic of the new style of learning, and Aristotelians, emblematic of the old. Between the 1720s and the 1740s, as Dupont notes, definitions of the philosophe by cafétistes and salonnières such as Terrasson, Mme de Lambert, and Trublet characterized the philosophe not as a heterodox radical, but as a man of letters exhibiting modest skepticism, wedded to observation over authority and the pursuit of logical rigour in literary matters, who possessed particular characteristics such as an even temper, a measured tone, and plenty of *esprit*.[72] In the *Dictionnaire Néologique*, Cartesianism, café learning, and the financial policies of the Regency were portrayed as parts of a programmatic embrace of novelty that had transformed the social sphere in tandem with the Republic of Letters, to no good effect. The café was an exemplary site for demonstrating the dangerous or absurd consequences of the new philosophy:

> However strange or revolting a paradox may be, our *Cafétistes* make no bones about maintaining it; the example of Descartes justifies everything. This great man came, banished the shades of the Philosophy of Aristotle, & renewed sciences & *esprits*. Monsieur de la Motte comes,

70. Dominique and Romagnesi 1730, 7–9.

71. For an earlier critique, see Jean-Baptiste Bertrand, review of Hugues Le Bon, *Dissertatio de hygieine* (1710), *Mémoires de Trévoux* (1712), 859–69, quoted on 868–69.

72. Dupont 1898, 102–5; see also Pekacz 1999, 66. In the article "Encyclopédie" in the eponymous work, Denis Diderot singled out La Motte and his *cafétiste* friends—Boindin, Fontenelle, and Terrasson—as individuals "under whom reason and the philosophical or sceptical spirit have made such great progress" (Gevrey and Guion 2002, 9).

> & declares, in a Preface which someone may have read, that his aim is to carry out the same revolution in Poetry that Descartes has produced in Physics.[73]

There were numerous ties of sociability between Cartesian philosophers and financial circles in the early decades of the eighteenth century. Many *cafétistes* were close to John Law and his circle: the abbé Jean Terrasson, for example, had made a fortune speculating on the Mississippi scheme and published letters in support of Law's System just before its collapse. He too was targeted by the *Dictionnaire Néologique*, which explicitly compared the advance of Cartesianism to the Regent's financial reforms: "All systems of Philosophy have ceded to that of Descartes, all systems of Finance must vanish before that of Law." The café poet César-Chesneau Dumarsais was, for a while, the tutor to Law's son; and even La Motte would publish an "Ode au Régent, sur le Systême de Mr Law [Ode to the Regent, on Mr Law's System]." Finally, it was a style of light poetry—what else?—that acquainted Parisians with the Law scheme itself and the financial neologisms associated with it. Thus worldly poetry and its protagonists were particularly linked with both Cartesian philosophy and the new finance as the purveyors of social and epistemological novelty.[74]

Financiers, in particular the tax farmers, were increasingly indispensable to Crown revenues at this time. The links between prominent *cafétistes* and financiers in the period after 1710 were numerous. Voltaire's vast fortune, which allowed him to live the life of a country gentleman, was acquired through financial speculation in 1729. Louis Racine, son of the famous playwright, invested in the Law scheme, was ruined by its collapse, but subsequently bought his way into the Fermes Généraux. Jean-François Melon, the advisor to a member of the Regency Conseil des Finances, acquired a post as *inspecteur général des fermes* before becoming Law's *premier commis* or chief administrator. He went on to publish perhaps the most significant French-language work of political economy of the first half of the eighteenth century, the *Essai politique sur le commerce*. Nicolas Boindin was attached to the Bureau des finances as a prosecutor, following in his father's foot-

73. [Bel and Guyot-Desfontaines] 1750, 320–21.

74. Ibid., 321. On support for Law, see Perrot 1992, 45–55; Cellard 1996, chaps. 22–24 and p. 279; Murphy 1997, chaps. 15–17; Murphy 2007, 5–6; Terrasson 1715, 1720; Goujet 1759, 351; *Biographie Universelle* 11:521–23. On chansons, see Raunié 1879–84, vol. 1, introduction; Adam 1920, 41.

steps. The father of both the La Faye brothers, Jean-Élie and Jean-François, was a *receveur général des finances*, one of the second main group of state financiers. The embrace of novelty and the access to luxury that the café represented echoed—both in their problems and in their opportunities—the shocking reversals of fortune, the possibilities of social upheaval, and the dangers of innovation and speculation associated with both the Law scheme and Cartesian philosophy.[75]

The café world, though firmly locked into the financial and political fabric of the Old Regime, thus emphatically stood for innovation in all spheres, the gustatory, literary, philosophical, and financial. However, it should not be understood as an *egalitarian* meeting place before 1750. If the sons of artisans could safely associate with, and even critique, nobles or clergymen within the literary world of the café, achieving acceptance there was no straightforward matter, but depended on conformity to standards of literary production and *honnêteté*.[76] One Brébiette haunted the Café Procope in oddly assorted and filthy clothes, boasting of his familiarity with all Europe and with six or seven trades. He passed his time composing insults in the form of epitaphs for people who were still living, one of several performative skills exhibited by men of letters. Yet his emulation of their behavior never made him anything other than a figure of fun among the rest of the café's literary clientele.[77] Mere presence at a literary café and participation in literary forms, then, did not guarantee membership of the literary élite. Individuals of many different types sought to participate in the growing world of letters, philosophie, and enlightenment. Yet many of these would suffer from problems of intellectual legitimacy. Among those disenfranchised from literary enlightenment by later generations, or whose literary status was challenged by contemporaries, were café proprietors themselves, several of whom sought to participate in learned life. Here I shall consider three in particular: Procope's eldest son Michel, raised within the combative literary atmosphere of the café, who became a physician of the Paris

75. See Besterman 1968, introduction, ii–iii; Melon 1734; *Biographie Universelle*, 22:447–48; 35:47–49; 11:521–23; *Nouvelle Biographie Universelle*, 27:588–89; 4:571–72. Melon advised Henri-Jacques de La Force, a member of the Académie Françoise since 1715, later implicated in the collapse of the Law scheme. Cf. http://www.academie-francaise.fr/immortels/base/academiciens, of June 26, 2007. On the Regency financial world and the effects of the Law scheme, see Durand 1971, bk. , pt. 1, chap. 1; Schaeper 1983, chap. 7; Haudrère 2005, 1:73–88.

76. See Lilti (2005) for a comparable argument on salons.

77. Fosca 1934, 60. Pekacz 1999, 19 represents *honnêteté* as an ideal of conduct which allowed for social mobility while preserving the principle of élitism.

medical faculty in 1708; Charlotte-Jacquéline Renyer, wife to two limonadiers, whose poetry and plays won her European renown; and Charles Manoury, employee and later proprietor of a café renowned for its draughts competitions.

THE DON QUIXOTE OF DIGESTION

Michel Procope Couteaux's younger brother Alexandre would inherit the café business, while Michel became a physician. This move into the medical profession indicates that Procope senior must have amassed a substantial fortune from his celebrated business: it cost many hundreds of livres to pay for the various degrees and examinations required to qualify as a member of the Paris medical faculty. Yet Procope's eldest son's café origins damaged his credibility as a commentator on natural matters of fact. In 1712, in the heat of the trituration debate discussed in chapter 1, Michel published a tract on the mechanism of digestion in which he took the side of the fermentationists. Supporters of trituration in the medical faculty accused him of using an inappropriate tone: "he prefers to sink to the level of jokes, & censure such a learned system in a silly buffoonish way, than to become better instructed about good sound [medical] practice," claimed Raymond Finot in his defense of Hecquet. The problem with Procope junior's approach to medical critique was precisely his heavy reliance on belletristic devices and comedic genres such as satire and parody. For his critics, style, credibility, and status all blurred marvelously into one another in attacking this self-titled Don Quixote of fermentation. They emphasized the inappropriateness of applying literary tactics to scrutinize natural knowledge-claims. For some medical men—though evidently not all—there was an incommensurability between literary production and natural knowledge: genre and style were fundamental to learned authority. Philippe-Bernard de Bordegaraye, for example, argued that Procope should not be taken seriously as a commentator on natural knowledge-claims, precisely because he adopted the satirist's role and a language more suited to a novel or to the stage. Procope's attempts to salvage his reputation by distinguishing his artful deployment of satirical modes from his learning did not succeed with this audience. Among other things, Bordegaraye charged him with making "a hotchpotch [*salmigondis*] of [celebrated physicians] and charlatans, sellers of mithridates, & the Paris Apothecaries." The term "*salmigondis*" was a translation of the Greek "*satiricon*," a mixed dish, the linguistic root of the word "satire." If Procope exemplified an age of *esprit* and satire, where the difference between learning and its parody was hard to discern, only systems could counteract *salmigondis*.[78]

The problem was compounded by the fact that Procope was well known to have one foot in each camp. His café upbringing had brought him into contact with countless men of letters, and for the remainder of his life he would alternate between writing medical works and writing satires and comedies, either on his own or in collaboration.[79] He repeatedly resorted to satire in polemical exchanges with medical and surgical opponents, but here it proved a double-edged sword, putting his own status and credibility at risk. For it was all too easy to draw ammunition from Procope's café origins and present him as a bad distiller of arguments: "far from developing, separating, extracting and exhibiting real, clear [and] evident principles," Bordegaraye charged, "he confounds, destroys, precipitates, obfuscates & composes a formless mixture." In a second telling line of attack, Bordegaraye compared Procope's style of reasoning with fashion, superficially persuasive for a particular audience: "provided one possesses the art of dressing it up in a pleasing fashion, one is almost sure to succeed; this is what one vulgarly terms whipped cream, on which scientific dandies nourish themselves without being satisfied." Procope's origins and literary activities thus pointed to the rise of a certain literary public that critics and reformers saw as typifying café learning. Only during the 1740s would he finally achieve eminence in the medical faculty, when he fought the guild of surgeons' attempt to achieve autonomy from physicians. He went on to become a prominent Freemason and even married into the nobility. But despite these social successes, his café origins continued to threaten his learned credibility: in 1747, at the height of the clash between the surgeons and physicians, Julien Offray de La Mettrie, materialist physician and supporter of the surgeons, would satirize Procope in *La Faculté Vengée* (The Faculty Avenged) under the name of "Bavaroise" (a hot drink made with tea, capillary syrup, and sometimes spirits), and had him address a café audience:

> All you Wits, my most worthy Colleagues, who like me occasionally refresh the Scene, while my Brother refreshes throats, if you cannot warm

78. Bordegaraye 1713, 2–8; Finot, unpaginated testimonial in Bordegaraye 1713; Moura and Louvet 1929, 41n. On the cost of entry to the Paris medical faculty, see Gillispie 1980, 216.

79. E.g., Romagnesi and [Procope] C[outeaux 1736]; P[rocope] C[outeaux] and de Merville 1746. See Florkin [1964], 31–32; on the significance of language in medicine, see Wenger 2007, 310–19.

> me up—since you yourselves have frozen minds [*esprits*]—at least transmit that indignation to my heart which, by occasionally turning you into Poets, helps you find good rhymes in the absence of good reasoning.

Such disputes show up the danger of the comedic in this period; it is a testament to the enduring political role of poetry, satire, and plays that La Mettrie's use of satire would lead to his expulsion from Paris, just as it had for Jean-Baptiste Rousseau fifty years before.[80]

THE LEMONADER MUSE

In some settings for enlightenment, such as salons and Masonic lodges, women held an equal or even superior social status. But their right to participate in literary life and in publication—to hold the status of *gens de lettres*—was never secure under the Old Regime. The Académie Françoise and the Académie Royale des Inscriptions et Belles-Lettres, the officially designated bodies for policing French literary output, excluded women. Even so, many women numbered themselves among the *gens de lettres*, and their writing was informally evaluated in other settings, including the periodical press and the salons.[81] If coffee drinking had by all accounts become a universal French habit by the mid-eighteenth century, the café itself, like the English coffee-house, had also become a masculine space. Fashionable women mostly drank coffee at home; their knowledge of cafés was limited to being served at the window of their carriages by a waiter bearing a coffee-pot.[82] There was one type of woman, however, who was invariably to be found inside the café: the limonadière. Often a mere background figure in images of café interiors, she entered print in the guise of the celebrated—or notorious—"Lemonader Muse": Charlotte-Jacquéline Renyer.[83]

80. Bordegaraye 1713, v, 60; La Mettrie 1747, 64–65. For Procope's activities on behalf of the medical faculty, see Delaunay 1906, 178–93; Jal 1872, 448. On La Mettrie and Le Sage's satires against Procope, see Florkin [1964], 25–32. Despite enduring claims that La Mettrie's flight from France was a consequence of his philosophical heterodoxy, contemporary correspondence demonstrates that it was his medical satires which led powerful physicians to request court patrons to exile him (Bibliothèque Publique et Universitaire, Geneva, Archives Tronchin, ms. 198, f°s. 42–44, Letters, François Quesnay to Théodore Tronchin, October 21, [174?] and undated).

81. Landes 1988; Goodman 1992; Terrall 1995; Eger et al. 2001; Hesse 1998, 2003, chapter 2.

82. Savary Des Brûlons and Savary 1723–30, 1:516. The gender balance of French cafés appears to have transformed definitively between 1700 and 1720, since earlier references mention polite women clients as well as men (M[ailly] 1702, 367–68; Obrist 1995, 19).

83. On Renyer, see Franklin 1887–1902, 13:259–63; Fosca 1934, 31; De Lancey [1933]; Helvétius 1981–2004, 4:301n–303n; Darnton 1984b, 8; Briquet 1804, 63. Her correspondence with Helvétius is in Renyer 1754, 2:14–17; Helvétius 1981–2004, vol. 4, letters 177bis and

Renyer was the mistress of the Café Allemand, later renamed the Café des Muses, on the rue Croix-des-Petits-Champs. Born in 1714, Renyer married twice, both times into the lemonader trade. After her first husband, Gilles Curé, died in 1751, she married her garçon or journeyman, Marc Bourette. She played two loopholes for female involvement in male domains off against one another. On the one hand, the café trade: most cafés were run by a male artisan who was responsible for the preparation of drinks and foodstuffs in a back room known as the laboratory. His wife or another female relation sat at the till in the front, managing the shop's finances and credit arrangements, buying in supplies and interacting with customers. In the café, women thus specialized in financial and social skills, while the men exercised the practical skills of the art. When a master lemonader died, his widow was legally entitled to continue the trade under her own name.[84] Thanks to an inventory of Gilles Curé's estate drawn up after his death to protect the interests of their son, Louis-Clair Curé, we know something of Renyer and of the Café Allemand. She was the daughter of a Paris limonadier who had brought to the marriage as part of her dowry the right to practice as a guild distiller in the city. Curé and his wife did not own their large town premises, several rooms of which were let to minor nobles, but their personal possessions were of the best quality. The shop outfittings were less costly, but were in keeping with standard furnishings: a marble-topped counter and ten marble-topped oak tables with needlepoint stools, chandeliers, and a liqueur cabinet painted yellow, which housed the credit notes; the walls were lined with crimson velvet damask, and there was the obligatory iron stove. The shop stock included Alicante, Muscat, and Malaga wine, claret, beer, Turin ratafia, a variety of liqueurs, both bought and manufactured, flavored syrups, apricots and peaches preserved in brandy, chocolate, coffee, almonds, sugar, tea (bohea and green), and the equipment for making and serving ices, *bavaroises*, and orgeat. From her writings it is also clear that the café served cooked food: she mentions omelettes and *boeuf à la vinaigrette*.[85]

Madame Curé also entered the world of letters. Hers was a literary café with a difference—she was herself a poet, adroitly combining commerce and literature: as one anonymous versifier put it,

---

177ter. Though her name often appears as "Renière" in secondary sources, Renyer was the orthography she used in legal documents.

84. On the involvement of women from artisanal families in family businesses, cf. Crowston 2001, 334–52.

85. Archives Nationales, Paris, Minutier Central, Étude XC/369, "Inventaire. 30. Juillet 1751." This also lists Renyer's clothes and jewels, plus the family silver. On cooked food served in the café, see Renyer 1754, 187–89: "Epître à Madame Curé par M. Taxil."

At her door she has her Sign,
Curé, *At the Caffé Allemand*!
As you come in you'll see her
With writing-case & desk;
Pen in hand, keeping a register
Of the homage she receives.[86]

La Muse Limonadière (The Lemonader Muse), published in 1754, reproduced Madame Curé's correspondence, predominantly with well-known men of letters and public figures. Most of these exchanges were in verse. Poetry, here, was a display of mental ingenuity, but also a social skill that classified Curé among the *gens de lettres*. In speaking their language, she achieved partial acceptance among them. This literary enterprise should also be understood as a commercial skill, since Curé used her poetry to lure elite high-profile clients to her café. As "front of house" at the Café Allemand, Renyer would have participated in literary and philosophical conversations. She viewed her feminine role as that of constituting order and sociability in her literary circle. In this and in other ways, such as the recruitment of promising new poets, playwrights, and savants to her café, her tactics resembled those of the salonnières.[87] The Café Allemand thus became a form of salon, where prominent figures from the world of letters attended poetry readings and plays.

In some eyes, at least, Madame Curé's literary activities conferred on her standing as a *femme de lettres*. Among those who responded in kind to her poetical sallies were numerous famous philosophes: Claude-Adrien Helvétius, Pierre-Louis Maupertuis, Voltaire, and Fontenelle. In *La Muse Limonadière*, Renyer would publish both sides of these verse exchanges. Moreover, to attempts to belittle her literary standing, she could oppose a pen every bit as sharp as those of the *cafétistes*. When Elie-Catherine Fréron, favorably reviewing her ode to the king of Prussia, wrote that her "Prose seemed very poetical to me, & [her] Verses very prosaic," she replied with a neat epigram which at once manifested and subverted the implied insult in Fréron's comment:

Woman is customarily
Contrary in all things;

86. Renyer 1754, 157–58, "Lettre d'un Inconnu . . . ."
87. Goodman 1994; Gordon 1988–89; Lilti 2005b.

As she's at odds with everything
In Prose, she writes in Verse,
In Verse, she writes in Prose.[88]

While favorably disposed *gens de lettres* accorded her polite status, Renyer was far from oblivious to the social ambition implicit in her venture, recalling in her dedicatory preface to Stanislaus, king of Poland, that both Virgil and Homer were of humble origin.[89] But her pretensions to participation in the polite literary world were compromised by her commercial activities. In adopting the ubiquitous form of learned self-expression in order to attract a clientele, and hence for the particular purpose of making a profit, Mme Curé was in essence perpetrating a capitalist satire against the world of letters. Celebrity clients were recognized "draws" for a business, and their presence in a café was cultivated and advertised. The famous authors and philosophes who frequented particular cafés on a regular basis were worked into the commercial gimmickry of the café itself. Indeed, when Jean-Jacques Rousseau visited the chess-playing Café de la Régence in the 1770s, his presence caused such a crowd that the police asked him to move on. Thus, Renyer stood to profit considerably from her philosophe clientele.[90]

Even more than Renyer's social origins or her blending of the literary and commercial, however, it was her gender that threatened the success of her enterprise. Those who associated with Mme Curé and became part of her café's regular literary circle paid a price, just like La Motte thirty-five years before. Contemporary sources portrayed limonadières in general as sexually available, often only one step beyond prostitution. As Rivière-Dufresny noted in 1709, "Each Café is an illuminated Palace, in the entrance of which appears an Armide or two who charms you to begin with, in order to lead you into debt up to your eyeballs." The limonadière's beauty could be a commercial asset for a café. Consequently, it became increasingly inappropriate for polite women to frequent cafés. Such considerations probably played a part in the refusal of Mme de Graffigny—Mme Helvétius's aunt—to acknowledge Mme Curé's invitations. In July 1751 she wrote to a correspondent: "The Curé woman has let me be for a long time, but she's furious with me for persistently refusing to answer her or receive her." In effect,

88. Renyer 1754, 63–65. Friedrich Melchior Grimm denied that a woman could have written the more inspired parts of the ode; cf. Tourneux 1877–82, 2:14.

89. Renyer 1754, iv–v.

90. Fosca 1934, 52; Dupont 1898, 9–10; anon. 1798, 58–60; Dulaure 1785, 90.

what Renyer found it hardest of all to achieve was respectability, an essential part of the polite salonnière's persona.[91]

Renyer's case shows that participation in a *politesse* based on the mastery of literary forms could become problematic for a social elite once those of lower social status began to lay claim to equal standing within the literary world. The café was in certain respects a compromised space of sociability, consumption, and performance. If Mme Curé's rise signaled the emergence of a new kind of woman of letters, socially inferior to the salonnières who had patronized men of letters since the days of the *précieuses* in the late seventeenth century, her status could be contested on the same basis as the café's.[92] The satirical pen of Charles Palissot de Montenoy, opponent of the philosophes, also showered venom upon women writers in his *Dunciade* of 1764, a tailoring of Pope's *Dunciad* to fit the French literary world. Where formerly the troupe of female authors had been led by the likes of Mlle Scudéry, nowadays they advanced in company with the philosophes, under Renyer's flag:

> In letters of gold, on their noble banner
> Is written: *The Lemonader muse*;
> And the owl who was once Le Mié,
> Served as guide to the warrior troop.
> Stupidity, who knows their value,
> Wants to invade Parnassus at their head.[93]

Learned pretensions by such a one as Renyer could be deftly cut down in spite of the favor shown toward her publishing efforts by prominent political and literary men, including the enlightened monarchs Stanislaus of Poland and Frederick the Great of Prussia. Nevertheless, she continued to write. At around the time when her play *La Coquette punie* (The Flirt Punished) opened at Maestricht in 1779, she sold her café. By this time, she was wealthy and socially successful; her daughter had married Marmet, *valet de chambre* to Monsieur, the king's brother, and her grandson had Monsieur

91. Quoted in Helvétius 1981–2004, 4:301. On Parisian cafés as sites of sexual attraction, see [Rivière-Dufresny] 1709, 62; Fosca 1934, 42; Chamfort 1929, 170; Haine 1996, 180; Garrioch 1986, 24; Brennan 1988, 148; Obrist 1995, 23.

92. Landes 1988, 7; Pekacz 1999, 89–92. On the problems of being a woman of letters in the Old Regime, see Goldsmith and Goodman 1995; Hesse 1998. On the précieuses, see Maître 1999.

93. [Palissot de Montenoy] 1771, 1:153.

and Madame as godparents.[94] For several reasons, however, her literary endeavors failed to procure her a lasting reputation. While men of humble origins and even those from limonadier families could hope to attain institutional status within the Republic of Letters, while women of high birth could host respected salons, Renyer was trapped in the satirical world of the café, where her gender and social status combined to delegitimate her attempts to participate in the literary life. After her death in 1784, her very identity became fragmented thanks to her different names, and the unique nature of her participation in the literary world—part salonnière, part author, part merchant—has never been commented on by scholars, for whom she remains one of the most obscure of eighteenth-century *gens de lettres*.

THE *ESPRIT* OF DRAUGHTS

By the mid- to late eighteenth century, many cafés relied upon a particular gimmick to attract clients, as at the Café du Caveau, also known as the Café du Sauvage, where a performer earned six livres to play the eponymous savage, grimacing and leaping and banging a kettle-drum before a clientele of up to 200.[95] Other cafés specialized in particular activities such as draughts and chess, philosophical discussions, or even prostitution. The café on the Quai de l'École where La Motte and his fellows used to meet was eventually taken over by Charles Manoury, who had been a "garçon de café" or journeyman distiller there during the 1730s.[96] It had become renowned as a center for chess and draughts players, headed by Manoury himself, whose skills as a draughts player made him one of the café's draws. In 1770 Manoury published his own treatise on a variant of the game as played in most Parisian cafés, Polish draughts.[97] He would later claim that this variant, despite its name, was invented in Regency Paris. His personal intellectual expertise thus centered upon an endeavor fashioned in the café, but one which, ultimately, possessed little standing outside it.

Manoury clearly did not place himself on a par with his elite clientele of philosophes, savants, and men of letters. This is evident from a brief eulogy

94. Renyer 1777, 1779.

95. Fosca 1934, 35–36.

96. Little biographical information is available for Manoury beyond his own publications. Anon. 1789, 143, suggests he was not a practicing distiller. On the Café Manoury, see Franklin 1887–1902, 13:281–83.

97. The board had 100, not 64, squares, and 40 pieces that could move both forward and backward.

in the second edition of his book in 1787, concerning one of his clients, Charles-Marie de La Condamine. This celebrated academician had participated in a Crown-funded voyage to measure the meridian in the 1730s and '40s. Like many philosophes, he was as closely involved in the belletristic world as in the natural scientific one; on the occasion of his reception into the Académie Françoise, an epigram attributed to him ran:

> Today La Condamine's received
> Among the immortal throng
> He's deaf, so much the better for him:
> But he's not dumb, so much the worse for them.[98]

Though a participant in the satirical world of *esprit*, La Condamine's learned status was well above that of Manoury, as the café proprietor acknowledged:

> There was such a distance between that justly famous man and me. . . . But similar tastes can sometimes narrow the gap; & it is to [La Condamine's taste] for the Game of Draughts alone that I owe the honour of having known him. I sometimes had [the honour] of playing against him. In truth, I was better than he; but given how many other advantages he had over me, he could well afford to let me have that one, if it was one.[99]

In spite of Manoury's humility, it is clear that his relationship with La Condamine was more than that normally subsisting between a café proprietor and his client. While beating La Condamine at draughts, Manoury consulted the philosophe and traveler for advice on preparing his book for publication. Exhibiting superior mental skills in a competitive situation before a social superior and a client, and then in public, was something that had to be negotiated with care. In print, Manoury's superior skill at the game had to be rendered harmless by categorizing draughts expertise as outside the realms of true intellectual endeavor, because unconnected with "the progress of human knowledge." The significance of his draughts-playing abilities was defused by presenting them as mental skills of a different order from those possessed by the true savant. "The good player," Manoury claimed, "must have several fairly rare qualities: accuracy of *esprit* in order to judge soundly,

98. La Condamine 1782, 170. La Condamine died in 1774. On his activities as a man of science, see especially Safier 2001; Mercier 1969.

99. Manoury 1787, 23.

the faculty of judging rapidly, breadth in order to embrace the different parts of a complicated move, wisdom so as not to sacrifice solidity to display, & above all clarity & precision so as not to confuse matters." Even so, draughts represented a type of mental endeavor distinct from true learning: "The talent of a great Draughts Player is not in itself proof of a superior genius outside the Game." And Manoury contrasted the famous draughts player Laclef, "a very limited man, without the knowledge or aptitude for anything else," with Jean-Jacques Rousseau, who gave up draughts "out of despair at being a mediocre player." The terms of draughts playing were simply different:

> It is generally supposed that a savant experienced in calculation, [or] a man skilled in algebra, geometry and all areas of mathematics, must possess the *esprit* of Draughts to a high degree. This is wrong; these two *esprits* are very different, perhaps indeed opposites. The geometrical *esprit*, for example, is indeed an *esprit* of calculation & combination, but it uses a scrupulous, slow combination which examines its subject from all angles, one after another, & compares them to one another in succession, taking care not to omit any of them, & to bring them together in all their aspects. . . . The *esprit* of Draughts is not like that; it is a spirit of combination of the instant, which entertains a great many possibilities in a single glance & in a manner which is vague yet certain. Some [possibilities] may escape it unproblematically, because it is less subject to rules [and] is [only] a type of instinct perfected by habit.[100]

Draughts, then, was nothing more than an instinct honed by frequent practice and a "mechanical memory," and the player was predisposed toward it by a "certain *esprit* which one must term the *esprit* of the Game": these "are the sources of the science of Games of combination, & do not point to any other talents or merit in the same man."[101] The problem confronted by Manoury was that of classifying types of mind and mental state, still, in the 1780s, denoted with the single term *esprit*. The terms "instinct" and "habit" to which he resorted were what naturalists used to distinguish the activities of spiders and bees from the rational intelligence of men. Manoury was explicitly defining draughts playing as falling *outside* the scope of Enlightenment, and echoing half a century of polemical claims over café knowledge: what was not an empty parade of trivial learning was a mechanical skill, an aptitude born of habit and physical predisposition, not a

100. Ibid., 43–49.
101. Ibid.

display of genius. His dilemmas reflect the increasing problems attached to pretensions to possess *esprit* in the final decades of the Old Regime, just as the academic world was being attacked for its exclusivity.[102]

CONCLUSION

Parisian cafés housed not one but many, sometimes conflicting, literary and philosophical enterprises. Yet as a whole they seem to exemplify certain critical shifts in the distribution of learning in the eighteenth century. Conceived by their proprietors and their clienteles as sites for *honnête* conduct, cafés offered comestibles and learning that fitted a wider program of public knowledge: rational, scientific, orderly, and above all new. They offered hitherto unavailable opportunities for the sons of hatters (La Motte), cutlers (Diderot) or clockmakers (Rousseau) to associate intimately with the wealthy, and for café owners themselves to enter print. In this sense, they were a locus in which the world of letters seemed to take on a leveling aspect. The rapid growth of printing and reading in the course of the eighteenth century converted the possession of literary good taste from a mark of membership in high society to a general attribute of literate persons.[103] In short, the contours of the learned world began to transform rapidly with the development of the public sphere, and this transformation would be most noticeable between 1740 and 1789.

Before the French Revolution, the natural and moral sciences were not clearly distinguished, and the term "science" was applied to all pursuits involving a formally structured body of knowledge underpinned by philosophical principles. To limit ourselves, in studying the early modern period, to the approach and content of modern science is to overlook much of what contemporary practitioners and philosophes considered scientific. Geoffrey Sutton, writing of the decades before 1750, has demonstrated the concern of La Motte's lifelong friend Fontenelle to reform natural philosophy into a worldly program of sociable, public, and literary learning.[104] The profound implications of his study for our understanding of scientific work in early eighteenth-century Paris have not been adequately addressed. In effect, no account of the sciences circa 1750 can be complete unless it takes the problem of literary form seriously. This means that historians of science cannot

102. Hahn 1971. Chess proved similarly difficult to accommodate within programs of Enlightenment. See Metzner 1998, 34–35, 46.

103. See Martin and Chartier 1984, esp. pt. 5; Goldgar 1992.

104. Sutton 1995.

afford to be insensitive to genre, style, figures of speech, and the other literary skills that underpinned the credibility of participants in debates over matters of fact as well as fiction. To single out only those aspects of contemporary writing that resemble today's science, or which emerged from recognizable centers of scientific practice such as the Académie Royale des Sciences, is to misrepresent "science" in the early modern period.

If we are to comprehend the nature of early modern scientific activity, therefore, we might begin by redrawing our map of the scientific to include the terms of engagement in the public sphere. Spang characterizes one new space for consumption, the restaurant, as a site where privacy and individual choice were made possible, features that she presents as central attributes in the formation of the modern self.[105] The café too permitted the exercise of individual choice over consumption, but differed from the restaurant in the theatricalized, public nature of its space. It was this that allowed it to mediate between individual knowledge-claims and public opinion, and which permitted certain categories of individual, such as merchants, to advance claims to participate in the world of learning by virtue of possessing literary skills, even though they were excluded from salons and academies. Renyer and Manoury formed literary relationships with elite men and women of letters, some of whom numbered among their clients. In different ways, however, each eschewed more extreme forms of egalitarianism. Though Renyer presented herself as on a par with celebrated poets of the Enlightenment, this self-presentation was limited to the literary sphere. When she remarried after the death of her husband in 1751, her second husband was no philosophe or poet, but her garçon de café, Marc Bourette. Her family ties thus remained firmly within the café business, suggesting that her poetic endeavor was indeed, as some suspected, subordinated to her commercial identity. While guild legislation did not prohibit her from continuing the business on her own (witness the Widow Laurent's café), there may have been several commercial advantages to remarriage, such as greater respectability, and a union of resources, a common benefit of marriage in urban artisanal milieux. In addition, the public skills and attractions of the limonadière complemented the private skills of the male distiller who prepared the café's wares at the back of the shop.

For his part, Manoury, though writing in the closing decades of the Old Regime, nevertheless maintained an intellectual divide between himself and his elite readership by downplaying the significance of his own mental skills. But within two years of the second edition of his book, the cafés of

105. Broman 1998; Spang 2000, 76–79.

Paris would become one of the principal political platforms of the French Revolution. Just as they had specialized in literary circles, cafés now specialized in clienteles of particular political persuasions. The Café Procope, now owned by Dubuisson, became a prominent meeting place for political orators. The Café Manoury was praised as a place where "many patriots gather daily, and where, more than anywhere else, one speaks without indecency or lapses, with truly republican liberty." Cafés were suitable homes for the new political world, not least because of their traditional role as mingling places for strangers with widely differing opinions, public spaces where contentious issues could be discussed with minimal violence. It is important to recall that only a few Parisian cafés had literary pretensions; most catered to a wide range of different constituencies, from draughts players in the mid-morning to modestly prosperous merchants or artisans taking their wives to dinner in the evening. They never offered a homogeneous public setting, and in this chapter I have not sought to offer a general picture of all Parisian cafés so much as a series of snapshots, illustrating moments when the relations between consumption, enlightenment, and epistemological authority were particularly acute.[106]

Anglophone historians' attention to the public prominence of Parisian cafés during the Revolutionary decades has come at the cost of interest in their earlier role.[107] Though some Old Regime cafés certainly did house clandestine political meetings and religious heterodoxy, the salient common feature of literary cafés before the 1780s was their role in fostering the playful and sometimes satirical uses of language. Poetry and philosophie were themselves sublimated forms of political commentary, however. From the late seventeenth to the mid-eighteenth centuries, Parisian literary cafés played an indispensable part, both in policing participation in enlightenment, and in forming the relationship between publicity and political and epistemological authority. During the 1780s, however, contemporaries remarked upon a shift in café clienteles. As one savant wrote in 1788, the cafés had originally replaced the cabarets precisely because they were centers of enlightenment, where polite people came to hear instructed individuals speak. "But these fine days are now past; as [the cafés] are nowadays filled with dubious people, polite company has condemned them & the cabarets alike; & the

106. Dulaure 1785, 89; Haine 1996, 211; Archives Nationales, Paris: F[11] 201, dossier A, pièce 209: letter, Guillaume Grivel, commissioner, to Conseil exécutif du département de Paris, 14 Ventôse, year II / March 4, 1794.

107. E.g., Smith 2002, chap. 5. On police surveillance of cafés, see Funck-Brentano 1905, chap. 5; *Biographie Universelle* 4:571–72. During the Old Regime, there were strict official prohibitions against public political debate and satire.

musées, recently established in Paris, have replaced them." The timing of this shift fits well with W. Scott Haine's study of the café as a meeting-place for politically engaged workers after 1789.[108]

In a sense, the propagation of a new, secular, public knowledge and the provision of a forum for conversation that crossed social divisions *was* the political task of the café before 1789. The café was critical as a space that, both in its form and in its refreshments, centered upon novelty. Its intellectual role was intimately tied to the consumption of particular commodities: news, drinks, and learning. Just as coffee itself came to stand for novelty, so Regency financial innovations and the transformations of the Republic of Letters denoted the rise of a new and perilous world of commerce and learning, in which the old rules of the Grand Siècle were flouted at society's peril. In the following chapter I shall move on to consider the production and consumption—both literary and literal—of innovative foods and drinks in mid-century Paris.

108. Buc'hoz 1788, 44. On the social and political shift in cafés during the 1780s, see Haine 1996, esp. chap. 8; Brennan 1988, 137; Isherwood 1986, 240–41; Funck-Brentano 1905, 237; Legrand d'Aussy 1783, 3:114. On the musées, see Lynn 1999; 2006, chap. 4; Goodman 1994; Guénot 1986.

CHAPTER FOUR

Distilling Learning

If cafés were sites for consuming and producing foods, learning, and Enlightenment, it was a contested Enlightenment.[1] In the last chapter, I explored the problematic status of the café as one of several new sites for crafting a public, worldly knowledge. The very publicity of cafés, and their association with commerce, novelty, and the rejection of tradition, meant that those who frequented them might find their attempts to lay claim to learned or literary authority undermined by criticism. Yet cafés provide an extraordinary case of how Enlightenment worked as a form of public knowledge and self-fashioning, for they were shops where the sons and daughters of artisans and merchants could lay claim to various forms of expertise involving the explicit use of mental skill. In this chapter, we turn to the wider commercial setting of the Paris luxury trade, exemplified in a case study of the production and sale of another of the café's principal goods: liqueurs. Moving on from the world of belles-lettres, the relationship between learning and commerce is here illustrated through merchant involvement in academic and non-academic chemistry. Though academic chemists had no monopoly on chemical practice, they were engaged on a different knowledge project from that of nonacademic chemists, one that replaced a connoisseurial expertise located within the body with a quantified and metrological authority situated in instruments, as the history of brandy distillation reveals. The two approaches would never be fully conciliated. However, the enlightened public world of the café created a space in which a union between scientific and connoisseurial knowledge was temporarily possible. To approach knowledge and reason from the standpoint of commerce is thus to shine a new light upon their construction and credibility, and on the rela-

1. An earlier version of this chapter has appeared as Spary 2010.

tionship between polite science, artisanal skill, and the more familiar realm of early modern academic natural knowledge.

Well-to-do Parisians in the 1750s and 1760s could take their pick of fashionable luxury comestibles. Mustard, lemonade powder, rum, candy, cake, and game pie jostled with a host of other goods, from fabrics, wigs, snuffboxes, natural history specimens, watches, medicaments, fireworks, lamps, and books to perfumes, prints, and an oyster fork, specially designed, which administered a measured volume of pepper to the mollusk in the act of prising it from its shell.[2] The shops that sold luxury food products formed a cluster stretching northwards from the Pont-Neuf, near other luxury boutiques owned by merchants such as the mercers. By the mid-eighteenth century, food shops had spread into the newly built-up areas of the wealthy Saint-Honoré district and the streets around the Palais-Royal with its gaming dens, cafés, and brothels. Carolyn Sargentson describes the mercers' shops as elaborately decorated; like cafés, they impressed visitors with their lavish outfitting in mirrored glass, giltwood and marble. Wares were displayed in ornate arrangements, although Parisian boutiques lacked the large windows that characterized English shopfronts.[3]

Sargentson contrasts this mastery of display, and the decorous conduct of shopowners toward their customers, with encounters between merchants, which often descended into physical or verbal violence. Traders in luxury goods needed this Janus-like quality. They faced fierce rivalry from commercial competitors, but their clients were those whose every gesture, item of dress, or habit was determined by courtly standards of politeness, even if they themselves would never attend at court. As a Lyons silk merchant complained, even the Parisian *petite bourgeoisie* behaved in matters of self-presentation as if it were personally related to the royal family, mourning when they mourned, and copying down to the last degree every innovation espoused by courtiers. And those, he added, were extremely delicate and discriminating in their tastes: they had "such an exact attention to and . . . such a perfect knowledge of" the mode, down to the last detail, that nothing smacking of last year's fashion could ever be sold to them. Merchants presented Paris as leading the world in matters of tasteful innovation.[4]

A very complex system of knowledge went into the construction of fashionable identity, and its experts were the connoisseurs: persons of taste and

2. *Avantcoureur* (1762), 186–87.

3. On the luxury shops of eighteenth-century Paris, see Sargentson 1996; Coquery 2003; Hilaire-Pérez 2000; Jones 2004. See also Coquery 1998, 96–105; Perrot 1995.

4. Sargentson 1996, 104; see also Jones 2004, chap. 1.

high social rank. Those who emulated them, and even those who sold to them, had to participate in the same system of knowledge, and this was as true of fashionable food items or even medicaments as it was of dress or gesture. This polite science was gleefully satirized by contemporaries, even those who practiced it. The Italian-born marquis Louis-Antoine de Caraccioli parodied the excessive variety of everything fashionable in Paris: "In one decade, how many ways of styling one's hair, bedizening oneself, applying beauty spots, gaudifying, perfuming oneself, dressing, swelling with conceit, introducing oneself, greeting, speaking, carving, eating, dancing, walking, blowing one's nose?"[5] Every detail of dress and gesture, every accessory, every table manner was part of polite science; knowledge could change every year, and only true experts—both sellers and buyers—could master the vast amount of information and detail required to remain ahead of the emulators, or distinguish among the "2000000000000" designs of fans that, Caraccioli claimed, were on offer in Paris in 1745. In this sense the marketplace was the locus for a conjuncture between at least two kinds of knowledgeable experts, the artisanal vendor and the polite client. In effect, the community that judged liqueurs and other fashion goods was a community of practitioners of polite science, headed by the connoisseurs.

As Caraccioli's parody suggests, however, expertise in worldly science was under attack during these decades. In his banned materialist work *De l'Esprit* (On Esprit), the Farmer General Claude-Adrien Helvétius devoted several chapters to polite science, protesting against the fact that its values were not universal but local. "If one understands by good *ton* the tone suited to pleasing in any society, in that sense there is no man of good *ton*. For there to be one, he would have to embrace all the types of knowledge, all the types of mind, and, perhaps, all the different jargons; an impossible supposition." In place of polite science with its infinite local variations, Helvétius proposed a homogeneous, public civic knowledge, concerned with social utility, governance, and economy.[6] For these reasons the title of his book should

5. [Caraccioli 1757]: vj–vij. On fashion, see Berg 2005, chap. 7; Roche 1994; Jones 2004; Ribeiro 1995. Poni 1998 argues for fashion as socially constructed rather than innate.

6. Helvétius 1988, 100, and cf. Discourse II, chaps. 4–10, especially chap. 9. [Caraccioli 1757] was, in part, a satire upon this work, e.g., xvij. Helvétius was drawing upon classical models of civic utility, widespread in the early modern period, and arguing for the replacement of courtly civility with a politeness derived from inner honesty rather than outward appearance. A "jargon" was a technical language. On the notion of a polite or worldly science, see Pekacz 1999, 33; Revel 1989; Elias 1983; Bury 1996, 175–94; Pocock 1985; Klein 1994; 2001, 162. In Académie Françoise 1714–87, 4:542, La Motte defined polite science as a peculiarly French form of knowledge.

also be read as a critique of polite uses of the term "*esprit*" to mean "wit" in all the various senses of the word, as discussed in the previous chapter.

As for other luxury fashion items, the manufacture of prepared foods involved skilled knowledge. Such goods, though luxury items, were comparatively inexpensive, part of the "move of predominance in the luxury markets from court and aristocracy to an educated and acquisitive bourgeoisie" described by Robert Fox and Anthony Turner.[7] Their manufacturers laid particular emphasis on aesthetic values that were shared by their clientele, presenting their range of goods as visually attractive, innovative, and diverse, capable of producing tastefulness, delicacy, and pleasure. Most items sold at a few livres apiece, so were within the reach of the urban well-to-do, not just the rich. A cost analysis, however, does little to locate foodstuffs within a particular lifestyle or knowledge system, and cannot explain how a given comestible was variably appropriated or contested in different social worlds. This is the aim of this chapter.

Food entrepreneurs have received scant historical attention. In one weekly newspaper, the *Avantcoureur*, which I shall argue played a particularly important role in uniting science and commerce, there were some forty prepared-food manufacturers advertising between 1761 and 1773.[8] They represented an eclectic range of Parisian guilds: the apothecaries and grocers' guild, including grocer-confectioners; the distillers and limonadiers; the culinary guilds (the traiteurs, pastrycooks, and roasters), one mercer, one *négociant* or long-distance trader, and a vinegar-maker. One advertiser described himself as a chocolate-maker (chocolatier) and one simply as "directeur de magasin" or shopkeeper. These vendors were united more by the range of goods they had on offer than by guild affiliation. The largest single category was the liqueurs, whose manufacture within city limits was legally restricted to the limonadiers' guild. However, they were also imported, sold, and even manufactured by members of other guilds. The vinegar-makers, grocers, and apothecaries were all licensed to distill wine into brandy, and the placiers or street vendors sold neat brandy or brandied walnuts and cherries from roadside stalls.[9] Other drink preparations were powders, pastes, tablets, essences, or syrups, sold for making up at home and used not only in

7. Fox and Turner 1998; Lewis 1998; Berg 1999; 2005, esp. introduction; Sewell 2010.

8. On the *Avantcoureur*, see Sgard 1991, 1:151–56. Its journalists included Anne-Gabriel Meunier de Querlon and Nicolas Bricaire de La Dixmerie, discussed in more detail in chapter 5 below.

9. *Avantcoureur* (1762), 786; (1764), 387; (1770), 38. On the placiers, first mentioned in legislation in 1678, see Legrand d'Aussy 1783, 3:69.

drinks (primarily lemonade and barley water) but also to compose ices and other refreshments. These products were advertised by grocers, confectioners, distillers, and limonadiers.

The prepared foods that were most heavily advertised included pastry goods, confectionery, chocolate, fortified wines, vinegars, mustards, meat products, ice cream, and syrups. Certain characteristics were shared by all of these. First, they were all products of skilled labor, in which materials such as wine, sugar, spices and other aromatics, meat, dairy products, fruit, and flowers were elaborated into different forms, textures, and flavors. Thus what stood out about them was their artistry or, negatively viewed, their artificiality; to many contemporaries they were, as will become clear, allied with the products of chemical operations. Second, many of them were also marketed as some form of extract or concentrate, indicating that the issue of preservation and transportability featured in their commercial success. Third, novelty and exoticism dominated the ingredients of such products, as we have already seen in chapter 3.

The pattern of advertising in the periodical press for prepared-food goods reflects the legal complexities of production and trade in Old Regime Paris. Certain prepared foods, such as coffee or liqueurs, straddled the boundaries of guild privileges or even lay entirely outside the terrain of privileged goods. Such commodities generated intense conflict among merchants, which drew in all the various bodies charged with implementing the capital's laws: the police, the Paris *parlement*, and the Crown's Conseil d'État. Foods that became fashionable stirred up particular commercial rivalry, and thus also publicity. Moreover, these same luxury foods attracted criticism from moralists and medical authors because manufacturers explicitly associated them in advertising literature with exoticism, artificiality, and pleasure. The struggle to capture the meaning of liqueurs, to produce them as epistemological as well as material objects, went on simultaneously on the commercial, scientific, and medical fronts. Chemistry, in particular, became an important weapon for both apothecaries and distillers moving between scientific institutions and polite print culture to further their commercial ends. Liqueurs came to signify an opposition between pleasure and reason, and debates about their use were, in effect, debates about the relationship between minds, bodies, and expertise in an Enlightened age.[10]

For an audience dominated by merchant manufacturers and their fashionable clienteles, the consumption of liqueurs signified pleasure and taste-

10. On commodities that caused legal conflict between guilds, see Spang 2000, 8–9; Davis 2004, chaps. 1 and 3; Sonenscher 1998; chapter 3 in this volume.

fulness. It is this view that I shall term "connoisseurship" in what follows. The physiological justification for liqueur consumption was that, like coffee, liqueurs nourished the nervous system and enhanced mental abilities. According to others, however, liqueurs were ingesta without being nutriment, "empty" foodstuffs consumed solely for their pleasurable qualities and supposed mental benefits. Especially for those medical authors who argued that everything non-nutritious should be be considered a medicament, liqueurs played a particularly problematic cultural role in their guise as the signifiers of fashionable life and of self-pleasuring. They reduced alimentary intake to pure symbolism and commercial transaction; moreover, they were substances explicitly consumed for the purposes of altering the healthy individual's moral state, potent substances whose consumption was not legislatively controlled during the eighteenth century. No wonder then that numerous individuals cited liqueurs as evidence of the moral and corporeal excesses of the modern age. As in the case of Philippe Hecquet's critique of luxurious eating (discussed in chapter 1), such denunciations of liqueurs were generally advanced in the name of health. Liqueur merchants too, however, could invoke health by appealing to older iatrochemical models of mind and body. The public debate over liqueurs as commodities, therefore, rested in part upon a continuing tension between iatrochemistry and *esprit* on the one hand, and attempts to use "health" and "nature" as a platform from which to reform the habits of French consumers on the other.

THE COMPOUND LIQUEURS

The present-day use of the English term "liqueurs" conjures up an image of flavored, spirituous drinks, usually consumed in small doses, and sold under an endless variety of names, colors, and bottle shapes. In the eighteenth century, the term applied to such beverages, but was also often used in a wider sense, to denote all the drinks produced and sold by the limonadiers, including coffee, tea, chocolate, and lemonade. Liqueurs were made for drinking, but also for use as cosmetics, perfumes, and medicaments.[11] Our present-day usage corresponds more closely with a particular group of drinks known as the "compound" liqueurs. The image we have today of liqueurs preserves one of their outstanding qualities for eighteenth-century consumers. Liqueurs epitomized the cornucopian, the embrace of Nature's treasury of comestibles. The distiller Déjean, author of a much-reprinted treatise on distillation, claimed that liqueurs could be made from "everything

11. Déjean 1759, viij, 3.

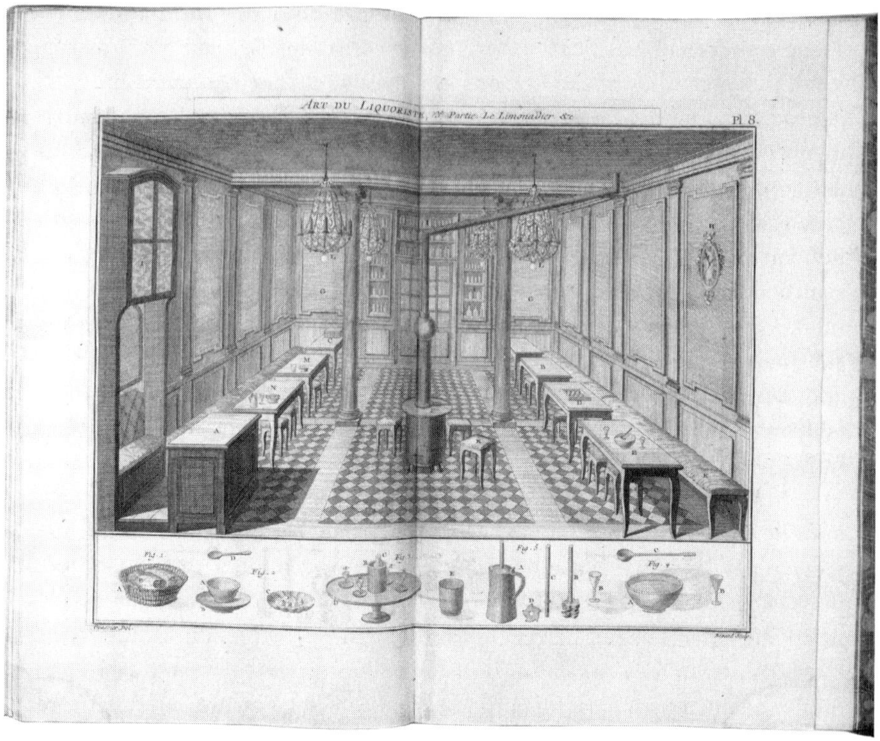

Figure 4.1. Jacques-François Demachy, *L'Art du distillateur liquoriste* (Paris, 1775), plate 8. The interior of a café in the 1770s. Copperplate engraving after Goussier. British Library.

the earth produces, flowers, fruits, seeds, spices, aromatic and vulnerary plants, odoriferous drugs, &c.," and he portrayed France as especially favored by nature for the manufacture of liqueurs. His book included recipes for liqueurs made using orange blossom, lilies, pinks, jasmine, violet, marjoram, lemon balm, aspic, thyme, basil, sage, rosemary, citrus, clove, aniseed, cinnamon, nutmeg, coffee, and cocoa. According to the official Académie Royale des Sciences publication describing the trade, a typical liquorist's laboratory was supplied with some thirty aromatic spirits, twenty to twenty-four essential oils, plus the same oils dissolved to saturation in spirit of wine, about thirty tinctures, and a supply of basic brandy in each of three types, one plain, one with a certain quantity of sugar suitable for the category of liqueurs called "essences," and a third with syrup in quantities sufficient to create an oily consistency, the basis for the category of liqueurs known as oils. Using these substrates, the liquorist could compose any liqueur quickly, creating a judicious balance of flavors and aromas.[12]

Compound liqueurs were produced in large households for domestic consumption, and recipes are to be found in manuscript receipt books as well as published cookbooks and domestic economy manuals.[13] The *officier d'office*, or steward, was the domestic counterpart of guild limonadiers and confectioners, preparing a range of liqueurs, pastries, and sweetmeats that adroitly combined flavors and spices. The rise of the liqueur trade was part of a general move of luxury food production into public commerce as domestic production declined and a new group of literate and professionally trained urban entrepreneurs emerged.[14] The changing definition of distillation in the *Dictionnaire de l'Académie Française* supports this transition. In 1694 a distiller was anyone "who distils flowers [and] herbs." By 1798 the definition had become "He *whose profession* is that of distilling flowers [and] herbs" (emphasis added).[15] By the early eighteenth century, liqueurs were already a highly competitive commercial terrain and a showpiece of Paris entrepreneurialism, as in the travel guide published by Louis Liger in 1715:

> It is well-established that Paris is a very delicious abode; everything is to be found here which might arouse the mouth's enjoyment, & flatter the most sensual. Pastry, Liqucurs, Confectionery & other things of that nature are not lacking here, everything prepared in the last [degree of] perfection.[16]

Liger went on to explain that "Under this term Liqueurs I understand the Cafés where they are sold," and to advertise the family business: "The Masters of these Cafés take the title of Distillers, because the majority dis-

12. Demachy 1775, 84. Déjean's real identity is uncertain. Ferchl 1937, entry 118, identifies him with Ferdinand Déjean, a Dutch colonial physician, but this seems unlikely. Two sources give unreferenced claims that Déjean was the pseudonym of the Parisian distiller Antoine Hornot, born in Burgundy (Caillet 1912, 2:279–80, entry 5259; Oberlé 1989, 599–600). However, the dedication of Déjean's book to the limonadiers' guild supports his membership of that body. The grocer and distiller Sauvel claimed to be Déjean's protégé, and the two appear to have shared the same address, the Magasin de Provence on the corner of rue Neuf des Petits-Champs and rue des Petits-Enfants (*Avantcoureur* (1762), 102; *Année Littéraire* 1764.iv.68–69; Déjean 1778, after title page).

13. E.g., Chomel 1740; [Menon] 1750.

14. Martin 1996; 1999, 49, 53–54; 2009; see also chapter 3 in this volume.

15. "Distillateur," Académie Françoise 1694, 1:336; "Distillateur," Académie Françoise 1798, 1:432.

16. Liger 1715, 352.

til on their own behalf & compose the liqueurs that they sell: & I may say that among those who work at this [trade], Liger is the one who excels. He lives in the rue de la Huchette."[17] Paris distillers like Déjean or his successor, Sauvel, were not large-scale brandy manufacturers. They specialized rather in the compound liqueurs, preparations or mixtures of brandy, sugar, and flavorings.[18] A few liqueurs are mentioned by name in the earliest legislation concerning the limonadiers' guild: the eponymous lemonade was a drink made with citrus fruit, sugar, and water, or occasionally brandy, but other traditional liqueurs were classic Italian imports such as Rossolis, Populo, or Frangipane, all reflecting the Italian origins of the liqueur trade in the seventeenth century. Most of these combined essences of spices such as aniseed, cinnamon, musk, and amber with brandy, sugar, and water. Imported or provincial sweet wines from Spain and the south of France were also named in the early legislation.[19] The name of "eaux" or waters was given to a class of liqueurs made by distilling water or brandy with aromatic herbs, spices, or fruits, such as strawberry water, cherry water, cinnamon water, and so on.[20] Global trade was also creating a new market for foods and drinks prepared with exotic flavoring substances. Two important new classes of spirituous liqueurs were invented in the early eighteenth century: the ratafias and oils. Ratafias resembled the eaux, but used only brandy in combination with fruit juices, such as peach, apricot, grape, pear, orange, or lemon, and exotic spices, especially clove, long pepper, mace, cinnamon, and nutmeg.[21] The oils, very fashionable from their invention in the 1720s but in decline by the 1770s, were loaded with sugar syrup at levels that produced an oily consistency. These too made use of exotic ingredients: there was oil of Barbados and star anise oil, for example. The use of flavoring and sweetening substances derived from global commerce and colonial cultivation attests to the falling price and increasing availability, across a broader social spectrum, of such goods.[22]

17. Ibid., 355–56.

18. Déjean 1759, ix.

19. See Delamare 1722–38, 3:797; Lespinasse 1886, 1:602–5. On their Italian origin, see Audiger 1692; Onfroy 1765, 5; Forbes 1948, 95, though some were already known outside Italy before the eighteenth century (Wilson 2006, 179).

20. "Eaux distillées," [Macquer] 1766, 1:373–76; Delamare 1722–38, 3:797.

21. Delamare 1722–38, 3:797.

22. Mintz 1985, 79–96; Flandrin 1996b. A royal act of January 1713 restricted French brandy producers to grapes as a raw material, a situation that prevailed for many decades (*Déclaration* [n.d.]; see also Schaeper 1983, 173). Colonists, by contrast, could manufacture brandies and liqueurs from other substances, such as sugar cane. The metropolitan trade in colonial

INNOVATION AND INVENTION

Liqueurs and other prepared foods were portrayed in advertisements as products whose manufacture required special ingenuity. The printed advertisement was itself a new invention, a valuable way of engaging with polite readers forming part of a large, upwardly mobile, wealthy, literate, health-conscious, urban population. Like other advertisements, those for food reified an abstraction, the middling world of public commercial transactions, even while they represented an aspiration to standards of tasteful and fashionable self-presentation that had its basis in the emulation of courtly conduct. Food advertising created a market ostensibly built around the consumer's *social* distinction, in practice increasingly permitting anyone with enough money to possess taste. Advertisements concealed corporate rivalries behind appeals to the civilizing power of commerce, as Martin and Jones show. Thus, they unite two of the themes prominent in Jürgen Habermas's *The Structural Transformation of the Public Sphere*, the expanding world of printing and reading and the world of social and financial commerce.[23]

Only a fraction of Parisian food and drink entrepreneurs exploited the new opportunities for marketing and self-promotion offered by print. In advertising materials for luxury goods, entrepreneurs constructed a specific clientele, deemed to be tasteful and discriminating, setting standards for health, fashion, and beauty that merchants merely emulated. Advertisers also constructed their own moral character as industrious, trustworthy, and inventive.[24] The *Avantcoureur*'s editor acknowledged the role played by distillers in facilitating the exercise of taste through the constant generation of novelty and variety, as in an advertisement for "Chinese Balm," "Royal Water," and "liquid Carmine" sold by one Fontaine on the rue du Roulle: "The Public should be grateful to our Distillers for seeking all means of delighting its taste." Newly invented liqueurs followed the same principles. When the grocer Rissoan promoted his new liqueur, cream of pineapples, as

---

liqueurs, which began in the 1740s, was variably regulated throughout the Old Regime (Meyer et al. 1991, 246–65; Legrand d'Aussy 1783, 3:72, 82–83).

23. Martin 1999, chap. 2; 2009, chap. 3; Jones 1996, 24–27; Habermas 1989. Coquery, discussing trade almanacs, names food entrepreneurs who also advertised in newspapers. As she remarks, "publicity sheds light not only on the growth in demand and the transformation of modes of consumption, but also on the techniques and methods used by entrepreneurs to create demand and stimulate desire" (2003, 193).

24. See analogous claims concerning Josiah Wedgwood in McKendrick, Brewer, and Plumb 1982, 100–145; also Jones 1996.

being "very fine & judged very agreeable by the gourmets," he also alluded to the diversity of his stock: "a great number of liqueurs no less remarkable perhaps for the singular names they have been given than for their different tastes."[25]

Diversity and innovation were key principles of the commercial aesthetic of consumption. Food and drink entrepreneurs presented their tireless innovation as a reaction to the needs of tasteful buyers, but they also included themselves in a broader artisanal ferment of French inventiveness. "It is necessary to invent ceaselessly in order to stimulate [piquer] the taste of the Public," ran one advertisement in the *Avantcoureur* for the confectioner Le Camus's pastilles and sugar jewels in 1765. Le Camus's fame had been earned by "exposing objects which are as gallant as they are new . . . to the eyes of the Public each year." Among his wares were sugar loaves that when broken open revealed surprises inside, and pastilles in all colors, especially pink. Such diversity was also evident in the range of products on offer: besides pastilles (rose, gooseberry, or citrus) and sugar surprises, Le Camus advertised lemonade paste, a cosmetic pearl vinegar, aniseed oil, a rose and jonquil perfume, and seasonal bonbons. Discovery narratives were part of this culture of innovation: in a notice inserted into the *Avantcoureur* in 1769, the merchant grocer-confectioner André, based in the rue des Fossés-Saint-Jacques, vaunted his discovery of "a means of extracting almond milk & working it together with sugar to make a dry powder which produces an excellent barley water, and melts easily in water without leaving any deposit." Such goods were sold, sealed and branded, to domestic consumers and cooks.[26]

The perception of merchants was thus that novelty was not merely a central commercial tactic—it was also a responsibility they had toward the French consuming public. Food advertisers emphasized the novelty and diversity of their range, and pursued policies of changing or enhancing their

25. *Avantcoureur* (1765): 147; (1770): 38. Rissoan's business was located in the rue de Bussy, at the sign of the *Grand Turc*. He may have been related to the apothecary Isaac Rissoan, who became a master in 1722. See Bouvet 1937, 109.

26. *Avantcoureur* (1765): 797–98; (1769): 342–43. See also Spary 2009; unpublished, chap. 4. On innovation and novelty, see Hoock and Lepetit 1987; Campbell 1992; Bianchi 1998, esp. papers by Bianchi and Gualerzi; Pennell 1999; Hilaire-Pérez and Garçon 2003; Bruland 2004; Berg 2005, chap. 3. David Edgerton critiques an "innovation-centric view" of the history of technology, but the history of *innovativeness*, into which I see debates over liqueurs as fitting, largely remains to be written. Nonetheless, the fact that liqueurs have been excluded from the history of technology underlines the importance of Edgerton's call to attend to "all inventions and innovations at a particular time, independently of their later success or failure" (Edgerton [2006]: xiv–xv; Klein and Spary 2010).

range at regular intervals. An advertisement of 1763 for "New liqueurs" promised visitors to Sauvel's shop, in the rue Neuve des Petits-Champs, "a complete range of everything that gourmands might desire in that line, whose richness augments in proportion to the increase in desires and luxury appetites." Progress in liqueurs was cumulative: Sauvel, a grocer and distiller, had begun by selling the liqueurs of the celebrated distiller Déjean, and judiciously added novelties to his range each year, becoming one of the leading Parisian liqueur-sellers in the 1760s.[27] This prominent liquorist and advertising virtuoso chose the *Avantcoureur* for advertising as part of a well-formulated commercial strategy. Prefacing the issue for January 1767 was the newspaper's agenda for reporting scientific and artistic news:

> Every day Savants make discoveries or useful attempts, the Arts give birth to stimulating [piquant] Novelties or interesting trials, individuals undertake new enterprises, the Merchant receives new products from the Manufactures and Industry of foreign countries. But often all these things, which their Authors, their Inventors, or those who store them in their warehouses have such a strong interest in making known, & which the public for its part desires with the greatest eagerness, remain unknown for a long time, or are announced in a faulty manner, which does not convey the right idea about them.
>
> The only way of avoiding all these inconveniences & of having the Savant, the man of genius, the Artisan, the industrious man, enjoy the fruit of their labours, would be for them to give the necessary indications themselves, which the Journal could immediately make known to the public without fear of any error.[28]

By publishing food entrepreneurs' advertisements, the *Avantcoureur* was participating in a mission of enlightenment: this was a way of correcting error and ensuring that only the "right idea" entered the heads of the public. The development of a commercialized public sphere, the beginnings of an industrial world, and the progress of scientific and artistic knowledge were here allied, supporting the argument that the existence of a consumer society was a prerequisite for the development of a manufacturing revolution.

27. *Avantcoureur* (1762): 102; (1763): 86. By a legal contract of March 28, 1751, an Antoine Sauvel was taken on as apprentice grocer and wax merchant by one Marc Broue (Archives Nationales, Paris, Minutier Central, Étude XXXIX/408). Possibly this was the individual who later worked with Déjean.

28. *Avantcoureur* (1767): unpaginated letter inserted before the first issue.

But more significantly, for the *Avantcoureur* and its advertisers, commerce, consumption, and novelty were forms of knowledge, and the commercial enlightenment of the public was an important social responsibility.[29]

Sgard describes the *Avantcoureur* as something of an experiment, an attempt to reconcile the interests of entrepreneurs with those of literary or scientific writers, and notes "the difficulty this periodical had in finding its identity, cultural or commercial." One might dwell instead upon the transformations of the polite and commercial worlds implied by the very existence of such an enterprise. The *Avantcoureur* demonstrates the erosion of boundaries between commerce and cultivation, the openness of print as a medium for making claims concerning discovery and invention and tying those to the possession of taste. Prepared foods could themselves be a form of news. When the marriage of Marie-Antoinette and the Dauphin was announced in 1770, the confectioner Faciot, a regular advertiser in the *Avantcoureur*, was swift to advertise the "portrait in sugar of Madame the future Dauphine in a medallion artistically boxed in by a gilded border" as an "interesting novelty." This edible publication appeared on the market even before a more orthodox plaster medallion of the new Dauphine could be advertised, later that month. Reading and consuming seemed interchangeable in the periodical press, as in one of Sauvel's many advertisements: "In Paris, Sir, bad Liqueurs are made just like bad Books, & one can count almost as many dull distillers in this Capital as dull writers. . . . Liqueurs after [Sauvel's] fashion, such as Hebe, Ambrosia, Pomona, Oil of Mocha, Orange Flower in St. Laurent wine, &c, are very esteemed by the most difficult gourmets." Food and drink products were marketed as part of the public world of consumption of knowledge; the entrepreneurs who manufactured them were placing themselves on a creative par with men of letters and savants. Though advertisements can tell us nothing about the uses of such goods, they provide suggestive evidence as to the nature of the relationship between producers and consumers.[30]

In equating innovation in the alimentary arts with invention in the sciences, the *Avantcoureur* was not unique among periodicals, but it was particularly explicit in declaring its agenda. Nor can its editors' claims to report from the cutting edge of invention and discovery be marginalized as relevant only to commercial issues or "popular" science, for this newspaper was also the first to publish some of Lavoisier's earliest experiments and was a leading forum for chemical controversies. However, the status of

29. McKendrick et al. 1982; Jones 1996; Berg 1994; Sonenscher 1989.

30. Sgard 1991, 1:155; *Avantcoureur* (1770): 230; (1766): 807; *Année littéraire* 1766, 287–88.

advertising and invention was far from stable, particularly with regard to food products. In one advertisement for pies made in Amiens, the *Avant-coureur*'s editor adopted a defensive tone: "We will not neglect any object of industry. Is it any more ridiculous to announce a good dish than a beautiful fabric? We exhort the scoffers to make use of all these things, if they can, rather than laughing at the advertisement."[31] Such concerns were well founded, given prevailing descriptions of the French national character. If French merchants lauded their nation as the one that set fashionable standards for the rest thanks to the power of the national imagination, critics portrayed the restless pursuit of novelty as a moral shortcoming peculiar to the French, the fickleness of fashion's devoted followers as a national failing. Such an accusation could threaten the whole project of a public Enlightenment by limiting knowledge to shallow and superficial outcomes, rather as the café had threatened the seriousness of scholarship in the 1730s. As Caraccioli scoffed,

> France . . . prefers a Marchande de modes who works tastefully, an Actress who perfects the art of declamation, a Varnisher who imagines a new varnish, a Cook who finds a new sauce, a Dandy who invents a neat quip, to all the discoveries of the German & Italian Scholars whose works are going to waste in the study of Law & Antiquities.[32]

The trouble with public knowledge was that, by addressing new objects, it could threaten the foundations of the social order. Liqueurs were a commercial domain that particularly suffered from the perceived public danger posed by innovation. As early as 1685, less than a decade after the creation of their guild, the limonadiers were attacked for unbridled experimental innovation in the alimentary domain in a report to the Paris police. On "the pretext that [they] have the right . . . to retail brandy, lemonade & other well-known and widely used liqueurs in their shops," limonadiers were taking their guild legislation as a license

> to invent, compose & sell, & serve to drink to anyone of the Public, as they do every day, other extraordinary and unknown liqueurs which they compose as seems good to them, of rectified brandy, spices & other, more violent drugs, which render furious those who use them fre-

31. Smeaton 1957; *Avantcoureur* (1766): 10.

32. [Caraccioli 1757]: 41; see also Legrand d'Aussy 1783, 3:81. For positive renderings of French taste, cf. Poni 1998, 610, 615–20.

> quently, & which have been judged to be bad & very dangerous, after an infinity of unfortunate accidents.[33]

There were several well-reported cases of liqueur-related accidents, such as the death of one competitor in a drinking competition held in a Paris café in 1756, which involved consuming one pint each of the liqueurs Cinnamomum, white Escubac, and Crême des Barbades.[34]

The risky business was thus the production of *new* liqueurs. From the earliest origins of their guild, the limonadiers had been professional innovators. Both their liqueurs and their other wares, such as coffee, tea, and chocolate, were novelties unknown to earlier generations, raising questions about how a new substance could enter everyday diet. Debates over new forms of consumption centered less on the formation of social spaces for new stimulants than on the significance of novelty as evidence for disruptive and potentially damaging social change. More than many food products, liqueurs exemplified the dietary transformations of Parisians since the previous century and the concomitant alterations in their physical and moral nature, including the generalized ill health of city dwellers. As the journalist Louis-Sébastien Mercier put it in his contentious *Tableau de Paris* (Picture of Paris):

> Our ancestors went to the cabaret, and it is said that they preserved their good humor: we hardly dare go to the café; and the black water that one drinks there, is more harmful than the generous wine on which our fathers got drunk: sadness and caustic humor reign in these ice parlors, and a despondent tone is manifest on all sides: is it the new drink which has produced this change? In general, the coffee one takes there is bad and over-roasted; the lemonade dangerous; the liqueurs unhealthy and made with spirit of wine: but the good Parisian, who stops at appearances, drinks, devours and swallows it all.[35]

33. Delamare 1722–38, 3:810. This stress on innovation as a dangerous characteristic of guild production contrasts with portrayals of the guilds as ossified (Root 1994, 132; Coornaert 1968, 272–73).

34. *Annonces, Affiches et Avis Divers* 1756.48, 191, December 1. Cinnamomum, as the name suggests, utilized cinnamon; Escubac or Scubac contained numerous spices including saffron, vanilla, mace, angelica seed, and coriander; Crême des Barbades, very fashionable in the 1750s, combined the peels of citron and Portugal orange with mace, cinnamon, and clove. Déjean 1759, chaps. 53, 90, and 88; Legrand d'Aussy 1783, vol. 3, sec. 6. The marquis d'Argenson attributed the death of the cardinal de Soubise in 1756 to liqueur drinking (D'Argenson 1997, 292).

35. [Mercier] 1781, 90–91.

The limonadiers' products could serve as pivotal points in discussions about the changing boundary between luxury and necessity. Why was alimentary and gustatory innovation occurring? Was it a necessary coda to civilization's progress, or evidence of the process of decline and degeneration? Were people physically and morally transfigured by their habits? Mercier singled out foods, and particularly liqueurs and spices, as formative elements of the Parisian mind:

> The air of Paris, if I am not mistaken, must be a unique air. What substances flow together in such a small space! Paris can be considered like a large saucepan, in which meats, fruits, oils, wines, pepper, cinnamon, sugar, coffee, [and] the most distant productions come to mingle; and stomachs are the furnaces which decompose these ingredients. The most subtle part must be exhaled and incorporate itself in the air which one breathes. . . . How deeply the soil must be imbued with all the salts which nature had distributed to the four corners of the earth! From all these juices, assembled and concentrated in the liqueurs which flow into every household in great streams, which fill whole streets (such as the rue des Lombards), how should attenuated parts in the atmosphere not be the result, which compress the [mental] fiber more than any other part? Perhaps that is [the cause of] that lively, light sentiment which distinguishes the Parisian, that carelessness, that flowering of spirit which is particular to him.[36]

Though manufactured in Paris, compound liqueurs and the limonadiers' products in general, like the products of fashionable cuisine, depended on exotic ingredients incorporated into the body's fabric and excreted to form a veritable local atmosphere, a bath of the exotic through which Parisian bodies moved every day. In this sense, the spread of liqueurs and other prepared foods throughout urban society was far more dangerous than other forms of fashionable consumption, for they altered the character of those who consumed them by directly affecting both body and mind.[37] Through the habitual consumption of exotic foods, the mental state of the inhabitants of France's capital city was acquiring a foreign quality, especially as

36. Ibid., pt. 1, p. 2.

37. Both compound liqueurs and the "wine of manipulators and chemists," produced according to the principles of scientific oenology, were viewed as the products of artifice and adulteration (Lachiver 1988, 11; Dion 1959, 603–4; for the twentieth century, see Fischler 1993, 217–19).

the Galenic quality of heat in foods and drinks was still widely explained as a product of climatic heat. Heating foods and drinks like spices or liqueurs fueled the imagination, but endangered serious mental endeavor, physical strength, and political freedom.[38] These discussions of the implications of liqueurs for French society thus rehearsed contemporary debates over French national character and its relationships with knowledge and government, connecting the nation of France with the wider natural world through a politicized medical geography.

Liqueurs themselves could be taken both to epitomize the exercise of French génie and to promote and fashion it. In a world of *esprit*, the pursuit of forms of knowledge that required an active imagination, such as poetry or geometry, had been prized. But after 1750, just such knowledge projects—and the foods that fueled them—became a focus for criticism as the mental faculty of imagination came under renewed attack as a threat to reason.[39] Liqueurs, especially commercially produced liqueurs, represented the dangers of an unbridled imagination in more than one way. Their manufacturers, as I have argued, celebrated them as examples of a specifically French innovativeness, a demonstration of the pleasures procured through the cultivation of artifice (in the form of chemical expertise). But what critics disliked in this celebration of artificiality was the way it redefined public taste. In commodifying their product, liqueur manufacturers were effectively performing an impossible feat: proclaiming the consumption of liqueurs to be a mark of gustatory and, thus, social superiority, while at the same time making liqueurs accessible to all with the means to buy them, no matter how discriminating or well educated their palate. Some even made this democracy of taste into a selling point; in one of his advertisements, Sauvel noted of his liqueurs: "It is not necessary to wonder what flower, fruit or plant forms the base of his chemical extracts; the dullest nose, the coarsest palate can straightaway distinguish their smell & taste." But in such formulations, connoisseurship was inevitably realigned with consumers' spending power rather than their personal expertise, thus removing its power to sustain social hierarchies grounded in anything other than wealth.[40]

38. Montesquieu (1998, 1:360–82, esp. 363) stressed that the function of the senses was affected by climate, and even conducted an anatomical experiment on the tongue demonstrating that its sensibility declined in cold conditions. See also Mably 1763. On medical geography, see especially Rupke 2000.

39. On the eighteenth-century critique of imagination, see especially Daston 2005; Goldstein 2005, chap. 1.

40. *Année littéraire* 1764, 68–69. On the capacity of an order of distinction founded on sensuous signification for "referential aberration," see Mah 2003, 51–57. Jones's 1996 portrayal

Because the consumption of liqueurs was riven by internal contradictions in this way, their polite status came under fire as the social profile of the consuming public and the moral freight attached to self-pleasuring altered over the course of the century. By the 1770s the apothecary Jacques-François Demachy could observe: "However agreeable these Liqueurs may be, at the time of writing they have lost some of their value. I do not know what coarseness in the palates of persons who were formerly the most delicate, led them to be no more difficult than the common people. They take out of sensuality what the latter only use through need." Only neat brandy or Andaye brandy, scented with fennel, were, according to the apothecary, "served without formality on our best tables, & . . . drunk there without blushing." Demachy's treatise on liqueurs was, as will be shown below, a polemic against the rival guild of distillers, but his comments nonetheless reveal that as objects of polite knowledge, compound liqueurs were unstable; they exemplified the local, contingent, and variable status of fashion objects and luxury consumption. It is in this light that both historical accounts of liqueurs and contemporary critiques and defenses of them should be read.[41]

Compound liqueurs usually contained brandy, a byproduct of wine manufacture and a measure of the failure of winemaking, since vintners only distilled poor-quality wine that was unacceptable to the consumer market. According to Cullen, two peaks occurred in European brandy commerce during the eighteenth century, in the 1720s and the 1760s.[42] The eighteenth-century flowering of the compound spirituous liqueurs relates quite closely to this chronology: Oil of Venus, the first of the new class of oily liqueurs, appeared contemporaneously with the first peak, and the proliferation of newspaper advertisements for new liqueurs correlates with the second. The compound liqueurs would thus appear to have significance as meters of the flourishing of French commerce and invention in the eighteenth century. However, they have received scant attention from historians. Cullen touches only very briefly upon the flavored liqueurs, probably because the work of composition took place in the fashionable urban milieu, away from the provincial production of brandy. Delamain, in his history of cognac, treats liqueurs as a temporary folly, an aberration during the rise of the

of advertisers as constructing an egalitarian public sphere thus represents only one side of the debate over consumption, as Martin (2009, 57–60) argues.

41. Demachy 1775, 98. See also Le Maître de Claville 1740, cited in Dornier 1997, 177. For secondary accounts of the luxury debate in this period, cf. Coquery 1998, 96–105; Berg and Eger 2003a, 2003b; Berg 2005; Perrot 1995; Margairaz 1999; Berry 1994; Morize 1970; Shovlin 2006, chap. 1; Maza 2003, chap. 2.

42. Lachiver 1988, 270; Cullen 1998, 1, 21, 47.

cognac industry. For his part, Lachiver portrays the creation of a French market for brandies and liqueurs as a perversion of the natural French taste for wines, and it is thus important to him to present the market as one founded entirely by outside forces: Dutch entrepreneurs capitalized on wine shortages in bad years to drum up trade in brandy, first in the French seaports, and later in cities, including Paris.[43]

For modern commentators, liqueurs have appeared the very opposite of Frenchness; they are represented as foreign marketing ploys, which distracted from the truly French drink of wine, and perverted tastes through the addition of substances foreign both to France and to wine. These modern formulations recapitulate eighteenth-century aspersions on liqueurs as adulterated products, and so efface liqueurs as a historical subject despite their central role in debates over luxury, French character, and innovation in the middle decades of the century. For manufacturers, liqueur production signified the flowering of French artistic skill and the richness of French natural resources. Liqueurs, in fact, were the very stuff of modernity, and it was the French who excelled in their production. In an advertisement for a new peach wine, Lecouvreur, owner of the Grand Café on the Pont Saint-Michel, commented that the art of distillation "seems now to have been brought to its highest degree. Every day sees it making some new discovery." A practice indispensable to attracting and retaining fashionable clienteles—the production of novelty—was here presented as the epitome of perfection in the mechanical arts, a sign of the progress of civilization. Both in their guise as the subject of medical and social critiques of luxury consumption, and in their guise as the pinnacle of artisanal endeavor in France, liqueurs thus played a role in characterizations of French identity and inventiveness in the last decades of the Old Regime.[44]

Certainly the liqueurs seem a good indicator of the development of eighteenth-century French consumerism.[45] The reviewer of one domestic liqueur manual commented: "One hundred and fifty years ago, only a few domestic ratafias were known among liqueurs; nor had their use become habitual or general. Today we have spirituous liqueurs of all kinds, colors and countries, and there is hardly a person alive who does not permit himself the

43. Cullen (1998, 99–100) only considers the addition of sugar and coloring to brandy; see also Delamain 1935, 26–33; Lachiver 1988, 255–71; Dion 1959, chap. 13; Sournia 1990, chap. 2. More recent works such as Paul 1996 or Brennan 1997 pass over liqueurs altogether.

44. *Avantcoureur* (1769): 6. Legrand d'Aussy 1783, 3:84, claimed that Parisian liqueur production had replaced the import trade.

45. Cullen (1998, 53) suggests brandy consumption be taken as a meter of the amount of superfluous cash available for the purchase of luxury goods in a given society.

liberty of tasting them, even if only out of politeness." According to Déjean, distillation was one of the most extensive and essential branches of French commerce, and he referred to the "immense consumption" of brandy in the nation. A 1773 advertisement in the *Avantcoureur* for liqueurs manufactured by a Lorraine distiller, Cheneval, described liqueurs as being "of nearly universal usage," and added that "the torch of Chemistry has contributed not a little to enlightening the theory & practice of distillation, and to accelerating the progress of that art."[46] All these readings of the art of distillation seemed, on the face of it, to credit distillers with considerable abilities in the practice of chemistry. Chemistry was the basis for distillers' claims to innovate, the source for their claims to possess enlightenment, and the resource that enabled them to develop a market for this particular luxury food. The next part of this chapter will address the chemical production of liqueurs and brandies.

THE DELIGHTS OF DISTILLATION

Idle browsers through *Élémens de pharmacie*, a textbook penned by the master apothecary Antoine Baumé, might be forgiven for thinking they were reading a cookbook or domestic economy manual. Perhaps half of the receipts it contained were as much alimentary as medicinal: chocolate, quince jelly, cherry wine, and barley sugar jostled with pills, plasters, and electuaries. Baumé in fact defined confectionery and distillation as arts dependent upon pharmacy; both were prominent among the alimentary arts in being the subject of scientific interest during the course of the eighteenth century.[47] An innkeeper's son from Senlis, Baumé became a master apothecary in 1751, after four years at the Geoffroy family dispensary in Paris. A royal dispensation allowed him to enter the guild without having served a full apprenticeship. Baumé eventually established a wholesale trade supplying other apothecaries' shops and hospitals with medicaments and laboratory apparatus. The leading historian of French pharmacy termed this shop "the first true pharmaceutical drugstore."[48]

Like many pharmacists, Baumé did not make categorical distinctions between the medicinal and the alimentary in his business or his publications. This astute pharmaceutical businessman also sought to participate in

46. *Année littéraire* 1756, 316–25 (review of Poncelet 1755); 1773, 147–48; Déjean 1759, ix.

47. Baumé 1762, 446–49, 531–32, 547–55; also Gabriel Venel, "Chymie" (1753), in Diderot and d'Alembert 1751–77, 3:420.

48. See Bouvet 1937, 128, 190.

the learned life. The combination of commerce and science was not atypical of apothecaries in eighteenth-century Paris. Several prominent apothecaries even founded dynasties within the Académie Royale des Sciences: the Geoffroy family (under whom Baumé worked as an apprentice), or the Lémerys, father and son.[49] Baumé taught courses and pursued extensive research in chemistry over many years, finally achieving election to the Académie Royale des Sciences in 1772. He collaborated with Pierre-Joseph Macquer in the chemistry course that formed the basis of the latter's famous *Dictionnaire de Chymie*, published in 1766. The course featured in various newspapers, including the *Avantcoureur*, where Baumé publicized his own inventions alongside the food advertisers: processes for producing or improving plant starch, borax, and earthenware, and a new remedy, "Crystals of Venus."[50] Baumé thus spanned the divide between commercial pharmacy and academic chemistry, actively involving himself in the reform of many arts, especially those concerned with alimentation. His much-cited memoir on distillation was reprinted several times, and accounts of his experiments on distillation and confectionery appeared in the *Avantcoureur*. On behalf of the Paris municipal authorities, he analyzed imported wines that had been confiscated as falsified, in collaboration with Macquer. Within the chemical community, before judicial authority and in the press, Baumé thus counted as an expert on distillation.[51]

The concerns of distinct types of practitioners thus intersected in distillation. Baumé represented big pharmaceutical business in the eighteenth century and was also firmly located within the chemical networks of Old Regime France, thanks to his ties to Macquer and the Académie Royale des Sciences. At the same time, however, he was a successful urban merchant, like Sauvel or Déjean; both groups shared an artisanal origin and a place in the developing business world of eighteenth-century France. Both apothecaries and distillers innovated in three domains, the medicinal, alimentary, and cosmetic, and both relied on representations of their art as involving

49. Sturdy 1995.

50. *Avantcoureur* (1761): 675; (1763): 178; (1766): 296–98; (1768): 24–27, 309–12, 391–94. On Baumé's earlier pursuit of academic status, see Poirier 1996, 28; "Baumé," *Dictionary of Scientific Biography*, 1:527. Macquer and Baumé's course was taught annually for sixteen years, beginning in 1762, from a laboratory in the rue Saint-Denis; see Bouvet 1937, 88–89; Lehman 2007; on chemistry courses in the capital, see Bensaude-Vincent 2007. On Baumé's relations with Macquer, see Julien 1992; on Macquer, see Anderson 1984.

51. Baumé's memoir on distillation is Baumé 1778b, previously published as Baumé 1778a. It was the prize-winning essay submitted to the Société Libre d'Emulation for a competition on alembic design; see Dujardin 1900, 159–61; "Eaux distillées," [Macquer] 1766, 1:376; [Cossigny de Palma] 1782. On wine analysis, see *Avantcoureur* (1766): 40; (1767): 13.

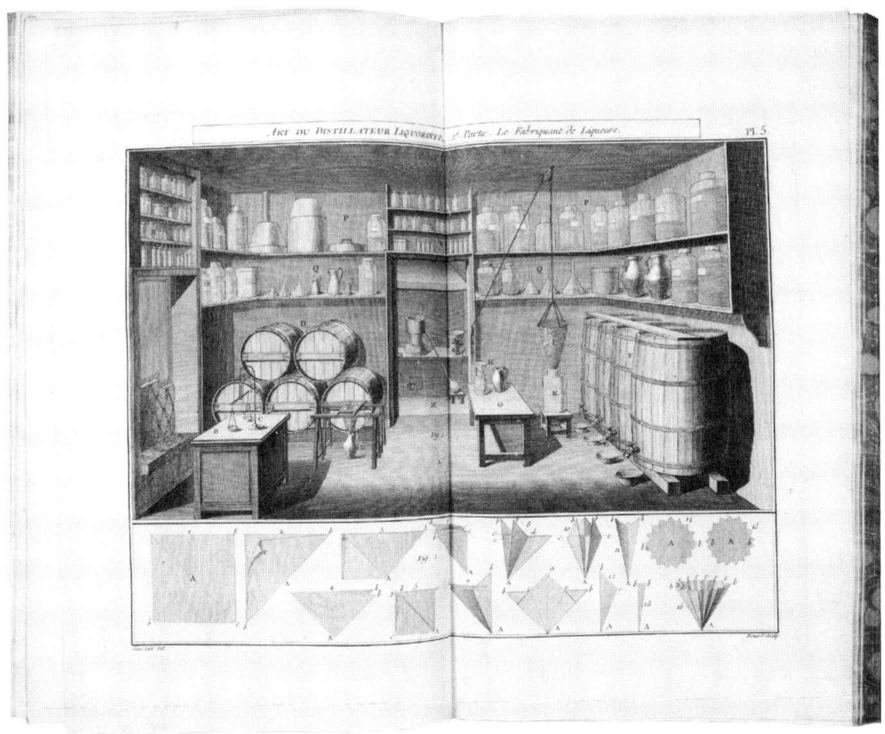

Figure 4.2. Jacques-François Demachy, *L'Art du distillateur liquoriste* (Paris, 1775), plate 5. A liquorist's workshop or laboratory. Copperplate engraving after Goussier. British Library.

expertise, ingenuity, and invention. Within that context, both groups also viewed themselves as engaged in scientific activity, albeit outside the well-studied confines of academies and scientific institutions. Like apothecaries, distillers worked in a laboratory, usually a room behind the public area of the café, where they prepared liqueurs of all kinds. The negotiations between apothecaries and distillers over chemistry, therefore, took the form of a debate over the boundaries between public and private knowledge and over the role of commercial involvement in attributions of expertise.[52]

When Baumé began his interventions in the distillers' trade, he was still a decade away from being an academician. In institutional, practical, social, and entrepreneurial terms, he was on a par with the liquorists in their labo-

52. Demachy 1775, 114. On the history of laboratories, see especially Crosland 2005; Klein 2005, 240–42.

ratories, and it would be wrong to represent the debate over distillation as a simple opposition between "artisans" and "scientific practitioners," as some uses of the term "scientific" for this period imply. In fact, the activities of apothecaries and distillers were hard to differentiate. Experimental protocol for distillation was discussed both in mid-century chemistry and pharmacy books and in didactic works written by distillers on their art. There were thus at least two categories of knowledgeable expert active in the realm of distillation, and both laid claim to public expertise through the medium of print—hence the importance of beginning this account in the world of commerce and publishing rather than in the scientific institution. A closer look at experimentation in this area will demonstrate that institutional chemists were actually less technically sophisticated than distillers, and that their publications provided formulaic and reductionist accounts of practice and instrumentation.[53]

Successful distillation demanded skill, expertise, and experience, as well as sophisticated chemical apparatus. Déjean's book, aimed at the apprentice distiller, describes an art subject to many difficulties, and with potentially deadly outcomes in the form of explosions and fires—problems edited out of other didactic works, such as Baumé's. Déjean defined distillation as the "art of extracting spirits from bodies." The insensible parts of a body were put into motion by heat, and the trapped spirits, freed of phlegm and earthy parts, were then able to volatilize. Déjean drew heavily on technical chemical terminology, referring to primary principles such as phlegm, fire, and earth. With his chemical explanation of distillation, he sought to confer epistemological nobility on the practice, which "may be worthy of the care & attention even of Savants." Distillation involved heating the substrate in an alembic, and allowing the vapor to rise up and escape the vessel by means of a spiral tube, the serpentine, which was cooled along its length. The condensate was collected in a receptacle attached to the serpentine. While most general chemical treatises represented three different arrangements of distillatory apparatus, Déjean described thirteen, all suited to particular products and employed by different artisanal groups. Each had its own name, taken from the particular alembic shape involved. Procedures ranged from distillation *per descensum*, used only by "Liquorist Distillers" to produce essences of clove, nutmeg, and mace, to the use of glass alembics in a bain-marie, which was restricted to the production of "quintessences,

53. As Lynn (2006, 149) notes, the status of savants was crucial in determining the type of audience from which they recruited legitimacy—academic, governmental, or public. However, status could alter, and a public lecturer become an academician, as with Baumé.

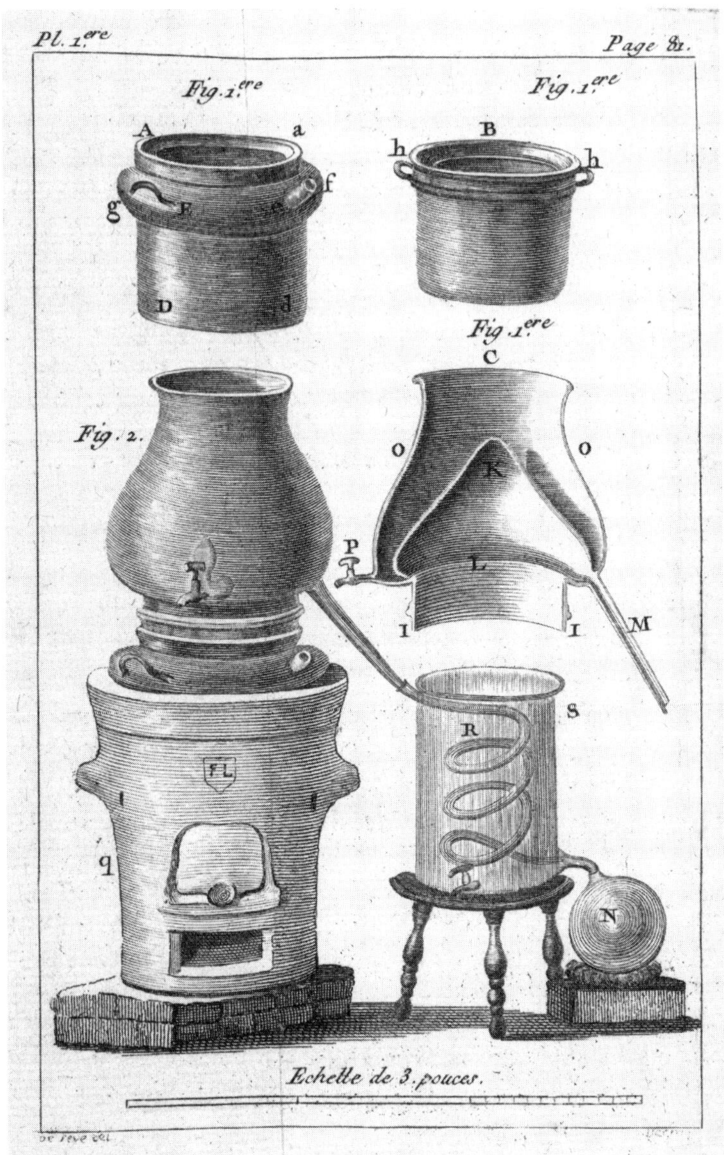

Figure 4.3. Antoine Baumé, *Elémens de pharmacie* (Paris: Veuve Damonneville, 1762), plate opp. p. 80. Distillatory apparatus. Copperplate engraving after a drawing by Jacques de Sève. Cambridge University Library.

simple waters, and anything of which one distils only a little at a time" because of their fragility. Twenty years of distilled practical knowledge allowed Déjean to recommend technical maneuvers for each raw material. His account, written for apprentices, acknowledged the technical complexity and multiple variants of distillation as used by the corporate distiller in a way which chemistry textbooks, written for polite audiences, failed to do.[54]

Conversely, Baumé's memoir on distillation systematically investigated all the apparatus used in distillation with the aim of *eliminating* variants. This was justified by theoretical claims about the processes occurring within the apparatus; for example, Baumé asserted that for greatest efficiency, the width of the alembic's neck should be correlated with the diameter of the still-head. Not surprisingly for a man who made his living as a bulk producer of chemicals, Baumé's primary goal was to speed up the distillation process, and he valued the cost of production and purity of the product over the careful manipulation of flavors and aromas.[55]

Spirit of wine was the twice-distilled product of vinous fermentation. The first distillation produced the more strongly flavored and aromatic brandy. In the manufacture of compound liqueurs, Paris-based distillers like Déjean or Sauvel might buy in supplies of brandy made by provincial distillers, though they also had the legal right to distill their own brandy from wine. The artisan combined brandy with a variety of flavoring and aromatic substances, and then redistilled the mixture to yield spirits, oils, and essences. Here, distillation thus served to extract and concentrate flavoring substances from individual herbs, spices, and fruits. Skill was deployed both in this technique and in the combination of different flavors so as to produce commercial liqueurs. The volumes produced by urban distillers were usually small.

For his part, Baumé criticized the distillers' techniques. Ordinary brandy was not adequate for making up liqueurs, nor ordinary spirit of wine for making remedies. He called on pharmacists to compose their liqueurs using only spirit of wine manufactured in their own shops, and not to buy product from other guilds. "It is on the purity of spirit of wine, & on the separation of its coarse essential oil, that the perfection of compound spirituous

54. Déjean 1759, 3, chap. 2. For some standard formulations of distillation, see, e.g., "Distillation," [Macquer] 1766, 1:354–57; Baumé 1773, 1:83–84, "De la Distillation." By contrast, a treatment of distillatory apparatus in the *Encyclopédie*, Venel 1763, only included stills invented by European academic chemists. Distillers were constantly reforming their apparatus; on the chemical practice and apparatus of distillation, see Dujardin 1900, chap. 9; Forbes 1948; Moran 2005.

55. Baumé 1778b. Baumé's reasoning did not go unchallenged even among academic distillers; see [Cossigny de Palma] 1782, 10–13.

waters, & table liqueurs, depends in large part." Baumé's was one of numerous contemporary suggestions for improving liqueurs, but it is typical of a trend running throughout his treatise, namely the denunciation of rival corporations as concerned with profit over quality. Claiming the epistemological high ground by promoting standardization was itself a competitive strategy: Baumé was asserting that his techniques for making liqueurs yielded better results for connoisseurs. In other words, he was entering the hotly contested arena of liqueur innovation.[56]

Macquer's *Dictionnaire de Chymie* was subtly keyed to Baumé's material technology. His article "Brandy" collapsed brandy into spirit of wine or "ardent spirit"—so that brandy, a substance in the production of which the distillers' guild specialized, ceased to exist in its own right. What the distillers produced in the single distillation of wine that yielded brandy, Macquer asserted, was merely an impure form of a different substance, spirit of wine: "It will be sensed that this [first] distillation, being very quick & poorly managed, can only provide a very impure spirit of wine, charged with many of the other principles of wine; thus brandy contains plenty of superfluous water, & oil of wine, substances totally foreign to spirit of wine, properly speaking." This ontology was not commercially neutral, for in the article "Rectification," describing the process of redistilling spirits to remove these impurities, Macquer referred to Baumé's invention of an experimental technique for rectifying large quantities at a time, thus saving fuel and labor. Since Baumé's speciality was precisely the manufacture of large quantities of chemical commodities, a call for pure spirit of wine as the substrate for chemical operations as well as medicinal, alimentary, and cosmetic production was an excellent advertisement for his enterprise.[57]

THE INFINITELY LIGHT

Even the matter theory underlying Baumé and Macquer's account of spirit of wine related subtly to Baumé's business enterprise. Macquer sought to represent spirit as a general substance produced by all forms of spirituous fermentation, not just wine. Again, we are apparently getting away from the commodity here toward a general chemical class of substances. There

56. Baumé 1762, 332–35. In suggesting that liqueurs be composed with spirit of wine instead of brandy, Baumé was probably echoing the academic apothecary Geoffroy 1741; see de Montigny 1770, 436. Déjean (1759, 75, 190) limited the use of spirit of wine to the manufacture of cordials and perfumes.

57. "Eau-de-vie," [Macquer] 1766, 1:396–97; "Rectification," [Macquer] 1766, 2:359–62.

were in fact two rival accounts of the nature of spirit of wine current in the European chemical community. In his *Elémens de chymie-pratique* (Elements of Practical Chymistry) of 1751, Macquer portrayed spirit of wine as a compound of oily, acidic, and aqueous principles. Stripping the spirit of its water rendered both its acidic and oily properties more evident. In this Macquer followed the German chemist Georg Stahl's account of spirit as a very attenuated and light oil, combined with water by the mediation of an acid. This oil, according to Stahl, was phlogiston itself. By 1766, however, Macquer's view had altered. Although not ruling out the possibility of discovering an oil principle, he now portrayed most oils as compound substances that emitted phlogiston during decomposition. Experiments by the Dutch physician Herman Boerhaave and the German chemist Johann Juncker had suggested that spirit was a simpler compound of phlogiston and water. After combustion, only the water remained behind. These medical chemists represented phlogiston and the fire principle as one and the same thing, a claim now strongly supported by Macquer, who remarked in his chemical dictionary that the combustion of spirit of wine contaminated with oil of wine—that substance which, as Baumé showed, it was so hard to remove from spirit of wine by distillation—might give misleading results favoring Stahl's interpretation.[58]

Macquer also described, in some detail, Baumé's well-known experiments in distilling ardent spirit with a concentrated acid. The aim was to strip the spirit of its water, thus getting closer, perhaps, to a substance that was pure fire. The acid first removed water in which the spirit was dissolved, then the water that was, as Macquer put it, "essential" to the spirit itself, that is, water held in combination with the fiery substance, that gave rise to the characteristic properties of spirit. The result was ether, a fluid more volatile and flammable than rectified spirit of wine, and which was completely consumed during combustion, leaving no residue. In a treatise on ether of 1757, Baumé claimed that the properties of ether placed it midway between oil and spirit of wine. Mercier's picture of a special, spirituous Parisian atmosphere was no figure of speech, for Baumé wrote in similar terms of the odor that dispersed from the shops of wine merchants and grocers: "it is Ether which the drinkers are forming naturally," he claimed.[59]

58."Esprit ardent," [Macquer] 1766, 1:407–14; "Huile," [Macquer] 1766, 574; Macquer 1751, quoted in Baumé 1757, 76.

59. "Ether," [Macquer 1766], 1:409, 455–63, gives Baumé's method for producing ether; see Baumé 1757, 104. Baumé's work was also discussed in "Vin, & Fermentation vineuse (Chimie)" (1765), in Diderot and d'Alembert 1851–77, 17:288. Ether was the subject of Baumé's first memoir to the Académie Royale des Sciences, read on June 11, 1755 (Baumé 1760).

From Baumé's treatise, it becomes clear that these experiments on spirit of wine were conducted as part of a wider inquiry among European chemists into the nature of fire. In his famous treatise on fire, Boerhaave had identified phlogiston in its purest state with "alkool," the most highly rectified form of spirit of wine, or in other words, with ether. This was the view toward which Macquer moved between the 1750s and the 1760s.[60] Although familiar with this explanation, which had its origins in the ether experimentation of German chemists during the 1730s, Baumé continued to defend Stahl's account of phlogiston as a compound between fire and vitrifiable earth. By 1773, in his *Chymie expérimentale et raisonnée* (Experimental and Reasoned Chymistry), he described phlogiston as a combustible compound able to exist in two forms, a carbonaceous solid or an oily vapor. He accorded it a prominent role in the natural economy: Nature, by means of vegetation, united fiery matter from the sun with vitrifiable earth in organized bodies, which were the only source for the distribution of fire, the principle of motion and transformation, throughout the natural world. The fire principle was thus now an entity distinct from phlogiston, a highly attenuated and possibly weightless body. Famously, Baumé claimed that during calcination phlogiston could combine with metals, while fire was evolved.[61]

Baumé and Macquer agreed on phlogiston's properties, if not its chemical nature. It had powerful effects on the nervous system, typified by toxic airs including sulphur vapor, coal gas, the vapors given off by fermenting bodies, and subterranean mephitical exhalations. Ether and spirit of wine shared the properties common to phlogistical substances in their extreme volatility and flammability, as well as their ability to affect the brain and nervous system, causing a range of dramatic effects, "drunkenness, dizziness, suffocation, unconsciousness & death." For Macquer, spirit of wine, "containing the phlogistical principle very developed, & almost free, acts

60. Both Macquer and Baumé referred to Boerhaave's experiments: [Macquer] 1766, 1:408; Baumé 1773, 1:128. The first French-language edition of Boerhaave's *Elementa chymiae* appeared in 1748, but more widely available were Boerhaave 1752 and 1754. On Boerhaave's view of ether as identical to the fire principle, see Heimann 1981, 70; though this view was contested ("Vin, & Fermentation vineuse (Chimie)" (1765), in Diderot and d'Alembert 1851–77, 17:286–87). On the chemical investigation of ethers, see Kopp 1843–45, 4:299–321; Priesner 1986, 130–32.

61. Baumé 1773:"Sur la matiere combustible dans l'état huileux" (1:125–38), "Sur le Phlogistique" (1:145–52); "Des propriétés du Phlogistique" (1:155–61). Thus, the view of Bensaude-Vincent and Stengers (1996, 58–61), that French chemists abolished Stahl's vitrifiable earth from phlogiston, identifying the latter with fire, is only partly correct; in fact, there appears to have been a change of emphasis in which fire became a main focus of experimental inquiry, with phlogiston taking various different forms.

on the nervous system, like all substances which contain a very attenuated and volatile flammable principle." Similarly, "in [ether's] quality as a very attenuated & very volatile flammable matter, it has a marked action on the nervous system, like all substances of this kind." Thus Macquer continued to view spirit as highly phlogistical.[62] In 1773 Baumé cited Boerhaave's definition of alcohol as the most highly rectified form of spirit of wine for the first time. Although he did not pass judgment upon Boerhaave's claim, it is likely that Baumé, like Macquer, had come to regard the fire principle as corresponding to the volatile part of spirit of wine and ether.[63] Thus, whether phlogiston was or was not identical with the fire principle, fire was for both chemists an important constituent of spirit and ether, reflecting a long tradition of identifying the two.

Ether should also be viewed as a simultaneously chemical and commercial object, despite the broader scientific claims made by Baumé and Macquer in their commentaries on it. Baumé's original experimentation had been prompted by the attempts of chemists at the Académie Royale des Sciences during the 1740s to develop methods of producing ether on a large scale. Following the success of the chemist Jean Hellot in replicating the German chemists' methods of ether production at the Académie Royale des Sciences in 1739, both Macquer and Baumé had pursued this avenue of inquiry, and in 1755 ether was the subject of Baumé's first memoir to the Académie. Not only was Baumé an acknowledged expert in the complex technical maneuvers involved in producing ether, he was also a bulk manufacturer of it, and one of the principal merchants selling it for medicinal purposes, which at this time were still very limited owing to the high cost of production. Its medicinal value stemmed from its effects on the nerves. Hoffman's celebrated anodyne mineral liqueur had been one of the first commercial uses of ether as a sedative and antispasmodic, but ether was now, Macquer claimed, far better known as a remedy, and was prescribed by many physicians. Ether thus linked Baumé's bid for academic recognition and his market entrepreneurialism.[64]

None of these transactions concerning purity, procedural improvement,

62. "Phlogistique," [Macquer] 1766, 2:222; 1:414, 463.

63. This has been almost the only aspect of Baumé's work discussed in histories of chemistry, where it has figured as an attempt to save the phenomenon of phlogiston against the attacks of Lavoisier. See, e.g., Legrand 1973; Flahaut 1995. But the picture is far more complex; see, among others, Allchin 1992; Musgrave 1976; Poirier 1996, 67, 113; Donovan 1993, 107–8, 295; Bensaude-Vincent 1993, 50, 268.

64. Baumé 1757, 2–20: "Discours historique sur l'Æther Vitriolique," presented to the Académie on June 28, 1755; [Macquer] 1766, 1:455–63.

and displays of technical expertise were truly distinct, therefore, from the strategies employed by distillers in their own self-promotion. The matter theory that underpinned experimentation on spirit was shared by Déjean, who drew upon Macquer's *Elémens de chymie* in defining spirit as the lightest part of bodies, by nature disposed to great mobility and possessing an igneous substance.[65] All three thus shared a single model of spirit. What differed was that, unlike Déjean and other distillers who wrote on the subject, Baumé and Macquer also sought to establish a general, systematic, and interconnected cosmology of principles through experimentation. Phlogiston, ether, and spirits were not only central to Baumé's cosmology, they were part of his self-presentation as experimenter and discoverer, which, like those of the distillers, sustained his commercial reputation. This goes some way toward explaining why he remained strongly committed to phlogiston and opposed Lavoisier's alternative chemistry. Here was a pharmacist perpetually at work with the fiery matter in the laboratory, and who had, moreover, made his scientific reputation through his daring tentatives in this regard.

THE EXPERIMENTAL BODY

Ontology was not the only domain in which the chemistry of distillers and pharmacists diverged. Déjean's suggested methods for judging brandy involved the distiller's own body as meter. Good brandy should be clean, sparkling, neither too white nor too cloudy; in a glass, it should bubble and foam, and each bubble should last for a long time. A small amount rubbed between the palms should quickly evaporate, and it should not soak into paper. The "best manner of judging it" was, however, by means of taste. The distiller should learn "to be a little gourmet in this respect: taste decides even better than all the above-mentioned proofs. Those who do not want to rely on themselves alone, or who mistrust their taste, can make use of the proofs above." For Déjean, noncorporeal proofs clearly took second place in a commercial world in which connoisseurship was central to the distiller's art, and not to possess connoisseurial skills was "shameful." According to the *Dictionnaire de Trévoux*, "gourmets" were "those who taste wine, and judge of its goodness and keeping qualities"; the gourmets numbered among the wider group of skilled connoisseurs.[66] The gourmet was thus in himself

65. Déjean 1759, 45, and chap. 15.

66. Quoted in Giaufret Colombani and Mascarello 1997, 60. The term included the *courtiers*, wine brokers who acted as intermediaries between rural vintners and urban wine merchants.

an accurate measure of the goodness and composition of distilled liqueurs. Indeed, this was the very model used by Voltaire to define the "man of taste" in the *Dictionnaire philosophique* in 1764: "The gourmet promptly senses and recognizes the mixing of two liqueurs. The man of taste, the connoisseur, will promptly notice the mixing of two styles." The polite connoisseur could be a liqueur expert, and vice versa.[67]

The connoisseur was perceived to possess a corporeal and gustatory expertise that the distiller needed to master; the most successful distiller was he who could match his sense of taste to that of his customers. Déjean advised the trainee distiller to emulate the connoisseur's palate, learning to discriminate between the different materials used in liqueur manufacture. His fellow distiller Dubuisson made the same argument: "only those who have received an exquisite taste from Nature . . . will be able to reform, enhance, prescribe & pronounce upon the just proportion of mixtures." Baumé's *Élémens de pharmacie* worked rather to efface connoisseurship. High-quality spirit of wine should be "perfectly pure," have "no foreign odor"; the "spirituous part should promptly evaporate, & leave neither humidity nor an odour approaching that of the phlegm of brandy": so far we are not too distant from Déjean's second-order criteria. But Baumé then added: "Perfectly rectified spirit of wine should not weigh more than six gross forty-eight grains in a bottle which holds an ounce of water, the temperature being ten degrees above freezing." This was typical of his redefinition of quality in terms of chemical purity and quantifiable criteria rather than corporeal skill, natural or acquired. Analysis and quantification were the primary devices for demonstrating the fundamental identity of different substances—in this case, fermented liqueurs. By such methods Baumé sought to pin down the elusive property of chemical identity and create a single category of flammable spirits. Here distillation was an instrument used for a purpose quite other than the production of new and pleasing tastes.[68] Writing of fermented liqueurs such as wine, beer, and cider, Baumé noted:

> All these flammable spirits are of the same nature, they have the same properties; they only differ among one another in the flavors & odors particular to each, & which cannot be entirely removed by reiterated

67. Voltaire, "Homme de goût," *Dictionnaire philosophique* (1764); quoted in Flandrin 1989, 300. Connoisseurs or gourmets were qualified to detect falsifications, a skill that fell within the remit of policing in early eighteenth-century France. See Giaufret Colombani and Mascarello 1997, 60–63; Sleeswijk 2004; "Gourmet," Furetière 1727, vol. 2, unpaginated.

68. Déjean 1759, 77–78, 252; Dubuisson 1779, 1:196–97; Baumé 1762, 332.

> rectifications; however, the thing may not be impossible. For example, I did everything possible to spirit of wine extracted from Spanish wine, to remove its odor & flavor, without succeeding: after a great number of rectifications carried out with different intermediaries, it retained the odor & flavor which are peculiar to that sort of wine.[69]

In fact, Baumé was *unable* to demonstrate experimentally that odor and flavor were accidental to flammable spirit, in other words to show that all flammable spirits were the same. Nevertheless, he continued to maintain that separating gustatory properties from spirit of wine was theoretically possible, thus upholding the possibility of a dissociation between connoisseurship and quality.

Baumé's search for chemical ways of measuring liqueur quality substituted the calibrated laboratory instrument for the gourmet's or connoisseur's body, transferring expertise from commercial distillers and their polite clientele to chemists. Toward the end of 1768 he announced his invention of an areometer, a device for measuring the spirit content of liqueurs by specific weight, in the pages of the *Avantcoureur*, explaining its design and calibration against water into which known weights of sea salt had been dissolved, and providing a table of figures against which the areometer's results could be compared at different temperatures. As in his interventions before the law courts concerning imported wines, Baumé played policeman to the distillation trade. However, Baumé's instrument worked best for his own product, purified spirit of wine. The sugar in flavored beverages containing brandy or spirit of wine, such as the compound liqueurs, affected the areometer's readings. The ideal of an instrumental control over the spirituous content of drinks remained elusive, but his experiments tied Baumé to an academic tradition half a century old. Etienne-François Geoffroy had written on brandy quality in the Académie Royale des Sciences's memoirs in 1718, while Etienne Mignot de Montigny published a design for an areometer in the same pages in 1768. The Société Royale des Sciences of Montpellier held a prize contest on the "best manner of determining the degree of spirituosity of brandies and spirits of wine," which was judged in 1773. The year after his final piece on the areometer appeared in the *Avantcoureur*, Baumé achieved election to the Académie Royale des Sciences.[70]

69. Baumé 1762, 326–27.

70. *Avantcoureur* (1768): 712–16, 793, 806–11; (1773): 38–41; [Cossigny de Palma] 1782, 46; Geoffroy 1741; de Montigny 1770. For Britain, see Ashworth 2001; Sumner 2001. I am grateful to Simon Schaffer for these references.

DISTILLATION, PUBLICATION, AND THE ACADEMY

Chemists in the eighteenth century struggled to raise the status of their discipline from a manual art to a philosophical science, as Meinel has shown. Others have argued that chemists were progressively liberating themselves from associations with pharmacy and other "dependent arts." Given that most individuals termed "chemists" in France before 1770 were apothecaries, such an enterprise was potentially jeopardized by commercial activities.[71] In their training and daily commercial practice, apothecaries used many chemical techniques, only some of which were shared with specialist distillers. Yet in their daily practice, distillers competed with apothecaries over chemical truth, disputing with them concerning apparatus, techniques, and the meaning of products. Distillers began to enter print culture from the 1750s onward in order to defend a chemical expertise increasingly central both to commercial production and to public self-promotion. This is evident in the readership for scientific and technical works, an unusual literary genre in that it united the worlds of commerce and polite consumption. Roche's study of book ownership shows that merchants and nobles formed largely distinct readerships. Nobles' tastes ran to literature, theology, and history—subjects largely neglected by merchants—but in the growing proportion of works on the sciences and mechanical arts in their libraries, they were converging on the merchants' favored reading material. Growing public interest in manufacturing technologies is evident from the many periodicals, dictionaries, encyclopedias, and manuals on individual arts or crafts penned in the second half of the century. As Robert Darnton once remarked of the *Encyclopédie*, "For every remark undercutting traditional orthodoxies, it contains thousands of words about grinding grain, manufacturing pins, and declining verbs."[72]

Déjean's publication of artisanal techniques, an unusual move, was part of an explicit attempt to reform and perfect the art of distillation before a polite audience familiar with chemistry. It inserted him within the program of useful, rational public knowledge pursued by the Académie Royale des Sciences. This was not least a response to a medical commonplace among his polite clientele—fostered by physicians—that liqueurs were dangerous to health.

71. See Meinel 1983. Crosland (1994, 109) claims that "the close association of chemistry with pharmacy was more a feature of seventeenth-century France," but numerous prominent chemists of the late eighteenth century were apothecaries. See also Court and Smeaton 1979; Simon 2005.

72. Roche 1978, 391; 1988, chap. 12; Lynn 2006, 7–12; Darnton 1984a, 191.

> Distillers had failed to destroy people's false opinion concerning the danger of using Liqueurs. The simple Exposition I give of composition and the various combinations, will undeceive many people who have believed up to now that [the consumption of Liqueurs] is pernicious; & they will consume them with that much more confidence, given that the mystery that had been affected [by distillers] was alarming to them in itself.

In using chemical terminology and theory, Déjean drew upon a literature familiar to his scientifically informed clientele. Most chemistry textbooks contained a discussion of distillation, and members of polite society had been attending the lecture courses of fashionable academic chemists since the start of the century. Distillers were thus well advised to keep abreast of chemical publications. Within the world of print, moreover, a distiller might engage on equal terms even with academic chemists. Déjean criticized the academician and celebrated public lecturer Nicolas Lémery for his account of the chemical operation occurring within part of the distillatory apparatus, the *vaisseau de rencontre*.[73]

Within the academy, the balance of power was different. Apothecaries had first entered the Académie Royale des Sciences in the late seventeenth century; distillers remained excluded. Membership of the academy conferred considerable social and political prestige. Particularly since the institution's reform in 1699, academicians had concerned themselves with the technical perfection of the arts, acting as consultants on various royal boards of commerce appointed to examine technical procedures and innovations in the mechanical arts. The academicians' communal publishing enterprise, the *Description des Arts et Métiers*, aimed to reform the mechanical arts throughout the kingdom by setting out the principles of their practice in print.[74] Such publications were often still interventions in corporative tussles, something generally overlooked in histories of eighteenth-century chemistry. This is clearly evident from the principal *Arts et Métiers* treatise on distillation, the official text on the subject produced under the academy's aegis. Where the series has received historical attention, it has been viewed as a neutral manifestation of Enlightenment enthusiasm for practical and utilitarian matters. *L'Art du Distillateur Liquoriste* (1775),

73. Déjean 1759, vol. 5, chaps. 11, 12 and 15. Lémery's *Cours de Chymie* (1675) went through eight editions during the eighteenth century. On the difference between defending scientific expertise in the academy and in the public domain, see especially Broman 1998, 135.

74. Hahn 1971; Garrigues 1998. On the "Description des Arts et Métiers" series, see Gillispie 1980, 344–56; Parker 1965, 92–93. In the terms of Klein (2003; 2005, 233–34), this is an example of "experimental history."

by Jacques-François Demachy, apothecary, satirist, and spy, attests to the contrary. Demachy became a master apothecary in 1761 and rose to prominence in the apothecaries' guild after the founding of the Collège de Pharmacie in 1777. But despite presenting himself on every possible occasion as a candidate for vacancies in the Académie Royale des Sciences's chemistry section, and giving several well-received memoirs at its meetings, Demachy would never be elected to the academy. His contribution to the *Descriptions des Arts et Métiers* series must be read as a product of the tangled interrelations between guild and academy as sites for the production of authoritative knowledge.[75]

Demachy began the foreword to his treatise by lamenting the resistance he had experienced from guild distillers to disclosing the secrets of their production. His account played on a well-rehearsed contemporary theme: the greed underlying secret artisanal knowledge, as opposed to the civic benefits of openness and publication. To support this dichotomy and suppress distillers' claims to epistemological equivalence, Demachy marginalized and localized the distillers' technical language by characterizing it as a "jargon" that needed translation into the "Chemists' terms that are generally known." All the technical terms used exclusively by distillers, but not by pharmacists, were printed in italics. Both distillers' experimental practice and their knowledge-claims fared similarly at the hands of the guild apothecary. Demachy indicated that the distillers' tinkerings with alembics and receptacles could not be counted as chemistry: only in fermentation did "the Liquorist become the imitator of the Chemist." This was a rank insult, since fermentation was the expert domain of vintners and brewers, not distillers. Moreover, Demachy split distillers into the large-scale producers, the "brandy boilers or burners," and a "species of *amphibious artisan* whose existence as a guild is extremely recent in France, and who titles himself *distiller liquorist*." Read in one way, Demachy's treatise is thus a sustained satire on the liquorists' claims to expertise and good taste. Among other things, he claimed that the class of compound liqueurs known as the

75. Demachy 1775. The Académie Royale des Sciences's minutes reveal that Demachy volunteered to write this account of the liquorist's trade and supplied the text in separate sections to the academy's reporters, Pierre-Joseph Macquer and Louis-Claude Cadet de Gassicourt (Académie des Sciences, "Procès-verbaux," XCII, August 21, 1773; XCIII, July 13, 1774). This strategy, elsewhere used to conceal the satirical purposes of a manuscript, here served to secure the academy's publishing privilege, tantamount to an official endorsement of the work. On Demachy, see Toraude's introduction to Demachy 1907, esp. chaps. 1 and 2; *Biographie Universelle*, 10:389–90. On his official guild involvement, see Bibliothèque Interuniversitaire de Pharmacie, Registre 39.

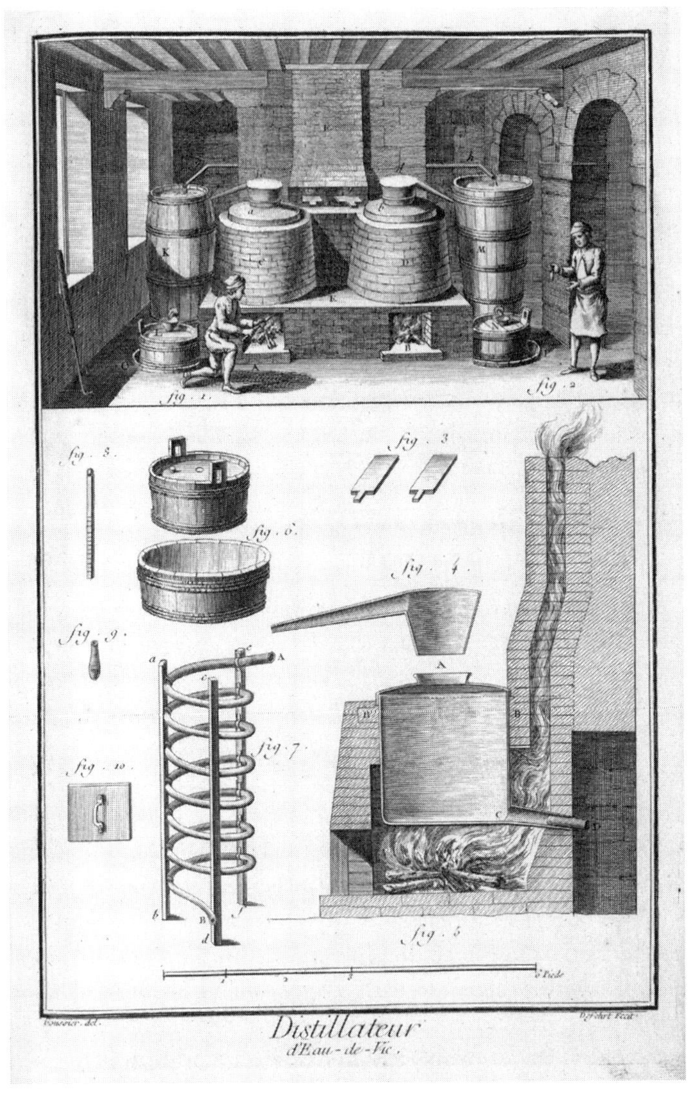

Figure 4.4. Denis Diderot and Jean Le Rond d'Alembert, eds., *Encyclopédie* (Paris: Briasson et al., 1763), 20:22. A large-scale brandy distillery of the sort becoming increasingly common in the second half of the eighteenth century. Copperplate engraving by Defehrt after Goussier. Cambridge University Library.

oils had been invented by an apprentice tanner, a snide reference to contemporary fears that spirits would harden and desensitize the palate and stomach.[76] The composition of liqueurs was nothing more than the skill of disguising revolting or flavorless ingredients through artifice:

> Star anise on its own smells of lice, [but] a little green aniseed saves it from this awkwardness; amber alone produces no odor, a little musk gives it the necessary relief; quince on its own is detestable, a little clove picks up & corrects its perfume; vanilla, associated with sugar, has more odor than if one did not grind it with that saline substance; the association of a little clove corrects the aftertaste of cinnamon; absinthe, even absinthe finds a place among the Liqueurs, as long as lemon zest associates itself with its aroma and makes its bitterness vanish. Could one believe, if Authors worthy of a certain confidence had not assured it to be so, that cow dung, combined with aromatics, could transform its disgusting denomination into the pompous title of Water of mille-fleurs? All this resembles in every point the Art of the Cook, seasoning saves all; & the great Lord who devoured his slippers made into a ragoût by his industrious Cook, proves that the Liquorist is an equal master of creating whatever illusion he wishes, as long as a fine palate, a discernment which is skilful in its mixtures, perhaps also a wise discretion, preside over his operations.[77]

Such attacks would not be taken lying down by the distillers. In 1779 François-René-André Dubuisson, a retired café proprietor, published his *Art du Distillateur* largely as a corrective to the presumption of Demachy in setting himself up as an authority on distillatory procedure. Dubuisson represented the peak of commercial prowess within the Paris distillers' guild. He had been a distiller since the early 1730s, and his business had flourished so well that by his retirement his son was running the Caveau, a celebrated café at the Palais Royal, while another cafetier, Cusin, was managing the café Dubuisson, formerly the still more famous Café Procope, opposite the Comédie Françoise. Both of these cafés served as outlets for the sale of Dubuisson's two-volume treatment of the distiller's art.[78]

76. Demachy 1775, 2, 9, 88, 56, 96–97. Original emphasis. The purported name of this inventor, "Bouillerot," was itself an insulting reference to a vulgar name for a distiller, bouilleur.

77. Demachy 1775, 68. The method for making water of mille-fleurs from cow manure and urine was described in Malouin 1750, 1:108–11; it was a purgative.

78. Dubuisson 1779: "Avant-propos," I. On Dubuisson's cafés, see Fosca 1934, 36; Isherwood 1986, 241. There was another, more famous Caveau: see Level 1988. A royal ruling of

Dubuisson's strategy for discrediting Demachy bears careful examination, since it challenges our usual assumptions about the history of chemistry. He invoked the twin authorities of the Académie Royale des Sciences and the medical faculty as supreme arbiters in the dispute. For Dubuisson, Demachy was a representative of the apothecaries' guild, not of the Académie Royale des Sciences. Indeed, he warned the academy that "that illustrious Company" was at risk of being swindled by Demachy's illegitimate claims to distillatory expertise. Placing himself on an epistemological par with the likes of Demachy, Dubuisson left the reader in no doubt that Demachy's "official" text was in fact just another tactic in the ongoing commercial war between the apothecaries and the distillers. Like Déjean, Dubuisson laid claim to chemical expertise: he termed the limonadier a "Chemist-Distiller" and claimed to have instructed himself, early in his career, by consulting leading chemical and medical publications "to find the principles which were necessary to direct my operations in such a manner as to obtain products capable of fulfilling the [medical] indications which might appear." His authority of first resort had been Nicolas Lémery, "because [in the 1730s] that Author still enjoyed the titles of Restorer of Chemistry in France, & Reformer of Pharmacy in the Capital."[79]

Lémery's chemical project had coupled a concern with the manipulation of material substances with a Paracelsian heritage that centered on the extraction of essences from natural bodies. Iatrochemists argued that essences or spirits, purified of their coarse and earthy parts, penetrated the body's fabric more readily to work their specific effects. Dubuisson's account of distillation adopted this model to legitimate his claims for the healthiness of his products. Well-made liqueurs "could not only create an agreeable sensation in the organs of the human body, but were also able to reestablish, & maintain movement & the circulation of our liquors, in the equilibrium which suits the state of health." Thus healthiness was an outcome of the distiller's skill in extracting the most volatile or spirituous part of aromatic substances, known as the spiritus rector. In Dubuisson's hands, distillation was a tool for separating the spiritus rector from "acrid & bitter salts" binding it in plant materials, using different techniques for different aromatics, including infusion, dilution and the addition of sugar. The artisan distiller's domain of expertise lay in his ability to discover, in each case, "sufficient

1777 had revoked the publishing monopoly held by the guild of Paris libraires, allowing Dubuisson to publish his book himself, a common strategy for extrainstitutional scientific practitioners in the last decade of the Old Regime. See Hesse 1989, 69–97; Censer and Popkin 1987.

79. Dubuisson 1779, "Avant-Propos"; 1:ix.

means to divest himself of the harmful parts, & . . . to appropriate those which are more suitable to fulfil his goals."[80]

This program would inform all of Dubuisson's experimentation, presented as a way of raising the standards of liqueur manufacture. In one set of experiments he replicated procedures described by medieval iatrochemists in which brandy was distilled six times before being set to circulate in a closed still for many weeks. The result was a brandy that became stronger but also purer, losing the "heterogeneous parts" of wine, its salts, acid, and oil. Dubuisson wholeheartedly agreed with Baumé that ordinary brandy was inadequate for manufacturing quality liqueurs. However, in his view, the highly rectified spirit produced by the big distillers produced a harsh, burning product, only suitable for "the fabrication of varnish," while his own lengthy manufacturing process generated a brandy that was both more flavorsome and "more spirituous than it had been before having undergone these different operations." Dubuisson's definition of a pure, high-quality brandy or spirit of wine was thus quite different from that of Baumé. It did not depend on spirit content as measurable by an instrument, nor was a tasteless and odorless spirit the ultimate goal of rectification; rather, rectification served to improve and even intensify flavor. Dubuisson's experimentation was thus entirely in keeping with the program of enhancing and managing flavors typical of the aims of guild liquorists at this time.[81]

The prevailing view in histories of French medical practice is that over the course of the eighteenth century pharmacists and physicians increasingly united to suppress all other traders in medicinal substances.[82] Dubuisson's appeal to the physicians nearly, if not quite, reversed the trend. For Dubuisson, distillation created pleasurable products, but it was also a technique that allowed the medicinal components of plants to be isolated and could thus facilitate more precise medical intervention. He portrayed himself as an ally of physicians, improving artisanal techniques for the benefit of public health. Citing both chemical publications on distillation and medical treatises on materia medica and dietetics, he classified his li-

80. Ibid., 1:v, 50, 175–76. The name "spiritus rector" was also used by chemists; see "Esprit recteur," [Macquer] 1766, 1:420–22; Baumé 1762, 302. The term "quintessence," in contemporary distillers' parlance, described a concentrated extract of the aromatic parts of a body. In Paracelsian medicine it had referred to the fifth element, or the ether. Aroma was still identified by many French chemists with the spirituous or volatile principle, the Paracelsian sulphur. See Déjean 1759, 140–41; Brock 1992, 45–46.

81. Dubuisson 1779, 1:126, 97. "Varnish" was the name under which brandies doped with resin had famously been smuggled into the city of Paris toll free in the 1760s. See de Montigny 1770, 439.

82. Ramsey 1988; Brockliss and Jones 1997, esp introduction.

queurs in the language of humoral medicine. That his advances were not rebuffed by physicians is clear from the medical reception of his book. The specialist medical periodical *Gazette de Santé* received it warmly:

> Someone has already said that the art of poisoning oneself agreeably had been reduced to principles. This reproach only refers to the abuse that is made of certain liqueurs. But when one only has in view the manner of perfecting or correcting, not only the spirituous liqueurs, but the majority of water-based drinks whose use is consecrated by habit & taste; then it is to render an evident service to the public to show them these means of perfection. This is the merit of the work we announce. It is the fruit of long experience, carried out in the town where the best Judges and those with the most delicate palates reside & by an Artisan whose reputation has survived longest, & still survives.[83]

At the Société Royale de Médecine, a presentation copy from the author was reviewed with great interest. In an unusually lengthy report, the society's two commissioners, Cornet and Caille, assented not only to distillation's status as a branch of chemistry, but also to its medicinal role, proposing the distillers' guild as, in effect, a *fourth* Parisian medical corporation, to rank alongside the apothecaries. Though this suggestion was erased from the final version of Cornet and Caille's report, in their first draft they enumerated legal reforms akin to those implemented in the recent reform of the apothecaries' guild, including inspection visits by physicians, public lecture courses, and a new criterion for entry to the guild, consisting of an examination, to be carried out before a consultant chemist or physician appointed by the lieutenant général de police. All these would, the commissioners wrote, prevent unchecked fraudulence and ignorance among the limonadiers from posing a threat to public health.[84] Elevating the scientific and medical institutions to the status of epistemological authorities thus facilitated Dubuisson's attempt to lay claim to a scientific status equal to that held by apothecaries. Where Baumé and other pharmacists, such as Gabriel Venel, author of the article "Chymie" in the *Encyclopédie*, defined distillation as dependent upon pharmacy, Dubuisson defined *both* pharmacy and

83. Review of Dubuisson 1779, *Gazette de Santé* 1780, 104–5 (June 25). On the *Gazette*, see Sgard 1991, I, entry 544; on medical journalism, see Delaunay 1906, chap. 14.

84. Bibliothèque de l'Académie Nationale de Médecine, fonds Société Royale de Médecine, ms. 98, dossier 20, pièce 1: Report by Cornet and Caille, March 21, 1780. On the reform of the apothecaries' guild and the foundation of the Société Royale de Médecine, see Gillispie 1980, 194–212.

distillation as theoretically underpinned by chemistry (the preserve of the Académie Royale des Sciences), and practically of service to medicine (the preserve of the Paris medical faculty and the Société Royale de Médecine). Thus the agendas, procedures, and authority claims of apothecary chemists were freely contested by rival guild members who also laid claim to the chemical heritage of the academy, and who did not accord innate epistemological superiority to the apothecaries.

The issues that were most controversial in commercial chemistry touched on matters that fitted best within Lémery's program for chemical inquiry. In rejecting Demachy's right to comment on distillation, Dubuisson construed academic chemistry to mean this longer-term project of analysis and extraction, which remained the primary published evidence of academic interest in distillation. New editions of Lémery's work throughout the century seemed to confirm the enduring importance of this program for chemical research. In this sense the program of extraction of essences remained alive outside the academy, even though academic chemists had switched as early as the 1710s to a more systematic inquiry into the general principles of chemical activity and the relations between different categories of chemical substances.[85] Dubuisson was representative of distillation's development into an increasingly technically and theoretically complex activity "in which, beside the old-fashioned distiller, more sophisticated distillers worked consciously to a higher standard." But he simultaneously opposed the conversion of distilling into a bulk industry, a phenomenon acknowledged by a new entry in the 1798 edition of the *Dictionnaire de l'Académie Française*: "Distillery," referring to a "place where one carries out distillations on the large scale." Dubuisson explicitly contrasted the luxury distiller of the Paris café with "our Gargotier-Liqueur-Makers," who supplied an impure brandy charged with "heterogeneous bodies" to make liqueurs that "have been imagined purely to satisfy the disordered appetite of the people." In effect, Dubuisson distanced compound liqueurs from the problem of public drunkenness on the basis of social distinction, appealing to the existence of precisely the sort of aspirational clientele for luxury goods that was fashioned in advertisements for prepared foods.[86]

Even though Déjean and Dubuisson accounted themselves chemical experts, only the names of Demachy and Baumé figure in histories of chemistry. In law, however, neither group had a prerogative where chemical prepa-

85. See especially Kim 2003, chap. 2; Klein 1996, 275–76; Holmes 1989, 61–83.

86. Cullen 1998, 100; Académie Françoise 1798, 1:432; Dubuisson 1779, 1:24. A gargotier was the owner of a cheap eaterie. On public drunkenness, see below, this chapter.

rations were concerned. Rather, these fell under the corporate privilege of a tiny guild, the distillateurs d'eaux-fortes. By a royal ruling of May 1746, the limonadiers were banned from "meddling in any of the operations belonging to the art of chemistry," as Baumé put it.[87] The apothecaries' claims to chemical superiority would also be undermined by the attempts of Lavoisier and his followers to ally chemistry with experimental natural philosophy rather than pharmacy. Commercial pharmacy remained distinct from both institutional chemistry and the alimentary trades to the Revolution and beyond.[88] The struggle over the nature and purpose of distillation in the second half of the eighteenth century can be viewed as a product of the attempts of practitioners of different arts to redefine their domain of expertise over certain skills and commodities.

HISTORIES OF PLEASURABLE MATTER

In his well-known history of stimulants in modern Europe, Wolfgang Schivelbusch proposes that coffee rose to prominence among the European elite because it denoted industriousness. For this reason, he argues, it was more important in those nations in which the Protestant work ethic reigned; Catholic, absolutist, and aristocratic cultures such as Spain or Austria favored chocolate. Schivelbusch's argument leaves France, perhaps the most famous nation of European coffee drinkers, in an anomalous position. It also flies in the face of the fact that tea, rather than coffee, dominated the eighteenth-century English market. The mapping of cultural styles onto particular comestibles in this way produces an account that is too coarse-grained to accommodate such anomalies.[89] Moreover, anachronistic categories such as "alcohol" or "stimulants" beg the question of what contemporaries experienced when consuming such substances, how they explained those effects, and how they themselves classified ingesta. Notwithstanding these basic difficulties, the principle of Schivelbusch's inquiry—that one ingestum can stand for a single worldview, emerging out of the concerns of a homogeneous culture—has lately assumed prominence as a model for writing histories of food and drugs, and in the substantial literature on the temperance

87. Antoine Baumé,"Distillateur," [Macquer] 1766–67, 1:500. The distillateurs d'eaux-fortes' struggles with both the apothecaries and the limonadiers are discussed in Scagliola 1943, 72–94; see also Bibliothèque Interuniversitaire de Pharmacie, registre 38, f°s. 5 r°.–9 r°. Their principal artisanal domain was the production of strong acids for assaying.

88. See Court and Smeaton 1979; Simon 2005; Levere 1994, chap. 4. For a comparable account for the case of cosmetics, see Lanoë 2008a–b.

89. Schivelbusch 1992, 38. On tea in Britain, see especially Ellis 2004a, 208–9.

movement.[90] Such claims, however, rest on two unexamined assumptions: that accounts of any foodstuff can be univocal to the extent that Schivelbusch's analysis demands, and that the composition and effects of foods and drinks, as understood in the eighteenth century, translate readily into today's categories. Neither of these premises bears close scrutiny. As the case of liqueurs reveals, alcohol and stimulants are not stable historical categories that can provide explanatory foundations for the history of food.

Historians of the temperance movement often construe their subject in terms of alcoholic consumption in the modern sense, attending little to eighteenth-century chemical and consumer categories. The familiar Anglocentric model, in which temperance was a religious movement aimed at repressing unruly behavior among the poor, provides an inadequate explanation for French debates over the polite consumption of liqueurs and spirits.[91] There were three ways in which compound liqueurs drew criticism in France. First, they were often made with brandy, and therefore figured in a critique of drunkenness that gained ground in the later eighteenth century. Second, they were subject to a medical critique of the inflammatory effect of certain foodstuffs, primarily the productions of hotter climates, such as spices. Third, as commodities sold for profit by experts in the manipulation of tastes, liqueurs were a target for attacks against the commercialization of food production. There was thus no single overarching French discourse of "temperance" or "anti-alcoholism." According to the *Encyclopédie*, "intemperance" was any form of alimentary overindulgence and was not limited to drinking, let alone to the consumption of alcoholic drinks.[92]

"Alcohol" was not, therefore, a stable category of ingestum throughout

90. See, for example, Hobhouse 1985, pt. 3; Walvin 1997. For approaches to "stimulants" as an historical category, see also Matthee 1985; Camporesi 1988; 1994; Rudgley 1993, introduction; Davenport-Hines 2002, chaps. 1–3; Walvin 1997, chap. 12; Porter and Teich 1985; Courtwright 2001; Sournia 1990; Blocker and Warsh 1994; Nahoum-Grappe 1991. A more fruitful approach, which identifies stimulation as merely one of several possible social and corporeal functions of pleasurable substances, is offered in Sandgruber 1994. The German term "Genußmittel" used here provides a more useful analytical category than the English "stimulants," though it is poorly translated by the unwieldy "recreational substances." See also Merki 2003; Onfray 1991.

91. Most studies concern Britain, e.g., Halimi 1988; Clark 1988; Porter 1985. In France, too, public disorder and drunkenness were blamed on the consumption of brandy by the poor. Sournia (1990, chap. 3) explains the comparatively low-key French temperance movement by claiming that spirit drinking was uncommon, an impression no doubt gleaned from French-language histories of winemaking. This essay, together with Cullen 1998, chap. 5, and Brennan 1988, contradicts that assumption.

92. See de Jaucourt 1765a. Sournia (1990, 37) notes this different usage, but explains it as a product of contemporary ignorance.

the early modern period, as historians of temperance have implicitly assumed. As late as the 1760s, the term still primarily referred to a chemical procedure for purification, or else to the quality of extreme subtlety, not to any sort of beverage. Even if one identifies spirit of wine with "alcohol," as most historians have, it is important to recognize that "spirit of wine" was an equivocal experimental object among chemical practitioners. There could be no general agreement about classifications of individual foods based on their chemical composition; even for Macquer or Baumé, spirits were one manifestation of a larger category of substances troubling the nerves and brain. At this time, therefore, there was a gap between the chemical account of spirits and the social critique that has implicitly been taken as founded on it.[93]

Nor did critiques of liqueurs necessarily relate to whether or not they contained spirit of wine. In many early eighteenth-century writings, liqueurs were allied not with wine but with a range of foods and beverages especially associated with the expertise of cooks and limonadiers. In this formulation, the limonadiers' sphere of expertise was primarily the manipulation of flavors and aromas, not of spirit of wine. Distillation using brandy or spirit of wine was merely one of several techniques employed by limonadiers for liberating the spiritus rector from aromatics. Other methods, specific to the substance being worked upon, relied upon water, heat, maceration, infusion, or grinding. This formulation created a category for liqueurs that encompassed coffee, tea, and chocolate as well as brandy, spirituous, and nonspirituous beverages. The polemical importance of that category is revealed by the fact that all the fashionable drinks made and sold by distillers, not merely the "alcoholic" ones, came under attack. Thus, the Paris medical faculty physician François Thierry classed tea, coffee, and chocolate among the liqueurs in the category of "slow, but universal poisons." His erstwhile colleague Etienne-Louis Geoffroy allied liqueurs as often with coffee or with spiced and salty dishes as with wine. Like numerous contemporaries, he grouped these particular foods and drinks together as heating substances, capable of engendering fever and inflammation if misused. In 1775 Demachy defined the limonadier as "by condition a vendor of all kinds of hot Liqueurs, of all those that are prepared with fruit juices & sugar and generally

93. For definitions of "alcohol," see [Hecquet] 1710a, vol. 1: "Explication de quelques termes de médecine," unpaginated; [Macquer] 1766, 1:10; Dujardin 1900, chap. 2; Giaufret Colombani and Mascarello 1997, 57. In "Alkool" (1751) it is noted, however, that the term was almost exclusively applied to highly rectified spirit of wine (Diderot and d'Alembert 1751–77, 1:277).

known under the name of *cold Liqueurs* & *Ices*, & lastly distilling, making & selling strong Liqueurs from Brandy to the most compound Liqueur." In Galenic medical terms, liqueurs were not distinct from other heating foods, and "spirit" denoted all volatile and aromatic parts of foods. Furthermore, each foodstuff had a distinct effect on the constitution, although medical practitioners rarely agreed about what these effects were. Physicians and apothecaries were themselves implicated in the liqueur trade, for they participated in the invention of new liqueurs, in technical reforms of distillation, and, not least, in the tasteful consumption of luxury goods.[94] The well-established medical literature attacking the unhealthiness of liqueurs is thus misinterpreted when read exclusively as an attack on alcohol drinking.

Liqueurs could also be critiqued in their role as symbols of artistic progress and artisanal expertise. In his health manual, the abbé Jacquin identified two kinds of spirituous liqueurs, "bourgeois" and "distilled." The former, less harmful, were composed by infusion, while the latter were fermented in wine or brandy, then extracted with an alembic. Jacquin warned in equal measure against distilled liqueurs and nonfermented liqueurs such as barley water or lemonade. Distilled liqueurs were "so many slow poisons, which erode health: they carry fire into our viscera & our vessels, which desiccates the vital organs, & destroys the springs which make the animal economy work," but nonfermented liqueurs upset the digestion by cooling the stomach excessively. Only the bourgeois or infusion liqueurs were spared, even though they too contained spirits. Jacquin's criticism was thus principally directed against *commercial* production, for it singled out the cluster of goods made and sold by the limonadiers, together with their guild-specific practice of distillation. As the alembic became the symbol of artificial intervention in drinks, so liqueurs epitomized contemporary fears about the denaturing of modern French bodies. Ending his didactic treatise with an account of the infusion liqueurs, Déjean noted that "the foremost" reason for studying their preparation was "that it is necessary to satisfy many people who are very convinced that anything which has passed through an Alembic is prejudicial to health, & who will never be disabused of their viewpoint [*esprit*]."[95]

The work of chemists like Baumé was central to the invention of alco-

94. Dubuisson 1779, vol. 1, chap. 1; Thierry 1755, chap. 7; Geoffroy 1997, passim; Demachy 1775, 109.

95. Jacquin 1762, 194–97; Déjean 1759, 458–59. The success of Poncelet 1755 attests to the flourishing of domestic liqueur production alongside the commercial market; compare, for England, Wilson 2006, esp. 230–43; Burnett 1999, chap. 5; 2000.

hol as a social and chemical category. Baumé's writings redefined spirituous liqueurs as a chemically homogeneous class of fluids, united by containing the same chemical substance, "alcohol." This maneuver was facilitated by importing Boerhaave's redefinition of alcohol as "the purest form of the flammable principle reduced to its greatest degree of simplicity" into late-eighteenth-century chemistry.[96] To replace a myriad spirituous drinks with a single category of spirit, identical in all fermented substances, which varied in (measurable) degree of purity, was to make an important epistemological assertion. In effect, spirit, a chemical substance, was elided with alcohol, formerly a value (purity) and a procedure (rectification). Such tautologous definitions explained alcohol as a substance that could be identified through the chemical procedures by which it was produced. Formulations of this sort aligned with a medical and moral literature that joined wine and liqueurs in critiques of drunkenness and blamed their consumption for numerous diseases.[97] Only in this literature can we find the temperance debate presented in familiar form, and identifiable with modern concepts of "alcohol."

Last, there was the way in which brandy related to the concerns of government. Academicians' involvement in the development and calibration of areometers was prompted by the attempts of royal, municipal, and fiscal authorities to generate absolute quantitative measures of the strength of brandy as a reliable means of combating smuggling. In the fiscal world, the 1760s marked the moment at which tax farmers and law courts abandoned brandy, a highly variable product, as the basic unit of taxation. The reification of the chemical entity of spirit, and later alcohol, provided the bases for a more homogeneous measure of the strength of drinks, and thus permitted greater fiscal control.[98] As legal definitions of strength became increasingly identified with metrological criteria, so legal definitions of goodness diverged from those used by the distillers. Criteria such as flavor could only remain primary for Parisian distillers, who were entitled to manufacture their own brandy within the city walls, and who were not liable for the customs charges paid by their corporate rivals, the grocers, in importing brandy

96. Baumé 1773, 1:cxlviij: "Vocabulaire."

97. Plagnol-Diéval 1997, 248. [Macquer] (1766, 2:642–43) also allied wine with brandy in attacking excess consumption.

98. See especially de Montigny 1770. On de Montigny as an academician, see Sturdy 1995, 383, 428; Hahn 1971, 119. His status as a trésorier de France would have given him a familiarity with taxation issues, while rendering him independent of one side in the dispute, the tax farmers (Durand 1971, esp. 48–50, 300; Bosher 1970, 90–91, 95). On the areometer in commerce, see Bensaude-Vincent 2000, 160–63.

from provincial distillers. Though academic chemists criticized distillers (as we have seen) for using once-distilled brandy in their liqueurs, Dubuisson denied outright that any distiller other than the gargotiers would make use of unrefined once-distilled brandy. He also insisted that a pure and properly rectified spirit of wine contained not only flavor, odor, and color but also water.[99] The academicians thus persistently downplayed the complexity and multifariousness of distillers' apparatus and practice, and they did so in the context of conflicts over legal standards that between the 1740s and the 1760s gradually shifted the scene of debate from the connoisseur's concern with taste to the assayer's reliance on quantifiability.

We are thus faced with several overlapping frameworks for classifying and ascribing value to liqueurs, considered as the objects of knowledge. As an alternative both to "stimulant histories" that chart the activities of potent substances through human history, and the linear narratives of commodity history that presume that things have a continuous and uninterrupted historical identity, I want to invoke certain models drawn from anthropology and sociology. These rest on the shared assumption that the meaning of things lies in their local use, and that their history can be written as a collection of such local appropriations, which may or may not be compatible, interchangeable, and comparable. It may thus result that a single material object or substance possesses completely distinct meanings and uses in different hands. For this reason, it behoves us as historians to scrutinize the strictly local uses of foods before we embark on grand narratives that presume their historical continuity. One principal methodological problem in the study of material substances concerns the reconciliation of the presumed identity of a given substance in space and time, and the actual variety of appropriations of that substance in different cultural settings. An approach that is beginning to emerge as an important alternative to "commodity biography" in the old style is actor-network theory, explored by Robert Foster in his outstanding anthropological study of the relationship between the local and global meanings of Coca-Cola.[100]

As this chapter has shown, liqueurs, spirits, and "alcohol" circulated within and between domains of epistemological possession, and between the realms of learning and commerce. The actor-network theorist Bruno Latour deploys Michel Serres's account of the "quasi-object" to explain how material objects can inhabit more than one social world of meaning and use at once, and how they can appear stable while transforming and being

99. Dubuisson 1779, 24–27.
100. Foster 2008, chap. 1; see also Spary 2005.

transformed: "A quasi-object should be thought of as a moving actant that transforms those which do the moving because they transform the moving object. When the token remains stable or when the movers are kept intact, these are exceptional circumstances which have to be accounted for." Contestations over the cultural role and significance of material substances show that the moments when stability of meaning or identity is attained are the result of agency, not the natural state of things. With this chapter I have eschewed the attempt to impose a singular historical meaning upon liqueurs, which were troublesome precisely because they eluded such categorizations for so long; where scientific explanation was concerned, they were matter in the wrong place. It is in investigating their parallel deployment by different actors in distinct epistemological projects relating to luxury and taste, iatrochemical and other models of health, that we can understand why liqueurs became the focus of debates over what it meant to be enlightened.[101]

I have also endeavored to avoid a second teleological trap, the foreknowledge of alcohol's emergence as a social and scientific reality, by beginning this chapter from the "wrong" starting point, namely the marketplace rather than the academy. From that standpoint it becomes clear that there was nothing inevitable about the stabilization of the category of alcohol. The new chemical terminology was adopted by Parisian chemists and pharmacists, and eventually by most literate groups in the capital. The pharmacist Antoine-Alexis Cadet de Vaux argued in the 1800s that the term's adoption was essential to the consolidation of chemical authority: "it is time that the language of science, which has too long been subjugated to an insignificant language, was spoken." The reality of alcohol would become a point of agreement on which practitioners could reform various arts and trades such as distillation and sugar manufacture, and forge new etiological categories and new regimens of chemical analysis. This marked a profound shift in French understandings of *esprit* in more ways than one, as the next chapter will show. In histories of distillation, Baumé, with his bulk production of chemicals, appears as one of the first of a new generation of distillers and chemists driven by economic concerns, not connoisseurial ones.[102] Yet when distillers perfected an apparatus for producing purified spirit on an industrial scale, the product attracted criticism for its lack of flavor, even though flavorlessness had been an explicit goal of chemist distillers between 1760 and 1800. Distillers in Cognac responded by inventing an exclusive

101. Latour 1993; 2011 plus quotation; Serres 1982; 1989; Myers 2001, esp. 6–8; Appadurai 1986; Star and Griesemer 1989. On the "quasi-object," see also Bensaude-Vincent 1992, 234.

102. Destouches 1809; Cadet de Vaux year VIII: 21n.

connoisseurial tradition of brandy distillation in which flavor played a central role. This was how brandy became the ultimate connoisseurial beverage, equipped with all the flavor, odor, and color that early industrial distillers were now highly skilled at removing. Indeed, in English, the word now denotes that beverage alone. Connoisseurial liqueur producers and consumers thus continued to flourish by assenting to the distinction between an alimentary and a chemical spirit that academic chemists were forging, but then reinventing the significance of their own skills in terms not amenable to scientific analysis.[103]

103. See Delamain 1935, esp. 34–37.

CHAPTER FIVE

The Philosophical Palate

In earlier chapters, I have discussed the changing locus of expertise over food and drink in the early eighteenth century, identifying the beginnings of a shift that would downplay the importance of the eater's body as the site of knowledge production in favor of instruments wielded by scientific practitioners working within institutions. Here I return to the world of letters a decade or so after the publications of La Motte and his contemporaries, in order to examine how the models of learning, expertise, and embodiment expressed in cuisine and alimentary chemistry related to attempts to craft philosophical identity between the 1730s and the 1750s. Culinary writing from this period may often be read as a commentary upon the state of learning. The point of conjuncture for mental and alimentary agency in the middle decades of the century, which was central to culinary discussions of creativity and philosophical discussions of cuisine, was appetite. The political and physiological stakes of eating were worked out in debates over the creation and satisfaction of bodily needs, and the role and reliability of taste. Contemporary discussions of the relationship between reason and consumption, I shall argue, supported certain models of habit formation that would later form the foundation of medical models of addiction. So at the heart of accounts of physiological taste was a moral, political, and social dilemma: were eaters in control of their appetites, or were they controlled by them? What role could reason and Enlightenment play in creating order out of consumption?

The epistemological status of expert eaters in early modern France was summarized in the first edition of the *Dictionnaire de l'Académie Françoise* of 1694: "*Gourmet*. s.m. He who knows [sçait] how to know [connoître] & taste wine well." "Sçavoir" and "science" derive from the same root, denoting certain knowledge. As a knowledgeable expert, the gourmet was to be on a par with scientific practitioners, knowing foods in the same way as the savant knew the truths of the natural or social world. The gourmet's tongue and palate were precision instruments, capable of generating the *connaissances*, or experiential knowledge, upon which *sçavoir*, or true knowledge, was founded. Then as now, the word "taste" denoted both a physiological faculty and the power of discrimination. Good taste was one of the chief characteristics attributed to polite individuals, underpinning other polite characteristics such as social superiority, learning, and sensibility. The link between taste and knowledge was also a feature of alimentary connoisseurship. The members of one seventeenth-century dining club, the Ordre des Côteaux (Order of the Slopes) were described in a contemporary poem as "the knowledgeable ones" [les connaissans] for their power to detect the geographical origin of wines, and, as we saw in chapter 4, the site of juridical expertise over the question of wine falsification continued to be the body of the gourmet or connoisseur until well into the eighteenth century.[1]

Though contemporaries described eighteenth-century Paris as a center of taste in both the physical and the moral senses, artistic taste has received extensive historical scrutiny, whereas physiological taste has been comparatively neglected.[2] In this chapter I will argue that the debate over physiological taste in the mid-century reveals one set of relationships between enlightenment and corporeality, grounded in some by now-familiar iatrochemical claims about the effects of particular foods on *esprit* (understood as mind, wit, and spirit). Physiological taste was thus the point of conjuncture between mind and matter, reason and the passions. Mid-eighteenth-century culinary writers invested physiological taste with credibility and social status by formulating rules for its proper cultivation that were explicitly compared to the rules of artistic good taste, even though some contemporaries denied the possibility of anything more than a strictly metaphorical relationship between the two forms of taste.

The debate over physiological taste also rehearsed concerns about the political implications of consumption and cuisine. From its origins in the late seventeenth century, French nouvelle cuisine had been described and defined in contemporary cookbooks. Stephen Mennell argues that eighteenth-century culinary literature charts the adoption of courtly styles of cookery and table service within a wider French polite society. Dishes became less substantial and more costly, and fewer spices and seasonings were used in their composition. Nouvelle cuisine was based around the extraction and

1. Académie Françoise 1694, 1:528; Franklin 1887–1902, 6:137–39.
2. See, e.g., Bayley 1991, pt. 1; Sekora 1977; Brewer and Porter 1992; Brewer 1997; Berry 1994.

concentration of alimentary essences, and the provocation of appetites by the masterly manipulation of flavors. Its skill was the skill of artful combination: in a good dish, none of the original ingredients should be readily identifiable, and no single flavor should predominate over others—in effect, good cooks produced an entirely new compound flavor, forming a harmoniously balanced whole. In other words, the skills demanded by cuisine were similar to those vaunted by the liquorists of mid-eighteenth-century Paris.[3]

However, cuisine differed from distillation in one crucial aspect. To a far greater degree than distilling, nouvelle cuisine became a subject of active debate and interest among Parisian men of letters from the 1730s onwards. Many cookbook prefaces and other printed discussions of cuisine were claimed by contemporaries—and are still held—to have been penned by literary men, not cooks. Mennell offers a possible social agenda for the rise to prominence of cuisine as a literary genre. He notes that during the eighteenth century "it has long been supposed that some of the leading figures in the land did actually venture into the kitchens themselves," to oversee the invention and execution of particular dishes. This personal involvement of the educated elite in cookery conferred on food preparation "the title of a science as much as an art," in the words of Beatrice Fink.[4] The social transformations of culinary literature thus engendered a new relation between cuisine and knowledge. Only by recruiting a polite readership could cookery writing as a genre become a matter of interest within the Republic of Letters, and thus have a fate very different from, say, the liquorists' manuals. In addition, cooks and liquorists left different historical traces. Liquorists were often guild-based merchants, who wrote in defense of their organization, or to advertise their wares to a reading public. Cooks, by contrast, worked within households, leaving few archival traces.[5] Perhaps as a result, the identity of even the most prolific authors of eighteenth-century

3. Spang 2000; Hyman and Hyman 1999; Flandrin, Hyman, and Hyman 1983, 14–99; Girard 1977; Bonnet 1983; Mennell 1996; Peterson 2006, 194–96, 199–201; Metzner 1998, 58–61; Rambourg 2005, 119–24; Takats 2011, chap. 5. Revel (1979, 206) identifies nouvelle cuisine as characterized by the practice of impregnating foods with flavors.

4. Mennell 1996, 81; Fink 1995, 8. In the 1720s, the young Louis XV occasionally prepared omelettes and chocolate in a kitchen and still-room he had added to his private apartments at Versailles. See Saule 1993, 58; Oberlé 1989, 90.

5. Cooks' biographies were considered of little literary interest before the early nineteenth century, while archival materials about them are rare because they worked in private houses. The most eminent kitchen servant, the maître d'hôtel, appeared only in the richest households; to have a male cook marked a household as wealthy, for middling households only employed female cooks. Cookbook authors were sensitive to these social distinctions. See Davis 2004; Gutton 1981, 23–45; Girard 1977, 511–12; Takats 2011, chaps. 1, 4.

French cookbooks remains doubtful and little is known of their lives. The problem is compounded by the fact that cookbooks have generally been treated as autonomous texts, mere resources to be plundered for historical information about dietary habits and the preparation, preservation, and presentation of food. The question of why and for whom cookbooks were written has remained unaddressed.

This chapter suggests an alternative reading, which situates cookbooks within the wider print culture of mid-eighteenth-century France, as contributions to a battle over the learned state and the new forms of knowledge made possible by print and commerce. Polite men of letters saw the literature of nouvelle cuisine as a forum for discussions of the significance of taste, connoisseurship, and consumption for eighteenth-century literate society; of the proper scope of learning and the validity of scholarly attention to new subjects; and of the status of philosophes as representatives of new styles of learning emerging in France from the end of the seventeenth century onwards. As both serious and satirical texts make clear, the state of the art of cookery was taken as a commentary upon the condition of French minds and bodies. During the middle decades of the eighteenth century, philosophical self-conduct was often legitimated through somatic practices, most notably through accounts of the cultivation of the tongue and palate as integral to the moderation of the passions by reason. Such concerns about consumption, self-construction, epistemological authority, and moderation were the obverse of discourses about self-indulgence, intemperance, and their political dangers that rose to prominence from the 1750s onwards. Particularly after 1760, many argued for the inevitable collapse of the expert eater into the greedy eater, the gourmet into the gourmand. By the time of publication of the fifth edition of the *Dictionnaire de l'Académie Françoise* in 1798, the food expert or "gourmet" had vanished from its pages; only the entry for "gourmand" remained, describing the individual "who eats avidly and to excess." Attempts to achieve a balance between pleasurable self-indulgence and rational self-control, a theme that had preoccupied philosophes up to the middle of the eighteenth century, would subsequently give way to pessimism about the power of reason to restrain bodily appetites.[6]

LEARNED COOKS, CULINARY SCHOLARS

Although the identity of the author(s) of *Les Dons de Comus* (The Gifts of Comus), a cookbook first published in 1739, was unknown to contempo-

6. Académie Françoise 1798, 1:651.

rary readers, one fact was clear to them: the preface was written by an educated member of polite society with extensive knowledge of the classics. Comus was the Roman god of cookery and comedy; the very title of the book was thus a play on the classical education of elite males.[7] The book's authorship is attributed to François Marin, chief cook in the high noble households of de Gèsvres and de Soubise, and later a protégé of the chief arbiter of taste in mid-eighteenth-century France, Jeanne-Antoinette Poisson, marquise de Pompadour, the king's mistress after 1745. The preface, on the other hand, is nowadays claimed to be the work of two Jesuits, Pierre Brumoy and Guillaume-Hyacinthe Bougeant.[8] Addressing polite society demanded familiarity with certain standards of literary style, hence the involvement of men of letters. The title itself recommended the book to those eager for knowledge about the newest methods of "being served delicately": it was a work for the curious and the socially ambitious. Riding on Marin's success, the prolific culinary writer Menon, whose first name is unknown, is also believed to have recruited a different author to write the preface of his *Science du Maître d'Hôtel Cuisinier* (The Science of the Head Cook).[9] This text is generally attributed to Etienne Laureault de Foncemagne, a member of the Académie Françoise. Polite collaborators of this sort could confer legitimacy upon cooks' claims to capture taste, and thus elevate the status of cookery from its humble role among the mechanical arts to a science or fine art, possessing rules and connoisseurs. Nor were these well-known culinary works the only ones in which men of letters involved themselves.[10]

French nouvelle cuisine authors constructed a readership with courtly

7. Quotations come from [Marin] 1750. The first edition, [Marin] 1739, was principally a treatise on the art of serving foods, with lists of dishes. [Marin] 1742 consisted of recipes with an additional preface, attributed to the journalist Anne-Gabriel Meusnier de Querlon. [Marin] 1750 combined the publications of 1739 and 1742 and their prefaces (Mennell 1996, 77–82; Oberlé 1989, 88–89). On Comus, see Smith 1996, 122.

8. Oberlé 1989, 88–89. Marin's first employer, the duchesse de Gèsvres, was probably the wife of François Potier de Gèsvres, who held the title from 1704 until 1739. The second, Charles, prince de Soubise, was a noted epicure. On Bougeant, see Sheridan 1993. From their publications, it appears that both these authors were Gallicans; Bougeant in particular satirized Jansenism in his works.

9. [Menon] 1768. The companion volume to this was [Menon] 1750, and the two were published as a pair throughout the second half of the eighteenth century. The recipes in the main text of [Menon] 1768 reveal a far less skillful handling of language than the preface, supporting the argument for different authorship.

10. Culinary works were a common genre for hacks in the pay of Parisian libraires, like François Aubert de La Chesnaye des Bois, who possibly cowrote [de La Chesnaye and Briant?] 1750, and certainly cowrote [de La Chesnaye et al.] 1762–64 with two physicians (Oberlé 1989, 91; Sue year VIII: 31). The apothecary Jacques-François Demachy may have been the author of [Demachy?] 1769. The agronomist Pons-Augustin Alletz was the probable author of [Alletz] 1760.

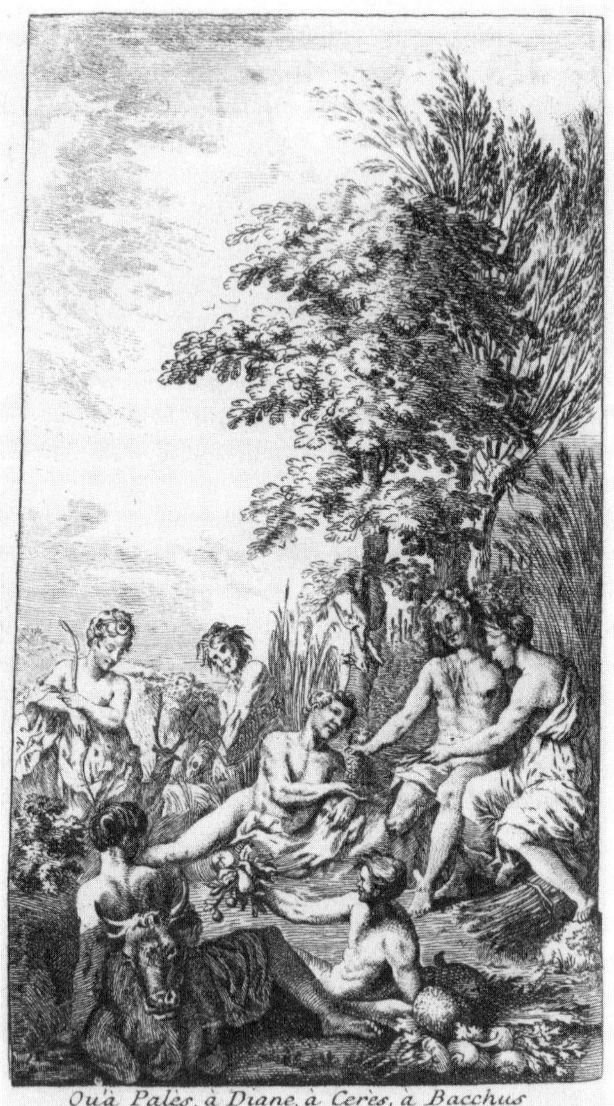

Figure 5.1. Marin, *Les Dons de Comus* (Paris: Veuve Pissot, 1750), frontispiece. The caption translates as: "Let Glaucus and Pomona join / With Pales, Diana, Ceres and Bacchus / All their gifts together are superfluous goods / Unless seasoned by Comus." Copperplate engraving, unknown artist. Berliner Staatsbibliothek, O♀6854/272. @ Bildarchiv Preußischer Kulturbesitz, Berlin, 2000

aspirations.[11] In early eighteenth-century France, the entry of elite employers into the kitchen and the rising social status of cuisine meant that chefs needed to become conversible with the language of taste and refinement. Prefaces and recipes catered for both cooks and their employers. In *Les Dons de Comus*, some recipes were simply named for their ingredients or mode of preparation ("with cucumbers"), or given some national identity ("Polish fashion," "Milan fashion"). But others could only be meaningful to members of a particular social and intellectual milieu, such as those named for specific individuals in high life ("Chirac fashion"). Some recipes described social categories from polite society ("Duke fashion," "Dandy fashion," "Bourgeoise fashion"). Such functions of social commemoration and classification overlapped with playful allusions to a select society of initiates. There were culinary jokes, in which the name combined with the ingredients, colors, preparation, and perhaps flavors to entertain and amuse the eater. Thus, for example, pigeons served "Sun and Moon style" consisted of a brace of birds, one fried golden in a batter, the other covered with a round leaf and dressed with a white sauce of eggs, cream, nutmeg, and lemon juice. There was "Nonpareils' Sauce," in which aphrodisiac ingredients predominated, and "Vestal" sauce, made purely of white ingredients. To get the joke, the connection between the dish and its name, both reader and eater needed *a priori* alimentary and social knowledge, most directly accessible in the act of eating, the moment of encounter with the cook's skill. This demanded membership of a particular social milieu. Above all, such playful culinary knowledge was presented, particularly in prefaces written by academicians and literary protégés, as suitable fare for anyone coupling politeness with learning: this was a cuisine for the philosophe and for the wit.[12]

Satirical responses to the scholarly pretensions in *Les Dons de Comus* were not long in coming. Rolland Puchot, comte Desalleurs, a courtier and future French ambassador to Constantinople, wrote an anonymous pamphlet challenging its author's claims about novelty, philosophy, and the mind-body relationship. *Les Dons de Comus* exhibited such a degree of erudition in history and metaphysics, Desalleurs argued, as to prove either that the pref-

11. The French situation is well summarized in Flandrin 1989, 302–6; in England, by contrast, culinary self-help guides predominated, aimed at the middling family concerned with household management. The success of [Menon] 1746, compared with his work on courtly cuisine, [Menon] 1755, reveals the turn toward English-style self-help publications. See Girard 1977; Sherman 2004; Thirsk 2007, 182–91.

12. [Marin] 1750, 1:39, 62, 65, 74, 75, 86, 87, 451; 2:203, 214, 395. Pierre Chirac was a Montpellier physician, the superintendant of Paris's Jardin des Plantes from 1718 (Sturdy 1995, 404; Brockliss and Jones 1997, 419–21).

ace had been written by someone who was not a cook, or that cooks had become very learned. This philosophical interest in cookery had characterized French polite society since the Regency, the self-styled "English pastrycook" scoffed. Yet modern philosophes who interested themselves in cookery were reducing themselves to the level of the *monde*, wasting their minds on shallow trivialities: fashion, novelty, hairstyles, and the discourse of "persiflage," at which latter, he claimed, members of the Académie Royale des Sciences and Académie Françoise were experts. "Thanks to the good taste of the century, our meals have become a School of civility and compliments, which would last through the whole of suppertime, if they were not interrupted by scientific Analyses of all the dishes and sauces, which, being very numerous, necessarily require plenty of time for discussion."[13] An interest in cookery, therefore, potentially undermined philosophes' claims to be taken seriously. But the "pastrycook" also made a more serious allegation, effectively taxing the author of *Les Dons de Comus* with downright materialism:

> According to your principles, all the education young people needed could be achieved by giving them food and nourishment appropriate to the condition in life for which they are destined. These foods would [need to] be dosed and seasoned by a skilful Cook, of consummate experience, who would know in depth the thoughts produced in the soul by the digestion of a *potage à la Nivernoise*, a *sauce à la Chirac*, and similar foods.

Desalleurs concluded his pamphlet with a reworking of the well-known passage in *Gulliver's Travels* in which Gulliver visits the Academy of Lagado and observes philosophers bottling sunbeams and transplanting the heads of political opponents to generate social harmony. Dean Swift's political commentary on English factionalism acquired, in Desalleurs's hands, a more specifically French and philosophical meaning. The purpose of switching heads was now to even out the supply of *esprit* (mind or wit) in the nation. Here the French term "*esprit*," unlike its English cognates, referred not only to mind but also to spirit, in both its material and mental senses.

Desalleurs's presentation of spirit as substance was more than a mere rhetorical ploy. In medical and culinary writings, foods had long been con-

13. [Desalleurs] 1739, 9, 12. See also [Desalleurs] 1981, XX–XXIII; Girard 1977, 519; Wheaton 1983, chap. 11. In persiflage, a victim, usually a social climber, was lured into conversational ambushes by an interlocutor, before an audience that was in on the joke; the politeness of the address concealed from the victim the fact that (s)he was being ridiculed. See Bourguinat 1998; Chartier 2005. For contemporary definitions of the beau monde, see Lilti 2005a, 161–63.

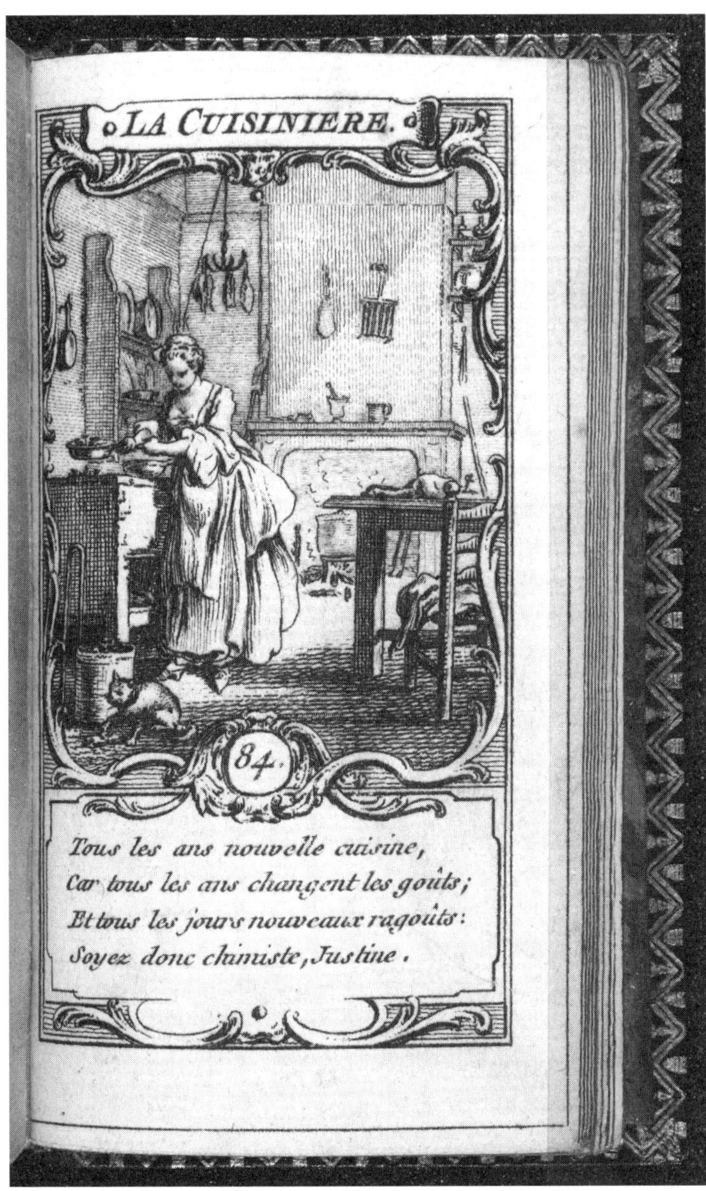

Figure 5.2. "La Cuisiniere." *Almanach utile et agréable de la Loterie de l'École Royale Militaire, pour l'année 1760* (Paris: Prault père and Laurent-François Le Clerc, 1760), plate 84. The (female) cook is advised to become a chemist in order to keep up with changing culinary tastes. Copperplate engraving, unknown artist. British Library.

strued in terms of essences and spirits. According to Louis Lémery, writing in 1700, cloves had beneficial effects in the body "through their volatile and exalted principles, which divide and attenuate the foods contained in the stomach, preserve the liquors in a suitably liquid state, and increase the quantity of spirits." Chemical analyses of foods and the identification of a spirituous principle had commenced in the sixteenth century, allied with the development of Paracelsian medicine and characterized by interest in fermentation and distillation as models for corporeal processes. The chemistry of spirits acquired particular significance from the late seventeenth century onwards with the writings of philosophers such as René Descartes and anatomists such as Thomas Willis on the question of mental physiology. If the intestines acted as the site of extraction of alimentary spirits, the brain too was a digestive organ, converting the spirits extracted from foods into the most subtle and refined of material substances, the animal spirits. Via the nerves, animal spirits reached every part of the body, acting as the vehicles of movement, thought, will, and sensory impressions.[14] Certain foods, such as fermented liqueurs, spices, and other highly flavored foods, possessed large quantities of penetrating volatile principles or volatile salts, which were easily converted to a spirituous principle in the blood during digestion. The brain then extracted the most subtle part of spirituous principles from the blood and secreted it into the nerves as animal spirits. Cookery writers claimed that the operations of nouvelle cuisine could facilitate mental function by extracting these principles and concentrating them in dishes. According to the preface to Menon's *Science du Maître d'Hôtel,*

> Cookery subtilises the coarse parts of foods, [and] strips the compounds it uses of the earthy juices that they contain: it perfects, purifies, and spiritualises them in some degree. The dishes it prepares must therefore bring a greater abundance of spirits into the blood, which will be purer and freer. Hence, more agility and vigour in bodies, more liveliness and fire in the imagination, more breadth and strength in the genius, more delicacy and finesse in our tastes.[15]

14. Lémery 1705, 198–99; Canguilhem 1955, 30–88; Clarke 1968; Johns 1996; Laudan 2000; Takats 2011, 119–24. As Clericuzio 1994 makes clear, Cartesian animal spirits were mechanically produced, but Willis invoked a ferment in the brain that separated and exalted a volatile salt, which constituted animal spirits. Lémery 1705 thus plainly borrowed from English Restoration, not just Cartesian and Paracelsian, natural philosophy.

15. "Dissertation préliminaire sur la Cuisine moderne," in [Menon] 1768, xvij. See also "Esprit," Furetière 1727, vol. 2, unpaginated. On nouvelle cuisine as the self-consciously modern art of stripping food of earthiness, see especially Spang 2000, 41–50; Duncan 1705.

Chemical cooks partially performed the digestive work that sapped physical strength and removed the "earthy juices" that encumbered the mind. They accordingly directed their attentions to producing concentrated extracts of foods, typified in the nouvelle cuisine repertoire by *jus* (gravy), *coulis, restaurants* (restoratives), and *quintessence* (concentrate) of ham. As Desalleurs parodied it, "A geometrically chemical dish, containing only reasoned quintessences, precisely liberated of all earthiness—what a ragoût for delicately sensual people. . . . It's very apparent that the digestion of such foods would only carry very sound ideas and very delicate thoughts to the head." The contemporary commonplace that *génie* was a product of the arrangement and function of the organs, the congenital strength of the senses and the constitution, was supplemented in some mid-century medical writings by a far more radical claim: that diet could be used to enhance genius. In satirizing nouvelle cuisine, Desalleurs presented arguments that were virtually identical with the genuine claims of materialist physicians like Julien Offray de La Mettrie or Antoine Le Camus about mind-body relations.[16] Of "that labourer accustomed to the hardest work . . . that mercenary with a sweaty forehead who contents himself with base vegetables at his meals," the Paris physician Antoine Le Camus observed that "their souls are exhausted by the labours of their bodies." He drew a sharp contrast with the effects of polite alimentation upon the mind:

> Now consider that delicate man who measures his work according to his strength, that citizen of policed towns, who chooses foods which are as agreeable to his palate as they are suitable to his constitution. . . . It is in such bodies that reason and judgement, never obscured by the vapors of coarse and indigestible juices [sucs], and never extinguished by exhausting their strength, exhibit themselves in their full vigour & exercise all their rights. An astonishing power of the regimen of living over minds [esprits].[17]

Culinary literature united philosophical accounts of mind and creativity with the chemistry and physiology of spirit in such a way as to legitimate the mental superiority of polite, literate city-dwellers. This tactic was only credible because in eighteenth-century France *esprit* was the common locus

16. [Desalleurs] 1739, 2–4; Le Camus 1769, 1:471; La Mettrie 1912, 21–22, 64. On eating and the mind-body problem, cf. Steinmetz 1988, who traces such concerns to Cartesian philosophy; also Figlio 1975.

17. Le Camus 1769, 1:450, 222. For earlier formulations of esprit as the (corporeal) source of taste and delicacy, cf. de Bellegarde 1702; de Vassetz 1704, 5, reviewed in *Mémoires de Trévoux* (1702): 104–13; (1704): 99–106.

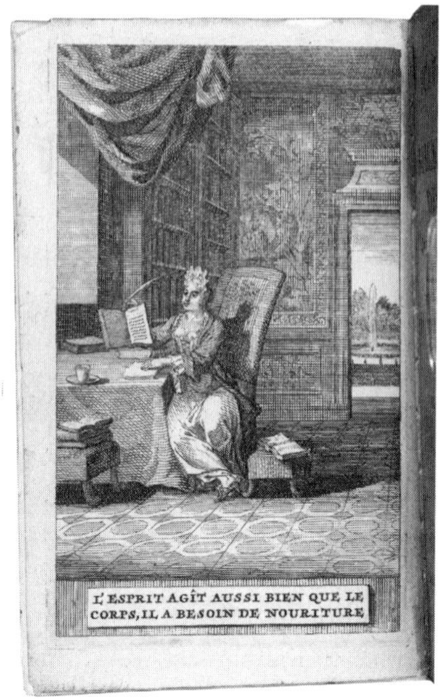

Figure 5.3. "L'Esprit agît aussi bien que le corps, il a besoin de nouriture." (The Mind acts as well as the body, it requires nourishment). N.C., *Les Femmes sçavantes ou Bibliotheque des Dames* (Amsterdam: Michel Charles le Cene, 1718), frontispiece. The epigraph of this book, almost certainly published for a French readership, was a play on contemporary iatrochemical models of mind. British Library.

of mental operations that we would nowadays differentiate into sensory impressions, mental skills, and moral habits. While disagreeing over the precise relations between these phenomena, writers tended to agree that mental phenomena were enabled and characterized by the state of the body, and that *esprit* was altered and shaped by physiology and in particular by the composition of the animal spirits.[18]

One particular model of taste would be a central focus for these eighteenth-century debates about the relations between corporeal and mental or spiritual activity. This was the model proposed by the Cartesian natural philosopher Jacques Rohault in the seventeenth century, and taken up by Claude-Nicolas Le Cat, a Rouen surgeon and physician. Le Cat's treatise on the senses, published in 1740, became a standard source for subsequent French-language accounts of taste and flavor. Le Cat explained the differences between flavors as resulting from the different shapes of food corpuscles. The

18. On the moral-physical relationship, see Staum 1980, chap. 2; Williams 1994.

surface of the tongue, palate, and throat (in some versions also the esophagus and stomach) was sprinkled with several categories of nervous papillae or protusions, each supplied with a ramification of the nerve from the ninth pair. The salivary juice exuded by these papillae leached flavor-bearing, soluble salts out of their earthy and insipid matrix in foods: "The active Principles of Savours, or of savoury Bodies, are Salts, as well fixed as volatile. Earths, Phlegm, and Sulphurs are no Part of savoury Compositions." This flavorsome liquid then soaked into the pores, where the variously shaped particles each imparted a distinctive movement to nervous papillae, which was propagated to the brain.[19] In the words of the *Encyclopédie* contributor Louis de Jaucourt,

> Why do things which have taste fortify one rapidly? When we are languid, there are substances whose agreeable & strong taste revives our strength to begin with. This comes from the fact that their parts agitate the nerves, & cause the nervous fluid to flow. . . . The subtle parts . . . insinuate themselves into the vessels to start with, agitate them by their action, & transmit themselves to the brain where they disturb the principle of the nerves; all this sets the nervous juice, which was virtually motionless, flowing in our machine.
>
> But what is it that gives so much taste and strength to these bodies . . . ? Almost nothing, the Chemists' spiritus rector. Sendivogius says that this subtle and restorative fluid . . . composes 1 part in 820 of every aromatic body. From one whole pound of cinnamon, one barely obtains 60 drops of ethereal oil; just one of these drops of oil, passing along the veins, much diluted by the blood, arrives there with all its virtue, by which the body feels itself suddenly animated.[20]

The Cartesian inheritance invoked here, with its emphasis on spirit and spice, was under attack by satirical writers in these very decades. In an equally satirical reply to Desalleurs, published in 1742, the journalist Anne-Gabriel Meusnier de Querlon mocked the "Philosophical spirit" without which one would "never have discovered that the different expressions which the Philosophes use have the same meaning at bottom," caricatured belles-lettres at the Académie Françoise, and parodied Le Cat's geometrical model

19. Rohault 1727, pt. 1, chap. 24; Le Cat 1750, 18. For other uses of Rohault's model, see, e.g., the master apothecary Rouvière 1708; review of Deidier 1708, *Mémoires de Trévoux* 6 (1710): 951–63; [Hennebert] 1765, pt. 1, 77–78. On the appropriation of Descartes by French chemists, see Principe 2007, 4–7; Metzger 1923. Rohault's model was bitterly attacked in *Mémoires de Trévoux* (1712): 868–69.

20. De Jaucourt 1757a, 760.

of taste. Great natural philosophers such as Newton, Descartes, Hartsoeker, Malpighi, and Musschenbroek had "mathematically demonstrated that mixtures and in general all bodies, both solid and liquid, only differ from one another in the configuration of their parts; from which it results that if one Ragoût does more harm than another, this arises purely from the shape and configuration of its parts." A "petit Pâté parallelipipede" (small parallelipiped Pie) must, therefore, have different properties from one of a different shape. "You apparently believe that a triangular Ramekin, a parabolic Pie and similar Ragoûts would be less healthy than the others: but pray disabuse yourself, not only would they be more agreeable to people of good taste, they might even be healthier." In the near future, de Querlon added, a modern physician would doubtless publish a book listing all human diseases with the ragoûts geometrically suited to cure them, which would be followed by an essay on human understanding that proved, in "a new and Metaphysico-geometric fashion," the political importance of the art of cookery as an instrument of public opinion and health. Such satires undermined optimistic views of geometry and chemistry as capable of resolving political and corporeal questions.[21]

PLEASURE AND PHILOSOPHIE

The union of corporeal and moral taste was celebrated in writings about cuisine as *esprit* became the characterizing feature of polite persons, *honnêtes gens*. As contemporary definitions and satires reveal, *esprit* referred to the whole system of mental faculties that permitted the cultivation of philosophy, poetry, and worldly wisdom—reason, imagination, and judgment. At the same time, *esprit* was a desirable possession in high society, a passport across the thresholds of the *beau monde*. Unlike "*ame*," the expression for soul, "*esprit*" referred uniquely to secular faculties of mind. It could also refer to various social personae. According to the 1694 *Dictionnaire de l'Académie Françoise, beaux esprits*, or wits, were those who "distinguish themselves from the common [run] by the politeness of their discourses & works." Analogous figures, uniting learning, politeness, and delicacy, were the philosophe and the persifleur or mystificator.[22] Early eighteenth-century

21. [Meusnier de Querlon?] 1742, reproduced in [Desalleurs] 1981, 25–42; quotes 34–37. Meusnier de Querlon has been suggested as a coauthor of [Marin] 1742, 1750, though these texts are stylistically very distinct from the cited satire. On the political function of cookbooks in eighteenth-century Britain, see Sherman 2003.

22. Académie Françoise 1694, 1:399.

authors contrasted the mental skills of the traditional scholar or savant unfavorably with those of the wit: "A wit knows everything without studying: he is savant by nature: the least opening serves him to develop [and] enlighten the whole. . . . The savant is only savant by virtue of ideas he has taken from others: the wit is a wit in his own right."[23] Later authors were more critical, suggesting a decline in the status and credibility of the worldly yet learned person between the 1700s and the 1750s. Caraccioli, writing in 1759, was far less complimentary about the *bel esprit*'s authority:

> But who is he, this wit? The product of the graces themselves, the elixir of pleasures, the volatile salt of our soul: . . . he knows how to concoct a tasteful outfit, prepare a meal with the utmost delicacy . . . how to make a merit out of raising his little finger, drawling his pronunciation, winking, nodding, shrugging, being cheerful or arrogant . . . ; lastly he knows how to write a Poem in a week, a Novel in three days, & satirize all of Religion & its proofs in a quarter of an hour.[24]

That the two alimentary metaphors for literary wit were elixir, a type of liqueur made by infusion, and volatile salts says much about the ways in which fashionable people and their foods were related. The products of the skills of limonadiers and cooks characterized not only fashionable consumption, but fashionable eaters themselves.

These models of corporeal and moral refinement inhabited a world of playful polite learning, in which the philosophe was contrasted with the erudite and solitary scholar, and actively participated in a worldly, even courtly society. Intellectual activity was fashionable, but to be polite was to know how to make a moderate rather than an exaggerated display of learning. Poetry and the new philosophy became exemplary mental activities for the polite individual, as the man of letters Charles-Georges Leroy attested. "Equidistant from cold Gravity, from sharp Satire, and from shameful Licentiousness," poetry supplied "the tone of good company," and "spreads that gentleness and urbanity which distinguish *honnêtes gens* from all others, Over the character and mores." A regular guest of Paris salons throughout the 1750s, Leroy befriended other philosophes and philosophical patrons, including Buffon, Diderot, d'Angiviller, and Helvétius; it was at his instigation that Helvétius would publish the radical materialist work *De l'Esprit*,

23. De Vassetz 1704, 65; similarly, [Marivaux] 1728, 1:525–27. The *bel esprit* as a literary figure is discussed in Russo 2007. On persiflage, see above, n. 13.

24. [Caraccioli 1759]: 19–21; likewise, Coyer 1757, 277–83.

which was condemned in 1759. The philosophe in the world thus needed to possess and exhibit the values of *délicatesse* and *politesse*. During the same period, certain forms of learning and mental activity such as philosophie and poetry were widely portrayed, like nouvelle cuisine, as activities at which the French excelled by virtue of their national character. The philosophe, the persifleur, and the wit or *bel esprit* thus represented what was most innovative about, or, depending upon one's point of view, what was most wrong with French society. So too did nouvelle cuisine.[25]

To be a *bel esprit* demanded both a particular approach to knowledge and a particular type of constitution. Le Camus began his medical treatise on mind by citing a definition of *esprit* as "a fire which a disease or accident sensibly extinguishes . . . a delicate temperament which disrupts itself, a fortunate conformation of organs which wear out, an assemblage and a particular movement of spirits which exhaust themselves and dissipate," and finally as "the most lively and subtle part of the soul which seems to age with the body." *Esprit* was both delicate and fragile, to be cultivated and preserved through lifestyle practices. The self-conduct of philosophes thus operated simultaneously at an alimentary and at a literary level; corporeal preservation and literary production could be aspects of the same problem. Reflecting on poetry before Paris's Académie Royale des Inscriptions et Belles-Lettres, Louis Racine, son of the famous playwright, remarked upon the fact that the activity in the animal spirits that stimulated poetic creativity, "poetic inebriation," differed only in degree from that produced by "natural inebriation," fever and madness, even if wine was not, as some claimed, absolutely indispensable to the creative process. Le Camus explicitly invoked the beneficial effects of wine upon creativity and polite table talk: "through the moderate use of this nectar, the blood circulates easily, the nerves obtain and preserve that irritability which is the first mobile of their entire play. Hence those *bons mots*, those conversations full of an Attic salt, those agreeable comments that one hears at tables served with prudence, which banish both stinginess and prodigality."[26]

25. Bibliothèque de l'Institut de France, ms. 1268, Letter, Charles-Georges Leroy to Pierre-Marie Hennin. On Leroy and Helvétius, see Anderson 1994; Hennin too was a regular guest of Helvétius and Voltaire. On the coupling of amusement with instruction in French polite society, see Riskin 2007; Pekacz 1999, chap. 1; Sutton 1995, esp. chaps. 3 and 4; Spencer 1984; Hecker 1979, 134–45. Lilti (2005a, 188–205) terms this conjuncture the "topique voltairienne," and argues that later in the century this concession to worldly manners appeared an unacceptable compromise.

26. Le Camus 1769, 1:xviij, 491; Racine 1808, 2:177–78: "Réflexions générales sur la Poésie." Yolton (1991, 66–69, 102, 106–9) suggests that physiology played a more important role in materialism in France than it did elsewhere in Europe.

More problematic was the status of brandy, spirit of wine, ratafias, and spirituous liqueurs. These Le Camus judged "very contrary to health" even if used soberly, tending to "harden the stomach's fibers, blunt the taste, diminish the appetite" and produce other evils. Even in such cases, however, occasional small doses posed no danger to the healthy; "they confer gaiety, increase the sallies of the imagination, and the facility of expressing one's ideas." By the mid-eighteenth century, medical writers, including Le Camus, cast doubt on late seventeenth-century assertions that the physiological phenomenon of rational thought was literally a flame of burning spirit. Nonetheless, few doubted that there were important relations between *esprit* in the animal and alimentary senses, especially since animal spirits were the ultimate and most refined product of the digestive process. Thus construed, *esprit* continued throughout the Old Regime to permit discussion about the relations between food or drink and knowledge. In her journal of Parisian high life in 1782, the baronne d'Oberkirch described the champagne-like properties of the worldly knowledge required by a guest at one of Madame de Boufflers' renowned suppers:

> Without *esprit*, elegance, worldly science, anecdotes, and the thousand nothings which make up news, you shouldn't dream of being admitted to these charming gatherings. There, you are only chatting: chatting on the lightest of propositions, and thus the most difficult to sustain; it is a real foam which evaporates and leaves nothing behind; but whose flavor is full of delight. Once you have tasted it, the rest seems dull and bland. The comtesse du Nord has often written to me that what she missed most about Paris was *esprit*. All intelligent foreigners say the same.[27]

Certain foodstuffs particularly embodied debates over how best to refuel the mind. Charlotte Renyer, Madame Curé, the celebrated "Muse limonadière" under whose banner the philosophes marched, announced at the start of her book of poems that she was inspired not by the waters of Hippocrene, like other authors, but by liqueurs. This was a significant departure from the Bacchic literary genre mentioned in chapter 3, which was fueled by, and celebratory of, the inspirational powers of wine. Another prominent candidate for a spiritual gasoline was coffee. François-Marie Arouet de Voltaire,

27. Le Camus 1769, 1:65–67, 121–23, 491–92; d'Oberkirch 1970, 209. "Comtesse du Nord" was the pseudonym used by the wife of the heir to the Russian throne on their European tour of 1782. See also Jacquin 1762, 180. Muchembled (1998, 211) takes this particular passage to encapsulate "a whole theory of French *esprit*, concentrated in Paris, exemplary for all of Europe."

that most famous of coffee drinkers, was a product of the Regency milieu of libertine philosophy whose physiology was characterized in contemporary writings on *esprit*. In his stormy relationship with those in power, Voltaire borrowed from Dutch medicine, English Newtonian natural philosophy, and Swiss religious tolerance to criticize the state of the French nation. Already a controversial figure in France by the time of Desalleurs's pamphlet in 1739, Voltaire was in disgrace at the French court by the late 1740s and fled to the court of Frederick II in Potsdam, where he remained for three years before settling in Geneva. This prominent and controversial philosophe generated a cult of massive proportions during his own lifetime; his poems were treated as news items, and bulletins were issued concerning his state of health. Contemporaries dubbed him the "father of philosophes."[28]

Voltaire was well known for his coffee habit. His physician, Théodore Tronchin, had been the favored student of the famous Dutch physician Herman Boerhaave.[29] Tronchin was no devotee of spirits or iatrochemistry but, like his teacher, viewed health as a state of equilibrium between the body's solids and fluids. Accordingly, he regarded all hot beverages as the principal cause of the degenerate state of the bodies and minds of modern Europeans: consumers were literally diluting their strength.[30] Almost all of his many medical recommendations between the 1750s and 1770s advised the sick, regardless of complaint, to renounce hot drinks, especially coffee. This piece of dietetic advice was a central tenet of his therapy. Nonetheless Voltaire persisted in his commitment to coffee, writing to his Lyon banker, who supplied the household with luxury goods, in 1757: "I learn that a bale of coffee has arrived for me from Lorient, in spite of the doctor. He will not succeed in ridding us of our bad habits."[31] Coffee's value for self-fashioning, in Voltaire's view, exceeded its dangers for his health. Here he was drawing upon iatrochemical doctrines fashionable during his youth, which prescribed coffee and other substances containing volatile salts, such as liqueurs and spices, as a way of replenishing the animal spirits used up during intensive mental activity.

28. Renyer 1754, 1:vij–viij; *Journal encyclopédique, passim*; Sutton 1995, 247–48.

29. Quoted in Gay 1966–69, 31; see also Tronchin 1906; Heller 1984, 18, 72–74; Lindeboom 1958.

30. Bibliothèque Publique et Universitaire, Geneva, Archives Tronchin, ms. 204, f°. 1: Letter, Théodore Tronchin to Jacques Pernety, September 4, 1756. For other medical warnings against coffee's suitability for men of letters, see Jacquin 1762, 189–90; Gentil 1787, 97.

31. Voltaire 1950, 196, Letter, Voltaire to Jean-Robert Tronchin (Théodore's cousin) from Mont-Riond, January 23, 1757.

Such claims were still being taken seriously in belles-lettres and culinary works at mid-century. As one author put it, coffee's salts were "so many irritant particles, which being all in a great movement, irritate the organs, & by this means open the conduits of the brain [and] procure a free and easy course for the animal spirits."[32] Voltaire's taste for coffee both forged and sustained the link between this drink, wit and philosophical creativity, as a poem by one of his chief protégés, Jean-François Marmontel, shows:

> The salt, the traits of fire with which a good Tale burns
> A coffee bean contains them.
> What, one says, wit [esprit] comes to us from Mocha?
> . . . so sad a view
> Shocks me at first glance
> But it's only too true:
> It's thanks to coffee that Voltaire created [enfanta].[33]

A hygienic writer from the mid-century corroborated this view: "Men of Letters like to reanimate their *esprit* and their eloquence with the sparkling fire of coffee." Coffee was thus an important part of philosophical and literary identity, and Voltaire's commitment to coffee over Tronchin indicates his commitment to a particular identity as philosophe and man of letters.[34]

Maintaining the existence of a physiological link between coffee and creativity was a useful weapon in the offensive against the opponents of philosophie. In the pages of contemporary periodicals, satires, and serious works of science and philosophy, the moral claims of playful, polite philosophie were widely challenged, especially its central tenet that pleasure and utility ought to be coupled in the practice of philosophie. The moral rifts opening up in the definition of "philosophe" are evident from the late seventeenth century onward in the *Dictionnaire de l'Académie Françoise*, which defined the philosophe in the first place as a seeker out of causes and a student of the sciences, next as a "wise man who leads a tranquil and retired life, beyond business worries" and finally as "a man who out of mental libertinism places himself above the ordinary duties & obligations of civil life," the irresponsible "man who refuses himself nothing, who constrains

32. [De La Chesnaye and Briant?] 1750, 1:236.

33. Marmontel 1972, 2:16: Letter 268, Marmontel to comte de Gilly (1781–82). See also, e.g., Tissot 1770, 1991, 128–29; La Mettrie 1912, 21.

34. Geoffroy 1774, 129.

himself with regard to nothing"—in short, as the ultimate self-indulger and free-thinker.[35] While free-thinking philosophes such as Denis Diderot, Voltaire, and others were conquering the prestigious royal academies during the 1750s, commentators such as Jean-Jacques Le Franc, marquis de Pompignan, Jacob-Nicolas Moreau, and Elie-Catherine Fréron relentlessly satirized the philosophes as poor writers and impious frauds. Reviewing Diderot's materialist *Pensées sur l'Interprétation de la Nature*, Fréron scoffed that "the Letters declined among the Romans, when they found themselves assailed by a swarm of Philosophes. The number became so great that they caused famine in Rome, and one was forced to expel them in order to let the good Citizens live." Readers of the works of Diderot, Marmontel, Voltaire, and others challenged the philosophical standing of these authors, as well as their claims about philosophie as a worldly pursuit coupling pleasure and utility. Their conduct was contrasted with models of the learned man derived from Christian asceticism and devotional literature, and of philosophie as a form of knowledge close to divine wisdom, requiring a pious withdrawal from worldly concerns. For such writers, the rise to fame of the philosophes as men of letters denoted the decline of taste and learning.[36] Fréron's bitter condemnations of their work in his newspaper *L'Année Littéraire* made him in turn a target for satirical attack by the philosophes. Voltaire's play *L'Ecossaise* caricatured him as "Frélon" or Hornet, who spent his days touting for literary commissions in cafés, selling libelles priced by the paragraph, and deluding himself that he was making the café famous.[37]

Voltaire was involved in discussions over the significance of both the new cookery and the new philosophy. He was quoted in the preface to *Les Dons de Comus*, and there is evidence that he was held to be its author.[38] The abbé Coyer imagined the poet and satirist tackling the history of the exact sciences of his day, and marveling over how

35. "Philosophe," Académie Françoise 1694, 2:229–30. The same definition, with minor variations, was given in Académie Françoise 1762, 2:364–65.

36. *Année Littéraire* 1754.i.1. For similar comments, see Fréron's reviews of Terrasson 1754, Goudar 1756, and [Deschamps] 1769 in *Année Littéraire* 1755.i.241–66, 1756.vii.3–20, 1769.v.85–92; de La Versane 1766; Pompignan 1763. This extensive literature has received little historical attention, apart from the excellent study by McMahon 2001.

37. Voltaire 1830, 17–18, 35–36, 61. The play was first performed in 1760. On *libelles*, see Darnton 1982.

38. [Desalleurs] 1739, 20. Voltaire had corresponded with Desalleurs since 1728, and in early 1739 responded critically to a long letter from Desalleurs on the question of fire. In 1738 Voltaire's enemy Jean-Baptiste Rousseau had spread rumors of his atheist convictions in Paris. See Voltaire 1968–77, 6:283–90: Letter D1936, Voltaire to Rolland Puchot Desalleurs, March 13, 1739; Besterman 1969; Sutton 1995, 253; Joly 1995, 825, 840.

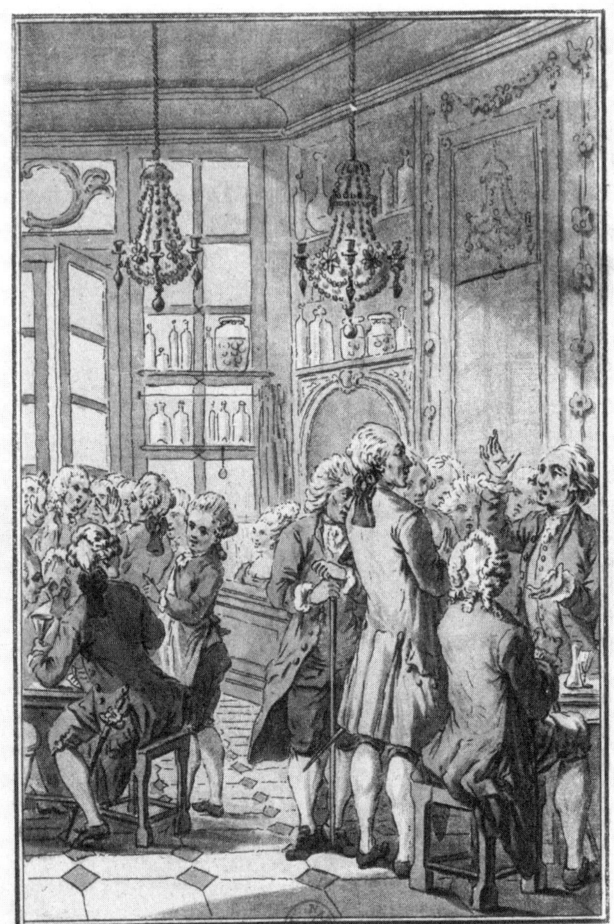

Figure 5.4. "Etablissement de la nouvelle Philosophie. Notre Berceau fut un Caffé." (Establishment of the new Philosophy. Our Nursery was a Café.) Pen and wash, unknown artist. Bibliothèque Nationale de France, de Vinck collection, XXIV:4152.

> a great Poet is suddenly changed into a Natural Philosopher, the Natural Philosopher suddenly becomes a wit. . . . But all the French are becoming, either Geometers, or Natural Philosophers; in a word, the philosophical spirit, by a species of electricity, [is] communicated to every brain, more or less; these are the efforts of nature which were reserved for our century. A modern Apicius produces an Essay on his art; Fable, History [and] Metaphysics unite to adorn his Book: the Cook hides behind the man of Letters; the Preface of a Cookbook becomes a piece of eloquence: & down to the very title of the Work, one recognizes the skilful Artisan of sauces, ingenious at disguising the vilest of meats, & at gently needling his Guests.[39]

In short, Voltaire's claim to be producing serious natural knowledge was as preposterous as the notion that cuisine warranted serious scholarly attention.

The attribution of the preface of *Les Dons de Comus* to Voltaire was not all that far-fetched. As a leading Voltaire scholar shows, Voltaire's writings were peppered with references to nouvelle cuisine. He referred to himself as an "elderly cook's apprentice," dishing up delicacies such as "little pâtés" or "rather salty ragoûts," in the form of pamphlets and satires. He contrasted the hearty food of freethinking with the dainty "meringues and whipped cream" favored in frivolous France, even deploying nouvelle cuisine's claims to facilitate digestion as a metaphor for the healthiness of the new philosophy. Every nouvelle cuisine reference was a play on philosophical innovation and the corporeal/mental double meaning of spirit, spice, or digestion.[40] Critics of philosophie like Desalleurs or Coyer also used nouvelle cuisine as a metaphor for the state of modern learning: were not the French merely making themselves ridiculous with the claim that cuisine merited serious philosophical attention? Writing in 1770, Nicolas Bricaire de la Dixmerie scoffed: "Among you a Cook is a precious man, & cookery a highly researched art.

39. Coyer 1757, 254–55; similarly, see [Neufville de Brunaubois-Montador] 1740, esp. 26–27. Such allusions to Voltaire as the author of the preface to [Marin] 1739, beginning with Desalleurs, seem to have been overlooked in culinary histories. Especially interesting is Coyer's suggestion that the whole preface was parodic. Though no modern source supports the view that Voltaire was the author of this preface, many anonymous satires were attributed to Voltaire during his lifetime (Hecker 1979, 76–77; Guiragossian 1963). Responses of this sort make it clear that food and consumption were such controversial topics as to make it virtually impossible to publish *any* reliable factual account of them; either the writing or the reading of such works was performed in satirical mode.

40. Mervaud 1998, 34–35. The expression "whipped cream" refers to the type of knowledge favored by wits (see La Mettrie 1747, 71; also p. 133, this volume.

It has principles, elements, treatises, dictionaries, an encyclopaedia."[41] An antiluxury writer of the following decade, the libraire Antoine-Prosper Lottin, scoffed at the positioning of "certain frivolous Arts that we owe to Luxury, alongside the sciences & masterpieces which immortalize the centuries that produced them," and insisted that the growth in public interest in learning was no more than a version of fanaticism, producing a multitude of "unbearable demi-savans (half-savants)": "There is not a house but has its library, not a society but has its poets; & on the strength of Dictionaries, Abridgements, and Newspapers, one thinks to know everything." And Lottin ended with a vehement denunciation of the whole *Encyclopédie* enterprise: "Let no-one say that this is the century of the Sciences [or] the Encyclopédie, that it is the century of Philosophy!" Enlightenment potentially supported new and worldly areas of learning such as cuisine, and new types of learned practitioners; but the very universality of such endeavors was what compromised them after 1750.[42]

From a culinary standpoint, an excessively serious attitude to learning and discourse could appear to be a form of extremism. In a health manual explicitly flagged as uniting pleasure and utility, Armand-Pierre Jacquin advised eaters, when at table, to

> avoid those political & dogmatic dissertations, in which people burble on drearily about the State & Religion, & reform everything except their own conduct; matters of this sort are too respectable to be discussed in the middle of the pleasing folly, the soul of repasts, & too serious to entertain companions whom joy brings together. . . . Indeed, if such conversations are not promptly stopped, the spirit of novelty, singularity or factionalism soon overtakes the participants.[43]

At the absolutist dinner table, both consumption and conversation had to be regulated, in the interests of moderation and social harmony.

41. [De la Dixmerie] 1770, 50–52, 64–65. On cuisine as a specifically French form of excellence, see *Avantcoureur* (1770): 22–23, advertisement by the pastry cook Bouchez; also Spang 2000, 4. On the longer history of debates over the learned status of cuisine, see Cowan 2007, 212–13.

42. De Saint-Haippy 1784, 15–17. This book was written for a prize contest at Toulouse's Académie des Jeux Floraux; see Margairaz 1999, 35. For portrayals of the new philosophie and mid-century didactic literature as trivial and unscholarly, see, e.g., *Année Littéraire* 1766.iii.20–23, 1768.viii.66–69, 1770.v.182–86.

43. Jacquin 1762, 372. On philosophical dinners, see Chartier 1997, a response to Goodman 1994.

THE SENSUAL SAGE

Technologies of chemical and spiritual alimentation fitted well with libertine and courtly self-presentations current in polite society. Late seventeenth-century libertine philosophers had celebrated pleasure, conversibility, delicacy, *volupté*, and wit. Charles de Saint-Evrémond, prominent among their number, classified forms of pleasure and pleasure-seekers according to their relationship with self-knowledge and self-control. The "*sensuels*" abandoned themselves to appetite and denied themselves nothing, the "*voluptueux*" experienced sensual impressions via the soul, while the "*délicats*" employed *esprit* in the service of good taste, and were thus responsible for the invention or refinement of gallantry, music, and cuisine. Saint-Evrémond also classified sensual experiences, from the gentle impressions of agreeable objects to the enervating but delicious experiences of *volupté*. The 1694 edition of the Académie Françoise's dictionary included terms such as "*délicat*" and "*délicatesse*" under a general subheading of "Délices," defined as pleasure or *volupté*. A "*voluptueux*" was "a man delicious in his drinking & eating." The word "*délicat*" referred both to the quality of a food, and to the quality of its eater: someone "who judges finely of that which concerns the senses or the *esprit*," or someone "difficult to satisfy, whether in matters of the senses or of the *esprit*." *Délices*, pleasures, thus conflated the operations of body and mind. There were, however, also negative connotations. "Délicater," the verb derived from *délices*,"meant "to treat with excessive softness" in matters of sensual self-indulgence. *Délicatesse* itself had a primary meaning of "discriminating, discerning," but could also be used in a pejorative fashion.[44] For Desalleurs, experts in *délicatesse* commanded little epistemological authority:

> Who is more suited to providing rules for an art than people who have made it their sole occupation all their lives, & who by means of vigilance, cares & research, have eventually acquired the reputation of being excessively delicate? . . . Are you not revolted, Sir, at the lack of respect

44. Saint-Evrémond 1725, 1:126–34;"Delices," Académie Françoise 1694, 1:311–12; "Volupté," Académie Françoise 1694, 2:659. On libertine philosophy, see Meeker 2006, chap. 2; Rivière 2004; Casenobe 1991; Morize 1970, 34–40; Féher 1997. Saint-Evrémond was, however, critical of nouvelle cuisine. *Volupté* in the eighteenth century did not have the predominantly sexual connotations that it has today, but was closer to "sensuality" or "sensual pleasure." Thus [Hennebert] 1765, pt. 1, 13, defined "*volupté*" as "*pleasure with seasoning*, in the sense that one calls esprit, *reason with seasoning*."

> & injustice the public shows towards excessively delicate people? They are ordinarily taken to be *voluptueux* plunged in pleasures, joy and good cheer. But alas! how wrong we have been on their account, & how different their way of life is to what we suppose! You can't imagine the troubles, pains & torments it costs to be excessively delicate.[45]

Negative formulations of delicacy would become more common during the second half of the century, when it came to be synonymous with physical frailty, denoting a person of weak health caused by soft living, as chapter 6 will argue. Early in the century, however, *délicatesse* was still most closely associated with social and tasteful distinction, and with the spread of politeness and enlightenment. In other words, it was seen as both the result and the precondition of polite society. Other than in reforming circles, as I showed in chapter 1, *délicatesse* largely lacked the pejorative associations with effeminacy, weakness, and political disenfranchisement it would acquire some decades later. The libertine philosophical legacy encouraged celebration of the cultivation of pleasure, rather than concern over the dangers of delicacy. After the Regency, such debates moved out of courtly circles and into the urban world of printing and reading, where cooks, physicians, and philosophes competed for the same readership. The ensuing search for a philosophical legitimation for gustatory pleasure underpinned attempts to elevate it to an art or science, with rules and connoisseurs.

The polite prefaces to cookbooks presented a corporeal model in which balance, variety, and moderation were central themes. Moderation of mind and body would be central to both philosophical and culinary self-presentations throughout the first half of the century, as in the introduction to the second edition of *Les Dons de Comus* in 1750: "Let those over whom reason has no power, who sacrifice everything to temperament, and who are not able to reconcile the pleasures of the table with that useful moderation which is their price, and which may itself only be a refinement of sensuality, fear the art of cookery with reason: it is a dangerous art for them." Such individuals should "reduce themselves to the coarse life of the first ages, . . . But those sensual sages, who, while satisfying nature, know they must listen to reason, and control . . . the means of making [their pleasures] last by avoiding satiety, may taste the delights of the table without fear." In effect, to lack the capacity to control appetite was a mark of unreason and incivility;

45. [Desalleurs] 1739, 16.

knowledge and politeness were here inextricably conjoined with pleasure. However, this coupling was by no means self-evident. Was it truly possible to be a "sensual sage"?[46]

An emphasis upon moderation was characteristic of contemporary writings celebrating pleasure as a philosophical mode of being. Advocates of sensual moderation drew upon claims about the production of pleasure advanced by nouvelle cuisine writers, and on a sensual physiology common to medical, natural historical, and culinary writings. According to Georges-Louis Leclerc de Buffon, salon habitué and coauthor of the monumental *Histoire naturelle, générale et particulière,*

> everything which acts gently on these [sense] organs, everything which moves them delicately, is a cause of pleasure; everything which shakes them violently, everything which agitates them strongly, is a cause of pain. All sensations are thus sources of pleasure when they are gentle, temperate and natural, but once they become too strong, they produce pain.

Pain was thus the extreme, rather than the converse, of pleasure, and therefore a symptom of excess. Buffon's example of moderate pleasure was, predictably, derived from nouvelle cuisine. He contrasted the unpleasantness of an "insipid or coarse dish" with a "fine flavor" and other moderate sensations which "delight & often move us deliciously." In man, the imagination, rather than the body, was the dominant source of both pleasure and pain, but also the source of frequent error. Happiness, Buffon concluded, was to be found within, in the calm exercise of the spirit, which only occurred in the lull between the storms of passion that imagination stirred up. "The happiest being in Nature" was the man who "joins to the pleasures of the body . . . the joys of the mind [esprit]." In this figuration of pleasure as at once spiritual and corporeal, Buffon was not alone. Other eighteenth-century authors advanced similar arguments, yoking pleasure and pain in scenarios of sensual moderation. In his health manual, the abbé Jacquin described how a contented mind and healthy body together produced the conditions for moderate enjoyment, when "the nervous fibers experience an agreeable & light oscillation, from which a delicious tickling results: then a gentle & voluptuous heat, drawing its principle from the vis-

46. [Marin] 1750, xxvj. This passage is not in the first edition. See also Malouin 1750, 1:334–35; Takats 2011, 121. Construed as a set of practices affording entry to the polite world, moderation was central to *honnêteté* (Pekacz 1999, chap. 1).

cera, spreads through the whole habit of the body, & produces the feeling of joy."[47]

For these authors, the truly philosophical individual was the person who was capable of exercising rational moderation in all things, but particularly in the cultivation of corporeal pleasure, including eating and sex. As Diderot, an early enthusiast of Shaftesbury, put it, "Unregulated passions remove the peace of the soul. The immoderate use of pleasures removes health. The calculation of the *voluptueux* is that of the moment, and only in that is he wrong. The *voluptueux* does not foresee the infirmities and annoyances which await him."[48] Enlightened eating reworked older debates about the relationship between reason and the passions in terms of a secular morality of self-conduct that fitted well with other contemporary uses of reason as a means of validating social and mental condition, and with critiques of excess as evidence of social inferiority, madness, or disordered imagination.[49] The inability to regulate one's tastes through moderation demarcated the social boundary between the polite and the impolite. Writing in 1763, Achille-Guillaume Le Bègue de Presle, author of a health manual, pointed out that those most likely to succumb to "pleasures which make a lively impression on the senses" were the lower orders, the unenlightened "*peuple*" who "makes no use of its reason for the preservation of health."[50] Many men of letters expressed faith in rational self-restraint as a means of sustaining sensual pleasure and health. Such self-government was often associated either with appeals to Stoic philosophers such as Seneca, or with Epicureanism. Simultaneously, however, moderation was a response to the moral and political problems accompanying the birth of a consumer society. In his fourth discourse on man, Voltaire sketched a man who, unable to attain a state of pleasure, filled the void with an unceasing consumption of foods and goods, and contrasted him with the sensual sage: "Moderation is the sage's treasure; / He knows to regulate his tastes, his labours, his pleasures; / To set a goal to his pursuits, a limit to his desires."[51]

47. Buffon et al. 1749–88, 4:42; Jacquin 1762, 357; see also Le Camus 1769, 1:24, 43–44. Diderot 1765 likewise celebrated the pleasurable passions, identifying those who did not as either hypocrites or badly organised. On pleasure and its management, see, e.g., [Hennebert] 1765, pt. 1, pp. 83–85, 114, pt. 2, pp. 86–109; [Le Maître de Claville] 1769.

48. Diderot 1955–70, 2:57–58: Letter, Denis Diderot to Sophie Christine Charlotte, Princess of Nassau-Saarbrücken, [May or June 1758]. On Shaftesbury and taste, see Gigante 2005, 5–7.

49. L. Wilson 1993; Schaffer 1992.

50. Le Bègue de Presle 1763, x–xij.

51. Quoted in Morize 1970, 140, 25–28; see also Gaffiot 1926. Morize represents Voltaire's moderate lifestyle, avoiding both luxury and austerity, as a mark of his bourgeois identity, and thus as a socially situated practice.

Just such a lifestyle, uniting pleasure, consumption, and learning, was exemplified by Charles-Georges Leroy, first introduced above as a fledgling philosophical poet. Leroy was *lieutenant des chasses* or keeper of the Hunt to the king from 1753, populating his apartments at Versailles with a succession of women. In letters which his cousin, Pierre-Marie Hennin, described as a "pleasant picture of your Epicureanism," Leroy celebrated hedonism, idleness, and *volupté* over marital love, industriousness, and erudition. Studying Locke and Malebranche in order to avoid seeming ignorant in polite company, Leroy described himself as "a Philosophe without pig-headedness, a Philosophe, in fact, as every *honnête homme* should be." But this was also an explicitly political stance: "in the country of Slavery"—absolutist France—"I am leading the Freest life that has ever existed," and he contrasted his own libertine philosophy with Condillac's treatise on sensations, which entailed automatism.[52] During the 1750s, Leroy turned from writing poetry to writing *Encyclopédie* articles, an example of mid-century philosophie's roots in the *bel esprit* culture of the preceding decades. Like other Epicurean philosophes of the 1750s, such as d'Holbach, Leroy integrated the practice of sensual pleasure into that of philosophie, serving his friends "delicate and philosophical suppers."[53]

At the other end of the theological spectrum was Buffon and Leroy's Académie Françoise colleague, the *cafétiste* abbé Jean Terrasson, for whom truly virtuous eating entailed hating and fleeing from even the pleasure attached to necessary foods, such as bread and water. Above this were three degrees of self-indulgence. Pleasure in necessary foods, or pleasure in seeking out those foods, like meat and wine, which "cause more pleasure" than foods that were absolutely necessary, constituted a venial and forgivable sin. A mortal sin was committed only by someone who sought pleasure for the sake of "pure delectation," and, driven by this urge to exceed "all the bounds of necessity and even Reason," transgressed both divine and churchly laws

52. Bibliothèque de l'Institut de France, ms. 1268, Hennin-Leroy correspondence, f°s. 20–22: Letter, Leroy to Hennin, January 19, 1754, and Hennin's response of February 16, 1754; f°s. 176 v°.–177 v°.: Letter, Leroy to Hennin, July 15, 1755; f°s. 144 r°.–144 v°.: Letter, Leroy to Hennin, March 15, [1754?]; f°s. 32 r°.–32 v°.: Letter, Leroy to Hennin, December 19, 1747; f°s. 166 v°.–167 v°.: Letter, Leroy to Hennin, December 28, 1757.

53. Jean-François Ducis, letter to Alexandre Deleyre, July 25, 1775; quoted in Leroy 1994, 22. On the cultivation of Epicureanism by Parisian philosophes and *cafétistes* of the previous generation, including numerous authors discussed in chapter 3, cf. Denis Diderot, "Epicuréisme ou epicurisme" (1755), in Diderot and d'Alembert 1751–77, 5:779–85.

in pursuit of enjoyment.[54] In moral terms, alimentary pleasure thus occupied a grey zone of permissible self-indulgence, always provided the eater was able to qualify as rational. For this enlightened philosophe, as for others, it was the failure to master the passions by reason that was politically, socially, and theologically impermissible. The relationship between the passions and reason thus formed a common moral ground on which both the theologically heterodox and the orthodox could agree circa 1750. In their writings, the theorization of pleasure enshrined the principles of moderation and the self-presentation of delicate and philosophical eaters. This secular reliance on reason tended to be expressed in an optimistic manner in the first decades of the eighteenth century, when eating right served as a marker for the progress of reason through society and as a distinguishing characteristic of its polite and philosophical members. At this time, cuisine became an emblematic art or science of rational hedonism.

In physiological discussions, moderate philosophes had much in common with learned cooks and tasteful connoisseurs. In his preface to Menon's work, de Foncemagne (if it was he) deployed a variety of treatises on the beautiful to explain the interaction of alimentary flavors. Particularly prominent was the *Théorie des Sentimens agréables* of Louis-Jean Lévesque de Pouilly, a friend of Shaftesbury who argued for moderation as the ideal moral and physical state.[55] The reasoned exercise of pleasure required detailed knowledge of the properties of foodstuffs, so that the eater could balance the effects of one with those of another. For cooks to demonstrate expertise, they required a suitable audience with properly cultivated corporeal skills: "delicate palates, as fine and learned [sçavantes] ears [are] for a profound Musician."[56] Only a select few eaters could be competent judges in culinary matters, namely those who adhered to rules of moderation and self-control, for only moderate pleasure left the body in a state of balance, with undiminished sensibility and thus capable of sustained enjoyment. This corporeal balance or harmony was characteristic of the construction of the connoisseur as a person of taste in both the sensible and aesthetic domains, as an individual in whom the exercise of reason over the passions, mind over body, was perfected to yield a lifestyle of calm philosophical pleasure.

54. Terrasson 1754, 220–34, "Essai d'un systeme philosophique et theologique sur le Plaisir & la Douleur." This sort of apologia for pleasure was typical of contemporary moral treatises; see Dornier 1997, 176–77.

55. Levesque de Pouilly 1749. This work was also cited in a later treatise on moderation: Changeux 1767, esp. chaps. 19 and 20. On the aesthetics of cuisine, see especially Knabe 1983.

56. [Menon] 1768, preface, vj.

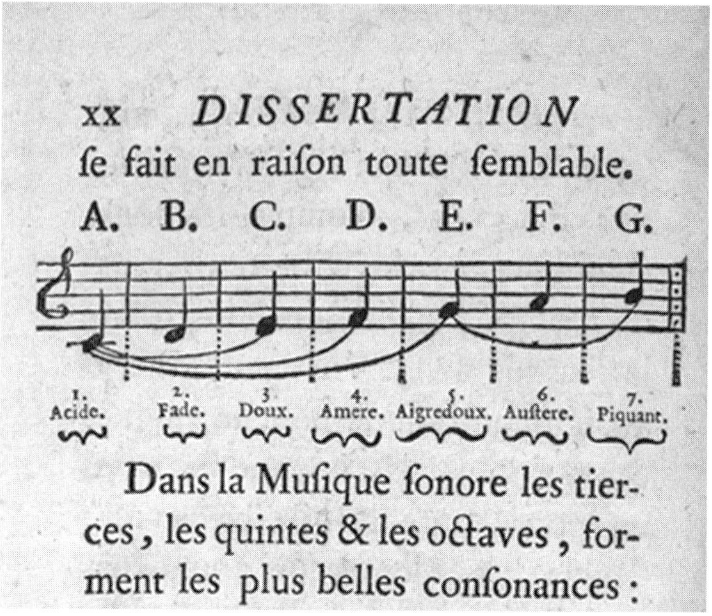

Figure 5.5. Abbe Polycarpe Poncelet, *Chimie du goût et de l'odorat* (Paris: P. G. Le Mercier, 1755), xx. The scale of flavors: acid, bland, sweet, bitter, bittersweet, astringent, hot. Copperplate engraving, unknown artist. British Library.

Corporeal harmony was no mere metaphor. De Foncemagne speculated about the possibility of a "harmony of flavors" analogous to the Jesuit Louis-Bertrand Castel's mechanical model of a harmony of colors.[57] Castel's "ocular harpsichord," described in 1725, was an attempt to identify natural analogies between sound harmonies and color relations, and an attack on Newtonian color theory that met with a skeptical reception from the philosophes. For Castel, the ocular harpsichord was also a demonstration of his "mathematical theory of pleasure." The same model was taken up by an Oratorian priest, Polycarpe Poncelet, in his *Chimie du goût et de l'odorat* (Chemistry of Taste and Smell) of 1750, a guide to the domestic production of liqueurs that went through several editions. Here a theory of producing pleasure through a harmony of flavors was to be embodied in a "taste organ" that combined different liqueurs. "As for the pleasure [agrément] of

57. Ibid., preface, v. Gustatory harmony was treated as a matter of expertise in the *Mémoires de Trévoux* (1749): 1988–99. On harmony as a principle of cookery, cf. Steinmetz 1988, 21; Peterson 2006, 194–201.

Liqueurs, it depends on the mixture of flavors, in a harmonic proportion. Flavors consist in the stronger or weaker vibration of the salts acting on the sense of taste . . . : thus there can be a Music for the tongue and for the palate, as there is one for the ears." Gustatory music depended on seven primitive flavors, acid, insipid, sweet, bitter, bittersweet, austere, and piquant, and their consonances or dissonances. Ultimately the liquorist was a composer: "In a word I regard a well-understood Liqueur, as a sort of musical Air; a Composer of Ragoûts, Preserves, [and] Ratafia Liqueurs, is a Symphonist after his fashion, and he must know the nature and principles of harmony at bottom, if he wishes to excel in his art, whose object is to produce agreeable sensations in the soul."[58]

THE DECLINE OF TASTE

Others too equated connoisseurship of food and cuisine with connoisseurship of the fine arts, and situated both capacities within the fabric of the body. Marin's preface connected taste in both domains:

> Since corporeal and spiritual taste both depend on the conformation of the organs [which are] destined to operate their diverse sensations, the acuity of these two sorts of taste reliably proves the acuity of their respective organs. Could one not rise from corporeal taste to a very delicate principle which it would, in some sense, have in common with purely spiritual taste?[59]

During these decades, "spiritual" taste was the subject of highly divisive debates in the literary world. Voltaire's article "Goût" in the *Encyclopédie* drew parallels between good and bad taste in the physical and moral senses; but only artistic taste was, he argued, capable of perfection through education.[60] This apparently stable categorization of physiological taste under the

58. Chouillet-Roche 1976, 142; Poncelet 1755, xviij–xxij, "Dissertation préliminaire sur la salubrité des Liqueurs, & l'harmonie des saveurs." See also Pluquet 1786, 1:214. On Castel's organ, see Gessinger 1996; Mortier and Hasquin 1995; Hankins 1994; Franssen 1991. The number of flavors recognized by eighteenth-century authors varied, but was always greater than those in use today: Poncelet identified seven, but the surgeon-physician Le Cat listed ten. The sense of smell was accorded only a minor role in tasting at this time, whereas the tongue and palate were assigned extensive discriminatory powers.

59. [Marin] 1750, preface, xxvij.

60. See Gigante 2005, chap. 1; Spang 2000, 15, 49, especially her reading of Voltaire, "Goût" (1757), in Diderot and d'Alembert 1751–77, 7:761.

rubric of nature and artistic taste under that of culture was challenged by materialist explanations of the origins of bad taste. "Avoid those people who find nothing good," exhorted de Foncemagne,

> it is often proof that the papillae of their tongue are worn and lacking in elasticity. Only the strong and piquant can move them, and in that way awaken their appetite. The just proportion of salts and sulphurous juices, distributed by a wise and skilful hand during the preparation of foods, is not capable of exciting an agreeable taste sensation in them, they need a dominant salt, proportioned to the sagging of the fibers of their organ, an acid and corrosive juice which alters its tissue, to make it feel. Is the palate of that sort of Person a competent Tribunal to judge the merit of an Artist in matters of Cookery?[61]

The deterioration of physiological taste was widely agreed to be a sign of moral shortcoming and weak reason. Succumbing to excess, to the unrestrained pursuit of gustatory pleasure, produced a decline in sensibility—the nervous fibers of the tongue and palate were weakened by sensory impressions of excessive duration or strength. Gluttons were thus on a downward spiral in which gustatory overindulgence corrupted physiological function, leading to a loss of sensibility and a corresponding need to use ever stronger flavors in order to produce the same level of pleasure. If for many, the cultivation of taste through reason raised man above animal needs, the moral consequences of ignorance or lack of self-control were thus similarly manifested through the exercise of taste.

Medical authors in particular elaborated this critique into a wholesale attack upon nouvelle cuisine and luxurious eating in general as sources of political, moral, and physical degeneracy. In a 1756 treatise on child-rearing, a regent doctor of the Paris medical faculty, Charles-Augustin Vandermonde, discussed in detail the nervous physiology upon which the spiral of taste degeneration was predicated. Rather than appealing to animal spirits, he adopted a mechanistic account of nerves as elastic bodies derived from the writings of seventeenth-century English natural philosophers. The whole body was a composite of nerves, each composed of a tightly interlocking network of spiraling nervous fibrils. Tension in the nerves was determined by the tightness of these tiny springs, which transmitted impressions to the brain as a vibration. Laxity in the spirals could reduce sensibility, but so too could the hardening of the fibers that was the end result of constant

61. [Menon] 1768, preface, vij.

stimulation and excess. The exemplary manifestations of this phenomenon, according to Vandermonde, were nouvelle cuisine and liqueurs: "Such are those people who indulge in a surfeit of wine or spirituous liqueurs. . . . So we see drinkers turning to spicy ragoûts, [or] to ardent drinks, in order to create a sort of sensation in themselves: impressions which are capable of exciting pain in other organs, only tickle them gently."

Excessive indulgence in strongly flavored or spirituous ingesta, notably those typical of nouvelle cuisine, produced an insensibility which the sufferer sought to combat through hyperstimulation, generating a closed circle of loss of sensibility and overindulgence. Moreover, the greater one's tendency to submit to one's desires and satisfy them, the more elastic the fibers became, creating still more forceful sensations of desire, up until the point when the fibers hardened into terminal insensibility. "The same pleasure which God has attached to our preservation, often becomes the instrument of our destruction. The more we seek to satisfy ourselves, the more we should doubt ourselves. Habit turns into nature, & pleasure into necessity." Because of this process, the body "bears in this life the sensible marks of the excesses it has committed. Habit gives nerves dispositions [or] tendencies to become irritated, which are virtually insurmountable; which gives rise to disgust and passions that are often extraordinary."[62] The fashionable Swiss physician Théodore Tronchin outlined a similar physiology of habituation in a 1756 letter to Madame d'Epinay about the logical flaws of materialism and the literary cult of the *bel esprit*:

> There are contagions of one or the other sort which triumph over morality and Medicine. Should we conclude from this my good friend, that one and the other are in vain, No, you will say that they have their limits. . . . These limits are not the same for Epictetus & for la Meterie [La Mettrie], for Hippocrates & for Chicoineau [Chicoyneau] . . . we will end by avowing that Sentiment quintessentialised in the Wit's alembic is but a narcotic which puts us to sleep during suffering, but which will never cure, and just like opium, it is necessary to augment the dose if one wants it to have an effect, one accustoms oneself to it in the end, the remedy no longer works, the ill remains.[63]

62. Vandermonde 1756, 1:377–86. For a similar formulation by another Paris medical faculty member, see Lorry 1781, 2:33. On Vandermonde, see *Biographie Universelle* 40:565; a more general formulation of his account of moral and physical degeneration is in Vila 1998, 88–91. On the shift to a "body made of fibers," see Vigarello 1999, 148–64.

63. Bibliothèque Publique et Universitaire, Geneva, ms. 204, f°s. 29–31: Letter, Théodore Tronchin to Madame d'Epinay, October 25, 1756. François Chicoyneau was a renowned Montpellier-trained physician who had died in 1752.

Tronchin's metaphor, in which the distiller's alembic stands for what is wrong with materialist philosophy, does double duty here. It undermines both the claims of chemists to generate a true account of mental function and polite morality, and the scholarly standing of the wit or free-thinking philosophe.[64]

Liqueurs, particularly brandy, were the target of some of the most devastating critiques by medical writers. According to Vandermonde, wine and spirits had the power to "retract, contract, & concentrate the nervous teats" of the tongue.

> Repeated [use of] the drink dries out the nervous teats, & destroys the whole sensation of taste. Thereafter the child only finds pleasure in that which strongly irritates his tongue or palate, & loses his taste for all foods which do not produce the same effect on his organ. He spoils his taste, & accustoms himself only to find that which is acrid and biting good and pleasant.

Although the first impression of brandy was very profound, "yet you habituate yourself to it insensibly, & when you make frequent use of it, you blunt your taste so much that nothing but spirituous liquors will please [your palate] any more. In this way, you manage to deprave the most pleasurable sense in life, & make it into the instrument of your destruction." Menon too urged consumers to "use anything which is composed of brandy soberly." Spices and strongly flavored foods such as ragoûts were the subject of similar comments. These were dire warnings indeed: for the loss of gustatory delicacy entailed the loss of health, but also the loss of the power to discriminate, which denoted the consumer's polite status. Those who gave way to their desires committed themselves to a lifetime of chasing increasingly elusive pleasures: "It is not in what [man] possesses that he finds his happiness; he places it in that which he desires."[65]

Such criticisms were explicitly countered by the liquorists. Poncelet's refutation of those "famous Physicians" who regarded liqueurs as "a cold

64. Fifty years later, the British physician Thomas Trotter would publish what is widely viewed as the first medical description of alcohol addiction (the term "alcoholism" only being coined in 1849, by Magnus Huss). Trotter's account, however, was clearly derived from eighteenth-century accounts of the "spiral of degeneration" of taste; see Porter 1988; 1985; Edwards 1992, 5; Berridge 1990, 4.

65. Vandermonde 1756, 2:296–98; [Menon] 1758, 154–55; *Avantcoureur* (1769): 795. For Condillac's views on the creation of desire from the habitual satisfaction of needs, along with the potential it offered for generating new forms of error, see Bates 1995–96, esp. 318–19.

poison, . . . invented by intemperance, proscribed by reason, and the more agreeable it is, the more to be feared," rested on the fundamental trustworthiness of moderate physical pleasure: "an agreeable sensation is almost always a certain sign of the goodness of the food which excites it." Liqueurs produced a "gracious sensation" on the nervous papillae of the tongue, which, transmitted to the brain, mingled with the animal spirits and was felt in the heart as an "impulse as surprising, I should almost say as miraculous, as it is lively and varied: could this delicious commotion . . . have a poison as its principle?" Expertise and moderation were central to this defense of liqueurs: they had to be consumed in moderation, and only by someone with a "well-constituted palate and a mediocrely sensual tongue." The healthiness of liqueurs was also guaranteed by expert knowledge of liqueur composition. Good liqueurs contained a balance of salts, oils, and spirits that served to facilitate digestion, fortify the nerves, and stimulate appetite, like all spirituous and salty foods in iatrochemical models of cuisine.[66]

In this sense, Poncelet could legitimately present his book as a contribution to public health. To refute medical claims that liqueurs harmed digestion by destroying the equilibrium between solids and fluids, impoverishing the blood, contracting the stomach, blunting the points of the villous tunic lining the intestines, intercepting the course of the animal spirits, and heating up the entire vascular system to the point of spontaneous combustion, Poncelet carried out his own chemical experiments, modeling the digestive process. Minced or whole cuts of meat, combined with water, spirit of wine, or a mixture of gravy, spirit of wine, spirit of vitriol, and saliva, were left in the open air or over a steam bath for a week. The preparation with mincemeat, steam, saliva, gravy, and spirits of wine and vitriol yielded the result closest to a "praiseworthy" digestion: "the meat from the jar placed in the steam bath, was changed into a sort of greyish chyle, with a very bearable odour." Thus the abbé could experimentally demonstrate the truth of claims by nouvelle cuisine supporters that spirits and meat essences produced the best digestions, in combination with mastication, body heat, and saliva.[67]

66. Poncelet 1755, iv–v, vij–ix. According to Lémery 1705, 484–89, spirit was a compound between volatile salts and exalted oil. The salts had "fine and cutting points" that stimulated the sense of taste and divided and also attenuated the oil, converting it to spirit. The spirit then aided digestion by warming the stomach. Spirit penetrated the brain from the blood, producing greater corporeal activity and "fine thoughts."

67. Poncelet 1755, v, viij, xj–xvj, xxvj. On chemical cookery as a method of producing artificial chyle, see [Desalleurs] 1981, 7; on "embodied knowledge" as a way of contesting health advice, see Keane 1997, 181–82.

In a science-fiction work published a decade later, Vandermonde's medical faculty colleague Charles-François Tiphaigne de la Roche underlined the absurdity of claims that a more perfect chemical knowledge would enable cooks and liquorists to overcome the health risks posed by their products. A savant explorer from the nation of "Babylone" [Paris], bearing up-to-date scientific exploration equipment—a compass, a glass mask against sand-storms, and nutritional tablets—reaches the nation of Giphantie, isolated within a vast desert. The population is made up of elementary immaterial spirits, who have invented numerous machines, including a device for overhearing comments on the current state of literature. Invited to dine, the explorer learns that the local chemists have succeeded in extracting the essences of quail, trout, oranges, and so on, in the form of salts, which produce the appropriate taste sensations when scattered onto a particular species of fruit. When he begs if it is "permitted for a mortal to enter into the mysteries of the physics of spirits [and] learn from you the inestimable secret of your saline powders," the elementary spirits explain the invention as a product of scientific concerns to make available "all that can delight the senses," since among the Babylonians "one of the things upon which emulation prides itself most, is having a delicately served table." And this was an occasion to take yet another swipe at Voltaire's renowned praise for cuisine.

Both literary interest in delicate eating and serious scientific attempts to explain its principles were, in this formulation, absurd and even immoral. The chemical solution to pleasing the sense of taste was "sensual & ambitious," and the scientific knowledge of essences and combinations vaunted by Giphantie's spiritual liquorists was, by implication, little better than the Babylonian addiction to imported foreign liqueurs and nouvelle cuisine, with all their attendant dangers for health:

> The most exquisite wines have not been able to fix [the Babylonians'] taste; they esteem only that which they owe to violence against the order of natural productions. They concentrate the most active parts of wine; they join to this all that the Indies sends them in aromatics; &, with such liqueurs, the seeds of fire gathered in all the countries of the world flow in their veins.

Tiphaigne de la Roche also toyed with the notion of an instrument for measuring animal spirits, since "different casts of *esprit*, different talents, different dispositions depend upon the heat & greater or lesser motion of the animal spirits: this is a matter that the natural philosophers have decided."

He imagined a thermometer filled with a suitable spirituous liquid, which would measure individual aptitude for various activities by a scale rising from cold-headed to hot-headed: "Fit for history, fit for natural philosophy, fit for poetry, fit for the robe, fit for the sword, fit for the mitre, fit for the marshall's baton, fit for the madhouse."[68]

If philosophes like Poncelet could mount sustained and experimentally supported challenges to prevailing medical accounts of the dangers of fashionable drinks, incorporated distillers deployed a different strategy, in which novelty and inventiveness were solutions to the fragility of taste. The distiller and grocer Sauvel, for example, confronted the health critique directly and, with typical aplomb, turned it to commercial advantage.

> Our factitious needs, which keep the inventive spirit of the artisans of luxury in constant torture, never render them more industrious than when it is a matter of modifying the aromatics of the Indies & of Arabia to please the worn palates of our Apiciuses. . . .
>
> The pleasing Coquette, the Bouquet of taste, the unknown Admirable, the Springtime or the Green-Gallant, the Bouquet of Bouquets, &c, &c. These are some of the baroque names that are given to drinks which make thousands of hundredweight of spices circulate in our veins, & make us older at thirty than our forebears were at forty-eight.
>
> —An ample assortment of these liqueurs, made with all possible art & care, is in the stock of sieur Sauvel merchant grocer & distiller rue neuve des Petits-champs, on the corner of rue neuve des bons Enfans; at the Provence shop.[69]

Such parodies suggest that the possible responses by connoisseurial consumers to dire medical prognostications might include an ironic, rather than a literal, interpretation of the health effects of liqueurs, a response entirely in keeping with the satirical mode characteristic of discourse in the spaces of connoisseurial consumption. The answer to the blunting of taste described by Vandermonde and other medical contemporaries was to challenge the palate with novelty—and who better to do so than artisanal en-

68. [Tiphaigne de la Roche] 1760, pt. 2, 3–14, 150; similarly, see [Desalleurs] 1739, 5. On Tiphaigne, cf. Marx 1981. This was a social as well as a learned hierarchy: the "robe" and "sword" were the two classes of nobles in Old Regime France, while the clergy is represented by the mitre. "Babylone" probably refers to an earlier satire, [de Montbron] 1759–60. Nutritional tablets were the subject of active experimentation at this time; see Spary 2009.

69. *Avantcoureur* (1761): 795–96. The names of liqueurs seem, here, to be invented, like those in Demachy 1775.

trepreneurs, renowned for the fertility of their imagination? Medical men, however, could respond to such claims by arguing that the distillers' very occupation dulled their own *esprit* and appetite, trenchant criticisms given distillers's attempts to enter the world of print, to present themselves as creatively inspired and to assert that their tastes were on a par with those of connoisseurs.[70]

If men of letters writing in the first half of the century sometimes allied diet with creativity on the basis of the chemical effects of foods and drinks upon physiology, the medical foundation for such claims was under attack by the 1750s. Simultaneously, the association between spirit, rational pleasure, and learning cultivated by men of letters was being challenged. The supporters of iatrochemical approaches to cuisine and learning had rested their arguments that the delicacy of taste could be preserved on the assumption that reason was strong enough to master the passions. This was a central feature of their claims about which individuals were capable of politeness and enlightenment, and it allied reason with health. Le Camus, for example, accorded rational moderation a significant role in the preservation of health:

> there is a middle point to everything, . . . everything is relative, & . . . in general a man who uses composed foods in moderation, will fare better than a man who uses a simple regimen to excess . . . doesn't man have reason as his guide, & wouldn't it be harmful to him if one were to doubt [reason] continually?

Vandermonde agreed that the exercise of the passions was legitimate as long as reason "guides us [and] holds the balance in equilibrium." His emphasis, however, was on the effects of transgression. "It is natural for man to be hungry [and] thirsty, to feel the impressions of love, as long as he . . . uses them with moderation; but if he gives himself over violently to his inclinations, hunger degenerates into gourmandise, thirst into drunkenness, love into libertinism. . . . Although all the passions are legitimate in principle, one step too far makes them illicit." Such a transgression could result from behavioral disorder or from the corporeal effects of ingesta, whereupon "our altered humors, our irritated organs cause us to find pleasure in passions which exhaust our body, stupefy our soul, & obscure our reason."[71]

For eighteenth-century writers, addiction could result from any form of

70. [Vandermonde] 1759, 2:46–47, "Maladies des Distillateurs."
71. Le Camus 1769, 480; Vandermonde 1756, 1:364–66.

passionate self-indulgence, particularly in food and drink. This was a model of addiction markedly different from today's accounts, in which certain chemical substances *within* ingesta produce changes in the brain chemistry that affect behavior. In these eighteenth-century writings, individual conduct was the primary trigger for addiction and habituation. For example, Déjean claimed that the abuse of liqueurs and spices produced ill health, rather than any quality intrinsic to those particular foods.[72] It was the pursuit of unbridled pleasure, the flight from reason, which caused the individual to become enslaved to particular ingesta. This was the central claim of Tiphaigne de la Roche's 1765 novel *Sanfrein* (Brakeless). The clergyman hero began by cultivating moderation until he was "almost a Philosophe," then engaged in libertine behaviors such as gambling to test the strength of his newly acquired morals. All too soon, he found that moderation yielded to excess. From a dispassionate attitude toward the pleasures of the table, he became "one of the great Wine connoisseurs, & one of those who made most use of it," before finally losing the capacity for sensual pleasure altogether.[73]

Alimentary innovators' defense of the healthiness of new foods, like their claims to expertise over matters of taste, hinged on the claim that the cultivation of taste and the embrace of new luxuries were unproblematic, even beneficial for society. But portrayals of a luxury lifestyle as harmful to health were increasingly common in antiphilosophical treatises and medical writings. A hygienic poem by the Paris faculty physician Etienne-Louis Geoffroy contrasted "table luxury & a debauchery which no brake can restrain" with "the wise precepts of Nature." Simple dishes no longer pleased blunted tastes, so that only "denatured foods" could please the modern eater. Above all, polite consumers prized the exotic and the unattainable. The French were "slaves to their mouths," and diseases were the inevitable consequence.[74] Ten years later, similar arguments allying cuisine and liqueurs with luxury and ill health were advanced by the bookseller Antoine-Prosper Lottin:

> In order to banish the monotony & boredom of the most sought-after pleasures, delights and *voluptés*, entertainments of all kinds succeed

72. Déjean 1759, 88.

73. Tiphaigne de la Roche 1765, 13. On nervous diseases as indicators of national decline, see Vila 1998, chap. 7; Mullan 1984; Moravia 1978.

74. Geoffroy 1774, 55–56; see also Tissot 1770. The clergyman Pluquet 1786, 1:96–97, argued that a man for whom happiness consisted in "the agreeable sensations that food produces" would be "incessantly occupied with the task of procuring [food]. . . . His need to be affected by agreeable flavors in order to be happy, equates to a constant need to eat."

> one another among these Sybarites [the Parisians] with astonishing variety and rapidity; such that these fortunate men seem only ever to have known laughter, games & a constant round of feasts. . . . Luxury . . . puts the goods which Providence has allocated to us to use in a way which is always detrimental to him who uses them . . . like those agreeable & perfidious liqueurs which man abuses, which cheer the spirit, arouse the imagination, & smooth the most wrinkled of foreheads, at the moment that one savours them; but which burn the blood & poison the days of those who indulge in them to excess.[75]

Just like nouvelle cuisine, luxury was a poison that procured fleeting pleasures for the imagination, but long-term decrepitude. It insinuated itself into all classes of society, even among the wise, producing a "universal uprising of men against their individual condition" so that people nowadays were ashamed to admit their true social rank. Nouvelle cuisine and liqueurs, those two domains of tasteful and peculiarly French excellence, were a particular target for fears about the power of consumption to overturn both reason and the social order.

By contrast, it was possible for the self-confessed sensualist Denis Diderot to represent the growth of appetites quite differently, as a form of social progress; any commerce that augmented the "mass of our pleasures" was beneficial, while any philosophy that "tends to hold man in a sort of brutalization, and in a mediocrity of pleasures and happiness" was contrary to nature.[76] Writing about cuisine was thus always a political act, insofar as it was a discourse about progress. Such writings, whether favorably or unfavorably disposed toward their subject, were ways of evaluating the significance of novelty, invention, consumption, and change for French society. Through the lens of cuisine, the political, economic, moral, and medical condition of the French could be critically examined.

THE POLITICS OF SELF-INDULGENCE

At the heart of the debate over consumption and alimentary delicacy was the question of the consequences of the proliferation of needs and the ex-

75. De Saint-Haippy 1784, 6–7. On the political implications of luxury and consumption, see also Pluquet 1786, vol. 2; Sekora 1977; Berry 1994; Miller 1995.

76. Duchet 1971, 436–37, quoting Diderot's contributions to Raynal 1770. Conversely, Pluquet (1786, 1:427) argued that luxury extinguished the faculty of reason, leaving the consumer an entirely sensual being.

perience of pleasure for French society. In his *Discours sur l'inégalité*, Rousseau argued for an undifferentiated progression from consumption to political vice: "in the first place it is a case of seeing to necessity, then to superfluity; then come pleasures, and then vast riches, then subjects, then slaves." "Needs" were strictly limited to the physical requirements—food, sleep, sex, and shelter—that preserved life. "Beyond physical necessity, everything is a source of evil. Nature gives us only too many needs; and it is, at the very least, extremely imprudent to multiply them unnecessarily, and so to put one's soul into a greater dependency." In his *Discours sur les sciences et les arts* of 1751, Rousseau associated the decline of mankind from the natural state with progress in the arts and sciences, which fueled a luxury that in turn engendered physical weakness. All practitioners of the sciences and arts thus toiled in the service of luxury and corporeal decline: "While the commodities of life multiply, while the arts perfect themselves and luxury spreads, true courage is enervated, the military virtues vanish."[77]

Many readers interpreted Rousseau's arguments as a disquisition on the relations between the passions and reason. In responding to him, they invoked the same arguments as the culinary authors about civilization as founded upon the rational experience of pleasure and the cultivation of the senses. The deposed ruler of Poland, Stanisław Leszczyński, defended *délicatesse* as commensurate with, even necessary to, the state of civilization. Following Hobbes, this philosophe king argued that primitive and civilized man were both governed by the passions. If certain peoples were less susceptible to their effects, it might be because they were physiologically closer to the brute: perhaps their "coarse senses" were merely "inaccessible to the attraction of pleasures?" Rousseau's equation between few needs and many virtues might thus be a misreading of physiology. A "primitive" society in which the senses were unregulated could be more liable to crime and vice than a civilized state, in which reason and pleasure were counterbalanced: "to what excesses might a volupté lacking all rules and knowing no restraints not lead?" In another "Refutation of the Observations of Jean-Jacques Rousseau of Geneva," the same point was made: "The more passions man has, the more the science of morals and philosophy is necessary to him in order to conquer them." Rousseau was quick to respond to such charges by turning the philosophes' self-appointed status as moderates against them: "I saw that men of letters were always talking about equity, moderation, [and] virtue, and that under the sacred safeguard of

77. Rousseau 1967–71, 2:62, 141–52, 252. On the distinction between need and pleasure in eighteenth-century moral philosophy, see especially Gronow 1997, chap. 1.

these fine words they gave themselves over to their passions and vices with impunity."[78]

In a manuscript fragment dating from circa 1753–54, concerning climate and history, Rousseau distinguished several types of need. Physical needs related to the physical conservation of the body: they "were given us by nature and . . . nothing can deliver us from them." A second category of need stemmed from bodily appetites, which were "sometimes so violent, that they torment more than the true needs; but it is never absolutely necessary to satisfy them. . . . The needs of this second class have the luxury of sensuality, softness, the union of the sexes and everything which delights our senses as their object." A third and final category related to worldly needs, such as the need for glory or recognition. Clearly, the sensual pleasure of food belonged in the second class, along with leisure, sex, and other socially degenerative forces. In these early discussions, Rousseau embedded needs within his broader political critique of French polite society. Needs threatened the health and moral standing of the individual, and were the product of enervating luxury, a characteristic of the enslaving absolutist state. As Duchet has argued, needs were also given a positive role in history by contemporaries, as the motor for the progressive unfolding of human faculties and thus of civilization. But by the 1760s many men of letters, philosophes, and medical men were suggesting that the exercise of reason might not be sufficient to rein in the progress of needs and save France from moral perdition. In a neoclassical moral treatise, the radical Republican Gabriel Bonnot de Mably warned that if the unnatural needs created by the indulgence of volupté were to increase any further, then the French might never again be capable of virtuous government, and charged those who urged the self-conscious pursuit of pleasure with sophistry. The political condition of France was thus implicated in the rational cultivation of pleasure, viewed by an earlier generation of men of letters as the mark of enlightenment, *politesse*, and indeed Frenchness.[79]

But not all philosophical authors subscribed to this crisis of reason. The *Encyclopédie* article "Homme Morale" was another direct response to Rousseau's *Discours*. Its author, Charles-Georges Leroy, went on to publish numerous letters on animal intelligence in newspapers between 1762 and

78. Rousseau 1967–71, 2:72–76, 173–76. This last comment was a direct response to Le Cat 1971.

79. Rousseau 1967–71, 2:183–84; Duchet 1971, 359, with quotation; Mably 1763, 77–85. See also, e.g., Pluquet 1786, 1:81–82; Mah 2003, introduction. In later writings, Rousseau appeared to view reason less negatively.

1768, which appeared in collected form as *Lettres sur les animaux* (1768). A prominent theme in this radical treatise was the question of the cumulation of needs and the future of the social condition. In society, sheltered from the immediate pressures of his animal needs for food, sex, and shelter, man's passions and needs were transformed beyond recognition and appeared to lose all connection with the basic animal needs. The natural and social were so thoroughly intermingled, Leroy argued, that "one cannot always distinguish without difficulty what [man] owes to his own constitution from that which he owes to the social condition. Natural needs are stifled by a host of factitious needs, and these last produce the most noticeable impulses and movements in him." Greater social complexity generated greater needs, which tended to create social unrest as individuals competed to meet their own needs. Paradoxically, therefore, both social cohesion and social disunity resulted from the pursuit of pleasures in order to satisfy both the natural and factitious needs.[80] Two needs that must be fulfilled for happiness operated in social man. The first was the need for rest, which could only be met at a certain social level. The second was what Leroy called "un besoin d'exister vivement," a need for a feeling of life, which if unsatisfied produced boredom. Only by two means, variety or excess, could boredom be assuaged.

> In order to be happy, we are thus forced either to change objects constantly or to experience sensations of the same kind to excess. This produces an inconstancy by virtue of which our wishes can never reach an end, and a progression of desires which, forever extinguished by being satisfied, but reawakened by memory, stretch to infinity. This disposition, which soon causes the disease of boredom to succeed the most interesting emotions, is the torment of idle civilized man.

Factitious needs drove the development of the arts and sciences, such as cookery: "It is not the starving man whom it is difficult to satisfy; it is the sickened [dégoûté] man whose desires it is a struggle to excite; the earth supplies natural man, perhaps without much effort, with the coarse foods that suffice to maintain his vigor." Leroy drew upon contemporary views of fashionable consumers as superficial and fickle, and of the evil consequences of overindulgence, extending a by now familiar argument about sensual pleasure and its role in the formation of needs and habits to the political constitution of human societies. Man suffered from a constant need for "extraordinary spectacles whose novelty shakes his hibernating organs," including the

80. Leroy 1994, 145–53.

extremes of gustatory sensation, but also more sinister manifestations of the pursuit of novelty, such as the thirst for bloodshed and violence. Where there was power, this drive for novelty and violence could develop unchecked, producing tyranny and barbarism—words with a fateful echo a few years later. Indeed, for Leroy, this physiology was the very mechanism whereby societies declined, for political evil was the outcome of an unchecked drive to consume. Yet in the end he fell back on a standard philosophical response to concerns about passionate excess: exercising rational moderation in the pursuit of pleasure would ensure that the state of satiation which created boredom was never attained. "Reason, which is to say experience, rectifies . . . the errors of judgement into which we may initially fall concerning what seems to us essential to our happiness . . . the enlightened desire for happiness restrains the blind desire." Reason was still the philosophe's best answer to the political dangers of self-indulgence.[81]

CONCLUSION

Diet and taste possess a complex epistemological status. Like pleasure, they appear to be innate corporeal experiences, so intimate as to take on the appearance of fundamental natural drives, not open to historiographical analysis or cultural explication. This is certainly how some eighteenth-century writers also accounted for taste. Voltaire, writing in the *Encyclopédie*, attributed bad corporeal taste to an incorrigible defect in the organs; for him, corporeal and aesthetic taste were only related at the level of metaphor.[82] For the abbé Jean-Baptiste du Bos, writing some years earlier, however, this distinction was far less clear-cut:

> Do we reason in order to know if a ragoût is good or bad, and do we ever, after having established the geometrical principles of flavor, and defined the qualities of each ingredient entering into the composition of that dish, undertake to discuss the proportions in which they are combined, in order to decide if a ragoût is good? We do nothing of the sort. There is a sense in us [which is] constituted to know whether the cook has operated according to the rules of his art. We taste the ragoût and even

81. Leroy 1994, 106, 147, 150–53. Compare Pluquet 1786, 1:430–31, 463–67, and Thomas Trotter's 1807 account of the nervous temperament, discussed in Porter 1988, esp. xxviii–xxxii. Berry (1994, 116–25) identifies this self-generating "dynamism of human desires," driven by imagination, in the writings of the late-seventeenth-century author Nicholas Barbon.

82. Voltaire 1757.

> without knowing these rules we know if it is good. It is the same, in a way, for works of the mind and pictures which are produced to please us by moving us.[83]

The display of taste is often taken nowadays as an unwitting manifestation of inner moral nature, perhaps because tastes are so integral to the fashioning of personal identity. Pierre Bourdieu's account of aesthetic taste as a logic of the economy of cultural goods has been seminal in weakening this long-standing reductionist argument. Bourdieu presented taste as dual: culturally produced, yet internalized and thus naturalized. In considering taste, "the area par excellence of the denial of the social," he thus demonstrated the necessity for economic and social explanations of taste, as well as its cultural situatedness.[84]

In many recent accounts of eating, appetite, and alimentary taste, even those of considerable sophistication, human biology is given explanatory priority. Commentators have often perpetuated medical polemics against cuisine, appealing to a corporeal domain over which reason has no power; what one might term the "Voltaire trick." Stephen Mennell, for example, does not analyze eighteenth-century claims about cooks as seducers of taste, but presents taste as an innate corporeal force whose outer expression can never be completely concealed. This is in spite of the fact that Mennell bases his sociology of eating upon Elias's account of the progressive concealment of bodily behaviors. As I have tried to show, however, such claims were not transparent in their origins. Even a statement such as Voltaire's reflected the contested nature of the terrain of polite taste. Jean-Louis Flandrin likewise argued against such biological reductionism, taking taste to be a cultural product, an expression of self subject to historical change. Medieval eaters, he suggested, possessed "a taste differing from our own because shaped by other dietetic beliefs, other alimentary habits." To rewrite the history of corporeal taste, we need a history of physiological explanations for taste and the various purposes such explanations could fulfill, from bolstering the status of a particular group of food producers to fueling the autocritique of French polite society in the later eighteenth century. Accordingly, past and present scientific or medical models of taste cannot be treated as objective, disinterested, or politically neutral. One program for such an inquiry is charted by Sidney Mintz, whose account of changing sugar consumption

83. Du Bos 1719, quoted in Menant 1981, 60. The same view of taste as the immediate, innate judgment of polite persons is evident in de Vassetz 1704, 3–4, 6, 32.

84. Bourdieu 1994, 11; see also Gronow 1997, chap. 2; Shilling 1993, 128–30.

in Britain during the eighteenth and nineteenth centuries is underpinned by an anthropological account of taste in which "meanings [do not] inhere in substances naturally or inevitably." Mintz notes: "Cross-cultural studies of dietary preferences reveal eloquently that the universes that human groups treat matter-of-factly as their 'natural environments' are clearly social, symbolically constructed universes." A symmetrical approach to the history of science should allow the accounts of taste produced within scientific and medical communities to be subject to inquiry and analysis in the same way as those generated in the arts.[85]

I have argued that nouvelle cuisine was a literary, somatic, and gustatory practice drawing its scientific credentials from the claim that chemistry and geometry provided the best models for representing true events within the body. This claim, however, was already under attack by the 1730s. In later decades, more elaborate rebuttals of the moral claims of supporters of nouvelle cuisine would take shape. These would rest not so much upon proving or disproving the healthiness of nouvelle cuisine, as upon different arguments about the power of reason over the corporeal passions or inclinations. The chemistry of spirit had made possible a nosology in which nervous, mental, and corporeal function were all on a par in ontological and causal terms; moreover, it supplied a heuristic for passing from behavior to mental function, to sensual pleasure, and thence to corporeal habits and composition. The body was a potential victim of its own passions; desires could rapidly transform the material fabric so as to become needs. Many savants of the 1740s were still confident of the philosophe's ability to practice moderation. But when the Prussian academy of sciences set a prize question for foreign savants in 1769 on the plasticity of natural inclinations, it was answered by an essay—in French—asserting the overwhelming power of nature over education. After Rousseau, this was an increasingly common line of argument among authors opposed to the status quo of French courtly absolutism, but it also reflected growing concern about consumption's power to remodel French morals. Indeed, as the consumption of luxury goods increased during the eighteenth century at all social levels, in response to Crown programs for encouraging domestic and international trade, so the problem of consumption and the problem of government increasingly came to seem one and the same. Reforming administrators, men of letters, physicians, and savants perceived the issue of proliferating needs to be bordering a national

85. Mennell 1996, 33; Flandrin 1989, 307; 1996a, 508; 1999; Mintz 1985, xxix, 8; Bayley 1991, 174–75; Teuteberg 1993.

political crisis. By the middle years of the century, the long-standing tension over whether alimentary innovation denoted European progress or decline had come to a head.[86]

In the case of liqueurs, ragoûts, pâtés, and other emblems of nouvelle cuisine, the expert maker's task was to compose a food that displayed the properties of a member of polite society. Its taste, like worldly manners, should be neither coarse nor extreme, but should express a harmonious balance of flavors, mirroring the balanced passions of the polite, rational person. Expertise in the manipulation of tastes thus depended upon the possession of knowledge about how to produce a harmonious product and even entirely new tastes, through perfectly balanced combinations. This was the principal role of the cook or liquorist but, increasingly, both their artful production of foods and the state of politeness itself were presented by commentators as morally bankrupt, politically as well as medically dangerous. The spread of luxury consumption to poorer sections of the city's population raised the specter of a society controlled by, rather than controlling, the flood of new goods pouring from the shops and workshops of merchants and artisans, and contaminated by the foreign substances on which they depended. Critics of luxury dwelt on ways in which the polite connoisseur could be deceived by artists with superior gustatory skills. The debate over food, drink, and taste thus served as a focus for discourse about the relations between the bodies of French consumers and their foods, and about the transformative effects of commerce on reason, government, and society. In this sense, models of bodily function in the eighteenth century must be addressed if we are to give a full account of Enlightenment, both as a product of mental function and as a project for the reformation of society. In a very profound way, the opposition between the natural and artificial, which Rousseau in particular would highlight as a political crisis for French readers, was being worked out in debates over cuisine in the middle decades of the eighteenth century.[87]

These polemics allying the formation of gustatory habits to the degradation and coarsening of the mind and body also shaped the language in which our models of addiction are still formulated today, as governments worldwide devote vast resources to controlling the consumption of "addictive" compounds. But the medical distinction between foods and "stimulant" or "psychoactive" substances invoked in recent histories is of nineteenth-century

86. Review of Kéralio 1769, in *Année Littéraire* 1769.vii.131–39.

87. Starobinski 1988, chap. 2.

origin.[88] This chapter has argued that taste, pleasure, and need themselves have a history, and that this history structures more recent debates over the economics of consumption. For this reason, past understandings of consumer choice and innovation (and their social significance) provide a better foundation for the history of early modern consumption than economic analyses of people as consuming agents. We need to evaluate the emergence of such models of consumption and invention within their culture of origin, rather than treating the consumer as a timeless economic agent; only then can the political legacy of the beginnings of consumerism and its role within more recent economic analyses be fully appreciated.[89] Early eighteenth-century models of need, excess, and habituation, for example, differed from today's models of addiction in that they prioritized individual behavior, not chemical, biological, or economic essences, to explain why consumption posed a social threat.

The distance between a model of need that looked to the eater's conduct as the cause of ill health, and our own culture, which proscribes particular substances for their exceptional effects upon the body, is evident in Philippe Hecquet's explanation of opium habituation in terms of the action of nervous fibers. Hecquet enthused over opium as a corrective to nervous disorders, proclaiming it to be no more dangerous than wine; it was, he said, "uniquely the abuse of Opium which should be attacked . . . the blame should neither fall on the quality of the Opium, nor be imputed to malignity on the part [of the drug]." In the age of Enlightenment, many if not all ingesta were viewed as potentially "addictive"; habituation to any particular foodstuff or flavor wrought havoc upon body and mind and became an irreversible need which it was dangerous to break. Alimentary risk thus lay with the eater, not the eaten. Above all, however, it lay with the departure from reason that disorderly eating represented.[90]

88. On stimulants as a historical category, see my discussion above in chapter 4. Berridge 1978 advances a similar argument for the medicalization of opium eating in nineteenth-century Britain; see also Berridge and Edwards 1987, introduction and chaps. 1–3; Parssinen and Kerner 1980; Davenport-Hines 2002, chaps. 1–3. Opium studies are one domain where the cultural complexity of attempts to classify recreational ingesta has been explored in some detail, though much of the literature still takes medical claims for granted, e.g., Booth 1996; Butel 1995; Musgrave and Musgrave 2000, 117–39.

89. Compare Bianchi 1998. In one leading source of the new theory of consumption, Scitovsky 1976, which presents consumers as pleasure-seeking individuals rather than the rational agents of neoclassical economic theory, the account of novelty bears strong resemblances to the eighteenth-century model (Rizvi and Sethi 1998).

90. [Hecquet] 1726a, 75. This continued to be the case in Britain until the 1830s; see Berridge 1978, 456–57.

CHAPTER SIX

Rules of Regimen

In 1754 the artist, monarchist and natural philosopher Jacques Gautier d'Agoty recorded his trials of an "alimentary powder" made of a mixture of semolina and dried salted meat or veal jelly, in his journal *Observations sur la physique*. Just six ounces a day were claimed to sustain "the most robust and hard-working man," and the mixture would keep for several years.

> I nourished myself with it for months on end in order to retire from the world and devote myself entirely to studying. . . . My books and instruments, and an eighteen-pound pot of this compound, were all my munitions of war and mouth. With the former I attacked Newton and Descartes on paper, and with the latter I made two good soups a day; during that time I did wonderfully. . . . I could have passed as a sorceror or a great saint in my district, if I had wanted to make a mystery of my regimen: for it was positively known that no-one brought me any food, no provisions were ever seen to enter my home, and I was never seen to leave my observatory. . . . To console my relations, I appeared at the window for half an hour a day.[1]

1. Gautier d'Agoty 1754, 131–32, § XXII. The powder was based on an invention of the Swiss military surgeon Bouèbe, proposed to the naval ministry in 1753 and trialed at the Hôtel Royal des Invalides on behalf of the army. See *Journal Œconomique* October 1754, 99; anon. 1755; Archives Nationales, Paris, Mar-D[3] 42, f°s. 210–39; Service Historique de l'Armée de Terre, ms. 3556; Bibliothèque de l'Académie Nationale de Médecine, Archives de la Société Royale de Médecine, ms. 201, dossier 9: Sabatier, "Mémoire sur La conservation des Equipages." The store of Bouèbe's powder was reopened in the 1780s and found to be still edible; see Parmentier 1781, 352–58; Legrand d'Aussy 1783, 1:110; anon. 1788, 251n–252n.

Observations sur la physique is better known as the *Journal de physique*. Edited after 1773 by the agronomist abbé François Rozier, the periodical has been held up as an early example of specialization in the natural sciences.[2] In the hands of d'Agoty, however, it was a unique testament to a one-man scientific crusade. The many articles in which he recounted experiments he had performed before the king, described his observations in natural history, optics, and astronomy, reviewed new books, intervened in current scientific disputes, and published useful secrets of the arts, all served to establish his scholarly credentials. But as the quote above suggests, d'Agoty's program for the manufacture of learned credibility also encompassed the conspicuous control of lifestyle.

Gautier d'Agoty's journal offers us just one among many eating strategies adopted by men and women of letters in eighteenth-century France in the attempt to present themselves as enlightened. The main focus of this chapter will be the heart of philosophical life in mid-eighteenth-century Paris, the salons and literary circles of urban polite society, at a time of notorious fights over materialism, deism, and theism. These highly public conflicts shook Paris and Geneva, filled the journals and theaters, and seemed at times to divide Parisian men of letters sharply into encyclopedists and antiencyclopedists. In seeking to capture a learned status for which many groups competed, salonnières and their guests made explicit choices among particular repertoires of lifestyle, in which eating played a prominent role. Accounts of personal regimen in correspondence, journals, and medical consultations demonstrate how the consumption choices of polite and lettered individuals were ways of negotiating the relationship between politeness, health, philosophical authenticity, and medical authority.

As chapter 5 has shown, mid-century reformers began to question the credibility of those who claimed that reason could be extended to the pursuit of sensory pleasure by cultivating the faculty of taste. French connoisseurship became embroiled in a politicized debate over the deleterious consequences of the creation of new needs for a society increasingly dominated by luxury consumption. The most vocal opponents of nouvelle cuisine were reformers who for one reason or another dissented from French courtly styles of eating and knowing—Swiss or French Protestants like Samuel-Auguste-André-David Tissot or Louis de Jaucourt, disgruntled diplomatic aides like Gabriel Bonnot de Mably. Reformers appealed to nature as the source of true government of the individual and the nation, and advocated abstinence, frugality, and extreme sobriety as lifestyle practices that

2. McClellan 1979, 427.

would allow French eaters to combat the adverse health effects of life in a luxurious, absolutist society. The rejection of fine eating in favor of abstemiousness had long been a way of rejecting the political status quo of the Old Regime, as I showed in chapter 1. However, during the 1750s, this opposition consolidated to offer a serious alternative to the system of patronage that dominated polite lives and conduct, with the monarch as its chief representative. Fashionable eating, with its courtly origins, now came under widespread attack in the name of nature and health. Paradoxically, this occurred at a time when nouvelle cuisine itself was becoming increasingly mainstream, and luxury foods were beginning to enter the everyday life of many urban inhabitants, not just the wealthiest.

Though advice literature concerning the lifestyle of men of letters flourished in the second half of the eighteenth century, medical models were far from being the only resource on which learned eaters could draw in constructing themselves as enlightened. The relationship between the scholarly state and eating was much older. Steven Shapin recounts a well-known tale of Isaac Newton keeping William Stukeley waiting for so long that Stukeley ate a chicken intended for Newton's dinner. When Newton finally arrived to find nothing but the bones, his first interpretation of events was that he had already eaten and forgotten the fact. Accounts like this, Shapin argues, draw our attention to enduring traditions of the disembodied scholar, and to the place of eating or abstinence in the fashioning of scholarly status. For contemporaries, the dietary conduct of men of letters was relevant to the evaluation of their knowledge-claims. But what was praiseworthy evidence of philosophical disembodiment in Newton bordered on a supernatural practice when adopted by his less famous rival, d'Agoty.

Learned styles of eating competed with alternative alimentary repertoires that conflicted and intersected in the lives of individuals who at some point presented themselves, or were presented, as learned. Even the best-known philosophes, writers of the order of Voltaire or Diderot, were acutely aware of the political stakes involved in the pursuit of health and the exercise of dietary choice. In their self-fashioning, the philosophes, like other literate medical clients, contended with older connoisseurial claims about the relationship between cuisine, chemistry, and creativity, but also with new medical programs for preserving the strong and natural body, both of which had particular relevance for a learned self-presentation. This chapter will address the responses of literate eaters themselves to the perceived political crisis of appetite. How did philosophes and polite readers reform their lifestyle practices when confronted by conflicting models of alimentary conduct in moral treatises and medical advice? Eaters selected among these alimentary styles as they were confronted with different performative settings that placed particular demands upon them. Thus, though eating was indeed central to self-fashioning, eaters inhabited multiple rather than singular personae.[3]

The relationship between eating and identity was fraught with ambiguity. On the one hand, the act of eating was artificial, a mannered act in which inner nature was to be concealed, just as the task of cooks in nouvelle cuisine was to disguise the identity of individual ingredients. On the other, eating habits were commonly also taken to display authentic inner nature, either by manifesting deviant appetites or through the adverse health effects of a bad diet. These issues of appetite, authenticity, and control—of the eater's engagement with foodstuffs, and of the transformations of both foods and eaters during that encounter—are the central concern of this chapter. Eating choices were part of a complex dialectic between alimentary advice, multiple scholarly identities, and the polite grammar of cuisine. If special categories existed for scholarly eating habits over many centuries, that is because they were perpetually reworked in new situations where a "scholarly" self-presentation continued to be valuable. The dietary choices of men and women of letters were thus the point at which questions of individual self-government translated into broader questions of national or enlightened identity.

Philosophes and salonnières were readers of medical and culinary literature, and formed part of the clientele of physicians and cooks. Their interest in matters scientific and medical, as well as their status as elite medical consumers, qualified them as expert lay commentators on medical matters. But the work done to confer meaning upon particular strategies of eating was not all done by scholars. They themselves were judged according to models of wise eating operating within their own culture. While they participated in making and enforcing such definitions, they were also subject to the expectations and exhortations of others, including medical practitioners, family members, cooks, even journalists. The state of the body was disclosed only to an audience meeting certain criteria of personal intimacy, such as relations and lovers, and to chosen medical practitioners. The latter thus played a key role in guiding eaters as to the link between food and self-fashioning. The tendency of medical authority to embrace lifestyle reflected the need of the literate elite to sustain enlightened and polite

3. Shapin 1998; see also Iliffe 1998, 123. On strategies of eating in relation to learning, see Onfray 1989, introduction; Steinmetz 1988, 22.

self-presentations. But in order to qualify as authoritative in polite society, physicians themselves needed to present a learned identity, mediated by publication and sociability.[4]

WHEN IN ROME

In Diderot and d'Alembert's famous *Encyclopédie*, the article "Goût" (Taste) was written by chevalier Louis de Jaucourt, scion of a French family that had never abjured Protestantism and continued to practice its faith clandestinely. As a young man, de Jaucourt had undertaken a tour of European Protestant centers of learning under a pseudonym. In Leiden he studied medicine under Herman Boerhaave, where his fellow student and lifelong friend was the Genevan Théodore Tronchin. De Jaucourt was a prodigious contributor to the *Encyclopédie*, whose output increased at a time when the project, in political trouble after 1759, was shedding many collaborators. His articles on taste and flavor were extracted verbatim from Le Cat's treatise on the senses; taken together with other articles he contributed on cookery, food, sobriety, and self-indulgence, they form a comprehensive polemic against French dietary habits that reflects de Jaucourt's Protestant medical training. In one of his early articles for the *Encyclopédie*, "Cuisine," de Jaucourt attacked by name the treatises of nouvelle cuisine and drew a historical portrait in which cooks participated in the progressive corruption of tastes:

> There is a pretty general agreement to disfigure the foods that nature supplies in a hundred different ways, which by this means lose their good quality, and are . . . so many flattering poisons prepared in order to destroy temperament and abridge the course of life. . . . Cookery, which was simple in the first ages of the world . . . , is now a science of the most laborious kind, on which we see new treatises . . . appearing every day.

The "experimental researches of sensuality" that scientific cookery undertook yielded nothing beyond ill health. De Jaucourt's critique drew heavily upon Seneca's picture of culinary excess in the Roman empire after its corruption by Asiatic luxury. Such comparisons were politically charged: as in

4. On the politics of personal transparency, see Starobinski 1988; on the "communication approach to consumption," see Douglas and Isherwood 1996, xiii; de Knecht–van Eekelen and van Otterloo 2000.

classical Rome, French adherents of *bonne chère* might eventually find that they formed a nation of degenerate weaklings.[5]

De Jaucourt's critique was not a salon commonplace before 1750. Mme de Graffigny, a salonnière, had commented to a correspondent in 1741 that nouvelle cuisine "does no harm to those who don't eat too much of it, and is good in itself," while the iatrochemist Antoine Le Camus deemed nouvelle cuisine necessary for mental labor. "A simple regimen which is always uniform, is not favorable for the mind," he observed. "Based on this principle, one should permit the moderate use of ragoûts and some succulent and spiced meats to men of Letters, be it to stimulate their tardy digestions or to volatilize their nervous juice [suc] which gradually hardens." By contrast, ragoûts, a dish of meat in sauce that formed a centerpiece of nouvelle cuisine, were singled out for criticism in cookbooks that emphasized health.[6] In general, the chemical pretensions of nouvelle cuisine attracted increasing criticism in cookbooks written after 1750. When the culinary writer Menon published his *Cuisine de santé* (Healthy Cookery) in 1758, Marin's version of nouvelle cuisine was specifically targeted as unhealthy for its emphasis on chemical knowledge. A reviewer noted that the book's contribution to health lay not in a different choice of foods, but rather in reforming "the gravies, *coulis*, consommés, restoratives & other ingredients of that nature, which make our kitchens resemble true chemical laboratories."[7]

Behind this abandonment of iatrochemistry were new portrayals of the ideal body as strong and robust, a composite of fibers rather than a collection of chemical principles. The chemical eater of the 1700s to 1740s differed in several fundamental ways from the health-conscious eater of the

5. Louis de Jaucourt, "Cuisine" (1754), "Goût" and "Gourmandise" (1757), "Intemperance," "Saveurs," and "Sobriété" (1765), all in Diderot and d'Alembert 1751–77, 4:537–39, 7:758–61, 7:754, 8:806, 14:708–10, 15:248 respectively. Morris (1979, ii–iii, 4–6) shows de Jaucourt used his *Encyclopédie* articles as a platform for a social, moral, and political critique of absolutist France; the quote here paraphrased an earlier reformer, Fénelon (Leplâtre 2008, 84–86). On de Jaucourt's culinary articles for the *Encyclopédie*, see Bonnet 1976; Spang 2000, 14–15; Flandrin 1989, 289. Famous Roman eaters, such as Lucullus, Apicius, or Heliogabalus, were well known to contemporary readers. On the opposition between alimentary pleasure and health, see Fischler 1993, chap. 8.

6. De Graffigny 1992, 3:262–63: Letter 418, Mme de Graffigny to Devaux, October 8, [1741]; Le Camus 1769, 1:480–83. Staum 1980, 61–63, and Vila 1998, 85–88, both mention Le Camus's argument that mental function could be enhanced by diet, but do not explore the chemistry on which it rested. On ragoûts, see [de La Chesnaye and Briant?] 1750, 3:235–36; 1:xiv–xv; Cowan 2007.

7. Review of [Menon] 1758 in *Suite de la Clef ou Journal historique sur les matières du tems* 1758.1, 183–84. See also Jacquin 1762, 163; [de La Chesnaye and Briant?] 1750, 2:107, 521.

1760s. This shift can be measured in the changing connotations of the term "*délicatesse*." As I argued in chapter 5, delicacy had been a distinguishing characteristic of polite and connoisseurial eaters since the late seventeenth century, and delicacy in matters of taste was a physical impossibility for the diseased body. By the 1750s, however, the connoisseur and the healthy eater were diverging. Moderation was gradually being superseded as a principle of dietary conduct, as models of alimentary delicacy were challenged by negative portrayals of sensual pleasure. The healthy eater of the 1760s was exhorted to be physically robust; delicacy, as the opposite of robustness, now acquired connotations of physical frailty and civic incapacity. Those who continued to espouse connoisseurial models of eating and delicacy viewed these new developments as a simple misapprehension. The author of the article "Gourmandise" in the Jesuit *Dictionnaire de Trévoux* of 1771 merely reasserted that rational choice and variety were sufficient checks to unregulated consumption, and charged the *Encyclopédie* article by the same name with confounding delicate eaters with gluttons. But there, as elsewhere in his writings on cuisine, de Jaucourt was in fact advocating a very different model of alimentary self-conduct: abstinence.[8]

Exhortations to abstinence featured in a long-standing medical and moral critique of alimentary excess. For many authors, abstinence was distinct from moderation in moral and practical terms. The author of *Dialogues entre Messieurs Patru et d'Ablancourt sur les plaisirs*, writing in 1701, asserted that it was "moderation and not abstinence which conforms to God's intention." Abstinence was personified by Luigi Cornaro, a sixteenth-century Venetian nobleman abandoned for dead by his physicians at the age of forty, who, thanks to the adoption of a strict regimen, lived on until the age of ninety-one. This originally antimedical story was revived as a medical cautionary tale in eighteenth-century discussions of Cornaro.[9] Like moderation, abstinence demanded self-restraint "in the pursuit of the pleasures of the table," but writers calling for abstinence tended to configure *appetite* differently. "The

8. Trévoux 1771, 4:567; de Jaucourt 1757b. The *Dictionnaire de Trévoux* continued to support the claim that choice and variety were sufficient checks upon unregulated consumption. For a contemporary medical view of delicacy as a nonpathological state of sensibility, see Lorry 1781, 2:16–24. On the shift from chemical to mechanical physiologies at this time, see especially Clarke 1968.

9. Dornier 1997, quoted 176. For mid-century familiarity with Cornaro, see Tissot 1991, 119–20; Jacquin 1762, 4n; "Non-naturelles (Choses)" (1765), in Diderot and d'Alembert 1751–77, 11:222; Le Camus 1769, 1:463–67. French-language editions of Cornaro's treatise had appeared in Ramazzini 1724 and as [Cornaro] 1701, 1703, two translations which were much reprinted. See also anon. 1702.

art of preparing dishes to irritate the appetite of men beyond true needs, is a destructive art," wrote de Jaucourt uncompromisingly of cuisine. The Lausanne physician Samuel-Auguste-André-David Tissot exhorted Élie de Beaumont, Voltaire's friend and a leading legal defender of philosophical causes, to "great sobriety; men of letters are often not enough on guard against their appetite," and another anonymous physician advanced the same argument: "The essential point is to be very severe about the quantity of foods. One should always rest On one's appetite, and insensibly accustom the Stomach to have but few needs." In practice, this meant waiting until the digestion of one meal had finished before eating again. Because that entailed undergoing the disagreeable experience of hunger, authors recommending abstinence tended to accord reason a more limited ability to subjugate bodily appetites than the writers of culinary and philosophical works discussed in chapter 5.[10]

Appetite was thus the somatic locus where powers of mind might be overwhelmed by bodily desires. The main point of disagreement between the supporters of rational moderation discussed in chapter 5 and the supporters of abstinence concerned the relative strength of reason and appetite. In a series of discourses read before the Société Royale des Sciences at Montpellier, Tissot presented the physician as the assistant of nature, understood as a harmoniously interacting system of vital powers in the body. Aligning himself with the "animists" against French "machinists" like La Mettrie, Tissot argued that human action was governed by "sensitive appetites" deriving from the body's needs. Only man possessed an immaterial soul, and the ability to reflect and reason enabled man to act in ways which might conflict with the immediate demands of bodily appetites. These powers of self-denial, which Tissot identified with the exercise of free will, could not be explained by materialists.

> Gourmandise is a shortcoming of the body and not of the soul. . . . One might say to a gourmand machinist, why do you not teach your soul this lesson. *My soul you like tasty morsels but experience has taught you that these liqueurs and ragoûts destroy the health of your body, which is the greatest good of life, read a fine chapter of Seneca you will see there that nature is content with bread and water and that Cornaro*

10. De Jaucourt 1765c. This was a paraphrase of Fénelon, who in his "Voyage à l'île des plaisirs" had written: "The art of irritating men's appetite beyond their true need is an art of poisoning men." On Elie de Beaumont, see Bibliothèque Centrale et Universitaire, Lausanne, fonds S.-A. Tissot, IS 3784/II/144.01.04.01: Anonymous *mémoire de consultation* for Jean-Baptiste Elie de Beaumont, January 1, 1765; 144.01.04.05: Samuel-André-Auguste-David Tissot, *mémoire de consultation* for Beaumont, November 1, 1769.

> *succeeded in living for nearly a century on this diet although badly constituted.*[11]

Materialists, who denied the existence of the soul, could not rank the directives of rational knowledge concerning healthy eating over the promptings of the bodily appetites; they therefore had no philosophical grounds for preserving health or avoiding corporeal excess. In essence, the materialist body lacked self-control. Appetite would lead the individual inexorably astray; only reason allowed free will to dominate over the bodily appetites. But for Tissot, reason, divine in origin, could only be situated in the soul, whose existence materialists denied.

The exercise of reason would, moreover, lead a Tissotian eater to quite different alimentary choices from a Le Camusian one. For Tissot, indulgence in physical pleasure and the gratification of sensuality risked irreversibly undermining health and becoming an obstacle to the enjoyment of normal pleasures.

> The more we seek out agreeable sensations, the further we get from them. The more we pleasure them, the more choosy the organs become, [and] it is only by remaining in an appropriate simplicity that we can be sure of experiencing continued pleasure; the drinker of water will always find it exquisite, the man who wants spicy wines is always wanting new ones, and it is the same for foods. Organs which are constantly irritated by acrid foods and drinks become calloused; their sensation is blunted, leading to indifference to everything that is not spicy and out of the ordinary, which makes it necessary to nourish ourselves with unhealthy foods and drinks, and finally, in some cases, makes it impossible to nourish ourselves, because the end of such regimens is often a total disgust against which we are protected by a simpler regimen.[12]

If this account at first sight resembles the spiral of excess discussed in chapter 5, on closer inspection there are crucial differences. In particular, two entirely different models of nature were at stake. Culinary authors presented

11. Bibliothèque Centrale et Universitaire, Lausanne, fonds S.-A. Tissot, IS 3784/I/60.1: "Dissertations concernant l'empire de l'ame sur le corps humain. Luês a la Societé royale des sciences." See also IS 3784/I/86: "Essay sur la Nature," where Tissot claimed that the physician should be guided by the sick person's appetites. Trained at Montpellier, Tissot clearly aligned himself with other Montpellier supporters of vital forces. See Williams 1994, 25–66; Emch-Dériaz 1992a; Barras and Louis-Courvoisier 2001.

12. Tissot 1770, 157–58.

Nature as cornucopian, filled with riches which the eater was invited to exploit: it was both natural and healthy to "use all [foods] indiscriminately, & lay our hands on all the delicacies that Providence offers us in profusion." Likewise, the materialist physician Julien-Joseph Offray de La Mettrie called for active gratitude toward nature for her sensory gifts, rather than Stoic indifference.[13] The nouvelle cuisine principle of alimentary variety was thus supported by Nature herself.

By contrast, Tissot, Rousseau, and de Jaucourt resorted to a much more impoverished image of a Nature "content with bread and water." All consumption beyond basic necessity immediately altered and transformed Nature; all culinary interventions and dietary innovations were forms of artificiality. The route to pleasure lay not in nouvelle cuisine and the cultivation of gustatory expertise, but in self-denial and satisfaction with what was already possessed.[14] So far from arguing that reason could contribute to alimentary enjoyment, such authors saw pleasure as a target missed when it was actively pursued, and they expressed pessimism about the extent of rational self-control. Tissot exhorted his readers to reject more sophisticated and more pleasing flavors altogether in favor of a "simpler regimen." Rousseau explained at length the pitfalls of departing from the minimum alimentary requirement imposed by Nature:

> The more we distance ourselves from the state of nature, the more we lose our natural tastes, or rather, habit forms a second nature which our prejudices substitute for the former to such an extent that none among us recognizes the latter.
>
> It follows from this that the most natural tastes must also be the simplest for it is those which are the most easily transformed, while in whetting themselves upon and being irritated by our fantasies they take on a form which no longer changes. The man who is not yet of any country will adapt himself readily to the customs of any country whatsoever, but the man of one country will not become [the man] of another.
>
> This seems to me to be true of all the senses and especially for taste itself. Our first food is milk. We only accustom ourselves by degrees to

13. [Marin] 1750, xvij; La Mettrie 1996, 86, "L'École de la volupté." Thomson (1981, 69–77) views this work as a product of La Mettrie's contacts with Parisian libertine circles. Like Voltaire and Diderot, La Mettrie oscillated between sensualist and dietetic self-constructions, treating proper self-management as a prerequisite for pleasure; see Teulon 1998. On La Mettrie, see also Wellman 1992; Hecht 2004.

14. The significance of this impoverished version of consumption for definitions of luxury is discussed in detail in Pluquet 1786, vol. 1.

strong flavors, at first they revolt us. Fruits, vegetables, herbs, perhaps some grilled meat without seasoning or salt composed the feasts of the first men; the first time that a savage drinks wine, he grimaces and rejects it. . . . Let us preserve the child's primitive taste for as long as possible, let his nourishment be common and simple, do not let his palate familiarize itself with anything but mild flavors, nor form an exclusive taste for itself.[15]

Most susceptible to overindulgence were not the *peuple* in their unenlightened, passionate state, but the very embodiment of Enlightenment, the polite and the philosophes. For such authors, eighteenth-century polite tastes were always already corrupted, in some cases through parental inheritance, in others through lifelong practices of gustatory excess. This thoroughgoing corruption meant that polite tastes were no longer capable of accurately metering bodily needs. That connoisseurial ideal of the perfectly balanced, trained tongue and palate was a fiction; indeed, the connoisseur was perhaps the most corrupt of all, precisely because he was an expert in the creation and evaluation of new pleasures. Any appeal to *délicatesse*, variety, or balance was suspect, as a product of artificial ways of life. If Montesquieu, the author of *L'Esprit des lois*, could argue in 1748 that the cultivation of alimentary *délicatesse* created "plenty of sensations unknown to the rest of us vulgar eaters," a decade later Rousseau described his "new Héloïse" as having to *quit* the coffee habit in order to preserve her gustatory sensibility. The artful cultivation and perfection of taste sat poorly within the new accounts of the natural advocated by Rousseau and others.[16]

REGIMEN AND SELF-RULE

By the 1760s, then, delicacy was becoming a pathological condition, denoting ill health and a condition of physical—and sometimes moral and political—disenfranchisement that contrasted sharply with earlier figurations of the delicate man as the supreme product of civilization and the ultimate self-registering device. Delicacy, sensibility, and imagination, formerly desirable attributes of the polite individual and hallmarks of French *génie*,

15. Tissot 1770, 157–58; Rousseau 1967–71, 2:471–72, from the Favée manuscript of *Emile* (1762).

16.Montesquieu 1757, 765; Rousseau, *Julie ou la Nouvelle Héloïse* (1758), quoted in Bonnet 1979, 136–37. Vigarello (1999, 164–65) sees this as a generalized move away from nouvelle cuisine and toward a "rustic" diet. On the complex relationship between medical and libertine writings after 1760, see Wenger 2007, 263–67.

were increasingly linked to effeminacy and pathologized as the cause for an epidemic of nervous disorders afflicting fashionable society.[17] The shift from delicacy to simplicity was evident not only in print, but also in dietary practice. Most regular members of salon circles construed their eating habits in terms of regimen, a tradition familiar to all literate Europeans from Hippocratic and Galenic medical practice. In contemporary medical literature, regimen advice constituted a hygienic prescription for lifestyle. Hygiene was that part of medicine concerned with prophylaxis, and hygienic writings covered the six nonnaturals: airs, food and drink, motion and rest, sleep and waking, retentions and evacuations, and the passions. Every person's constitution, determined by the balance of the humors, indicated the rules of conduct he or she should follow in everyday life so as to maintain health. While regimen potentially addressed many aspects of everyday life, before around 1780 it was overwhelmingly concerned with diet, though some fashionable therapies like exercise and ventilation also featured prominently.[18]

With regimen, the mid-century eater participated in a total system of alimentary information, replicated and endorsed in dictionaries and cookbooks, in health manuals and medical advice. But because regimen was unique to the individual body in a way that chemical claims were not, the first requirement of eaters was to know themselves. One needed to counter the effects of disease, age, sex, climate, and season with the appropriate foodstuffs; one needed to know one's own constitution and, to some degree, act out the medical role it demanded. The mastery of such knowledge, moreover, allowed one to retain bodily autonomy in exchanges with medical men. Mme Geoffrin, leading salonnière of the 1750s and 1760s, ascribed her own sustained good health to the regimen she followed. In 1766, this "true philosophe of women" outlined her lifestyle to her daughter, the marquise de La Ferté-Imbault:

> I rise every day at five o'clock; I drink my two large glasses of hot water; I take my coffee. I write when I am alone, which is rare; I do my hair in company; I dine every day with the king. . . . I make calls after dinner; I go to the theatre; I come home at ten o'clock; I drink my hot water,

17. Rousseau 1976, 152; 1991b, 230–31; Vidal 2004; Vila 1993; 1998, esp. 94–107, 231–47; Spang 2000, 38; Flandrin 1989, 289–91; Vincent-Buffault 1991, 99–104; Russo 2007, prologue. On the critique of nouvelle cuisine as a critique of civilization, see Spang 2000, 50–57; Morton 1994, chap. 4.

18. On the eighteenth-century health literature, see Parkin 1996, mentioned by kind permission of the author; also Rey 1991; Spang 2000, 39–44; on the nonnaturals, see Engelhardt 1993; Emch-Dériaz 1992b; Turner 1982; Niebyl 1971; Rather 1968.

> and I go to bed. . . . I eat so little at these great dinners that I am often obliged to drink a third glass of water to appease my hunger. I owe my good health to the severity of this diet. I shall be faithful to it till I die.[19]

Mme Geoffrin's final illness and death were attributed by one of her philosophe guests, the abbé Morellet, to an error of regimen, though not of alimentary regimen—sitting in the cold in Notre-Dame cathedral. "It seems that the poor and excellent woman confirmed by her own example the adage which was frequently on her lips, that one never died but through stupidity." Central to the conduct of health, then, was the possession of knowledge: the mastery of the complexities of regimen and a particular understanding of one's own temperament were necessary preconditions for a successful maintenance of health.[20]

Neither the abstinence nor the claims to learning of salonnières were necessarily taken seriously.[21] Charles Palissot de Montenoy's play *Les Philosophes*, first performed in 1760, caricatured Mme Geoffrin together with Diderot, Rousseau, and Helvétius. The central character was a salonnière, Cydalise, who considered herself to have reached the age of wisdom. Embracing the new philosophy, Cydalise welcomes the *Encyclopédie* into her library, but is largely ignorant of classical learning. Her pet philosophes secretly mock the moral treatise she is about to publish. In order to win the hand of her daughter Rosalie, the hero must disabuse her of her illusions about the learned state. Accordingly, his manservant Crispin waits upon her on all fours, as a convert to Rousseau's state of nature (like Cydalise, he has read the *Discours sur l'inégalité*): "A taste for Philosophy before which all must cede / Has particularly made me choose the state of quadruped." Conjuring a lettuce from his pocket, Crispin parodies Rousseau's claims about modern civilization:

> In civilising ourselves, we have lost all,
> Health, happiness, and even virtue.
> Thus I enclose myself in animal life
> Here is my cookery, simple and frugal.

19. Letter, Mme Geoffrin to Marie-Thérèse, marquise de La Ferté-Imbault, July 8, [1766], quoted in Goodman 1994, 82 (Goodman's translation). The hot water diet was fairly well known in mid-century Paris.

20. Morellet 1988, 216. On another characterization of death as a product of (willful) error in regimen, see Marmontel 1972, 1:244.

21. On the salons, see Goodman 1994; Lilti 2005a–b; Pekacz 1999; Kale 2004, chap. 1, 2002; Landes 1988, chap. 2; on Mme Geoffrin's circle in particular, cf. Maison de Chateaubriand 2011.

Cydalise, meanwhile, proclaims: "For my part, I'd taste a pure delight [volupté]/To see us return to the state of nature." Here volupté was a purely philosophical pleasure, for, Palissot implied, Cydalise had become too old to experience sensual pleasure. In contrast with hearty convivial dinners, her salon suppers were decidedly dull:

> Not long ago Madame reformed her house.
> We no longer gossip except by means of reason.
> To begin with, that coarse gaiety,
> The delight of Guests [Traitans] and the food of the Vulgar, was banned;
> At your suppers one smiles, nothing more.
> If one is bored, at least it is with Mind [Esprit].[22]

Mme Geoffrin's displays of conspicuous abstinence at princely banquets were part of her self-fashioning as moral and learned individual. The *Encyclopédie* article "Envie," or craving, described "an immoderate desire to take solid or liquid foodstuffs of a particular kind, of good or bad quality, which are not usual or out of season, in preference to all others." This "depraved appetite" was defined as a "spiritual malady," a "lesion of the imagination" to which women were especially subject because of their more delicate organs. Female bodily weakness thus threatened at any moment to become a mental illness exhibited in excessive or unusual appetites. In contemporary medical writings, moreover, women were coming to be portrayed as more sensible, their bodies more delicate and their minds less forceful.[23] For these reasons, learned women needed to adopt far more extreme displays of self-restraint than did males. Mme Geoffrin's salon suppers were famously frugal: as another guest, Marmontel, recorded, "Their good cheer was succinct: it was commonly a chicken, spinach, an omelette."[24]

In eighteenth-century medical regimen advice, alimentary abstinence continued to be presented by authors as a secular virtue, fueled by the constant reprinting of works describing the attainment of longevity and good

22. Palissot de Montenoy 1975, ll.1105–6, 1111–14, 1093–94, 27–32; see also Barling's introduction to Palissot 1975, XII–XVII. Rousseau's claim that wild children went on all fours attracted widespread satirical attention (Meijer 1999, 126).

23. Arnulphe D'Aumont, "Envie" (1755), in Diderot and d'Alembert 1751–77, 5:735–38. Attacks on feminine learning were not new, but by the later eighteenth century women's exclusion from the political domain was being justified by appealing to female mental and physical frailty (Lougee 1976; Williams 1994, 54–56; Schiebinger 1989; Azouvi 1981; Vila 1995).

24. Marmontel 1972, 1:169.

health through strict regimen, such as the Cornaro case. Conversely, the visible consequences of greedy or luxurious eating served as an example of personal vice: educating his daughter Angélique, Denis Diderot "showed her the envious man with his hollow eyes and his pale, thin face; the intemperant man with his ruined stomach and his gouty legs; the luxurious man with his asthmatic chest and the remnants of numerous diseases that can't be cured."[25] Such characters exhibited the long-term moral and physical consequences of disordered appetites. But ascriptions of alimentary virtue or vice to specific individuals were almost always polemical. Many biographical sources attribute La Mettrie's death in 1751 to the consumption of a pâté or pie (a nouvelle cuisine speciality) at the court of Frederick the Great. Antimaterialist contemporaries dwelt with delight on the details of his demise. Antoine-René Ferchault de Réaumur regretted that the "monster" had died in his bed, but "at least he died there like a madman [enragé], crying, sobbing, howling, when he recognized that he had killed himself by having himself bled twice to cure himself of an indigestion." Most modern sources never ask why the pie figures so prominently in this necrography; the story is repeated as local color.[26] But La Mettrie, as perhaps the most outspoken materialist of the early eighteenth century, was abhorred by many French savants, including Réaumur, sometime president of the Académie Royale des Sciences and a committed supporter of natural theology, who saw him as representing learning without moral commitments, a world with no guarantee of ethical and spiritual standards. Réaumur's remark was by way of a morality tale: as La Mettrie was a true materialist, it was morally appropriate that he should die after a fashion that emphasized his corporeality and lack of self-control.[27] The anecdote undermined

25. Diderot 1875–77, 19: Letter CXXV, Diderot to Sophie Volland, Paris, September 11, 1769. See also Quinlan 2007, 35.

26. Quoted in Torlais 1961, 279. Voltaire wrote to the duc de Richelieu that La Mettrie "has just died of eating a whole pheasant pie with truffles" (Voltaire 1968–77, 12:313: Letter D4605, Voltaire to Louis-Armand-François du Plessis, duc de Richelieu, November 13, 1751); see also *Biographie Universelle*, 28:143–46. Gay (1966–69, 1:8–9) treats the anecdotes as gossip rather than a critique of materialism, while Wellman (1992, 6) interprets the death in Kochian terms, claiming that La Mettrie died "after eating contaminated pâté." In his eulogy of the dead philosophe, Frederick II of Prussia, more neutrally, claimed La Mettrie's death was caused by a "burning fever" (La Mettrie 1912, 9). Compare Onfray 1991, 275.

27. Similarly, the heterodox Voltaire was described in the *Gazette de Cologne* as dying "in frightful agitations, crying with fury, I am abandoned by God and men; he bit his arms, and putting his hands in his chamberpot and seizing what was in it, he ate it." Quoted in Bonnet 1982, 180. Compare La Mettrie 1996 for an account of the calm, philosophical death.

La Mettrie's claims to learning, even though he too had defended sobriety as the sign of a good life, and good regimen as the basis for mental development and the acquisition of "the knowledge of truth and virtue."[28]

Both supporters and opponents of materialism held that the successful practice of good regimen served as a secular, corporeal guarantee of right thinking; likewise, both sides treated indigestion as an indicator of personal laxity in mind and body. The diagnoses of La Mettrie's cause of death are significant because they aligned his specific physical disorder, indigestion, with a general mental disorder that must have produced both his beliefs in the materialism of the soul and his lack of alimentary self-control. Materialist philosophes inverted the relationship, identifying indigestion as a cause of poor mental performance. As Diderot wrote in November 1759, "I've tormented myself all morning, chasing after an idea which got away. I came down [to dinner] sad; . . . I sat down to a sumptuous table with no appetite; I had a stomach laden with foods from the day before; I overloaded it with the volume of food I ate. . . . But I see that I am digesting badly, and that all this sad philosophy is born from a burdened stomach."[29]

Réaumur was a reasonably wealthy man, whose dining room played an important role in his social life. At his hôtel in Paris and later in Charenton, he hosted dinners for gatherings of savants and polite society that were not noted for their frugality.[30] The point is thus not that there was some essential connection between philosophical commitment and alimentary conduct, but that charges of gluttony or self-restraint played an important polemical role in undermining or supporting the eater's claims to scholarly credibility. Conflicting demands on sociability and self-presentation ensured that polite eaters were constantly in situations of temptation and fall. Regimen was sometimes viewed as a penance, adopted to atone for earlier excesses; the language of sin and self-restraint used to describe its practice lent itself to such treatment. Health-manual writers might exhort their readers to pay ongoing attention to their diet, but most of them, unlike Mme Geoffrin, dieted in an expiatory, intermittent fashion. Diderot described how

> Damilaville invited me to supper with him, I accepted; I'm a glutton; I ate a whole pie; on top of it I put three or four peaches, ordinary wine, [and] Malaga wine, with a big cup of coffee. It was one o'clock in the

28. La Mettrie 1912, 64 (my translation).

29. Diderot 1955–70, 2:319: Letter 156, Denis Diderot to Sophie Volland, Grandval, November 3, 1759. Similar claims were made by La Mettrie 1912, 22.

30. On Réaumur's domestic arrangements, see Torlais 1961, 222–37.

> morning when I returned; I burnt in my bed and couldn't sleep a wink. I had the best conditioned indigestion. I spent the day taking tea; the day after that I was well enough to go to *Tancrède* [Voltaire's latest play].

The cycle of weakness, temptation, fall, penance, and absolution was here transacted via the gut.[31]

Such quasi-religious trajectories were present in many accounts of the eating self. In his *Mémoires* of 1802, Jean-François Marmontel, a second-generation philosophe, protégé of Voltaire, and leading light of the Académie Françoise after his election in 1763, recounted his journey from nutritional innocence, living on dairy products and fruits as a tailor's son in the notoriously poor Limousin, to lavish dining as a successful Parisian author, then finally to sobriety and self-control. This was a tale of alimentary redemption that served the *Mémoires'* wider agenda of shoring up Marmontel's political and literary reputation.

In Marmontel's childhood home, "order, economy, work, a little trade, and above all frugality, kept us in comfort." The familial alimentary resources included turnips, chestnuts, quinces, apples, pears, honey, buckwheat pancakes. "The excellent mountain butter and the most delicate cheeses were common and cost little; wine was not expensive, and my father himself used it soberly." Besides beef, the family also ate lard, ham, sausages, honey, rye, peas, and broad beans: an idealized version of a peasant diet. Marmontel recorded his grandmother's simple faith: "see the gifts that Providence has given us; how many honest folk have not received as much as us!" and her culinary skills: "While one was at mass, broth with green cabbage, black pudding, sausage, chitterlings, the most vermilion morsel of salt pork, cakes, apple fritters fried in lard, were all prepared mysteriously by her and one of her sisters." Marmontel's initiation as scholar was a parable of the triumph of frugality and devotion to learning over worldly engagement; abandoning a career in commerce, he lived in lodgings with a bed, table, and chair, an "anchorite's vessel" and a supply of bread, water, and prunes. This austere lifestyle at first characterized his Parisian existence as a poor man of letters, but after his play *Denis le Tyran* made him a wealthy man, he was swept away by the "whirlwind of Paris": "Invited every day to dinners and suppers whose hosts and *convives* were equally new to me, I let myself be abducted, as it were, from one society to another." Like Charles-Georges Le Roy, Marmontel consorted with "Diderots, d'Alemberts, Buffons, Turgots,

31. Diderot 1875–77, 18:447: Letter XXXIV, Denis Diderot to Sophie Volland, Paris, September 5, 1760.

d'Holbachs, Helvétius, Rousseaux" in Paris salon society, coming to roost in the salon of a wealthy financier, de La Pouplinière.[32]

> With neighbors like this, it was hard for me to husband my hours of either sleep or . . . work. The pleasures of the table also contributed to obscuring my intellectual faculties. I hadn't suspected that temperance was the nurse of genius, and yet nothing is more true. I awoke with a troubled head and ideas weighed down with the vapors of an ample supper. I was amazed that my spirits were not as pure and free as in the rue des Mathurins or des Maçons. Oh! that's because the imagination at work doesn't wish to be hampered by the action of the other organs. The muses, it is said, are chaste; it should have been added that they are sober.[33]

After the (resulting) failure of Marmontel's play *Les Funérailles de Sésostris*, Mme de Pompadour got him a post as *sécretaire des bâtiments* at court. Over the next years, up to his marriage, the playwright and poet alternated between philosophical and theatrical circles; in his *Mémoires* he identified the former as characterized by frugality and the latter by frivolity: "Yes, I admit, it was all good, the pleasure, study, the table, philosophy; I had a taste for wisdom with the sages; but I freely lent myself to folly with the fools." This happy state of things was not to endure, for his health suffered from the obligation to participate in Court life with its rich dinners. Only at the royal castles of Marly and Compiègne could he live "solitary and sober. Once at Compiègne I spent six weeks on milk for the pleasure of it, and in full health. My soul was never more calm or peaceful than during this regimen." Marmontel's frequent headaches led him to consult Genson, stable manager to the Dauphine, who recommended a healthy regimen:

> Dine wisely today, no ragoûts, no pure wine, coffee, or liqueurs; and, rather than eating supper tonight, drink as much clear cold water as

32. Marmontel 1972, 1:6–8, 17–18, 26, 79, 119, 220–26. On Marmontel's self-presentation as an exemplar of simplicity and naturalness, see Proust's introduction to Diderot 1964, XXX–XXXI; on his artisanal origins and entry to Parisian salon circles, see Kors 1976, 172–75, 207–13. On Alexandre-Jean-Joseph Le Riche de la Pouplinière, see Cucuel 1913, chap. 11; Durand 1971, esp. 523–25. His regular salon guests included, for example, Edmé-François Guyot-Desfontaines and Jacques Vaucanson. See Doyon and Liaigre 1966, 129, 141, 154.

33. Marmontel 1972, 1:106.

> your stomach can support without fatigue. . . . Observe this regimen for a few days, and I predict that tomorrow the attack will be weaker, that the day after tomorrow it will barely be sensible, and the day after that it will no longer exist.

Marmontel's dietetic self-accounting thus took the form of a passage from primordial alimentary innocence in his parental household, through a trial by fire in the world of urban temptations and courtly artifice, to a state of ill health that had to be combated by self-conscious sobriety—here specifically meaning the abandonment of foods from the chemical cuisine repertoire. The narrative was simultaneously a moral emplotment of the political options open to a man of letters in the Old Regime.[34]

Medical doctrines such as Hippocratic regimen partly replaced, then, the more orthodox religious codes abandoned by numerous philosophes. Christian moral structures of sin, guilt, and atonement were transcribed almost unaltered into the corporeal domain in a secular language of eating and, as Fernando Vidal has shown, sex. Now, however, the priests who could administer alimentary absolution were physicians. Eaters might protest at the strictness of the diets imposed upon them by physicians, but medical men could point to the earthly afterlife and the painfully immanent consequences of disobedience. According to Tissot, indigestion ranked high among the medical conditions typical of men of letters: "The man who thinks the most is he who digests the worst, all other things being equal." Their worst habit was reading at mealtimes: if "the busy soul suspends the distribution of animal spirits during the time when they are necessary to [the stomach], digestions are necessarily contaminated." However, men of letters tended to be willful: "all oppose to the physician an obstinacy that they take for firmness, on which they congratulate themselves and whose victims they become . . . one can say that in general men of letters are the most difficult sick men to guide [conduire]." Of the many men of letters, most produced work of little worth, Tissot argued; if one or two were Newtons or Montesquieus, the greatest number "do not even have the public in view and merely devour study as the *gourmand* devours meat to assuage

34. Ibid., 1:119, 132, 149–50. This tale of urban corruption and simple rural food fits well Rousseau's critiques of artificiality, but Marmontel was in fact a bitter opponent of Rousseau whose praise for moderation was denounced by Rousseau supporters as the ultimate in artifice and *politesse*; see Marmontel 1972, 1:XXIX–XLII; Diderot 1964, XXXI. For another autobiographical formulation of diet as redemption by a surgeon, see Pressavin 1986, "Discours préliminaire." On the ideal of the "natural" diet, cf. Pinkard 2009, chap. 6.

his passion." These learning addicts could be safely torn from their books by the physician.[35]

Men of letters' lack of exercise also adversely affected digestion: "The stomach weakens, the nature of the digestive juices alters, the digestion becomes slower, laborious, imperfect, because when the action of the digestive forces is diminished, rather than undergoing those changes which make a good digestion, foods scarcely do more than corrupt." These weak bodies required gentle foods: Tissot advised men of letters to avoid fatty, pasty, viscous, and windy foods, as well as dried or hard meats. Thus doughnuts, eel, pork, and beans were all banned. Permitted were tender young meats, most fish, cereals, chicory, root vegetables, bread, eggs, milk, fruit, and chocolate. A vegetable diet was especially recommended. Savants were allowed to use some seasonings, such as marjoram, thyme, basil, nutmeg, or cinnamon, but stronger flavors like pepper, garlic, and mustard were to be avoided. The Swiss physician also warned against variety, so prominent in the pleasure theory of nouvelle cuisine: the thinking man should "avoid mixtures of different foods, and never permit himself more than two or at the most three dishes at each meal."

This discussion of suitable regimen for the man of letters ended with a warning to the sensualists:

> Those who are attached to the pleasure of eating, might be tempted to envisage these rules as austere precepts which have never been followed exactly, and which it would perhaps be dangerous to follow to the letter; it is easy to reassure them with a host of examples which prove that a far greater sobriety than that which I have prescribed, is the sole means of preserving perfect health.

And Tissot cited a series of exemplary abstinent lives, including Anacreon, Paul the Hermit, St. Anthony, Arsenius, St. Epiphanius ("All lived for more than a century, by nourishing themselves only on bread, dates, some roots, a few fruits and water") . . . not forgetting Newton, who "during the time of his greatest meditations, lived only on a little bread and water, [and] occasionally a little Spanish wine; and during the course of his life, he took virtually nothing else but for a little chicken."[36]

35. Vidal 2004; Tissot 1770, 33, 75, 95, 97; compare Le Camus 1769, 1:474. On the secular morality of health and moderation, cf. Smith 2002, chap. 4; Stolberg 1998. On Tissot's treatise on the health of men of letters, see Godonnèche 1976; Vila 1998, 94–107.

36. Tissot 1770, 59, 108–21. Arsenius, Paul the Hermit, Epiphanius, and Saint Anthony of Egypt were prominent early Christian ascetics. Anacreon, the Greek poet of the sixth cen-

POLITICS OF THE PHILOSOPHER'S BODY: VOLTAIRE AND DIDEROT

The practice of sobriety in the eighteenth century involved eaters in certain types of bodily self-discipline that also structured the relations between the individual and the medical practitioner. In his letters to Théodore Tronchin, Voltaire frequently aligned himself with sober eaters: when ill, he described himself as trying "to vanquish the vile passion of gourmandise" with the "Sobriety which sustains me."[37] Yet such self-presentations are unlikely to have been neutral. In a well-known passage, Voltaire contrasted nouvelle cuisine with the food he served his guests, which was "more simple than delicate." His favored diet was explicitly philosophical in nature, "very ancient and good nourishment, on which all the sages of antiquity always fared well." The philosophe made the same links between delicacy and nouvelle cuisine as those discussed above, anathemizing substances—essences, flavorings, sauces, mushrooms, sweetbreads—which figured largely in other nouvelle cuisine critiques.

> I avow that my stomach does not cope well with nouvelle cuisine. I can't abide veal sweetbreads swimming in a salty sauce which rises fifteen lines above that little sweetbread. I can't eat a meat loaf composed of turkey, hare and rabbit which they try to make me take for a single meat. I don't like pigeon *à la crapaudine* (flattened and grilled to look like a toad), or bread without its crust. I drink wine in moderation, and I find those people who eat without drinking, and don't even know what they are eating, very strange. . . . As for the cooks, I can't bear the essence of ham, nor the surfeit of morels, mushrooms, pepper and nutmeg, with which they disguise dishes that are very healthy in themselves, and which I wouldn't even want to have larded.[38]

Like Voltaire's other writings on nouvelle cuisine, this text has been claimed to function on more than one level, in this case as a systematic parody of religious orthodoxy in which the diet of the "sages of antiquity" was deism,

---

tury BC, wrote bacchanalian and erotic poetry at the court of Polycrates of Samos, but in old age adopted an austere lifestyle.

37. Bibliothèque Publique et Universitaire, Geneva, Archives Tronchin, ms. 166, f°s. 9–10: Letter, Voltaire to Théodore Tronchin, June 18, [1756?]; f°. 13: Letter, Voltaire to Théodore Tronchin, undated.

38. Voltaire 1968–77, 29:287: Letter D12871, Voltaire to Henri-Jean-Baptiste Fabry de Moncault, comte d'Autrey, September 6, 1765. On culinary deception, see Davis 2009.

Voltaire's own creed. Voltaire's discussions of nouvelle cuisine were also part of his subversive appropriation of categories of health and disease, sobriety and delicacy, medical and political authority.[39]

Tronchin returned to his native Geneva in 1754, and Voltaire followed him soon afterwards, settling on the outskirts of Geneva in a country house, Les Délices, and later moving back across the French border to the feudal demesne of Ferney. This was a political move. Both illness and philosophical solitude served as justification for a strategic retreat from the demands of absolutism. Voltaire's medical self-presentation permitted him to avoid offending monarchs by a direct refusal of their requests. Rejecting the "invitation" of Frederick II to return to Prussia, the philosophe insisted: "I need nothing on earth save health. All my ambition is limited to not having colic." As he explained it in a letter to Tronchin, "I prefer my Switzerland[;] I will not go to Petersburg whither the autocratrix calls me, nor to Berlin whence the despot has written me a touching letter. I prefer my doctor in spite of his consistory." Voltaire's autonomy was thus in part attained and managed through an appeal to ill health. Tronchin's medicopolitical authority was acceptable only because it did not erode Voltaire's sovereignty over himself.[40] At Les Délices and at Ferney he established his own pastoral realm, producing much of his own food from the estate's farm and garden. Throughout the 1750s Voltaire represented his corporeal life as a constant encroachment upon the rules of healthy living. Oscillating between the demands of health and delicacy, he presented the philosophe now as hearty banqueter, now as reticent sage eating simply and soberly. When faced with political and philosophical opposition, Voltaire could retreat to a model of the philosophe as solitary and self-denying eater: "the horrors of the so-called men of letters make me despair, formal dinners are killing me. One

39. Mervaud (1998, 33–34) argues that this letter represents a coded attack on orthodox Christian theology, not Voltaire's actual culinary preferences. But several of the nouvelle cuisine references cannot easily be explained as religious metaphors, seeming rather to echo medical critiques of nouvelle cuisine as an art of deception. Given Voltaire's familiarity with Tronchin's Boerhaavian medical precepts, Spang's reading of this passage as a play on theology and chemical cookery operating at two levels seems most plausible (Spang 2000, 45). Voltaire's household accounts, published as Besterman 1968, suggest that he preferred the recommended foods for elderly valetudinarians—fowl, fish, crayfish, and fruit. Though the culinary treatment of these ingredients is not indicated by this source, there are few references in the household accounts to spices, strongly flavored foods or standard nouvelle cuisine accessories such as ham, truffles, liqueurs, or sweetbreads.

40. Bibliothèque Publique et Universitaire, Geneva, Archives Tronchin, ms. 167, f°. 94: Voltaire's annotation on a letter from Mme Denis to Théodore Tronchin, Monrion, February 7, [1757]. This in spite of the fact that Frederick himself assiduously cultivated the status of philosophe. For another account of Voltaire's deployment of health and illness, see Dawson 1999.

must be a philosophe in mind [esprit] and in stomach." Medical, political, and alimentary choices and judgments were thus inextricably linked in Voltaire's self-accounting.

If Voltaire refused to abandon coffee, he nevertheless complied with Tronchin's other recommendations. In 1757 he requested "liqueur wines . . . for my guests, and . . . cassia [a laxative favored by Tronchin] for me" from his Lyon supplier. His experience of embodiment was described in terms that subscribed to Tronchin's model of luxurious urban living as a principal cause of disease, contrasting "my frail Parisian body" with the "young and vigorous" body of a Swiss protégé. The characteristic dryness and inflexibility of the aging humoral body was a touchstone for his many descriptions of his own body as "dry" and "thin" and his understanding of his stubborn constipation as a product of "dry entrails."[41] Such attempts to inhabit the valetudinarian role were not always successful, however. Voltaire's friends praised his delicate table, but his enemies accused the philosophe of living a luxurious, even libertine, lifestyle. Some made use of his lavish hospitality to portray him as intemperant, while others sneered at attempts to link his eating habits to genius. The marquis de Luchet's six-volume *Histoire littéraire de M. de Voltaire* described Voltaire's daily life at Ferney in detail: "the great man remained in bed until midday . . . never dined and took coffee or chocolate, worked until eight o'clock, and then showed himself for supper when his health permitted." Reviewing this biography, Fréron the younger, editor of the *Année Littéraire*, scoffed: "It's a great pity that the Historian has not told us if his hero ate with a good appetite, whether he digested promptly, &c." Alimentary conduct was an intimate matter, whose disclosure to a wider reading public might be criticized as inappropriate or even demeaning.[42]

The self-accounting of Denis Diderot, editor of the *Encyclopédie*, reveals how social and political conditions shaped the philosophe's deployment of different medical and philosophical models of eating. Diderot, lack-

41. Voltaire 1950, 110: Letter, Voltaire to Théodore Tronchin, [September 29, 1755?]; 138: Letter, Voltaire to Théodore Tronchin, from Mont-Riond, January 8, 1756; 190: Letter, Voltaire to Jean-Robert Tronchin, Les Délices, December 22, 1756; 263: Letter, Voltaire to Jean-Robert Tronchin, October 12, [1757]; 266: Letter, Voltaire to Jean-Robert Tronchin, Lausanne, October 20, 1757. On dryness as a model of masculinity and asceticism, see Schivelbusch 1992, 49; Lorry 1781, 2:201–15.

42. Review of Luchet 1780, *Année littéraire* 1781.2: 97–98. Luchet (1780, 2:190) was quoting from a letter describing Voltaire's lifestyle in 1774. On Voltaire as libertine, see Sabatier de Castres 1781, 4:456–512; Fréron, review of Jean-Marie-Bernard Clément, "Satyre sur les abus du Luxe," in *Année Littéraire* 1770.v.108–15. On literature describing the bodily condition of the philosophes, especially Rousseau, cf. Vila 2007.

ing independent wealth, was a habitué of the salon of the baron Paul Thiry d'Holbach, a minor German noble of extraordinary wealth and a clandestine author of materialist books. If Voltaire was the father of philosophes, d'Holbach is often dubbed their maître d'hôtel, or chef.[43] In Diderot's correspondence with his lover Sophie Volland over two decades, he described his alternation between the lavish luxury of d'Holbach's households at Grandval and Paris and his own more modest Parisian lodgings with his wife and daughter. Life at Grandval was depicted as a continuous cycle of overindulgence: "We dine, well and for a long time. The table is served here as in town, and perhaps even more sumptuously. It is impossible to be sober, and it is impossible not to be sober and to be well."[44]

Diderot was well aware of the potentially invidious moral position of a philosophe who attached himself to the table of a rich man as a "parasite," and in his *Neveu de Rameau*, finished in 1773 or 1774, he borrowed from Horace's *Saturnalia* to present the two alternatives that lay before the poor man of letters. "He," Rameau, and his interlocutor "I," defended, respectively, the parasitic and the self-denying lifestyle. According to "I," sensuality was almost irresistible; the only person capable of living according to principle was "the philosopher who has nothing and who asks for nothing," like Diogenes, naked and feeding on nature's bounty alone.

> Rameau: Poor fare.
> I: It is abundant.
> R: But badly served.
> I: Yet it's the one whose remains are used to set our tables.
> R: But you'll admit that the ingenuity of our chefs, pastry cooks, caterers, restaurateurs, and confectioners put something of their own into it. With that austere diet, your Diogenes must have had very tractable organs.[45]

43. This cognomen appears to originate in a letter from the abbé Ferdinand Galiani, the Neapolitan critic of the économistes, to d'Holbach. See Sauter and Loos 1986, 61, Letter 42, Naples, April 7, 1770. Roche (1988, chap. 9) is one of the few authors to take the alimentary significance of d'Holbach's title seriously; compare, e.g., Boulad-Ayoub 1992. On Diderot's relations with d'Holbach, see Kors 1976, 14–15; on the salons as sources of patronage affording access to prestigious academic posts, Lilti 2005a, 170–78.

44. Diderot 1955–70, 2:264: Letter 146, Denis Diderot to Sophie Volland, [Grandval, October 1, 1759].

45. Quoted and translated in Gay 1966–69, 1:175. The tale of the famous Renaissance "parasite" Montmaur, a perpetual guest at the tables of the wealthy, was well known to contemporaries (Oberlé 1989, 216). In the passage quoted here, Rameau was a servant eating leftovers from the master's table. On the *Neveu de Rameau*, see Chouillet 1991.

The writings of the ancients, particularly Seneca, Horace, and Socrates, provided Diderot with two different versions of sociability and consumption in the "good" philosophical life: convivial overindulgence versus abstinence, simplicity, and solitude. Pleasures were to be sought in everyday life by a calm and philosophical fulfillment of the urgings of the natural passions; reason would check excesses and any descent into disorder mental, moral, or corporeal. Although Diderot was able to find models in Seneca's life for both frugal and lavish lifestyles, the Stoic type of the solitary, frugal sage represented by Socrates was also tempting. This is exemplified in both his own self-conduct and his patronage of other men of letters. In 1762 Diderot described to Sophie Volland the lifestyle of a copyist who might have been a model for Darnton's "gutter hacks." "My man was naked as a worm, dry, but serene, saying nothing, eating his morsel of bread with appetite, and occasionally squeezing his neighbour on the miserable pallet which took up two-thirds of his room. If I hadn't known that happiness is in the soul, my Epictetus of the rue Hyacinthe would soon have taught me." Diderot procured the support of d'Holbach's entire "Epicurean society" for his protégé: "Grimm, Mme d'Epinay, Damilaville, the Baron, all my friends interested themselves in him. He appeared to be the most honest man [*honnête homme*] in the world." But his patronage impulse toward his ragged-trousered philosopher, his personal "Rousseau du ruisseau," was to end in sad disillusionment. When he gave Glénat a sensitive manuscript on religion and government to copy, the text ended up in the hands of the chief of police, de Sartine. The solitary sage turned out to be no more than a Grub Street spy, paid by the police to hand over anything potentially offensive to morals, government, or public order. With bitter memories of his spell in prison at the château de Vincennes, Diderot angrily recoiled from Glénat.[46]

Glénat was apparently an increasingly common phenomenon in the world of literary production. Darnton depicts a horde of would-be philosophes descending upon Paris during the last decades of the Old Regime in the attempt to scrape a living by writing. However, it was hard to be free and independent as a man of letters: the demands of family life, patronage, and

46. Diderot 1875–77, 17:337–536; 18:129: Letter LXIX: Diderot to Sophie Volland, August 4, 1762; 19:130–31, Letter LXXIX, Paris, September 19, 1762. On gutter journalism at the end of the Old Regime, cf. Darnton 1982, chap. 1. On Diderot's use of ancient philosophers as role models, see Gay 1966–69, vol. 1, chap. 3; Seznec 1957, chap. 1. Epictetus's manual of moral conduct, advocating a self-denying lifestyle, was much read in the period; on philosophical biography in general, see Ribard 2003. D'Holbach himself described his salon as an "Epicurean society" (Sauter and Loos 1986, 45: Letter 29, d'Holbach to Cesare Beccaria, Paris, March 15, 1767).

friendship conflicted with it even if, like Diderot, one was able to achieve financial independence without losing political independence. Neither the role of parasite at d'Holbach's table nor that of host at his own exactly fulfilled Diderot's conditions for freethinking and social virtue.[47] In 1765 he experimented with the type of philosophical solitude adopted by d'Agoty. Engrossed in his writing, he wrote to Volland, "I've acquired such a lively taste for study, application and living alone that I am not far off planning to stick to it." Retreat and solitude prohibited the pleasures of social intercourse, but also freed one from "injured self-love, revolted delicacy, and an infinity of other small unpleasantnesses." "Another month of this sedentary life," he commented a month later, "and Pacomius's deserts will not have seen a better conditioned Anchorite." Relapses into gluttony were paid at a high, if predictable price: "The day's work had given me a devouring appetite. I wanted to eat supper; once, twice, all went well, but the third time paid for all. I had the best-conditioned of indigestions; with hot water, diet and [your] mother's medicines, it's all cured." Going without supper and drinking hot water at night were two commonplace pieces of contemporary dietetic advice for the preservation of health.[48]

Diderot's ambivalence about his alimentary experiences reflects his concerns about his status in d'Holbach's house. In accounting for his daily life to Sophie Volland, he gave diet a particular moral place in his two ways of life. "What a difference between the life at Grandval and the one I lead here [at home]! My health has felt it too: [at Grandval] I sleep badly; I can't digest; I had a migraine to drive one mad. All that has dissipated." The moral imperatives of healthy living and medical self-knowledge, which promised sensible consequences for transgressions in the form of the dreaded indigestion, continued to signify Diderot's unease at the lifestyle in d'Holbach's household even while his favored philosophical model permitted self-indulgence.[49]

Diderot's persistent indigestions and stomach problems during the late 1750s and early 1760s, particularly after visits to Grandval, led him to

47. See Roche 1988, chap. 10. On Diderot's resentment of the role of host, see Diderot 1875–77, 19:66: Letter LXIII, Diderot to Sophie Volland, Paris, October 12, 1761. Lilti 2005a, 196–207 argues for Rousseau as a leading creator of the figure of the independent writer and casts Diderot's rupture with him as a moment of choice between two lifestyles.

48. Diderot 1875–77, 19:188–90: Letter XCIV, Diderot to Sophie Volland, October 20, 1765; 200: Letter XCVII, Diderot to Sophie Volland, Paris, November 21, 1765; see also Tissot 1770, 118. St. Pacomius was a desert-dwelling ascetic who founded cenobitism.

49. For Diderot's consultations of Tronchin, mostly on his father's behalf, see, e.g., Bibliothèque Publique et Universitaire, Geneva, Archives Tronchin, ms. 167, f°. 323: consultation of March 31, 1760; ms. 204, f°s. 220–22, April 9, 1759; Diderot 1955–70, 2:129: Letter 111, Denis Diderot to Friedrich Melchior Grimm, [late April 1759].

consult various physicians, including Théodore Tronchin. To cure a fever, Diderot renounced purging in true Tronchinian style:

> Since then I have lived soberly, I have taken tea, moistened myself and I will get better, unless I am mistaken, by regimen alone. I dine alone; however frugal my meal, it is followed by a headache, mild indeed, but a sign of a stomach which is becoming tired, and which is digesting with difficulty.[50]

During much of his life, Diderot experimented with different diets to combat illness: in the 1750s and 1760s, he tried the so-called *diète lactée* or milk diet:

> I have had my chest quite paralysed. Dry cough. Terrible sweats. Difficulty in speaking and breathing. But I am doing much better, thanks to a cruel remedy: bread, water and milk as my sole nourishment. Milk in the morning, milk at noon, milk for tea, milk for supper. That's a lot of milk![51]

During the later 1760s he adopted a different preservative regimen: "I drink milk in the morning, lemonade at night; I am doing well and the Baron [d'Holbach] proves to me, from Stahl and Beccher, that I am wrong to be surprised." On this latter diet he fared so well that for the first time he could risk intemperance: after heavy drinking at a dinner with Naigeon and others, "there I was on my morning milk and my evening lemonade, fresh as a slightly faded rose," and he reassured Volland: "I have never felt so well as the day after our orgy, and it's lasting. A little libertinism from time to time does no harm." This dietary auto-experimentation was typical of the period. It was a lifetime's personal experience which led Diderot to proclaim: "To date there are only a few general remedies in which one can have confidence, such as regimen, exercise, distraction, time and nature. The rest may often do more harm than good, pace Mr Le Camus." A generalized faith in regimen as a heuristic device, as a means of making sense out

50. Diderot 1875–77, 17:463: Letter XXXIX, September 1760; 19:2: Letter L, Paris, November 3, 1760; 32: Letter LV, Diderot to Sophie Volland, Paris, November 25, 1760; 72: Letter LXV, Paris, October 25, 1761; 263: Letter CIX, Diderot to Sophie Volland, Paris, October 11, 1767.

51. Diderot 1955–70, 1:198: Letter 52, Denis Diderot to Caroillon La Salette, September 22, 1755; 204: Letter from Friedrich Melchior Grimm to anon., January 24, 1756; Rousseau 1965–85, 2:349: Letter, Deleyre to Rousseau, October 13, 1756. The milk diet, well known in the period, is discussed in Lorry 1781, 2:178, and Malouin 1750, I, pt. 2, chap. 2.

of the corporeal experiences of everyday life, drove Diderot's dietetic decisions, rather than faith in any one medical practitioner. Regimen seemed self-evidently natural; its status as true knowledge could be independently tested and replicated by every literate individual.[52]

That being so, how did eighteenth-century physicians seek to exert authority over the alimentary habits of their clients? Under what circumstances did the knowledge-claims of physicians successfully translate into changes in what the client ingested? One answer is that physicians utilized a form of mimicry. In order to appear authoritative, leading physicians presented themselves as learned also, as men of letters or philosophes.

THE PHYSICIAN AS PHILOSOPHE

Tronchin and Tissot stand out among eighteenth-century physicians for their ties to Parisian circles of philosophes and *gens de lettres*. Voltaire was only one of many French sufferers who rejoined Théodore Tronchin in Geneva, and the number increased after Tronchin inoculated the children of the Duc d'Orléans in 1756. Prominent in the controversial inoculation campaign, Tronchin was also notorious among Paris physicians for his attempts to reform medical practice, abolishing phlebotomy and purgatives and emphasizing regimen.[53] While food only represented part of Tronchin's therapeutic repertoire, it played a central role. His status as the epitome of enlightened medicine in the 1750s was supported by his social position. He belonged to a collateral branch of a Genevan patrician family whose politically prominent members maintained very close ties with Parisian polite society, and especially with the *encyclopédistes*. Into the 1770s and 1780s, individuals such as Diderot, Grimm, and Mme d'Epinay continued to correspond with various Tronchins. Voltaire's involvement with the family was especially close. The magistrate François Tronchin purchased Voltaire's house, Les Délices, when Voltaire decamped to Ferney, and in Lyon Jean-Robert Tronchin was his banker. Théodore, the physician, numbered among his clients many philosophes and their families, including Diderot, Voltaire, Rousseau, Buffon, Mme d'Epinay, and La Condamine. Voltaire persistently

52. Diderot 1875–77, 19:280: Letter CXII, Denis Diderot to Sophie Volland, Paris, August 28, 1768 (Georg Stahl was the German animist physician, while Johann Becker was an iatrochemist); 292: Letter CXVI, Denis Diderot to Sophie Volland, Paris, October 26, 1768; 295: Letter CXVII, Denis Diderot to Sophie Volland, Paris, November 4, 1768; IX, 427. See, similarly, Rousseau 1966, 60–61.

53. Tronchin 1906, chaps. 2–3.

referred to Théodore as "my dear philosophe"; like Tissot, he was regarded as epitomizing the spirit of Enlightenment in medicine.

Tronchin shared many of Rousseau's perspectives on the difference between Genevan and Parisian life, seeing the latter as exemplifying the modern cultivation of artificiality, and the attendant degeneration of morals and health that stemmed from a rejection of nature. His pathology was predicated upon the luxurious lifestyle of his clients in cities and at court, in the cabinet or the convent. The fortification of the dilapidated nervous systems of the modern French was to be effected by the avoidance of hot drinks and by adherence to a strict diet: in most cases Tronchin favored one of two strategies, prescribing either the "white diet" of "milk . . . which should merely be warmed, rice, pearl barley, gruel, millet, freshwater fish, and white meat . . . , fresh eggs, and tender vegetables," or a "dry diet" of solid foods to rid the body of the excess humors caused by consuming hot drinks, in which "roast [meat], cold or hot, is preferable to boiled, Milk and fruits are forbidden. The crust of bread, well chewed, is worth more than the crumb." For such conditions, Tronchin also banned all hot drinks, soups, and broths, along with humid, floury, or glutinous foods. While scholars suffered from many specific conditions such as strained eyes and hunched back in consequence of their lifestyle, the "excesses of the table and the Sedentary life" were particularly liable to produce serious illness in them. A full belly compressed the hypochondria, the liver, or other inner organs adjacent to the stomach, and a host of symptoms developed as humors were obstructed and forced into acrid stagnation. The solution was "sobriety": eating little but often, and avoiding all foods that might contribute to the acridity of the stagnating humors, including highly flavored, sour, or salted foods, meat essences, undiluted wine, and liqueurs. Voltaire's account of himself as eating only "the gentlest of foods in the smallest quantity" bore the hallmark of Tronchin's recommendations to his clients.[54] Tronchin's alimentary advice, unlike Tissot's, did not specifically target nouvelle cuisine. However, his theological commitments sharply opposed the iatrochemical explanations favored in sensualist models of alimentary choice. Responding to a correspondent anxious about how to ensure an ideal chemical balance in his diet, he emphasized naïve faith in Providence over chemical autoexperimentation:

54. Bibliothèque Publique et Universitaire, Geneva, Archives Tronchin, ms. 204, f°. 58: Letter, Théodore Tronchin to anonymous client, December 24, 1756; f°. 152: Consultation by Théodore Tronchin for the comtesse de Jumilhac's nun, April 19, 1758; f°s. 53–54, 85, 113, 162–64, 166, e.g.

> Consult the simplest men, artisans and labourers, they will tell you that they put neither art nor finesse [into the choice of foods], that they know neither alkali nor acid, that they eat[,] they digest, and that nature sees to all. She only uses two means to do her job, sobriety and exercise, she has no need of Physicians nor of Chemists. The acid of bread, the alkali of meat turn into a neutral salt without the Labourer worrying about it or the artisan getting involved. . . . He who has made your Body has endowed it with everything it needs to Preserve itself.[55]

The sober eater, unlike the sensualist, was not to be a chemical expert; excessive knowledge led people to second-guess God. Tronchin's call for faith in nature was a central part of his appeal for Voltaire and other philosophes with deist inclinations.[56]

The Swiss physicians of the Enlightenment are of value not only because they were the physicians of choice for many enlightened eaters, but also because their geographical location meant that Parisian clients approached them through correspondence. Epistolary relations shaped medical discourse in particular ways. Tronchin presented himself as his clients' equal and friend, deploying polite forms of address and emphasizing the status of *honnête homme* over that of physician: "The first quality required in a physician, is that he should be an *honnête homme*, the science comes afterwards." He contrasted medical rivals as dangerous and greedy charlatans with himself as sensible, polite, tolerant, humane, and learned.[57] The illness of Louise-Florence-Pétronille Delalive d'Épinay, wife of a tax farmer and mistress of Diderot's friend Friedrich Melchior Grimm, demonstrates how far Tronchin's ability to reform everyday life depended on his ability to master polite codes. As her health declined from 1755 onwards, Mme d'Epinay's perspective on Tronchin altered. Initially, she resisted the role of sick woman. Writing to Tronchin in 1756, her protégé Rousseau, at that time living in a house owned by the d'Epinay family, ascribed Mme d'Epinay's poor health to uncontrolled appetites. "There is also that difference [between us] that in giv-

55. Bibliothèque Publique et Universitaire, Geneva, Archives Tronchin, ms. 204: Letter, Théodore Tronchin to Baron d'Aigunes, November 27, 1758. On the iatrochemical incorporation of acidity and alkalinity into humoral theory, see especially Boas Hall 1956.

56. See, e.g., Tronchin's correspondence with the naturalist Georges-Louis Leclerc de Buffon over his wife's final illness in 1768–69: Bibliothèque Publique et Universitaire, Geneva, Archives Tronchin, ms. 167, f°s. 389–97.

57. Bibliothèque Publique et Universitaire, Geneva, Archives Tronchin, ms. 204: Letter, Théodore Tronchin to d'Argenlieu, March 4, 1757. On the physician as philosophe and man of letters, see Wenger 2007, chap. 9; on eighteenth-century French medical correspondence more generally, see Pilloud et al. 2004; Brockliss 1994.

ing herself over without scruple to all the leanings that *honneteté* justifies, she is at least in agreement with herself, whilst I, floating between nature and reason, am in a perpetual contradiction and do nothing that I want." For his own part, Rousseau strategically distanced himself from medical authority, begging his patron in 1755: "By God! Madam, don't send me Mr Malouin [a prominent Parisian iatrochemist] any more," and he wrote to Tronchin in the same year that "For three years I have renounced all medical aid, since long experience has shown me its uselessness in my case." But he did not ignore medical knowledge-claims, writing to Tronchin that "I am instructing myself from your Letters to Madame d'Epinay; whilst she combats your maxims, I try to profit from them."[58]

By 1757 Mme d'Epinay had become a convert to dieting, under pressure from Grimm and Rousseau. In a letter to Grimm, she dutifully recorded:

> I started on ass's milk yesterday, it went down very well: I am more severe about my regimen than you would be yourself. I sleep passably well; I don't expose myself to sun or dew; I don't walk without having my carriage follow me. That's everything you recommended and that the physicians are requiring of me; I am following it exactly, you can count on that.

At first, continuing on milk seemed successful: "I have never been so well." But her health was still shaky when she wrote to Grimm to relay the contents of a letter from her husband's brother-in-law, "in a pleasant enthusiasm about his Geneva. He was ill on arrival, and as it is Tronchin who cured him, he solicits me, with an urgency that would make you laugh, to come and place myself in his hands." In response, her lover promised to "add my voice to his, if occasion arises, to make you promise to seek out that great physician. But I hope, however, that your health will not require it, if you continue to husband yourself." He warned her against excessive participation in salon life, and particularly against excessive literary activities, chastising her for copying out two books of her novel to send to him.

Finally, the appearance of more alarming symptoms, coupled with the pressure of family and friends, led Mme d'Epinay to partial capitulation. "I have finally given way to persecution from my mother and M. Grimm to

58. D'Epinay 1865, 2:71; Bibliothèque Publique et Universitaire, Geneva, Archives Tronchin, ms. 165: Letter, Rousseau to Théodore Tronchin, Paris, December 22, 1755; letter, Rousseau to Théodore Tronchin, L'Hermitage, August 18, 1756. For Rousseau's scepticism about medicine, see Thériault 1979, esp. Bonnet 1979; Neumann 1991.

make me see Tronchin. But I'll start by sending him the history of the ills which have overwhelmed me since he returned to Geneva; and, if he judges it to be indispensable for me to make the journey, I shall have to make up my mind to it." Tronchin's response "does not console me much," she wrote in her journal, but "it gives me more confidence than I had before in his wisdom [*lumières*] and prudence." Even so, she remained resistant:

> can I take it upon myself to leave so many people who are dear to me? Perhaps never to see them again! Barely reunited with M. Grimm, from whom I have been separated for six months! Can I leave my mother at her age? My children? . . . This picture terrifies me. . . . It's decided, I'll tell them that I shall never make my mind up to do it, and I'll insist they shan't speak of it any more.

But a further crisis left her so weak that, within a week, she had decided to undertake the journey.[59]

Mme d'Epinay's detailed account of her negotiations over her own state of health reveals how family members and friends cooperated in the manufacture of a network of powers that tied polite clients to physicians and conferred authority and credibility on them. This process simultaneously involved imposing control over appetites, aligning self-discipline with medical obedience, and (literally) internalizing medical authority by transforming consumption through the adoption of medical regimen. Tronchin's medical authority was enhanced in Mme d'Epinay's eyes by his ability to participate in her polite literary world, as evidenced in his allusive references to the failure of belles-lettres to resolve the problem of morals under an absolutist government in his surviving letter to her.[60]

At the same time, Tronchin kept his distance from the *Encyclopédie* and from publication in general, comparing his situation with that of de Jaucourt: "The poor Chevalier who thought quite differently on that subject [the eternity of the material world] when we lived together, has become the champion of this chimera, he wanted to enrol me in the Regiment [of *encyclopédistes*] that has been formed to defend it!"[61] Yet Tronchin found

59. D'Epinay's journal, September 1757 (D'Epinay 1865, 2:240, 250, 274, 290, 300, 348, 359, 361).

60. Bibliothèque Publique et Universitaire, Geneva, Archives Tronchin, ms. 204, f°s. 29–31: Letter, Théodore Tronchin to Mme d'Epinay, Paris, October 25, 1756 (see also chapter 5, n. 63). Similar arguments to my own are advanced by Broman 1995, 1998, 134.

61. Bibliothèque Publique et Universitaire, Geneva, Archives Tronchin, ms. 204, f°s. 75–76: Letter, Théodore Tronchin to comte d'Argenlieu, Paris, March 4, 1757; f°. 109: Letter, Théodore

himself forced to deal with fallout from the *Encyclopédie*. Its famous article "Genève," written by D'Alembert, painted the Republic in glowing colors as a realm of religious tolerance, and incidentally attributed a belief in the Socinian heresy to the three Genevan pastors who had been D'Alembert's interlocutors. Tronchin, the secretary at a meeting of the Genevan council concerning the article's implications for the Republic, was the individual who had to mediate between D'Alembert and the other *encyclopédistes*, including Voltaire, the three outraged and frightened pastors, and the council. In general, however, heterodoxy posed less of a problem in Geneva than in Paris. Since the early decades of the eighteenth century, the Republic had embraced religious tolerance as an official policy. Intellectual disagreement over religious matters still left room for reasoned persuasion, and the truth would inevitably emerge in the afterlife. Tronchin was thus able to maintain friendships with numerous French materialists and religious dissenters by dint of shifting the emphasis onto the conduct of daily life and away from the public expression of radical views. This meant that, for example, the news of Rousseau's abandonment of his own children disgusted him, where Diderot's open discussions of materialism did not.[62]

Like Voltaire, like Rousseau, like Tissot, Tronchin presented himself as leading an isolated, moral lifestyle, which preserved his happiness and moral purity, and consequently his health. In 1766, however, the political tension provoked in Geneva by the condemnation of Rousseau's *Emile* and the exile of its author led Tronchin to accept a post in that corrupt city, Paris. The unrest pitted the patrician city rulers (including the Tronchins) against the politically disenfranchised bourgeois (who supported Rousseau). The disturbances were only suppressed by inviting the French to send in military reinforcements, headed by a relation of de Jaucourt; for a period of time, Geneva was effectively under the rule of the French ambassador

---

Tronchin to marquise de Jaucourt, October 21, 1757. While studying under Boerhaave, Tronchin and de Jaucourt had cohabited.

62. Diderot 1955–70, 2:139–40: Letter 113, Denis Diderot to Théodore Tronchin, Paris, [May 20, 1759]. On Tronchin's support for La Mettrie, see Bibliothèque Publique et Universitaire, Geneva, Archives Tronchin, ms. 198, f°. 42: Letter, François Quesnay to Théodore Tronchin, October 21, [174?]; for his view of Rousseau, see Bibliothèque Publique et Universitaire, Geneva, Archives Tronchin, dossier ouvert: Letter, Théodore Tronchin to Paul Moultou, June 17, [1762?]. On the *Encyclopédie* scandal in Geneva, see Gargett 2004. After 1706, the Genevan government effectively endorsed the Arminian heresy, a mid-seventeenth-century reform movement that rested on the claim that empirical observation would reveal Providence in action, and that Christian truth was not the same for all, with only a few truths being fundamental to salvation. Tronchin's ancestor had been a prominent Arminian. See Dawson 1987, 56–60; Voltaire 1950, XXV–XXIX.

Pierre-Marie Hennin, Charles-Georges Leroy's cousin. From a Genevan perspective, the philosophe connections of the Tronchin family were thus taking political sides, even though such divisions were effaced in the philosophes' rosy portrayals of Geneva as an "alternative France" where climate, government, and morals combined to preserve innocence, good health, and social harmony.[63]

"ORDONNANCE" AND OBEDIENCE

Unlike Tronchin, Tissot turned down all offers to leave the tiny Bernese dependency of Lausanne.[64] Nonetheless, the wide readership for his many books ensured that he became an even more significant figure in the creation of a new French medical hygiene in the second half of the eighteenth century than Tronchin, who published little. Among the numerous clients who requested his diagnoses, remedies, and regimen advice in the 1760s and 1770s, several emphasized Tissot's authoritative status in Europe as the epitome of the enlightened, philanthropic medical man with a genuine understanding of nature. As one of his clients claimed in 1769, "you are the philosophe-physician of our century."[65] Correspondents frequently attributed medical expertise and philosophical status to Tissot based upon familiarity with his printed works rather than himself. If clients approached Tissot as something of a hero of the literary world, Tissot himself regarded Rousseau in the same light. Soon after the publication of *Emile*, he wrote to Rousseau that he, Tissot, would "learn the only useful art in medicine, that of observing, from you," adding that they shared views about the harmfulness of medicine in the hands of most physicians.[66] Like Rousseau, Tissot suffered the indignity of having his masterpiece, *L'Onanisme*, a treatise on the health dangers of masturbation, banned in Paris. And he espoused Rous-

63. Théodore Tronchin's cousin Jean-Robert was closely involved in Rousseau's disgrace ([Tronchin] 1765; Rousseau 1764).

64. He did visit Paris, attending Mme du Deffand's salon in 1779 or 1780 (Lilti 2005a, 148).

65. Bibliothèque Centrale et Universitaire, Lausanne, fonds S.-A. Tissot, IS 3784/II/144.01.07.09: Letter, De Croyer, *capitaine aide-major* in the La Fère artillery corps, to Tissot, Laon, Picardy, December 10, 1772. Compare, e.g., IS 3784/II/144.01.07.02: Letter, Chevalier de Belfontaine to Tissot, Paris, November 25, 1772. For an overview of this correspondence, see Stolberg 1986, esp. 401; Teysseire 1995; Pilloud 1999; Rieder and Barras 2001; Louis-Courvoisier 2001; Pilloud and Louis-Courvoisier 2003. Tissot corresponded with Rousseau and La Condamine, and treated Maupertuis's niece; see, e.g., 144.01.09.03: Letter, Bougourd to Tissot, Saint Malo, August 2, 1773. On Tissot's involvement in constructing the figure of the "enlightened physician," see Benaroyo 1989; see also Roche 1988, chap. 13.

66. Rousseau 1965–85, 11:238–39: Letter 1966: Tissot to Rousseau, Lausanne, July 8, 1762.

seau's own self-presentation as the Christian sage opposed to the unbelieving philosophes, claiming to his correspondent Johann Caspar Hirzel that he found the truths of Christianity presented in *Emile* "with a clarity which I have sought in vain elsewhere." Rousseau's converse was "V[oltaire]. whose works are infinitely more dangerous . . . [and] whose example has augmented luxury, perverted morals; the poison has been savoured and the antidote rejected. *Oh tempora*." From Rousseau, Tissot appropriated a radical critique of lifestyle as well as a philosophical ideal.[67]

The perception that Tissot's status as a man of letters qualified him as enlightened also contributed to his medical authority. As one of the men of letters who numbered among his clients remarked, "It will not be difficult for a man as enlightened as you to decide, from this picture, what course I must take to sustain my feeble remains of health. What regimen should I observe, of what foods should I make use, Must I limit myself to a single meal, and renounce my dear Library entirely to reduce myself to the country. I can promise you docility at least."[68] The physician's expertise was taken as a sufficient reason for repressing corporeal appetites. In a letter thanking Tissot for his counsel in 1784, his client Larrey asked for further enlightenment on his diet: "Deign to tell me what You think of the use of Coffee, and don't be afraid you are being too harsh. If an ordinary Physician imposed privations on me, They would seem hard, because a doubt concerning the necessity of this Regimen would remain, but You have all My Confidence Sir."[69]

The language of regimen was consistently a language of government. Consultants wrote of leading a "regulated" or "unregulated" life; they spoke of the degree of order or disorder in their animal economy, and they awaited Tissot's "orders" concerning their diet. The physician's *ordonnance* or medical prescription was a type of text in which the normal self-abasement of polite

67. Rousseau 1965–85, 12:32–33: Letter 1994: Tissot to Hirzel, July 14, 1762; 19:276–79: Letter 3206, Rousseau to Madeleine-Elisabeth Roguin, Motiers-Travers, April 6, 1764 (Rousseau advised her to consult Tissot). On Tissot's view of Rousseau as clashing with "the modern philosophes, Buff[on]. Dider[ot]. D'Al[embert]. Volt[aire]" see Rousseau 1965–85, 12:140–41: Letter 2052, Tissot to Albrecht von Haller, [circa August 2, 1762]. On Rousseau as sage, see Rousseau 1965–85, 12:178–79: Letter 2071, Isaac-Ami Marcet de Mézières to Rousseau, Geneva, August 13, 1762; Emch-Dériaz 1992a, 61: Letter, Tissot to Zimmerman, July 13, 1762.

68. Bibliothèque Centrale et Universitaire, Lausanne, fonds S.-A. Tissot, IS 3784/II/144.01.07.34: Letter, abbé de Saint-Veran to Tissot, from Carpentras, August 12, 1772; 144.01.07.35: "Memoire adressé à Mr. Tissot Docteur et Professeur en Medecine à Lausanne, Par L'Abbé de St. Veran Bibliotheqre. de Carpentras." On the questions of medical authority raised by Tissot's correspondence, see Louis-Courvoisier 2001, 283–84.

69. Bibliothèque Centrale et Universitaire, Lausanne, fonds S.-A. Tissot, IS 3784/II/144.03.04.16: Letter, Larrey to Tissot, La Clergère[?], January 5, 1784.

epistolary language was abandoned in favor of commandment. Prescribing for an older man suffering from shortness of breath and edema, Tissot ordered, in a language duplicated otherwise only in government legislation:

> Foods are to be taken at regulated meals, chocolate with water or coffee with egg yolk is to constitute breakfast,
> —soup with herbs or turnips, onions, leeks, parsnips, Celery, White of Fowl, lean of mutton roast rather than Boiled, lightly poached fish without sauce, eggs[,] Cooked vegetables prepared with egg yolks or a light veal juice, cooked fruits, Sweetmeats, is to Constitute dinner
> —Monsieur is to sup lightly on fish, vegetables, cooked fruit.[70]

Many clients asked in minute detail about the advisability of their alimentary choices. As his regular client Madame de Chastenay of Chartres remarked, sick people wanted to know how they should use *"such things* from *such a time to—such another* . . . the number of *grains of salt in an egg."*[71] Memoirists often supplied regimen information in a separate section of their document, and as a diary-like record of their day. Take for example the memoir of Monsieur Lavergne, aged fifty-seven:

> I rise at half past 6 and take a Spoonful of scillitic syrup composed simply of sugar and a Bulb of Squill. . . . After half to three quarters of an hour I eat a fair-sized piece of bread with a cup of chocolate with water, without vanilla. My Stomach is constantly disposed to give them a good welcome. Sometimes for variation I eat a brioche which is equivalent to a good-sized piece of bread, but which is kneaded with butter and eggs. I accompany it with a goblet of sugared water and I always digest it wonderfully.
>
> At Eleven o'clock a glass of cinnamon water neither too weak nor too strong with a spoonful and a half of Absinthe salt infused in the water labelled Alkaline water.
>
> At one o'clock I dine with or without soup, on roast veal or fowl, or else boiled fowl or mutton, some vegetables or carp roes, sometimes 3

70. Bibliothèque Centrale et Universitaire, Lausanne, fonds S.-A. Tissot, IS 3784/II/144.03.04.08, Tissot's ordinance for M. Martine of Lyons, February 18, 1784; see also 144.03.04.07 and 144.03.04.09.

71. Bibliothèque Centrale et Universitaire, Lausanne, fonds S.-A. Tissot, IS 3784/II/144.03.05.05, Letter, Mme de Chastenay to Tissot, December 15, 1784. Original emphasis. The salt-and-egg joke is from Molière's *Le Malade imaginaire* (1673). Detailed descriptions of diet were standard in medical consultations; see, e.g., Le Thieullier 1739–47.

> or 4 asparagus or small turnips . . . , 2 or 3 half glasses of beer water, and two glasses of water with about one fifth of wine.
>
> At 5 o'clock a glass of Cinnamon water with one and a half spoonfuls of alkaline water.
>
> At 7 o'clock . . . dose of quinine, and half an hour later a biscuit if I need it.
>
> Then I begin my milk which I finish at 9 o'clock in 4 glasses, one every half hour. . . .
>
> The milk goes down wonderfully as if [given] to a child, and I always find it delicious. At 10 o'clock in the evening before going to bed I present myself at the garderobe and there I render either some wind, or nothing at all, or a small stool.[72]

This insistence on the regularity of lifestyle was also marked in Tissot's ordonnances.

Tissot's alimentary advice was in keeping with standard views of the effects of different categories of foods. For chest diseases caused by the accumulation of acrid humors, he recommended a gentle regimen, avoiding all acrid foods. Cases of onanism or nocturnal pollutions were attributed to overindulgence in succulent foods, ragouts, and sauces—the luxury foods of the nouvelle cuisine. Clients of Tissot seeking to present themselves as healthy eaters emphasized their avoidance of certain foods, thus confirming the unhealthiness of particular alimentary categories. Charte des Galerans, a *conseiller du roi* suffering from hemorrhoids, described himself (in the third person) as an "*homme de Cabinet,*" and claimed to have "always led a frugal life; and he has even totally abstained from prepared dishes in the last few years. he has only made use of Liqueurs, including Coffee, very moderately . . . lastly, the Counsel is requested to fix in the greatest detail the Regimen that The Consultant should observe, both in food and Drink, and in occupation and exercise."[73] Clients thus participated in forging an opposition between nouvelle cuisine and healthy eating; as Larrey, a victim of nocturnal pollutions, remarked: "what are all the gifts of Comus, and the Nectar of the Gods at the price of health!"[74]

72. Bibliothèque Centrale et Universitaire, Lausanne, fonds S.-A. Tissot, IS 3784/II/144.01.07.20: "Memoire" for Lavergne, undated (probably 1772).

73. Bibliothèque Centrale et Universitaire, Lausanne, fonds S.-A. Tissot, IS 3784/II/144.01.07.16: Letter, Charte des Galerans to Tissot, Crest (Dauphiné), July 1772; 144.01.07.17: "Mémoire" for Charte des Galerans.

74. Bibliothèque Centrale et Universitaire, Lausanne, fonds S.-A. Tissot, IS 3784/II/144.03.04.16: Letter, Larrey to Tissot, La Clergère[?], January 5, 1784.

Diets, like the two vehicles for much medicinal treatment, whey and broth, were where the authority of medical practitioners, cooks, and consumers intersected. Contemporary culinary literature reveals that cooks had extensive knowledge of the medical properties of foods. The medical recommendations of physicians generally required the cooperation of domestic cooks, who, though invisible in ordonnances, were responsible for preparing broth, buying whey, cooking eggs to the right degree of hardness, and omitting spices from invalid dishes. Medicinal broth was usually an infusion of herbs in ordinary stock, made in the kitchen on the orders and to the taste of the polite eater. Menon and Marin used a broadly similar palette of foodstuffs: meat (beef, lamb, veal, chicken, duck), vegetables (peas, lentils, cabbages, lettuce, turnips, carrots, parsnips), and seasonings (salt, black pepper, bay, onion, shallots, chives).[75] But in terms of their handling of *medical* knowledge, there were telling distinctions between *Les Dons de Comus* in the first half of the century, and Menon's books, which dominated the second half. Menon's later cookbooks, in particular, abound with regimen information on foods, a subject hardly broached by *Les Dons de Comus*. The relative authority of cooks and doctors over diet was also treated differently. The preface to *Les Dons de Comus* portrayed the long-standing enmity between the two groups in light-hearted vein:

> We are being made war upon in our homes, should we yield without a struggle? Though the match is unequal, at least we have something in common with our adversaries. We are paid the same honor as the Physicians; . . . everyone decries cookery, and no-one can do without it. If we work for the Physician, the Physician in turn works for us. . . . Besides, who is unaware that the Cook is often called to the counsel of the Physician, and, lastly, that Cookery serves Medicine?[76]

Annotations to the recipes, however, reveal that the extent of culinary medical responsibility was considerably underplayed by the flippant preface; the cook's role in preparing medical prescriptions was taken for granted by Marin himself. Thus, in a recipe for a "refreshing broth with crayfish,"

75. [Menon] 1750; [Marin] 1750. See also, e.g., [Alexandre] 1716, 46. For medical prescriptions using broth, see, e.g., Le Thieullier 1739–47; Jourdan de Le Cointe 1790, 1:181–82. Vigarello (1999, 94, 122–25) claims that physicians began to supervise their clients' diet more closely in seventeenth-century high society, creating heightened conflict between cooks and physicians.

76. [Marin] 1750, 1:xviij–xix; on the relations between cooks and physicians, see Spang 2000, 29; Cowan 2007, 230; Takats 2011, chap. 5.

Marin referred to the "four seeds," a central feature of the French pharmacopeia, which listed four seeds for each category of hot (minor or major), or cold (minor or major). It was taken for granted that readers would comprehend the significance of this fleeting medical reference. Similarly, in discussing recipes for refreshing and purgative broths, Marin noted that the main ingredient was usually veal or pullets, but that "calves' liver, calves' lung, vipers, scarabs, frogs and others are also used, according to the prescription." As one of those groups charged with the execution of medical prescriptions, cooks inevitably became medically knowledgeable.[77]

The author of the preface to the *Science du Maître d'Hôtel*, by contrast, explicitly subjugated cooks to medical practitioners, but also emphasized cooks' medical status. "The Art of preparing foods necessarily belongs to *Dietetics*, which has always been regarded as a very important part of Medicine. . . . If Cooks ever form a Regulated Body, I believe I can assure, in the name of my Fellows, that it will never occur to them to escape from the subordination in which they exist with regard to Physicians."[78] Medical concerns permeated the book, far more so than in *Les Dons de Comus*. A separate table of contents at the end of the book referred health-conscious readers to discussions of the medicinal properties of individual foodstuffs. But the shift was visible even between the first edition of *Les Dons de Comus* in 1739 and the second, published in 1750, when the dietetic discussion was moved higher up the preface and was more heavily documented. Similarly, the 1750 *Dictionnaire des Alimens*, probably written by a former Capucin turned hack author, François-Alexandre de La Chesnaye des Bois, and/or the prince de Conti's pastrycook, Nicolas Briant, flagged its medical content: "Here is what is new and most interesting about this Dictionary: skilful Physicians have written on the nature, properties and choice of Foods; that which is dispersed among several Books, is brought together here from a single point of view." This work borrowed liberally from different cookbooks and medical treatises, from Lémery and Andry to Cheyne, Boerhaave, Hoffman, or Arbuthnot. The *Dictionnaire* was one of the despised works of compilation, but it points toward a new tendency to conflate medical and culinary knowledge.[79]

77. [Marin] 1750, 1:127–32. The substances named here had a range of medicinal uses; see, e.g., [Alexandre] 1716. On the major and minor seeds, see, e.g., Chomel 1712, though the apothecary Baumé (1762, 49) claimed these denominations to be "virtually abolished from current medical practice."

78. [Menon] 1768, xxij–xxiij; on this issue, see Cowan 2007.

79. [De La Chesnaye and Briant?] 1750, 1:xiv; [Desalleurs] 1981, 6–7; [Marin] 1750, xi–xxviij. For earlier, nonmedical attacks on ragoûts and strong flavors, see, e.g., "Goust" in Furetière 1727, vol. 2, unpaginated; Morize 1970, 40n.

If the growing number of health manuals penned by authors such as Tissot, Vandermonde, Le Bègue de Presle, and Jacquin was any guide, healthy eating was becoming a central concern of the literate elite in France. As one Toulouse doctor remarked of cuisine, "there is no subject, especially in the [polite] world, about which [Medicine] is more often consulted."[80] It became expedient, not to say essential, for culinary writers to exploit this medicalization of their readership. Menon's *Cuisine de santé* of 1758 was hardly distinct from a health manual in its own right. He presented a heavily medicalized cookery that rehearsed the central tenets of the health literature: "I think it superfluous to warn that, as regards [food] choice, everyone must before anything else have studied & learnt his temperament. What is healthy for one person, is not so for another: & in the case of indisposition one ought not so much to resort to foods, as to abstain from them with care." Nonetheless the book was a compendium of regimen advice, with medical qualities ascribed to each dish or ingredient. Sometimes Menon explicitly bowed to physicians' authority, as in the type of broth known as "eau de poulet," where he recommended seeking medical advice before consumption. But he *offered* medical advice too, prescribing eau de carottes for cases of bile in the blood, on the basis that "I have several times seen the cure of this malady effected by eau de carottes." The emphasis on cookery's medical role came at the expense the chemical cuisine of previous decades. "The select preparations of cookery, those elaborate, complicated ragoûts, those quintessences, so to speak, those new Elixirs that refinement has introduced" were clearly harmful to health; yet "the utility of the art of cookery for the preservation of health should also be recognised. How many foods might not become dangerous if, by means of different preparations, the secret of depriving them of harmful acrimony, & of damaging qualities which are natural to them had not been found, which demonstrates the error of those who, guided by misplaced economy, or by excessive prejudice, criticise all culinary preparations."[81]

The incorporation of medical advice into cookbooks enabled cooks to appear as expert participants in the medical marketplace, and also allowed

80. Thouvenel 1780, 60. To take just one example of philosophical interest in health manuals, Charles-Georges Leroy's library contained Tissot 1770 and Vandermonde 1759, an iatrochemical classic (Malouin 1750), three books by the faculty physician Lieutaud, and two translations, William Buchan's health manual *Domestic Medicine* (1769), and Antonio Cocchi's *Régime de Pythagore* (1762), a vegetarian treatise with a life of Cornaro. See Leroy 1994, appendix.

81. [Menon] 1758, 10–11, 60, 83, 6–7; see also Flandrin 1996a, 506–7. "Eaux" of carrots or chicken were made in a similar manner to vegetable or meat stock today.

them to keep up with the new fashion for "natural" medicine developing among their readers. Conversely, the explicit presentation of cuisine as a quasi-medical transaction created an opportunity for physicians to medicalize the alimentary choices of individuals in everyday life, not merely during illness. Hyacinthe-Théodore Baron, the Paris faculty physician who wrote the censor's report on Menon's *Cuisine de Santé*, praised him for having "entered so well into the views of Medicine" in his critique of seasonings and ragoûts.[82] Depicting food choices in stark terms as moral decisions between right and wrong, healthy and unhealthy, natural and unnatural meant that the penetration of daily life by health concerns, presented as an enfranchisement of the eater, was also an enrollment of the eater within a medical polity that conferred supreme authority upon physicians. The medicalization of French society marked the consolidation of medical authority over spheres of everyday life, in which the blame for diseased states was to be ascribed to the conduct of the sick person.

Medicalization was, however, a two-way street. The gain in authority among physicians was made possible by a growing attention to health among polite eaters as "the natural" became an increasingly indispensable part of self-presentation after 1750, while chemistry (including iatrochemistry) was relegated to the realms of artifice and deception. But medicine itself was by no means the prerogative of physicians; dieting for health was frequently undertaken by literate individuals without medical advice.[83] After a voyage to Bengal, one Monsieur Gaspary fell ill, and put himself on an "austere regimen" to sweeten his acrid blood for six months, initially on the advice of a Dutch physician. Abstaining "totally from Spices and even salt in [my] Broth, I nourished myself With Rice [cooked] in water instead of bread, a broth made from a grain-fed pullet Without Salt and another small roast pullet." Left with only "the Dictionnaire de Santé [Vandermonde's health manual] and Old wives' Counsel" for assistance, "I put myself on Rice and Light fish as my only nourishment and on rhubarb as a remedy." Only later, encountering Tissot's work, did this client address himself to the Swiss physician. Regimen was thus not monopolized by trained physicians, as the cases of Diderot and Marmontel, discussed above, reveal. Indeed, doctors possessed a doubly mediated authority in the home, since domestics, including the cook, were closest to the client and prepared many foods and medicines.[84]

82. Baron, unpaginated endorsement in [Menon] 1758, January 27, 1757.

83. Jewson 1976; Shapin 2003; Lachmund and Stollberg 1995, esp. 60–66; Rey 1991, 420.

84. Bibliothèque Centrale et Universitaire, Lausanne, fonds S.-A. Tissot, IS 3784/II/144.02.02.05: "Mémoire a Consulter," by Gaspary, May 26, 1773.

Last, of course, the world of medical publishing was not homogeneous. The medical faculty of Paris itself was constantly split by disputes between different factions, and medical manuals were penned by an even more diverse set of authors. Medical clients had to choose among experts with vastly different therapeutic and theoretical principles, from Malouin or Le Cat's chemical medicine to the emphasis on dieting and exercise in Tronchin's ordonnances. The curé of Curchy's medical history, as recounted by a surgeon treating him, shows how clients interwove medical advice, personal experience, and reading when tailoring diet to constitution. This forty-year-old sufferer from a nervous disease had noticed while studying in Paris, aged eighteen, that "Eggs and almost all lean foods caused him indigestions, pains and heaviness of the Stomach, which obliged him to live according to a regimen from early on." The condition was exacerbated by his profession, which placed him on a par with men of letters. Tronchin recommended that he should stop work, take exercise, and eat "cold roast meat, [and] no soup, boiled [meat] or ragoûts," but in spite of this, his condition worsened. At this juncture Pomme's *Traité des Vapeurs* was published. The curé revolutionized his regimen: warm domestic baths, watery drinks, whey, bouillons, "white tender meat, boiled or roast, melting ripe fruits, no wine, nor spirits, mineral waters etc. which was followed to the letter for more than two years without relief." "Finally tiring of continuing such an inconvenient regimen Without Success, the sick man returned himself to ordinary life . . . in the meantime The excellent treatise on the Health of men of Letters by M. Tissot has fallen into our hands, after having read it M. le curé subjected Himself to the regimen that he believed he observed in it for his condition." Literate medical consumers took health manuals as literal programs for conducting daily life, akin to corporeal scriptures or devotional literature.[85]

For an individual to adopt a particular regimen, the consulting physician needed to capture a variety of different factors successfully. The physician's ability to represent Nature or Enlightenment was extremely important in making his regimen advice into an obligatory passage point for eaters, but such control was still only partial or ephemeral. Mme de Chastenay did not hesitate to reject unpalatable commands: "you have caused me much dismay by forbidding me Burgundy or Bordeaux wine at meals, I shall drink it

85. Bibliothèque Centrale et Universitaire, Lausanne, fonds S.-A. Tissot, IS 3784/II/144.02.04.14: "Mémoire" for the curé of Curchy, by Berthier, master surgeon, Curchy, May 10, 1774. See Wenger 2007, 109–13.

until further orders."[86] Medical governance, in spite of its forceful language, was far from perfect. And in spite of their abject promises of obedience to physicians, eaters regularly disobeyed, ignored, or tinkered with regimen advice; particular symptoms, newly appearing or hitherto undisclosed, could serve as legitimation for doing so, as could individual tastes and preferences. Moreover, the physician was rarely the sole player in a field shaped by reading, advice from friends and family, recommendations from rival medical practitioners, the promises of medical advertisements, and the client's own habits. In the medical marketplace, undesirable advice from one physician could be played off against the recommendations of some medical competitor. Madame de la Ville Gille wrote to Tissot complaining: "Every day I broke my fast with a cup of Coffee with Water and Without Sugar which usually made Me go to Stool, My Physician Has forbidden it, I admit that I have Not yet had the Courage to Prevent Myself." In a later letter she added: "pray tell me your Feeling on the Use of Coffee, If it is absolutely Contrary to me, I will Renounce it But If it is Not Harmful for Me I would be very pleased Not to deprive Myself of it. I will observe The Regimen that you have ordered precisely."[87]

Nor were clients ignorant of the commercial stakes underlying medical descriptions of cuisine. When Raymond, a Besançon physician and native of Autun, defended a thesis before the Paris Medical Faculty on the subject "Are ragoûts contrary to health?," the journalist Meusnier de Querlon observed: "This question will always be decided in the affirmative by Physicians, whose business is to undermine [contreminer] the maker of sauces; but experience establishes the pro & contra, & is not clearly decisive against the use of ragoûts, except in cases of excess, or of a ruined complexion."[88] In a regimen world, personal experience was the final court of appeal for all medical transactions, so that all medical procedures became forms of autoexperimentation, with physicians a source of reference rather than an absolute authority.

86. Bibliothèque Centrale et Universitaire, Lausanne, fonds S.-A. Tissot, IS 3784/II/144.03.05.05: Letter, Mme de Chastenay to Tissot, December 15, 1784. On obligatory passage points, see Callon 1986.

87. Bibliothèque Centrale et Universitaire, Lausanne, fonds S.-A. Tissot, IS 3784/II/144.02.03.24: Letter, Mme de la Ville Gille to Tissot, from Saint Malo, [1773]; 144.02.03.24: Letter, Mme de la Ville Gille to Tissot, from Saint Malo, October 3, 1773. See also 144.02.04.02: Letter, de Bouju to Tissot, from Angers, January 5, 1774. On lay intermediaries among Tissot's correspondents, see Pilloud 1999.

88. *Annonces, Affiches et Avis Divers* (Paris), 1765.14, 54, April 3.

The power structure of medical autonomy was described in detail by Madame de Myrmont. During an illness in her twenties,

> they wanted to make me try ass's milk cut with barley water, buttermilk, broths of chicken, of tender of veal, of frogs mixed with herbs. but as all these liquids only produced a Spasm, I took the firm resolution to stall evils for which I could find no remedies, and limited myself to studying which foods were contrary to me. always on water, I never allowed myself wines or liqueurs, nor coffee[;] I even withdrew Salted meats[,] cheese; and all that seemed to me able to carry acridity. besides this[,] in ordinary life, I still gave preference to vegetables, soft fruits, and cold dairy foods. . . . It was thus that I lived from the age of 26 to 31 without any remedies.[89]

A worsening of her condition led this woman to fire off a volley of memoirs to various physicians, "in spite of all my reluctance to be preoccupied with my ills. . . . The variety of opinions was as great as that of the means indicated. nonetheless always firm and tranquil[,] accustomed to reasoning, I . . . contented myself with trying all the different remedies that were prescribed in succession. " What prompted her approach to Tissot was her dissatisfaction with an unsuitable regimen, prescribed by another practitioner, which had left her stomach severely weakened. For this woman, the exercise of reason concerning her own body took the form of an informed fashioning of regimen that reconciled conflicting medical advice with lived corporeal experience. Licensed physicians were fond of citing Hippocrates or Galen to the effect that temperament could be known only through experience, and also that temperamental types were blurred both by intermediate forms and by the infinite diversity of individual cases. Medical literature for the polite consumer, however, tended to contradict such statements. Particular temperaments or diseases tended to be allied with a particular age, gender, nationality, or occupation, and temperaments were still often linked to a particular physical appearance.[90] Readers could thus shop around among corporeal identities and find one to suit themselves—exactly what several medical clients I have already discussed were clearly doing.

89. Bibliothèque Centrale et Universitaire, Lausanne, fonds S.-A. Tissot, IS 3784/II/144.02.04.21: "Mémoire" concerning Madame de Myrmont, Paris, February 20, 1774.

90. See, e.g., Jacquin 1762.

CONCLUSION

In describing their own health in these medical memoirs, individuals did not offer some unifying account of "the body" corresponding to a single thread of somatic experience. Rather, they tended to represent themselves as a collection of discrete body parts or experiences bound together by a singular identity, as in the "narrative enclaves" proposed by Katharine Young.[91] Such identities, however, were often temporarily assumed for particular ends, as in the case of both Voltaire and Diderot, for whom health became an epistemological and micropolitical strategy of self-construction. Such plays of the self problematize the widespread tendency to treat regimen as a homogeneous body of knowledge, virtually unaltered in Western Europe over many centuries. Each use of regimen was an *interpretation* of a medical tradition firmly rooted in institutions, prescribed by medical practitioners and appropriated by their clients, in a world where medical consumers had considerable control over the content of therapy. In other words, regimen may be seen as a negotiated and temporary set of agreements about the self as identity and body, a heuristic of practice rather than a body of knowledge. It might be regarded as a classificatory grid into which individuals fitted themselves, or alternatively as akin to a game, with fixed rules but no predetermined outcomes. The continuing output of regimen literature through the early modern period should thus be seen as a constant reworking of knowledge-claims in response to new settings and problems. By the eighteenth century, regimen advice was also mediated through a flourishing print culture. The publication of dietetic advice in cookbooks and the proliferation of health manuals for the lay reader simultaneously denoted the appropriation of medical knowledge by consumers—the "medicalization of the old regime"—and, through the fulfilment of medical commands, the strengthening of medical authority in everyday life. In effect, all members of polite society became valetudinarians.[92]

A fruitful way of working with such questions can be derived from Sahlins's study of mythopraxis, in which the prevailing narratives of a culture are flexible and permit of innovation and alteration through usage, rather than confining action absolutely. Although Sahlins was concerned with Hawai'ian culture, these European medical consumers exhibit similar propensities to treat regimen as a prescriptive ideal that actual behavior man-

91. Young 1989, 1997, 32–45; see also Shilling 1993, 4–8, on body projects.
92. Goubert 1982.

ifested only imperfectly. Therefore, medical knowledge did not exhibit a perfect "fit" with the practices of everyday life. Nonetheless, the torrent of medical writings and prescriptions in which regimen was enshrined were highly relevant to the practice of everyday life. Even a loose "fit" permitted regimen to figure in debates over national morality, individual self-conduct, medical authority, and philosophical materialism. While the meaning of particular foods, dishes, and culinary practices depended upon their deployment within such debates, every dietary choice which referred back to the nonnaturals served to confirm regimen as a *general* methodology of health, described by one contemporary hygienist as the most certain part of all medicine. Adaptable to new narratives of enlightenment and the natural, regimen was a system of corporeal power relations with knowledge at its heart.[93]

By the 1770s the type of philosophical optimism discussed in chapter 5, where chemical models of taste offered a reliable guide to the healthiness of foods, and reason an unproblematic route to self-control and health, had largely vanished. Even the culinary tradition came to reflect the now-fashionable health concerns among the eating public. In 1776 a young medical student, Jourdain de Le Cointe, wrote to Tissot from Montpellier complaining about the teaching there and asking for reading suggestions on the basis of the "Restorative Genius of your Works." Tissot responded with a complete course of medical literature. One of the few cookbooks to be published during the Revolutionary years was a certain Jourdan-Lecointe's *Cuisine de santé*, complete with an extensive preface on healthy eating; it ran to numerous editions in the nineteenth century, becoming part of the gastronomic canon.[94] This disciple of Tissot thus entered the domain of cookery specifically to affirm the primacy of health over culinary pleasure. New alimentary spaces and concerns would emerge as this hierarchy became generalized in Parisian polite society after 1760.[95]

Mennell has claimed that "there is little evidence to suggest that [physicians'] opinions had had much effect on people's daily eating habits in the past. Still less is it safe to assume that philosophers like Rousseau had great

93. Pressavin 1786, j–ij; Sahlins 1981, esp. 51–55, 67–68; see also Wittgenstein 1958, 1:§§198–99.

94. Bibliothèque Centrale et Universitaire, Lausanne, fonds S.-A. Tissot, IS 3784/I/130.1.29: Letter, Jourdain de Le Cointe to Tissot, Montpellier, August 26, 1776; 130.1.48: Letter, Tissot to Jourdain de Le Cointe, Lausanne, October 13, 1776; Jourdan de Le Cointe 1790.

95. In particular the restaurant (Spang 2000, 1–2; Rambourg 2005, 154–56). Wenger (2007, chap. 8) shows that a tradition emphasizing the beneficent effects of cultivated pleasure did persist after the 1760s, notably in the medical and pornographic writings of the Turin-trained physician Amédée Doppet.

practical impact on such mundane behavior." This assertion is, I think, substantially refuted, at least for the case of the polite elite, by a study of a category of material that has failed to penetrate canonical culinary history or more recent anthropological approaches to cuisine: the daily practices of polite eaters as recorded in correspondence, memoirs, and journals. The turn toward health and the natural constituted a micropolitics of the self, built upon Rousseau's claim that modern urban eaters, and Parisians in particular, were all valetudinarians. Thus, during the closing years of the Old Regime, polite eaters would treat regimen as a political praxis, a means of forming or reforming politically fit bodies. In the 1780s, Mme de Genlis, governor to the sons of the duc d'Orléans, raised both boys on a regimen of rigorous exercise, hard beds, and a diet of bread and milk, a program she derived from Rousseau's educational treatise *Emile*. The elder would go on to become the constitutional monarch Louis-Philippe.[96]

96. Mennell 1996, 35; Broglie 1985, 136. Rousseau (1967–71, 2:491–92) had Emile dislike nouvelle cuisine's "fine ragoûts" and prefer "good vegetables, good cream and good people."

CONCLUSION

Food is a domain in which everybody is an expert. On a daily basis, ordinary eaters are responsible for choosing which foods they will consume, and articulating reasons for those choices. As an audience member astutely put it to me at one seminar: "Why did anyone *need* alimentary experts anyway?" The complex urban world of eighteenth-century Paris, just like many Western societies today, confronted individual eaters with many competing systems of alimentary knowledge, from health manuals and satires to dietaries and cookbooks. In deciding how to constitute their diet, eaters might appeal to personal preference, habit, cultural circumstances, family background, medical advice, or political priorities. Every anthropological study of food consumption suggests that as soon as there is even limited flexibility in the food supply, eaters exercise choice.[1] And yet eaters, now as in the eighteenth century, alter those choices in response to the knowledge-claims of publicly authoritative figures. I am particularly interested by this phenomenon in societies in which there is a public domain constituted in such a way that experts and eaters have no personal knowledge of one another. Then the problem of authority becomes even more acute, and is related to the question of how credit and credibility can be mediated through text.[2] How is trust in another's knowledge-claims developed to such a degree that an individual's most intimate practices might be altered in response to the dictums of a stranger? For that is, in essence, what the modern system of public nutritional advice requires of eaters, and it is one of the principal

1. Caplan 1997; Oddy and Miller 1976; Mintz 1985, chap. 1. Sociologists such as Lupton 1996 espouse similar views.

2. Shapin 1984, 1995; Shapin and Schaffer 1985; Broman 1998, 128–29.

dilemmas afflicting the relationship between eaters, experts and foods in modern times.[3] In early modern humoral medicine, there was widespread agreement concerning the autonomy of elite medical clients, such that polite individuals were deemed best qualified to identify the foods most suited to their own constitutions. The transition described by Nicholas Jewson in his 1976 article on the "disappearance of the sick man from medical cosmology" can thus justifiably be viewed as a transfer of the locus of knowledgeable expertise.[4] Learned authority over eating may have been, as it continues to be today, an imperfect enterprise, but this is not to claim, as some historians have, that the sciences and medicine had no effect upon eating practices in the early modern period. Rather, it is to call for an historical approach along the lines proposed by historians of the book: eating, especially in complex, urbanized, cosmopolitan cultures, is not a passive process of consumption, but an active process of choice and assimilation, and its history should reflect that. It is because most eaters are knowledgeable that the history of food and the history of scientific authority in the eighteenth century intersect at critical points.

We have now reached the very last course of the meal. Enlightenment has been consumed and, to some extent, digested. Like other universals, "the" Enlightenment is often proclaimed to be a construct, yet enlightenment as process or state cannot be dismissed as an empty historical category on that basis, for the *state* of enlightenment was frequently invoked by the scientific and medical practitioners involved in making eating scientific between 1670 and 1760, in order to legitimate the participation of some actors in the making of knowledge while excluding others.[5] In this book I argue against starting historical explanation from the standpoint of large categories such as gender or class. History, when understood in terms of agency and action, practice and print, association and credibility, becomes an account of the social and geographical positioning of particular knowledge-claims, not a biography of disembodied and decontextualized ideas. Nicholas Jardine has written of the importance of both historical accounts and institutions as knowledge technologies, which form a resource in particular debates. Though his concern is with change, he also demonstrates that apparently stable, traditional or transhistorical knowledge is only that which has happened to have been appropriated by successive generations of users, often

3. See especially Coveney 2006, xii–xviii; Keane 1997; Furst 1992.

4. Jewson 1976.

5. See, e.g., Goodman 2001.

for highly localized polemical purposes. Moreover, that process of reuse is a normal part of the legitimation of scientific truth-claims.[6]

Like enlightenment, the meaning of foods is always contingent and local, and often polemical. It is a commonplace of anthropologically informed accounts of food and eating to assert that foods cannot be treated merely as material substances serving nutritive purposes: they must be viewed as part of broader systems of communication, social distinction and self-fashioning. Often such approaches also reflect structuralist borrowings, making individual foods and acts of eating into representatives of larger symbolic categories. Anthropologists have addressed the ways in which meaning is constructed by social transactions such as festive dinners, home cooking, gifts of food, sacrifices. Most famously, Claude Lévi-Strauss coined the term "gustemes" to describe the individual food ingredients composing a meal, arguing that foods formed a cultural "grammar."[7] Historians who have turned to anthropology to provide a methodology for writing about food often place the foodstuff or the occasion of its consumption at the center of analysis, not the actor. In such renderings of the history of food, as in commodity histories, it is rare to find attention paid to foods as the subject of conflict and contestation between eaters. Yet it is apparent that if foods are to have any instrumental function in human cultures beyond that of basic nourishment, then a given foodstuff is unlikely to possess a univocal, agreed-upon meaning except in an entirely homogeneous culture. This is certainly not the condition of any culture with a public sphere of contestation and exchange, such as that existing in eighteenth-century Paris. In *Eating the Enlightenment*, foods are not a grammar but an instrument; if eating is to be represented in linguistic terms, eighteenth-century Paris might be seen as a patchwork of dialects.[8]

Eating as communication is no more straightforward than making any other sort of knowledge-claim, and equally contested. Eating practices and foods do not connote inherent meanings and significances; rather, their meaning and significance are *attributed* by multiple actors, who are far from composing a homogeneous constituency. Those meanings are, accordingly, constantly subject to challenge, questioning, and revision, particularly in a culture like eighteenth-century Paris, where food production and consump-

6. Jardine 1991.

7. Lévi-Strauss 1997, 1970; see the analyses in Morton 1994; Mennell et al. 1992, 1–19; Goody 1982, chap. 2; Fischler 1993; Caplan 1997; Coveney 2006. See also Douglas and Isherwood 1996, xiii; de Knecht–van Eekelen and van Otterloo 2000.

8. On sociological and anthropological approaches to food and how these differ from the nutrition sciences, see Prättälä 1991.

tion was subject to fashions and innovation. To say, with Deborah Lupton, that norms of alimentary conduct "are generally adhered to by most people most of the time" or that "men are typically associated with red meat and large helpings of food" is to leave unaddressed several issues of specifically historical, rather than sociological or anthropological, importance.[9]

In the first instance, how can we explain a culture's uptake, whether eager or reluctant, of new foods? For precisely what distinguished Paris as an alimentary culture, in the eyes of contemporaries, was its population's readiness to embrace novelty. In the second instance, under what circumstances can certain sorts of norms, notably those generated by political authorities or alimentary experts, take on universal force; under what circumstances are they rejected; and what happens when there is a division of opinion? This is to paraphrase a question posed by Ophir and Shapin in asking under what circumstances scientific knowledge-claims move from being local to becoming universal.[10] Anthropological and sociological histories of food and eating always present us with a done deal. It is only by unpicking this alimentary knowledge in the making that we can see how alimentary standards might come to be fashioned as political projects: how the association between red meat and masculinity, for example, might be the outcome of past polemics over corporeal delicacy and political empowerment. It behoves us to ask just how meaning can be said to inhere in material objects, specifically in foods, and what happens to meaning during consumption, when food integrates into our bodies and hence becomes part of our self and identity.[11] This book thus underlines the historical importance and the historiographical unwieldiness of matter. More than many other historical topics, food is marked out by its transience; so far from supporting a *longue durée* perspective on the past, food reminds us forcibly of its ephemeral, transient, and perishable quality. Food is, by definition, a sort of matter liable to vanish; the history of food as knowledge demands attention to the changing historical relationship between matter, knowledge, and meaning.

Almost all historical assertions about food and meaning draw their most fundamental level of interpretation from modern nutritional science, medicine, and biology. Gerald Mars and Valerie Mars epitomize the general view; people have "loaded, encrusted and elaborated upon the biological

9. Lupton 1996, 29, 104.

10. Ophir and Shapin 1991; also Latour 1992.

11. On materiality and meaning in the history of science, see, e.g., Daston 2004; Klein and Spary 2010. Turner (1996, 37–43) notes the absence of material questions of embodiment from politico-economic theories of the regulation of bodies.

need to eat with socially derived and culturally validated rituals and symbolic repertoires. It is this mixture of nature and culture that gives food such power."[12] At the very least, the agenda of a sociologically informed history of science would require that we place these various interpretative levels on a par and do not privilege modern or past scientific meanings over other types of meaning that foods might possess. These scientific accounts of food and diet themselves possess a history that was fashioned through interaction with rival accounts, and the various past accounts of food connoted different politics of knowledge about food that were sometimes incompatible. Why then should we view one set of accounts as amenable to historical interpretation, while another set on the "science" side acquires an ahistorical transcendence and an immunity to historical analysis? *Eating the Enlightenment* rejects biological reductionism for the very specific reason that natural-scientific accounts of food were themselves not yet authoritative during the period covered; to take them as the foundation of inquiry is to assume an epistemological stability that could not be taken for granted in 1670 or even in 1760. To defend alimentary knowledge-claims required labor, and could only be accomplished within certain bounded spaces, such as laboratories and academies. Outside these privileged settings, no epistemological superiority could be assumed for scientific objects over everyday ones during much of the early modern period, nor for scientific knowledge-claims over everyday assertions.[13]

Yet alimentary standards often appear to be embedded in a timeless and mysteriously inaccessible culture of tradition and convention, even if they are in fact the product of earlier regimes of knowledge and practice. Within a static anthropology or an ahistorical sociology of foods, such practices, standards, and preferences are then often represented as parts of "culinary tradition"; they appear to possess an intrinsic authority that requires no scholarly investigation or analysis. An example here might be the practice of parboiling eggs, which continues to this day, having long since shed its humoral underpinnings. Only a historicist approach can disclose the fact that Renaissance and early modern dietetic treatises routinely recommended this method of preparation, since liquid egg-white or solid egg-yolk were deemed to be indigestible.[14]

12. Mars and Mars 1993, 11–13; also Rebora 2001; Goody 1982, 1.

13. With this claim, I extend Pinch and Bijker 1984's principle of symmetry, the claim that the same kind of explanation must be advanced for both the success and the failure of knowledge-claims.

14. Lémery 1705, 345–46; D[u] F[our de La Crespelière] 1671, 70; Albala 2002.

As this book has endeavored to demonstrate, eaters were and are surrounded by numerous different possible repertoires from which they might appropriate meanings for individual foods or for particular eating practices. Eating choices were usually retrospectively constructed into a narratival unity, but that unity was a social event, performed in response to a particular audience of critics, in other words an act of self-fashioning that joined private action to public self-presentation. The multiplicity of narratives involved in self-fashioning is sensitively explored by the medical ethnographer Katharine Young for the case of the body.[15] Eaters may act in accordance with the particular alimentary plots they deem to be most appropriate in different situations. Thus, it is possible to argue that sugar was invested with a particular meaning during a specific transaction (eating, debate, legislation), but not that it universally signified "health" or "disease." In the modern West, eating is argument, but we still lack a history of what the argument has been about.

The approach I am advocating here is closer to a poststructuralist reading of the ways in which individuals employ foods for self-fashioning, understanding such activities as part of a dialectic between agency and authority.[16] "When one person speaks and another acts": such is the definition of authority proposed by Bruno Latour. In exploring these local contestations about eating, we are scrutinizing some of the ways in which the micropolitics of individual self-governance translates into the macropolitical structure of government and authority relations. This dialectic was expressed by Foucault as a process of internalization of behavioral standards, rules of self-governance, and emotions that are subsequently applied in everyday life.[17] Ultimately, this book is less concerned with how enlightened eaters consumed food than with how they stomached learning. The act of swallowing one substance rather than another was itself a micropolitical decision, a vote for one form of authority over another: that of chefs or connoisseurs, that of physicians or apothecaries? The same food could be at one and the same time the property of different groups of experts and users.

Within a literate culture, food practices were thus always under tension, poised between multiple authoritative advisors and internalized personal preferences. As Pierre Bourdieu pointed out, taste is the site of execution of social distinction; yet his account also explored mobility within that system, an issue of particular importance in societies where food habits are

15. Young 1997; see also Coward 1989, 146; Lupton 1996, 75.

16. Lupton 1996, 13.

17. Latour 1986, 2000; Bachelard 1975; Foucault 1988; Rose 1996.

rapidly changing, where innovation and fashion are defining principles of self-presentation, and where governments and scientific or medical practitioners are actively intervening to alter diet.[18]

One of the most interesting events in French food history between 1670 and 1760 was that the courtly embrace of fine dining and gustatory connoisseurship became implicated in debates over the extent, scope, and validity of new forms of knowledge. Cuisine entered public debate primarily because diet particularly showcased the pervasive question of social change and innovation; new forms of knowledge and new foods were both equally disturbing to the moral economy of French society. These sorts of innovations placed government at the forefront of concern, whether it be self-government, the public authority of alimentary experts, or the relations between Crown and consumer. The terrain of disputes over foodstuffs then took the form of a conflict between rival groups of scientific practitioners in the broadest sense—that is, all those who laid claim to expertise based on knowledge.

The wide reach of scientific lectures and entertainments from the 1710s to the end of the century ensured that many people could credibly appeal to scientific legitimation in making alimentary knowledge-claims. This general deployment of scientific credibility by a wide learned and literate public was a condition that was at one and the same time a prerequisite for stabilizing scientific practice as an authoritative public and political resource, and a threat to that same process. If we now narrow the focus to those individuals who more closely resemble the scientific practitioners who figure in most histories of science, it is not possible to find conclusive victories for the natural sciences within the period covered by this book. Rather, we find very local disputes, conducted in universalizing language. From the point of view of medical practitioners like Macquer or Baumé, the appeal to chemical expertise made by distillers or grocers was a case of "too many cooks spoiling the broth"; instead, they presented institutional chemists as the authentic and legitimate guardians of scientific truth. *Eating the Enlightenment* calls for a more even-handed consideration of the specific conditions under which certain categories of learned persons, both individually and severally, attempted to engineer positions of public expertise in regard to alimentary knowledge and conduct; something explored here in the case of several different individuals, from Hecquet and de Jussieu to Sauvel and Baumé.

As in Bruno Latour's account of the manufacture of scientific truth, the

18. Bourdieu 1984; Gronow 1997, chap. 2.

process of cultural adoption of a particular alimentary truth or custom is one-way.[19] Food practices, like scientific truth-claims, can become "black-boxed" within cultures and thereby hard to reverse. The recognition of the distance between expert recommendations and public predilections was one of the issues contributing to the debate over habits and needs, which, I have argued, gave rise to the dual nature of modern accounts of addiction. In order to justify interventions to food habits conducted on the basis of expert knowledge-claims, it was absolutely necessary to naturalize such behaviors, and portray them as appetites springing from within the body, which could not be mastered by reason. This was one reason why, during the eighteenth century, the regulation of eating would change from a personal and private matter into a public and political one, and from a matter of satire and poetry to one of chemistry and physiology.

Eating the Enlightenment calls for a historicist approach to be applied with equal enthusiasm both to satire and to physiology. In short, it calls on historians of science to attend more closely to past uses of language, and on historians of food to attend more closely to past accounts of embodiment. The historical study of food and eating places knowledge about the body at center stage. Perhaps to the regret of some of my readers, I have nowhere suggested, either directly or by the implicit maneuver of including recipes in this book, that the food historian's task should include the replication of past culinary practice. Setting aside the fact that recipes published before 1760 rarely utilized measures, and the fact that, in countless ways, today's ingredients bear little resemblance to their eighteenth-century equivalents, there is also the fact that polite connoisseurs regarded themselves, and were regarded, as finely honed instruments with a sense of taste created by a lifetime's experience and practice. When the "Gascon Cook" called on his readers to season oysters "in good taste" without providing any more specific definition, it calls to mind Jean-Louis Flandrin's salutary reminder of the vast historical transformations affecting judgments about taste in particular. In other words, we cannot have a history of foods without having a history of eaters and their accounts of embodiment.[20]

Where the production of learned accounts of food was concerned, the way in which particular foods were used to bolster particular self-presentations, to define cultural groups, and to mark out transgression was fought out largely at the local level. Although this study pays close attention to the local

19. Latour 1987.

20. Flandrin 1996a; anon. 1740, 49. On the body, see Lawrence and Shapin 1998; Shilling 1993, 2007; Lupton 1996; Ferguson 2001, 17–18.

in considering how alimentary expertise could be produced, it also shows the extent to which issues of global significance resided at the heart of the local. Between the 1710s and the second half of the eighteenth century, daily diet at all social levels within the city came to depend upon access to vastly distant and different cultures. The new habits of daily life acquired by Europeans after 1650 drove a lasting reconfiguration of political and commercial relations between Europe and the rest of the world.[21] Eighteenth-century Parisians could hardly take a bite without affecting cultures and natures in other parts of the world. The dark side of Enlightenment, too, was embedded in debates over eating and globalization. Commentators were all too well aware not only of the pernicious effects of luxury consumption in maintaining the slave trade but also of the converse problem, the increasing failure of governments to control domestic desires. Reflection on the problem of habituation, desire, and need became an autocritique built into the beginnings of capitalism, and in which a need to consume certain substances became the engine for political transformation, both at home and abroad.[22]

Addiction is our chief legacy from the politics of taste that was at the heart of controversies over reason, learning, and Enlightenment in 1750. The close connection between the moral, political, and physiological in today's public debates and policies on addictive substances derives from the common ground underlying these eighteenth-century discussions over taste. These debates were, of course, ways of explaining the consequences of the growth of new consumption for eighteenth-century societies. Hence they are also at the origin of a particular economic model that still serves to explain the interdependency of capitalist accumulation and the increasingly global reach of Western consumption. The cumulative model of consumer desires would become a key tenet of subsequent economic, political, and social theory. In Collins's words, J. Edgar Hoover accounted for the mechanism of American prosperity as "the stimulation and satisfaction of human wants to the point where 'the great mass of consumers will never for a moment know what it means to be content.'"[23] This malaise of ever-expanding desires stimulated by commerce continues to be attacked as the major moral

21. Mintz 1985.

22. See especially Kilgour 1990; Baudrillard 1994; Heller 1976; Finkelstein 1989.

23. Collins 1976, 39; see also Finkelstein 1989, 102; Gardiner 2000, 94–99; Heller 1976, esp. chap. 2. Berry (1994, 188–95) locates the origins of Marx's theory of the historical production of needs in the writings of Adam Smith and Hegel, though the claim that needs were historically generated was, as chapter 5 shows, already current in French philosophical circles by the mid-eighteenth century. Similarly, my argument here diverges from implicit assumptions about the relationship between capitalism, industrialization and habituation in Sherratt 1995.

failing of modern society, and the peculiar characteristic of what many have taken to be the most fully developed capitalist economy in the world.[24] It is not always recognized, however, that modern commerce and the critical discourses about it arose simultaneously.

Even in the eighteenth century, as this book has shown, critics asserted that consumption perverted bodies and minds, and generated global and local inequality. Today's critics tend to portray the moral dilemmas posed by modern commerce as a recent problem, where in fact the main change since 1720 is one of scale.[25] A critique developed during the eighteenth century in response to the spread and global implications of luxury consumption generated a political physiology of need that continues to serve a variety of purposes into our own time. Concerns about the relationship between governments, experts, and consumers, the evil consequences of mass consumption, or the dependency of individual consumers upon opaque systems of food production, are thus not recent inventions but, on the contrary, precisely as old as the modern commercial world itself.

24. See Miller 1995, 1987, chaps. 8–10; Appleby 1993; Gronow 1991.

25. An example here is Birken 1988, 22–34, though such views are increasingly challenged by recent history of consumption.

BIBLIOGRAPHY

ARCHIVAL AND MANUSCRIPT REFERENCES

Archives de l'Académie des Sciences, Paris: dossier "Réaumur"; "Procès-verbaux."

Archives de Paris: mss. D^5B^6 685; D^5B^6 1635.

Archives de la Chambre de Commerce de Marseille: mss. B 152; H 112.

Archives Nationales, Aix-en-Provence: mss. C^2 14; C^2 285; C^3 3; C^3 4; C^{8A} 21; C^{8A} 26; C^{8A} 27; C^{8A} 33.

Archives Nationales, Paris: mss. Mar-D^3 42; F^{11} 201; F^{12} 55; T160 19; T160 22; V^7 167; AJ^{15} 502.

Bibliothèque Centrale et Universitaire, Lausanne, fonds S.-A. Tissot: IS 3784/I, mss. 60, 86, 130; IS 3784/II, ms. 144.

Bibliothèque de l'Académie Nationale de Médecine, fonds Société Royale de Médecine: mss. 98; 201.

Bibliothèque de l'Institut de France: ms. 1268.

Bibliothèque Interuniversitaire de Pharmacie: registres 32, 38.

Bibliothèque Publique et Universitaire, Geneva, Archives Tronchin: mss. 165; 166; 167; 168; 198; 204.

Minutier Central, Paris: études XXXIX/408; XC/369; LXV/381.

Service Historique de l'Armée de Terre, Vincennes: ms. 3556.

Service Historique de la Marine, Brest: ms. 50.

ELECTRONIC DOCUMENTS

Académie Française. 2011. "Les immortels" [database of academicians]. http://www.academie-francaise.fr/immortels/.

D'Argenson, René-Louis Voyer, marquis. 1997. *Journal et mémoires du marquis d'Argenson* (1755–57), vol. 9, pt. 2. Edited by E.-J.-B. Rathery. Electronic document. Paris: INALF. http://visualiseur.bnf.fr/ark:/12148/bpt6k873364.

Fénelon, François de Salignac de La Mothe. 2011. "Voyage dans l'île des Plaisirs." http://platea.pntic.mec.es/~cvera/aplicacion/telemaque/fables.html (accessed March 31, 2011).

Geoffroy, Étienne-Louis. 1997. *Manuel de médecine pratique: Ouvrage élémentaire auquel on a joint quelques formules*. Paris: INALF. http://visualiseur.bnf.fr/ark:/12148/bpt6k884537.

Latour, Bruno. 2011. "On Actor Network Theory: A Few Clarifications." http://www.nettime.org/Lists-Archives/nettime-l-9801/msg00019.html (accessed November 25, 2011).

Murphy, Antoin E. 2007. "Law and Turgot: The Importance of Money." Paper presented at the Conference on French Political Economy, 1650–1850, at Stanford University, April 16–19, 2004. http://www-library.stanford.edu/depts/hasrg/frnit/pdfs_gimon/murphy.pdf (accessed June 5, 2011).

PRINTED WORKS

Abad, Reynald. 2002. *Le grand marché. L'approvisionnement alimentaire de Paris sous l'Ancien Régime*. Paris: Fayard.

Abdel-Halim, Moham ed. 1964. *Antoine Galland, sa vie et son oeuvre*. Paris: A. G. Nizet.

Académie Française. 1970. *Histoire des membres de l'académie française morts depuis 1700 jusqu'en 1771*. Geneva: Slatkine Reprints.

Académie Françoise. 1694. *Le Dictionnaire de l'Académie françoise, dedié au Roy. Dictionnaire des Arts et des Sciences*. 4 vols. Paris: Jean-Baptiste Coignard.

———. 1714–87. *Recueil des Harangues prononcées par Messieurs de l'Académie Françoise*. 2nd ed., 8 vols. Paris: Jean-Baptiste Coignard, Veuve Brunet, Regnard and Demonville.

———. [1762]. *Dictionnaire de l'Académie Françoise*. 4th ed., 2 vols. Paris: Veuve de Bernard Brunet.

———. 1798 / year VI–VII. *Dictionnaire de l'Académie Françoise, revu, corrigé et augmenté par l'Académie elle-meme*. 5th ed., 2 vols. Paris: J. J. Smits et Cie.

ACE. [1692]. *Arrest du Conseil d'Estat du Roy. Concernant la vente du Caffé, du Thé, du Sorbec & du Chocolat*. [N.p.].

———. 1723. *Arrest du Conseil d'Estat du Roy, pour la prise de possession par la Compagnie des Indes du Privilege de la Vente exclusive du Caffé*. [N.p.].

———. 1736. *Arrest du Conseil d'Estat du Roy, Portant Reglement sur les Caffez provenant des plantations & cultures des Isles Françoises de l'Amérique*. Marseille: D. Sibié.

Adam, Pierre. 1920. *Etude sur le vocabulaire du chansonnier historique. La Régence (1715–1723)*. Jarville-Nancy: Imprimerie Arts Graphiques.

Aguilà Sorana, Irène. 1997. "Le vin dans le théâtre de la foire." In *Le Vin*, ed. Jean Bart and Élisabeth Wahl. Special issue of *Dix-huitième siècle* 29:211–25.

Albala, Ken. 2002. *Eating Right in the Renaissance*. Berkeley: University of California Press.

Albrecht, Peter. 1988. "Coffee-Drinking as a Symbol of Social Change in Continental Europe in the Seventeenth and Eighteenth Centuries." *Studies in Eighteenth-Century Culture* 18:91–103.

Alem, André. 1900. *Le marquis d'Argenson et l'économie politique au début du XVIIIe siècle. Pratiques mercantiles et théories libérales*. Paris: Arthur Rousseau.

[Alexandre, Nicolas]. 1716. *Dictionnaire botanique et pharmaceutique*. Paris: Laurent Le Conte.

Allchin, Douglas. 1992. "Phlogiston After Oxygen." *Ambix* 39:110–16.

[Alletz, Pons-Augustin]. 1760. *L'Agronome. Dictionnaire Portatif du Cultivateur*. Paris: Veuve Didot, Nyon, Savoye and Durand.

Ames, Glenn J. 1990. "Colbert's Indian Ocean Strategy of 1664–1674: A Reappraisal." *French Historical Studies* 16 (3): 536–59.

———. 1992. "Colbert and the World Market Economy, 1661–1683: Bourbon Absolutism and the Compagnie Royale des Indes Orientales." *Proceedings of the Annual Meeting of the Western Society for French History* 19:57–65.

———. 1996. *Colbert, Mercantilism, and the French Quest for Asian Trade*. DeKalb: Northern Illinois University Press.

———. 2003. "Mughal India during the Age of the Scientific Revolution: François Bernier's Travels and Lessons for Absolutist Europe." In *Distant Lands and Diverse Cultures: The French Experience in Asia, 1600–1700*, ed. Glenn J. Ames and Ronald S. Love, 147–62. Westport, CT: Praeger.

Anderson, Elizabeth. 1994. "Introduction." In Charles-Georges Leroy, *Lettres sur les animaux*, 1–71. Oxford: The Voltaire Foundation at the Taylor Institution.

Anderson, R. G. W., J. A. Bennett, and W. F. Ryan, ed. 1993. *Making Instruments Count: Essays on Historical Scientific Instruments presented to Gerard L'Estrange Turner*. Aldershot: Variorum.

Anderson, Wilda A. 1984. *Between the Library and the Laboratory: The Language of Chemistry in Eighteenth-Century France*. Baltimore: Johns Hopkins University Press.

[Andry de Boisregard, Nicolas]. 1710. *Le regime du Caresme, consideré par rapport a la nature du corps, & des alimens*. Paris: Jean-Baptiste Coignard.

Andry de Boisregard, Nicolas. 1713. *Traité des Alimens de Caresme*. 2 vols. Paris: Jean-Baptiste Coignard.

Anon. 1696. "Eloge et utilité du Café." *Mercure Galant* 15–55 (May).

———. 1702. *L'Anti-Cornaro ou Remarques critiques sur le Traité de la vie sobre de Louis Cornaro venitien*. Paris: Claude Borré.

———. [1711?] *Chanson sur l'usage du caffé, sur ses propriétez, & sur la manière de le bien préparer*. Paris: Jacques Estienne.

———. 1740. *Le Cuisinier Gascon*. Amsterdam: [n.p.].

———. 1743. "Dissertation sur la nature & les propriétés du Levain de l'estomach." *Mémoires de Trévoux*, 2374–93.

———. 1773. "Lettre à Louis Guillaume Lemonnier . . . sur la culture du Café." *Année littéraire* 1773.viii.276–86.

———. 1774. "Lettre à l'Auteur de ces Feuilles sur un Article concernant le Café." *Année littéraire* 1774.v.282–88.

———. 1789. *Tableau général des Maîtres Distillateurs Limonadiers et Vinaigriers de la Ville, Fauxbourgs & Banlieue de Paris; Pour l'Année 1789*. Paris: Chardon.

———. 1798 / year VI. *Traité du Café, Contenant l'Histoire, la Description, la Culture et les Propriétés de ce Végétal*. Paris: Rue Saint-André-des-Arts, no. 46.

Appadurai, Arjun. 1986. "Introduction: Commodities and the Politics of Value." In *The*

Social Life of Things: Commodities in Cultural Perspective, ed. Appadurai, 3–63. Cambridge: Cambridge University Press.

Appleby, Joyce. 1992. "Consumption in Early Modern Social Thought." In *Consumption and the World of Goods*, ed. John Brewer and Roy Porter, 162–73. London: Routledge.

Ashworth, William J. 2001. "'Between the Trader and the Public': British Alcohol Standards and the Proof of Good Governance." *Technology and Culture* 42:27–50.

Assaf, Francis. 1987. "La deuxième Querelle (1714–1716): Pour une genèse des Lumières?" In *D'un siècle à l'autre: Anciens et Modernes*, ed. Louise Godard de Donville and Roger Duchêne, 277–92. XVIe Colloque (Janvier 1986). Marseille: A. Robert.

Astruc, Jean. 1711. *Mémoire, sur la cause de la digestion des Alimens*. Montpellier: Honoré Pech.

———. 1714. *Traité de la cause de la digestion, ou l'on refute le nouveau Sistéme de la Trituration & du broïement*. Toulouse: Ant. Colomiez.

Aublet, Jean-Baptiste-Christophe Fusée. 1775. "Observations sur la Culture du Café." In *Histoire des Plantes de la Guiane Françoise*, 4:49–56. 4 vols. London: Pierre-François Didot le jeune.

[Audiger?]. 1692. *La Maison réglée, et l'art de diriger la maison d'un grand Seigneur et autres, tant à la Ville qu'à la Campagne, et le devoir de tous les Officiers, et autres domestiques en général*. Paris: Michel Brunet, 1692.

Audiger. 1995. *La maison reglée et l'art de diriger la maison d'un grand seigneur tant à la ville qu'à la campagne*. In *L'art de la cuisine française au XVIIe siècle*, ed. Gilles Laurendon and Laurence Laurendon, 439–565. Paris: Editions Payot & Rivages.

Azouvi, François. 1981. "Woman as a Model of Pathology in the Eighteenth Century." *Diogenes* 115:22–36.

Babelon, Jean-Pierre, ed. 1993. *Versailles et les tables royales en Europe XVIIème–XIXème siècles*. Paris: Réunion des musées nationaux.

Bachelard, Gaston. 1975. *Le nouvel esprit scientifique*, 13th ed. Paris: Presses Universitaires de France.

Badinter, Elisabeth. 1999–2007. *Les passions intellectuelles*. 3 vols. Paris: Fayard.

Baker, Keith Michael, ed. 1987. *The Political Culture of the Old Regime*. Vol. 1 of *The French Revolution and the Creation of Modern Political Culture*. Oxford: Pergamon.

———. 1990. *Inventing the French Revolution: Essays on French Political Culture in the Eighteenth Century*. Cambridge: Cambridge University Press.

Ball, Daniela U., ed. 1991. *Coffee in the Context of European Drinking Habits*. Veröffentlichungen des Johann Jacobs Museums zur Kulturgeschichte des Kaffees 2. Zürich: Johann Jacobs Museum.

Banier, abbé Antoine. 1732. *Les Métamorphoses d'Ovide, traduites en français, avec des remarques, et des explications historiques*. 3 vols. Amsterdam: R. & J. Wetstein & G. Smith.

Banks, Oliver T. 1977. *Watteau and the North: Studies in the Dutch and Flemish Baroque Influence on French Rococo Painting*. New York: Garland.

Banzhaf, H. Spencer. 2000. "Productive Nature and the Net Product: Quesnay's Economies Animal and Political." *History of Political Economy* 32 (3): 517–51.

Barbier, Antoine-Alexandre. 1875. *Dictionnaire des ouvrages anonymes*. 3rd ed., 4 vols. Vol. 6. Paris: Paul Daffis.

Barbier, Edmond-Jean-François. 1857–66. *Chronique de la Régence et du règne de Louis XV (1718–1763) ou Journal de Barbier, avocat au parlement de Paris.* 8 vols. Paris: Charpentier.

Barras, Vincent, and Micheline Louis-Courvoisier, ed. 2001. *La médecine des Lumières: Tout autour de Tissot.* Geneva: Georg.

Barrère, Pierre. 1743. *Nouvelle Relation de la France Equinoxiale.* Paris: Piget and Durand.

Bates, David. 1995–96. "The Epistemology of Error in Late Enlightenment France." *Eighteenth-Century Studies* 29:307–27.

Baudrillard, Jean. 1994. "The System of Collecting." In *The Cultures of Collecting*, ed. John Elsner and Roger Cardinal, 7–24. London: Reaktion Books.

Baumé, Antoine. 1757. *Dissertation sur l'Æther, dans laquelle on examine les différens produits du mêlange de l'Esprit de Vin avec les Acides Minéraux.* Paris: Jean-Thomas Hérissant.

———. 1760. "Mémoire sur l'Éther vitriolique." *Mémoires de Mathématique et de Physique, Présentés à l'Académie Royale des Sciences, par divers Savans, & lûs dans ses Assemblées* 3:209–32.

———. 1762. *Élémens de Pharmacie theorique et pratique.* Paris: Veuve Damonneville et al.

———. 1773. *Chymie expérimentale et raisonnée.* 3 vols. Paris: P. François Didot le jeune.

———. 1778a. "Les Météores aqueux sont de vrais exemples de la distillation en grand." *Observations et Mémoires sur la Physique, sur l'Histoire naturelle et sur les Arts et Métiers* 12 (2): 1–37.

———. 1778b. *Mémoire . . . sur cette question: quelle est la meilleure manière de construire les fourneaux et les alambics propres à la distillation des vins.* Paris: Clousier.

Bayle, Pierre. 1685. Review of Philippe Sylvestre Dufour, *Traitez nouveaux & curieux du café, du thé et du chocolate* (1684). *Nouvelles de la République des Lettres* 3:497–520.

Bayley, Stephen. 1991. *Taste: The Secret Meaning of Things.* Boston: Faber and Faber.

Beaune, Jean-Claude. 1989. "The Classical Age of Automata: An Impressionistic Survey from the Sixteenth to the Nineteenth Century." In *Fragments for a History of the Human Body*, 3 vols., ed. Michel Féher, Ramona Naddaff and Nadia Tazi, 1:430–80. New York: Zone.

Becq, Annie. 1984. *Genèse de l'esthétique française moderne. De la Raison classique à l'Imagination créatrice, 1680–1814.* 2 vols. Pisa: Pacini Editore.

[Bel, Jean-Jacques, and Edme-François Guyot-Desfontaines]. 1750. *Dictionnaire Neologique à l'usage des beaux esprits du siècle, avec l'Eloge historique de Pantalon-Phoebus, par un avocat de province.* 6th ed. Amsterdam: Arkstee and Merkus.

Benaroyo, Lazare. 1989. "Tissot et la conception de la médecine savante au 18e siècle." *Gesnerus* 46:229–38.

Bensaude-Vincent, Bernadette. 1992. "The Balance: Between Chemistry and Politics." In *The Chemical Revolution: Context and Practices.* Special issue of *The Eighteenth-Century: Theory and Interpretation* 33:217–37.

———. 1993. *Lavoisier: Mémoires d'une révolution*. Preface by. Michel Serres. Paris: Flammarion.

———. 2000. "'The Chemist's Balance for Fluids': Hydrometers and Their Multiple Identities, 1770–1810." In *Instruments and Experimentation in the History of Chemistry*, ed. Frederic L. Holmes and Trevor H. Levere, 153–83. Cambridge, MA: MIT Press.

———. 2007. "Public Lectures of Chemistry in Mid-Eighteenth-Century France." In *New Narratives in Eighteenth-Century Chemistry*, ed. Lawrence M. Principe, 77–96. Dordrecht: Springer.

Bensaude-Vincent, Bernadette, and Christine Blondel, eds. 2007. *Science and Spectacle in the European Enlightenment*. Aldershot: Ashgate.

Bensaude-Vincent, Bernadette, and Isabelle Stengers. 1996. *A History of Chemistry*. Translated by Deborah van Dam. Cambridge, MA: Harvard University Press.

Berg, Maxine. 1994. *The Age of Manufactures, 1700–1820: Industry, Innovation and Work in Britain*. 2nd ed. London: Routledge.

———. 1999. "New Commodities, Luxuries and their Consumers in Eighteenth-Century England." In *Consumers and Luxury: Consumer Culture in Europe, 1650–1850*, ed. Maxine Berg and Helen Clifford, 63–85. Manchester: Manchester University Press.

———. 2005. *Luxury and Pleasure in Eighteenth-Century Britain*. Oxford: Oxford University Press.

Berg, Maxine, and Elizabeth Eger. 2003a. "Introduction." In *Luxury in the Eighteenth Century: Debates, Desires and Delectable Goods*, ed. Maxine Berg and Elizabeth Eger, 1–4. Basingstoke: Palgrave Macmillan.

———. 2003b. "The Rise and Fall of the Luxury Debates." In *Luxury in the Eighteenth Century: Debates, Desires and Delectable Goods*, ed. Maxine Berg and Elizabeth Eger, 7–27. Basingstoke: Palgrave Macmillan.

Berridge, Virginia. 1978. "Victorian Opium Eating: Responses to Opiate Use in Nineteenth-Century England." *Victorian Studies* 21:437–61.

———. 1990. "Dependence: Historical Concepts and Constructs." In *The Nature of Drug Dependence*, ed. Griffith Edwards and Malcolm Lader, 1–18. Oxford: Oxford University Press.

Berridge, Virginia, and Griffith Edwards. 1987. *Opium and the People: Opiate Use in Nineteenth-Century England*. New Haven, CT: Yale University Press.

Berry, Christopher J. 1994. *The Idea of Luxury: A Conceptual and Historical Investigation*. Cambridge: Cambridge University Press.

Bertrand. 1712. "Lettre de Mr. Bertrand Medecin aggregé au College de Marseille, à Mr. Deidier Professeur en Medecine de l'Université de Montpelier, sur le mouvement des muscles." *Mémoires de Trévoux*, 704–22.

Besterman, Theodore, ed. 1968. *Voltaire's Household Accounts 1760–1778*. Facs. ed. New York: The Pierpont Morgan Library.

———. 1969. *Voltaire*. London: Longman and Harlow.

Biagioli, Mario. 1993. *Galileo, Courtier: The Practice of Science in the Culture of Absolutism*. Chicago: University of Chicago Press.

Bianchi, Marina, ed. 1998. *The Active Consumer: Novelty and Surprise in Consumer Choice*. London: Routledge.

Bien, David. 1987. "Offices, Corps, and a System of State Credit: The Uses of Privilege Under the Ancien Régime." In *The Political Culture of the Old Regime*, ed. Keith Michael Baker, 89–114. Vol. 1 of *The French Revolution and the Creation of Modern Political Culture.* Oxford: Pergamon Press.

Birken, Lawrence. 1988. *Consuming Desire: Sexual Science and the Emergence of a Culture of Abundance.* Ithaca, NY: Cornell University Press.

Bléchet, Françoise. 1997. "Les interprètes orientalistes de la Bibliothèque du Roi." In *Istanbul et les langues orientales. Actes du colloque organisé par l'IFÉA et l'INALCO à l'occasion du bicentenaire de l'École des Langues Orientales. Istanbul 29–31 mai 1995*, ed. Frédéric Hitzel, 89–104. Varia Turcica 31. Paris: L'Harmattan.

Blocker, Jack S., Jr., and Cheryl Krasnick Warsh, eds. 1994. *Social History of Alcohol.* Special issue of *Histoire Sociale/Social History* 27:225–445.

Boas Hall, Marie. 1956. "Acid and Alkali in Seventeenth-Century Chemistry." *Archives Internationales d'Histoire des Sciences* 34:13–28.

Boerhaave, Herman. 1752. *Elémens de chymie.* Translated by J.-N.-S. Allamand. 2 vols. Amsterdam: J. Wetstein.

———. 1754. *Elémens de chymie.* Translated by J.-N.-S. Allamand. 6 vols. Amsterdam: J. Wetstein.

Bonnet, Jean-Claude. 1976. "Le réseau culinaire dans l'Encyclopédie." *Annales: Economies, Sociétés, Civilisations* 31:891–914.

———. 1979. "Le système de la cuisine et du repas chez Rousseau." In Serge A. Thériault, *Jean-Jacques Rousseau et la médecine naturelle*, 117–50. Montréal: L'Aurore.

———. 1983. "Les manuels de cuisine." *Dix-huitième siècle* 15:53–63.

———. 1998. *Naissance du Panthéon. Essai sur le culte des grands hommes.* Paris: Fayard.

Booth, Martin. 1996. *Opium: A History.* New York: Simon and Schuster.

Bordegaraye, Philippe-Bernard de. 1713. *Réponse à Monsieur Procope Couteaux, sur sa prétendue analyse du systême de la Trituration.* Paris: François Fournier.

Bosher, John F. 1970. *French Finances, 1770–1795: From Business to Bureaucracy.* Cambridge: Cambridge University Press.

Bossenga, Gail. 1988. "Protecting Merchants: Guilds and Commercial Capitalism in Eighteenth-Century France." *French Historical Studies* 15:693–703.

Bots, Hans, and Françoise Waquet. 1997. *La République des lettres.* Paris: Belin.

Boulad-Ayoub, Josiane. 1992. "D'Holbach, le 'maître d'hôtel de la philosophie.'" *Corpus* 22–23:7–11.

Boulanger, P. 1980. "Sources et ressources de la Chambre de Commerce de Marseille pour une histoire du café." In *Le café en Méditerranée. Histoire, anthropologie, économie XVIIIe–XXe siècle*, ed. J.-L. Miège, 1–15. Aix-en-Provence: Institut de Recherches Méditerranéennes.

Bourdieu, Pierre. 1994. *Distinction: A Social Critique of the Judgement of Taste.* London: Routledge.

Bourgeon, Jean-Louis. 1985. "Colbert et les corporations: l'exemple de Paris." In *Un nouveau Colbert. Actes du Colloque pour le tricentenaire de la mort de Colbert*, ed. Roland Mousnier, 241–53. Paris: Editions Sedes.

Bourguet, Marie-Noëlle, and Christophe Bonneuil. 1999. "De l'inventaire du monde à la mise en valeur du globe: botanique et colonisation (fin XVIIe siècle—début XXe siècle)." *Revue Française d'Histoire d'Outre-Mer* 86 (1): 5–38.

Bourguinat, Elisabeth. 1998. *Le siècle du persiflage, 1734–1789*. Paris: Presses Universitaires de France.

Bouvet, Maurice. 1937. *Histoire de la pharmacie en France des origines à nos jours*. Paris: Editions Occitania.

Brennan, Thomas. 1988. *Public Drinking and Popular Culture in Eighteenth-Century Paris*. Princeton, NJ: Princeton University Press.

Brennan, Thomas. 1997. *Burgundy to Champagne: The Wine Trade in Early Modern France*. Baltimore: Johns Hopkins University Press.

Brentjes, Sonja. 1999. "The Interests of the Republic of Letters in the Middle East, 1550–1700." *Science in Context* 12 (3): 435–68.

Brewer, Daniel. 2002. "Le philosophe, l'intellectuel et l'éclipse du nouveau." In *Le travail des Lumières*, ed. Caroline Jacot Grapa, Nicole Jacques-Lefèvre, Yannick Séité and Carine Trevisan, pour Georges Benrekassa, 805–21. Paris: Honoré Champion.

Brewer, John. 1997. *The Pleasures of the Imagination: English Culture in the Eighteenth Century*. London: Harper Collins.

Brewer, John, and Roy Porter, ed. 1992. *Consumption and the World of Goods*. London: Routledge.

Briquet, Fortunée. Year XII / 1804. *Dictionnaire Historique, Littéraire et Bibliographique des Françaises, et des Etrangères naturalisées en France*. Paris: Gillé, Treuttel & Würtz.

Brock, William H. 1992. *The Fontana History of Chemistry*. London: Fontana Press.

Brockliss, L. W. B. 1978. "Medical Teaching at the University of Paris, 1600–1720." *Annals of Science* 35:221–51.

———. 1987. *French Higher Education in the Seventeenth and Eighteenth Century: A Cultural History*. Oxford: Clarendon Press.

———. 1989. "The Medico-Religious Universe of an Early Eighteenth-Century Parisian Doctor: The Case of Philippe Hecquet." In *The Medical Revolution of the Seventeenth Century*, ed. Roger French and Andrew Wear, 191–221. Cambridge: Cambridge University Press.

———. 1994. "Consultation by Letter in Early Eighteenth-Century Paris: The Medical Practice of Etienne-François Geoffroy." *Clio Medica* 25:79–117.

———. 1998. "Before the Clinic: French Medical Teaching in the Eighteenth Century." In *Constructing Paris Medicine*, ed. Caroline Hannaway and Ann La Berge, 71–115. Amsterdam: Rodopi.

———. 2002. *Calvet's Web: Enlightenment and the Republic of Letters in Eighteenth-Century France*. Oxford: Oxford University Press.

Brockliss, Laurence, and Colin Jones. 1997. *The Medical World of Early Modern France*. Oxford: Clarendon Press.

Broglie, Gabriel de. 1985. *Madame de Genlis*. Paris: Librairie Académique Perrin.

Broman, Thomas H. 1995. "Rethinking Professionalization: Theory, Practice, and Professional Ideology in Eighteenth-Century German Medicine." *Journal of Modern History* 67:835–72.

Broman, Thomas H. 1998. "The Habermasian Public Sphere and 'Science in the Enlightenment.'" *History of Science* 36:123–49.

Brown, Theodore M. 1968. "The Mechanical Philosophy and the 'Animal Oeconomy': A Study in the Development of English Physiology in the Seventeenth and Early Eighteenth Century." Doctoral diss., Princeton University.

Bruland, Kristine. 2004. "New Technologies and the Industrial Revolution: Some Unresolved Issues." In *Artisans, industrie: Nouvelles révolutions du Moyen Âge à nos jours*, ed. Natacha Coquery, Liliane Hilaire-Pérez, Line Sallmann and Catherine Verna, 55–68. Lyon: ENS Editions.

Buc'hoz, Pierre-Joseph. 1788. *Dissertations sur l'utilité, et les bons et mauvais effets du tabac, du café, du cacao et du thé.* Paris: Buc'hoz, De Bure l'aîné, Veuve Tilliard & fils.

Buchwald, Jed Z. ed. 1995. *Scientific Practice: Theories and Stories of Doing Physics.* Chicago: University of Chicago Press.

Buffon, Georges-Louis Leclerc de, Louis-Jean-Marie Daubenton, Philibert Guéneau de Montbeillard and Gabriel-Léopold-Charles-Aimé Bexon. 1749–1788. *Histoire Naturelle, Générale et Particulière, avec la description du cabinet du roy.* 36 vols. Paris: Imprimerie Royale.

Burke, Peter. 1992. *The Fabrication of Louis XIV.* New Haven, CT: Yale University Press.

Burnett, John. 1999. *Liquid Pleasures: A Social History of Drinks in Modern Britain.* London: Routledge.

———. 2000. "From Cordial Waters to Coca-Cola: Soft Drinks and Health in Britain." In *Order and Disorder: The Health Implications of Eating and Drinking in the Nineteenth and Twentieth Centuries*, ed. Alexander Fenton, 299–311. East Linton: Tuckwell Press.

Bury, Emmanuel. 1996. *Littérature et politesse. L'invention de l'honnête homme 1580–1750.* Paris: Presses Universitaires de France.

Butel, Paul. 1995. *L'Opium: histoire d'une fascination.* Paris: Perrin.

Buti, Gilbert. 2001. "Marseille entre Moka et café des îles: espaces, flux, réseaux. XVIIe–XVIIIe siècles." In *Le commerce du café avant l'ère des plantations coloniales. Espaces, réseaux, sociétés (XVe–XIXe siècle)*, ed. Michel Tuchscherer, 213–44. Cairo: Institut Français d'Archéologie Orientale.

Cabanis, Pierre-Jean-Georges. Year X / 1802. *Rapports du physique et du moral de l'homme.* 2 vols. Paris: Crapelet.

Cadet de Vaux, Antoine-Alexis. Year VIII / 1799–1800. *Instruction sur l'art de faire le vin . . . Publiée par ordre du Gouvernement.* Paris: H. Agasse.

Caillet, Albert L. 1912. *Manuel bibliographique des sciences psychiques ou occultes.* 3 vols. Paris: Lucien Dorbon.

Calaresu, Melissa. In press. "Making and Eating Ice-cream in Early Modern Naples: Rethinking Consumption and Sociability in Southern Europe." *Past and Present.*

Calhoun, Craig, ed. 1992. *Habermas and the Public Sphere.* Cambridge, MA: MIT Press.

Callon, Michel. 1986. "Some Elements of a Sociology of Translation: Domestication of the Scallops and the Fishermen of St. Brieuc's Bay." In *Power, Action and Belief: A New Sociology of Knowledge?*, ed. John Law, 196–233. London: Routledge and Kegan Paul.

Callot, Emile. 1965. *La Philosophie de la vie au XVIIIe siècle. Etudiée chez Fontenelle, Montesquieu, Maupertuis, La Mettrie, Diderot, D'Holbach, Linné*. Paris: Editions Marcel Rivière et Cie.

Campbell, Colin. 1987. *The Romantic Ethic and the Spirit of Modern Consumerism*. Oxford: Basil Blackwell.

———. 1992. "The Desire for the New: Its Nature and Social Location as Presented in Theories of Fashion and Modern Consumerism." In *Consuming Technologies: Media and Information in Domestic Spaces*, ed. R. Silverstone and E. Hirsch, 48–64. London: Routledge.

Camporesi, Piero. 1988. *Bread of Dreams: Food and Fantasy in Early Modern Europe*. Translated by David Gentilcore. Cambridge: Polity.

———. 1994. *Exotic Brew: The Art of Living in the Age of Enlightenment*. Cambridge: Polity.

Canguilhem, Georges. 1955. *La formation du concept de réflexe aux XVIIe et XVIIIe siècles*. Paris: Presses Universitaires de France.

Caplan, Pat. 1997. "Approaches to the Study of Food, Health and Identity." In *Food, Health and Identity*, ed. Pat Caplan, 1–31. London: Routledge.

[Caraccioli, Louis-Antoine, marquis de]. 4444 [1757]. *Le Livre de quatre couleurs*. Aux Quatre-Éléments: De l'Imprimerie des Quatre-Saisons [Paris: n.p.].

———. [1759]. Le livre à la mode. Verte-Feuille: L'Imprimerie du Printemps [Paris: n.p.].

Carrière, Charles. [1973]. *Négociants marseillais au XVIIIe siècle. Contribution à l'étude des économies maritimes*. 2 vols. [Marseille:] Institut Historique de Provence.

Carrière, Charles, and Marcel Courdurié. 1975. "L'espace commercial marseillais aux XVIIe et XVIIIe siècles." In *Aires et structures du commerce français au XVIIIe siècle*, ed. Pierre Léon, 75–106. Colloque national de l'association française des historiens économistes, Paris, C.N.R.S., 4–6 Octobre 1973. Lyon: Centre d'Histoire économique et sociale de la Région lyonnaise.

Cary, Edmond. 1963. *Les Grands traducteurs Français. Etienne Dolet—Amyot; Mme Dacier, Houdar de la Motte et les traducteurs d'Homère; Galland et les traducteurs des Mille et une Nuits; Gérard de Nerval—Valery Larbaud*. Genève: Georg & Cie.

Casenobe, Colette. 1991. *Le Système du libertinage de Crébillon à Laclos*. Studies on Voltaire and the Eighteenth Century 282. Oxford: The Voltaire Foundation at the Taylor Institution.

Cassan. 1789. "Mémoire sur les cultures de l'isle de Sainte-Lucie." *Mémoires d'Agriculture, d'Économie rurale et domestique, publiés par la Société Royale d'Agriculture de Paris* (Summer): 60–109.

Cellard, Jacques. 1996. *John Law et la Régence*. Paris: Plon.

Censer, Jack R., and Jeremy D. Popkin, ed. 1987. *Press and Politics in Pre-Revolutionary France*. Berkeley: University of California Press.

Chamfort, Nicolas de. 1929. *Maximes et Pensées. Anecdotes et caractères*. Paris: Larousse.

Changeux, abbé Pierre-Nicolas. 1767. *Traité des Extrêmes ou Éléments de la Science de la Réalité*. 2 vols. Amsterdam: Darkstée and Merkus / Paris: Panckoucke.

Chantin, Jean-Pierre. 1996. *Le Jansénisme. Entre hérésie imaginaire et résistance catholique (XVIIe-XIXe siècle)*. Paris: Les Editions du Cerf.

[Chanvalon, Jean-Baptiste Thibault de]. 1763. *Voyage a la Martinique, contenant diverses Observations sur la Physique, l'Histoire Naturelle, l'Agriculture, les Moeurs, & les Usages de cette Isle.* Paris: Cl. J. B. Bauche.

Chardin, Jean. 1686. *Journal du voyage du chev.[r] Chardin en Perse & aux Indes Orientales par la Mer Noire & par la Colchide.* 2nd ed. Amsterdam: A. Wolfgangh.

———. 1927. *Sir John Chardin's Travels in Persia.* With an Introduction by Brigadier-General Sir Percy Sykes, K.C.I.E., C.B., C.M.G. London: Argonaut Press.

Chartier, Pierre. 2005. *Théorie du persiflage.* Paris: Presses Universitaires de France.

Chartier, Roger. 1987a. *The Cultural Uses of Print in Early Modern France.* Translated by Lydia G. Cochrane. Princeton, N. J.: Princeton University Press.

———. 1987b. "Distinction et divulgation: la civilité et ses livres." In Chartier, *Lectures et lecteurs dans la France de l'Ancien Regime,* 45–86. Paris: Seuil.

———. 1989. "Texts, Printings, Readings." In *The New Cultural History,* ed Lynn Hunt, 156–75. Berkeley: University of California Press.

———. 1997. "The Man of Letters." In *Enlightenment Portraits,* ed. Michel Vovelle, trans. Lydia G. Cochrane, 142–89. Chicago: University of Chicago Press.

Chaudhuri, K. N. 1985. *Trade and Civilisation in the Indian Ocean: An Economic History from the Rise of Islam to 1750.* Cambridge: Cambridge University Press.

Chaussinand-Nogaret, Guy. 1972. *Gens de finance au XVIIIe siècle.* Paris: Bordas.

Cheung, Tobias. 2004. "Motus Tonicus: Georg Ernst Stahl's Formulation of Tonic Motion and Early Modern Medical Thought." *Bulletin of the History of Medicine* 78:767–803.

———. 2006. "From the Organism of the Body to the Body of an Organism: Occurrence and Meaning of the Word Organism from the Seventeenth to the Nineteenth Centuries." *British Journal for the History of Science* 39:319–39.

Chisick, Harvey. 1984. *The Limits of Reform in the Enlightenment: Attitudes Toward the Education of the Lower Classes in Eighteenth-Century France.* Princeton, NJ: Princeton University Press.

Chomel, abbé Noël. 1740 [1709]. *Dictionnaire Œconomique, contenant divers moyens d'augmenter son Bien, et de conserver sa Santé.* 4th ed., 2 vols. Paris: Veuve Etienne.

Chomel, Jean-Baptiste. 1712. *Abregé de l'histoire des Plantes usuelles.* Paris: Charles Osmont.

Chouillet, Anne-Marie, ed. 1991. *Autour du "Neveu de Rameau" de Diderot.* Paris: Librairie Honoré Champion.

Chouillet-Roche, Anne-Marie. 1976. "Le Clavecin oculaire du Père Castel." *Dix-huitième Siècle* 8:141–66.

Clacquesin, Paul. 1900. *Histoire de la communauté des distillateurs. Histoire des liqueurs.* Paris: L. Cerf.

Clark, Peter. 1988. "The 'Mother Gin' Controversy in the Early Eighteenth Century." *Transactions of the Royal Historical Society,* 5th ser., 38:63–84.

Clarke, Edwin. 1968. "The Doctrine of the Hollow Nerve in the Seventeenth and Eighteenth Centuries." In *Medicine, Science and Culture: Historical Essays in Honor of Owsei Temkin,* ed. Lloyd G. Stevenson and Robert P. Multhauf, 123–41. Baltimore: Johns Hopkins University Press.

Clément, Nicolas. 2002. *L'abbé Alary (1690–1770). Un homme d'influence au XVIIIe siècle.* Paris: Honoré Champion.

Clément, Pierre, ed. 1861–82. *Lettres instructions et mémoires de Colbert, publiés pour le Ministère des Finances.* 8 vols. Paris: Imprimerie Nationale.

Clericuzio, Antonio. 1994. "The Internal Laboratory: The Chemical Reinterpretation of Medical Spirits in England (1650–1680)." In *Alchemy and Chemistry in the Sixteenth and Seventeenth Centuries*, ed. Piyo Rattansi and Antonio Clericuzio, 51–83. Dordrecht: Kluwer Academic.

Cole, Charles Woolsey. 1964. *Colbert and a Century of French Mercantilism.* 2 vols. London: Frank Cass and Co.

Collins, E. J. T. 1976. "The 'Consumer Revolution' and the Growth of Factory Foods: Changing Patterns of Bread and Cereal-Eating in Britain in the Twentieth Century." In *The Making of the Modern British Diet*, ed. Derek Oddy and Derek Miller, 26–43. Totowa, NJ: Rowman and Littlefield.

Condren, Conal, Stephen Gaukroger, and Ian Hunter. 2006. "Introduction." In *The Philosopher in Early Modern Europe: The Nature of a Contested Identity*, ed. Conal Condren, Stephen Gaukroger and Ian Hunter, 1–16. Cambridge: Cambridge University Press.

Connery, Brian A., and Kirk Combe. 1995. "Introduction." In *Theorizing Satire: Essays in Literary Criticism*, ed. Brian A. Connery and Kirk Combe, 1–15. Basingstoke: Macmillan.

Coornaert, Emile. 1968. *Les corporations en France avant 1789.* 2nd ed. Paris: Les Éditions Ouvrières.

Coquery, Natacha. 1998. *L'hôtel aristocratique: Le marché du luxe à Paris au XVIIIe siècle.* Paris: Publications de la Sorbonne.

———. 2003. "Mode, commerce, innovation: La boutique parisienne au XVIIIe siècle. Aperçu sur les stratégies de séduction des marchands parisiens de luxe et de demi-luxe." In *Les chemins de la nouveauté: Innover, inventer au regard de l'histoire*, ed. Liliane Hilaire-Pérez and Anne-Françoise Garçon, 187–206. Paris: Editions du CTHS.

Corcos, Alain F. 1983. "Jean Astruc (1684–1766) on Old Age: A Man of His Time?" *Clio Medica* 18:141–54.

[Cornaro, Luigi]. 1701. *De la sobriété et de ses avantages, ou, Le vray moyen de se conserver dans une santé parfaite jusqu'à l'âge le plus avancé.* Translated by d[e] L[a] B[onodière]. Paris. Loüis Coignard.

———. 1703. *Conseils et moyens très assûrez & faciles pour vivre plus de cent ans dans une parfaite santé* (1701). Translated by d[e Premont]. Amsterdam: Estienne Roger.

[Cossigny de Palma, Joseph-François Charpentier de]. 1782. *Supplément au Mémoire sur la fabrication des Eaux-de-vie de sucre.* Isle de France: Imprimerie Royale.

Cottom, Daniel. 1999. "The Work of Art in the Age of Mechanical Digestion." *Representations* 66:53–74.

Cottret, Monique. 1983. "La cuisine janséniste." In *Aliments et cuisine*, ed. Jean-Claude Bonnet and Beatrice Fink. Special issue of *Dix-huitième Siècle* 15:107–14.

Courdurié, Marcel. 1980. "Du café du Yemen au café des Antilles, ou renversements de courants commerciaux sur la place de Marseille (XVIIe-XVIIIe siècles)." In *Le café en*

Méditerranée. Histoire, anthropologie, économie XVIIIe–XXe siècle, ed. J.-L. Miège, 73–85. Aix-en-Provence: Institut de Recherches Méditerranéennes.

Court, Susan, and W. A. Smeaton. 1979. "Fourcroy and the Journal de la Société des Pharmaciens de Paris." *Ambix* 26:39–55.

Courtwright, David T. 2001. *Forces of Habit: Drugs and the Making of the Modern World*. Cambridge, MA: Harvard University Press.

Coveney, John. 2006. *Food, Morals and Meaning: The Pleasure and Anxiety of Eating*. 2nd ed. London: Routledge.

Cowan, Brian. 2005. *The Social Life of Coffee: The Emergence of the British Coffeehouse*. New Haven, CT: Yale University Press.

———. 2007. "New Worlds, New Tastes: Food Fashions After the Renaissance." In *Food: The History of Taste*, ed. Paul Freedman, 197–231. Berkeley: University of California Press.

Cowans, Jon. 1999. "Habermas and French History: The Public Sphere and the Problem of Political Legitimacy." *French History* 13 (2): 134–60.

Coward, Rosalind. 1989. *The Whole Truth: The Myth of Alternative Health*. Boston: Faber and Faber.

Coyer, abbé Gabriel-François. 1757. *Bagatelles morales et dissertations . . . avec le Testament litteraire de Mr. l'Abbé Desfontaines*. London [Paris?]: Knoch and Eslinger.

Crosland, Maurice. 1994. *In the Shadow of Lavoisier: The Annales de Chimie and the Establishment of a New Science*. Oxford: British Society for the History of Science.

———. 2005. "Early Laboratories c. 1600–c. 1800 and the Location of Experimental Science." *Annals of Science* 62:233–53.

Crow, Thomas E. 1985. *Painters and Public Life in Eighteenth-Century Paris*. New Haven, CT: Yale University Press.

Crowston, Clare Haru. 2001. *Fabricating Women: The Seamstresses of Old Regime France, 1675–1791*. Durham, NC: Duke University Press.

Cucuel, Georges. 1913. *La Pouplinière et la musique de chambre au XVIIIe siècle*. Paris: Librairie Fischbacher.

Cullen, L. M. 1998. *The Brandy Trade Under the Ancien Régime: Regional Specialisation in the Charente*. Cambridge: Cambridge University Press.

D'Epinay, Louise-Florence-Pétronille de La Live. 1865. *Mémoires de Madame D'Epinay*. Annotated by Paul Boiteau. 2 vols. Paris: Charpentier.

D'Oberkirch, Henriette-Louise de Waldner de Freundstein, baronne. 1970. *Mémoires de la Baronne d'Oberkirch sur la cour de Louis XVI et la société française avant 1789*. Annotated by Suzanne Burkard. [N.p.]: Mercure de France.

Dacier, André. 1771. *Bibliothèque des Anciens Philosophes, contenant La vie de Pythagore; ses Symboles; la vie d'Hiéroclès, & ses Vers dorés* (1706). Paris: Saillant and Nyon, Pissot and Desaint.

Dacier, Anne. 1711. *L'Iliade d'Homere, traduite en françois, avec des remarques*. Paris: Rigaud.

———. 1714. *Des causes de la corruption du goust*. Paris: Rigaud.

Dagognet, François. 1987. "L'Animal selon Condillac." In Etienne Bonnot de Condillac, *Traité des animaux*, with an introduction by François Dagognet, 7–131. Paris: Librairie philosophique J. Vrin.

Darnton, Robert. 1979. *The Business of Enlightenment: A Publishing History of the "Encyclopédie."* Cambridge, MA: Belknap Press.

Darnton, Robert. 1982. *The Literary Underground of the Old Regime.* Cambridge, MA: Harvard University Press.

———. 1984a. *The Great Cat Massacre and Other Episodes in French Cultural History.* New York: Basic Books.

———. 1984b. "Policing Writers in Paris Circa 1750." *Representations* 5:1–31.

———. 1995. *The Corpus of Clandestine Literature in France, 1769–1789.* New York: W. W. Norton.

———. 1996. *The Forbidden Best-sellers of Pre-revolutionary France.* London: HarperCollins.

———. 2010. *Poetry and the Police: Communication Networks in Eighteenth-Century Paris.* Cambridge, MA: The Belknap Press of Harvard University Press.

Daston, Lorraine. 1991. "The Ideal and Reality of the Republic of Letters in the Enlightenment." *Science in Context* 4 (2): 367–86.

———. 2005. "Fear and Loathing of the Imagination in Science." *Daedalus* 134 (4): 16–30.

Daston, Lorraine, and Katharine Park. 1998. *Wonders and the Order of Nature, 1150–1750.* New York: Zone Books.

Davenport-Hines, Richard. 2002. *The Pursuit of Oblivion: A Social History of Drugs.* London: Phoenix Press.

Davis, Jennifer. 2004. "Men of Taste: Gender and Authority in the French Culinary Trades, 1730–1830." Doctoral diss., Pennsylvania State University.

———. 2009. "Masters of Disguise: French Cooks between Art and Nature, 1651–1793." *Gastronomica: The Journal of Food and Culture* 9 (1): 36–49.

Dawson, Deirdre. 1999. "Voltaire's Complaint: Illness and Eroticism in La Correspondance." *Literature and Medicine* 18:24–38.

Dawson, Virginia P. 1987. *Nature's Enigma: The Problem of the Polyp in the Letters of Bonnet, Trembley and Réaumur.* Philadelphia: American Philosophical Society.

De Bellegarde, abbé Jean-Baptiste Morvan. 1702. *Lettres curieuses de Littérature & de Morale.* Paris: Jean and Michel Guignard.

De Blégny, Nicolas. 1687. *Le Bon Usage du Thé du Caffé et du Chocolat pour la preservation & pour la guerison des Maladies.* Paris: Estienne Michallet.

[De Caylus, Jean-Baptiste]. 1719. *Histoire naturelle du Cacao, et du Sucre.* Paris: Laurent d'Houry.

De Clieu, Gabriel-Mathieu d'Erchigny. 1774. "Lettre de M. de Clieu . . . à l'Auteur de ces Feuilles." *Année littéraire* 6:217–24.

De Graffigny, Françoise d'Issembourg d'Happoncourt. 1992. *Correspondance de Madame de Graffigny.* Edited by N. R. Johnson. Oxford: Voltaire Foundation.

De Knecht–van Eekelen, Annemarie, and Anneke H. van Otterloo. 2000. "'What the Body Needs': Developments in Medical Advice, Nutritional Science and Industrial Production in the Twentieth Century." In *Order and Disorder: The Health Implications of Eating and Drinking in the Nineteenth and Twentieth Centuries,* ed. Alexander Fenton, 112–44. East Linton: Tuckwell Press.

[De La Chesnaye des Bois, François Aubert, and Nicolas Briant?]. 1750. *Dictionnaire des Alimens, Vins et Liqueurs, leurs qualités, leurs effets, relativement aux différens âges, & aux différens tempéramens.* 3 vols. Paris: Gissey.

[De La Chesnaye des Bois, François Aubert, Jean Goulin, and Augustin Roux]. 1762–64. *Dictionnaire Domestique Portatif, contenant toutes les connoissances relatives à l'Oeconomie domestique & morale.* 3 vols. Paris: Vincent.

[De la Dixmerie, Nicolas Bricaire]. 1770. *Le Sauvage de Taïti aux Français, avec un envoi au philosophe ami des sauvages.* London: Lejay.

[De La Roque, Jean]. 1716. *Voyage de l'Arabie Heureuse, par l'Ocean Oriental, & le Détroit de la Mer Rouge.* Amsterdam: Steenhouwer and Uytwerf.

De La Versane, Louis Lesbros. 1766. *Le Philosophe soi-disant. Comédie en vers et en trois actes.* Amsterdam: n.p.

De Lancey, Cornelius Ver Heyden. [1933]. *Coup d'oeil sur deux figures curieuses de la vie parisienne au XVIIIe siècle: Jean Ramponeaux, cabaretier, et Charlotte Renyer, veuve Curé, puis dame Bourette, connu sous le sobriquet de "La Muse limonadière."* Preface by Robert Morche. Paris: Edition de la Revue des indépendants.

[De Montbron, Jean-Louis Fougeret]. 1759–60. *La Capitale des Gaules ou la Nouvelle Babilone.* 2 vols. La Haye: n.p.

De Montigny, Etienne Mignot. 1770. "Mémoire sur la construction des Aréomètres de comparaison." *Histoire de l'Académie Royale des Sciences. Année M.DCCLXVIII,* "Mémoires," 435–59.

De Saint-Haippy [Antoine-Prosper Lottin]. 1784. *Discours sur ce sujet: le Luxe corrompt les Moeurs, & détruit les Empires,* new ed. Amsterdam and Paris: Desauges, Belin and Mequignon.

De Vassetz, abbé. 1704. *Traité du mérite.* La Haye: Guillaume de Voys.

Debus, Allen G. 1987. *Chemistry, Alchemy and the New Philosophy, 1550–1700.* London: Variorum Reprints.

———. 1991. *The French Paracelsians: The Chemical Challenge to Medical and Scientific Tradition in Early Modern France.* Cambridge: Cambridge University Press.

———. 2001. *Chemistry and Medical Debate: Van Helmont to Boerhaave.* Canton, MA: Science History Publications.

Déclaration. [1732]. *Déclaration du Roy, Concernant les Cafez provenant des plantations & culture de la Martinique & autres Isles Françoises de l'Amérique, y dénommées.* [N.p.].

Déclaration. [N.d.]. *Déclaration . . . qui fait défenses de fabriquer aucunes eaux de vie de sirops, mélasse, grains, lies, bières, baissières, marc de raisin, hydromel et toutes autres matières que de vin . . .* [N.p.].

Deidier, Antoine. 1708. *Physiologia, tribus Dissertationibus comprehensa.* Montpellier: Honoré Pech.

Déjean [pseud. Antoine Hornot?]. 1759. *Traité raisonné de la Distillation, ou la Distillation réduite en Principes, avec un Traité des Odeurs.* 2nd ed. Paris: Nyon and Guillyn.

———. 1778. *Traité raisonné de la Distillation, ou la Distillation reduite en Principes.* 4th ed. Paris: Guillyn, J. Saugrain and Bailly.

Delamain, Robert. 1935. *Histoire du cognac.* Preface by Gaston Chérau. Paris: Librairie Stock.

Delamare, Nicolas. 1722–38. *Traité de la Police.* 2nd ed. 4 vols. Paris: Michel Brunet and Jean-François Herissant.

Delaunay, Paul. 1906. *Le monde médical parisien au dix-huitième siècle.* 2nd ed. Paris: Librairie Médicale et Scientifique Jules Rousset.

[Demachy, Jacques-François?]. 1769. *Economie rustique, ou notions simples et faciles sur la Botanique, la Médecine, la Pharmacie, la Cuisine & l'Office.* Paris: Lottin le jeune.

Demachy, Jacques-François. 1775. *L'Art du distillateur liquoriste.* Académie Royale des Sciences. Descriptions des Arts et Métiers 15. [Paris: n.p.].

———. 1907. *Jacques-François Demachy. Histoires et contes précédés d'une étude historique, anecdotique et critique sur sa vie et ses oeuvres.* Edited and with an introduction by L.-G. Toraude. Paris: Charles Carrington.

[Desalleurs, Rolland Puchot, comte]. 1739. *Lettre d'un Patissier Anglois au Nouveau Cuisinier François, avec un extrait du Craftsman.* [Paris: n.p.].

———. 1981. *Lettre d'un Pâtissier Anglois, et autres contributions à une polémique gastronomique du XVIIIe siècle.* Introduction by Stephen Mennell. Exeter: University of Exeter.

[Deschamps, Léger]. 1769. *Lettres sur l'Esprit du Siècle.* London [Paris]: Edouard Young.

Destouches, P.-R. 1809. "Observations sur la rectification de l'alcohol." *Bulletin de Pharmacie* 1:19–23.

Dew, Nicholas. 2006. "Reading Travels in the Culture of Curiosity: Thévenot's Collection of Voyages." *Journal of Early Modern History* 10 (1–2): 39–59.

———. 2009. *Orientalism in Louis XIV's France.* Oxford: Oxford University Press.

Diderot, Denis. 1875–77. *Oeuvres complètes.* Edited by Julien Assézat and Maurice Tourneux. 20 vols. Paris: Garnier frères.

———. 1955–70. *Correspondance.* Edited and annotated with a preface by Georges Roth. 16 vols. Paris: Les Editions de Minuit.

———. 1964. *Quatre Contes.* Geneva: Droz.

Diderot, Denis, and Jean Le Rond d'Alembert. 1751–77. *Encyclopédie, ou Dictionnaire raisonné des sciences, des arts et des métiers.* 17 vols. Paris: Briasson et al. Searchable full text at http://portail.atilf.fr/encyclopedie/

Dierig, Sven, Jens Lachmund, and J. Andrew Mendelsohn. 2003. "Introduction: Toward an Urban History of Science." In *Science and the City,* ed. Dierig, Lachmund and Mendelsohn. *Osiris* 18:1–19.

Dion, Roger. 1959. *Histoire de la vigne et du vin en France des origines au XIXe siècle.* Paris: Flammarion.

Doe, Janet. 1960. "Jean Astruc (1684–1766): A Biographical and Bibliographical Study." *Journal of the History of Medicine and Allied Sciences* 15:184–97.

Dominique [P.-F. Biancolelli], and Jean-Antoine Romagnesi. 1730. *La foire des poètes, l'isle du divorce, et la Sylphide, comédies. Représentées pour la première fois par les comédiens italiens ordinaires du Roy, le 11 septembre 1730.* Paris: Louis-Denis Delatour.

Donovan, Arthur. 1993. *Antoine Lavoisier: Science, Administration, and Revolution.* Cambridge: Cambridge University Press.

Dornier, Carole. 1997. "Le vin, cette liqueur traîtresse . . ." In *Le vin,* ed. Jean Bart and Élisabeth Wahl. Special issue of *Dix-huitième siècle* 29:167–84.

Douglas, Mary, and Baron Isherwood. 1996. *The World of Goods: Towards an Anthropology of Consumption.* London: Routledge.

Doyle, William. 1996. *Venality: The Sale of Offices in Eighteenth-Century France*. Oxford: Clarendon Press.

Doyon, André, and Jacques Liaigre. 1966. *Jacques Vaucanson: mécanicien de génie*. Paris: Presses Universitaires de France.

Drayton, Richard. 2000. *Nature's Government. Science, Imperial Britain, and the "Improvement" of the World*. New Haven, CT: Yale University Press.

Du Bos, abbé Jean Baptiste. 1719. *Réflexions critiques sur la poésie et sur la peinture*. Paris: [n.p.].

D[u]F[our de La Crespelière, Claude-Denis]. 1671. *Commentaire en Vers François, sur l'École de Salerne*. Paris: Gervais Clouzier.

Dubuisson, François-René-André. 1779. *L'Art du Distillateur et Marchand de Liqueurs. Considérées comme Alimens médicamenteux*. 2 vols. Paris: Dubuisson.

Duchesneau, François. 1976. "G. E. Stahl: antiméchanisme et physiologie." *Archives Internationales d'Histoire des Sciences* 26 (98): 3–26.

———. 1982. *La physiologie des Lumières. Empirisme, modèles et théories*. The Hague: Martinus Nijhoff.

Duchet, Michèle. 1971. *Anthropologie et histoire au siècle des lumières. Buffon, Voltaire, Rousseau, Helvétius, Diderot*. Paris: François Maspero.

Dufour, Philippe Sylvestre. 1671. *De l'Vsage du Caphe du Thé et du Chocolate*. Lyon: Jean Girin, Barthélémy Rivière.

———. 1679. *Instruction morale d'un Pere a son Fils, qui part pour un long voyage*. Basle: Jean Hermann Widerhold.

———. 1684. *Traitez nouveaux & curieux du café du thé et du chocolate*. Lyon: Girin and Rivière.

———. 1685. *Tractatus novi de potu caphe, de chinensium thé et de chocolata*. Translated by Jacob Spon. Paris: Muguet.

Dujardin, Jules. 1900. *Recherches rétrospectives sur l'art de la distillation. Historique de l'Alcool de l'Alambic et de l'Alcoométrie*. Paris: J. Dujardin.

Dulaure, Jacques-Antoine. 1785. *Nouvelle Description des curiosités de Paris*. Vol. 1. Paris: Lejay.

Dulieu, Louis. 1973. "Jean Astruc." *Revue d'Histoire des Sciences* 26:113–35.

Duncan, Daniel. 1705. *Avis salutaire a tout le monde, contre l'abus des choses chaudes, et particulierement du Café, du Chocolat, & du Thé*. Rotterdam: Abraham Acher.

Dupont, Paul. 1898. *Un poète-philosophe au commencement du dix-huitième siècle: Houdar de La Motte (1672–1731)*. Paris: Librairie Hachette et Cie.

Durand, Yves. 1971. *Les fermiers généraux au XVIIIe siècle*. Paris: Presses Universitaires de France.

Duval, Hippolyte. 1912. "Note sur les diverses éditions du traité de Philippe-Dufour de l'usage du café, du thé et du chocolat." *Annales de la Société botanique de Lyon* 37:8–14.

Eagleton, Terry. 1984. *The Function of Criticism: From "The Spectator" to Post-Structuralism*. London: Verso.

Edgerton, David. [2006]. *The Shock of the Old: Technology and Global History since 1900*. London: Profile Books.

Edwards, Griffith. 1992. "Problems and Dependence: The History of Two Dimensions." In *The Nature of Alcohol and Drug Related Problems*, ed. Malcolm Lader, Griffith Edwards and D. Colin Drummond, 2–13. Oxford: Oxford University Press.

Eger, Elizabeth, Charlotte Grant, Clíona Ó Gallchoir, and Penny Warburton. 2001. *Women, Writing and the Public Sphere, 1700–1830*. Cambridge: Cambridge University Press.

Ehrard, Jean, and Jacques Roger. 1965. "Deux périodiques français du 18e siècle: 'Le Journal des Savants' et 'les Mémoires de Trévoux.'" In Geneviève Bollème, Jean Ehrard, François Furet, Daniel Roche, and Jacques Roger, *Livre et société dans la France du XVIIIe siècle*, 33–59. Paris: Mouton and Co.

Elias, Norbert. 1983. *The Court Society*. Translated by Edmund Jephcott. Oxford: Blackwell.

Elkin, P. K. 1973. *The Augustan Defence of Satire*. Oxford: Clarendon Press.

Ellis, Markman. 2004a. *The Coffee-House: A Cultural History*. London: Weidenfeld and Nicolson.

———. 2004b. "Pasqua Rosee's Coffee-House, 1652–1666." *London Journal* 29 (1): 1–24.

Ellis, Stewart Lee. 2000. *The Devil's Cup: Coffee, the Driving Force in History*. Edinburgh: Canongate.

Emch-Dériaz, Antoinette. 1992a. *Tissot: Physician of the Enlightenment*. New York: Peter Lang.

———. 1992b. "The Non-Naturals Made Easy." In *The Popularization of Medicine 1650–1850*, ed. Roy Porter, 134–59. London: Routledge.

Engelhardt, Dietrich von. 1993. "Hunger und Appetit. Essen und Trinken im System der Diätetik—Kulturhistorische Perspektiven." In *Kulturthema Essen. Ansichten und Problemfelder*, ed. Alois Wierlacher, Gerhard Neumann and Hans Jürgen Teuteberg, 137–49. Berlin: Akademie Verlag.

Eurich, S. Amanda. 2003. "Secrets of the Seraglio: Harem Politics and the Rhetoric of Imperialism in the *Travels* of Sir Jean Chardin." In *Distant Lands and Diverse Cultures: The French Experience in Asia, 1600–1700*, ed. Glenn J. Ames and Ronald S. Love. 47–70. Westport, CT: Praeger.

Evans, R. J. W., and Alexander Marr, eds. 2006. *Curiosity and Wonder from the Renaissance to the Enlightenment*. Aldershot: Ashgate.

Fairchilds, Cissie. 1992. "The Production and Marketing of Populuxe Goods in Eighteenth-Century Paris." In *Consumption and the World of Goods*, ed. John Brewer and Roy Porter, 228–48. London: Routledge.

Faroqhi, Suraiya. 1994. "Crisis and Change, 1590–1699." In *An Economic and Social History of the Ottoman Empire*, ed. Halil İnalcık and Donald Quataert, 411–636. Cambridge: Cambridge University Press.

———. 1995. *Kultur und Alltag im Osmanischen Reich. Vom Mittelalter bis zum Anfang des 20. Jahrhunderts*. München: C. H. Beck.

Faure, Edgar. 1977. *La banqueroute de Law. 17 juillet 1720*. Paris: Gallimard.

Featherstone, Mike H., and Bryan S. Turner, eds. 1990. *The Body: Social Process and Cultural Theory*. London: Sage.

Féher, Michel. 1997. "Libertinisms." In *The Libertine Reader: Eroticism and Enlightenment in Eighteenth-Century France*, ed. Féher, 10–47. Cambridge, MA: MIT Press.

Féher, Michel, Ramona Naddaff, and Nadia Tazi, eds. 1989. *Fragments for a History of the Human Body*. 4 vols. New York: Zone.

Ferchl, Fritz. 1937. *Chemisch-pharmazeutisches Bio- und Bibliographikon*. Mittenwald: A. Nemayer.

Ferguson, Priscilla Parkhurst. 2006. *Accounting for Taste: The Triumph of French Cuisine*. Chicago: University of Chicago Press.

Figlio, Karl. 1975. "Theories of Perception and the Physiology of Mind in the Late Eighteenth Century." *History of Science* 13:177–212.

Fink, Beatrice. 1995. *Les liaisons savoureuses. Réflexions et pratiques culinaires au XVIIIe siècle*. Saint-Étienne: Publications de l'Université de Saint-Étienne.

Fink, Beatrice, and Gerhardt Stenger, eds. 1999. *Être matérialiste à l'âge des lumières. Hommage offert à Roland Desné*. Paris: Presses Universitaires de France.

Finkelstein, Joanne. 1989. *Dining Out: A Sociology of Modern Manners*. Cambridge: Polity Press.

Fischler, Claude. 1993. *L'Homnivore. Le goût, la cuisine et le corps*. [Paris:] Editions Odile Jacob.

Fish, Stanley. 1980. *Is There a Text in This Class? The Authority of Interpretative Communities*. Cambridge, MA: Harvard University Press.

Flahaut, Jean. 1995. "Lavoisier et les pharmaciens parisiens de son temps." *Revue d'histoire de la pharmacie* 42:349–55.

Flandrin, Jean-Louis. 1989. "Distinction through Taste." In *Passions of the Renaissance*, ed. Roger Chartier, 267–307. Vol. 3 of *A History of Private Life*, ed. Phillippe Ariès and Georges Duby. Cambridge, MA: The Belknap Press of Harvard University Press.

———. 1996a. "Assaisonnement, cuisine et diététique." In *Histoire de l'alimentation*, ed. Jean-Louis Flandrin and Massimo Montanari, 491–509. Paris: Fayard.

———. 1996b. "Choix alimentaires et art culinaire." In *Histoire de l'alimentation*, ed. Jean-Louis Flandrin and Massimo Montanari, 657–81. Paris: Fayard.

———. 1999. "Préface." In *Tables d'hier, tables d'ailleurs. Histoire et ethnologie du repas*, ed. Jean-Louis Flandrin and Jane Cobbi, 17–36. Paris: O. Jacob.

Flandrin, Jean-Louis, Philip Hyman, and Mary Hyman, eds. 1983. *Le cuisinier françois*. Paris: Montalba.

Florkin, Marcel. [1964]. *Médecins, libertins et pasquins*. Liège: Librairie Fernand Gothier.

Fontaine, Laurence. 2003. "The Circulation of Luxury Goods in Eighteenth-Century Paris: Social Redistribution and an Alternative Currency." In *Luxury in the Eighteenth Century: Debates, Desires and Delectable Goods*, ed. Maxine Berg and Elizabeth Eger, 89–102. Basingstoke: Palgrave Macmillan.

Fontenelle, Bernard Le Bovier de. 1717. "Eloge de M. de Tournefort." In Joseph Pitton de Tournefort, *Relation d'un Voyage du Levant, fait par ordre du Roy*, vol. 1, unpaginated preface. 2 vols. Paris: Imprimerie Royale.

———. 1718. "Observations botaniques."*Histoire de l'Académie Royale des Sciences. Année M.DCCXVI*, "Histoire," 34.

———. 1721. "Sur la Digestion." *Histoire de l'Académie Royale des Sciences. Année M.DCCXIX*, "Histoire," 33–37.

Forbes, R. J. 1948. *Short History of the Art of Distillation from the Beginnings Up to the Death of Cellier Blumenthal*. Leiden: E. J. Brill.

Forth, Christopher E., and Ivan Crozier, ed. 2005. *Body Parts: Critical Explorations in Corporeality*. Lanham, MD: Lexington Books.

Fosca, François. 1934. *Histoire des cafés de Paris*. Paris: Firmin-Didot & Cie.

Foster, Robert J. 2008. *Coca-Globalization: Following Soft Drinks from New York to New Guinea*. Houndmills: Palgrave Macmillan.

Foucault, Michel. 1988. "Technologies of the Self." In *Technologies of the Self: A Seminar with Michel Foucault*, ed. Luther H. Martin, Huck Gutman and Patrick H. Hutton, 16–49. London: Tavistock.

Foucher-Wolniewicz, Christiane. 1992. *La fête—le pouvoir—le prince. Partage des nourritures, manières conviviales et art de la table comme instruments de gouvernement*. Doctoral diss., Université Charles de Gaulle. Lille: Atelier National de Reproduction des Thèses.

Fox, Robert, and Anthony Turner. 1998. "Introduction." In *Luxury Trades and Consumerism in* Ancien Régime *Paris: Studies in the History of the Skilled Workforce*, ed. Fox and Turner, xvi–xviii. Aldershot: Ashgate.

France, Peter. 1992a. *Politeness and Its Discontents: Problems in French Classical Culture*. Cambridge: Cambridge University Press.

———. 1992b. "The Language of the Gods: Uses of Verse 1650–1800." In *Poetry in France: Metamorphoses of a Muse*, ed. Keith Aspley and Peter France, 106–21. Edinburgh: Edinburgh University Press.

Franklin, Alfred. 1887–1902. *La vie privée d'autrefois*. 27 vols. Paris: E. Plon and Nourrit.

Franssen, Maarten. 1991. "The Ocular Harpsichord of Louis-Bertrand Castel: The Science and Aesthetics of an Eighteenth-Century Cause Celebre." *Tractrix* 3:15–77.

Froeschlé-Chopard, Marie-Hélène, and Michel Froeschlé. 2001. "'Sciences et arts' dans les *Mémoires de Trévoux*, 1701–1762." *Revue d'Histoire Moderne et Contemporaine* 48 (1): 30–49.

Frye, Northrop. 1990. *Anatomy of Criticism: Four Essays*. London: Penguin Books.

Fryer, David M., and John C. Marshall. 1979. "The Motives of Jacques de Vaucanson." *Technology and Culture* 20:257–69.

Funck-Brentano, Frantz. 1905. *Les nouvellistes*. 2nd ed. Paris: Hachette.

Furet, François. 1965. "La 'librairie' du royaume de France au 18e siècle." In Geneviève Bollème, Jean Ehrard, François Furet, Daniel Roche and Jacques Roger, *Livre et société dans la France du XVIIIe siècle*, 3–32. Paris: Mouton and Co.

———. 1988. *Interpreting the French Revolution*. Translated by Elborg Forster. Paris: Editions du Maison des Sciences de l'Homme.

Furetière, Antoine. 1727. *Dictionnaire universel*. Edited by Henri Basnage de Beauval and Jean Baptiste Brutel de la Rivière. 4 vols. La Haye: Pierre Husson et al.

Furst, Lilian R. 1992. "Introduction." In *Disorderly Eaters: Texts in Self-Empowerment*, ed. Lilian R. Furst and Peter W. Graham, 1–9. University Park: Pennsylvania State University Press.

[Gacon, François]. [N.d.] *Les Fables de Mr Houdart de La Motte Traduittes en Vers François*. Asinus ad liram: Café du Montparnasse [Paris: n.p.].

Gaffiot, Maurice. 1926. "La théorie du luxe dans l'oeuvre de Voltaire." *Revue d'histoire économique et sociale* 14:320–43.

Galland, Antoine. 1992. *De l'origine et du progrès du café. Extrait d'un manuscrit arabe de la Bibliothèque du Roi.* [Paris]: Editions La Bibliothèque.

———. 2002. *Voyage à Constantinople: 1672–1673.* Annotated by Charles Schefer; preface by Frédéric Bauden. Paris: Maisonneuve et Larose.

Galliani, Renato. 1989. *Rousseau, le luxe et l'idéologie nobiliaire: étude socio-historique.* Studies on Voltaire and the Eighteenth Century 268. Oxford: The Voltaire Foundation at the Taylor Institution.

Gardiner, Michael E. 2000. *Critiques of Everyday Life.* London: Routledge.

Gargett, Graham. 2004. "Genève au dix-huitième siècle: de la cité de Calvin au foyer des Lumières." In *The City in French Writing: The Eighteenth-Century Experience*, ed. Síofra Pierse, 136–61. Dublin: University College Dublin Press.

Garrigues, Frédéric. 1998. "Les Intendants du commerce au XVIIIe siècle." *Revue d'histoire moderne et contemporaine* 45:626–61.

Garrioch, David. 1986. *Neighborhood and Community in Paris, 1740–1790.* Cambridge: Cambridge University Press.

Gasking, Elizabeth B. 1967. *Investigations into Generation, 1651–1828.* London: Hutchinson.

Gautier d'Agoty, Jacques. 1754. *Magazin Philosophique ou Supplément des Observations sur l'Histoire Naturelle, sur le Physique & sur la Peinture.* In Gautier d'Agoty, *Observations sur l'histoire naturelle, sur la physique et sur la peinture, avec des planches imprimées en couleur.* 6 vols. Part 11, 123–54. Paris: Delaguette.

Gay, Peter. 1966–69. *The Enlightenment: An Interpretation.* 2 vols. New York: W. W. Norton.

Genç, Mehmet. 2001. "Contrôle et taxation du commerce du café dans l'Empire ottoman fin XVIIe—première moitié du XVIIIe siècle." In *Le commerce du café avant l'ère des plantations coloniales*, ed. Michel Tuchscherer, 161–67. Cairo: Institut Français d'Archéologie Orientale.

Gentil, Claude-Joseph. 1787. *Dissertation sur le caffé, et sur les moyens propres à prévenir les effets qui résultent de sa préparation communément vicieuse.* Paris: Gentil.

Geoffroy, Claude-Joseph. 1741. "Méthode pour connoître & déterminer au juste la qualité des Liqueurs Spiritueuses qui portent le nom d'Eau de Vie & d'Esprit de Vin." *Histoire de l'Académie Royale des Sciences. Année M.DCCXVIII*, "Mémoires," 37–50.

Geoffroy, Étienne-Louis. 1774. *L'Hygieine, ou l'art de conserver la santé.* Paris: Pierre-Guillaume Cavelier.

Gessinger, Joachim. 1996. "Visible Sounds and Audible Colors: The Ocular Harpsichord of Louis-Bertrand Castel." In *Languages of Visuality: Crossings Between Science, Art, Politics, and Literature*, ed. Beate Allert, 49–72. Detroit: Wayne State University Press.

Gevrey, Françoise, and Béatrice Guion, ed. 2002. *Houdar de La Motte. Textes critiques: Les raisons du sentiment.* Paris: Honoré Champion.

Giaufret Colombani, Hélène, and Maria Teresa Mascarello. 1997. "De Dictionnaires en *Encyclopédie*: Le savoir oenologique et sa diffusion." In *Le vin*, ed. Jean Bart and Élisabeth Wahl. Special issue of *Dix-huitième siècle* 29:51–68.

Gigante, Denise. 2005. *Taste: A Literary History.* New Haven, CT: Yale University Press.

Gillispie, Charles Coulston. 1980. *Science and Polity in France at the End of the Old Regime.* Princeton, NJ: Princeton University Press.

Gillot, Hubert. 1914. *La querelle des anciens et des modernes en France.* Nancy: Crépin-Leblond.

Girard, Alain. 1977. "Le triomphe de 'La Cuisinière Bourgeoise': Livres culinaires, cuisine et société en France aux XVIIe et XVIIIe siècles." *Revue d'histoire moderne et contemporaine* 24:497–523.

Godonnèche, Jean. 1976. "La dégradation de la santé des gens de lettres d'après Tissot." *99e Congrès national des sociétés savantes, Besançon, 1974, Section des sciences* 5:235–42.

Goffman, Daniel. 2002. *The Ottoman Empire and Early Modern Europe.* Cambridge: Cambridge University Press.

Goldgar, Anne. 1992. "The Absolutism of Taste: Journalists as Censors in Eighteenth-Century Paris." In *Censorship and the Control of Print in England and France, 1600–1910,* ed. Robin Myers and Michael Harris, 87–110. Winchester: St. Paul's Bibliographies.

———. 1995. *Impolite Learning: Conduct and Community in the Republic of Letters, 1680–1750.* New Haven, CT: Yale University Press.

Goldsmith, Elizabeth C., and Dena Goodman, ed. 1995. *Going Public: Women and Publishing in Early Modern France.* Ithaca, NY: Cornell University Press.

Goldstein, Jan. 2005. *The Post-Revolutionary Self: Politics and Psyche in France, 1750–1850.* Cambridge, MA: Harvard University Press.

Golinski, Jan. 1992. *Science as Public Culture: Chemistry and Enlightenment in Britain, 1760–1820.* Cambridge: Cambridge University Press.

———. 1998. *Making Natural Knowledge: Constructivism and the History of Science.* Cambridge: Cambridge University Press.

Gooding, David, Trevor Pinch, and Simon Schaffer, eds. 1989. *The Uses of Experiment: Studies in the Natural Sciences.* Cambridge: Cambridge University Press.

Goodman, Dena. 1992. "Public Sphere and Private Life: Towards a Synthesis of Recent Historiographical Approaches to the Old Regime." *History and Theory* 31:1–20.

———. 1994. *The Republic of Letters: A Cultural History of the French Enlightenment.* Ithaca, NY: Cornell University Press.

———. 2001. "Difference: An Enlightenment Concept." In *What's Left of Enlightenment? A Postmodern Question,* ed. Keith Michael Baker and Peter Hanns Reill, 129–47. Stanford, CA: Stanford University Press.

Goody, Jack. 1982. *Cooking, Cuisine and Class: A Study in Comparative Sociology.* Cambridge: Cambridge University Press.

Gordon, Daniel. 1988–89. "'Public Opinion' and the Civilising Process in France: The Example of Morellet." *Eighteenth-Century Studies* 22:302–28.

Gordon, Daniel, David A. Bell, and Sarah Maza. 1992. *The Public Sphere in the Eighteenth Century.* Forum, *French Historical Studies* 17 (4): 882–956.

Goubert, Jean-Pierre, ed. 1982. *La Médicalisation de la société française, 1770–1830.* Special issue of *Historical Reflections/Réflexions historiques* 9:1–2.

Goudar, Ange. 1756. *Les intérêts de la France mal entendus, dans les branches de l'agriculture, de la population, des finances, du commerce, de la marine, et de l'industrie.* 3 vols. Amsterdam: Jacques Coeur.

Goujet, abbé Claude-Pierre. 1759. "Article de Monsieur de la Motte." In abbé Nicolas-Charles-Joseph Trublet, *Mémoires pour servir a l'Histoire de la Vie et des Ouvrages de M^r. de Fontenelle*, 2nd ed., 331–57. Amsterdam: Marc Michel Rey.

Greenbaum, Louis S. 1981. "Science, Medicine, Religion: Three Views of Health Care in France on the Eve of the French Revolution." *Studies in Eighteenth-Century Culture* 10:373–91.

Grell, Ole Peter. 2007. "Between Anatomy and Religion: The Conversions to Catholicism of the Two Danish Anatomists Nicolaus Steno and Jacob Winsløw." In *Medicine and Religion in Enlightenment Europe*, ed. Ole Peter Grell and Andrew Cunningham, 205–21. Aldershot: Ashgate.

Gronow, Jukka. 1991. "Need, Taste and Pleasure: Understanding Food and Consumption." In *Palatable Worlds: Sociocultural Food Studies*, ed. Elisabeth L. Fürst, Ritva Prättälä, Marianne Ekström, Lotte Holm and Unni Kjærnes, 33–52. Oslo: Solum Verlag.

———. 1997. *The Sociology of Taste*. London: Routledge.

Guénot, Hervé. 1986. "Musées et lycées parisiens (1780–1830)." In *Dix-huitième siècle* 18:249–67.

Guerrini, Anita. 1987. "Archibald Pitcairne and Newtonian Medicine." *Medical History* 31:70–83.

Guery, Alain. 1989. "Industrie et Colbertisme: origines de la forme française de la politique industrielle?" *Histoire, Economie et Société* 8:297–312.

Guiragossian, Diana. 1963. *Voltaire's* Facéties. Genève: Librairie Droz.

Gutton, J.-P. 1981. *Domestiques et serviteurs dans la France de l'Ancien Régime*. Paris: Editions Aubier Montaigne.

[Guyot-Desfontaines, Pierre-François, and François Granet, eds.]. 1731. *Le Nouvelliste du Parnasse, ou reflexions sur les ouvrages nouveaux*. Vols. 1–3. Paris: Chaubert.

Habermas, Jürgen. 1989. *The Structural Transformation of the Public Sphere: An Inquiry into a Category of Bourgeois Society*. Translated by Thomas Burger. Cambridge: Polity.

Hahn, Roger. 1971. *The Anatomy of a Scientific Institution: The Paris Academy of Sciences, 1666–1803*. Berkeley: University of California Press.

Haigh, Elizabeth L. 1976. "Vitalism, the Soul, and Sensibility: The Physiology of Théophile Bordeu." *Journal of the History of Medicine and Allied Sciences* 31:30–41.

Haine, W. Scott. 1996. *The World of the Paris Café: Sociability among the French Working Class, 1789–1914*. Baltimore: Johns Hopkins University Press.

Halimi, Suzy. 1988. "La bataille du gin en Angleterre dans la première moitié du XVIIIe siècle." In *Toxicomanies: Alcool, tabac, drogues*. Special issue of *Histoire, économie et société* 7:461–73.

Hamilton, Earl J. 1991. "Prices and Wages at Paris under John Law's System." In *Pre-Classical Economists. 3: John Law (1671–1729) and Bernard Mandeville (1660–1733)*, ed. Mark Blaug, 51–79. Aldershot: Elgar.

Hammer, Stephanie Barbé. 1990. *Satirizing the Satirist: Critical Dynamics in Swift, Diderot, and Jean Paul*. New York: Garland.

Hankins, Thomas L. 1994. "The Ocular Harpsichord of Louis-Bertrand Castel; or, The Instrument That Wasn't." *Osiris* 9:141–56.

Harkness, Deborah E. 2007. *The Jewel House: Elizabethan London and the Scientific Revolution.* New Haven, CT: Yale University Press.

Haskell, Francis. 1987. *The Painful Birth of the Art Book.* London: Thames and Hudson.

Hattox, Ralph S. 1991. *Coffee and Coffeehouses: The Origins of a Social Beverage in the Medieval Near East.* Seattle: University of Washington Press.

Haudrère, Philippe. 1989. *La Compagnie française des Indes au XVIIIe siècle (1719–1789).* 4 vols. Paris: Librairie de l'Inde.

———. 1993. "The 'Compagnie des Indes' and Maritime Matters (c. 1725–1770)." In *Ships, Sailors and Spices: East India Companies and Their Shipping in the Sixteenth, Seventeenth and Eighteenth Centuries,* ed. Jaap R. Bruijn and Femme S. Gaastra, 81–97. Amsterdam: Neha.

———. 2005. *La Compagnie française des Indes au XVIIIe siècle.* 2nd ed., 2 vols. Paris: Les Indes Savantes.

Hecht, Hartmut, ed. 2004. *Julien Offray de La Mettrie: Ansichten und Einsichten.* Berlin: Berliner Wissenschafts-Verlag.

Hecker, Kristine. 1979. *Die satirische Epigrammatik im Frankreich des 18. Jahrhunderts.* Romanistik 16. [N.p.]: Schäuble Verlag.

[Hecquet, Philippe]. 1710a. *Traité des dispenses du carême.* 2nd ed., 2 vols. Paris: François Fournier.

[———]. 1710b. *De la digestion des alimens, pour montrer qu'elle ne se fait pas par le moyen d'un levain, mais par celui de la trituration ou du broyement.* Paris: François Fournier.

———. 1712. *De la Digestion et des maladies de l'Estomac, suivant le systeme de la Trituration & du Broyement.* Paris: François Fournier.

[———]. 1726a. *Reflexions sur l'usage de l'Opium, des Calmants, et des Narcotiques, Pour la guerison des Maladies. En forme de Lettre.* Paris: Guillaume Cavelier fils.

[———]. 1726b. *Réponse à la question si les Medecins peuvent ou doivent prendre part dans les affaires de l'Eglise.* [Paris: n.p.].

———. 1730. *De la Digestion et des Maladies de l'Estomac, suivant le systeme de la Trituration & du Broyement.* 2 vols. Paris: Guillaume Cavelier.

———. 1740. *La Medecine, la Chirurgie et la Pharmacie des Pauvres.* 3 vols. Paris: Veuve Alix.

Hegyi, Klára. 1989. *The Ottoman Empire in Europe.* Budapest: Corvina.

Heimann, P. M. 1981. "Ether and Imponderables." In *Conceptions of Ether: Studies in the History of Ether Theory 1740–1900,* ed. G. N. Cantor and M. S. Hodge, 61–84. Cambridge: Cambridge University Press.

Heller, Agnes. 1976. *The Theory of Need in Marx.* London: Allison and Busby.

Heller, Sabine. 1984. *Boerhaaves Schweizer Studenten: Ein Beitrag zur Geschichte des Medizinstudiums.* Zürich: Juris Druck and Verlag.

Helvétius, Adrien. 1707. *Traité des Maladies les plus frequentes.* New ed. Paris: Pierre-Augustin Le Mercier.

Helvétius, Claude-Adrien. 1981–2004. *Correspondance générale d'Helvétius.* Preface by Charles-Antoine d'Andlau, introduction by Alan Dainard, Jean Orsoni, David Smith and Peter Allan. 5 vols. Toronto: University of Toronto Press.

———. 1988. *De l'Esprit* (1758). Paris: Fayard.

Helvétius, Jean-Claude-Adrien. 1721. "Observations Anatomiques sur l'Estomac de l'Homme, Avec des Reflexions sur le Systême nouveau, qui regarde la Trituration dans l'Estomac, comme la cause de la Digestion des Aliments." *Histoire de l'Académie Royale des Sciences. Année M.DCCXIX*, "Mémoires," 336–49.

[Hennebert, Jean-Baptiste-François]. 1765. *Du plaisir, ou du moyen de se rendre heureux.* Lille: J. B. Henry.

Hesse, Carla. 1989. "Economic Upheavals in Publishing." In *Revolution in Print: The Press in France, 1775–1800*, ed. Robert Darnton and Daniel Roche, 69–97. Berkeley: University of California Press.

———. 1998. "French Women in Print, 1750–1800: An Essay in Historical Bibliography." In *The Darnton Debate: Books and Revolution in the Eighteenth Century*, ed. Haydn T. Mason, 65–82. Studies on Voltaire and the Eighteenth Century 359. Oxford: Voltaire Foundation.

———. 2003. *The Other Enlightenment: How French Women Became Modern.* Princeton, NJ: Princeton University Press.

Highet, Gilbert. 1962. *The Anatomy of Satire.* Princeton, NJ: Princeton University Press.

Hilaire-Pérez, Liliane. 1997. *L'expérience de la mer. Les Européens et les espaces maritimes au XVIIIe siècle.* Preface by Daniel Roche. Paris: Editions Seli Arslan.

———. 2000. *L'invention technique au siècle des Lumières.* Preface by Daniel Roche. Paris: Albin Michel.

Hilaire-Pérez, Liliane, and Anne-Françoise Garçon, eds. 2003. *Les chemins de la nouveauté: innover, inventer au regard de l'histoire.* Paris: Editions du CTHS.

Hobhouse, Henry. 1985. *Seeds of Change: Five Plants that Transformed Mankind.* London: Sidgwick and Jackson.

Hobson, Marian. 1982. *The Object of Art: The Theory of Illusion in Eighteenth-Century France.* Cambridge: Cambridge University Press.

Hohendahl, Peter Uwe. 1982. *The Institution of Criticism.* Ithaca, NY: Cornell University Press.

Holmes, Frederic L. 1974. *Claude Bernard and Animal Chemistry: The Emergence of a Scientist.* Cambridge, MA: Harvard University Press.

———. 1989. *Eighteenth-Century Chemistry as an Investigative Enterprise.* Berkeley: Office for History of Science and Technology, University of California.

———. 1996. "The Communal Context for Etienne-François Geoffroy's 'Table des rapports.'" In *Fundamental Concepts of Early Modern Chemistry*, ed. Wolfgang Lefèvre. Special issue of *Science in Context* 9 (3): 223–320.

Holub, Robert C. 2003. *Reception Theory: A Critical Introduction.* London: Routledge.

Hoock, Jochen, and Bernard Lepetit. 1987. "Histoire et propagation du nouveau." In *La Ville et l'innovation. Relais et réseaux de diffusion en Europe 14e—19e siècles*, ed. Bernard Lepetit and Jochen Hoock, 7–28. Paris: Editions de l'École des Hautes Etudes en Sciences Sociales.

Hossain, Mary. 1990. "The Chevalier d'Arvieux and *Le Bourgeois Gentilhomme.*" *Seventeenth-Century French Studies* 12:76–88.

———. 1992. "The Employment and Training of Interpreters in Arabic and Turkish under Louis XIV: France." *Seventeenth-Century French Studies* 14:235–46.

———. 1993. "The Training of Interpreters in Arabic and Turkish Under Louis XIV: The Ottoman Empire 1." *Seventeenth-Century French Studies* 15:279–95.

Huard, Pierre, Marie-José Imbault-Huart, Maurice Genty and Geneviève Nicole-Genty. 1972. *Biographies médicales et scientifiques. XVIIIe siècle. Jean Astruc (1684–1766); Antoine Louis (1723–1792); Pierre Desault (1738–1795); Xavier Bichat (1771–1802).* Paris: Les Editions Roger Dacosta.

Huetz de Lemps, Alain. 1996. "Boissons coloniales et essor du sucre." In *Histoire de l'alimentation*, ed. Jean-Louis Flandrin and Massimo Montanari, 629–41. Paris: Fayard.

Hyman, Philip, and Mary Hyman. 1999. "Printing the Kitchen: French Cookbooks, 1480–1800." In *Food: A Culinary History from Antiquity to the Present*, ed. Jean-Louis Flandrin and Massimo Montanari, 383–93. New York: Columbia University Press.

Iliffe, Robert. 1995. "Material Doubts: Hooke, Artisan Culture and the Exchange of Information in 1670s London." *British Journal for the History of Science* 28:285–318.

———. 1998. "Isaac Newton: Lucatello Professor of Mathematics." In *Science Incarnate: Historical Embodiments of Natural Knowledge*, ed. Christopher Lawrence and Steven Shapin, 121–55. Chicago: University of Chicago Press.

İnalcık, Halil. 1994. "International Trade: General Conditions." In *An Economic and Social History of the Ottoman Empire*, ed. Halil İnalcık and Donald Quataert, 188–217. Cambridge: Cambridge University Press.

Institut de France. 1979. *Index biographique de l'Académie des Sciences 1666–1978.* Paris: Gauthier-Villars.

Isherwood, Robert. 1986. *Farce and Fantasy: Popular Entertainment in Eighteenth-Century Paris.* New York: Oxford University Press.

Israel, Jonathan I. 2001. *Radical Enlightenment: Philosophy and the Making of Modernity, 1650–1750.* Oxford: Oxford University Press.

———. 2006. *Enlightenment Contested: Philosophy, Modernity, and the Emancipation of Man, 1670–1752.* Oxford: Oxford University Press.

Jacob, Margaret C. 1991. *Living the Enlightenment: Freemasonry and Politics in Eighteenth-Century Europe.* New York: Oxford University Press.

Jacquin, abbé Armand-Pierre. 1762. *De la Santé. Ouvrage utile a tout le monde.* Paris: Durand.

Jal, Augustin. 1872. *Dictionnaire critique de biographie et d'histoire.* 2nd ed. Paris: Plon.

Jardine, Nicholas. 1991. *The Scenes of Enquiry: On the Reality of Questions in the Sciences.* Oxford: Clarendon Press.

Jeannin, Pierre. 1995. "Distinction des compétences et niveaux de qualification: Les savoirs négociants dans l'Europe moderne." In *Cultures et formations négociantes dans l'Europe moderne*, ed. Franco Angiolini and Daniel Roche, 363–97. Civilisations et Sociétés 91. Paris: Editions de l'E.H.E.S.S.

Jenner, Mark S. R., and Patrick Wallis. 2007. *Medicine and the Market in England and Its Colonies, c. 1450–c. 1850.* New York: Palgrave Macmillan.

Jettot, Stéphane. 2010. "La compréhension et la traduction des débats parlementaires à Londres par les diplomates de Louis XIV." In *Cultural Transfers: France and Britain in the Long Eighteenth Century*, ed. Ann Thomson, Simon Burrows, and Edmond Dziembowski, 205–18. Oxford: Voltaire Foundation.

Jewson, Nicholas. 1976. "The Disappearance of the Sick-Man from Medical Cosmology, 1770–1870." *Sociology* 10:225–44.

Johns, Adrian. 1996. "Dolly's Wax: The Historical Physiology of Interpretation in Early Modern England." In *The Practice and Representation of Reading in England*, ed. James Raven, Helen Small, and Naomi Tadmor, 138–61. Cambridge: Cambridge University Press.

———. 1998. *The Nature of the Book: Print and Knowledge in the Making.* Chicago: University of Chicago Press.

———. 2006. "Coffeehouses and Print Shops." In *Early Modern Science*, ed. Katharine Park and Lorraine Daston, 320–40. Vol. 3 of *The Cambridge History of Science*. Cambridge: Cambridge University Press.

Joly, Bernard. 1995. "Voltaire chimiste. L'influence des théories de Boerhaave sur sa doctrine du feu." *Revue du Nord* 77:817–43.

Jones, Colin. 1989. *The Charitable Imperative: Hospitals and Nursing in Ancien Régime and Revolutionary France*. New York: Routledge.

———. 1996. "The Great Chain of Buying: Medical Advertisement, the Bourgeois Public Sphere, and the Origins of the French Revolution." *American Historical Review* 101:13–40.

Jones, Jennifer M. 2004. *Sexing la Mode: Gender, Fashion and Commercial Culture in Old Regime France*. Oxford: Berg.

Jones-Davies, M. T., ed. 2005. *Culture, collections, compilations: Actes du colloque de Paris, 2001–2002*. Paris: Champion.

Jonsson, Fredrik Albritton. 2005. "The Physiology of Hypochondria in Eighteenth-Century Britain." In *Cultures of the Abdomen: Diet, Digestion, and Fat in the Modern World*, ed. Christopher E. Forth and Ana Carden-Coyne, 16–30. London: Macmillan Palgrave.

Jourdan de Le Cointe. 1790. *La Cuisine de Santé, ou moyens faciles & économiques de préparer toutes nos Productions Alimentaires de la maniere la plus délicate & la plus salutaire*. 3 vols. Paris: Briand.

Julia, Dominique. 1995. "L'éducation des négociants français au 18e siècle." In *Cultures et formations négociantes dans l'Europe moderne*, ed. Franco Angiolini and Daniel Roche, 215–56. Civilisations et Sociétés 91. Paris: Editions de l'E.H.E.S.S.

Julien, Pierre. 1992. "Sur les relations entre Macquer et Baumé." *Revue d'histoire de la pharmacie* 39:65–77.

Kaeppelin, Paul. 1967. *La Compagnie des Indes Orientales et François Martin*. Facsimile ed. New York: Burt Franklin.

Kale, Steven D. 2002. "Women, the Public Sphere and the Persistence of Salons." *French Historical Studies* 25:115–48.

———. 2004. *French Salons: High Society and Political Sociability from the Old Regime to the Revolution of 1848*. Baltimore: Johns Hopkins University Press.

Keane, Anne. 1997. "Too Hard to Swallow? The Palatability of Healthy Eating Advice." In *Food, Health and Identity*, ed. Pat Caplan, 172–92. London: Routledge.

Kennedy, Emmet. 1989. *A Cultural History of the French Revolution*. New Haven, CT: Yale University Press.

Kenny, Neil. 1998. *Curiosity in Early Modern Europe: Word Histories*. Wiesbaden: Harrassowitz.

———. 2004. *The Uses of Curiosity in Early Modern France and Germany*. Oxford: Oxford University Press.

Kéralio, Louis-Félix Guinement. 1769. *Discours sur la Question suivante: Si l'on peut détruire les penchans qui viennent de la nature*. Paris: Grangé.

Kernan, Alvin. 1959. *The Cankered Muse: Satire of the English Renaissance*. New Haven, CT: Yale University Press.

Kiel, Machiel. 2004. "Ottoman Sources for the Demographic History and the Process of Islamisation of Bosnia-Hercegovina and Bulgaria in the Fifteenth–Seventeenth Centuries." In *Ottoman Bosnia: A History in Peril*, ed. Markus Koller and Kemal H. Karpat, 93–119. Madison: University of Wisconsin Press.

Kilgour, Maggie. 1990. *From Communion to Cannibalism: An Anatomy of Metaphors of Incorporation*. Princeton, NJ: Princeton University Press.

Kim, Mi Gyung. 2003. *Affinity, That Elusive Dream: A Genealogy of the Chemical Revolution*. Cambridge, MA: MIT Press.

King, Lester S. 1978. *The Philosophy of Medicine: The Early Eighteenth Century*. Cambridge, MA: Harvard University Press.

Kiple, Kenneth F., and Kriemhild Coneè Ornelas, eds. 2000. *The Cambridge World History of Food*. 2 vols. Cambridge: Cambridge University Press.

Klein, Lawrence E. 1994. *Shaftesbury and the Culture of Politeness: Moral Discourse and Cultural Politics in Early Eighteenth-Century England*. Cambridge: Cambridge University Press.

———. 1997. "Coffeehouse Civility, 1660–1714: An Aspect of Post-Courtly Culture in England." *Huntingdon Library Quarterly* 59:30–51.

———. 2001. "Enlightenment as Conversation." In *What's Left of Enlightenment? A Postmodern Question*, ed. Keith Michael Baker and Peter Hanns Reill, 148–66. Stanford, Calif.: Stanford University Press.

Klein, Ursula. 1996. "The Chemical Workshop Tradition and the Experimental Practice: Discontinuities Within Continuities." In *Fundamental Concepts of Early Modern Chemistry*, ed. Wolfgang Lefèvre. Special issue of *Science in Context* 9 (3): 251–87.

———. 2003. "Experimental History and Herman Boerhaave's Chemistry of Plants." *Studies in the History and Philosophy of the Biological and Biomedical Sciences* 34:533–67.

———. 2005. "Technoscience *Avant la Lettre*." *Perspectives on Science* 13 (2): 226–66.

Klein, Ursula, and Emma Spary, eds. 2010. *Materials and Expertise in Early Modern Europe: Between Market and Laboratory*. Chicago: University of Chicago Press.

Knabe, Peter-Eckhard. 1983. "Esthétique et art culinaire." In *Aliments et cuisine*, ed. Jean-Claude Bonnet and Beatrice Fink. Special issue of *Dix-huitième siècle* 15:125–36.

Knight, Charles A. 2004. *The Literature of Satire*. Cambridge: Cambridge University Press.

Kopp, Hermann. 1843–45. *Geschichte der Chemie*. 4 vols. Braunschweig: Friedrich Vieweg und Sohn.

Kors, Alan. 1976. *D'Holbach's Coterie: An Enlightenment in Paris*. Princeton, NJ: Princeton University Press.

Krauss, Werner. 1967. "La néologie dans la littérature du XVIIIe siècle." *Studies on Voltaire and the Eighteenth Century* 56:777–82.

Kümin, Beat, and B. Ann Tlusty, eds. 2002. *The World of the Tavern: Public Houses in Early Modern Europe*. Aldershot: Ashgate.

La Condamine, Charles-Marie de. 1782. "Épigramme faite par M. de La Condamine, le jour de sa Réception à l'Académie Françoise." In [Claude-Sixte Sautreau de Marsy,] *Poésies satyriques du dix-huitième siecle*. 2 vols. London: [n.p.].

La Mettrie, Julien-Joseph Offray de. 1747. *La Faculté vengée*. Paris: Quillau.

———. 1912. *Man a Machine*. Annotated by Gertrude Carman Bussey. La Salle, IL: Open Court.

———. 1996. *De la volupté. Anti-Sénèque ou le souverain bien—L'École de la volupté—système d'Épicure*. Edited by Ann Thomson. Paris: Editions Desjonquères.

La Motte, Antoine Houdard de. 1714. *L'Iliade: poëme. Avec un discours sur Homere*. Paris: G. Dupuis.

———. 1715. *Réflexions sur la Critique*. La Haye: Henri du Sauzet.

La Varenne, Pierre-François de. 1651. *Le cuisinier françois, enseignant la manière de bien apprester et assaisonner toutes sortes de viandes*. Paris: P. David.

Labat, Jean-Baptiste, ed. 1735. *Memoires du Chevalier d'Arvieux*,. 6 vols. Paris: Charles-Jean-Baptiste Delespine fils.

Lachiver, Marcel. 1988. *Vins, vignes et vignerons. Histoire du vignoble français*. Paris: Librairie Arthème Fayard.

Lachmund, Jens, and Gunnar Stollberg. 1995. *Patientenwelten: Krankheit und Medizin vom späten 18. bis zum frühen 20. Jahrhundert im Spiegel von Autobiographien*. Opladen: Leske and Budrich.

Lacroix, Alfred. 1936. "Opinion d'Antoine de Jussieu au sujet du cafe indigène de Bourbon et de quelques autres drogues de cette île." *Recueil trimestriel de documents et travaux inédits pour servir à l'histoire des Mascareignes françaises* 2:203–14.

Laissus, Yves. 1986. "Les cabinets d'histoire naturelle." In *Enseignement et diffusion des sciences en France au XVIIIe siècle*, 2nd ed., ed. René Taton, 342–84. Paris: Hermann.

Lamarck, Jean-Baptiste-Pierre-Antoine de Monnet, chevalier de. 1783. *Botanique. Encyclopédie méthodique*. Vol. 1 of 13 vols. Paris: Panckoucke.

Landes, Joan B. 1988. *Women and the Public Sphere in the Age of the French Revolution*. Ithaca, NY: Cornell University Press.

Lanoë, Catherine. 2008a. *La poudre et le fard. Une histoire des cosmétiques de la Renaissance aux Lumières*. Seyssel: Champ Vallon.

———. 2008b. "Images, masques et visages. Production et consommation des cosmétiques à Paris sous l'Ancien Régime." *Revue d'Histoire Moderne et Contemporaine* 55 (1): 7–27.

Lansard, Monique. 1991. "Der Kaffee in Frankreich im 17. und 18. Jahrhundert: Modeerscheinung oder Institution?" In *Coffee in the Context of European Drinking Habits*, ed. Daniela U. Ball, 127–43. Zürich: Johann Jacobs Museum.

Latour, Bruno. 1986. "The Powers of Association." In *Power, Action and Belief: A New*

Sociology of Knowledge?, ed. John Law, 264–80. Sociological Review Monographs 32. London: Routledge and Kegan Paul.

———. 1987. *Science in Action: How to Follow Scientists and Engineers Through Society*. Milton Keynes: Open University Press.

———. 1988. *The Pasteurization of France*. Cambridge, MA: Harvard University Press.

———. 1992. "One More Turn after the Social Turn . . ." In *The Social Dimensions of Science*, ed. Ernan McMullin, 272–94. Notre Dame, IN: University of Notre Dame Press.

———. 1993. *We Have Never Been Modern*. Translated by Catherine Porter. New York: Harvester Wheatsheaf.

———. 1999. *Pandora's Hope: Essays in the Reality of Science Studies*. Cambridge, MA: Harvard University Press.

———. 2000. "On the Partial Existence of Existing and Nonexisting Objects." In *Biographies of Scientific Objects*, ed. Lorraine Daston, 247–69. Chicago: University of Chicago Press.

Laudan, Rachel. 2000. "Birth of the Modern Diet." *Scientific American* 283 (August): 62–67.

Laurioux, Bruno. 1996. "Cuisines médiévales (XIVe et XVe siècles)." In *Histoire de l'alimentation*, ed. Jean-Louis Flandrin and Massimo Montanari, 459–77. Paris: Fayard.

LaVopa, Anthony J. 1992. "Conceiving a Public: Ideas and Society in Eighteenth-Century Europe." *Journal of Modern History* 64:79–116.

Lawrence, Christopher, and Steven Shapin, eds. 1998. *Science Incarnate: Historical Embodiments of Natural Knowledge*. Chicago: University of Chicago Press.

Le Bègue de Presle, Achille-Guillaume. 1763. *Le Conservateur de la santé, ou avis sur les dangers qu'il importe à chacun d'éviter, pour se conserver en bonne santé & prolonger sa vie*. Yverdon: [n.p.].

Le Camus, Antoine. 1769. *Médecine de l'esprit*. 2nd ed. Paris: Ganeau.

Le Cat, Claude-Nicolas. 1750. *A Physical Essay on the Senses*. London: R. Griffiths.

———. 1767. *Traité des Sensations et des Passions en général, et des Sens en particulier*. 2 vols. Paris: Vallat-La-Chapelle.

———. 1971. "Réfutation du Discours qui a remporté le prix à l'Académie de Dijon en 1750, par un académicien de Dijon qui lui a refusé son suffrage." In Jean-Jacques Rousseau, *Oeuvres complètes*, 3 vols., preface by Jean Fabre, introduction by Michel Launay, 2:153–73. Paris: Éditions du Seuil-L'Intégrale.

Le François, Alexandre. 1723. *Reflexions critiques sur la medecine, ou l'on examine ce qu'il y a de vrai & de faux dans les jugemens qu'on porte au sujet de cet Art*. 2 vols. Paris: Guillaume Cavelier fils.

Le Gentil de la Barbinais, Guillaume-Joseph-Hyacinthe-Jean-Baptiste. 1779. *Voyage dans les Mers de l'Inde, fait par ordre du Roi*. 2 vols. Paris: Imprimerie Royale.

Le Gentil de la Barbinais, Guy. 1728. *Nouveau voyage autour du monde*. 3 vols. Amsterdam: Pierre Mortier.

Le Maître de Claville, Charles-François-Nicolas. 1740. *Traité du vrai mérite de l'homme, considéré dans tous les âges & dans toutes les conditions*. 4th ed., 2 vols. Paris: Saugrain père.

[Le Maître de Claville, Charles-François-Nicolas]. 1769. "De l'utilité, du choix et de l'usage des plaisirs." In *Le Temple du Bonheur, ou Recueil des plus excellens Traités sur le Bonheur, extraits des meilleurs Auteurs anciens et modernes*, vol. 3. Bouillon: Société Typographique.

[Le Sage, Alain-René]. 1715. *Histoire de Gil Blas de Santillane*. 4 vols. Paris: Pierre Ribou.

———. 1740. *La Valise trouvée. Premiere partie*. [N.p.].

Le Sage-de l'Hydrophonie [Alain-René Le Sage]. 1745. *Le Controlleur du Parnasse, ou Nouveaux Mémoires de Littérature Françoise et Etrangère*, vol. 1. Berne: Wolfs and Fleischmans.

Le Thieullier, Louis-Jean. 1739–47. *Consultations de medecine*. 4 vols. Paris: C. Osmont, J. Clousier and L. Durand.

Leclant, Jean. 1951. "Le café et les cafés à Paris (1644–1693)." *Annales: Économies, Sociétés, Civilisations* 6:1–14.

[Lefèvre de Saint-Marc]. 1740. *La Vie de M. Hecquet, Docteur Regent, & ancien Doyen de la Faculté de Médecine de Paris*. In Philippe Hecquet, *La Medecine, la Chirurgie et la Pharmacie des Pauvres*, III. Paris: Veuve Alix.

Legrand, Homer E. 1973. "The 'Conversion' of C.-L. Berthollet to Lavoisier's Chemistry." *Ambix* 22:58–70.

Legrand d'Aussy, Pierre-Jean-Baptiste. 1783. *Histoire de la vie privée des Français, depuis l'origine de la Nation jusqu'à nos jours*. 3 vols. Paris: Ph.-D. Pierres.

Lehman, Christine. 2007. "Between Commerce and Philanthropy: Chemistry Courses in Eighteenth-century Paris." In *Science and Spectacle in the European Enlightenment*, ed. Bernadette Bensaude-Vincent and Christine Blondel, 103–16. Aldershot: Ashgate.

Lémery, Louis. 1705. *Traité des aliments* (1700). 2nd ed. Paris: Pierre Witte.

Léon-Miehe, Anne. 2004. "Discours sceptique et art de jouir chez La Mettrie." In *Matérialisme et passions*, ed. Pierre-François Moreau and Ann Thomson, 67–77. Lyon: ENS Editions.

Leplâtre, Olivier. 2007. "'Un doux repas': Politique de l'alimentation chez Fénelon." *Food and History* 5 (2): 71–93.

Leroy, Charles-Georges. 1994. *Lettres sur les animaux*. Introduction by Elizabeth Anderson. Oxford: The Voltaire Foundation at the Taylor Institution.

Les Petits poètes du XVIIIe siècle. [1911]. London: J. M. Dent and Sons.

Lespinasse, René de. 1886. *Histoire générale de Paris. Les Métiers et corporations de la ville de Paris*. I: *XIVe–XVIIIe siècle: Ordonnances générales, métiers de l'alimentation*. Paris: Imprimerie Nationale.

Létoublon, Françoise, and Catherine Volpilhac-Auger, eds. 1999. *Homère en France après la Querelle (1715–1900)*. Paris: Honoré Champion.

Level, Brigitte. 1988. *A travers deux siècles. Le Caveau, société bachique et chantante 1726–1939*. Paris: Presses de l'Université de Paris-Sorbonne.

Levere, Trevor H. 1994. *Chemists and Chemistry in Nature and Society, 1770–1878*. Aldershot: Variorum.

Levesque de Pouilly, Louis-Jean. 1749. *Théorie des Sentimens agréables*. Dublin: S. Powell.

Levine, Joseph M. 1991. *The Battle of the Books: History and Literature in the Augustan Age*. Ithaca, NY: Cornell University Press.

Lévi-Strauss, Claude. 1970. *The Raw and the Cooked.* Vol. 1 of *Introduction to a Science of Mythology.* Translated by John Weightman and Doreen Weightman. London: Cape.

———. 1997. "The Culinary Triangle." In *Food and Culture: A Reader,* ed. Carole Counihan and Penny Van Esterik, 28–35. London: Routledge.

Lewis, Gillian. 1998. "Producers, Suppliers, and Consumers: Reflections on the Luxury Trades in Paris, c. 1500–c. 1800." In *Luxury Trades and Consumerism in* Ancien Régime *Paris: Studies in the History of the Skilled Workforce,* ed. Robert Fox and Anthony Turner, 287–98. Aldershot: Ashgate.

Liger, Louis. 1700. *Œconomie generale de la Campagne, ou Nouvelle Maison Rustique.* 2 vols. Paris: Charles de Sercy.

———. 1715. *Le Voyageur fidele, ou le Guide des Etrangers dans la Ville de Paris, qui enseigne tout ce qu'il y a de plus curieux à voir.* Paris: Pierre Ridou.

Lilti, Antoine. 2005a. *Le monde des salons. Sociabilité et mondanité à Paris au XVIIIe siècle.* Paris: Fayard.

———. 2005b. "Sociabilité et mondanité: Les hommes de lettres dans les salons parisiens au XVIIIe siècle." *French Historical Studies* 28:415–45.

[Limojon de Saint-Didier, Ignace-François]. 1716. *Le Voyage du Parnasse.* Rotterdam: Fristch and Bohm.

Linand, Barthélemy. 1700. *L'Abstinence de la Viande rendue aisée ou moins difficile à pratiquer.* Paris: Pierre Bienfait.

Lindeboom, G. A. 1958. "Tronchin and Boerhaave." *Gesnerus* 1:141–50.

Linton, Marisa. 2001. *The Politics of Virtue in Enlightenment France.* Basingstoke: Palgrave.

Lister, Martin. 1699. *A Journey to Paris in the Year 1698.* 3rd ed. London: Jacob Tonson.

Lorry, Anne-Charles. 1767. "Eloge historique de M. Astruc." In Jean Astruc, *Mémoires pour servir à l'histoire de la Faculté de Medecine de Montpellier,* xxxiij–lvj. Paris: P. G. Cavelier.

———. 1781. *Essai sur les alimens, pour servir de commentaire aux livres diététiques d'Hippocrate* (1757). 2nd ed., 2 vols. Paris: P. Théophile Barrois le jeune.

Lougee, Carolyn. 1976. *Le Paradis des Femmes: Women, Salons, and Social Stratification in Seventeenth-Century France.* Princeton, NJ: Princeton University Press.

Lougnon, Albert. 1939. *Voyages anciens à l'île Bourbon.* Tananarive: Imérina.

Lougnon, Albert. 1956. *L'île Bourbon pendant la Régence. Desforges Boucher, les débuts du café.* Paris: Editions Larose.

Louis-Courvoisier, Micheline. 2001. "Le malade et son médecin: Le cadre de la relation thérapeutique dans la deuxième moitié du XVIII siècle." *Canadian Bulletin of Medical History* 18:277–96.

Lovrenović, Ivan. 2001. *Bosnia: A Cultural History.* London: Saqi Books.

Luchet, Jean-Pierre-Louis, marquis de. 1780. *Histoire littéraire de Monsieur de Voltaire.* 6 vols. Kassel: P. O. Hampe.

Lupton, Deborah. 1996. *Food, the Body and the Self.* Thousand Oaks, CA: Sage Publications.

Lynch, Michael. 1993. *Scientific Practice and Ordinary Action: Ethnomethodology and Social Studies of Science.* Cambridge: Cambridge University Press.

Lynn, Michael R. 1999. "Enlightenment in the Public Sphere: The Musée de Monsieur and Scientific Culture in Late Eighteenth-Century Paris." *Eighteenth-Century Studies* 32 (4): 463–76.

———. 2006. *Popular Science and Public Opinion in Eighteenth-Century France*. Manchester: Manchester University Press.

Mably, abbé Gabriel Bonnot de. 1763. *Entretiens de Phocion sur le rapport de la Morale avec la Politique*. 2nd ed. Amsterdam: [n.p.].

[Macquer, Philippe], ed. 1766–67. *Dictionnaire portatif des arts & métiers, contenant en abrégé l'histoire, la description & la police des arts et metiers, des fabriques et manufactures de France & des Pays étrangers*. 3 vols. Yverdon: [n.p.].

Macquer, Pierre-Joseph. 1751. *Elémens de chymie-pratique, contenant la description des opérations fondamentales de la chymie, avec des explications et des remarques sur chaque opération*. 2 vols. Paris: [n.p.].

[Macquer, Pierre-Joseph]. 1766. *Dictionnaire de Chymie, Contenant la Théorie & la Pratique de cette Science, son application à la Physique, à l'Histoire Naturelle, à la Médecine & à l'Economie animale*. 2 vols. Paris: Lacombe.

Mah, Harold. 2000. "Phantasies of the Public Sphere: Rethinking the Habermas of Historians." *Journal of Modern History* 72:152–82.

———. 2003. *Enlightenment Phantasies: Cultural Identity in France and Germany, 1750–1914*. Ithaca, NY: Cornell University Press.

M[ailly], Louis de, chevalier. 1702. *Les Entretiens des Cafés de Paris, et les Diferens qui y surviennent*. Trevoux: Etienne Ganeau.

Maison de Chateaubriand. 2011. *Madame Geoffrin, une femme d'affaires et d'esprit*. Milan: Silvana Editoriale.

Maître, Myriam. 1999. *Les précieuses. Naissance des femmes de lettres en France au XVIIe siècle*. Paris: Honoré Champion.

Malleret, Louis. 1974. *Pierre Poivre*. Paris: École Française d'Extrême-Orient.

Malouin, Paul-Jacques. 1750. *Chimie médicinale*. 2 vols. Paris: D'Houry père.

Manoury, Charles. 1787. *Le Jeu de Dames a la Polonoise*, 2nd ed. Paris: Manoury.

Mantran, Robert. 1977. "La transformation du commerce dans l'empire ottoman au XVIIIe siècle." In *Studies in Eighteenth-Century Islamic History*, ed. Thomas Naff and Roger Owen, 220–35. Papers on Islamic History 4. Carbondale: Southern Illinois University Press.

———. 1984. *L'empire ottoman du XVIe au XVIIIe siècle: Administration, économie, société*. London: Variorum Reprints.

———. 1986. "Monsieur de Guilleragues, ambassadeur de France à Constantinople, et le commerce français au Levant (1679–1685). Documents et notes." In *L'Empire Ottoman, la République de Turquie et la France*, ed. Hâmit Batu and Jean-Louis Bacqué-Grammont, 59–72. Istanbul: Editions Isis.

Margairaz, Dominique. 1999. "La querelle du luxe au XVIIIe siècle." In *Le luxe en France du Siècle des Lumières à nos jours*, ed. Jacques Marseille, 25–37. Paris: ADHE.

[Marin, François]. 1739. *Les Dons de Comus, ou les Délices de la table*. Paris: Prault.

———. 1742. *Suite des Dons de Comus, ou l'Art de la cuisine, réduit en pratique*. 3 vols. Paris: Veuve Pissot, Didot and Brunet fils.

———. 1750. *Les Dons de Comus, ou l'art de la Cuisine, reduit en pratique*. 2nd ed., 2 vols. Paris: Veuve Pissot.

Marin, Louis. 1988. *Portrait of the King*. Translated by Martha M. Houle. Basingstoke: Macmillan.

[Marivaux, Pierre-Carlet de Chamblain de]. 1728. *Le Spectateur François*. New ed. Paris: Pierre Prault.

Marmontel, Jean-François. 1972. *Correspondance*. Edited by John Renwick. 2 vols. Clermont-Ferrand: Institut d'Etudes du Massif Central.

Mars, Gerald, and Valerie Mars. 1993. "Introduction." In *Food, Culture and History*, ed. Gerald Mars and Valerie Mars, 11–13. London Food Seminar 1. London: London Food Seminar.

Martin, Henri-Jean, and Roger Chartier, eds. 1984. *Le livre triomphant 1660–1830*. Vol. 2 of *Histoire de l'édition française*. 4 vols. Paris: Promodis.

Martin, Morag. 1996. "Il n'y à que Maille qui m'aille: Advertisements and the Development of Consumerism in Eighteenth Century France." *Proceedings of the Western Society for French History* 23:114–21.

———. 1999. "Consuming Beauty: The Commerce of Cosmetics in France, 1750–1800." Doctoral diss., University of California–Irvine.

———. 2009. *Selling Beauty: Cosmetics, Commerce, and French Society*. Baltimore: Johns Hopkins University Press.

Martin-Allanic, Jean-Etienne. 1964. *Bougainville navigateur et les découvertes de son temps*. Paris: Presses Universitaires de France.

Martino, Pierre. 1970. *L'Orient dans la littérature française au XVIIe et au XVIIIe siècle*. Geneva: Slatkine Reprints.

Marx, Jacques. 1981. *Tiphaigne de la Roche: Modèles de l'imaginaire au XVIIIe siècle*. Bruxelles: Editions de l'Université de Bruxelles.

Masseau, Didier. 1994. *L'invention de l'intellectuel dans l'Europe du XVIIIe siècle*. Paris: Presses Universitaires de France.

[Massialot]. 1698. *Le Cuisinier Roial et Bourgeois, qui aprend a ordonner toute sorte de Repas, & la meilleure maniere des Ragoûts les plus à la mode & les plus exquis*. 3rd ed. Paris: Charles de Sercy.

Massieu, Guillaume. 1740. "Carmen Caffaeum." In *Poetarum ex academia gallica, qui latinè, aut graecè scripserunt, carmina*, 273–82. Hagae-Comitum: Joannem van Duren.

Masson, Paul. 1912. *Marseille et la colonisation française. Essai d'histoire coloniale*. 2nd ed. Paris: Hachette & Cie.

Matthee, Rudi. 1985. "Exotic Substances: The Introduction and Global Spread of Tobacco, Coffee, Tea, and Distilled Liquor, Sixteenth to Eighteenth Centuries." In *Drugs and Narcotics in History*, ed. Roy Porter and Mikulás Teich, 24–51. Cambridge: Cambridge University Press.

Maza, Sarah. 2003. *The Myth of the French Bourgeoisie: An Essay on the Social Imaginary, 1750–1850*. Cambridge, MA: Harvard University Press.

Mazauric, Simone. 2007. *Fontenelle et l'invention de l'histoire des sciences à l'aube des Lumières*. Paris: Fayard.

McClaughlin, Trevor. 1975. "Sur les rapports entre la Compagnie de Thévenot et l'Académie royale des Sciences." *Revue d'histoire des sciences* 28:235–42.

McClellan, James E., III. 1979. "The Scientific Press in Transition: Rozier's Journal and the Scientific Societies in the 1770s." *Annals of Science* 36:425–49.

McKendrick, Neil, John Brewer, and J. H. Plumb. 1982. *The Birth of a Consumer Society: The Commercialization of Eighteenth-Century England*. London: Europa Publications.

McMahon, Darrin M. 2001. *Enemies of the Enlightenment: The French Counter-Enlightenment and the Making of Modernity*. New York: Oxford University Press.

Meeker, Natania. 2006. *Voluptuous Philosophy: Literary Materialism in the French Enlightenment*. New York: Fordham University Press.

Meignen, Louis. 1976. "Esquisse sur le commerce français du café dans le Levant au XVIIIe siècle." In Jean-Pierre Filippini, Louis Meignen, Claude Roure, Daniel Sabatier and Georges Stéphanidès, *Dossiers sur le commerce français en Méditerrannée orientale au XVIIIe siècle*, 103–50. Paris: Presses Universitaires de France.

Meijer, Miriam Claude. 1999. *Race and Aesthetics in the Anthropology of Petrus Camper (1722–1789)*. Amsterdam: Rodopi.

Meinel, Christoph. 1983. "Theory or Practice? The Eighteenth-Century Debate on the Scientific Status of Chemistry." *Ambix* 30:121–32.

Melon, Jean-François. 1734. *Essai politique sur le Commerce*. New ed. [N.p.].

Melton, James Van Horn. 2001. *The Rise of the Public in Enlightenment Europe*. Cambridge: Cambridge University Press.

Memoire [1692?]. *Memoire de ce qui est à faire dans la Generalité de Pour établir Maistre François Damame Bourgeois de Paris, en possession du Privilege de vendre seul, à l'exclusion de tous autres, . . . Tous les Caffez, Thez, Sorbecs, & le Chocolat, avec les drogues dont il est composé*. [N.p.].

Menant, Sylvain. 1981. *La chute d'Icare: la crise de la poésie française, 1700–1750*. Génève: Librairie Droz.

Mennell, Stephen. 1996. *All Manners of Food: Eating and Taste in England and France from the Middle Ages to the Present*. 2nd ed. Urbana: University of Illinois Press.

[Menon]. 1746. *La Cuisinière bourgeoise, suivie de l'Office*. Paris: Guillyn.

———. 1750. *La Science du maître d'hôtel, à l'usage des Officiers*. Paris: Paulus-du-Mesnil.

———. 1755. *Les Soupers de la Cour, ou l'art de travailler toutes sortes d'alimens*. 4 vols. Paris: Guillyn.

———. 1758. *Cuisine et Office de Santé, propre à ceux qui vivent avec œconomie & régime*. Paris: Le Clerc, Prault père and Babuty père.

———. 1768. *La Science du maître d'hôtel cuisinier, avec des observations sur la connoissance & les propriétés des Alimens* (1749). New ed. Paris: Leclerc.

[Mercier, Louis-Sébastien]. 1781. *Tableau de Paris*, part 1. London [Paris: n.p.].

Mercier, R. 1969. "Les Français en Amérique du Sud. La mission de l'Académie des Sciences, 1735–1745." *Revue d'Histoire de la France d'Outre-Mer* 16 (205): 327–74.

Merki, Christoph Maria. 2003. "Zwischen Luxus und Notwendigkeit: Genußmittel." In *"Luxus und Konsum": Eine historische Annäherung*, ed. Reinhold Reith and Torsten Meyer, 83–95. Münster: Waxmann.

Mervaud, Christiane. 1998. *Voltaire à table. Plaisir du corps, plaisir de l'esprit*. Paris: Éditions Desjonquères.

Metzger, Hélène. 1923. *Les doctrines chimiques en France du début du XVIIe à la fin du XVIIIe siècle.* Paris: Presses Universitaires de France.

Metzner, Paul. 1998. *Crescendo of the Virtuoso: Spectacle, Skill, and Self-Promotion in Paris during the Age of Revolution.* Berkeley, Los Angeles and London: University of California Press.

[Meusnier de Querlon, Anne-Gabriel?]. 1742. *Apologie des modernes ou réponse du Cuisinier françois auteur des Dons de Comus, à un pâtissier anglois.* [N.p.].

Meyer, Jean, Jean Tarade, Annie Rey-Goldzeiguer and Jacques Thobie. 1991. *Histoire de la France coloniale des origines à 1914.* Paris: Armand Colin.

Miller, Daniel. 1987. *Material Culture and Mass Consumption.* Oxford: Blackwell.

———. 1995. "Consumption as the Vanguard of History. A Polemic By Way of an Introduction." In *Acknowledging Consumption: A Review of New Studies*, ed. Miller, 1–57. London: Routledge.

Minard, Philippe. 1998. *La fortune du colbertisme. État et industrie dans la France des Lumières.* Paris: Fayard.

———. 2004. "Les corporations en France au XVIIIe siècle: métiers et institutions." In *La France, malade du corporatisme? XVIIIe–XXe siècles*, ed. Steven L. Kaplan and Philippe Minard, 39–51. Paris: Belin.

Mintz, Sidney W. 1985. *Sweetness and Power: The Place of Sugar in Modern History.* New York: Elisabeth Sifton Books and Viking.

Mokyr, Joel. 2002. *The Gifts of Athena: Historical Origins of the Knowledge Economy.* Princeton, NJ: Princeton University Press.

Molière, Jean-Baptiste Poquelin de. 1962. *Le Bourgeois Gentilhomme.* In Molière, *Oeuvres complètes*, preface by Pierre-Aimé Touchard, 506–41. Paris: Editions du Seuil.

[Montesquieu, Charles-Louis de Secondat, baron de La Brède et de]. 1721. *Lettres Persanes.* 2 vols. Cologne: Pierre Marteau.

Montesquieu, Charles-Louis de Secondat, baron de La Brède et de. 1757. "Essai sur le goût dans les choses de la nature & de l'art." In Denis Diderot and Jean Le Rond d'Alembert, ed., *Encyclopédie, ou Dictionnaire raisonné des sciences, des arts et des métiers*, ed. Denis Diderot and Jean Le Rond d'Alembert, 7:762–71. 17 vols. Paris: Briasson et al.

———. 1954. *Lettres persanes*, annot. Antoine Adam. Genève: Librairie Droz / Lille: Librairie Giard.

———. 1998. *De l'Esprit des Loix.* Facsimile ed., 2 vols. [Paris?:] Éditions Mollat.

Moran, Bruce T. 2005. *Distilling Knowledge: Alchemy, Chemistry and the Scientific Revolution.* Cambridge, MA: Harvard University Press.

Moravia, Serge. 1978. "From Homme Machine to Homme Sensible: Changing Eighteenth Century Models of Man's Image." *Journal of the History of Ideas* 39:45–60.

Morellet, André. 1988. *Mémoires de l'abbé Morellet de l'Académie française sur le dix-huitième siècle et sur la révolution.* Annotated and with an introduction by Jean-Pierre Guicciardi. Paris: Mercure de France.

Morize, André. 1970. *L'apologie du luxe au XVIIIe siècle et "Le Mondain" de Voltaire.* Geneva: Slatkine Reprints.

Morris, Madeleine F. 1979. *Le Chevalier de Jaucourt, un ami de la terre (1704–1780).* Genève: Librairie Droz.

Mortier, Roland, and Hervé Hasquin, eds. 1995. *Autour du Père Castel et du clavecin oculaire*. Special issue of *Études sur le XVIIIe siècle* 23:1–220.

Morton, Timothy. 1994. *Shelley and the Revolution in Taste: The Body and the Natural World*. Cambridge: Cambridge University Press.

Moura, Jean, and Paul Louvet. 1929. *Le Café Procope*. Paris: Librairie Académique Perrin et Cie.

Muchembled, Robert. 1998. *La société policée. Politique et politesse en France du XVIe au XXe siècle*. Paris: Seuil.

Mukerji, Chandra. 1997. *Territorial Ambitions and the Gardens of Versailles*. Cambridge: Cambridge University Press.

Mullan, John. 1984. "Hypochondria and Hysteria: Sensibility and the Physicians." *Eighteenth Century: Theory and Interpretation* 25:141–74.

Murphy, Antoin E. 1997. *John Law: Economic Theorist and Policy-Maker*. Oxford: Clarendon Press.

Murphy, Terence D. 1989. "The Transformation of Traditional Medical Culture under the Old Regime." *Historical Reflections/Réflexions Historiques* 16: 307–50.

Musgrave, Alan. 1976. "Why did Oxygen Supplant Phlogiston? Research Programmes in the Chemical Revolution." In *Method and Appraisal in the Physical Sciences: The Critical Background to Modern Science, 1800–1905*, ed. Colin Howson, 181–209. Cambridge: Cambridge University Press.

Musgrave, Toby, and Will Musgrave. 2000. *An Empire of Plants: People and Plants That Changed the World*. London: Cassell.

Myers, Fred R. 2001. "Introduction: The Empire of Things." In *The Empire of Things: Regimes of Value and Material Culture*, ed. Myers, 3–61. Santa Fe, NM: School of American Research Press.

Nahoum-Grappe, Véronique. 1991. *La Culture de l'ivresse. Essai de phénoménologie historique*. Paris: Quai Voltaire.

Nathans, Benjamin. 1990. "Habermas's 'Public Sphere' in the Era of the French Revolution." *French Historical Studies* 16:620–44.

Nemeitz, J. C. 1727. *Séjour de Paris, c'est à dire, Instructions Fidéles, pour les Voiageurs de Condition*. 2 vols. in 1. Leiden: Jean van Abcoude.

Nestlé, Marion. 2002. *Food Politics: How the Food Industry Influences Nutrition and Health*. Berkeley: University of California Press.

[Neufville de Brunaubois-Montador, Jean-Joseph-Florent]. 1740. *La nouvelle Astronomie du Parnasse François, ou l'Apothéose des Écrivains vivans dans la présente année 1740*. Parnasse: Vérologue [Paris?: n.p.].

Neumann, Josef N. 1991. "Rousseaus Kritik an der Heilkunde seiner Zeit: Zur Frage nach der handlungstheoretischen und ethischen Begründung medizinischen Handelns." *Medizinhistorisches Journal* 26 (3–4): 195–213.

Niebyl, Peter H. 1971. "The Non-Naturals." *Bulletin of the History of Medicine* 45:486–92.

Oberlé, Gérard. 1989. *Les fastes de Bacchus et de Comus, ou histoire du boire et du manger en Europe, de l'antiquité à nos jours*. Paris: Belfond.

O'Brien, Karen. 2011. "The Return of the Enlightenment." *American Historical Review* 115 (5): 1426–35.

Obrist, Gabrielle. 1995. "Die Frau als Gastgeberin und Gast im Pariser Café." In *Gesellschaft—Literatur—Politik. Das Pariser Café als Spiegel sozialen und kulturellen Wandels*, 19–28. Zürich: Johann Jakobs Museum.

Oddy, Derek, and Derek Miller, eds. 1976. *The Making of the Modern British Diet*. London: Croom Helm.

Olivier-Martin, François. 1938. *L'organisation corporative de la France d'ancien régime*. Paris: Librairie du recueil Sirey.

Omont, Henri. 1902. *Missions archéologiques françaises en Orient aux XVIIe et XVIIIe siècles*. 2 vols. Paris: Imprimerie Nationale.

Onfray, Michel. 1989. *Le ventre des philosophes: Critique de la raison diététique*. Paris: Bernard Grasset.

Onfray, Michel. 1991. *L'art de jouir: pour un matérialisme hédoniste*. Paris: Bernard Grasset.

Onfroy, Jean. 1765. *Observations sur la Nature et les Procedés de quelques Liqueurs ou Compositions usuelles*. Paris: [n.p.].

Ophir, Adi, and Steven Shapin. 1991. "The Place of Knowledge: A Methodological Survey." *Science in Context* 4:3–22.

Orland, Barbara, and E. C. Spary. In press. "Introduction." *Studies in the History and Philosophy of Biological and Biomedical Sciences*.

Ozouf, Mona. 1987. "L'opinion publique." In *The Political Culture of the Old Regime*, ed. Keith Michael Baker, 419–34. Vol. 1 of *The French Revolution and the Creation of Modern Political Culture*. Oxford: Pergamon.

———. 1988. "Public Opinion at the End of the Old Regime." In *Rethinking French Politics in 1788*. Supplement to *Journal of Modern History* 60:1–21.

[Palissot de Montenoy, Charles]. 1771. *La Dunciade: Poème en dix chants*. 2 vols. London: [n.p.].

Palissot de Montenoy, Charles. 1975. *Les Philosophes*. Introduction by T. J. Barling. Exeter: Exeter University Printing Unit.

Panzac, Daniel. 1996. *Commerce et navigation dans l'Empire ottoman au XVIIIe siècle*. Istanbul: Isis.

Pappas, John N. 1957. *Berthier's Journal de Trévoux and the philosophes*. Genève: Institut et Musée Voltaire.

Pardailhé-Galabrun, Annik. 1988. *La naissance de l'intime: 3000 foyers parisiens XVIIe–XVIIIe siècles*. Paris: Presses Universitaires de France.

Parker, Harold T. 1965. "French Administrators and French Scientists During the Old Regime and the Early Years of the Revolution." In *Ideas in History: Essays Presented to Louis Gottschalk by his Former Students*, ed. Richard Herr and Harold T. Parker, 85–109. Durham, NC: Duke University Press.

Parkin, Chloë. 1996. "Rousseau and Tissot and the Revolution in Health." Master's thesis, University of Warwick.

Parmentier, Antoine-Augustin. 1781. *Recherches sur les végétaux nourrissans, qui, dans les temps de disette, peuvent remplacer les alimens ordinaires*. Paris: Imprimerie Royale.

Parssinen, Terry M., and Karen Kerner. 1980. "Development of the Disease Model of Drug Addiction in Britain, 1870–1926." *Medical History* 24:275–96.

Paul, Harry W. 1996. *Science, Vine and Wine in Modern France.* Cambridge: Cambridge University Press.

Pekacz, Jolanta T. 1999. *Conservative Tradition in Pre-Revolutionary France: Parisian Salon Women.* New York: Peter Lang.

Pendergrast, Mark. 2001. *Uncommon Grounds: The History of Coffee and How It Transformed Our World.* New York: Texere.

Pennell, Sara. 1999. "Consumption and Consumerism in Early Modern England." *Historical Journal* 42 (2): 549–64.

Perrot, Jean-Claude. 1992. *Une histoire intellectuelle de l'économie politique.* Paris: Editions de l'École des Hautes Etudes en Sciences Sociales.

Perrot, Philippe. 1995. *Le luxe. Une richesse entre faste et confort XVIIIe–XIXe siècle.* Paris: Editions du Seuil.

Peterson, T. Sarah. 2006. *The Cookbook That Changed the World: The Origins of Modern Cuisine.* Stroud: Tempus.

Pettet, Deirdre. 2003. "A Veritable Bedouin: The Chevalier d'Arvieux in the Camp of the Emir Turabey." In *Distant Lands and Diverse Cultures: The French Experience in Asia, 1600–1700*, ed. Glenn J. Ames and Ronald S. Love, 21–46. Westport, CT: Praeger.

Pickering, Andrew, ed. 1992. *Science as Practice and Culture.* Chicago: University of Chicago Press.

———. 1995. *The Mangle of Practice: Time, Agency and Science.* Chicago: University of Chicago Press.

Pilloud, Sévérine. 1999. "Mettre les maux en mots, médiations dans la consultation épistolaire au XVIIIe siècle: Les malades du Dr Tissot (1728–1797)." *Canadian Bulletin of Medical History* 16 (2): 215–45.

Pilloud, Sévérine, and Micheline Louis-Courvoisier. 2003. "The Intimate Experience of the Body in the Eighteenth Century: Between Interiority and Exteriority." *Medical History* 47 (4): 451–72.

Pilloud, Sévérine, Stefan Hächler, and Vincent Barras. 2004. "Consulter par lettre au XVIIIe siècle." *Gesnerus* 61:232–53.

Pinch, Trevor J. and Wiebe E. Bijker. 1984. "The Social Construction of Facts and Artefacts: Or How the Sociology of Science and the Sociology of Technology Might Benefit Each Other." *Social Studies of Science* 14:399–441.

Pincus, Steve. 1995. "'Coffee Politicians Does Create': Coffeehouses and Restoration Political Culture." *Journal of Modern History* 67 (4): 807–34.

Pinkard, Susan. 2009. *A Revolution in Taste: The Rise of French Cuisine, 1650–1800.* Cambridge: Cambridge University Press.

Plagnol-Diéval, Marie-Emmanuelle. 1997. "Vin canaille et vin moral sur les scènes privées." In *Le Vin*, ed. Jean Bart and Élisabeth Wahl. Special issue of *Dix-huitième siècle* 29:237–53.

Pluchon, Pierre. 1991. *Le Premier empire colonial des origines à la Restauration.* Vol. 1 of *Histoire de la colonisation française.* Paris: Librairie Arthème Fayard.

Pluquet, abbé François-André-Adrien. 1786. *Traité philosophique et politique sur le luxe.* 2 vols. Paris: Barrois and Barrois.

Plutarch. 1785. *Les règles et préceptes de santé de Plutarque*. Translated by Jacques Amyot, annotated by abbé André-Charles Brotier. Paris: J.-B. Cussac.

Pocock, J. G. A. 1985. *Virtue, Commerce and History: Essays on Political Thought and History, Chiefly in the Eighteenth Century*. Cambridge: Cambridge University Press.

Poirier, Jean-Pierre. 1996. *Lavoisier: Chemist, Biologist, Economist*. Translated by Rebecca Balinski. Philadelphia: University of Pennsylvania Press.

Pomeau, René, and Jean Ehrard. 1984. *De Fénelon à Voltaire 1680–1750*. Littérature française 5. Paris: Arthaud.

Pomet, Pierre. 1694. *Histoire generale des Drogues, traitant des Plantes, des Animaux, & des Minéraux*. Paris: Jean-Baptiste Loyson and Augustin Pillon.

Pomian, Krzysztof. 1990. *Collectors and Curiosities: Paris and Venice, 1500–1800*. Translated by Elizabeth Wiles-Portier. Cambridge: Polity.

Pommier, Henriette. 1993. "Bibliographie de Jacob Spon." In *Jacob Spon: Un humaniste lyonnais du XVIIe siècle*, ed. Roland Étienne and Jean-Claude Mossière, 53–78. Lyon: Bibliothèque Salomon-Reinach.

Pompignan, Jean-Georges Le Franc de. 1763. *Instruction pastorale sur la prétendue philosophie des incrédules modernes*. Le Puy: Clet.

Poncelet, abbé Polycarpe. 1755. *Chimie du goût et de l'odorat, ou Principes pour composer facilement, & à peu de frais, les Liqueurs à boire, & les Eaux de senteurs*. Paris: P. G. Le Mercier.

Poni, Carlo. 1998. "Mode et innovation: Les stratégies des marchands en soie de Lyon au XVIIIe siècle." *Revue d'histoire moderne et contemporaine* 45:589–625.

Porphyry. *Traité de Porphyre, Touchant l'Abstinence de la chair des Animaux*. Paris: De Bure l'aîné, 1747.

Portal, Antoine. 1770–73. *Histoire de l'Anatomie et de la Chirurgie, contenant l'origine & les progrès de ces Sciences*. 6 vols. Paris: P. Fr. Didot le jeune.

Porter, Roy. 1985. "The Drinking Man's Disease: The 'Pre-history' of Alcoholism in Georgian Britain." *British Journal of Addiction* 80:385–96.

———. 1988. "Introduction." In Thomas Trotter, *An Essay Medical, Philosophical, and Chemical on Drunkenness and Its Effects on the Human Body*, ix–xl. London: Routledge.

Porter, Roy, and Mikuláš Teich, eds. 1985. *Drugs and Narcotics in History*. Cambridge: Cambridge University Press.

Poulot, Dominique. 1997. "Une nouvelle histoire de la culture matérielle?" *Revue d'histoire moderne et contemporaine* 44 (2): 344–57.

Prättälä, Ritva. 1991. "Outlining Multidisciplinary Food Research." In *Palatable Worlds: Sociocultural Food Studies*, ed. Elisabeth L. Fürst, Ritva Prättälä, Marianne Ekström, Lotte Holm and Unni Kjærnes, 17–31. Oslo: Solum Verlag.

Pressavin, Jean Baptiste. 1786. *L'Art de prolonger la Vie et de conserver la Santé; Ou Traité d'Hygiene*. Lyon: J. S. Grabit.

Priesner, Claus. 1986. "Spiritus Aethereus—Formation of Ether and Theories of Etherification from Valerius Cordus to Alexander Williamson." *Ambix* 33:129–52.

Principe, Lawrence M. 2007. "A Revolution Nobody Noticed? Changes in Early Eighteenth-Century Chymistry." In *New Narratives in Eighteenth-Century Chemistry*, ed. Principe. Dordrecht: Springer, 1–22.

Pris, Claude. 1977. "La glace en France aux XVIIe et XVIIIe siècles. Monopole et liberté d'enterprise dans une industrie de pointe sous l'Ancien Régime." *Revue d'Histoire Economique et Sociale* 55:5–23.

Procope Couteaux, Michel. 1712. *Analyse du Systême de la Trituration tel qu'il est décrit, par Mr Hecquet, dans son Traité de la Digestion & des maladies de l'estomach.* Paris: Veuve Muguet.

———. 1727. *Analyse du Systême de la Trituration tel qu'il est décrit, par Mr Hecquet, dans son Traité de la Digestion & des maladies de l'estomach.* Paris: Guillaume Cavelier.

P[rocope] C[outeaux], [Michel], and G. de Merville. 1746. *Le Roman.* Paris: Jacques Clousier.

Quérard, J.-M. 1869. *Les supercheries littéraires dévoilées. Galerie des Ecrivains français de toute l'Europe qui se sont déguisés sous des anagrammes, des astéronymes, des cryptonymes, des initialismes, des noms littéraires, des pseudonymes facétieux ou bizarres, etc.* Vol. 1, Paris: Paul Daffis.

Quesnay, François. 1736. *Essai phisique sur l'oeconomie animale.* Paris: Guillaume Cavelier.

———. 1748. *Essai phisique sur l'œconomie animale.* 2nd ed., 3 vols. Paris: G. Cavelier père.

Quinlan, Sean M. 2007. *The Great Nation in Decline: Sex, Modernity and Health Crises in Revolutionary France c. 1750–1850.* Aldershot: Ashgate.

Racine, Louis. 1808. *Oeuvres.* 6 vols. Paris: Le Normant.

Rafeq, Abdul-Karim. 2001. "The Socioeconomic and Political Implications of the Introduction of Coffee into Syria, Sixteenth–Eighteenth Centuries." In *Le commerce du café avant l'ère des plantations coloniales. Espaces, réseaux, sociétés (XVe-XIXe siècle),* ed. Michel Tuchscherer, 127–42. Cairo: Institut Français d'Archéologie Orientale.

Ramazzini, Bernardino. 1724. *L'Art de conserver la Santé des Princes, et des Personnes du Premier Rang.* Translated by Etienne Coulet. Leiden: Jean Arnoult Langerak.

Rambourg, Patrick. 2005. *De la cuisine à la gastronomie. Histoire de la table française.* Paris: Audibourg.

Ramsey, Matthew. 1988. *Professional and Popular Medicine in France, 1770–1830: The Social World of Medical Practice.* Cambridge: Cambridge University Press.

Rather, L. J. 1968. "The 'Six Things Non-Natural': A Note on the Origins and Fate of a Doctrine and a Phrase." *Clio Medica* 3:337–47.

Raunié, Marie-André-Alfred-Émile. 1879–84. *Chansonnier historique du XVIIIe siècle.* 10 vols. Paris: [n.p.].

Raymond, André. 1984. *The Great Arab Cities in the Sixteenth–Eighteenth Centuries: An Introduction.* New York: New York University Press.

———. 1999. *Artisans et commerçants au Caire au XVIIIe siècle.* 2nd ed., 2 vols. Cairo: IFAO/IFEAD.

———. 2002. *Arab Cities in the Ottoman Period.* Variorum Collected Studies Series. Ashgate: Variorum.

Raynal, Guillaume-Thomas-François. 1770. *Histoire philosophique et politique des établissemens & du commerce des Européens dans les deux Indes.* 6 vols. Amsterdam, [n.p.].

———. 1774. *Histoire philosophique et politique des établissements & du commerce des Européens dans les deux Indes.* New ed., 7 vols. La Haye: Gosse fils.

Réaumur, René-Antoine Ferchault de. 1756. "Sur la digestion des oiseaux. Premier Mémoire." *Histoire de l'Académie Royale des Sciences. Année M.DCCLVI,* "Mémoires," 266–307, 461–95.

Rebora, Giovanni. 2001. *Culture of the Fork: A Brief History of Food in Europe.* Translated by Albert Sonnenfeld. New York: Columbia University Press.

Reddy, William M. 1984. *The Rise of Market Culture: The Textile Trade and French Society, 1750–1900.* Cambridge: Cambridge University Press.

Regourd, François. 1999. "Maîtriser la nature: un enjeu colonial. Botanique et agronomie en Guyane et aux Antilles (XVIIe–XVIIIe siècles)." *Revue française d'histoire d'outre-mer* 86:39–64.

Renyer, Charlotte, Madame Curé, afterwards Madame Bourette. 1754. *La Muse Limonadiere, ou recueil d'ouvrages en vers et en prose.* Paris: Sebastien Jorry.

Renyer, Charlotte, Madame Curé, afterwards Madame Bourette. 1777. *A Monsieur et à Madame, sur l'honneur qu'ils ont fait de donner leurs noms au fils de ma fille, l'épouse de Marmet, un des valets de chambre de Monsieur.* [Paris:] Jorry.

———. 1779. *La coquette punie: comédie en un acte et en vers.* Paris: J. Fr. Bastien.

Revel, Jacques. 1979. *Un festin en paroles. Histoire littéraire de la sensibilité gastronomique de l'antiquité à nos jours.* Paris: Pauvert, 1979.

———. 1989. "The Uses of Civility." In *Passions of the Renaissance,* ed. Roger Chartier, 167–205. Vol. 3 of *A History of Private Life,* ed. Philippe Ariès and Georges Duby. Cambridge, MA: Belknap Press of Harvard University Press.

Rey, Roselyne. 1991. "La vulgarisation médicale au XVIIIe siècle: Le cas des dictionnaires portatifs de santé." *Revue d'histoire des sciences* 44:413–33.

———. 2000. *Naissance et développement du vitalisme en France de la deuxième moitié du 18e siècle à la fin du Premier Empire.* Oxford: Voltaire Foundation.

Ribard, Dinah. 2003. *Raconter, vivre, penser. Histoires de philosophes 1650–1766.* Paris: Vrin and E.H.E.S.S.

———. 2005. "Pratique(s) Jésuite(s) de l'écrit: le P. Tournemine, les *Mémoires de Trévoux* et Fénelon." *Dix-septième siècle* 57 (3): 513–26.

Ribeiro, Aileen. 1995. *The Art of Dress: Fashion in England and France, 1750 to 1820.* New Haven, CT: Yale University Press.

Richard, Jacques. 2001. "La bibliothèque de Jean Astruc, médecin des Lumières (1684–1766)." *Histoire des sciences médicales* 35 (1): 99–108.

Richardot, Anne. 2002. *Le rire des Lumières.* Paris: Honoré Champion.

Richardt, Aimé. 2005. *Les médecins du Grand siècle.* Paris: François-Xavier de Guibert.

Rieder, Philip, and Vincent Barras. 2001. "Ecrire sa maladie au siècle des Lumières." In *La médecine des Lumières. Tout autour de Tissot,* ed. Vincent Barras and Micheline Louis-Courvoisier, 201–22. Geneva: Georg.

Riley, James C. 1986. *The Seven Years War and the Old Regime in France: The Economic and Financial Toll.* Princeton, NJ: Princeton University Press.

Riskin, Jessica. 2003a. "The Defecating Duck, or, the Ambiguous Origins of Artificial Life." *Critical Inquiry* 29:599–633.

———. 2003b. "Eighteenth-Century Wetware." *Representations* 83:97–125.

———. 2007. "Amusing Physics." In *Science and Spectacle in the European Enlightenment*, ed. Bernadette Bensaude-Vincent and Christine Blondel, 43–63. Aldershot: Ashgate.

Rivière, Marc Serge. 2004. "Philosophical Liberty, Sexual Licence: The Ambiguity of Voltaire's Libertinage." In *Libertine Enlightenment: Sex, Liberty and Licence in the Eighteenth Century*, ed. Peter Cryle and Lisa O'Connell, 75–91. Houndmills: Palgrave Macmillan.

[Rivière-Dufresny, Charles]. 1709. *Amusemens serieux et comiques.* 5th ed. Amsterdam: Estienne Roger.

Rizvi, S. Abu Turab, and Ravij Sethi. 1998. "Novelty, Imitation and Habit Formation in a Scitovskian Model of Consumption." In *The Active Consumer: Novelty and Surprise in Consumer Choice*, ed. Marina Bianchi, 198–212. London: Routledge.

Robbins, Louise E. 2001. *Elephant Slaves and Pampered Parrots: Exotic Animals in Eighteenth-Century Paris.* Baltimore: Johns Hopkins University Press.

Robertson, John. 2005. *The Case for the Enlightenment: Scotland and Naples, 1680–1760.* Cambridge: Cambridge University Press.

Roche, Daniel. 1978. "Négoce et culture dans la France du XVIIIe siècle." *Revue d'histoire moderne et contemporaine* 25:375–95.

———. 1983. "Cuisine et alimentation populaire à Paris." In *Aliments et cuisine*, ed. Jean-Claude Bonnet and Beatrice Fink. Special issue of *Dix-huitième Siècle* 15:7–18.

———. 1987. *The People of Paris: An Essay in Popular Culture in the Eighteenth Century.* Translated by Marie Evans and Gwynne Lewis. Leamington Spa: Berg.

———. 1988. *Les Républicains des lettres. Gens de culture et Lumières au XVIIIe siècle.* Paris: Fayard.

———. 1994. *The Culture of Clothing: Dress and Fashion in the Ancien Régime.* Cambridge: Cambridge University Press.

———. 2000. *A History of Everyday Things: The Birth of Consumption in France, 1600–1800.* Cambridge: Cambridge University Press.

Roe, Shirley A. 1981. *Matter, Life and Generation: Eighteenth-Century Embryology and the Haller-Wolff Debate.* Cambridge: Cambridge University Press.

Roger, Jacques. 1997. *The Life Sciences in Eighteenth-Century French Thought.* Edited by Keith R. Benson, translated by Robert Ellrich. Stanford, CA: Stanford University Press.

Rohault, Jacques. 1727. *Rohault's System of Natural Philosophy, illustrated with Dr. Samuel Clarke's Notes* (1671). 2 vols. London: James Knapton.

Romagnesi, Jean-Antoine, and [Michel Procope] C[outeaux]. [1736]. *Les Fées, Comedie en trois Actes.* Paris: Briasson.

Root, Hilton L. 1994. *The Fountain of Privilege: Political Foundations of Markets in Old Regime France and England.* Berkeley: University of California Press.

Rose, Nikolas. 1996. *Inventing Our Selves: Psychology, Power, and Personhood.* Cambridge: Cambridge University Press.

Rothkrug, Lionel. 1965. *Opposition to Louis XIV: The Political and Social Origins of the French Enlightenment.* Princeton, NJ: Princeton University Press.

Rousseau, George S. 1976. "Nerves, Spirits and Fibres." *Studies in the Eighteenth Century* 3:137–57.

———. 1991a. "Nerves, Spirits and Fibres: Towards an Anthropology of Sensibility." In *Anthropological*, 122–41. Vol. 1 of *Perilous Enlightenment: Pre- and Post-modern Discourses*, ed. Rousseau. 3 vols. Manchester: Manchester University Press.

———. 1991b. "Towards a Semiotics of the Nerve: The Social History of Language in a New Key." In *Language, Self and Society: A Social History of Language*, ed. Peter Burke and Roy Porter, 213–75. Cambridge: Polity Press.

Rousseau, Jean-Baptiste. 1694. *Le Caffé, comédie*. Paris: P. Aubouyn, P. Emery and C. Clouzier.

Rousseau, Jean-Jacques. 1764. *Lettres écrites de la montagne*. Amsterdam: Marc-Michel Rey.

———. 1965–85. *Correspondance complète de Jean Jacques Rousseau*. Edited and annotated by R. A. Leigh. 44 vols. Oxford: Voltaire Foundation.

———. 1966. *Émile, ou de l'éducation* (1762). Edited by Michel Launay. Paris: Flammarion.

———. 1967–71. *Oeuvres complètes*. Preface by Jean Fabre, introduction by Michel Launay. 3 vols. Paris: Éditions du Seuil-L'Intégrale.

Rouvière, Louis-Henri. 1708. *Réflexions sur la Fermentation et sur la nature du feu*. Paris: Jean Baptiste Coignard.

Rudgley, Richard. 1993. *The Alchemy of Culture: Intoxicants in Society*. London: British Museum Press.

Rupke, Nicolaas, ed. 2000. *Medical Geography in Historical Perspective*. Supplement to *Medical History* 20.

Russo, Elena. 2007. *Styles of Enlightenment: Taste, Politics, and Authorship in Eighteenth-Century France*. Baltimore: Johns Hopkins University Press.

Sabatier de Castres, abbé Antoine. 1781. *Les Trois Siècles de la Littérature Françoise*. 5th ed., 4 vols. La Haye: Moutard.

Safier, Neil. 2001. "Unveiling the Amazon to European Science and Society: The Reading and Reception of La Condamine's *Relation abrégée d'un voyage fait dans l'intérieur de l'Amérique Méridionale* (1745)." *Terrae Incognitae* 33:33–47.

Sahlins, Marshall. 1981. *Historical Metaphors and Mythical Realities: Structure in the Early History of the Sandwich Islands Kingdom*. ASAO Special Publications 1. Ann Arbor: University of Michigan Press.

Said, Edward. 1978. *Orientalism*. London: Routledge and Kegan Paul.

Sainte-Beuve, Charles-Augustin. 1926–32. *Port-Royal*. 10 vols. Paris: La Connaissance.

Saint-Evrémond, Charles de. 1725. *Oeuvres*. 7 vols. London: Jacob Tonson.

Saint-Germain, Jacques. 1960. *Samuel Bernard, le banquier des rois; d'après de nombreux documents inédits*. Paris: Hachette.

Sandgruber, Roman. 1991. "Kaffeesuppe und 'kleiner Brauner.' Sozialgeschichte des Kaffeekonsums in Österreich." In *Coffee in the Context of European Drinking Habits*, ed. Daniela U. Ball, 53–67. Zürich: Johann Jacobs Museum.

———. 1994. "Genußmittel. Ihre reale und symbolische Bedeutung im neuzeitlichen Europa." *Jahrbuch fur Wirtschaftsgeschichte* 1:73–88.

Santschi, C. 1993. "De Zurich à Vevey en passant par Genève et Lyon: Le réseau familial de Jacob Spon." In *Jacob Spon: Un humaniste lyonnais du XVIIe siècle*, ed. Roland Étienne and Jean-Claude Mossière, 187–206. Lyon: Bibliothèque Salomon-Reinach.

Sargentson, Carolyn. 1996. *Merchants and Luxury Markets: The Marchands Merciers of Eighteenth-Century Paris*. London: Victoria and Albert Museum.

Saule, Béatrix. 1993. "Tables royales à Versailles, 1682–1789." In *Versailles et les tables royales en Europe XVIIème–XIXème siècles*, ed. Jean-Pierre Babelon. 41–68. Paris: Réunion des musées nationaux.

Saunders, Stewart. 1991. "Public Administration and the Library of Jean-Baptiste Colbert." *Libraries and Culture* 26 (2): 283–300.

Sauter, Hermann, and Erich Loos, eds. 1986. *Paul Thiry Baron d'Holbach. Die gesamte erhaltene Korrespondenz*. Stuttgart: Franz Steiner Verlag.

Savary Des Brûlons, Jacques, and Philémon Savary. 1723–30. *Dictionnaire universel de Commerce: d'Histoire naturelle, & des Arts & Metiers*. 3 vols. Paris: Jacques Estienne.

Savary Des Brûlons, Jacques, and Philémon Savary. 1759–65. *Dictionnaire universel de Commerce: d'Histoire naturelle, & des Arts & Metiers*. 2nd ed., 5 vols. Copenhagen: Cl. & Ant. Philibert.

Scagliola, Robert. 1943. *Les apothicaires de Paris et les distillateurs*. Clermont-Ferrand: [n.p.]

Schaeper, Thomas J. 1983. *The French Council of Commerce 1700–1715: A Study of Mercantilism After Colbert*. Columbus: Ohio State University Press.

Schaffer, Simon. 1992. "Self Evidence." *Critical Inquiry* 8:328–62.

———. 1999. "Enlightened Automata." In *The Sciences in Enlightened Europe*, ed. William Clark, Jan Golinski, and Simon Schaffer, 126–65. Chicago: University of Chicago Press.

Schatzki, Theodore R., and Karin Knorr Cetina, eds. 2001. *The Practice Turn in Contemporary Theory*. London: Routledge.

Schiebinger, Londa. 1989. *The Mind Has No Sex? Women in the Origins of Modern Science*. Cambridge, MA: Harvard University Press.

Schivelbusch, Wolfgang. 1992. *Tastes of Paradise: A Social History of Spices, Stimulants, and Intoxicants*. Translated by David Jacobson. New York: Pantheon Books.

Scitovsky, Tibor. 1976. *The Joyless Economy: An Inquiry Into Human Satisfaction and Consumer Dissatisfaction*. New York: Oxford University Press.

Scott, Katie. 1995. *The Rococo Interior: Decoration and Social Spaces in Early Eighteenth-Century Paris*. New Haven, CT: Yale University Press.

Scoville, Warren C. 1950. *Capitalism and French Glassmaking, 1640–1789*. Berkeley: University of California Press.

Secord, Anne. 1994a. "Corresponding Interests: Artisans and Gentlemen in Nineteenth-Century Natural History." *British Journal for the History of Science* 27:383–408.

———. 1994b. "Science in the Pub: Artisan Botanists in Early Nineteenth-Century Lancashire." *History of Science* 32:269–315.

Secord, James A. 2000. *Victorian Sensation: The Extraordinary Publication, Reception, and Secret Authorship of* Vestiges of the Natural History of Creation. Chicago: University of Chicago Press.

Sekora, John. 1977. *Luxury: The Concept in Western Thought from Eden to Smollett*. Baltimore: Johns Hopkins University Press.

Serres, Michel. 1982. *Parasite*. Baltimore: Johns Hopkins University Press.

———. 1989. *Statues*. Paris: Flammarion.

Sewell, William H. 1980. *Work and Revolution in France: The Language of Labor from the Old Regime to 1848*. Cambridge: Cambridge University Press.

———. 2010. "The Empire of Fashion and the Rise of Capitalism in Eighteenth-Century France." *Past and Present* 206:81–120.

Seznec, Jean. 1957. *Essais sur Diderot et l'Antiquité*. Oxford: Clarendon Press.

Sgard, Jean. 1991. *Dictionnaire des journaux, 1600–1789*. 2 vols. Paris: Universitas.

Shapin, Steven. 1984. "Pump and Circumstance: Robert Boyle's Literary Technology." *Social Studies of Science* 14:481–520.

———. 1988. "The House of Experiment in Seventeenth-Century England." *Isis* 79:373–404.

———. 1998. "The Philosopher and the Chicken: On the Dietetics of Disembodied Knowledge." In *Science Incarnate: Historical Embodiments of Natural Knowledge*, ed. Christopher Lawrence and Steven Shapin, 21–50. Chicago: University of Chicago Press.

———. 2003. "Trusting George Cheyne: Scientific Expertise, Common Sense, and Moral Authority in Early Eighteenth-Century Dietetic Medicine." *Bulletin of the History of Medicine* 77:263–97.

Shapin, Steven, and Christopher Lawrence. 1998. "Introduction: The Body of Knowledge." In *Science Incarnate: Historical Embodiments of Natural Knowledge*, ed. Lawrence and Shapin, 1–19. Chicago: University of Chicago Press.

Shapin, Steven, and Simon Schaffer. 1985. *Leviathan and the Air-Pump: Hobbes, Boyle and the Experimental Life*. Princeton, NJ: Princeton University Press.

Sheridan, Geraldine. 1993. "*Les Amusements d'un Jésuite*: Père Bougeant, Physiognomy and Sensualist Theories." *Australian Journal of French Studies* 30:292–310.

Sherman, Sandra. 2003. "Gastronomic History in Eighteenth-Century England." *Prose Studies* 26 (3): 395–413.

———. 2004. "'The Whole Art and Mystery of Cooking': What Cookbooks Taught Readers in the Eighteenth Century." *Eighteenth-Century Life* 28:115–35.

Sherratt, Andrew. 1995. "Introduction: Peculiar Substances." In *Consuming Habits: Drugs in History and Anthropology*, ed. Andrew Sherratt, Jordan Goodman, and Paul E. Lovejoy, 1–10. London: Routledge.

Shilling, Chris. 1993. *The Body and Social Theory*. Newbury Park, CA: Sage Publications.

———, ed. 2007. *Embodying Sociology: Retrospect, Progress and Prospects*. Malden, MA: Blackwell.

Shovlin, John. 2006. *The Political Economy of Virtue: Luxury, Patriotism, and the Origins of the French Revolution*. Ithaca, NY: Cornell University Press.

Sibum, H. Otto. 1998. "An Old Hand in a New System." In *The Invisible Industrialist: Manufactures and the Production of Scientific Knowledge*, ed. Jean-Paul Gaudillière and Ilana Löwy, 23–57. Basingstoke: Macmillan.

Simon, Jonathan. 2005. *Chemistry, Pharmacy and Revolution in France, 1777–1809*. Aldershot: Ashgate.

Sleeswijk, Anne Wegener. 2004. "Du nectar et de la godaille: qualité et falsification du vin aux Provinces-Unies, XVIIIe siècle." In *La sécurité alimentaire, entre santé et marché*, ed. Martin Bruegel and Alessandro Stanziani. Special issue of *Revue d'histoire moderne et contemporaine* 51 (3): 17–43.

Smeaton, W. A. 1957. "*L'Avantcoureur*: The Journal in Which Some of Lavoisier's Earliest Research Was Reported." *Annals of Science* 13:219–34.

Smith, Pamela H. 2004. *The Body of the Artisan: Art and Experience in the Scientific Revolution.* Chicago: University of Chicago Press.

Smith, Pamela H., and Paula Findlen, eds. 2002. *Merchants and Marvels: Commerce and the Representation of Nature in Early Modern Europe.* New York: Routledge.

Smith, William. 1996. *The Wordsworth Classical Dictionary.* London: Wordsworth Editions.

Smith, Woodruff D. 2002. *Consumption and the Making of Respectability, 1600–1800.* London: Routledge.

Sonenscher, Michael. 1989. *Work and Wages: Natural Law, Politics and Eighteenth-Century French Trades.* Cambridge: Cambridge University Press.

———. 1998. "Fashion's Empire: Trade and Power in Early Eighteenth-Century France." In *Luxury Trades and Consumerism in* Ancien Régime *Paris: Studies in the History of the Skilled Workforce*, ed. Robert Fox and Anthony Turner, 231–54. Aldershot: Ashgate.

Sournia, Jean-Charles. 1990. *A History of Alcoholism.* Introduction by Roy Porter, translated by Nick Hindley and Gareth Stanton. Oxford: Basil Blackwell.

Spallanzani, Lazzaro. 1784. *Experiences sur la digestion de l'homme et de différentes espèces d'animaux.* Genève: Barthélémi Chirol.

Spang, Rebecca Lee. 2000. *The Invention of the Restaurant: Paris and Modern Gastronomic Culture.* Cambridge, MA: Harvard University Press.

Spang, Rebecca Lee, and Colin Jones. 1999. "Sans-Culottes, *Sans Café, Sans* Tabac: Shifting Realms of Necessity and Luxury in Eighteenth-Century France." In *Consumers and Luxury: Consumer Culture in Europe 1650–1850*, ed. Maxine Berg and Helen Clifford, 37–62. Manchester: Manchester University Press.

Spary, E. C. 2000. *Utopia's Garden: French Natural History from Old Regime to Revolution.* Chicago: University of Chicago Press.

———. 2004. "'Peaches which the Patriarchs Lacked': Natural History, Natural Resources, and the Natural Economy in Eighteenth-Century France." In *Oeconomies in the Age of Newton*, ed. Neil De Marchi and Margaret Schabas, 14–41. Supplement to *History of Political Economy* 35. Durham, NC: Duke University Press.

———. 2005. "Of Nutmegs and Botanists: The Colonial Cultivation of Botanical Identity." In *Colonial Botany: Science, Commerce, and Politics in the Early Modern World*, ed. Londa Schiebinger and Claudia Swan, 187–203. Philadelphia: University of Pennsylvania Press.

———. 2009. "Self Preservation. French Travels Between *Cuisine* and *Industrie.*" In *The Brokered World*, ed. James Delbourgo, Kapil Raj, Lissa Roberts and Simon Schaffer, 355–86. Canton, MA: Science History Publications.

———. 2010. "Liqueurs and the Luxury Market-Place in Eighteenth-Century Paris." In *Materials and Expertise in Early Modern Europe: Between Market and Laboratory*, ed. Ursula Klein and E. C. Spary, 225–55. Chicago: University of Chicago Press.

———. Unpublished. "Economic Chemists / Industrial Eaters. French Food and the Sciences, 1750–1815."

Spencer, Colin. 1993. *The Heretic's Feast. A History of Vegetarianism*. London: Fourth Estate.

Spencer, Samia I. 1984. "Women and Education." In *French Women and the Age of Enlightenment*, ed. Spencer, 83–96. Bloomington: Indiana University Press.

Spon, Jacob, and George Wheler. 1724. *Voyage d'Italie, de Dalmatie, de Grece et du Levant, fait aux années 1675. & 1676* (1678). 2 vols. La Haye: Rutgert Alberts.

Stafford, Barbara Maria. 1991. *Body Criticism: Imaging the Unseen in Enlightenment Art and Medicine*. Cambridge, MA: MIT Press.

———. 1994. *Artful Science: Enlightenment Entertainment and the Eclipse of Visual Education*. Cambridge, MA: MIT Press.

Stallybrass, Peter, and Allon White. 1986. *The Politics and Poetics of Transgression*. London: Methuen.

Stanziani, Alessandro. 2007. "Negotiating Innovation in a Market Economy: Foodstuffs and Beverages Adulteration in Nineteenth-Century France." *Enterprise and Society* 8 (2): 375–412.

Star, Susan Leigh, and James R. Griesemer. 1989. "Institutional Ecology, 'Translations,' and Boundary Objects. Amateurs and Professionals in Berkeley's Museum of Vertebrate Zoology, 1907–1939." *Social Studies of Science* 19:387–420.

Starobinski, Jean. 1988. *Jean-Jacques Rousseau: Transparency and Obstruction*. Translated by Arthur Goldhammer, introduction by Robert J. Morrissey. Chicago: University of Chicago Press.

Staum, Martin S. 1980. *Cabanis: Enlightenment and Medical Philosophy in the French Revolution*. Princeton, NJ: Princeton University Press.

Stearn, William T. 1962. "The Influence of Leyden on Botany in the Seventeenth and Eighteenth Centuries." *British Journal for the History of Science* 1:137–59.

Steinmetz, Rudy. 1988. "Conceptions du corps à travers l'acte alimentaire aux XVIIe et XVIIIe siècles." *Revue d'histoire moderne et contemporaine* 35:3–35.

Stella, Alain. 1997. *The Book of Coffee*. Preface by Carlo Fruttero and Franco Lucentini. Paris: Flammarion.

Stewart, Larry. 1992. *The Rise of Public Science: Rhetoric, Technology, and Natural Philosophy in Newtonian Britain, 1660–1750*. Cambridge: Cambridge University Press.

———. 1999. "Other Centres of Calculation, or, Where the Royal Society Didn't Count; Commerce, Coffee-Houses and Natural Philosophy in Early Modern London." *British Journal of the History of Science* 32:133–53.

Stewart, Philip. 1985. "L'Ambigu ou la nourriture spectacle." In *Littérature et gastronomie, huit études*, ed. Ronald Tobin, 85–111. Paris: Papers on French Seventeenth Century Literature.

Stolberg, Michael. 1986. "'Mein äskulapisches Orakel!' Patientenbriefe als Quelle einer Kulturgeschichte der Krankheitserfahrung im 18. Jahrhundert." *Österreichische Zeitschrift für Geschichtswissenschaften* 7:385–404.

———. 1998. "Der gesunde und saubere Körper." In *Die Erfindung des Menschen: Schöpfungsträume und Körperbilder 1500–2000*, ed. Richard van Dülmen, 305–17. Wien: Böhlau.

Stroup, Alice. 1990. *A Company of Scientists: Botany, Patronage and Community at the Seventeenth-Century Parisian Royal Academy of Sciences*. Berkeley: University of California Press.

Sturdy, David J. 1995. *Science and Social Status. The Members of the Académie des Sciences, 1666–1750*. Woodbridge, Suffolk: The Boydell Press.

Sue, Pierre. Year VIII / 1799–1800. *Memoire historique, littéraire et critique, sur la Vie et sur les Ouvrages tant imprimés que manuscrits de Jean Goulin*. Paris: Blanchon.

Suleiman, Susan R., and Inge Crosman, eds. 1980. *The Reader in the Text: Essays on Audience and Interpretation*. Princeton, NJ: Princeton University Press.

Sumner, James. 2001. "John Richardson, Saccharometry and the Pounds-Per-Barrel Extract: The Construction of a Quantity." *British Journal for the History of Science* 34:255–73.

Sundeen, Glenn. 2003. "Thévenot the Tourist: A Frenchman Abroad in the Ottoman Empire." In *Distant Lands and Diverse Cultures: The French Experience in Asia, 1600–1700*, ed. Glenn J. Ames and Ronald S. Love, 1–19. Westport, CT: Praeger.

Sutton, Geoffrey V. 1995. *Science for a Polite Society: Gender, Culture, and the Demonstration of Enlightenment*. Boulder, CO: Westview Press.

Takats, Sean P. E. 2011. *The Expert Cook in Enlightenment France*. Baltimore: Johns Hopkins University Press.

Taveneaux, René. 1973. *La Vie quotidienne des Jansénistes aux XVIIe et XVIIIe siècles*. Paris: Librairie Hachette.

Tavernier, Jean-Baptiste. 1679. *Les six voyages de Jean-Baptiste Tavernier*, part 1. [Paris]: [n.p.].

Teply, Karl. 1978. "Kundschafter, Kuriere, Kaufleute, Kaffeesieder. Die Legende des Wiener Kaffeehauses auf dem Röntgenschirm der Geschichte und der Volkskunde." *Österreich in Geschichte und Literatur* 22:1–17.

Ter Minassian, Anahide. 1997. "Les 'Arméniens' du Roi de France." In *Istanbul et les langues orientales*, ed. Frédéric Hitzel, 215–34. Paris: L'Harmattan.

Terrall, Mary. 1995. "Gendered Spaces, Gendered Audiences: Inside and Outside the Paris Academy of Sciences." *Configurations* 2:207–32.

Terrasson, abbé Jean. 1715. *Dissertation critique sur l'Iliade d'Homere, où à l'occasion de ce Poëme on cherche les regles d'une Poëtique fondée sur la raison*. 2 vols. Paris: François Fournier and Antoine-Urbain Coustelier.

———. 1720. *Lettres sur le nouveau systême des finances*. [Paris?: n.p.].

———. 1754. *La Philosophie applicable a tous les objets de l'Esprit et de la Raison*. Paris: Prault fils.

Terry, Jennifer, and Jacqueline Urla, eds. 1995. *Deviant Bodies: Critical Perspectives on Difference in Science and Popular Culture*. Bloomington: Indiana University Press.

Teulon, Fabrice. 1998. "Le voluptueux et le gourmand: économie de la jouissance chez La Mettrie et Brillat-Savarin." *Symposium* 52 (3): 176–92.

Teuteberg, Hans Jürgen. 1993. "Prolegomena zu einer Kulturpsychologie des Geschmacks." In *Kulturthema Essen. Ansichten und Problemfelder*, ed. Alois Wierlacher, Gerhard Neumann and Hans Jürgen Teuteberg, 103–36. Berlin: Akademie Verlag.

Teysseire, Daniel. 1993. "Le réseau européen des consultants d'un médecin des Lumières:

Tissot (1728–1797)." In *Diffusion du savoir et affrontement des idées 1600–1770*, 253–67. Montbrison: Association culturelle du centre culturel de la ville de Montbrison.

Thelamon, Françoise. 1992. "Sociabilité et conduites alimentaires." In *La sociabilité à table: Commensalité et convivialité à travers les âges*, ed. Martin Aurell, Olivier Dumoulin and Françoise Thelamon, 9–15. [Rouen]: Publications de l'Université de Rouen.

Thériault, Serge A., ed. 1979. *Jean-Jacques Rousseau et la médecine naturelle*. Montréal: L'Aurore.

Thierry, François. 1755. *Médecine Expérimentale, ou Résultat de nouvelles Observations Pratiques & Anatomiques*. Paris: Duchesne.

Thirsk, Joan. 2007. *Food in Early Modern England: Phases, Fads, Fashions 1500–1760*. New York: Hambledon Continuum.

Thomson, Ann. 1981. *Materialism and Society in the Mid-Eighteenth Century: La Mettrie's* Discours Préliminaire. Geneva: Droz.

———. 2008. *Bodies of Thought: Science, Religion, and the Soul in the Early Enlightenment*. Oxford: Oxford University Press.

Thouvenel, Pierre. 1780. *Mémoire chimique et médicinal sur la nature, les usages et les effets de l'Air et des Airs, des Alimens et des Médicamens, relativement a l'Économie animale*. Paris: Ph.-D. Pierres and Didot le jeune.

[Tiphaigne de la Roche, Charles-François]. 1760. *Giphantie*. Babylone [Paris: n.p.].

[Tiphaigne de la Roche, Charles-François]. 1765. *Sanfrein, ou mon dernier Séjour à la campagne*. Amsterdam: [n.p.].

Tissot, Samuel-Auguste-André-David. 1770. *Essai sur les maladies des gens du monde*. Lausanne: François Grasset & Cie.

———. 1991. *De la santé des gens de lettres* (1758). Preface by Christophe Calame. Paris: Editions de La Différence.

Torlais, Jean. 1936. *Réaumur: Un esprit encyclopédique en dehors de l'Encyclopédie*. Paris: Desclée de Brouwer.

———. 1961. *Un esprit Encyclopédique en dehors de "L'Encyclopédie." Réaumur*. 2nd ed. Paris: Blanchard.

Tourneux, Maurice, ed. 1877–82. *Correspondance littéraire, philosophique et critique par Grimm, Diderot, Raynal, Meister, etc.* Paris: Garnier Frères.

Trévoux. 1771. *Dictionnaire universel françois et latin, vulgairement appelé Dictionnaire de Trévoux*. New ed., 8 vols. Paris: Compagnie des Libraires Associés.

Tronchin, Henry. 1906. *Un médecin du XVIIIe siècle. Théodore Tronchin (1709–1781) d'après des documents inédits*. Paris: Librairie Plon.

[Tronchin, Jean-Robert]. 1765. *Lettres écrites de la campagne*. Geneva: [n.p.].

Trouillot, Michel-Rolph. 1982. "Motion in the System: Coffee, Color, and Slavery in Eighteenth-Century Saint-Domingue." *Review* 5 (3): 331–88.

Tuchscherer, Michel. 2003. "Coffee in the Red Sea Area from the Sixteenth to the Nineteenth Century." In *The Global Coffee Economy in Africa, Asia, and Latin America, 1500–1989*, ed. William Gervase Clarence-Smith and Steven Topik, 50–66. New York: Cambridge University Press.

Turner, Anthony. 2004. *Coffee: An Essay*. Paris: Blusson.

Turner, Bryan S. 1982. "Government of the Body: Medical Regimens and the Rationalisation of Diet." *British Journal of Sociology* 33:254–69.

———. 1992. *Regulating Bodies: Essays in Medical Sociology*. London: Routledge.

———. 1996. *The Body and Society: Explorations in Social Theory.* 2nd ed. London: Sage.

Van Kley, Dale. 1975. *The Jansenists and the Expulsion of the Jesuits from France, 1757–1765*. New Haven, CT: Yale University Press.

Vandal, Albert. 1900. *L'Odyssée d'un ambassadeur. Les voyages du marquis de Nointel (1670–1680)*. Paris: Librairie Plon.

Vandermonde, Charles-Augustin. 1756. *Essai sur la manière de perfectionner l'espèce humaine*. 2 vols. Paris: Vincent.

[Vandermonde, Charles-Augustin]. 1759. *Dictionnaire portatif de santé*. 2 vols. Paris: Vincent.

Vaucanson, Jacques. 1738. *Le Mécanisme du Fluteur Automate*. Paris: Jacques Guerin.

Venel, Gabriel. 1763. "Chymie." In *Recueil de planches, sur les sciences, les arts libéraux, et les arts méchaniques, avec leur explication*, vol. 2. Paris: Briasson et al.

Venturino, Diego. 2002. "L'historiographie révolutionnaire française et les Lumières, de Paul Buchez à Albert Sorel." In *Historiographie et usages des Lumières*, ed. Giuseppe Ricuperati, 21–83. Berlin: Berlin Verlag.

Vess, David M. 1975. *Medical Revolution in France, 1789–1796*. Gainesville: University Presses of Florida.

Vicaire, Georges. 1890. *Bibliographie gastronomique*. Preface by Paul Ginisty. Paris: P. Rouquette.

Vidal, Fernando. 2004. "Onanism, Enlightenment Medicine, and the Immanent Justice of Nature." In *The Moral Authority of Nature*, ed. Lorraine Daston and Fernando Vidal, 254–81. Chicago: University of Chicago Press.

Vieussens, Raymond. 1710. "De la nature et des proprietez du levain de l'estomac." *Mémoires de Trévoux*, 134–51.

Vigarello, Georges. 1999. *Histoire des pratiques de santé. Le sain et le malsain depuis le Moyen Age*. Paris: Editions du Seuil.

Vila, Anne C. 1993. "Enlightened Minds and Scholarly Bodies from Tissot to Sade." *Studies in Eighteenth-Century Culture* 23:207–20.

———. 1995. "Sex and Sensibility: Pierre Roussel's *Système Physique et Morale de la Femme*." *Representations* 52:76–93.

———. 1998. *Enlightenment and Pathology: Sensibility in the Literature and Medicine of Eighteenth-Century France*. Baltimore: Johns Hopkins University Press.

———. 2005a. "The *Philosophe*'s Stomach: Hedonism, Hypochondria, and the Intellectual in Enlightenment France." In *Cultures of the Abdomen: Diet, Digestion, and Fat in the Modern World*, ed. Christopher E. Forth and Ana Carden-Coyne, 89–104. London: Macmillan Palgrave.

———. 2005b. "Getting Cultural: New Perspectives in Eighteenth-Century Science Studies." In *The Eighteenth Century Now: Boundaries and Perspectives*, ed. Jonathan Mallinson, 281–91. Studies on Voltaire and the Eighteenth Century 10. Oxford: The Voltaire Foundation at the Taylor Institution.

———. 2007. "Somaticizing the Thinker in Eighteenth-Century France." In *Littérature et médecine: approches et perspectives*, ed. Andrea Carlino and Alexandre Wenger, 89–111. Geneva: Librairie Droz.

Vincent-Buffault, Anne. 1991. *The History of Tears: Sensibility and Sentimentality in France*. Basingstoke: Macmillan.

Viridet, Jean. 1735. *Traité du bon chyle pour la production du sang*. 2 vols. Paris: Fréres Osmont.

Voltaire, François-Marie Arouet de. 1752. *Le Micromégas de M. de Voltaire, avec une Histoire des croisades, et un Nouveau plan de l'histoire de l'esprit humain par le même*. London [Paris: n.p.].

———. 1830. *L'Écossaise, comédie en cinq actes, par M. Hume, traduite en français par Jérome Carré*. In Voltaire, *Oeuvres complètes*, vol. 5. Paris: Armand-Aubrée.

———. 1950. *Correspondance avec les Tronchin*. Edited and annotated by André Delattre. Paris: Mercure de France.

———. 1968–77. *The Complete Works of Voltaire. Correspondence*, ed. Theodore Besterman. 51 vols. Oxford: The Voltaire Foundation at the Taylor Institution.

Walvin, James. 1997. *Fruits of Empire: Exotic Produce and British Taste, 1660–1800*. Basingstoke: Macmillan.

Weinberg, Bennett Alan, and Bonnie K. Bealer. 2001. *The World of Caffeine: The Science and Culture of the World's Most Popular Drug*. London: Routledge.

Wellman, Kathleen. 1992. *La Mettrie: Medicine, Philosophy and Enlightenment*. Durham, NC: Duke University Press.

Wenger, Alexandre. 2007. *La fibre littéraire. Le discours médical sur la lecture au XVIIIe siècle*. Geneva: Droz.

Wheaton, Barbara Ketcham. 1983. *Savoring the Past: The French Kitchen and Table from 1300 to 1789*. Philadelphia: University of Pennsylvania Press.

Wijnands, D. Onno. 1983. *The Botany of the Commelins*. Wageningen: Balkema.

———. 1988. "Hortus Auriaci: The Gardens of Orange and Their Place in Late Seventeenth-Century Botany and Horticulture." *Journal of Garden History* 8:61–86, 271–304.

Wild, Antony. 2004. *Coffee: A Dark History*. New York: Fourth Estate.

Williams, Elizabeth A. 1994. *The Physical and the Moral: Anthropology, Physiology, and Philosophical Medicine in France, 1750–1850*. New York: Cambridge University Press.

———. 2007. "Neuroses of the Stomach: Eating, Gender, and Psychopathology in French Medicine, 1800–1870." *Isis* 98:54–79.

Williams, Raymond. 1999. "Consumer." In *Consumer Society in American History: A Reader*, ed. Lawrence B. Glickman, 17–18. Ithaca, NY: Cornell University Press.

Wilson, C. Anne. 2006. *Water of Life: A History of Wine-Distilling and Spirits 500 BC–AD 2000*. Totnes: Prospect Books.

Wilson, Lindsay. 1993. *Women and Medicine in the French Enlightenment: The Debate Over "Maladies des Femmes."* Baltimore: Johns Hopkins University Press.

Wintroub, Michael. 2006. *A Savage Mirror: Power, Identity, and Knowledge in Early Modern France*. Stanford, CA: Stanford University Press.

Withers, Charles W. J. 2007. *Placing the Enlightenment: Thinking Geographically about the Age of Reason*. Chicago: University of Chicago Press.

Wittgenstein, Ludwig. 1958. *Philosophische Untersuchungen*. 3rd ed. New York: Macmillan.

Yeo, Richard. 2006. "John Locke and Polite Philosophy." In *The Philosopher in Early Modern Europe: The Nature of a Contested Identity*, ed. Conal Condren, Stephen Gaukroger and Ian Hunter, 254–75. Cambridge: Cambridge University Press.

Yolton, John. 1984. *Thinking Matter: Materialism in Eighteenth-Century Britain*. Minneapolis: University of Minnesota Press.

———. 1991. *Locke and French Materialism*. New York: Oxford University Press.

Young, Katharine. 1989. "Narrative Embodiments: Enclaves of the Self in the Realm of Medicine." In *Texts of Identity*, ed. John Shotter and Kenneth J. Gergen. 152–65. London: Sage Publications.

———. 1997. *Presence in the Flesh: The Body in Medicine*. Cambridge, MA: Harvard University Press.

Zirojević, Olga. 2004. "On the Distinctive Features of the Bosniacs." In *Ottoman Bosnia: A History in Peril*, ed. Markus Koller and Kemal H. Karpat, 167–70. Madison: University of Wisconsin Press.

INDEX